Mark Redmond places an emphasis on both communication theory and skill building, using clear language and a unique structure that presents alternating theory and skills chapters. This logical approach to interviewing and public speaking and to interpersonal, small group, organizational, and mass communication gives instructors the flexibility to focus on skill building or theory, depending on their preference.

Ask Yourself sections in every chapter prompt students to consider how the material applies to their personal lives.

Think about some of your interpersonal relationships. How have the dialectical tensions affected the development of those relationships? How comfortable were you in giving up some of your independence to become closer? How open or closed have you been in sharing information about yourself? What has happened in relationships when they became very predictable?

Connect Yourself sections are Internet-based activities that lead students to further exploration of ideas presented as they relate to technology.

Log on to a chat session. You don't have to participate; simply read the messages as people chat with one another. How much variety of self-disclosure is occurring (breadth)? How evaluative are the self-disclosures that are taking place (depth)? In what ways is self-disclosure on the Internet the same as disclosing face to face? In what ways is it different? To what degree does the type of chat group affect self-disclosure?

Use the following summary of initiation strategies to identify your skill at using each one. Record your responses on a scale from 1 (for a strategy you find very hard to use) to 5 (for a strategy you are adept at using):

1. Be honest and sincere.   1 2 3 4 5
2. Use free information in opening remarks.   1 2 3
3. Look for some common element to discuss.   1 2 3
4. Watch for signals of a willingness to interact.   1 2 3
5. Follow up on the other person's responses.   1 2 3
6. Ask questions, and then watch and listen to the answers
   for cues about the person's willingness to talk.   1 2 3
7. Follow the traditional, expected pattern for initial
   interactions.   1 2 3
8. Provide an appropriate amount of information about
   yourself.   1 2 3
9. Present yourself in a positive manner.   1 2 3
10. Listen actively.   1 2 3

Add up the numbers you have circled. If your total score is less than 30, the strategies that you marked with less than a 3 and try applying them interactions.

Students have the opportunity to assess their understanding of the material in **Test Yourself** sections.

Each application area includes a discussion of relevant theory and a set of suggestions and guidelines for skill improvement.

Summary and Self-Analysis sections list key ideas and give students another opportunity for self-assessment.

Summary and Self-Analysis:

Skills for Developing Relationships

Use the following summary of skills for developing relationships to identify your strongest skills and those that you could improve.

Affinity Seeking: Getting Another Person to Like You

- Self-presentation: Present an attractive and interesting image.
- Mutual trust: Show yourself to be trustworthy and trusting of the other.
- Politeness: Display good conversational behavior.
- Listening: Be attentive, supportive, and sensitive.
- Other involvement: Include the other in your activities.
- Self-involvement: Get yourself invited to be included in the other perso[n's] activities.
- Commonalities: Point out how similar you are to the other person.

Coordinating Relational Perspectives and Process Trajectory Cognitions

- Be willing to discuss your
- Be receptive to your partn
- Appropriately time relatio

Self-Disclosure: Sharing In

- Appropriately time when
- Watch for reciprocation o

Key Terms at the end of each chapter provide additional review.

Key Terms

approachability cues   Indications that a person is receptive to interpersonal communication.

free information   Information that is easily observed about another person and utilized in conversations.

affinity-seeking strategies   Behaviors we enact in an attempt to increase another person's liking for us.

maintenance strategies   Conscious attempts to "recharge" a relationship or help a relationship remain at a given level of intimacy.

compliance gaining   Interpersonal persuasion; the interpersonal process of overcoming another

door-in-the-face   A compliance-gaining strategy in which you initially make a very large request and then bargain down to a much smaller request, which is actually the one that you wanted.

mutual de-escalation   An effort by both parties to terminate a relationship or reduce its level of intimacy.

unilateral de-escalation   An effort by only one party to terminate a relationship or reduce its level of intimacy.

direct de-escalation strategies   Relational de-escalation efforts that involve explicitly stating a desire to terminate or redefine the relationship.

[indirect de-escalation] **strategies**   Relational de-[escalation efforts that] avoid any specific indica-[tion of a desire to t]erminate or redefine the

Cultural Bias in the Employment Interview

This article excerpt demonstrates why interviewers need to be sensitive to the cultural background of interviewees. The article describes the difficulties that Native Americans, specifically Navajo students, face in a typical U.S. employment interview.

It's important to understand the unfortunate dynamic of interview bias and [how it] impacts judgments made of traditional Native Americans. Some typical cr[iteria] used to evaluate students during on-campus interviews are:

- Self-Confidence: Strong handshake, good eye contact.
- Goal Orientation: Able to express short- and long-term goals.
- Enthusiasm: An animated conversationalist with an easy smile.
- Leadership: Able to provide examples of specific individual achievements a[nd] strengths.

What many recruiters fail to consider is that these may be false indicators [of] desired qualities and more a matter of style than of substance. Despite the Am[erican] "ideal," traits of confidence, commitment to the job, and even leadership c[an be] deeply woven into a quiet and unpresumptuous character. The challenge for recr[uiters] is to discover the qualities that are really there, perhaps hidden by cultural norms.

Feature Essays throughout the text address different points of communication including diversity, culture, and relationship issues.

Communication: Theories and Applications

Communication:
Theories and Applications

Mark V. Redmond

Iowa State University

Houghton Mifflin Company   *Boston*   *New York*

■ Dedication

As you will read in this text, the way we think, behave, and communicate is influenced by a variety of factors such as the people with whom we interact. A significant source of that influence are those who teach us. I am indebted to those who have taught me throughout my life not only for the knowledge they have imparted but for teaching me how to learn, think, and communicate. To the degree that you learn from this text, you will also be learning from these teachers. Regretfully I have forgotten the names of many of my elementary and high school teachers, but I would like to cite those college instructors who have had a significant impact on my understanding of communication; I humbly dedicate this book to those teachers. They include, from my undergraduate and graduate student days at Purdue University, Henry Ewbank, Gus Friedrich, Rod Hart, Mark Knapp, Brenda Logue, John Monsma, Charles Redding, Jo Sprague, Charles Stewart, and especially Ralph Webb. And during my continued graduate studies at the University of Denver, Alton Barbour, Frank Dance, Al Goldberg, and Carl Larson.

Photo Credits:
Part One: p. 1, Spencer Grant/Photo Edit.

Chapter 1: p. 9, Shamsi-Bash/The Image Works; p. 12, Ted Goff; p. 19, Michael Newman/Photo Edit.

Chapter 2: p. 34, Michael Jantze/King Feature Syndicate; p. 45, Randy Glasbergen. (continued on page 449)

Executive Editor: George Hoffman
Associate Editor: Jennifer Wall
Project Editor: Rachel D'Angelo Wimberly
Senior Production/Design Coordinator: Carol Merrigan
Manufacturing Manager: Florence Cadran
Senior Marketing Manager: Pamela J. Laskey

Cover Design: Minko T. Dimov, MinkoImages
Wassily Kandinsky "Orientalisches" 1909 Lenbachhaus Gallery, Munich, Germany

Printed in the U.S.A.

Library of Congress Catalog Card Number: 99-71918
ISBN: 0-395-88855-7

1 2 3 4 5 6 7 8 9 - DW - 03 02 01 00 99

Contents

Chapter 11

Small Group Communication: Skills for Members and Leaders 283

Chapter 12

Presentational Communication: Purposes, Theory, and Principles 306

Chapter 13

Presentational Communication: Research and Preparation 336

Chapter 14

Presentational Communication: Skills for Delivery 366

Chapter 15

Organizational Communication: Descriptive and Prescriptive Theories 391

Chapter 16

Organizational Communication: Skills for Employees and Managers 417

Preface

Communication: Theories and Applications is designed for introductory courses in communication. The aim is to help students understand the dynamics of human interactions, learn alternative strategies for coping with communication issues, and develop and refine their communication skills.

For students, the basic question is: Who needs a *textbook* on communication? Especially for a student who has plenty of friends and who works well with other people, the reasons for studying the subject may not be obvious. One goal of this book is to convince students of both the fascination and the practicality of communication as a field of study.

For an instructor, the main question is somewhat different: Why choose this book rather than one of the other numerous communication texts already available? That is, how does this book differ from the others? To answer that, let me explain the book's several distinguishing features.

■ The Book's Interactive Approach

This book endeavors, first of all, to be engaging and interactive. As much as possible I have tried to keep students involved in what they are reading. The text is written in such a way as to draw readers into each type of communication situation, prompting them to consider their own thoughts and reactions.

The interactive nature of the text appears most clearly in the three integrated features called *Ask Yourself*, *Connect Yourself*, and *Test Yourself*.

- The *Ask Yourself* features in each chapter consist of questions for the student to ponder while reading—questions that link the material to the student's own experiences.
- The *Connect Yourself* features include suggestions for using the Internet as a learning and application environment, often through search activities on the World Wide Web.
- The *Test Yourself* features include activities that allow students to assess their own communication skills and determine how well they understand the material they have read.

A second, related difference between this book and traditional communication texts is its conversational style. To the reader, it should feel like a conversation with the author rather than a lecture. The writing is meant to be friendly and enjoyable as well as informative. Readers are welcome to pretend that I am there with them, that they are asking me questions and telling me their ideas. This will translate, I hope, into lively discussions in the classroom as well as conversations among the students outside class.

A third distinguishing feature of this book is the large number of examples drawn from a wide variety of communication situations. I have deliberately included scenarios that appeal to a broad spectrum of student backgrounds. These examples are intended to both help students understand the content and to make it more personal and meaningful for them.

Along with its special elements, *Communication: Theories and Applications* includes traditional pedagogical features, such as Chapter Objectives, Review Questions, Key Terms with definitions, and excerpts from relevant magazine articles and other sources. Together, these multiple facets of the text are meant to complement the experience provided in the classroom. They offer, for example, a large variety of opportunities for class discussion. Teachers can engage the entire class in sharing responses to the *Ask Yourself* or *Connect Yourself* features. Or the end-of-chapter questions can be used for an effective in-class review of the chapter's content.

To gain full benefit from the book, students will need to be open and honest about who they are and the skills they possess, and they will need to apply and practice what they read. The text is designed to encourage such responses in every way possible. I hope that it will inspire students to find the study of human communication as exhilarating and challenging as I do.

▊ The Book's Content and Organization

In deciding what material to include, I asked myself this question: "If students are exposed to only one course in communication, what material should they be taught?" The material covered in this text is both fundamental and practical. It reflects some of the best information the field of communication has to offer in helping individuals understand and improve their skills across the full range of communication situations.

The text is divided into two parts. Part One, Chapters 1–5, covers communication basics—fundamental theories and concepts that are applied throughout the text. Part Two, Chapters 6–16, focuses on the specific communication contexts and applications that are treated in most introductory communication courses.

Part One, in addition to including traditional concepts, makes a strong effort to reflect contemporary communication scholarship. Theories such as uncertainty reduction and nonverbal expectancy violation theory are presented here. Chapter 5—unique in a text of this sort—examines common communication challenges, such as misunderstanding, conflict, and deceit.

Part Two is organized to reflect the way many fundamental courses are taught and at the same time to make understanding theory and skills easier for students. As in other texts, each major field of application is addressed in turn: interpersonal communication, interviewing, small group communication, presentational communication, and organizational communication. In this text, however, the first chapter devoted to each field discusses theory, and then a second chapter focuses on skills. (In the case of presentational communication, there are two chapters on skills.) The skills chapters are direct extensions of the theory chapters.

This format—first theory, then skills—makes assimilation of the theory material easier for students, and it also helps establish clear strategies for skill development. From a pedagogical perspective, the design will help teachers adapt the book to their instructional goals. For instance, a teacher can format the course into clearly distinguishable theory and skill units, if you choose to do so.

▌ Ancillary Materials

Instructor's Resource Manual with Test Items
Computerized Test Bank for Macintosh and Windows
Video
Multicultural Workbook for the Speech Communication Classroom
Speech Preparation Workbook
Houghton Mifflin Communication Web Site

▌ Acknowledgments

I cannot take sole credit for this textbook. It is a team project and many people have contributed to its development and production. I am greatly indebted to the valuable input and aid of a number of people who I would like to acknowledge. Amy Slump was an undergraduate research assistant who cheerfully and skillfully helped me find various resources such as the cartoons and articles that are included in each chapter; her help was invaluable. Several of my colleagues have also helped in the development of material for this text. Specifically, Dr. Denise Vrchota and Dr. Terry Pickett have shared their insights into presentations, teams, and organizations. Dr. Mei Zhong was always willing to provide me with intercultural communication examples. Dr. Scott Chadwick helped enormously in identifying the concepts to include in the organizational chapters and provided feedback that greatly improved their quality. Dr. Kim Smith and Dr. Eric Abbott diligently helped in developing material for the mass communication content that has been posted online for reader access. To all of these colleagues I express the greatest appreciation.

I have benefited, too, from working with an exceptional editorial and production team from Houghton Mifflin. First and foremost, I want to express my gratitude to George Hoffman, Senior Sponsoring Editor, who had the faith to pursue this project and has continued to provide encouragement and support. Thank you, George. Part of my success working with George is due to the effective communication that was maintained throughout by his associate editor, Jennifer Wall. Thank you, Jennifer. Many improvements to my verbiage stem from the insights of Doug Gordon, Developmental Editor (he should probably get second author credit for all of his contributions); Rachel Wimberly, Project Editor (who stuck with me even when I was lost among the various deadlines); and Monica Hincken, Editorial Assistant (whose fine eye and attention to detail helped so much).

Finally, I would like to thank those reviewers from colleges and universities who read over the first drafts of my chapters and gave invaluable feedback. Their encouragement and suggestions have had an immeasurable impact on improving the text.

Cherie C. White, Muskigum Area Technical College; Jan Courtney, University of Texas-Pan American; Edward C. Brewer, Northwestern Oklahoma State University; W. Steven Brooks, Missouri Western State University; Terrence A. Doyle, Northern Virginia Community College; Maureen Minielli, Saint Joseph's College; Scott T. Paynton, Humboldt State University; Scott Tucker, Kentucky Christian College/Midway College; John Guzalak, University of West Florida; Ann Cunningham, Bergen Community College; and Thomas B. Harte, Southeast Missouri State University.

M. R.

Communication: Theories and Applications

Part One

Basic Communication Theories

Chapter 1

Fundamentals of Human Communication

Objectives

Studying this chapter will allow you to:
1. Define human communication.
2. Distinguish among three models of communication.
3. Explain why we communicate.
4. Identify and explain the components of human communication.
5. Identify and define several different categories of human communication.

A number of newspapers now list their employment advertisements on the Internet. It's a quick and easy way to look at job opportunities across the country. Besides finding the types of jobs available, you can get a sample of the qualifications companies are looking for in potential employees. Here are some of the phrases related to communication that have recently appeared in job ads in the *Indianapolis Star and News,* the *Denver Post,* and the *Seattle Times:*

- Must have strong effective oral and written communication skills
- Outstanding communication skills
- Excellent written and verbal communication, organizational, and supervision skills
- Seeking individuals with good communication and people skills
- Seeking the right candidate with strong interpersonal, organizational, and communication skills
- Possess strong interpersonal and group facilitating skills
- Strong interpersonal and communication skills, ability to lead teams
- Systems engineers: Good interpersonal and communication skills
- Strong communication and team development skills

Needless to say, communication skills are important to employers. More and more employers are expressing concern about the quality of their employees' communication skills.[1] Companies want individuals who can express themselves effectively both in writing and in face-to-face interaction. College graduates with interpersonal, organizational, team, and presentational communication skills will have a decided advantage over their counterparts who lack such competencies. This text is designed to provide you with an opportunity to enhance a variety of communication skills.

Do your own search of the employment ads that appear in newspapers around the country. Most include a keyword search that allows you to identify certain job characteristics. Use *communication* as a keyword. Try another term related to your interests, such as *sales, human resources,* or *engineer.*

What kinds of jobs did you discover?

What qualifications are employers looking for?

Effective communication is important not just in the workplace. Our relationships with friends and family also depend on effective communication. You may believe that you are already a pretty good communicator and that reading this book will not make a major difference in your life. However, communication skills, like all other skills, can be improved.

To begin the process of improvement, you must first understand the nature and complexity of communication. Then, you must apply and practice effective communication skills. This text is designed to help you do both. To get started, let's look at some of the basic concepts related to communication.

▌ What Is Communication?

Here's a little self-quiz on communication. For each of the following scenarios, indicate whether or not communication is occurring:

1. Yes   No   You're walking down the sidewalk and you see someone approaching that you'd rather avoid, and so you quickly duck into a nearby building before the other person sees you.

2. Yes   No   You turn on your computer to check your electronic mail (email). The following appears on the computer screen:
"Login Name: _____
    Password: _____."

3. Yes   No   A man and a woman are walking along a riverbank under a full moon. They are not talking. They stop, gently kiss, and then continue walking.

4. Yes   No   You are waiting at a bus stop when a stranger walks up to you and speaks to you in a foreign language that you do not recognize. You shrug your shoulders and say, "I'm sorry, I don't understand you," and then turn away.

5. Yes   No   An instructor is lecturing to a class of five hundred students. One student in the back row is taking careful notes, but the instructor does not even notice this student among the other students.

6. Yes   No   The morning sun rises and begins to shine on a plant. The plant unfolds its leaves and almost imperceptibly adjusts them for maximum exposure to the sun's rays. Throughout the day, the plant continues to adjust its leaves in accordance with the sun's movement.

7. Yes   No   Watching a very close game on the TV show *Jeopardy*, you are waiting for the participants' final responses when the show is interrupted for a special newsbreak. After the five-minute break, the station reverts to commercials, and you never get to see what happened. You are particularly mad and upset.

Pat yourself on the back if you answered yes for all seven scenarios. They all represent communication, although they are not all examples of *good*, or *effective*, communication. The remainder of this section will help you understand why they are all forms of communication.

You may have answered no for scenario 6 because it doesn't involve people interacting. But **communication** in its most global usage, simply means acting on information.[2] How do you know if something has acted on information? Because there is change. Change occurs in response to information. The plant moves to follow the sun's path because the plant is acting on information.

The sun, of course, does not change as a result of the plant. This is an example of the **actional model of communication** (See Figure 1.1.), in which there is simply an action followed by a reaction. One thing reacts to another without a reciprocal effect; thus, the communication is a one-way process.

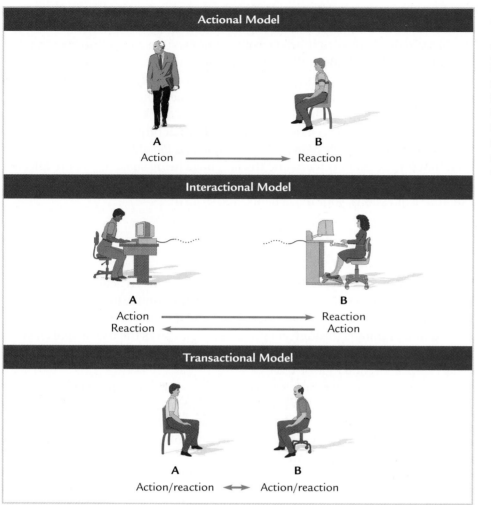

Figure 1.1

Models of Communication

In the *actional model,* B reacts to A, but A remains unaffected by B. In the *interactional model,* each reacts to the other's actions in sequence. In the *transactional model,* A and B react to each other simultaneously.

Communication in this most global sense also does not require intention. The sun has no intention of affecting the plant. The plant is simply in a position to collect information and respond to that information. Scenario 1 is similar, even though it involves two people. When you spot the other person and change your direction, you are acting on information, but the other person is unaffected by you. Therefore, one-way, actional communication is taking place. The same applies to scenario 5, in which the student responds to the instructor, who remains unaffected by the student.

In scenario 2, you are prompted to enter certain information. After typing in your name and password, you would access your email account. This scenario represents a *series* of actional, one-way, linear communication events. You do something, the computer reacts to your behavior, you react to what the computer shows, and the computer then acts on what you type. This sequence of events represents an **interactional model of communication.** (See Figure 1.1.) Each action is a response to a prior action; and each action evokes a new response. Thus, the model proceeds from an action to a reaction/action to another reaction/action, and so on.

In scenarios 3 and 4, a third type of communication comes into play. In these scenarios, the individuals are not just communicating in an actional or interactional fashion; they are communicating transactionally. The **transactional model of communication** (See Figure 1.1.) applies when two things affect one another simultaneously.[3] The couple holding hands and kissing are affecting each other at the same time. In essence, they are both acting on information at the same time, although their reactions are unique and individualistic. In scenario 4, even though you don't understand the language being spoken, you are affected by the stranger's actions, and the stranger likewise is affected by what you look like, your expressions, your movements, and so forth.

▮ What Is Human Communication?

You might have been tricked by scenario 6 in the quiz if you defined communication as having to do with people. In fact, **human communication** is a special form of communication that occurs between and among people. The connection made among humans through communication involves the use of spoken symbolic language—the words we speak—as well as nonverbal cues such as gestures, facial expressions, and tone of voice.

As with any other communication, communication among people is identifiable by change. You know that human communication has occurred when one individual's message affects or changes another person. You clearly are engaging in human communication when you express in spoken words your friendship for a person ("Thanks for being my friend"). However, smiling at someone you pass on the sidewalk and watching a mother hug her child good-bye are also examples of human communication, because these actions, too, involve some effect.

The way we interact with other people is reflected in the three models of communication presented earlier:

- *Actional communication.* We are constantly giving meaning to the behaviors we observe in other people—behaviors that may not have been intended as a message. If a man coughs repeatedly while we are talking to him, we may conclude that he has a cold. We react to what we have observed.
- *Interactional communication.* Internet chat sessions are a prime example of interactional communication. Each participant types in a message and waits to read what other users type in response. After reading the responses, the original poster submits another message. This sequence of actions and reactions continues until the users log off.
- *Transactional communication.* A face-to-face conversation between you and a friend is a clear example of transactional communication. But so is a committee member's decision to speak up during a meeting. The member's decision is influenced by the actions and reactions of the other members. In fact, each committee member influences and is influenced by the others at the same time. Thus, a member might decide to add more detail to an explanation after noticing the blank looks from other members.

■ Signs and Symbols

In human communication, we use both signs and symbols to communicate our meanings. **Signs** are stimuli that have fixed and concrete meanings. That is, the meaning of a sign remains constant regardless of who observes it or when it's observed.

Many of our sensory observations fall into this category: smelling smoke (knowing there must be a fire), hearing a dog howl, feeling a person's pulse, seeing lightning and hearing thunder, tasting the sweetness of sugar, or hearing a baby cry from hunger. One easy way to identify signs is that their meaning is unaffected by the culture in which they are observed. Hearing someone cough means that the person has a tickle in the throat to both Peruvians and Zambians.

Symbols, on the other hand, are stimuli that have abstract, arbitrary, flexible, and changing meanings. A symbol's meaning is culture specific. The phrase "Sprechen zie Deutsch?" is a set of symbols that has a meaning to those who speak German. The set does not have the same meaning in another culture.

Now, let's see how clever you are. If someone in your class coughs to catch another student's attention, is that cough a sign or a symbol? It's a symbol, because the cough is being used to mean "Look my way, pay attention to me." In the culture of the United States, we understand that symbol; in some cultures, however, the cough would not be interpreted in the same way.

Decide whether each of the following is a sign or a symbol, and say why. Discuss your answers with your classmates.

1. Showing one finger when asked how many hot dogs you want at the concession stand
2. Smiling at someone new whom you find attractive
3. Waving good-bye to a friend
4. Yelling "Ooowwweee" after hitting your finger with a hammer
5. Falling asleep during a lecture because you haven't slept in thirty-six hours
6. Groaning in class when your instructor announces an additional assignment
7. Patting someone on the back for doing a good job during a game
8. Crying while a doctor is sewing up a cut in your hand

■ Why Do We Communicate?

"I'd like a quarter-pound burger, a large order of fries, and a chocolate shake, please."

"Hey, Juan, do you want to come over to my place and watch the game tonight?"

"This amazing product will cut your potato-cooking time in half."

"What do you mean you don't love me anymore?"

Each of these statements reflects some of the reasons we communicate. We use communication to satisfy our needs, whether they are for food or friendship. We try to gain things from other people by creating persuasive messages. We ask questions to gain information. We can also coordinate activities or simply communicate for pleasure. In fact, communication is one of the fundamental tools we use to affect, influence, and shape the world around us, including ourselves.[4]

■ *To Satisfy Needs*

Needs are forces that motivate humans to act. Needs include physiological needs (food and sex, for example), social needs (such as relationships and acceptance by others), and psychological needs (esteem, self-fulfillment, and so on). One of the most effective ways humans have found to satisfy their needs is through communication.

Some experts suggest that humans developed communication as a way of meeting their need for food and protection. Hunting parties needed to coordinate their actions if they were to be successful, and communication provided this coordination. We can never know the exact reason humans starting talking to one another, but we do know that the overriding reason we now communicate with others is to satisfy needs. In Chapter 2, we'll explore this idea further.

■ *To Gain Information*

Many of our needs are satisfied because communication provides us with information. We gain information from others by asking questions, by interacting, by listening to speeches, and by watching news programs.

We can gain information either actively or passively. Sometimes we recognize a need for information and seek it out. For example, you might go see your advisor because of a question about a certain requirement for graduation, or you might seek out your supervisor with a question about some procedure.

However, we often acquire information passively; that is, we are receptive to learning without really having a particular question we are trying to answer. Watching the six o'clock news provides you with lots of information, but you don't necessarily know what news you're going to learn. Similarly, you sit through a lecture and gain information without knowing beforehand what it's going to be about.

■ *To Manage Relationships*

Our relationships with others are managed through communication. We initiate, maintain, and terminate relationships through the use of communication. We talk to those we like and avoid those we don't. We develop trust and intimacy by sharing information and learning about other people.

We can use communication both directly and indirectly to manage our relationships. For instance, to display your interest in another person indirectly, you can simply increase your communication with that person. Or you can express your interest directly: "I really like you and would like us to become closer."

■ *To Derive Pleasure and Entertainment*

Communication in and of itself can be a pleasurable pastime. Think about those times when you have had really intense and in-depth conversations with other

These two friends are using communication to manage their relationship, to provide enjoyment, and to validate each other's value.

people. These "peak" communication experiences provide satisfaction in and of themselves. Watching television, listening to a performer at the local comedy club, or shooting the breeze with friends about a hot new rock group—these are all forms of communication that provide pleasure and entertainment.

■ To Get Self-Validation

Have you ever walked by someone you knew and said hi, only to be ignored? How did you feel? You probably felt a little offended. You wondered if the other person was mad at you, disliked you, or felt too good for you. On a philosophical level, you failed to have your "self" validated. Like everyone else, you want other people to confirm your existence and value.

Making connections with others through communication validates your sense of self. Communication is one of the ways you tell other people you appreciate them and accept who they are.

■ To Coordinate and Manage Tasks

Communication allows us to give and receive directions so that we can coordinate our actions with those of others. Coaches continually tell players to talk to one another because they recognize that communication promotes coordination—team play.

Organizations rely on their members and units to use communication to co-ordinate various activities. The sales staff gets an order and transmits it to the manufacturing floor. The manufacturing unit uses the specifications from the sales staff in constructing the product. The shipping department is asked to deliver the product at a particular time and place. All of these actions require communication. When the messages are distorted or lost, coordination breaks down and chaos breaks out. Have you ever placed an order for something and never received it until you called two or three times? One reason might be ineffective internal communication within the organization.

■ *To Persuade and Gain Something from Others*

We can organize our messages in such a way as to gain things from other people. Your boss might try to motivate you to work harder by offering you a bonus. You might try to persuade a professor to extend the deadline on a paper because of some personal crisis. You might offer to wash your dad's car if he'll let you borrow it Friday night. You might give a presentation to persuade a company president to hire your firm to maintain the company's computers. All of these are examples of how we use communication to persuade and gain compliance from other people.

■ Components of Human Communication

The examples in the preceding section covered many types of situations, from personal relationships to teams to presentations. Despite their differences, these various communication situations share some basic components: a context; a source, or sender; a receiver; messages; noise; and channels, or modes.[5] Understanding these components can help us gain a fundamental understanding of the communication process as a whole. Let's look at the different components one by one.

■ *Context*

Have you ever heard the question: Which falls faster in a vacuum, a feather or a steel ball? The answer is that they both fall at the same rate—but only if the experiment is truly in a vacuum. When air is present, the rates of descent are extremely different.

Human communication never occurs in a vacuum. Rather, it always occurs in a context, and the presence of that context—like the air in the experiment—affects how we talk to others and what we talk about.

A **context** is a variable that surrounds and influences communication. The easiest context to identify is the environmental context. The environmental context includes the physical surroundings, the temperature, the presence of others, and the location of the interaction. For instance, if you talk to the president of your corporation while walking to the parking lot after work, the conversation will be substantially different than if you were called into the president's office. Other contexts (to be discussed in Chapter 2) include the psychological, relational, situational, and cultural.

■ Source (Sender) and Receiver

For communication to occur, there must be a **source** of information that is perceived by someone. When the source is *unintentional*, we call it an object. **Objects** are simply those stimuli around us that we perceive that were not intentionally directed toward us. People are objects when you watch them walking by your window; the clouds are objects as you watch them floating in the sky; and cars passing by as you walk are objects. In these situations, you are the perceiver of the objects. A **perceiver** is someone who attends to, perceives, decodes, and is affected by objects in the environment. (See Figure 1.2.)

When the source of information is *intentional*, we call it a sender. A **sender** is someone who engages in a process of encoding and delivering a message to produce some effect.[6] People waving at you from across the street are senders because they intend to communicate with you. Advertisers who put advertisements in the newspaper are senders; your friend who emails you is a sender. To **encode** the message means to decide on the words and actions that will be used to reflect the thoughts that the person is trying to communicate.

A **receiver,** as you have probably guessed by now, is someone who attends to, perceives, decodes, and is affected by a message transmitted by a sender. You can tell if someone is a receiver in the same way you can tell if communication has occurred: The receiver is affected or changed as a result of having received the message. As shown in Figure 1.2, receivers **decode** the message by attributing meaning to what they have perceived. Messages are sent with the intention of being transmitted to receivers.

Sometimes other people besides the intended receiver pick up the message, as in eavesdropping situations. In these cases, the unintended hearers are perceivers rather than receivers, and the message becomes an object to be perceived. For instance, I recently received an email from a male student that was intended for one of the female students in the class I was teaching. The message suggested that the

Figure 1.2   Sources of Information: Objects and Senders

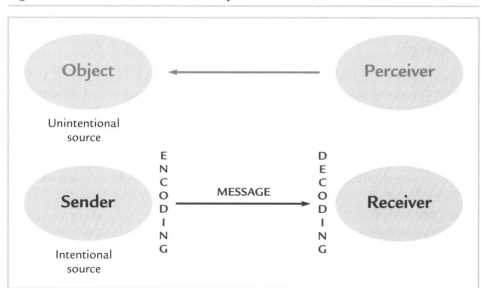

"Couldn't you give us less drastic feedback?"

woman needed to get out more on the weekends. The message was obviously not intended for me, but I received it, attended to it, and was affected by it. (I responded to the message, thanking the student for his concern and assuring him that I indeed would try to get out more on the weekends.)

Depending on the type of communication, the receiver's reaction to the original message might be perceived by the original sender. In essence, the original receiver's reaction then becomes a new message. Sometimes the receiver's reaction is called **feedback.** Feedback is easy to identify in the interactional communication model, in which one message responds to a previous message. In the transactional model, the sender and receiver are both sending and receiving messages at the same time, and feedback is more difficult to discern, but it does occur.

■ *Messages*

We have been using the term *messages* to refer to what it is that we send and receive in communication. More formally, **messages** are the units of information that we intentionally convey to one another. Messages involve the creation of a patterned and ordered set of verbal and nonverbal behaviors.[7]

Imagine this scenario: You go into a McDonald's and look up at the menu over the counter. Having decided what you'd like, you encode this thought into a verbal message that will effectively communicate what you want. So you say, "I'd like a Big Mac, Coke, and fries, please." The counterperson asks, "Would that be a large Coke and large fries?" Without saying a word, you nod your head up and down, a motion that in U.S. culture means yes. Thus, throughout this exchange, you have used both words and nonverbal gestures to convey your messages.

Senders intentionally create messages to affect receivers in some particular way. Messages are not always effective, however (see Figure 1.3); senders don't al-

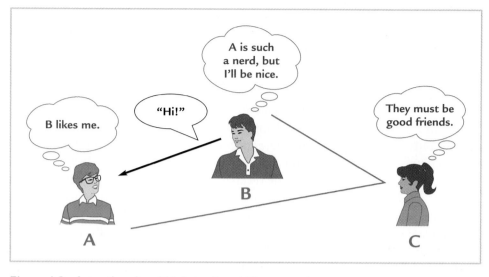

Figure 1.3 Intentional and Unintentional Messages

ways evoke the effect they intended. In Figure 1.3, person A, the receiver, gains information by attending to and decoding the message from sender B. However, person C also gains information (in this case, wrongly interpreted information) by observation.

Culture specificity.   Messages are culture specific. This means that a thought encoded in one culture is not encoded in the same way in another culture. If you've taken a foreign language, you have learned a second set of words to describe concepts for which you already have words.

Moreover, what we learn as the formal language of a country often differs from the language in everyday use. There are lots of special words and meanings used in everyday interactions that are not covered in language classes. International students attending college in the United States often find that the first challenge they face in communicating with U.S. students is learning slang and idiomatic phrases. Telling a Japanese student that you are "boiling over with anger" might evoke a strange look as the student watched for steam coming from your ears.

Content and relationship dimensions.   Messages are composed of two dimensions: content and relationship.[8] The *content dimension* is the one we most easily recognize. The content dimension represents the face value of a message, the information that is explicitly stated.

But every message also reflects the sender's feelings about his or her relationship with the receiver. This *relational dimension* conveys feelings about the other person, reflects power, and reinforces a certain communication pattern.

In the following dialogue, the content dimension concerns a project that two people are doing together. Can you discern the relational dimension?

PERSON A   Do you have your part of the project done yet?
PERSON B   No. But, but, um, I should have. I mean, I'll have it by the end of the day.

PERSON A   I'm getting kind of tired of your empty promises.

PERSON B   I know, I know. I'll have it done today, I really will. I've just been swamped.

PERSON A   I hope that I can trust you. I really don't want to jeopardize our relationship.

You should be able to tell that person A has a bit more power than person B. A is controlling the interaction and apparently has supervisory responsibility over B. The content in the final speech actually addresses the relationship explicitly.

Each message you create and communicate to other people reflects your perception of the relationships and the receivers. You've probably noticed speakers who act "uppity" or seem to look down on the audience. As an audience member, you also convey your view of the relationship with the speaker. For instance, do you sit back with your arms folded, gazing out the window, or do you lean forward, watching the speaker intently, frequently nodding in agreement? These behaviors reflect your attitude toward the speaker—your relational message.

According to the discussion in the text, which of the following situations involve messages and which do not?

1. A billboard sign advertising a hotel
2. A friend who waves at you from across the street
3. A flyer about a charity car wash, left on your car's windshield
4. Watching a referee throw up a penalty flag during a college football game
5. A referee signaling that you committed a foul during a basketball game
6. Listening to a conversation that your parents are having in the front seat of the car
7. Watching from the sidewalk as someone in front of you hails a cab
8. Someone hailing down the cab you are driving

■ Noise

A lot of things interfere with the degree of accuracy with which our messages get through to other people. No two people ever have exactly the same meaning for the same message; there is always an element of distortion, or noise.

Noise is anything that causes a message to get lost or be decoded in a manner different from the way it was intended. There are essentially three types of noise: external, or environmental; internal, or psychological; and physiological.

You are already well acquainted with the concept of *external* noise. You have confronted external noise as you talked to friends over the blaring sounds of a rock concert or a loud party. You have missed parts of instructors' lectures as jets or trains passed by the classroom. External noises really are stimuli that compete with a speaker for your attention. Many of us have tried to carry on a conversation while a TV or radio is on in the same room, only to be frustrated by the other person's failing to listen to us. Sights, sounds, feelings, and smells that fill our environment are all potential sources of noise. Speakers, too, can be a source of external noise that interferes with their own messages. You have probably found yourself distracted by another person's particular speech mannerisms: for instance, fidgeting, speaking in a monotone, or taking long pauses.

Internal, or *psychological,* noise is similar to external noise, except that the stimuli that distract us derive not from the surrounding environment but from our own thoughts. Listening to someone while you are thinking about what you are fixing for dinner tonight might prevent you from hearing the message accurately. Your thoughts about dinner are a form of psychological noise. Daydreaming during a class lecture or as your boss conducts the weekly staff meeting is another example of noise created by your own internal thought process.

Some noise is actually caused by physical breakdowns, handicaps, or impairments. Such *physiological* noises include speech disorders, accents, hearing loss, fatigue, and illness. The source of the physiological noise can be either the speaker or the listener.

What external, internal, or physiological noises can you identify that occur during a class period, preventing you from accurately receiving the instructor's message?

■ *Channels (Modes)*

You know the word *channel* from television. This text will use the term in a somewhat similar way. **Channels,** or **modes,** are the pathways on which our messages travel.

In everyday life, just as on TV, you can choose one of several channels, or modes, to relay your message. If you want to encode the feeling of love for another person, you can use the sound mode, saying, "I love you." Or you can remain silent and use touch as your mode by giving a warm hug. Or, using the smell mode, you could put on the special cologne that he or she likes. Or you might use the visual mode and send a written note that says, "I love you."

You can use more than one mode at a time to communicate your message. For instance, you could say, "I love you" while hugging the other person. Most of our communication tends to be multichanneled. Many of our messages contain both a verbal element, communicated through sound or light, and a nonverbal message communicated through various other modes.

■ Categories of Human Communication

A situation in which two people are having a conversation is significantly different from one in which a million people happen to be watching the same TV show. The communication components that we have identified—context, sender, receiver, message, noise, and channel—are present in both of these situations, but with differences. For example:

- The TV is limited to two modes (sound and light), while the two people can use the additional modes of touch and smell.
- The TV show is unchanging and unaffected by viewers' immediate reactions to it. In contrast, the flow of the conversation between the two people is very much affected by their responses to each other.

Because situations can be so different, people who study communication often divide it into several major categories. In this section, you will read about the qualities that define each of these categories.

Talk to the Animals

This excerpt from a magazine article discusses a talking parrot named Alex. Do you think Alex is engaging in human communication as it is defined in this chapter? Do you think animals other than humans are capable of human communication?

At first sight Alex appears out of place, somebody's pet brought in for the day and plopped down in a corner of the modern research laboratory at the University of Arizona. But the impression is wrong. Alex *is* the research. An African Grey, *Psittacus erithacus*, he lacks the gaudy greens and yellows of many species. Despite his silky sheen and crimson tail feathers, he seems duller than the average parrot. Perched on the back of a metal folding chair with newspapers unceremoniously spread underneath, he shifts his feet nervously and turns an owlish eye toward anyone who approaches.

"Alex, how many?" A researcher holds up a purple metal key and a larger green plastic key. The parrot stares, turning his head slowly: The question hangs for fifteen silent seconds. Why expect an answer? Doesn't "to parrot" mean "to mimic mindlessly"? But then the parrot says, "Two."

The same two keys are held up with a different question. "Which is bigger?" Again the parrot stares, pauses, then says, "Green key." Next is a wooden Popsicle stick. "What matter?" Again the long pause, again a correct answer: "Wood."

Getting the stick as a reward, Alex splinters it in his massive beak. It's strange to watch this bird perform—especially strange for anyone with a background in traditional science. For years the assumption had been that "talking" birds are nothing but mimics, attaching no meaning to their "words." But this parrot seems to crush that assumption as easily as he crushes Popsicle sticks. . . .

The researcher, Irene Pepperberg, describes earlier experiments in which birds solved problems based on numbers.

"In all these tests the birds 'responded' by picking a certain item. There was no vocal response. In the 1940's and 1950's a psychologist named Mowrer tried to teach parrots to use words for objects, and that effort failed. But I thought it should be possible to teach a bird to use at least a few vocal labels. The vocal behavior of birds is such a rich subject. Some individual march wrens, for example, will use hundreds of different songs, and a lot is known about how some birds learn their songs in different contexts—suggesting that they attach some meaning to the sounds. So why not see if those meanings could be attached to specific objects?" . . .

Next question: "What color?" Alex eyes the blue toy truck and reaches for it. Pepperberg pulls it away. "No. Tell me what color?" Alex pauses and then says, "Want a nut." Pepperberg speaks sharply and turns away: "No! Bad parrot! Pay attention. What color?" Finally he gets it out ("Blhoo"), and gets to play with the truck.

Then he has a request of his own: "Want pah-ah." "Better!" says Pepperberg. "Say it better." Alex tries again. "Want pah-ssdah." "Okay, that's pretty good," says Pepperberg, and hands him a piece of raw pasta. He crunches it hard, sending a shower of fragments to join the accumulation of crushed shredded-wheat squares, Popsicle sticks, and grapes on the newspaper below.

Then Pepperberg holds up three spools of different sizes and colors. "Which is smaller?" Show Alex a paper triangle and ask, "What shape?" and he'll say, "Three-corner." Show him five Popsicle sticks dyed red and ask, "What color?" and he'll say, "Rose." Then ask, "How many?" and he'll say, "Five." He is clearly responding to the question itself, as well as to the objects. He understands "different" and "same" and can answer questions about relationships: Show him a blue-dyed cork and blue key and ask, "What's the same?" he will answer, "Color." Show him two identical squares of rawhide and ask, "What's different?" and he will say, "None." Substitute a pentagon for one square, and he will answer, "Shape."

To do these things, Alex must understand the question, analyze several qualities, compare them, and search his vocabulary; he is processing information on several levels. None of this is simple memorization. On questions of size or color or shape, "different" or "same," Alex scores slightly better with new objects than with familiar ones; novelty seems to focus his attention. . . .

Alex does not seem to know the meaning of "bad parrot" or "good parrot" or "pay attention" but tones of approval and disapproval are enough to influence him. Another factor to reinforce learning: appropriate rewards. Past experiments with birds had rewarded "correct behavior" with food. But when Alex names an object correctly he is rewarded with the object itself; he may examine it, scratch himself with it, or chew it for several minutes before he loses interest and drops it. . . .

The author describes the interaction in Pepperberg's laboratory among people from different scientific disciplines.

The multidisciplinary feeling and constant lively debate are like a microcosm of Pepperberg's field. Researchers trying to open two-way communication with animals are caught in the crossfire of a controversy that has been running for decades. On one side are the strict behaviorists, who suggest that animals have no real thought processes, no consciousness, no awareness of their own actions. At the other extreme are those who maintain that animals may indeed be thinking and that science should inquire what they are thinking about. Joining this far-reaching debate are psychologists, linguists, and philosophers who ask: What is awareness? What is language? Do things like "belief" and "desire" really exist, even in humans?

The arguments continue, but the study of animal minds—now dignified with the name "cognitive ethology"—is gaining stature as a legitimate field. Researchers have managed to open limited dialogues with various mammals: chimpanzees, gorillas, orangutans, dolphins, sea lions. And joining this cast of "smart" mammals on stage is one Grey parrot. "We haven't gone as far as the chimpanzee or marine mammal studies," says Pepperberg. "But up to this point Alex has performed as well as the chimps or dolphins." No other researcher has taken bird communication to this level.

Source: Reprinted from the September/October 1991 issue of *Audubon Magazine*. Byline: Kenn Kaufman. To subscribe to Audubon, call 800-274-4201.

■ *Intrapersonal Communication*

It's almost noon, and you are just finishing up with a customer's order. You start thinking about what you are going to do for lunch and about whether you will have enough time to run some errands during your lunch hour. As you consider these issues, you are engaging in intrapersonal communication.

Intrapersonal communication is communication within ourselves; in essence, it is our thoughts, our self-discussions, our talk directed to ourselves. You might not think about this as a form of human communication, but it is.

What makes this communication? It has all the usual elements: Something stimulates a message that we send (to ourselves) and respond to. What makes it specifically *human* communication is the use of symbols to represent ideas and the formation of specific message units.[9] In our prelunch scenario, the message is similar to any message we might convey to another person, except that it is unspoken. As a matter of fact, sometimes we unconsciously vocalize our thoughts—we literally talk to ourselves.

As you read this text. you may be engaging in intrapersonal communication that sounds something like the following: "I'm getting tired of reading this; maybe I should take a break. Let me see how many more pages there are in this chapter. If it's not too many, I'll keep reading. I could use a snack about now, though." Intrapersonal communication often takes the form of cognitive analysis. We analyze situations, relationships, and even ourselves. We also use intrapersonal communication as a way to solve problems, evaluate issues, resolve conflicts, and contemplate an interaction with someone.[10]

Sometimes intrapersonal communication acts as noise during other forms of communication. We can get caught up in our own intrapersonal communication while interacting with others. We sometimes refer to this as "spacing out." Another problem with intrapersonal communication occurs when we deliver *egocentric* messages to other people without realizing the need to adapt the message.[11] We might use terms or phrases that have unique meaning to us, unrecognized by others. Have you ever talked with someone who continually mentioned the names of people you didn't know, clearly assuming you knew those people? This is an example of egocentric communication.

■ *Interpersonal Communication*

When we bring another person into the communication situation, we potentially have interpersonal communication.

Interpersonal communication occurs when two or more people transactionally influence one another. Remember from our earlier discussion of communication models that *transactional* means that the process is mutual and simultaneous. Thus, in interpersonal communication, two or more people have a mutual and simultaneous effect on one another.[12]

For example, you are sitting in a doctor's waiting room. You notice the person sitting across from you who is reading a magazine. So far, this is not interpersonal communication. However, you both reach for the same magazine that lies on the table between you. You look up, smile, and let the other person take the magazine. Interpersonal communication has occurred, albeit at a very impersonal level. Interpersonal communication has occurred because both of you affected and were affected by the other person at the same time. At this point, you may start talking about the cover of the magazine or some other issue, in which case it is much easier to see that interpersonal communication is taking place.

Two people make a **dyad.** Therefore, when only two people are involved in the interaction, it is sometimes referred to as a special form of interpersonal communication called **dyadic communication.**

Chapters 6 and 7 present a more detailed discussion of interpersonal communication, from the simple occurrence of mutual awareness at one end of a continuum to intimate disclosures and mutual confirmations of value at the other end. You will also see how interpersonal communication is used as the primary method for developing and managing interpersonal relationships.

■ *Interviewing*

Interviewing is a goal-structured form of interpersonal communication in which one party plays the role of interviewer and the other party plays the role of interviewee. The interviewer is the person who primarily asks the questions, and the interviewee is the person who primarily responds.

There are many types of interviews, including employment interviews, problem-solving interviews, and information action interviews (in which the interviewer seeks information to aid in a certain action). You probably think of

In interviews, one person typically asks questions and another person provides answers.

interviews primarily in the context of getting a job. However, you will participate in far more information-gaining and problem-solving interviews than employment interviews during the course of your career.

You will frequently find yourself in need of some piece of information, for example, and will seek out people who have the information and ask them questions to gain it. That is, you will conduct an interview. You may visit an instructor to find out about an upcoming assignment; you may seek information about recent manufacturing developments from someone you work with; or you may ask potential sales prospects about their product needs and requirements.

In Chapter 8, you will learn more about interviews, including the nature of the information obtained, how we respond to questions, and how to phrase questions effectively. Chapter 9 includes tips for being effective as both an interviewer and an interviewee.

■ *Small Group Communication*

When a third person is added to a dyad, a funny thing begins to happen to the dynamics of the interaction. In a dyad, both individuals are potentially equal in power and responsibility for listening and speaking. But when three or more people get together, they can begin to form coalitions, associating with one member rather than another. As the number of group participants increases, speaking time becomes more limited, and responsibility for listening increases.

Small group communication involves interpersonal communication among three or more people who view themselves as a group and who are working toward a shared purpose or goal. It is interpersonal communication because there is mutual and simultaneous influence or interaction occurring among the members.[13] Small groups have a common purpose that unites the individuals and gives them a sense of group identity.

When the group includes more than about twenty people, the opportunity for mutual and simultaneous influence is lost. The format of interaction becomes more like a discussion forum or business meeting, and this type of situation is not considered small group communication.

Small groups can be classified according to where they fall on a continuum from social orientation to task orientation.[14] There are groups whose main goal is to have a good time, to be social. There are also groups whose main goal is to accomplish some rigorous task, solve a problem, or make a decision. Of course, nearly all groups tend to demonstrate a blend of those two qualities. Even social groups have to make decisions and solve problems (What time shall we start the party? Where do we want to go for dinner?). Task groups, on the other hand, often spend time before a meeting discussing personal issues. During meetings, in fact, task groups deal with relational issues among members and frequently engage in activities with a social dimension (the power lunch, office parties, cocktails at the boss's house).

Chapter 10 will focus on the dynamics and forces that affect group process. Particular attention will be placed on problem-solving and decision-making groups. Chapter 11 will provide you with guidelines for being an effective group member and for planning, organizing, and leading decision-making groups.

Jot down a list of groups that you belong to, including formal organizational groups and informal social groups. Are some predominantly task oriented? Do these have a social element as well? Are some predominantly socially oriented?

Think about the roles that you play in each group. How does your role differ from group to group? Why?

▪ Organizational Communication

Organizational communication can simplistically be defined as communication that occurs in organizations.[15] Despite the accuracy of this definition, it is rather circular. We can improve on it by specifying what we mean by an organization. An **organization** is a group of interdependent individuals brought together in a hierarchical structure to perform a variety of structured tasks toward the accomplishment of some goal.[16]

You have probably noticed that the definitions of small groups and organizations are similar. In fact, there are organizations that are small groups. When an organization is small (three to fifteen members), the members often interact as a small group. Larger organizations are distinctly different from small groups, but often rely on small groups to perform certain tasks. A school, for instance, is an organization made up of a complex structure of interdependent units that rely on groups such as committees to plan, make decisions, and implement policies.

Some of the theories associated with organizational communication will be covered in Chapter 15. You will read about formal and informal organizational communication networks as well as vertical and horizontal hierarchies. Chapter 16 discusses ways in which you can use communication more effectively in an organization, with a particular focus on effective managerial communication.

▪ Presentational Communication

Presentational communication is primarily an actional form of communication in which one person speaks most of the time and other people listen. In general, presentational communication involves a speaker who is face to face with an audience. Presentations have a general purpose to inform, persuade, or entertain. The specific goal is determined by the speaker, the audience, and the situation.

Variations in topic, goals, audience size, and audience composition require speakers to adapt their presentations. The nature of the presentation varies from informal and spontaneous to formal and well-planned. You might be called upon, without prior notice, to informally update board members about an ongoing project. Or you might be required to formally address the annual stockholders meeting and provide a year-end review. The amount of interaction between you and your audience creates unique speaking challenges. In the informal presentation, members of the audience might interrupt you with questions and comments, creating an interaction almost interpersonal in nature. In the formal presentation, the audience might react with laughter or applause (or heckling) but would likely not ask questions or provide much feedback.

Chapters 12, 13, and 14 are devoted to presentational communication. To provide you with enough resources to develop and present an effective speech, these chapters discuss the basic issues related to effectively informing and persuading an audience, including guidelines for analyzing an audience, developing a topic, researching a topic, organizing and developing an outline, and delivering the presentation.

■ *Mass Communication*

Mass communication is the development and transmission of messages to a large (mass) audience through electronic or mechanical means. Mass communication encompasses newspapers, magazines, radio, television, movies, and now computer-mediated communication, such as the Internet. In mass communication, a common message is transmitted to a large audience simultaneously.

Like public speaking, mass communication typically involves a speaker and a listener, except that both roles are usually played by groups. Feedback is limited in mass communication because of the lack of an interactive environment, but this is changing with the onset of interactive TV and Internet applications.

Mass communication has the same purposes as presentations—to entertain, inform, and persuade:

- *Entertainment.* Soap operas, situational comedies, and dramatic series are designed to entertain us (though there are many shows people would claim are far from entertaining).
- *Information.* Newscasts and news magazines are designed to inform us, but there is also a strong element of entertainment associated with informative broadcasts as they attempt to gain and hold our attention.
- *Persuasion.* The most apparent use of the media for persuasive purposes is through advertising, commercials, and "infomercials." The media are used persuasively to get viewers to purchase products, support some principle or cause, or change viewer behavior in some other way (as in "Don't Drink and Drive" campaigns).

Although this text does not treat mass communication in depth, you'll find that many of the principles you learn in other chapters apply to mass media, as well.

■ *Intercultural and Multicultural Communication*

Each of us has been influenced by the culture in which we were raised. We have internalized the values, attitudes, traditions, customs, and language of a given culture.

In general, we associate culture with nationality. People from different countries are said to be from different cultures. There are also subcultures within each country that affect our communication. Subcultures usually develop because of some shared or common denominators: religion, race, ethnicity, and even sex. Some argue that men represent a different subculture from women. People who share a culture or subculture often develop unique ways of thinking and communicating. John Gray has made a fortune trying to teach men and women to understand each other's subculture with his book *Men Are from Mars, Women Are from Venus.*

Intercultural communication is the communication that occurs between or among individuals from different cultures or subcultures.[17] If you travel to a foreign country, your interactions with the natives of that country are intercultural. Such interactions are sometimes difficult and challenging, especially when the communication rules and meanings are considerably different in the two cultures. You may create extra communication problems by failing to recognize the cultural differences and communicating ethnocentrically—that is, assuming that people from another culture have the same cultural values that you do or that your culture is superior to another. This is a source of problems in communication between men and women, too.

The problems of intercultural communication are compounded when we have **multicultural interaction,** in which members of several cultures are interacting. You have probably been in a classroom where several different cultures are represented. Multicultural communication requires the participants to be especially sensitive to the diverse backgrounds of the other members.

Intercultural communication is not really a separate communication category because it never occurs outside the categories already discussed. For example, we can have interpersonal, small group, organizational, and mass communication involving participants from many cultures. Still, communication between individuals from different cultures does have unique characteristics that you should appreciate. Given the presence of intercultural dynamics in all of the communication categories, the topic of intercultural communication will be integrated throughout this text.

Try connecting with someone from another country through the Internet. There are a number of pen pal services that can be found by entering *pen pal* in a search engine. See if you can find three differences between the way you communicate in your culture and the way the other person communicates in his or her culture.

If the differences aren't apparent after interacting with the individual, ask your pen pal a few specific questions about communication behavior. For example, you could ask:

- How do you communicate liking for another person?
- What is communication like between an employer and an employee?
- If you are upset with a friend about something, what do you say or do?
- What is the dating process like in your country?

Summary

Effective communication is an important quality for success in both your professional and your personal life. Communication is acting on information: When communication has occurred, some change results. The actional communication model involves one thing acting on another; the interactional communication model reflects a series of actions and reactions; and the transactional communication model represents simultaneous action and reaction.

Human communication is a special form of communication between and among humans using signs and symbols. Signs are stimuli with fixed meanings, whereas symbols are stimuli with arbitrary and abstract meanings.

Why do we communicate? Satisfying needs is the most overriding reason. We also communicate to gain information, to manage relationships, to derive pleasure and entertainment, to get self-validation, to coordinate and manage tasks, and to persuade someone or gain something.

There are six components often identified with human communication: context, source (sender), and receiver, messages, noise, and channels (modes). Context refers to the circumstance and surroundings in which communication occurs. The sender is the origin of encoded messages. The receiver is the recipient and decoder of the messages. Messages are the units of information we intentionally convey to one another—patterned and ordered sets of words and nonverbal behaviors. Noise is anything that interferes with a communication or causes a message to be decoded in a manner different from the way it was intended. Channels, or modes, are the pathways we use to convey messages.

Human communication can be classified into several categories, each with its own unique qualities: intrapersonal communication, interpersonal communication, interviewing, small-group communication, organizational communication, presentational communication, mass communication, and intercultural and multicultural communication.

Key Terms

communication   Acting on information.

actional model of communication   Communication that involves a one-way process of action followed by a reaction.

interactional model of communication   Communication in which an action is followed by a reaction, which in turn becomes an action that leads to another reaction.

transactional model of communication   Communication in which two things simultaneously affect one another, both acting and reacting at the same time.

human communication   A special form of communication that occurs between and among people, involving the use of symbolic language as well as nonverbal cues.

signs   Stimuli with fixed and concrete meanings.

symbols   Stimuli with abstract, learned, arbitrary, flexible, and changing meanings.

context   A variable that surrounds and influences communication, including environmental, psychological, relational, situational, and cultural factors.

source   A person or object that intentionally or unintentionally becomes the origin of information.

objects   Stimuli we perceive that were not intentionally directed toward us.

perceiver   A person who attends to, perceives, decodes, and is affected by objects in the environment.

sender   A person who engages in a process of encoding and delivering a message to produce some effect.

encode   To put thoughts into the form of a message by selecting the words and actions that reflect the thoughts.

receiver   A person who attends to, perceives, attempts to decode, and is affected by another person's message.

decode   To translate a message by attributing meaning to what has been perceived.

feedback   A receiver's reaction to a message that then functions as a new message in and of itself.

messages   Units of information that we intentionally convey to one another.

noise   Anything that causes a message to be decoded in a manner different from the way it was intended.

channels   The pathways on which our messages travel; modes.

modes   The pathways on which our messages travel; channels.

intrapersonal communication   Communication that occurs within ourselves.

interpersonal communication   Communication in which two or more people transactionally influence one another.

dyad   Two people interacting as a pair.

dyadic communication   Communication between two people.

interviewing   A goal-structured form of interpersonal communication in which one party plays the role of interviewer and the other party plays the role of interviewee.

small group communication   Interpersonal communication among three or more people who view themselves as a group and who are working toward a shared purpose or goal.

organizational communication   Communication that occurs in organizations.

organization   A group of interdependent individuals brought together in a hierarchical structure to perform a variety of structured tasks toward the accomplishment of some goal.

presentational communication   An actional form of communication in which one person speaks most of the time and other people listen.

mass communication   The development and transmission of messages to a large audience through electronic or mechanical means.

intercultural communication   Communication that occurs between or among individuals from different cultures or subcultures.

multicultural interaction   Interaction among members of several cultures.

Review Questions

1. Define communication.
2. Explain the differences between the three models of communication.
3. Explain the similarities and differences between communication and human communication.
4. Explain why humans communicate.
5. What are the basic components of human communication?
6. Identify two of the categories of human communication, and explain how they are different.

Chapter 2

Context and Principles of Communication

Objectives

Studying this chapter will allow you to:
1. Identify and define the five contexts in which communication occurs.
2. Explain how various psychological qualities and personal characteristics affect communication.
3. Define four dimensions of culture.
4. Explain five general principles that connect context to communication.
5. Identify and explain four basic perspectives on human communication.

You have been up all night studying for a big exam. You are sitting by yourself in a remote corner of the student union or lounge having a cup of coffee and doing some last-minute review. An older man you don't know in rather ragged clothes comes up to you and asks for fifty cents so that he can buy coffee. You don't have time to deal with him, so you tell him to bug off.

A few minutes later, a student from another country—a young woman in the same class you are studying for—sits down next to you. You look up and smile, and she smiles back. New to the school, she asks you questions about what the food in the student union is like. With some degree of frustration about being interrupted again, you begin talking to her.

Why did you act differently toward these two individuals? What affected your communication with them?

This scenario actually reflects the effect of *context* on communication. There are five contexts at play in the student union scenario: psychological, relational, situational, environmental, and cultural:

- *Psychological.* The psychological context includes those personal, internal factors that affected you—lack of sleep, need to study, impending exam. Each of these influenced your reaction to the communication situation.
- *Relational.* The relational context involves your relationship or reaction to other people because of who they are. From the man's attire and demeanor, you reached certain conclusions that led to your sending him away. On the other hand, your preexisting relationship with the young woman, and her decision to sit down, influenced you to react in a different way.
- *Situational.* The situational context is the purpose for the interaction. The man wanted money; the student wanted friendship. These represent different purposes, or reasons, for interacting with you.
- *Environmental.* The environmental context in this scenario would be the student union or lounge, and more specifically, the remote corner where you were sitting. Student unions are public places that permit open and easy access to people. Choosing a remote corner, however, would normally signal to others that you do not want to be disturbed. However, someone from another culture might not know this social protocol.
- *Cultural.* The cultural context leads to different interpretations of communication. The young woman might have seen you as lonely and isolated, not as seeking privacy to study.

This chapter will discuss each of these types of context. It will also cover other basic principles of communication, such as uncertainty reduction and face, that will be relevant to the material presented in Part Two of this book. By understanding the basics presented in this chapter, you will have a foundation from which to improve your communication skills.

■ The Psychological Context

The **psychological context** (See Figure 2.1.) represents who we are and what we bring to any communication situation. In essence, the psychological context is your "self." Your psychological context represents the sum of your experiences—

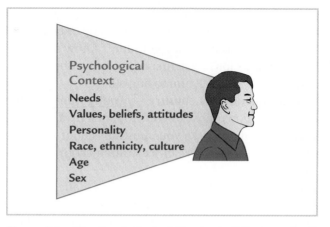

Figure 2.1   The Psychological Context of Communication

your upbringing, your education, your previous interactions. It is the product of your collective encounters with the world.

To decide what constitutes your psychological context, think about anything that you bring to a communication situation that affects the way you interpret, analyze, encode, or decode a message. Each person sees the world differently and communicates accordingly. The way you see the world is determined by your psychological context.

We can think of the psychological context as consisting of psychological qualities and personal characteristics. Let's first consider the psychological qualities.

■ *Psychological Qualities*

Psychological qualities include your needs, values, beliefs, attitudes, and personality. All of these factors affect your communication in many interesting ways.

Needs.   Whenever you engage in communication, you are satisfying some need. For instance, you might talk to your boss about getting an extra day off because of a social need to spend time with your family. If you hear a radio report about a flood in an area where you have family, you may turn on the TV news because of a need for more information. You may say "Hi" to a neighbor as you leave for school in the morning because you have a need to maintain a friendly relationship and to feel good about yourself as a friendly person.

Our needs vary in their intensity. Some needs, like saying "Hello" to a passerby, are relatively minor. In contrast, if you were making a presentation to a group of fellow citizens, trying to convince them to create a neighborhood watch, that might represent a rather intense need on your part—the need to protect yourself and your family.

Abraham Maslow classified and ranked the needs that motivate humans. His classification begins with very basic human needs and ends with a somewhat abstract notion of self-actualization. **Maslow's hierarchy of needs** is illustrated in Figure 2.2. The theory suggests that we work to fulfill our needs, starting with those at the bottom of the pyramid. After those needs are generally satisfied, we

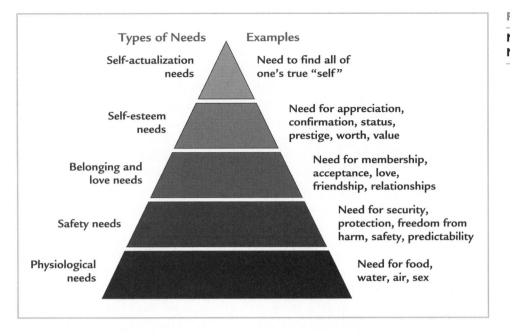

Figure 2.2

Maslow's Hierarchy of Needs

Types of Needs · Examples

Self-actualization needs — Need to find all of one's true "self"

Self-esteem needs — Need for appreciation, confirmation, status, prestige, worth, value

Belonging and love needs — Need for membership, acceptance, love, friendship, relationships

Safety needs — Need for security, protection, freedom from harm, safety, predictability

Physiological needs — Need for food, water, air, sex

move up to the next level. Communication is one of the tools we use in attempting to satisfy our needs.[1]

The satisfaction of needs may appear indirectly and implicitly in our behaviors. For instance, why are you taking a course in communication? What needs are being satisfied? At first you might say, "To get credits toward my degree," and you might not see how that motivation relates to Maslow's hierarchy. But then the question becomes: Why do you want a degree? The answer probably includes securing a job. You want a good job in order to get an income to buy food, provide shelter, and support and protect a family—in other words, to satisfy what Maslow called physiological and safety needs. Your answer might also include a desire to become a better person and to discover who you are and what you can be—in Maslow's terms, self-esteem and self-actualization needs. Fulfilling all these types of needs motivates you to communicate with others.

Flattery Will Get You Everywhere

Flattery in advertising? Oh, yes!

When done right, flattery works well in advertising. Many times it is so subtle, however, you don't notice it. But it is there, and it makes people feel good. See if you notice it in this catalog copy:

(Product: Women's Black Suit) "There are two kinds of people: those who emit light and those who absorb it. Luminosity is randomly inborn, of course. But anyone can increase the wattage by standing up straight, smiling, and wearing the

Advertisers create messages that try to persuade us and affect our buying decisions. This article demonstrates how messages can be constructed to appeal to the types of needs identified by Maslow.

right clothes. This really stunning suit is as right as you can get."—J. Peterman Company, catalog

(Product: Women's Dress) "Women instinctively understand the possibilities: midnight blue silk, swirling to fullness just above their ankles. See themselves advancing toward, then retreating from, the absolutely responsive Mr. K. or Mr. A. This isn't an MGM fantasy, this is real. Princess seams emphasizing a shapely waist flare to the full, sweeping skirt."—J. Peterman Company, catalog

In print advertising, good flattery resembles a compliment and is motivating. You probably noticed in these two examples that both descriptions give catalog readers an opportunity to feel good about herself. This is important in order to encourage the reader to visualize more than just another dress or suit in her closet; the good feelings offer the buyer a chance to fulfill a basic human need or desire.

Motivating Human Needs: Psychological

Naturally and instinctively, people will care for their psychological needs after their physiological needs—such as food, drink and rest—have been met. Psychological needs include security, power, love, curiosity, companionship, family preservation and many more.

Below, I have listed four psychological needs with an example. In each example notice how, in a complimentary fashion, the product or service helps the buyer satisfy a particular need.

- *Affiliation*. "Your membership dues (along with the dues of other members) enable the Society to fund the ventures of scientists such as Robert Ballard, Eugenie Clark, and Jane Goodall. So for you . . . and for the important research it fosters, isn't your membership in the National Geographic Society worth it . . . again? And we deeply appreciate your support."—National Geographic Society, direct mail piece
- *Belonging*. "Chances are, you've heard about something new coming down the pike here at Saturn . . . although our launch plans are a few years away—the news is true. We're very excited. And since you're part of the Saturn family, we thought this would be a good time to formally let you in on what's going on."—Saturn Corporation, letter
- *Independence*. "It's your money. Your future. Your retirement. Now, with the MarketPlace Variable Annuity, it's your decision how to make the most of all three. Invest for retirement on your terms."—John Hancock Variable Life Insurance Company, direct mail brochure
- *Pride*. "New Tomato. Park's OG 50 Whopper Improved, VFFNT Hybrid. It takes an extraordinary tomato to replace Park's Whopper. After only 65 days . . . you'll start harvesting big, red tomatoes . . . so they just won't let you down."—Park Seed Company, catalog

Motivating Human Needs: Desires

And then there are desires. Desires include sympathy, respect, happiness, comfort, fame, recognition, achievement and many more. Below, I have listed two desires with an example. Notice, again, how in each example the product or service helps the buyer satisfy a particular desire.

- *Prestige.* "Inside, you'll find a wealth of gift-giving options, each uniquely designed to impress, to inspire, to communicate your commitment to good business—and good taste. To ensure your satisfaction, your Personal Shopping Consultant will oversee your order from beginning to end."—Godiva Chocolatier, catalog
- *Status.* "If you're ready to make the leap from aspiring writer to published writer . . . let us show you the way! Become a published writer!"—Writer's Digest School, direct mail piece

Are you looking for a new direction for your next direct mail piece? Perhaps one of these motivating needs or desires can offer a new approach.

First, identify a list of needs or desires that your product or service could fulfill. Then, write a few lines of copy for your top two or three. Finally, develop a mail piece or response ad, and then test, test, test. Good luck.

Source: Linda Westphal, "Flattery Will Get You Everywhere," *Direct Marketing Magazine,* March 1998, p. 62. Copyright © 1998 by Linda Westphal, www.lindawestphal.com.

Think about how you use communication to accomplish each of the needs presented in Figure 2.2. For instance, to meet your need for food, you might use communication to order a Big Mac and fries or to place an order for lunch meat at a deli counter. What about the other needs?

Values, beliefs, and attitudes. As you have grown up, you have developed a number of values, beliefs, and attitudes. These are predispositions you have toward things: a set of preferences that you carry around in your head and apply to the world around you. Each of these affects your communication with other people.

- **Values** are deep-rooted conceptual responses about the worth or importance that you give something. Each person has a set of values that reflect what is important or valuable to him or her. You might value education, a close family, or having friends. Concepts that you hold as important are also values, such as religion, privacy, freedom of expression, or democracy.
- **Beliefs** are judgments concerning how things are or how they should be.[2] Beliefs are the convictions we have that something is true or not true. You might believe that the earth is relatively round, that people are basically good, and that a college education will get you a good job. You might also believe that there are no such things as ghosts, UFOs, or reincarnation.
- **Attitudes** are predisposed evaluative responses that we have developed toward persons, objects, or issues.[3] You might have a positive or negative attitude toward a TV program, a person you have met, or a job you have. Your

behavior toward people and things is affected by the attitudes you have toward them. This means that your attitude affects your communication. For instance, you try to talk more to people you like and less to people you don't like.

Values are the most embedded predispositions you hold. They influence your behavior the most, and they are the slowest to change. Beliefs, next in strength, are extensions of your values. Attitudes are the least ingrained of your predispositions. Attitudes reflect your values and beliefs but are more susceptible to change. Overall, you have more attitudes than beliefs and more beliefs than values. The relationship among these three sets of predispositions is illustrated in Figure 2.3.

For each of the following statements, decide the degree to which it reflects a belief, an attitude, or a value. Some statements reflect more than one quality. To what degree does each statement apply to you?

1. Without an education, you cannot succeed in today's world.
2. Corporations need to be more responsible to the environment and society.
3. Politics are corrupt.
4. I don't trust anyone who doesn't look me in the eye.
5. I like country music.
6. I won't take a job that interferes with my family time.
7. I think it's terrible that athletes are paid such incredible salaries compared to everyone else.
8. I wouldn't trade my time with my friends for anything.

Personality. **Personality** is the collection of qualities that people associate with how you behave and who you are. You might be described as aggressive or quiet, funny or serious, outgoing or shy, smart or shallow, caring or carefree.

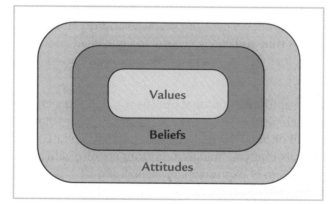

Figure 2.3

The Relationship between Values, Beliefs, and Attitudes

Values form the "core" of your predispositions; they are the fewest in number but the strongest in influence and the slowest to change. Beliefs are more numerous but less influential. Attitudes are the most numerous, the least influential, and the most susceptible to change.

A related concept is the symbolic self. George Herbert Mead coined the term **symbolic self** to represent a self that is the product of our symbolic interactions with others and that is defined or conceptualized through symbols. Your symbolic self includes your personality and other characteristics. It is how you think of yourself, how you describe yourself. For instance, I think of myself as funny, a bit boisterous, imaginative, a procrastinator, sensitive, musical, fatherly, an educator, and an author. Your body size, color of skin, nationality, interests, hobbies, and roles all contribute to your symbolic self.

On a piece of paper, create a list of ten terms to describe yourself. (Save this list for another exercise later in the chapter.) Where did these self-concepts come from? Think about how each one might affect your communication with others—and their communication with you.

For instance, if you are six feet eight inches tall and 300 pounds, do people act differently toward you than toward other people? If you are smart, how does that affect how you act in a team problem-solving situation?

■ *Personal Characteristics*

Your **personal characteristics** include your age, sex, race, ethnic background, and culture.

Age.   Age is generally a good measure of the amount of your life experience. The older you get, the more experiences you have had that affect who you are and how you think. Of course, simply having more and more experiences doesn't necessarily mean that you will gain from them. You also need the abilities to observe, analyze, recall, and understand the nature of your experiences.

Think about how the accumulation of experiences in going to school year after year has changed who you are. When you first started school, you didn't know what to expect. The first years of your education involved learning the rules of classroom behavior—when to talk, when to sit still, when to raise your hand. As you advanced through your education, you experienced different teachers and teaching styles. Your first days in college were probably considerably different from your previous educational experiences. Seniors act differently than first-year students because they have accumulated four or five (sometimes more) years of college experience. Similarly, nontraditional college students (for instance, those who have returned to school after working for many years) experience college in a different way than traditional students.

Connect to a chat room through the Internet. As you interact with the others online, see if you can guess their ages by the way they are communicating. After you have made your guesses, ask them to tell you (realizing, of course, that not everyone is open and honest online!). How far off were you? Why? What cues did you use to judge age? How does interacting with someone a lot older or younger than you affect the way you communicate?

Sex. Cultures vary in the way they define the roles of men and women. A **sex role** is a set of behaviors associated with a particular sex. In the United States, there are a number of traditional qualities associated with the roles that men and women play, and these affect how we communicate.

As you must have noticed, people treat women and men differently. When people are consistently treated a certain way because of their sex, they develop sex-based behaviors and attitudes. Each person varies, however, in how much he or she adopts these culturally defined sex roles. Think about your own upbringing. Were there strong female and male role models for you to follow? Were you prevented from playing with, or encouraged to play with, dolls, guns, model airplanes, or toy kitchen sets? To what degree did those influence the development of a sex role?

Men and women often differ in their beliefs, attitudes, values, and personalities. Many studies have found differences between men and women in such matters as level of self-disclosure, use of "powerful" or "powerless" language, and use of touch, as well as in aggressiveness, competitiveness, directness, and bluntness. However, the findings of such studies are often contradictory.

One scholar developed a theory that classifies people by their psychological sex type rather than by their physiology.[4] The **psychological sex types** of "masculine" and "feminine" include social stereotypical behaviors associated with male and female sex roles. For instance, aggression is considered a masculine trait and sensitivity a feminine trait. Thus, an aggressive person would be considered psychologically masculine, at least on that one dimension, regardless of whether the individual was actually male or female. Similarly, a sensitive person would be labeled psychologically feminine irrespective of his or her biological sex.

One problem with this approach is the arbitrariness of classifying aggression as a masculine trait and sensitivity as a feminine trait. We all have characteristics that can be classified as masculine or feminine, although sometimes we are embarrassed to admit that we have qualities that contradict our sex roles.

In this book, rather than trying to identify a variety of possible differences between men and women, the concern is more with how the behaviors typically associated with sex roles affect communication. For instance, a person's aggressive orientation—whether the person is a man or a woman—would affect the communication in a team. If a team member says something like, "I really don't feel right about this, but if it's what everyone else wants, I guess I'll go along," an aggressive person might react by saying, "Good, let's get to the next issue." However, a sensitive team member might say, "You don't seem very comfortable with the decision. What can we do to make you feel better about it?" These different responses may have substantially different effects on the group's subsequent progress. Remember, though, that some people will interpret the same message differently, depending on whether it was said by a women or by a man.

Go back to the list of terms you wrote down earlier to describe yourself. For each one, decide whether that quality would be viewed as "masculine" or "feminine" in the United States. If you are female, how would you feel about having a large number of qualities that are labeled "masculine"? If you are male, how would you feel about having a large number of qualities that are labeled "feminine"? What has happened to you in the past when you displayed a quality associated with the other sex?

Race, ethnicity, and culture.   Just as a person's sex can affect communication, so can race, ethnicity, and culture. In fact, your values, beliefs, and attitudes reflect your racial, ethnic, and cultural background.

The degree to which a group has a unique influence on its members depends on how much a group has distinguished itself from the larger cultural or social entity. In the past (and still today), large cities like New York, Chicago, and San Francisco have had separate communities associated with a single ethnic group, such as Chinese Americans, Italian Americans, and Polish Americans. These ethnic groups have maintained their distinct cultures even within the boundaries of the larger community. They have continued to speak their native languages and patronize their own schools, churches, and stores.

You might not recognize it, but you have been affected by the racial, ethnic, and cultural factors in your upbringing. If you are from a small town in Iowa, you have developed different ways of looking at the world than people from other communities. If you are from the multicultural islands of Hawaii, you have a different set of values than others. Even if you have moved around a lot, each place you have lived has a culture that has influenced how you view the world and how you communicate.

One researcher identified four dimensions on which cultures differ: individualism/collectivism, uncertainty avoidance, masculinity/femininity, and power distance.[5] These dimensions are a convenient way of thinking about how cultures can affect our communication. Let's look at each of them in turn.

1. *Individualism/collectivism.*   Some cultures emphasize the individual, while others emphasize the larger social group. In essence, some cultures are "I" oriented, while others are "we" oriented. In an *individualistic* culture, people are concerned first with their own personal enjoyment and enrichment. They are less influenced by in-groups (such as religious or social groups) than are members of collectivistic cultures. *Collectivistic* cultures, in contrast, place the common good of the group above that of the individual. Family, company, community, and country might be the most significant values held by members of a collectivistic culture. Overall, the United States is considered a highly individualistic culture, but there are certainly elements of collectivism present as well. Among other things, the degree of individualism or collectivism in a culture affects people's willingness to communicate with others, to participate in teams, and to join organizations.

2. *Uncertainty avoidance.* Uncertainty avoidance has to do with how much tolerance a given culture has for ambiguity and uncertainty. In cultures with a high level of uncertainty avoidance, there are often many rules, laws, and rituals that promote clarity and conformity. These cultures are very nationalistic and repress dissension.[6] Also, in cultures with high uncertainty avoidance, people tend to avoid aggressive and competitive behaviors, have a lower motivation for achievement, see loyalty to an employer as a virtue, and worry about the future.[7]

The United States generally falls in the middle range for uncertainty avoidance, though people have their own individual levels of tolerance. Take a moment to think about your own level of uncertainty avoidance. Do you have a high need for knowing all the rules of a game before you start? Are you uncomfortable when an instructor doesn't have a syllabus for a course and doesn't explain what your grade will be based on? If so, you are demonstrating a low tolerance for uncertainty. As another example, how well would you tolerate listening to a presentation from an individual from another country who, despite being articulate and fluent, didn't seem to have any clear structure or purpose to the speech? How would your tolerance or intolerance impact the speaker's effectiveness?

Because communication helps us gain information, it serves to reduce uncertainty. To increase our understanding and certainty, we can ask questions, seek information, and provide feedback—options that will be explored throughout this book.

3. *Masculinity/femininity.* The notion of masculinity and femininity is essentially the same one that was considered in the earlier discussion of sex roles. The point here is that entire cultures can be classified according to the degree to which they embody masculine or feminine characteristics. Feminine cultures value flexibility in sex roles, quality of life, service, and interdependence.[8] Masculine cultures value power, assertiveness, strong definition of sex roles, ambition, independence, achievement, and work.

The United States, as you might guess, is considered a masculine culture. Masculine cultures tend to place more value on male work than on female work—a characteristic reflected in the continued discrepancy in pay between males and females doing the same jobs in the United States.[9]

4. *Power distance.* The fourth and final cultural variable is called power distance. **Power** generally means the ability of people to influence other people in order to accomplish their goals. *Power distance* has to do with how a culture distributes power among its members. Cultures with high power distance clearly define and distinguish among their members on the basis of power. There is an expectation of obedience, servitude, conformity, and authoritarianism. Cultures with low power distance show a greater respect for equality of power.

You may have noticed that some Asian students are reluctant to ask questions in class or respond to questions from an instructor. Some of that reluctance could be attributed to the way power distance defines relationships in their cultures: Teachers might be defined as figures of authority and students as people subject to authority. Thus, students would see their role as remaining quiet and respectful.

Differences in power affect whom you talk to and how you talk. The United States tends to fall just below the midrange on scores of power distance, but there are many variations among individuals. When you interact with a boss who maintains strong power differences, you keep your distance and limit how much you talk. On the other hand, you may have had bosses who are very "approach-able" and try to reduce the power difference between you and them. You would probably spend more time with these bosses than with the others, reveal more about yourself, and talk about a wider variety of topics.

Think about how each of the four cultural dimensions applies to you. Then consider how your own values compare with those for the United States in general. What factors (family, education, traveling, and so forth) may have caused you to differ from mainstream U.S. culture?

Ask Yourself

■ The Relational Context

As you have seen, the psychological context involves what we bring to a communication situation regardless of who the other person is. The relational context, in contrast, involves our reactions to the specific person with whom we are communicating. That is, the **relational context** is how we behave and react because of who the other person is.

In every communication activity, there is a relationship between those who are communicating. We act differently toward different people, altering our communication behavior in accordance with the nature of the relationship. For instance, you act differently toward your employers, friends, family, teachers, coaches, and classmates. Each relationship has a defining set of communication expectations that makes up the context.

■ *Effects of the Relational Context*

The relational context affects the way you encode and decode messages. For example, to communicate your love for your mother, you might give her a hug and say, "Love ya, Ma." To communicate your love for your spouse, you might kiss and cuddle while whispering, "Darling, I love you so much." In these cases, your relationship affects the way you communicate your love.

Similarly, the relational context alters the meanings you attribute to the messages you receive. The meaning you derive from your mother's saying "I love you" is different from the meaning of the same phrase uttered by your spouse. The meaning is based on who the other person is; it is based on the relationship.

As these examples show, the effect of the relational context is easy to recognize in an interpersonal interaction. In other communication situations, the relational context may not be so apparent, but it is still a vital influence. Imagine a team of five people. Each of them is affected by the presence of the other four. The role each person gets to play is greatly affected by the roles the other people play. Suppose that two members want to play the role of leader. The ability to emerge as leader is dependent upon the other members' being followers. If the three nonleader members begin following the direction of one of the two leader candidates, the other candidate has no choice but to accept a nonleader role.

The relational context even affects mass communication. Think of two people, one who likes late-night TV host David Letterman and one who does not. Each person has a certain "relationship" with him, a relationship that is defined by the person's impression of, regard for, attraction to, and attitude toward David Letterman. It is a unilateral relationship, of course, in that Letterman does not have a specific impression or level of attraction to either of the viewers. But the viewer who likes Letterman will probably laugh at his jokes, even ones that the viewer wouldn't find funny if someone else told them. Similarly, the viewer who dislikes Letterman will probably think that his jokes are lame and unfunny, even though that viewer might like some of those jokes if told by another TV host. The two viewers' reactions are affected by the relationship each has with David Letterman.

■ *Factors Influencing the Relational Context*

A number of factors influence the relational context, including each of the psychological context factors discussed earlier. The personality, attitudes, values, beliefs, age, sex, race, ethnicity, and culture of the person with whom you are communicating affect your interpretation of and reaction to that person's messages. Each individual has a set of stereotypes, prejudices, and biases that are based on these personal qualities and characteristics.

For instance, you talk differently to a man than to a woman, albeit sometimes minutely. How would you react to the following statement if it were made by a male politician? "Daycare centers need to be established in major companies for the children of the employees." Now, how would you react to that same statement made by a female politician? Clearly, the sex of the speaker affects how we interpret the message.

The relational context depends on a variety of other factors as well, including relational history, attraction or liking, power, trust, and intimacy. If you have never seen David Letterman before, you have no relational history to bring to your interpretation of his communicative behavior. As you watch him for a while, however, you begin to develop that history. You develop an impression and attitude that then affect your future viewing. Similarly, our positive or negative feelings toward someone will obviously influence our interpretations of what that person says.

▌ The Situational Context

The needs of individuals in any communication interaction dictate the purpose, or reason, for the interaction, creating the **situational context.** If you are a waiter at a restaurant and an instructor of yours comes in for dinner, the situation dictates a different type of interaction than when the two of you are in a classroom. Your instructor depends on your taking the order accurately and bringing out the proper entrée. Power has shifted in the relationship because of the change in situational context.

Your perception of the situation affects your interpretation and understanding of the other person's communication as well as the way you communicate.

You have probably experienced the embarrassment of perceiving a situation differently than the person with whom you are interacting. For instance, imagine that a person you know and like, but have never dated, calls you up and asks you to meet for dinner. Your definition of the situation might include the anticipation of developing a romantic relationship. What if you then find out that the other person merely wants your advice as a friend about how to proceed in a romantic relationship with a third party? This misdefinition of the situation has served as the comic premise of more than one episode of TV shows like *Friends* and *Seinfeld*.

The difficulty occurs when the people involved have different reasons for communicating with each other. Sometimes the reasons are quite compatible, and communication progresses smoothly. At other times the reasons are incompatible, and this can produce conflict. For communication to flow effectively, participants need to reach some agreement about the reason for their interaction. In the date-advice situation, they would need to discuss and clarify their reason for interacting.

Knowing how each party views the situation has a strong impact on communication effectiveness. Giving a presentation to an audience that has "chosen" to attend is considerably different from speaking to an audience that has been "required" to attend. Think about your own attitude toward "required" courses as compared to those that you choose to take. The motivation to participate in a communication interaction is an important factor in the situational context.

■ The Environmental Context

You are working on a class project with a group of four other students. Do you meet in a library study room or at someone's apartment? Do you meet at seven o'-clock in the morning or eleven o'clock at night? Do you meet on Monday night or Friday night? The answers to these questions probably reflect how productive you anticipate the meeting to be. Meeting in the library at seven on a Monday morning will probably produce a more task-oriented, productive meeting than gathering at someone's apartment at eleven on a Friday night. In other words, the communication that occurs in your team is affected by a number of environmental factors, such as location and time of day.

The **environmental context** consists of those factors outside the individuals involved in the communication that nonetheless affect the communication. The environmental context includes such physical factors as location, furnishings (and their arrangement), room size, windows, decorations, temperature, humidity, lighting, and surrounding sounds (traffic, radio, TV, stereo). Temporal factors such as time of the day or day of the week are part of the environmental context, too.

You are not at the mercy of the environmental context. Indeed, humans, better than any other animal, manipulate their environment to suit their needs. You can arrange furniture to enhance or restrict interactions. (Think about how furniture has been arranged in some of the offices you have visited.) You can play the stereo when you have company, choosing the music that you think will create the right "mood." You can adjust lighting, temperature, and even smells with the use of deodorants, perfumes, and potpourris. Some home sellers will have fresh bread or cookies baking to create a homey smell when their house is being shown to prospective buyers.

■ The Cultural Context

The place where communication takes place generally dictates the cultural norms that are in effect. When you are interacting with someone in Cincinnati, Ohio, you expect U.S. cultural norms to be applied. For example, you expect that the conversational distance between you and the other person will be between eighteen inches and four feet.[10] If the interaction is taking place between two men in Riyadh, Saudi Arabia; however, the appropriate distance for interacting is smaller, and the men will stand closer together.

Culture has been defined as "a learned set of shared interpretations about beliefs, values, and norms, which affect the behaviors of a relatively large group of people."[11] The **cultural context** encompasses all of those culturally defined factors that impact human communication. Each time you communicate, you enact your culture; your behaviors are direct extensions of the beliefs, values, and norms that your culture has taught you. At this point, our discussion of contexts has come full circle, because culture, as you'll remember, also exists in each individual's psychological context. Your culture is both around you and within you, and you bring it to every communication situation. Figure 2.4 illustrates how the cultural context and the four other contexts relate to one another.

Our films and TV shows reflect the values and norms of our culture. Think about any foreign films you have seen or foreign TV shows you happened across on cable. What differences can you recall noticing about the way the people interacted or communicated as compared to your own cultural expectations? What communication norms were reflected in those shows? For example, were people animated or reserved in their manner? Were they formal or informal? Were women and men treated differently than in your culture?

■ *Intercultural Interactions*

One implication of the cultural context is that we need to be flexible when participating in intercultural interactions. Inflexibility creates *ethnocentric communication,* in which one person communicates to another person under the assumption that they share the same values and beliefs. Such an assumption can result in misunderstanding, confusion, stress, and even hostility.

To be an effective communicator, you need to recognize that each person you communicate with has been affected by a culture that might be markedly different from your own. The greater the degree of difference, the more you need to adapt your communication. Intercultural interactions really involve creating a blended culture, drawing from the different cultures of the participants to create a new "third" culture.[12]

Similarly, companies and organizations are made up of a diverse group of people, fusing their cultures to form a unique "organizational culture." Think about the kind of "culture" that exists at your college or university. How friendly is the campus? How important are academics, athletics, the Greek system, campus politics? In what ways does this culture differ from that of other colleges or universities? Table 2.1 reviews what you have learned about the intercultural context as well as the other four contexts.

■ Principles Related to Context

Some general principles apply to the five communication contexts just discussed. These principles have been implicit in the discussion so far, but now are presented.

1. ***All communication occurs within the five communication contexts.*** Whenever communication occurs, these contexts are present. Communication doesn't occur in a vacuum, but is affected by the factors identified in the five contexts. Each of the contexts affects every communication.

2. ***The way you communicate, the way you behave, and the meanings you attribute to what you perceive are all affected by the contexts.*** The contexts affect how you encode messages and how you decode messages. The meanings you give to words, your interpretations of other people's nonverbal behaviors, and your general behavior toward others are all influenced by the five contexts.

3. ***Each person is affected differently by a given context.*** Your reactions to each communication situation are unique to you. In general, most of our reactions are fairly similar to those of other members of our culture. However, no one else has had exactly the same experiences as you, and therefore nobody will have exactly the same reactions.

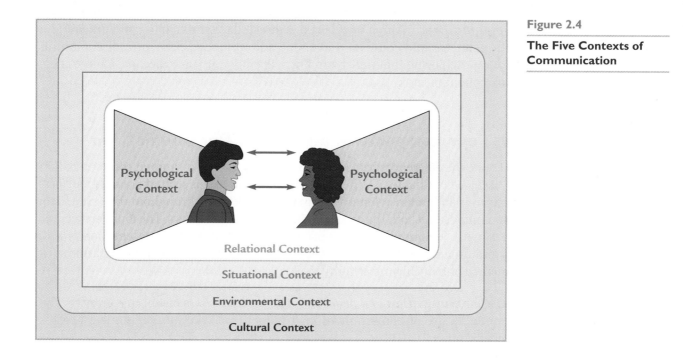

Figure 2.4

The Five Contexts of Communication

Table 2.1   Summary of Communication Contexts

Context	Description
Psychological context	Who you are and what you bring to any communication situation. Includes psychological qualities and personal characteristics.
Relational context	How you behave and react because of who the other person is; essentially, who you can be, given who the other person is. Includes issues of relational history, attraction, power, trust, and intimacy.
Situational context	The purpose or reason for the communication, dictated by the needs of the individuals in the communication.
Environmental context	Those factors outside the individuals involved in the communication that nonetheless affect the communication. Includes furnishings, time, temperature, presence of others, location, and outside sounds.
Cultural context	The impact of culturally defined factors such as beliefs, values, and norms on human communication. Culture exists in each person's psychological context and is enacted in each interaction. Communication interactions involve the merging of the participants' cultures.

*4. **The contexts are interactive; they affect one another.*** A change in one context changes the other contexts. Being in a bad mood (psychological context) might cause you to be short and temperamental toward a fellow employee (relational context) when that employee asks you a simple question (situational context).

*5. **You can improve your communication effectiveness by developing an awareness of how the contexts affect you and the people with whom you communicate.*** Much of this text is directed toward helping you understand the elements and contexts that shape and influence each form of communication. Achieving that understanding will empower you to become a more effective communicator.

▌ Four Perspectives on Human Communication

Despite the differences between the various categories of human communication (discussed in Chapter 1), there are commonalties. This section presents four perspectives on human communication that will be used throughout this text to help you understand both the commonalties and the differences. The four perspectives deal with communication as a process, communication as presentation of self, communication as a product of costs and rewards, and communication as a method of reducing uncertainty.

*1. **Communication is a process.*** The term *process* is meant to convey the dynamic nature of communication. The fact that communication is a process means that it is:

- Ongoing over time
- Continually changing
- Irreversible
- Nonrepeatable
- Cumulative

These qualities are interrelated. Think about the first two, for instance. Being *ongoing over time* means that communication is not a single, static moment, but rather a *continually developing and changing event*. This is important because it means that change occurs during the entire time people are communicating. People change, psychological contexts change, relationships change, and therefore communication must also change. Failure to recognize and adapt to change usually creates problems.

Sometimes people fail to recognize the ongoing nature of communication and treat it as a static event. For instance, you might tune people out after they start talking if you think you already know what they are going to say. You see the communication as a repetition of a prior moment, failing to recognize the changing nature of the communication. As a result, not only do you sometimes miss important new information, but you risk alienating the speaker as well.

Because of the changing, ongoing nature of communication, communication is *irreversible.* Once a moment in time has passed, it can never be relived. You have seen courtroom dramas in which a witness confesses under duress while answering a prosecutor's question, only to have the question objected to by the defense attorney and the objection sustained by the judge. At this point, the judge instructs the jury to "disregard that testimony." Can the jury erase its memory like a videotape? The jury might avoid discussing what was said, but the communication cannot be reversed or undone. Similarly, if you are giving a speech and you make a mistake, you can tell the audience members to forget that point, but in reality they will still remember it.

Similar to the irreversibility of communication is its *nonrepeatability.* You have probably had a friend who missed class ask you what she missed. While you can give a summary, you cannot actually repeat what occurred. Even if you had tape-recorded the class and replayed it, the experience would not be the same as having been there in person. Perhaps you have tried to reenact a particularly enjoyable experience, trying to recapture a moment. Such attempts are usually disappointing because you have changed, others have changed, and the situation has changed. You can have only one first date with someone; you can have only one sixteenth birthday.

Finally, communication is *cumulative* because, throughout this process of change, you continually add experiences to your psychological context. As communication proceeds over time, you accumulate information, you develop relationships, and you develop understanding and appreciation. When a speaker begins a presentation, you will probably be reluctant to interrupt with a question; but as the speech progresses and you get a sense of the openness and friendliness of the speaker, you are more likely to ask a question. Your accumulated experience with the speaker changes you and your relationship with the speaker. This means that history is important to interactions. Communication occurs in the context of relationships, and the relational history includes the cumulative effect of prior communications.

2. *Communication involves presenting an image of your "self" that you wish to have valued and confirmed.* Earlier in this chapter, you read about the symbolic self and about how the psychological context affects your actions and reactions. One goal of interacting with other people is to have your sense of self confirmed and accepted; this is often called an identity goal.[13]

In discussing self-image in communication, some researchers use the notion of face. People have a **face** that represents their self-concept. There are actually two types of face: positive face and negative face.[14] Your **positive face** is the image of yourself that you present to other people in hopes of having it liked, confirmed, and valued. Your **negative face** is the desire to go about your life with freedom from constraint or interference; it's your desire to do what you want without other people getting in your way.

Face is a key element in all communication activities. You are involved in presenting yourself to other people all the time, in both personal and professional situations. Each interaction with other people involves wanting to have your positive face accepted. Think of any new situation that you have entered—a new friendship, a new organization, a new class. In any such situation, you are probably quite sensitive to how other people are reacting to you. Are you being accepted? Do they like you? You modify your behavior and communicate in a way that you hope will maximize your acceptance. This exemplifies the effect of positive face on communication with other people.

On the other hand, think about the times when you were busy doing some project and your boss or some other figure of authority came in and told you to do something else. You probably felt some frustration because your negative face was being threatened; you were being prevented from finishing your project. Communication such as commands, requests, or advice will often cause you to alter your intended activity. Thus, communication can be a direct threat to your negative face.

Most of the research on face has dealt with *face-threatening acts*, those actions by which your positive or negative face is threatened, either by your own behavior or by other people's. In Chapter 5, you will read about how threats to face affect the way people deal with deceit and conflict. Generally, people try to "save face" when confronted with a face-threatening act.

The times when you feel embarrassed usually involve face-threatening acts. Tripping on the stairs while you are with a friend might threaten your image as a coordinated, agile individual. In such situations, other people can either help us save face or exacerbate the problem. Your friend can either laugh at you and call you a klutz or help you save face by saying something like, "Watch that step, I trip on it all the time, too."

Humans are actually pretty fragile when it comes to face. For example, someone giving a speech will worry about seeming foolish, inarticulate, and disorganized. And recent graduates looking for a job will often find the process very discouraging, partly because they internalize the lack of immediate job offers as a rejection of their face; that is, they believe that they are not valued. Understanding the many ways that face affects communication—both our own and other people's—can help us improve our communication skills.

3. *We often evaluate communication in terms of rewards and costs.* A well-known theory called social exchange theory has been developed to explain people's behaviors and decision-making. According to **social exchange theory,** people weigh the costs and rewards associated with a given situation or decision. Behavior can then be explained by the principle that people generally seek to maximize rewards while minimizing costs.

This means that in each of your communication situations, you are asking yourself whether or not it is "worth" it. Would you rent a movie you want to see from a video store, even if it's going to be on network TV in the next week? Your answer probably reflects an application of social exchange theory. Do you have the money to rent the video (costs)? How eager are you to see the movie (rewards)? How annoying do you find commercial interruptions (costs)? How much do you value the convenience of seeing the movie when it fits your schedule (rewards)?

We apply this type of evaluation to many communication settings. Obviously, you are still reading this chapter of the book. You are doing it because you believe that the rewards (either the intrinsic value of the knowledge you are gaining or doing well on an exam) outweigh the costs (the time and energy to plow through the material or getting a poor grade on the exam). Social exchange theory can be used to explain why we develop and maintain interpersonal relationships, stay in a job, attend meetings, work in teams, listen to speeches, and participate in interviews.

Of course, there are times when you engage in communication even when the costs seem to exceed the rewards. Sometimes we "hang in" when we believe that things will improve. Perhaps there have been times when you thought that going to college wasn't worth it, but you decided to hang on because you believed that it would get better. You might do this because you have certain **forecasted rewards**—for instance, your belief that a degree will lead to a good job.

You can also put excess rewards into a type of savings bank that you draw from when the costs increase. Think about your relationship with your best friend. This relationship has probably been quite rewarding for some period of time. These good periods result in **accumulated rewards.** There are times,

"Every time you say something right, you'll get 10 points. When you say something wrong, you'll lose 50 points. If you score 10,000 points, you'll win a second date."

though, when the relationship gets rocky and the costs exceed the rewards. You don't immediately drop the relationship, but rather you draw from your "savings" account to offset the costs. The size of your "savings" will determine how long you tolerate the high cost—low reward situation. Generally, the more you have invested in the relationship, the longer it takes to end.

4. *Communication provides information that reduces uncertainty.* Think about some of the new experiences in your life: coming to college for the first time, moving to a new community, or starting a new job. Each of these situations evokes a certain amount of stress. The stress is partially caused by the uncertainty you are feeling. You don't know what to expect; you don't know much about the people, community, or organization.

To reduce this stress, you engage in **uncertainty reduction,** actively seeking information to increase predictability. People like to be able to predict and control their environment,[15] and information helps them do this.

How do we seek information to reduce uncertainty? (You know the answer by now.) Through communication. One of the basic motives for communicating with others is to gain information. The acquisition of information is represented in all three forms of communication discussed in Chapter 1: actional, interactional, and transactional.

Imagine that you are sitting in a meeting when a guest is brought in to speak to the group. A number of questions go through your mind: Why is this person here? What does this person want? What is he going to talk about? Is this going to be worth listening to? What am I expected to do? Will I like him? All of these questions represent the initial uncertainties you have. Usually, some introduction is provided that gives you information about the speaker, and this helps reduce your uncertainty. As the speaker begins the presentation, you observe his behaviors, listen to his message, and make some conclusions about him. As you continue to reduce uncertainty, you are more prepared to focus on the message and allow a relationship to develop.

This example illustrates two types of uncertainty that exist in our dealings with other people: cognitive uncertainty and behavioral uncertainty.[16] **Cognitive uncertainty** has to do with our uncertainty about an individual's personal qualities—the person's attitudes, beliefs, and values. **Behavioral uncertainty** is our uncertainty about how another person will behave. Sometimes we can understand another person's attitude, but not predict his or her reactions. At other times, we can predict how someone will behave but not understand his or her values and beliefs.

■ *Applying the Four Perspectives*

The four perspectives on communication serve as a foundation for understanding the dynamics of human interaction. Each perspective can help you in making strategic communication choices that will increase your effectiveness. Many of the recommendations made in the remainder of the text are based on these perspectives. For example:

- ■ Knowing that persuading an audience is part of a process can help you develop appropriate appeals as a speaker.

- Understanding how evaluation of subordinates threatens their positive face can improve your effectiveness as a manager.
- Judging the rewards and costs of participating in a group can assist you in planning the degree and type of your involvement.
- Understanding people's need for uncertainty reduction can help you work out problems in a relationship with a friend.

Later chapters will offer more detail about communication situations like these, as well as practical advice for improving your skills.

Summary

Understanding how contexts affect communication helps you to become more effective in your communication. All communication occurs within five contexts: psychological, relational, situational, environmental, and cultural. These contexts affect how you behave, how you encode messages, and how you decode messages. Even though two people might be communicating within the same context, each person is affected differently. Moreover, the contexts do not act independently; rather, each affects the others.

The psychological context includes who you are and what you bring to any communication situation. All of your experiences and background are part of this context. It includes your psychological qualities—your needs, beliefs, attitudes, values, and personality. Needs can be considered as a hierarchy, progressing from basic physiological needs to needs for belonging and love and finally to the need to self-actualize and discover your "self." The psychological context also includes personal characteristics such as age, sex, race, ethnicity, and culture. Each of these characteristics affects how you communicate and react to the world around you.

The relational context represents how you behave and react because of who the other person is. A relationship exists each time you communicate, and you act differently toward different people. The relationship is affected by such factors as attraction, power, trust, and intimacy, as well as by the relationship's own history.

The situational context is an extension of your needs in that it represents the purpose or reason for the communication. Individuals have different reasons for communicating with one another, and these reasons can be compatible or in conflict.

The environmental context represents factors from the surroundings that affect the communicators. Physical factors such as the location, furnishings, presence of other people, lighting, and external noises all affect your communication. Even things like time of day and day of the week can change the nature of your communication.

Cultural context exists because communication occurs within a culture. In addition, each person's psychological context reflects the cultures to which he or she has been exposed. During communication, your cultural experiences interact with those of other people. The degree to which your cultural experiences are similar or different will dictate the degree to which a new cultural code (a third culture) must be developed for the communication.

Human communication can be viewed from several perspectives: as a process, as a presentation of self, as an evaluation of rewards and costs, and as uncertainty reduction.

As a process, communication is ongoing over time, continually changing, irreversible, nonrepeatable, and cumulative.

As presentation of self, communication involves presenting a "face," an image of your self, that you wish to have valued and confirmed. Your positive face is the sense of self that you want other people to like and value. Your negative face is the desire not to be interfered with, to continue unimpeded. In each communication situation, you are sensitive to face-threatening acts and seek to have others confirm and accept your face.

As an evaluation of rewards and costs, communication reflects people's attempt to maximize rewards while minimizing costs. Rewards are accumulated over time and act as a reservoir when costs rise. People also try to forecast whether something will ultimately be more rewarding than costly.

Finally, communication as uncertainty reduction involves the use of communication to acquire information. Uncertainty creates stress in your life, and you seek to reduce that stress by gaining information that increases your ability to predict and control the world around you.

Key Terms

psychological context The communication context that represents who we are and what we bring to any communication situation.

psychological qualities The part of the psychological context that includes our needs, values, beliefs, attitudes, and personality.

Maslow's hierarchy of needs A progressive listing of five levels of human needs that begins with very basic needs and ends with the need to self-actualize.

values Deep-rooted conceptual responses about the worth or importance that we give something.

beliefs Convictions we have that something is true or not true.

attitudes Our predisposed evaluative responses toward things.

personality The collection of qualities that people associate with how we behave and who we are.

symbolic self A self that is the product of our symbolic interactions with others and that we define or conceptualize through symbols.

personal characteristics That part of the psychological context that includes age, sex, race, ethnic background, and culture.

sex role A set of behaviors associated with a particular sex.

psychological sex types Masculine and feminine categories based on psychological orientation rather than physiology.

power The ability of people to influence other people in order to accomplish their goals.

relational context The communication context that deals with relationships and how we behave and react because of who the other person is.

situational context The communication context that reflects the purpose, or reason, for the interaction, as determined by the needs of the individuals.

environmental context The communication context that consists of those factors outside the individuals involved in the communication that nonetheless affect the communication.

cultural context The communication context that includes all of the culturally defined factors that affect the communication.

face Our sense of self.

positive face The image that we present to others in hopes of having it liked, confirmed, and valued.

negative face A desire to go about our lives with freedom from constraint or interference—to do what we want without others getting in our way.

social exchange theory The theory that people evaluate a situation or decision by weighing its rewards and costs.

forecasted rewards Rewards that we expect to receive in the future.

accumulated rewards The sum of rewards minus costs over some period of time.

uncertainty reduction Actively seeking information to increase predictability.

cognitive uncertainty Uncertainty about another person's personal qualities (attitudes, beliefs, and values).

behavioral uncertainty Uncertainty about how another person will behave.

Review Questions

1. Identify and define the five communication contexts.
2. Discuss how the qualities that constitute the psychological context affect communication.
3. In what ways do the relational and situational contexts affect each other?
4. How do the four dimensions of culture affect communication?
5. Discuss the five general principles related to context.
6. Explain the four perspectives on human communication.

Chapter 3

Perceiving, Listening, and Responding

Objectives

Studying this chapter will allow you to:

1. Define the three stages of perception.
2. Explain what attribution is.
3. Identify biases that affect the attribution process and ways to overcome them.
4. Discuss several principles that apply to listening.
5. Explain the differences between the various types of listening.
6. Understand how a response can be confirming or disconfirming.

ake a moment to survey the various stimuli that you are currently experiencing. What sounds do you hear: radio, stereo, talking, buzzing from a fluorescent fixture, engine noise from passing cars, birds whistling, dogs barking, telephones ringing, or passing jet planes? What do you feel through your sense of touch: the temperature, your clothes, the hardness or softness of the chair, a breeze in your face, the floor against your feet? What do you smell: stale air, lunch or dinner cooking, sweaty gym clothes, perfume, flowers in bloom, car exhaust, cows in the pasture? What do you see: words on a page, smudges in the margins, hair on your hands, a desk, light, note paper, a clock or watch?

Perception means being aware enough of a stimulus to attach meaning to it. The awareness comes from an arousal of one or more of your senses. Your senses have focused on some stimulus to which they are sensitive.

You are always engulfed in a deluge of stimuli. And yet you don't notice a lot of the stimuli around you because your senses have not been aroused enough or because you have chosen not to notice them. For example, you may have answered that you do not smell anything. In reality, you do smell something, but you are so used to smelling it that it is no longer arousing. On the other hand, if something begins burning nearby, that odor will arouse your sense of smell. At that point you might attach meaning to the smell: "It smells like burning paper." You will now have perceived the odor: It will have aroused your sense of smell and you will have associated a meaning with that arousal.

How does perception relate to communication? Perception serves as the basis for understanding people and their messages. It is the input or receptive half of the communicative process. Communication cannot occur without perception. Understanding the perceptual process, particularly as it applies to our perceptions of people, provides one of the cornerstones for improving communication effectiveness.

In this chapter, you will read about perception, especially about how it relates to your awareness of other people. Then you will find out about the process you use to explain what you perceive in the behaviors of other people. Next you will read about a particular type of perception—listening. Finally, the chapter ends with a discussion of how you react to what you perceive and hear—responding.

■ Perception

Perception involves three basic steps:

1. Selecting among the stimuli to which you are exposed
2. Organizing the stimuli you have selected
3. Interpreting the meaning of those stimuli

The overall goal of these three stages of perception is to improve the efficiency of managing information. Each stimulus around you is a potential source of information; therefore, you have to deal with an enormous and overwhelming amount of information. You handle this task by being selective in what you perceive, organizing the information into manageable chunks, and interpreting the information in the simplest ways.

Think about the stimuli that you were asked to focus on a moment ago. Each stimulus actually gives you information on which you can choose to act or not act. If the temperature is too cool, you might turn up the heat. If the chair is too hard, you might move to a more comfortable chair. If there is too much noise coming from outside, you might close the door and windows. Each time you act in response to a stimulus, you are showing that you received information.

You can also receive information and choose *not* to act—but this is a form of action as well. Perhaps the room is too cold, the chair too hard, or the room too noisy, but you decide not to do anything about it. The fact that you have made a decision is a form of action. You have collected information and decided on a course of action, or more accurately, a course of inaction.

As you will see, human communication provides a great deal of information, and the way you handle the perceptual process has a vital effect on the way you communicate.

■ *Selecting*

Earlier, you were probably unaware of most of the stimuli around you until your attention was called to them. Being unaware of your chair doesn't mean that you didn't know of its existence. Rather, you were able to select from among the stimuli that surrounded you and focus only on those that you believed warranted your attention. Perhaps your eyes were so glued to this text that you were oblivious to the world around you.

Selection is the process of focusing attention on specific stimuli while ignoring others; in essence, it is choosing from the available pool of stimuli. You would probably have a mental breakdown if you tried to maintain complete focus on all the sources of information surrounding you. Therefore, like other people, you have developed two mechanisms that help you focus on a limited number of stimuli at any one time: filtering and attending.

Filtering. The process of **filtering** involves setting threshold levels for the arousal of our senses. Think of each sense as having a filter, like the air filter on a furnace or automobile. Your sensory filter lets small pieces of information through but captures or reacts to large pieces, just as an air filter captures pieces of dirt. Arousal of the sense is like having an alarm that signals you each time a large piece of dirt has struck the filter. But you can choose whether to use finer or coarser filters—that is, you can vary the size of the dirt that is allowed to pass through. In this way, you set the threshold level at which the sense will be aroused.

Attending. The process of **attending** involves heightening our attention to particular sensory input. On most of the *Star Trek* TV shows, the characters have sensors that can be set to detect various fictional elements. You have the same capability with your senses. You can set them to detect, or attend to, certain stimuli.

You can probably remember playing outside as a kid and listening for your mom or dad to call you in for dinner. You had your hearing set to pick up a certain cue, and you could attend to that cue over and above other stimuli. Do you remember the *Where's Waldo?* books and posters? When you first look at the picture, finding Waldo seems like an impossible task. As you begin to focus your attention on the picture, however, the task of finding Waldo and the other hidden items becomes easier.

One way of increasing our attention to one sort of stimulus is to decrease attention to other stimuli. Each of your senses is being bombarded with potential information. You can reduce your focus on some senses so that you can more easily discern the information being received by other senses. You may have heard that blind people have more acute hearing or feeling. It probably isn't true that their sensitivity is increased, but they are not distracted by the competing information provided by sight.

Generate a list in your head of some of the times when you have tried to increase your attention to one stimulus or to focus on one thing. What did you do to increase your sensitivity?

Do you suppose that some people close their eyes when they are kissing because it allows them to focus more attention on the feeling? Do musicians close their eyes when they are playing intensely so they can focus more attention on the sound?

Biases in selection. Our selection process is inherently biased. The fact that we filter out information and attend to certain other information means that we have a distorted view of the world. This is particularly true when it comes to our interactions with other people.

Think about a close relationship that you chose to end. In such situations, people often notice many negative points about the other person that they hadn't seen when they were most attracted to him or her. This is the basis of the old adage "Love is blind." But when the relationship takes a turn for the worse, we start to select those stimuli that are negative.

A **halo effect** occurs when we consider someone good or attractive and therefore tend to see only positive qualities. In essence, we see the other person as perfect or saintly. On the other hand, the **horn effect** causes us to see only negative qualities in those we dislike or view as bad.

Selection is only the first stage of the perception process. Selection determines the stimuli to which we are going to attend, but it does not determine what the stimuli mean. The next two stages, organizing and interpreting, are where we put various pieces of information together and attach meaning to the stimuli.

■ Organizing

There are a number of reasons why perception requires organizing.

1. Information is received through the various senses simultaneously. Some parts of the information relate to each other, and some do not. To make sense of the information, the different sensory inputs have to be combined and organized before they can be interpreted.

2. So much information is being received that we need ways to simplify it. One major way of simplifying is to organize information into categories, which allow us to deal with general points rather than minute details.

3. Information is received in bits and pieces. Messages are rarely complete. The meaning of a message often depends on our ability to fill in blanks or provide additional information. The ability to fill in the blanks depends on how the information is organized.

Organizing, then, is the second step in perception, in which we combine information, categorize it, and fill in the missing pieces.

Categorizing.   Putting information into categories provides an efficient way of organizing a lot of information. Suppose you have a friend named Jane who is from Iowa. If you want to retain information about Jane's background, you could try to remember that she was born in Clear Lake, Iowa, a summer resort area featuring the Surf Ballroom, where the early rock-and-roller Buddy Holly last played, located in north central Iowa, just west of Interstate 35, about 113 miles north of Des Moines and 24 miles south of the Iowa-Minnesota state border. Of course, you usually don't need to remember such detailed information about someone, and therefore you don't. In the case of Jane's geographical background, you might simply categorize her as "an Iowan."

There are two steps to this categorizing process. First, we create categories based on the information we have collected. Second, we apply the information stored in a category to anything that we associate with the category. A **category** is a collection of information that is placed under a single, simplified label. We categorize almost everything we perceive. We create categories for movies, TV shows, speeches, cars, foods, stores, weather, places we visit, and so on.

For each of the following, generate a list of some categories that you personally use:

Movies   Teachers
Food   Family members

For example, you might classify movies as romantic, thrilling, or funny.
How do these categories affect your perceptions? How do they affect your communication with other people?

Stereotypes.   The categories that are probably most important to communication are those we create to describe people: stereotypes. A **stereotype** is a category in which we place individuals on the basis of some attribute or quality.

Take the example of "Jane the Iowan." "Iowan" is a category you have created on the basis of previous information you have collected or inferred about people from Iowa. You apply this category to Jane as a way of simplifying your perceptual process. What does this category mean to you? Depending on your experiences, your stereotype might lead you to think of Jane as a farm girl, used to working with pigs and cows, probably strong, hardworking, a little bit "hickish," and not very sophisticated. To the degree that these really are true attributes of Jane, your stereotype can be beneficial.

Stereotypes are not inherently bad. They help us organize and simplify our perceptions. Problems arise, however, when a stereotype is based on inaccurate or

What labels would you use to describe the various people pictured in this photograph?

biased information or applied to a population that is quite diverse.[1] In particular, a stereotype causes trouble when the target of your stereotyping proves to be an exception to the category. For example, Jane may have been raised in the suburbs of Des Moines, with a population approaching half a million people. Her father may be a professor at Drake University and her mother a vice president for finance at one of the many insurance headquarters located in Des Moines. Jane may never have set foot on a farm in her life. In this case, your stereotype of Jane would lead you to incorrect perceptions and probably some embarrassing comments.

Most of our categories tend to be *dichotomous,* or *bipolar;* that is, they come in pairs: good-bad, hot-cold, like-dislike, attractive-nonattractive, black-white, easy-hard, athletic-nonathletic, smart-dumb, passing-failing. Bipolarization simplifies perception: We have to gain only enough information to put something in one of two categories. However, bipolarization tends to oversimplify reality. People don't really fall into neat either-or categories.

Race is a good example. We tend to categorize people by their skin color—for instance, black or white. The reality is that there is a continuum of skin color in which people have varying degrees of blackness and whiteness. Given the multicultural mix that most of us are, it is misleading to categorize individuals in this way. Some people refer to golfer Tiger Woods as a black athlete, but he refers to himself as a "Cablinasian" because of a mixed cultural heritage of Caucasian (Ca-), black (-bl-), Indian (-in-), and Asian (-asian).

Filling in information. Another way we organize perceptions is by filling in missing information. In essence, we see things that aren't there because experience tells us they are. You don't have to see it raining to know that it has rained. You can conclude that it has been raining if you notice that the streets, sidewalks, cars, and roofs are all wet. You are able to make conclusions about causes and effects because of this ability to infer a cause from knowledge of an effect, and vice versa.

In communication, people are continually filling in missing pieces of information. You hear things people didn't really say because you assume that they did. This tendency creates a major dilemma in dealing with eyewitness accounts. Movies or TV shows that focus on witness testimony often present witnesses who think they saw or heard something that they eventually realize they didn't. For instance:

DEFENSE	So how do you know that Maurice killed John?
WITNESS	Because I heard Maurice through the door.
DEFENSE	What did you hear?
WITNESS	I heard him say, "I'm going to kill you," and then I heard a gunshot.
DEFENSE	So you didn't actually see the murder?
WITNESS	No.
DEFENSE	Have you heard lots of gunshots before?
WITNESS	No.
DEFENSE	Could the noise you heard have been a light bulb breaking?
WITNESS	I guess it could have been.

Participate in a chat session with strangers in which only a few people are online. After a few minutes, think about the impression you have drawn about one or two of the participants. How would you categorize these people? What conclusions can you make about their educational background, ethnicity, age, culture, and so forth? What information did you rely on to form these impressions and conclusions?

Now seek information from the other participants to either confirm or refute your impression (recognizing that not everyone is totally honest and disclosing online).

■ *Interpreting*

The final stage of perception involves interpreting the stimuli we have selected and organized. **Interpretation** is the process by which we attribute meaning to the stimuli we have selected and organized. Meaning is not inherent in the stimuli; rather, we carry meaning in us and attach it to our perceptions.

Memory provides an important base for our interpretations. If a person waves his hand at you, you know that he is probably saying hello or good-bye, depending on the situation. The wave, in and of itself, has no meaning; it is simply a visual stimulus. You put meaning on what you have observed because you have stored similar, previous experiences in your memory. These memories make up part of your psychological context. You have learned that a waving hand is a symbol in U.S. culture associated with greetings and departures.

Attaching meaning to stimuli is not just a matter of recalling a dictionary-like definition. Interpretation evokes both a cognitive and an emotional response. How do you feel about someone waving good-bye to you? The answer is, it depends. You may think "good riddance" and feel relieved and happy if it is a person you don't like. On the other hand, you may have a rush of warm memories and feel sad if it is someone you love.

In communication, we are particularly interested in the interpretation of messages. The next chapter features a detailed discussion of how we attribute meaning to messages, including both their verbal and nonverbal components.

■ Attribution Theory

In the interpretation stage, our perception of people goes beyond a singular attachment of meaning to the stimuli. The perception of people includes extrapolating from what we have observed about their previous behavior to current or predicted behavior.

People like to explain why things happen. We perceive human behavior, then seek to explain why it happened—to attribute some cause. The tendency of people to develop explanations for why people behave the way they do is called **attribution.**

One theorist observed that attribution involves people acting like *naive psychologists*[2] because they believe that they understand the reasons behind other people's behaviors. Imagine, for instance, that your teacher stomps into the classroom, slams her books down on the desk, and stomps back out of the room. What would your reaction be to perceiving this series of actions? You would probably wonder why she acted this way and would try to generate an explanation. You might conclude that she was angry about something that had just happened, maybe a run-in with a student before class began. If she was returning an exam to the class, you might infer that the class had done terribly and she was upset with the students. Maybe you would simply dismiss her behavior because that's the way she always comes to class.

This generation of an explanation represents the process of attribution. Your ability to create an explanation for the teacher's behavior depends on the available information you have to accompany your immediate perceptions. That information includes your own personal experiences in observing teachers in general and your knowledge about this teacher in particular.

■ The Causal Theory

In the scenario with your teacher, you ask yourself what caused the observed behavior. According to the **causal theory of attribution,** there are three potential explanations for people's actions: the stimulus, the circumstance, and the person.[3]

1. *The stimulus.* You might interpret your teacher's behavior as a specific reaction just to your class—the stimulus. You might feel confident about your stimulus attribution if you had seen this teacher in a number of other classes always maintaining her composure.

2. *The circumstance.* Perhaps you observed the teacher in the hallway, right before class, being accosted by a group of students from her previous class. You probably would attribute the anger she displayed toward your class to that hallway circumstance. Attributing to circumstance means seeing some previous external factor as the cause of the observed behavior.

3. *The person.* If you had observed this teacher being angry in several classes as well as when you visited her in her office, you would probably conclude that her anger was part of her personality (the person). Attributing to the person means that the behavior is seen as representative of the nature and personality of the individual.

Two of these three explanations, the stimulus and the circumstance, involve factors external to the individual. Only the third explanation, the person, relates to factors within the individual. As you will see in the next section, however, we tend to use that third explanation all too often in our attributions.

■ *Attributional Biases*

Your ability to make accurate attributions depends on how good you are at selecting, organizing, and interpreting relevant information. The more you interact and observe other people, the greater the potential for improving your attributions. We all rely on personal attribution theories in everyday life; that is, we have our personal ways of explaining why people behave the way they do. Unfortunately, our personal theories are always somewhat oversimplified or distorted. We all have **attributional biases** that cause us to make inaccurate attributions.

Many of these biases cause us to place too much meaning on certain information while ignoring the meaning of other information. This can occur through selective perception, by organizing the information according to a stereotype, or by interpreting what we have perceived according to our preconceptions. Here are a few of the more significant and common types of biases.

1. Overemphasis on the obvious, the irrelevant, and the negative. When you first meet someone, what do you notice immediately? You probably notice the person's sex, age, skin color, height, and weight. You focus on the most obvious and readily available information, often ignoring other information, such as a smile, nervous body movements, or a soft-spoken tone of voice. Stereotypes are often based on these most obvious characteristics.

Part of the error inherent in such attributions is the tendency to treat irrelevant information as relevant. A person's hair color is not relevant to his or her level of intelligence; yet there is a popular assumption that "blondes are dumb."

A related problem is our tendency to overgeneralize from limited information; that is, we take a small piece of information and assume that it is representative of a broader set of information. Perhaps you place a lot of significance in the strength of a person's handshake; or you disregard a speaker's message because of a lack of eye contact with you; or you avoid interactions with people who smoke cigarettes. These are all examples of overgeneralizing from one piece of information without taking the opportunity to find out more.

We also tend to weigh negative information disproportionately, making it more important than positive information. In an employment interview, an interviewee may have ten positive qualities and a single negative one, a low grade point average. Yet the employer often will decide against that candidate on the basis of the one piece of negative information, despite the larger number of positive characteristics.

2. *Overdependence on the simple.* One of the basic premises of the perceptual process is the tendency to simplify our perceptions by reducing, collapsing, and encapsulating what we have perceived. As you have seen, that is a vital and necessary part of the process. The problem, though, is that vital information can be ignored or left out.

This preference for simplifying perceptions often occurs in our attributional explanations of other people's behaviors. We prefer simple explanations to complex ones and so develop personal attribution theories that explain behavior in the simplest terms. Why are there such bad programs on television? The simple explanation: The people who develop and broadcast the programs are nitwits. This is probably an explanation most of us would accept. A more complex explanation would include multiple factors: Economics limits the amount of money that can be spent on script development, casting, and pilot testing; the programmers are under strong pressure from advertisers to create a nonoffensive, "safe" program; polls indicate that such programs draw large audiences; and so on.

3. *Sticking to preconceptions.* Strong preconceptions can cause us to see what we expect to see. Suppose you are getting a new boss who is being transferred from another part of the company. You have heard from his former subordinates that he is a closed-minded taskmaster. This could create a preconception that results in your perceiving all his actions as consistent with this perspective. He might call you into his office and ask for your advice. Your biased perception might lead you to believe that he is going to ignore the advice, so you decide not to tell him anything. Your own behavior might then induce him to act like a taskmaster, thus providing support for your preconception.

We also have preconceptions about which causes go with which effects, and vice versa. We then draw on those preexisting explanations rather than collecting more information. For example, you might assume that you were stood up for a date (effect) because the other person didn't like you (cause). The next time you see that person, you interpret his or her behaviors (for instance, how far the person stands away from you or the lack of a smile) as indicative of that dislike. This selective perception causes you to ignore information—such as a legitimate reason for missing the date—that might challenge your preconceptions.

4. *Incorrect causal attribution.* Deciding whether a person's behavior is the result of stimulus, circumstance, or the person is not easy. Making the correct attribution requires a concentrated effort to gain and process information. We therefore employ ways to make the process easier while risking greater inaccuracy.

In general, we have a preference for attributing other people's behavior to internal causes (the person's own personality) rather than to external causes (called the **fundamental attribution error**). On the other hand, we attribute our own negative behaviors to external causes rather than believing they are a reflection of our personality.[4] This is one reason students tend to blame the instructor for a poor exam grade (external cause), rather than accept that they just didn't study enough (internal cause).

Our bias in attributing causality is affected by our likes and dislikes. When people we like display negative behavior, we attribute it to external causes (stimulus or circumstance); however, that same behavior displayed by someone we dislike results in an attribution to internal cause (the individual's personality). On the other hand, we attribute the positive behaviors of those we like to internal causes, while attributing the same behaviors by those we dislike to external causes.

Think about a politician you like and one you dislike. How would you explain a rumor of misuse of campaign funds by both candidates? You'd probably say that the politician you liked was being railroaded and that the system was corrupt anyway. On the other hand, you'd probably declare that such behavior was typical of the lying, cheating, corrupt politician you disliked.

See if you can generate a list of some of your attributional biases. To do this, you have to be very honest with yourself. The following questions may help you.

- What information do you most readily respond to about other people: their sex, age, race, religion, political views, smoking habits?
- What minor elements about people do you tend to generalize from and treat as significant?
- Think about the last time you doubted someone's explanation for his or her behavior. Did the complexity or simplicity of the explanation influence its believability?
- Think about a time when you had preconceptions about a person (for instance, a teacher, new acquaintance, new work colleague). How did the preconceptions affect your perceptions? Was your preconception sustained or modified over time?

■ Overcoming Attributional Biases

Everyone suffers from biased perception and attribution. One of the first steps in overcoming these biases is to recognize their presence. Failure to admit that you are biased in your perception probably means that you are not aware of how such bias is distorting your interpretations.

The following suggestions parallel the attributional biases that were just discussed. These suggestions, in and of themselves, will not eliminate bias. To truly overcome attributional biases requires effort, commitment, time, and practice. After all, you have had a lifetime to learn them.

1. Appreciate subtle, relevant, and positive information. Try to look beyond the obvious information that blinds you to the deeper, more subtle information. Ask yourself questions that turn your attention to the subtle cues. Watch a person's face, eyes, body movement. Listen as completely as you can to what the other person is saying.

Overall, examine the bases for your attributions about other people. Are you basing them on obvious, irrelevant, or negative information? How much are you weighing the various pieces of information you have gained? What additional information should you seek to help ensure a correct attribution?

2. *Appreciate complexity.* This is an easy thing to say and a difficult thing to do. Again, to apply this suggestion, you need to examine the explanation you have generated for another person's behavior. Are you jumping at the first, most obvious, and simplest explanation available? If so, then you probably should reexamine your explanation.

Try to brainstorm a variety of possibilities. Then gather information to confirm or dispel each. Think about how Sherlock Holmes would develop explanations for the way a crime was committed. To paraphrase the famous detective, if you rule out all but one possible explanation, then the remaining explanation, no matter how complex, must be the one.

3. *Treat preconceptions cautiously.* Realize that you have preconceived notions and that they are directing your attention and biasing your interpretations. Try to assess how those preconceptions are affecting your perception. Consciously develop alternative explanations that challenge your preconceptions.

Above all, you need to maintain an open mind and be sensitive to information that you might otherwise cast off as irrelevant to your preconceptions. Your preconception of your new supervisor as a closed-minded taskmaster might lead you to see his request for advice as insincere. To overcome this bias, look for evidence to confirm that the request is sincere. Provide the requested advice and make open-minded observations of how he responds. Try to generate alternative explanations for his toughness rather than negatively categorizing him as a taskmaster. Perhaps he's receiving a lot of pressure from his supervisor to increase productivity, or perhaps he would like to be more people oriented but just doesn't know how. At some point you might need to check out your attributions by directly seeking confirmation or disconfirmation. You might have a heart-to-heart chat with your boss about his "taskmaster" behavior. In this way, you might gain insights into the underlying causes of his actions.

4. *Seek correct causal attributions.* Incorrect causal attributions generally occur because of incomplete information. Sometimes that information is incomplete because you choose to ignore information you already have or because you choose not to seek further information that might contradict what you want to believe.

For instance, people assume devious motives for a person they dislike who does nice things. They choose to ignore information that might require them to reassess their regard for the person. Put yourself in the other person's shoes, and think about the explanation you would generate if the actions were your own.

■ Principles of Listening

Perception encompasses all the stimuli to which you are exposed. Learning about perception helps you understand some of the dynamics that occur when you are trying to make sense of the world around you. However, just understanding perception does not give you a complete picture of the process by which you decode spoken messages; to gain that, you need to examine the process of listening.

Listening is a special form of perception that focuses on spoken messages. Listening involves focusing our perception on specific sounds that we believe have been generated for the purpose of conveying some particular information. *Hearing,* the sensory stimulation received by the ears, is not the same as listening. Because listening is a form of perception, the listener goes through the process of selecting, organizing, and interpreting. A reaction happens when listening occurs. Speakers watch for such reactions to determine whether their audience is listening and understanding.

Although listening depends only on a single sense—hearing—it does not occur in isolation. We listen in the context of other accompanying perceptions derived from our ears and from all our other senses. We interpret the meaning of what we hear in conjunction with how the words are spoken, the facial expression and eye contact of the speaker, the speaker's gestures and body posture, and so on.

Now let's look at some general principles of listening.

1. *Listening is a skill.* To say that listening is a skill implies that our listening abilities can be improved through training and practice. Listening is often identified as one of the most important skills a manager can have. And one research study found listening to be the second most troublesome communication situation for employees (motivating people was number one).[5] That listening is recognized as important can be seen in the investment that corporate America makes in trying to improve employee listening skills. Fifty-nine percent of the Fortune 500 companies that responded to a survey indicated that they provided listening training to their employees.[6]

You may be a good listener, but you probably could be a better one. It is common for students to identify listening as one of their personal communication strengths and at the same time identify it as an area that needs the most improvement.

"Remember when I told you that our company is going downhill fast? One reason is because nobody around here listens very carefully."

Your skills at listening no doubt vary according to the situation and the type of listening required. Some people are very good at picking up facts and information, while other people are good at making others feel better by listening to their personal problems.

2. *Listening involves reducing input and expanding output.* Listening, like other forms of perception, is an information process in which we take a large amount of information and simplify it. Think about all the information you have read in this chapter up to this point. You cannot remember every word—and you don't need to remember every word. Instead, you create an outline in your mind of what you have read, and you reduce complex sentences to short phrases that can easily be remembered. The same process applies when you are listening to someone speak. When asked to recall what was said, you take the core idea and elaborate on it by reattaching words. Look at the following example:

> Kris says to Chad, "Later on I thought you and I could go to a movie. I really want to see that new action flick with Stallone and Schwarzenegger as two old, washed-up spies. It's supposed to be real funny."
>
> Chad simplifies what he hears to the following: "Kris—Stallone—action movie—later."
>
> Chad runs into Sal and says, "Hey, Sal. Kris and I are going to a movie later on, the one with Stallone and that other guy, some action-adventure thing. Would you like to go along?"

Kris's original message did not have to be memorized word for word for Chad to capture the underlying meaning. Chad needed only the main points. When Chad later met Sal, he reattached information to the main points to make them intelligible to Sal. Notice that Chad added the notion of "adventure" that had not been in the original message from Kris. Such additions can create inaccuracies and distort the original message.

3. *Listening takes energy.* How do you feel after a day of listening to lectures or after spending several hours listening to a friend tell you his or her personal problems? Tired, right? You are tired because you exerted energy while listening. We sometimes take listening for granted and assume that it doesn't involve any work, but that's not true. Listening requires attention, cognitive processing, and sometimes responding to the speaker.

When we do a lot of listening, we become fatigued, and then we find it difficult to listen well. Sometimes, when we are tired, we tend to "pseudolisten." **Pseudolistening** means pretending to be listening to someone when we really aren't. If you are pseudolistening, you may nod your head occasionally, maintain eye contact, and say "uh-huh"—but your mind has drifted away from the spoken messages.

A corollary to this principle is that we control the amount of energy we invest in listening. We decide to pay attention or tune out a speaker. We tend to quit attending to a speaker when the topic isn't very interesting, when the information is repetitive, or when we have something more important on our mind. We can increase our level of attentiveness by focusing on the spoken message and tuning out surrounding noise. You've tuned out surrounding conversations when you really wanted to hear what an instructor was saying or when you were watching a favorite TV program. If the conversations persisted, you may have asked the other people to quiet down, because keeping your listening focused solely on the instructor or the TV required a lot of energy.

4. ***We listen faster than we talk.*** The cognitive speed at which we process information is considerably faster than the rate at which we speak. People speak at around 125 to 150 words per minute, yet we can mentally process between 850 and 1,000 words per minute. This means that our mind has to keep the brakes on while listening to someone talk.

The mind tries to keep itself occupied by checking other information sources. You may watch TV while another person is talking, read during lectures, or totally drift off into your own thoughts. Unfortunately, this can sometimes cause you to miss what is being said. To be an effective listener, you need to use the thought/speech rate differential to your advantage. Use the extra cognitive time to:

A. Think about the message.
B. Look for additional information from the speaker that is associated with the spoken message.
C. Analyze what you are hearing, but remind yourself to stay tuned to the speaker.

5. ***Listening is intermittent, not continuous.*** Language is repetitive, and speakers often add a lot of extra information that we really don't need to remember. As a result of these factors, as well as the thought/speech rate differential, our listening tends to represent a sampling of a speaker's message. We continually tune in and out. We take little "vacations" from listening, but we can still capture the essence of what a speaker says.

Of course, we have to be careful about how quickly we do the tuning in and tuning out. Figure 3.1 shows two patterns of intermittent listening. When the curve is above the horizontal line, the listener is tuned in; when it falls below the horizontal line, the listener is tuned out. As you can see, pattern A represents very short periods of tuning out, whereas pattern B shows long periods of tuning out. Listeners who follow pattern B are likely to miss quite a lot.

As listeners, we need to monitor our listening behavior to be sure that we don't take long mental vacations and thus miss critical information. As speakers, we also need to be aware of this listening principle. We can adapt our spoken message to accommodate intermittent listening. We can repeat important information to ensure that it is heard during one of the tuned-in cycles. We can use nonverbal cues, such as RAISING OUR VOLUME OR PITCH, to recall listeners' attention to our message. Obviously, we try to do similar things in our writing. We can also use NoVeLtY to regain and hold attention.

Figure 3.1

Two Patterns of Intermittent Listening

Pattern A is more effective than pattern B. Do you see why?

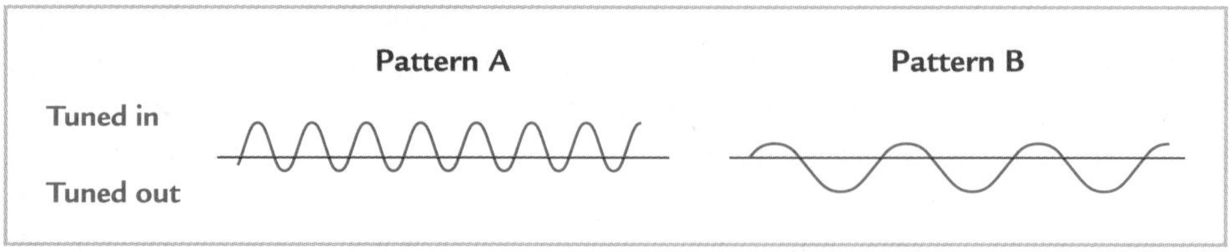

Pattern A   Pattern B

Tuned in

Tuned out

6. *Listening is biased.* As a form of perception, listening is subject to the same sorts of distortions and biases discussed earlier. Two forms of bias that particularly affect listening are listening for self-interest and primacy/recency.

In Chapter 1, communication was defined as need driven; that is, we communicate to satisfy needs. As part of the communication process, listening, too, is need driven. We listen to gain information; we listen to show that we care about a relationship; we listen to maintain a polite image. However, these needs also tend to bias the way we listen. We listen mainly for information that we regard as important to our self-interest, often missing other information that is being conveyed. Guess what happens when an instructor announces to the class that the material she is presenting is important but won't be on the exam? Most of the students tune out the rest of the lecture because they don't believe that listening to it is important to their self-interest.

The principles of primacy and recency have to do with the order and timing of information. **Primacy** is the tendency to recall the first part of what we hear. **Recency** is the tendency to recall the last or most immediate thing we have heard. Together, these tendencies mean that you probably can recall the first and last parts of a lecture better than the middle. Primacy and recency affect a variety of your interactions. In employment interviews, for instance, the impressions you create at the very beginning of the interview and as the interview concludes are recalled more easily by the interviewer than the middle section.

Listening effectiveness can be improved by putting more effort into attending to and remembering the information that is presented in the middle of any interaction. Good class notes involve writing about the entire lecture, not just the beginning and end. And, as a speaker adapting to this listening principle, you would want to put the most important information at the beginning and end of a presentation.

7. *Effective listening requires a willingness and commitment to listen.*
You probably receive a number of phone calls that interrupt what you are doing. If the caller begins rambling about things you consider unimportant, you may try to continue what you were doing and feign attention. In essence, you are not really committed to listening. If you are not willing to listen, you tune out the speaker or engage in pseudolistening.

In a situation like this, is it better to (a) tell the caller you don't want to listen or (b) pretend to listen? Telling people you don't want to listen to them implies that you don't value them or consider them important; in doing this, you challenge the speaker's feelings of worth. Pseudolistening allows speakers to maintain a feeling that you value them and the interaction. However, it is a form of deceit.

You need to decide if you are willing and committed to listening. Sometimes the decision involves determining the consequences of not listening or of pseudolistening. Often there may be a tactful way out of the predicament. In interpersonal situations, most people are responsive to your saying something like, "I really want to hear what you have to say, but right now I've got to finish up this report. Let's get together in an hour." This kind of statement conveys the desire to listen to the other person at a time when you can provide a true commitment to listening.

■ Listening Methods

There is more than one way to listen. The way you listen corresponds to your reason for communicating. For instance, you may listen to gain information, to derive enjoyment, or to nurture a relationship, and each of these reasons may require a different type of listening.

In this section, you'll read about several methods of listening. Each method places a different emphasis on how you listen, the type of information you seek, and how you use the information you acquire. Each method has appropriate and inappropriate times for its use. As you read, evaluate how adept you are in using each of the methods. Which ones need improvement?

■ *Listening Objectively*

Listening objectively involves listening to gain information and achieve understanding. In objective listening, you are trying to openly receive the information another person is conveying to you. Objective listening requires a nonjudgmental attitude. You do not evaluate or criticize what you are told; instead, you simply try to absorb it so that you can recall it as completely as possible.

You would probably try to listen objectively to lectures, to a boss's instructions, to directions from a coach, or to a friend's description of a new restaurant. One study called this method "listening with accuracy" and found that it included the ability to distinguish facts from opinions and to recall details from conversations.[7]

To gain and retain as much information as you can, you need to practice the following skills:

1. Listen for and remember the key points.
2. Try to get both the big picture and the supporting information.
3. Focus on the message and avoid being distracted by the speaker's mannerisms or qualities.
4. Avoid arguing in your mind about the points the speaker is making.
5. Be an active listener: Ask questions, seek clarification, and provide a summary of the speaker's points from time to time.

■ *Listening Critically*

You are continually bombarded by persuasive attempts to get you to do something or buy something: "Elect me as your senator," "Buy my company's insurance policy," "Let me borrow your class notes." It would be naive to be an objective listener in these situations. What is called for is critical listening.

Listening critically means analyzing and evaluating messages. It involves initially listening for information and then evaluating the integrity of the information. People often create misleading messages in an attempt to gain your compliance. The critical listener is able to identify the fallacies in a speaker's arguments and reject unreliable or inaccurate claims.

For each of the following typical lines from advertising, what weaknesses do you see in the claim or logic?

Test Yourself

1. Five out of every six doctors surveyed recommend our product.
2. This is the lowest-priced vehicle in its class.
3. The American team came in second from the top, while the Russian team came in second from the bottom.
4. With a suggested retail price of $1,999, it's yours for only $1,599.
5. Low, low price. Only four payments of $19.99!!!, plus shipping and handling of $8.99.
6. This is your last chance to buy at this year's prices. (Advertisement in December)
7. Buy now while the price is the lowest it has been.
8. Some people even believe that this tonic can improve your memory by 50 percent.
9. Dr. Whitesand, a noted researcher, recommends this toothpaste over all others.
10. Without your support, we can no longer broadcast our messages of love and peace.
11. This policy will give your family the security they deserve. You'll have peace of mind knowing that if something happens to you, they'll be provided for.

Critical listening requires critical thinking. You must listen carefully to the message and watch for irrational or unsubstantiated claims. Sometimes a speaker's deception makes use of perceptual biases. The halo effect often comes into play when an advertiser uses a likable celebrity to endorse a product. In this situation, the advertiser is hoping that your liking for the person will transfer to a liking for the product. Another method is to use emotional appeals that overshadow logic, as in Test Yourself items 10 and 11.

Listening critically to persuasive messages means stepping back from the emotion of the moment and rationally evaluating the request and evidence. Listening critically requires you to:

1. Collect as much relevant information as possible.
2. Evaluate the information in a systematic and objective manner.
3. Evaluate the sender, the evidence, the logic, and the reasoning.
4. Determine the degree to which emotion is driving your response.
5. Consider as many conclusions and interpretations of the information as you can.

■ Listening Appreciatively

Listening appreciatively occurs when you listen for pleasure and enjoyment. You listen appreciatively to storytellers, comedians, and other entertaining communicators. Your goal is not to acquire information or to learn, but to enjoy the moment.

Listening appreciatively sometimes means making yourself vulnerable. You let down your critical-listening guard for the purpose of being absorbed by the telling.

In contrast to the cautions about the impact of emotions on critical listening, listening appreciatively allows emotions to be aroused and triggered by the message.

Imagine what it would be like to listen to a comedian either objectively or critically. You would probably never laugh. A typical joke might begin, "A dog goes into a bar and asks the bartender for a cold beer." Listening objectively might evoke an inquiry like "What kind of dog was it? What time of day did this happen? What kind of bar was it?" On the other hand, listening critically might evoke a response like "Wait a minute, dogs can't talk!" Both types of listening prevent letting the information amuse and entertain you.

Listening appreciatively requires you to:

1. Put aside objective and critical listening.
2. Willingly suspend disbelief—not worry about the reasonability or the soundness of logic.
3. Be open-minded and let images develop and connect freely.
4. Block out noise, distractions, and competing stimuli.
5. Be open to emotional reactions.

■ *Listening Personally*

A friend of yours who is struggling in school is confused about whether he should continue or drop out. How would you listen to him? You might listen objectively, trying to understand all the facts. You might listen critically, trying to evaluate the situation. Or you might listen appreciatively, admiring your friend's storytelling. On the other hand, you might listen personally.

Listening personally means listening for the purpose of helping other people more effectively understand their own situation. Listening personally often entails using empathy as a tool. **Listening empathically,** in its broadest sense, involves understanding and feeling another person's reaction to a given situation.[8] Empathy equips us to ask questions and provide feedback that will ultimately be of some therapeutic value.

One study found this method of "listening to show support" to be important even in the workplace.[9] Think about times in your life when you have been particularly troubled and have had the chance to talk to someone you considered a really good listener. What did that person do that helped you? He or she probably listened personally, completely focusing on you and what you had to say. Sometimes it doesn't even matter whether the other person understands you, so long as he or she is there for you to talk to.

To listen personally, you should:

1. Focus on the other person, letting him or her talk with a minimal amount of interruption.
2. Ask questions to help sort out the situation.
3. Seek clarification and elaboration of points that are muddled or unclear.
4. Paraphrase back to the other person what you think you have heard. This helps a person gain perspective on the situation.
5. Help create an orderly analysis of the situation by organizing and periodically summarizing what's being talked about.

Lakeside Counsel: Plenty of Takers for Amateurs Giving Free Advice

There was a time when free advice was considered to be worth about what it cost, but now a pair of amateur gurus have discovered a vein of humanity hungry for priceless counsel. Nearly every Sunday for the past three years, Roderick MacElwain and Neal Caldwell have spread their blanket under a blue-and-white striped canopy beside the bike path on the shores of White Rock Lake and hung out their shingle: "Free Advice." They continue to be amazed by the number of takers.

For several hours each weekend, the lost, the lovelorn, the bewildered and the clueless pause for consultation, for tips on tax deductions, mending frayed relationships, dealing with troublesome neighbors or obnoxious bosses or replacing the grout in their bathroom tile.

"It's not a comedy act," says MacElwain. "It is serious stuff. Some guy suspects his wife is cheating. . . . That's a real problem for him."

Three years ago, MacElwain and Caldwell, both 47, were lounging by the lake and, on a whim, wrote the words "Free Advice" on a piece of cardboard and propped it against a water cooler. That day, 15 passers-by visited their clinic.

"We thought it would be a one-time deal," Caldwell says. "But it became a real challenge. We were almost giddy."

In the early days, they were sometimes greeted with sneers and jeers. Occasionally, a motorist would make an obscene gesture or a jogger would offer his own advice: "Get a job." But as they became fixtures by the lake, the hostility waned. Caldwell and MacElwain say their weekend avocation plays to a basic human need—not just for guidance, but for affirmation and a sense that someone cares about their problems. Often, a line forms in the shade of a nearby oak and cars crowd into the small parking lot 30 yards away.

For four, five, seven hours—whatever the weather allows and the traffic demands—the two men listen to the problems of strangers. Neither has formal training in most of the areas about which they are consulted, but they think they perform a service simply by listening and responding with detached common sense.

"We've had lawyers stop by for advice," said MacElwain, a self-employed financial consultant with an education in accounting, finance and history. He also has devoted considerable time to the study of dream analysis.

Do they ever worry that they might give the wrong advice and screw up somebody's life? Nah. Most people become preoccupied with problems that don't carry such serious consequences, they say. Such as: A young woman alights from her bike, approaches tentatively and asks the two strangers what to do about her boyfriend, who communicates in grunts and channel-surfs like a junkie. Slap him? Cancel his cable service? Might work, but MacElwain and Caldwell suggest something less provocative. Talk to him. Tell him how you feel. Help him to understand that the relationship is threatened by his behavior. Problem solved, maybe. Next!

A middle-aged woman in tennis shoes believes that her mother, who lives in another state, has been scammed by a mortician. After shelling out $12,000 to prepay

This newspaper article demonstrates how much people value a good listener.

her burial, the mother received a contract from the funeral home with suspicious small print: "Prices and terms subject to change at any time." Instead of that satin-lined bronze box she selected, Mom could spend eternity in fiberboard while the mortician demanded more money from her heirs.

MacElwain and Caldwell suggest that she request a refund on the grounds of unacceptable fine print. If that fails, she should complain to the consumer protection division of the attorney general's office in her mother's home state. Problem solved, definitely. The woman returned a few months later and showed them the $12,000 refund check she had received on her mother's behalf.

"We don't tell them what they must do," Caldwell says. "We explore different ways of looking at their problem."

"We build a model," MacElwain adds, "and give them some options."

One young man asked their opinion of a career move he was contemplating: giving up a reliable and good-paying job in Dallas to go to Hollywood and try to become an actor. Caldwell, a wine store manager and musician (he plays in local clubs with a band called the Enablers), briefed him on the hardships and high mortality rate of show business and suggested that he wait until he had a day job and a roommate on the West Coast and enough money to see him through lean times.

"He came back a few months later," Caldwell says. "He had organized things as we suggested, and he was ready to make the move."

"We get a lot of repeats," MacElwain says. "Or people will come by just to thank us. One woman baked a pie for us."

Source: Houston Chronicle October 12, 1998; byline: Jim Henderson. Copyright 1998 Houston Chronicle Publishing Company. Reprinted with permission. All rights reserved.

■ *Listening Passively or Actively*

Sitting in a large lecture hall or watching TV alone does not provide much opportunity for interaction with the speaker. In these situations you adopt a fairly passive listening style. **Listening passively** means that the listener remains quiet and focuses primarily on independently absorbing or evaluating information.

At other times, you take a more interactive role in the development of shared meaning and understanding. **Listening actively** means the listener asks questions, guides the flow of information, and seeks clarification. An active listener shares responsibility with a speaker for reaching understanding, rather than assuming that it is totally the speaker's job.

To listen actively, you should:

1. Be willing and committed to listen as well as conveying a desire and receptiveness to listening.
2. Focus on the speaker and convey this focus by eye contact, body posture, and reactions to the speaker's messages.
3. Probe by asking questions that seek more information and clarification.
4. Ask for confirmation or correction of your perceptions.
5. Paraphrase by restating in your own words what you think the speaker has said and asking for correction.
6. Summarize by periodically providing the speaker with a brief summary of the main points the speaker has covered.

Which types of listening are you best at: objective, critical, appreciative, personal, passive, or active? Which types of listening are you poorest at? What hampers your effectiveness in each type of listening? What improves your listening?

▌Responding

Consider this conversational scenario:

CHRIS	I can't believe I bombed that test. I don't think the questions were very fair.
TIFFANY	Uh-huh.
CHRIS	That instructor really doesn't write very good exams; he even admits that.
TIFFANY	Really?
CHRIS	I guess I shouldn't feel too bummed out. Nobody did well.
TIFFANY	Have you seen that new movie about a conspiracy to take over the IRS?

Was Tiffany listening in this conversation? You might say no, because her responses were so limited and tangential. Actually, we can't tell whether she was listening on the basis of her responses. Whether she was listening or not, however, her responses did little to foster effective communication.

Part of the listening process includes how we respond to a speaker. Tiffany's responses can be interpreted by Chris as a reflection of Tiffany's listening. Of course, Chris has the advantage of observing Tiffany's nonverbal responses. Tiffany might be very focused on Chris, using strong eye contact, leaning forward, nodding her head, and so forth. These nonverbal cues contribute to an assessment of whether someone is listening.

■ *Disconfirming Responses*

The way you respond to a speaker can have a dramatic effect on the interaction, the relationship, and the individual. In the example of Chris and Tiffany, what do you think would happen if Tiffany didn't display many nonverbal signs of listening and always responded to Chris with such tangential words? The relationship would probably come to an end, or at least be severely strained. The reason is that Tiffany is implicitly conveying to Chris that she doesn't care about what Chris is saying and, by inference, that she doesn't care about Chris. Tiffany is displaying disconfirming responses.

Disconfirming responses are behaviors exhibited by listeners that convey a lack of listening, a lack of interest in what another person is saying, and a lack of interest in the other person.[10] Disconfirming responses can create a negative communication climate. This climate can seriously hamper the flow of information or even cause an interaction to be terminated. Disconfirming responses can also cause speakers to devalue themselves. What effect do you think there would be on a six-year-old child's self-esteem if every time the child tried to talk, the parents conveyed a lack of interest in what was being said—ignoring, interrupting, or turning away?

Most of us are not faced with continual disconfirming responses, but we receive some from time to time. Any behavior that can be seen as indicating an unwillingness to listen can be considered disconfirming. The situation determines whether a behavior is disconfirming or not. Remaining silent during a lecture would not necessarily be disconfirming; however, remaining silent after the lecturer directly asked you a question would be disconfirming. The following are some typical types of disconfirming responses:[11]

> *Verbal silence:* giving no spoken response to what another person has said
> *Nonverbal silence:* remaining inanimate, with little change in facial expression or gesturing
> *Nonverbal rejection:* looking away, turning away, sitting askew, avoiding eye contact
> *Diverted attention:* performing unrelated tasks, (such as reading the newspaper, shuffling papers, or watching TV) while the other person is talking
> *Interrupting:* not permitting the other person to finish statements and imposing your own information as implicitly more important or pressing
> *Impervious response:* making statements that fail to recognize what the speaker was just talking about, especially when it would be appropriate to respond in a relevant fashion (for example, Tiffany's final comment in the earlier example)
> *Taking over:* responding to what someone has said by going off on a monologue about your own situation; sometimes referred to as stage hogging[12] because the other person no longer gets a chance to talk
> *Tangential response:* "Yes, but . . .": changing the focus or direction of the speaker's message or focusing on incidental issues while ignoring the main ones

■ Confirming Responses

Think about the times when you have talked and other people have really, really listened to you. They asked questions, made relevant comments, asked for more details, looked at you, leaned toward you, and seemed to hang on

LEMONT BROWN *by Darrin Bell*

your every word. They were *interested* in what you had to say. How did you feel in those situations?

Such listening behaviors create a feeling of importance, value, and confirmation. **Confirming responses** are listening behaviors that demonstrate that you are listening, that you have an interest in what is being said, and that you value the person speaking.[13] Confirming responses let speakers know that you are committed to listening to them. The strongest confirming responses are those that convey an understanding of what the speaker was saying. Confirming responses are a form of active listening because you directly react to what is said by asking for more information and clarification.

The following are some of the behaviors that provide confirmation:

Listening actively: attending, probing, perception checking, paraphrasing, and summarizing

Displaying interest: conveying to the speaker an interest in what is being said, both verbally and through nonverbal behaviors (for example, good eye contact, leaning forward, directly facing the other person, and making statements like "That sounds really neat, tell me more about what happened")

Reflective responses: statements that show you have processed what you have heard ("So what you're saying is that you like me, but you're afraid of getting too involved?")

Direct confirming responses: explicitly stating that you want to hear what the other has to say or that you have a genuine concern for the other person

This chapter has discussed the processes by which you perceive stimuli around you, interpret the behavior of other people, and listen and respond to messages. The next chapter focuses on the nature of those stimuli and messages by examining verbal and nonverbal communication. In essence, Chapter 4 involves in-depth examination of the process of interpretation—how you attach meaning to words and nonverbal stimuli.

This chapter has focused on three interrelated elements concerning how you deal with the information that surrounds you: perception, listening, and responding.

Perception involves the process of selecting, organizing, and interpreting the stimuli around you. As part of the selection stage, you filter and attend to specific stimuli; and because of your pattern of filtering and attending, you inevitably have a biased and incomplete picture of the world around you. After you have selected information, you organize it. You fill in blanks, attach additional information, put information into categories, and use stereotyping. Finally, you interpret the information you have selected and organized. Interpretation involves attributing meaning to what you have perceived. You draw from your recalled experiences to understand the new information you have encountered.

One application of perception research, called attribution theory, has to do with our explanations of why people behave the way they do. We strive to develop an explanation for the behaviors we observe. We can attribute the cause of a person's behavior to the stimulus, the circumstance, or the person. Unfortunately, our attributions are subject to many biases. Attributional biases include overemphasizing obvious, irrelevant, and negative information; overdependence on simple explanations; sticking to preconceived explanations; and making incorrect causal attributions. Overcoming these biases requires a deliberate effort.

Listening is perception that focuses on spoken messages, and as such it is a skill that can be improved. Listening involves simplifying what we have heard and then adding information back when we recall it. Listening requires energy and effort. One potential source of problems in listening derives from the fact that our mind can process information faster than the person we are listening to can speak. Because of this speed difference, we listen intermittently, sampling what is being said and taking occasional mental vacations. Listening is biased, partly because we listen to serve our self-interest and partly because we are influenced by the primacy or recency of information. To be effective listeners, we must be willing and committed to listening.

There are a number of listening methods. Listening objectively involves listening to gain information and reach understanding. Listening critically means that we analyze and evaluate the messages we hear. Listening critically is particularly important when we are exposed to attempts to influence or persuade us. We listen appreciatively when we listen for pleasure and enjoyment. When the goal of our listening is to help speakers effectively understand their own situation, we listen personally. Among the tools we use while listening personally are asking questions, paraphrasing, and organizing the information. Listening passively involves remaining silent as we absorb and evaluate information. This is in contrast to listening actively, in which we ask questions and guide the flow of information to ensure that we get the information we need.

We watch people's reactions to what we are saying to determine if they are listening and how well they are listening. Responses reflect what has occurred during the perceptual and listening process. The way we respond either enhances or restricts the flow of information. Disconfirming responses convey to a speaker that we are not interested in what is being said or in the person who is speaking. Among the responses that are disconfirming are poor eye contact, performing unrelated tasks, interrupting, changing the subject, and dominating the discussion. On the other hand, we can demonstrate that we are listening and that we value the speaker by the use of confirming responses. Confirming responses include listening actively, displaying interest, reflective statements, and direct expressions of concern for the other.

Key Terms

perception   Being aware enough of a stimulus to attach meaning to it.

selection   The first step in perception, in which we focus our attention on specific stimuli while ignoring others.

filtering   Setting threshold levels for the arousal of our senses, so that stimuli below the threshold are filtered out.

attending   Heightening our attention to particular sensory input.

halo effect   A bias that occurs when we consider someone good or attractive and we see only positive qualities.

horn effect   A bias that causes us to see only negative qualities in those we dislike or view as bad.

organizing   The second step in perception, in which we combine sensory information, categorize it, and fill in the missing pieces.

category   A collection of information that is placed under a single, simplified label.

stereotype   A category in which we place individuals on the basis of some attribute or quality.

interpretation   The third step of perception, which involves attributing meaning to stimuli we have selected and organized.

attribution   The inclination of people to develop explanations for why people act the way they do.

causal theory of attribution   A theory of the attribution process stating that we choose among three general causes for people's actions: the stimulus, the circumstance, and the person.

attributional biases   Factors that cause us to make inaccurate attributions.

fundamental attribution error   The tendency to explain other people's behaviors on the basis of internal causes (personality) rather than on external causes (circumstance).

listening   A special form of perception that focuses on spoken messages.

pseudolistening   Pretending to listen when we really aren't.

primacy   The tendency to recall the first part of what we hear more than other parts.

recency   The tendency to recall the last or most immediate thing we have heard.

listening objectively   A type of listening that focuses on gaining information and achieving understanding.

listening critically   A type of listening in which you listen for the purpose of analyzing and evaluating messages.

listening appreciatively   A type of listening that occurs when you listen for pleasure and enjoyment.

listening personally   A type of listening in which the purpose is to help other people more effectively understand their own situation.

listening empathically   A type of listening that involves understanding and feeling another person's reaction to a given situation.

listening passively   A type of listening in which the listener remains quiet and focuses primarily on independently absorbing or evaluating information.

listening actively   A type of listening in which the listener asks questions, guides the flow of information, and seeks clarification.

disconfirming responses   Listening behaviors that convey a lack of listening, a lack of interest in what another person is saying, and a lack of interest in the other person.

confirming responses   Listening behaviors that demonstrate that we are listening, that we have an interest in what is being said, and that we value the person speaking.

Review Questions

1. Identify and explain each of the three basic stages of perception.
2. Define attribution.
3. What are some of the biases that affect the attribution process?
4. How can you overcome attribution biases?
5. Identify and explain some of the principles that apply to listening.
6. Explain the differences between listening objectively, critically, appreciatively, personally, passively, and actively.
7. Define confirming responses and disconfirming responses.

Chapter 4

Attribution of Meaning in Verbal and Nonverbal Communication

Objectives

Studying this chapter will allow you to:

1. Distinguish between symbols, signs, verbal communication, and nonverbal communication.
2. Explain the general principles of how we attribute meaning.
3. Understand some basic ways in which language and words affect us.
4. Describe each of the categories of nonverbal communication.
5. Explain the principles that apply to nonverbal communication.
6. Explain how verbal and nonverbal communication relate to each other.

Shelly concluded her presentation by saying, "And finally . . . uh, an analysis of the impact of our proposal shows . . . um, shows the company can increase its market share by twenty cents, I mean 20 percent, and . . . um, 25 percent profits increase over the next five years." She spoke softly and in a monotone; her eyes were tied to her notes, avoiding contact with her colleagues seated around the conference table; and her body was rigid and inflexible.

If you were one of the people seated at the conference table, how would you react? Assuming that you heard the entire presentation, would you be inclined to support the proposal? What meaning would you attribute to Shelly's behaviors? You might feel that she lacked confidence in her proposal. You might have doubts as to whether she really believed what she was saying.

This scenario demonstrates how we respond to both verbal and nonverbal cues in interpreting what we perceive. The hesitations and mistakes in Shelly's language would have a definite effect on you as a listener. You can also imagine how Shelly's nonverbal qualities of tone, eye contact, and gesturing would influence how you responded to her verbal message. The impact would be much stronger if you actually saw and heard the scenario in person.

Chapter 3 dealt with our perception of the stimuli around us. This chapter is about the nature of those stimuli and how we go about attributing meaning to them. As you saw in Chapter 1, those stimuli can be categorized as symbols or signs. To refresh your memory, **symbols** are stimuli that have abstract, arbitrary, flexible, and changing meanings,[1] whereas **signs** are stimuli that have fixed and concrete meanings.

One way to determine if a stimulus is a symbol or a sign is to ask whether the meaning would be the same in different cultures. The meaning of symbols might easily change from one culture to another; signs, however, have the same meaning regardless of the culture in which they occur.

We can also divide stimuli into vocal and nonvocal types. **Vocal stimuli** include all sounds that emanate from the mouth. For example, vocal stimuli include gasps, coughs, and whistles as well as spoken words. **Nonvocal stimuli** include all stimuli except oral sounds. In other words, this category encompasses everything we perceive that is not vocal. Nonvocal stimuli greatly outnumber vocal stimuli.

Combining these two classifications, we can place any stimulus into one of four categories, as shown by the four quadrants in Figure 4.1: vocal symbols, vocal signs, nonvocal symbols, or nonvocal signs. Classifying stimuli into a given quadrant is not always as straightforward a task as you might expect. Something that is a sign in one culture can be viewed symbolically by another. Early Native Americans viewed things like rain, snow, and wind as symbols from their gods, though most of us see these phenomena as signs of certain atmospheric conditions. Coughing is a sign when it occurs because a person has a cold (the cough has a fixed meaning); but if we intentionally make a coughing sound to attract someone's attention, the cough becomes a vocal symbol. Determining whether something is a sign or symbol sometimes requires understanding the intention of the sender.

The information represented in the four quadrants of Figure 4.1 is generally reduced to two types of communication: verbal and nonverbal. **Verbal**

Figure 4.1

Classification of Stimuli

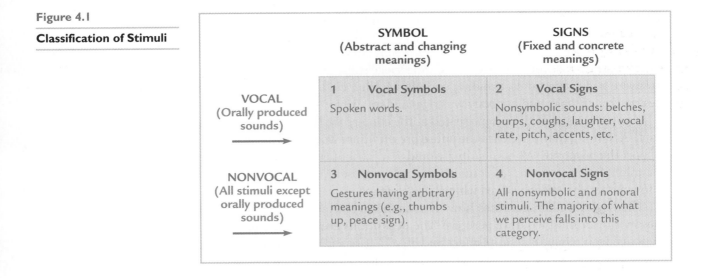

communication refers to communication that is based on the stimuli identified in the first quadrant of Figure 4.1—vocal symbols. **Nonverbal communication** refers to communication reflected in quadrants 2, 3, and 4—vocal signs, nonvocal symbols, and nonvocal signs. This chapter will examine both verbal and nonverbal communication and the relationship between the two.

■ General Principles of Attributing Meaning

So far, our discussion of stimuli has reflected many of the principles introduced in Chapter 3 with respect to the first two stages of perception: selecting and organizing. In this section, the focus shifts to the interpretation stage—attaching meaning to what we have perceived. Of course, the way we classify stimuli affects the meaning we attach to them. Our discussion of a cough shows how classification influences the attribution of meaning.

In this section, the term *attribution* has a slightly different meaning than when it was used in Chapter 3. When we make *attributions about people,* we are seeking to explain their behaviors. To say that we *attribute meaning* to something means that we attach some meaning to, or associate meaning with, the stimulus. There is a subtle difference between the two processes, as shown by the following statement: We attribute meaning to people's behaviors, and we make attributions about the causes of those behaviors.

We can identify six general principles that govern the ways we attribute meaning.

1. We attribute meaning to what we perceive. This principle should be familiar from Chapter 3. In this chapter, we will explore its implications further. Since people attribute meaning to both the verbal and the nonverbal stimuli they perceive, we cannot stop someone from attaching meaning to our words or actions. Attributing meaning to what is perceived is one of the reasons for the irreversibility of communication that was discussed in Chapter 2. We cannot undo someone's perception, and we cannot stop the resulting attribution of meaning. In addition, the meaning we intend by our words and actions is not always the meaning other people attribute.

2. *Meaning is in people, not in what is perceived.* The meanings we attach to what we perceive come from our psychological context, not from the objects of our perception. We sometimes act as if the spoken word itself has meaning, but the word is only a stimulus. It stimulates our perceptual process, and we attach meaning to the sound.

Let's look at an example. Try to visualize what comes to your mind when you see or hear the word *dog.* What color is the dog? How big is the dog? What breed is the dog? Is it a long- or short-haired breed? As you develop your image of a dog, see if you can identify what caused you to have that image. Meanings are based on our experiences. You may have pictured a dog you have now or one you had while growing up. Perhaps you pictured a friend's or neighbor's dog. Whatever the basis of your image, the image exists in your mind, not in the visual cue of the inked letters spelling out *dog.*

The Triangle of Meaning,[2] shown in Figure 4.2, was developed by linguistic theorists to illustrate the relationship between the symbol (word), the thought, and the referent (the actual thing). The referent is that which is perceivable, such as a person or object. As the lines in the figure indicate, there are direct links between symbols and thoughts and between referents and thoughts, but only an indirect link between symbols and referents.

In other words, when you hear the word *dog,* (the symbol), it evokes a thought. That thought is based on your experiences with dogs, the referent. The symbol itself (the spoken word *dog*) is linked only indirectly to the referent (a real dog). This is true whether the symbol or the referent comes first. Your thought process might be triggered by the perception of a dog while you are out for a walk, and you would then label your thought by using the symbol *dog.* On the other hand, if someone says, "Look at that dog," the symbol occurs first, then the thought, which finally leads you to look around for the referent, a dog.

We sometimes operate as though there is a direct link between the symbol and the referent; that is, we assume that the symbol is the same thing as the referent. This means that we assume that other people have the same referent for the symbol that we are using. We make statements as if the meaning is in the words,

Figure 4.2

The Triangle of Meaning

Solid lines indicate direct links; the dashed line shows an indirect link.

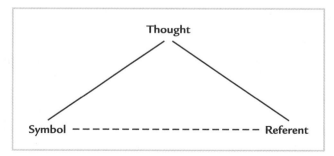

without recognizing that the words simply trigger a response. Usually, we have a pretty good idea of what response a given word or action will evoke, but we do err. For example, you might be talking about your dad, totally oblivious that the person with whom you are talking never knew his dad. You intend a positive statement, but you trigger feelings of anger or pain in the other person. In essence, once you say or do something, you have no control over the reaction that it might evoke in other people.

To avoid communication problems, we need to be cautious in our expectation that other people understand everything we say and do. The more we know about our audience, the more effective we can be in predicting reactions and effects.

3. ***Each person attributes a different meaning to what he or she perceives.*** Each person's psychological context represents a unique collection of experiences that affect interpretations. The word *dog* does not evoke a universally shared meaning. Earlier in the chapter, when you were asked to visualize a dog, you may have pictured a small white poodle, while some of your classmates visualized a large Great Dane and still others a pit bull. Each person attributes a slightly different meaning to both words and nonverbals.

One skill that helps us recognize these differences is social decentering. **Social decentering** represents the degree to which we understand the other person's psychological context. It allows us to understand someone else's interpretations and therefore create more effective communication. When we socially decenter, we move from being self-centered to being other-centered.

In contrast, we sometimes communicate in an egocentric fashion, creating messages that make sense to us without considering how other people will interpret those messages. In **egocentric communication,** we fail to recognize differences between ourselves and others and therefore fail to adapt our communication. Because we tend to interact with people who are similar to us, or at least from similar cultural backgrounds, we may manage to communicate fairly well despite our egocentric tendencies. In some situations, however, those tendencies get us into trouble.

4. ***Communication varies in terms of the degree to which meaning is shared.*** The degree to which you and another person have the same interpretation for a word or act represents **shared meaning.** Each part of Figure 4.3 shows two circles, one representing the meaning that you might associate with a word or nonverbal cue, and the other representing the meaning for another person. The degree to which the two circles overlap represents the amount of shared meaning.

When the two circles are totally apart (Figure 4.3A), there is no shared understanding, even though actional communication has occurred. If you say, "I was bitten by a mean dog yesterday" to a woman from Germany who does not speak English, she may give you a baffled look and say, "Ich nicht verstehe Sie." (I don't understand you). While no shared meaning of the words has occurred, you have gained some information, such as the realization that the person is from another country.

The more the two circles overlap, the greater the shared understanding (Figures 4.3B and C). The two circles can never *totally* overlap, but as relationships develop, we usually achieve more and more overlap in our circles of shared

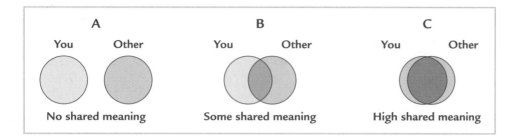

Figure 4.3

Degrees of Shared Meaning

A — You — Other — No shared meaning

B — You — Other — Some shared meaning

C — You — Other — High shared meaning

meaning. Think about when you started a new job. Did much of the terminology and behaviors of the other people at work baffle you? As time passed, you shared experiences with those people, and the circles of meaning increasingly overlapped.

5. *Meanings are culturally influenced.* We learn to associate meanings with what we perceive in two ways: We are taught by other people, and we deduce meanings from repeated exposure. In both instances, the cultural context has a lot to do with the meanings we associate with perceptions. Those who teach us, are teaching meanings that correspond to their cultural backgrounds. In this way, cultural meanings are passed on from one generation to the next. The less variation there is among those who teach us, the more our meanings will be aligned with theirs. Imagine a student being taught by the same teacher from kindergarten through high school. That student's understanding of the world probably would be quite similar to the teacher's.

Avoiding Cultural Blunders

In Hungary, men customarily walk on the left side of women or anyone of greater status, like a boss. When eating, keep both hands above the table, never in your lap. Never ask a man from the Middle East about his wife or family. A woman should not pour wine in Italy.

They do things differently over there. In fact, people do things differently everywhere in the world. And if you're a casual tourist, you'll likely to be forgiven the occasional faux pas as you pass through a foreign country. But if you're a business traveler, expectations are greater. And the fall-out from a miscue can have financial repercussions. Similarly, a sensitivity to local customs can enhance a visiting businessperson's stature and make doing business easier.

Some mistakes can be worse than embarrassing. In her book *Fascinating Arabs,* Margaret Nydell tells of an American woman in Saudi Arabia who slid into the front passenger seat of a car and planted a friendly kiss on the cheek of the man at the wheel. Public displays of affection don't play well there. The gesture was spotted by a captain of the Saudi National Guard who demanded to know if the couple was married. They were, but not to each other.

This article for business travelers illustrates the problems that occur because of the cultural nature of language and communication.

The woman was expelled from the country and the man, who argued with the lawman, spent some time in jail.

The stories of miscues and missteps are many and varied. No one in recent history has quite equaled the unfortunate incident when then-President George Bush, exhausted and clearly ill, threw up at a state dinner in Japan. But in Washington, there's a story that may be apocryphal about the American diplomat who thought the small finger bowl at his place setting was some kind of soup.

As he raised the bowl to his lips to drink, his Asian hosts did likewise for fear of offending him should he discover his error.

In 1995, Bill Richardson, then a congressman from New Mexico, traveled to Baghdad to meet with Saddam Hussein to try to secure the release of two Americans who had been imprisoned after accidentally straying into Iraqi territory. Richardson greeted Hussein with a handshake, then sat down and crossed his legs. Hussein stood up abruptly and left the room, ending the meeting before it began. Richardson's offense? He'd displayed the sole of his shoe, a serious insult in many Arabic and Eastern countries because the bottom of the foot is considered to be the dirtiest part of the body. (The Americans were eventually released, but Richardson's opening gambit didn't speed the process.)

Non-verbal communication can be as much a source of misunderstanding as verbal, says American business consultant Elizabeth Ulrich, author of *Speaking Globally*.

"The classic example is the 'A-OK' gesture which is positive in the United States," says Ulrich, "but obscene in much of the rest of the world."

Mary Murray Bosrock, author of a series of international etiquette books called *Put Your Best Foot Forward,* says showing up on time for a dinner party in South America could also be a disaster—no one expects anyone to be less than a half hour or hour late. She says you're liable to find your host or hostess still in the process of dressing if you actually adhere to the time on an invitation.

But the Middle East and Asia are faux pas minefields for American business travelers. Consider the simple issue of calling cards. In the States, a proffered card is usually quickly pocketed. But that's not the way things are done in most Asian countries. Like a Japanese tea ceremony or highly stylized Chinese opera, presenting a business card can be an elaborate exercise.

When presenting a card, always face the recipient and hold your card on the upper two corners as you offer the card face up. If you're the recipient, you are expected to take the card with studied seriousness and examine it before carefully and respectfully putting it in your cardholder. And everyone expects a business card, not just the principal person with whom you're meeting. Where the heck everyone in Asia stashes all the cards they've received is a mystery to me, but they sure collect a lot; experts advise an American traveling to Asia on business have enough cards to hand out 200 a week. You'll get bonus points if your card is translated into the local language on the reverse side. Make sure your translation is precise.

Ulrich's company's name, "Speak for Yourself," once turned up as "Speak Up or Shut Up" in Mandarin.

Oh, and if you need to scrawl your cell phone or hotel number on the card, never use red ink—it symbolizes death.

You've probably heard or read about the elaborate rituals of gift-giving in Japan, where just about everything except the changing of a streetlight seems to warrant an exchange of presents. You know some numbers are unlucky in China. That women in

Middle Eastern countries shouldn't wear mini-skirts or display bare arms. But the rules are many and varied, so if you're going to a new part of the world to try to make money—or even to visit—you might want to study up on the local customs.

Source: Rudy Maxa, "How to Avoid Cultural Blunders" [online], MSNBC, December 23, 1998. Reprinted with the permission of the author.

The process of deducing meaning from exposure is also culturally bound, because your experiences occur within a given culture. You would not have to be told what a Seder is in a Jewish household if your family took part in this traditional Passover meal. You would learn the meaning through observation. But someone who was never exposed to this Jewish tradition or to the term would have no meaning for the word *Seder.* The experiences you observe occur within a cultural context, creating a set of culturally based meanings that are associated with words and actions.

Groups of individuals who share certain common experiences are more likely to have a closer understanding of some words or actions than other people. The phrase *being in labor* refers to a female in the process of giving birth. Women who have been in labor share a common experience and are likely to have a specific meaning attached to that phrase that is different from the meanings attached by those who have not had the experience. Throughout your life, your shared experiences with others have created greater shared meanings for certain words and actions. Those experiences may have occurred in any number of social groups—classes, workplaces, family, friends, and church, for instance.

Your race, ethnicity, religion, regionality, hometown, sex, and age are all characteristics that can serve as common denominators that enhance shared meaning. As an African American, you may share some experiences with other African Americans, such as certain types of racism and prejudice not experienced by European Americans. Likewise, you share experiences with those of a similar age. Sometimes this produces problems for older, nontraditional students who have a different set of experiences than the typical undergraduate. As a college student, too, you have different meanings for what you hear than do noncollege students.

Social decentering is one way to bridge the gap with those who are different from you. Your social decentering skills can be used to evaluate the cultural elements that contribute to another person's psychological context. In this way, you can better understand the other person's reactions and meanings.

Think of three people you know who differ from you in some significant way, such as sex, age, race, religion, or where they were raised. Now try to identify three things about each that causes him or her to attribute different meanings to things than you do. For example, perhaps your grandmother gets very upset with you at dinner if you don't eat everything on your plate. Why? She might see this behavior as wasteful because she was raised during the Great Depression, when food was scarce.

6. *Meanings are attributed within contexts.* Think back to the scenario at the beginning of this chapter in which Shelly was making a presentation to a small group. Perhaps you thought that you really couldn't make much of an interpretation of the presentation because you were missing too much information. Some of the information you were missing was about the context.

How would your interpretation be affected if you knew that Shelly was the twenty-four-year-old daughter of the company president? Or if she *was* the company president? Or if she was not the one who was supposed to be giving the presentation, but was asked at the last minute to fill in for her sick boss? Each of these additional pieces of information would cause you to interpret the same observations in a different way.

As this example shows, we do not attribute meaning in a vacuum. Rather, we depend on the additional information we perceive, recall, or even imagine. Nonverbals add a context to the spoken words. Words themselves provide a context for other words. The statement "You've taken that out of context" reflects the problems that occur when we try to interpret words or phrases outside the full context.

Words and actions have multiple meanings, and it is through knowledge of the context that we are able to decide which meaning to apply. The word *dog* appearing by itself might be taken to mean the sort of domestic animal that typically has four legs and barks. But *dog* can take on different meanings when appearing in the context of other words:

"Boy, are my dogs sore."
"I'm dog-tired."
"My little brother has been dogging me all day."
"You will be dogged by your sins."

Even if you aren't familiar with these expressions, you can probably deduce their meaning from the context in which they occur. The first example may be the most difficult to figure out, and having a larger context would give you more help in attributing meaning: "I've been walking around Disneyland for eight hours now. I knew I shouldn't have worn these new shoes; they're too tight. Boy, are my dogs sore." In this use, dogs are feet.

In the same way, we use context to develop an understanding for nonverbal stimuli. For instance, a smile can mean something positive or negative, depending on the context. You can smile at someone you are attracted to and accompany the smile with a warm "Hello." Or you can smile with evil intent as you say, "Heeeere's Johnny!"

■ Verbal Communication and Language

The six principles just discussed all apply to verbal communication and language. Verbal communication has been used in this text as a general reference to any communication that utilizes words. Words are the components of language.

A **language,** formally speaking, is a set of words and the rules that govern the connection of those words. Languages are learned. Most of us acquire language by being exposed to it from birth as people communicate with us. We can also consciously try to learn languages through high school and college courses. Language acquisition involves learning both the vocabulary and the syntactic rules—the rules that govern sentence structure. We derive meaning from the combination of the words and the language rules.

The rules of a language govern its sentence structure, grammar, use of verb tenses, gender, and so on. For example, the sentence "Will you marry me?" takes on different meanings as the order of the words is changed. Look at the same words in different arrangements:

"You will marry me."
"Marry me, will you?"
"Me? You marry Will!"

In the last example, the meaning could be "Don't marry me, marry some guy named Will" or "I'm not marrying Will. You marry him." Clearly, learning the rules that govern word order is as important as learning the words themselves.

Words vary in more than just their meaning. The following sections explain more about the nature of words to help you better understand their intricacies. You have a multitude of choices for the words you use to express yourself, and your word selection can have a dramatic impact on how effectively you communicate. You will learn about how words vary in terms of power, abstraction, impact on how we think, denotation, and connotation.

■ *The Power of Words*

Words have power. We can evoke a variety of emotional reactions from other people, such as sadness, fear, pain, depression, anger, love, worry, and joy, simply by producing sounds—vibrating air. We can rally troops, motivate employees, gain favors, create relationships, deflate self-esteem, sell encyclopedias, start fights, or get a job simply by the words we choose to say. Language is a tool that allows us to meet our goals. However, other people are also using words to satisfy their needs, and sometimes these needs conflict with ours. Often, the person who is more adept at using words is more effective at wielding power and satisfying needs.

Power derived from listeners' reactions.   Words have power because we respond to them. We feel hurt and angry if someone calls us a name. Calling someone a liar, a blubbering fool, or an idiot usually evokes anger. But think about what gives those words power. Words, in and of themselves, do not have power; we give words power by reacting to the meanings we associate with them (remember, meaning is in people). Has anybody ever called you a name that failed to make you angry or upset? If so, it's probably because you didn't give the words power over you. Your reaction was tempered and controlled.

Write down several names that people have called you that made you angry, upset, or embarrassed. What is it about those words that produces that effect? Where does the power come from? What can you do to minimize the impact of such name-calling on you?

Powerful and powerless language. We can communicate our own power or powerlessness to other people through our language. As stated in Chapter 1, messages have both a content and a relational dimension. One of the ways we communicate the definition of a relationship is through our language.

Listen to the communication between instructors and students after class. Generally, instructors make declarative statements; students ask questions. Instructors control the conversation; students follow the instructor's lead. Students will typically use more hedges and qualifiers than their instructors, such as "I think you said we could hand the papers in tomorrow, um, is that right?"

Table 4.1 lists forms of powerless language and then shows the same forms translated into more powerful language. Examine this list and think about your own communication. When do you use powerful language, and when do you use powerless language?

Your use of powerful or powerless language is affected by the relational and situational contexts. For instance, your level of power in an interpersonal interaction is directly related to the amount of power the other person displays—the relational context. The situational context has similar effects: Hesitations would not necessarily mean powerlessness if used by a speaker who was talking about a very personal and distressful situation.

Table 4.1   Powerless and Powerful Language

Type	Powerless Language	Rephrased in Powerful Language
Hedges/Qualifiers	"I *think*, *maybe*, it *might* be okay."	"That will be great."
Hesitations	"*Um*, five percent, *ah*, is, *ah*, too low."	"Five percent is too low!"
Polite forms	"*Sir*, *please* tell me how I might help."	"How might I help?"
Tag questions	"It's on page 33, *isn't it?*"	"It's on page 33."
Disclaimers	"*I'm probably wrong*, but let's try anyway."	"Let's try."
Added baggage	"*My grade point average has fluctuated a lot. One term I had a 3.3 and another term it was 2.0. But* overall my grade point average is *now* 2.8, *which isn't too bad considering I had a part-time job.*"	"My grade point average is 2.8."
Intensifiers	"*So*, it was *really* nice meeting you. I had a *very* good time. It was *quite* a good movie."	"It was nice meeting you. I had a good time. It was a good movie."

Note: The words in italics are those that diminish the power of the message.
Source: Derived from J. J. Bradac and A. Mulac, "A Molecular View of Powerful and Powerless Speech Styles: Attributional Consequences of Specific Language Features and Communicator Intentions", *Communication Monographs,* 51 (1984) 307–319; and D. A. Infante, A. S. Rancer, and D. F. Womack, *Building Communication Theory* (pp. 216–217) (Prospect Heights, Il.: Waveland Press, 1990).

■ *Level of Abstraction*

Words vary in their level of abstraction. The triangle of meaning in Figure 4.2 shows the relationships between thought, symbol, and referent. However, not all words have referents that are as easy to perceive or visualize as a dog. What images come into mind when you think of the following terms?

mature white oak tree / timber / forest / national park /
health / welfare / peace / love / respect

The terms in the first line are more concrete—that is, the connection between the symbol and the referent is clearer. The likelihood that each of us pictures a similar image is fairly high. In contrast, the words in the second line are more abstract. They do not evoke clear mental images or have definitive referents.

Abstraction and misunderstanding.   The more communication incorporates abstract language, the more it becomes confusing and prone to misunderstanding. Telling someone "I love you" is not as clear as telling someone "I want to kiss you." *Love* is more abstract and ambiguous, thus lending itself to broader interpretation. The action represented by the word *kiss* has a more defined referent and is therefore less abstract and ambiguous than the word *love.*

Reaching shared meaning is harder to do when we are dealing with abstract concepts and language. For this reason, the process of resolving conflicts often begins with individuals moving from an abstract discussion to identifying specific behaviors and observable referents. Instead of telling your roommate or spouse "You are a pig," it is more constructive to say, "I am upset that you keep leaving your dirty clothes all over the living room."

Abstraction and equivocation.   We can intentionally use abstract language to avoid negative consequences or to help achieve our personal goals. An instructor might respond abstractly to a student's request for permission to miss a class by saying, "You're an adult. You can make decisions about your own behavior." So did the instructor say yes or no?

We often make statements that are intentionally ambiguous. Think of the line "Let's get together some time." Our intention might really be to never get together, but we don't want to belittle someone by making such a direct declaration. The use of intentional ambiguity allows us to avoid threatening or negative situations.

Creating intentionally ambiguous messages is called *equivocation.* Equivocal messages include messages that can be interpreted in a number of ways—messages that are self-contradictory, ambiguous, or evasive.[3] When your boss asks, "How do you like my proposal?" you might respond with an equivocal message:

"You really presented it well."
"I've never heard a proposal like that before."
"With a little bit of polishing, it will be great."

The language in these replies gives the appearance of having responded to the question without really doing so.

How ethical is it to respond to someone with an equivocal response? Should you respond clearly and unambiguously when the response is likely to hurt people's feelings or embarrass them? Are equivocal responses lies?

If someone recognizes that you are responding equivocally, he or she may ask you to be more direct. Is it okay then to give a direct response, even if you know that the person won't like what you say?

■ *The Interconnection of Language and Thought*

Language and thought are interconnected. Humans have the ability to think symbolically; that is, we can think with words rather than just with images. This enables us to think abstractly. We can think about things that don't have easily observable referents, like concepts and values.

While words give us the ability to think abstractly, they also limit our ability to think. We cannot think symbolically beyond the symbols we have. You can't think about the value of existentialist philosophy if you don't know what existentialism is. On the other hand, when we encounter something new for which we have no term, we often invent one. The influx of personal computers has created a need for a whole new set of terms, such as *surfing the net, email, PCs, the Internet, RAM, CD-ROM,* and *chat rooms.* But notice how many of these new terms actually rely on existing terms. *Surfing* is not a new term, nor is *net,* but the combination of them is new, and it reflects the essence of the experience that you have when on the Internet.

Much of your college education consists of learning symbols—learning words and their definitions. Those words then have an impact on how you think. People also judge the way you think on the basis of the language you use.

A boy and his father were driving late one night on some back roads. They had a terrible accident, and both were seriously injured. They were taken to the nearest hospital, and a surgeon was called to operate on the boy. Upon seeing the boy, the surgeon exclaimed, "I can't operate on him, he is my son!" How can this be? (Read on for the answer.)

The Whorfian hypothesis. The obvious connection between language and thought has led to various notions about how each influences the other. One famous theory is known as the Whorfian hypothesis, or the Sapir-Whorf or Whorf-Sapir hypothesis, after its two originators, Benjamin Whorf and Edward Sapir. The **Whorfian hypothesis** maintains that how we think is determined by the language with which we think. As a corollary, since languages are culture specific, the way one culture thinks can be expected to differ from the thinking of another culture.

Much confusion and distortion have occurred over the years since the hypothesis was developed. Benjamin Whorf, who was considered an amateur linguist, drew on the language of the Hopi Indians and Eskimos to support his theory. However, a number of errors have been discovered in his interpretations, leading to a tempering of the support for the hypothesis.[4] The issue becomes one of the chicken and the egg: Is it language that shapes culture and thought, or is it the culture and thought that form the language?

Biased language: sexism and racism.   Despite the uncertainties, the overriding principle of the Whorfian hypothesis deserves our attention. Language can have a dramatic impact on how we perceive and think about the world. This impact can be seen in the way that certain linguistic pitfalls affect our impressions of other people. For instance, the existence of sexist bias in our language has a variety of negative effects. It isn't clear if the existence of sexist terminology creates a sexist attitude or if those who are sexist simply employ sexist language. We do know that sexist language is offensive to people and therefore should be avoided.

Many of us use *he, him, his, man,* or *guy* as a general reference to people when we don't know their sex. We may not intend to be sexist, but such language does perpetuate a certain level of male dominance in a culture. The solution to the earlier Test Yourself riddle is rather simple. The surgeon was the boy's mother. If you concluded this without having heard the puzzle before, congratulate yourself. Most people don't see this obvious solution. Most assume that the surgeon is a male, and this assumption prevents them from seeing any other alternative.

In essence, then, the sexism in language restricts the way we think. We talk about doctors, lawyers, judges, even college professors as "he," thus failing to recognize that such positions are also held by women. Much of the language of the U.S. has been carried over from a time in which males dominated the culture. There are efforts to desex language by changing *chairman* to *chair, salesman* to *salesperson, stewardess* to *flight attendant,* and so on. However, we still have many words and phrases in our language that place the focus on men: for example, *freshmen, manned space station,* and "Caution: Men at Work."

Our language is also racist. We label people according to characteristics such as skin color or presumed racial background: *black, white, Anglo, Asian American, African American, Chicano.* We also create sets of derogatory words to distinguish amongst groups, and the meanings carry an array of demeaning effects. You may not think that mere labels carry much weight, but history is filled with examples in which the word or label was paramount. American baseball went though a time when an individual would be excluded from playing in the major leagues if he claimed he was Negro, but not if he claimed he was Cuban. The label was the predominant factor, not the skin color. The label defined the individual.

Biased language: polarization and overgeneralization.   These problems are extensions of the attribution bias discussed in Chapter 3, whereby we attribute meaning and categorize people according to the most obvious information—sex, skin color, age, and so forth. These perceptual biases often result in the application of terms that are by their very nature dichotomous and polarizing.

Polarization is the tendency in language to divide things into two groups: for instance, blacks and whites, men and women, gays and straights, rural and urban (farmers and townies), rich and poor. In addition, we tend to associate positive attributes with one group and negative attributes with the other (similar to the halo and horn effects discussed in Chapter 3).

In Whorfian terms, the use of bipolar language means that we are doomed to perceive the world inaccurately. That is why in the 1920s, a Cuban with dark skin color could play baseball and a black with lighter skin color could not. Cubans were of Spanish descent and therefore were seen as European or white. The reality is that polarization is an artificial way of classifying that is created by the inadequacies of our language. What would you call someone who has three Anglo-American grandparents and one African American grandparent? Our language forces us to categorize this person as either black or white; there really isn't any in-between. Individuals from bicultural or biracial backgrounds frequently find themselves forced by the culture and language to identify with one group or the other.[5]

Similar effects occur because of our tendency to use inclusive language. Inclusive language leads us to ignore important individual differences. We use language that is filled with overgeneralizations and allness statements. **Overgeneralizations** claim broader truth than is reasonable to assume. **Allness statements** claim the existence of a common characteristic for an entire category.

As the parent of teenagers, I have learned to watch for these types of language errors. My children make such claims as "Everyone else will be wearing shorts to school today" or "All of my friends get to stay up past eleven." The problem with such overgeneralizations and allness statements is the use of "every" or "all." We need to be cautious about such statements because they discount individual variations and oversimplify reality. They generally mislead a listener into forming an incorrect belief. Fortunately, they are often easy to disprove. As I drop my daughter off for school after her initial overgeneralization about shorts, I point out every kid wearing long pants.

In writing this text, I have tried to avoid making overgeneralizations or allness statements. One way to do this is to add qualifiers. **Qualifiers** are words or phrases that indicate probabilities, tendencies, restrictions, and limitations. Rather than overgeneralizing by saying, "Everyone always overgeneralizes," we can qualify that statement as "Most of us tend to overgeneralize." We can easily temper our generalizations and allness statements with words and phrases like *most, almost all, a lot, practically, probably,* and *possibly.* My teenagers might more accurately state, "Almost everyone else will be wearing shorts" and "Practically all my friends. . . ."

■ *Connotations and Denotations*

You already know that words elicit a response, but we actually respond in two ways. Let's say that you were bitten by a dog when you were a child and therefore have a fear of dogs. As you imagined a dog earlier in this chapter, you would have had two responses, as illustrated in Figure 4.4. Your first would have been the denotative meaning: A dog is usually a four-legged, domesticated animal that barks and growls. The second would have been the connotative meaning—a feeling of fear and anxiety. **Denotative meanings** are the objective, cognitive, dictionary-like, commonly defined meanings associated with words. **Connotative meanings** are the nonobjective, intrinsic, and often emotional responses associated with or implied by words.

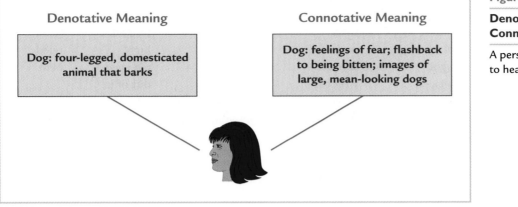

Denotative Meaning

Dog: four-legged, domesticated animal that barks

Connotative Meaning

Dog: feelings of fear; flashback to being bitten; images of large, mean-looking dogs

Figure 4.4

Denotative and Connotative Meanings

A person's possible response to hearing the word *dog*.

We accumulate both denotative and connotative meanings in our psychological context. Denotative meanings are more likely to have a commonly held meaning among various individuals, whereas connotative meanings are more individualistic. Words like *for, that, of,* and *among* are by nature fairly denotative. On the other hand, certain words elicit a large number of connotative responses from individuals—words like *love, death, tumor,* and *racist.* These words are loaded with emotional and individualistic meanings derived from our particular experiences.

Osgood's three dimensions. One researcher in semantics, Charles E. Osgood, has gone beyond denotation and connotation to identify three dimensions by which words vary: evaluation, potency, and activity.[6] His system involves determining the degree to which a word has each of these three qualities and then plotting the word in "semantic space." The advantage of such a system is that it allows us to see clearly how words differ from one word to another.

Osgood's *evaluative* dimension represents the degree to which a word reflects a sense of good versus bad, pleasant versus unpleasant, and positive versus negative. The *potency* dimension utilizes the scales of strong to weak, heavy to light, and hard to soft. The *activity* dimension is reflected in scales of fast to slow, active to passive, and excitable to calm.

Data have been collected to map hundreds of words along these three dimensions. In some ways, these data are of limited value because words change, meanings are often unique to each person, and meanings are situationally and culturally determined. Nevertheless, understanding that words vary in terms of the three dimensions should make you more sensitive to the potential impact of your word choices. The meaning that someone attributes to your words is affected by their evaluation, potency, and activity. To tell someone that you are "a bit tipsy" is different on all three dimensions from saying that you are "smashed."

Look at the following list of synonyms for *intoxicated.* Each word reflects a different level of potency, activity, and evaluation. Which words are the strongest? Weakest? Which are the most active? Passive? Which reflect a sense of good? Bad?

Ask Yourself

bombed	trashed	plastered	stewed	ripped
wiped out	tipsy	stoked	snockered	smashed
drunk	fried	juiced	tanked	loose
mashed	wasted	tittled	high	oiled
tight	torqued	messed up	pie-eyed	bent
pickled	wrecked	blotto	out of it	
plowed	blitzed	on a bender	a bit tiddly	
feeling good	three sheets to the wind	drowning your sorrows		

There may be more synonyms for *intoxicated* in U.S. English than for any other word. What does that reflect about U.S. society? What other words can you think of that have many synonyms? How might these reflect on the society?

■ Nonverbal Communication

Remember our earlier discussion about meaning being contextual? That discussion included the notion that meaning comes from interpreting both the verbal and the nonverbal cues. Now that you have a better understanding of the dynamics of language and verbal communication, let's turn to nonverbal communication.

Much of what we perceive falls within the category of nonverbal communication. Some nonverbal communication is symbolic in nature, such as the use of specific hand gestures to say "Hello" or "Peace." Some nonverbal communication is vocal, such as coughing, sneezing, pitch, tone, and accents. But most nonverbal communication is neither symbolic nor vocal; it consists of nonvocal signs such as yawning, looking away, holding hands, furniture arrangements, and perfumes.

■ *Types of Nonverbal Communication*

We are affected by a wide variety of nonverbal stimuli. Examining the different categories of nonverbal stimuli should heighten your awareness of their effects and potentially improve your use of them.

Physical characteristics, clothing, and possessions. People attribute meaning to our physical appearance. Physical characteristics include body shape (height, weight, muscle tone), physical aids (canes, wheelchairs, glasses), skin color, hair, and general facial features (the shape of our eyes, nose, and mouth). Any physical quality with which we associate some meaning constitutes a form of nonverbal communication.

We also add adornments to our bodies to which meaning is attributed. These include clothing (including hats and shoes), jewelry (all body piercing included), tattoos, perfumes, deodorants, and watches. We choose these adornments on the basis of our taste, and people interpret them as though they reflect who we are. We also attach meaning to other possessions, such as a red convertible sports car, a North Face backpack, a stereo, or an apartment. All these items represent forms of nonverbal communication. Knowing this, we sometimes carefully choose our attire in an attempt to manipulate the impressions others form of us.

This used to be a problem for me, because all through graduate school I had no money, and my mother frequently sent me clothes that I gladly wore. However, the impression I was generating was not who I was, but rather how my mother saw me. Each of us is limited by resources or other factors that might restrict our ability to choose clothing and possessions that make a statement about who we are.

Face and eyes (oculesics).   The face and eyes are part of our physical characteristics, but they deserve special attention because they are utilized extensively in nonverbal communication. As one researcher puts it, the face conveys information regarding "personality, your interest and responsiveness during interaction, and your emotional states."[7] We use facial expressions to convey a wide array of emotions through very subtle changes in facial muscles.

There are six emotions that seem to be the most easily recognizable through facial expression: surprise, fear, anger, disgust, happiness, and sadness. Other emotional displays are thought to involve combinations or variations of these six. The faces in the following photos represent these emotions. What facial qualities vary from one expression to another? Look at the mouth, eyebrows, eyelids, and lips and the skin on the forehead, around the nose, and on the cheeks.

We use facial expressions to express ourselves and to accompany our verbal messages. The face provides feedback to speakers about our reactions to what they are saying. In essence, our thoughts are reflected in our faces. We may display disapproval or approval, interest or disinterest, and understanding or misunderstanding toward a message.

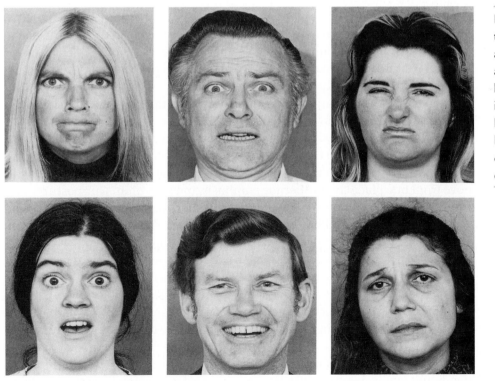

Faces displaying the emotions of surprise, fear, anger, disgust, happiness, and sadness are shown here. Can you tell which is which? Researchers believe these may be the six basic emotions that we display through facial expressions.

Suppose you were giving a presentation to a small group of coworkers and all you got were blank looks. Would those expressions affect you? What would you assume the looks meant? Obviously, the context would affect your interpretation; however, you might assume that your listeners did not understand or that they had already heard everything you were saying. It would be a good idea to find out exactly what those looks meant by directly asking your audience.

A great deal of research has been done on how the eyes affect how we communicate. The research has even investigated pupil dilation as a reflection of our interest or arousal.[8] We react to someone's staring at us, and we also react to someone who doesn't look at us during an interpersonal conversation. We increase our eye contact with those to whom we are attracted and reduce our eye contact when talking to someone of higher status.

Eye contact is one of the primary ways we regulate our interpersonal interactions. It's how we initiate contact, signal when it's the next person's turn to talk, and signal an end to the interaction. As we talk we might gaze away, but as we are about to finish what we are saying, we typically return to making eye contact with our listener, thereby signaling that the other person's turn to talk is approaching.

Maintaining eye contact with an audience is important in presentations. Presidential candidates are generally instructed to look into the camera when answering questions and to resist the natural temptation to look at either the other candidate or the reporter who has asked the question. The reason for this instruction is that the "audience" is the viewers at home, not the reporters. The importance of maintaining eye contact probably inspired the development of teleprompters, devices that allow individuals to read a scripted speech while still looking at the camera and audience.

Gestures and body movement (kinesics).   Earlier we discussed the use of symbolic gestures to communicate specific messages, such as "Hello" and "Peace." Gestures are also used in nonsymbolic ways to accompany verbal messages. One study found that the perceived sociability of a speaker related to the use of illustrator gestures (gestures that convey such things as size or location), a relaxed posture, and random body movements.[9]

We use our entire body for communicating nonverbally. We move toward things that we find interesting (test this yourself by watching people at parties or museums). Speakers increase and decrease their distance from an audience and move from one place to another for emphasis and attention. Our posture, too, communicates information. We lean forward in our chair when talking to people we are attracted to or when our interest is piqued. We slouch and droop our shoulders when we are tired, depressed, dejected, or bored.

We also communicate by changing our body orientation toward people. We tend to stand sideways with a shoulder toward another person when we are not really interested in carrying on a meaningful conversation. In essence, this is a disconfirming response because it doesn't show a commitment to listening. If we were committed to listening, we would more likely face the person directly.

Touch (haptics).   We shake hands with people as a form of greeting; we hug friends and family members of whom we are particularly fond; we pat people on the back for a job well done; and we kiss those we love. These are just a few of the ways we use touch to communicate.

Touch probably has more social mores attached to it than any other form of nonverbal communication because some forms of touch are part of sexual expression. The context, relationship, and culture are critical in determining the appropriateness and meaning of touch. In some cultures, members of the same sex continue to hold hands after they have greeted one another as they carry on a conversation. In the United States, such touch behavior is generally considered inappropriate and creates anxiety for the recipient.

One study identified seven major categories of touch:

- Positive-affect touches (kisses, embraces, fondling)
- Playful touches (tickling, wrestling, punching)
- Control touches (firm grasps, shoves)
- Ritualistic touches (handshakes, pats on the shoulder or arm)
- Hybrid touches (hugging hello or good-bye)
- Task-related touches (doctor's touches, helping someone hold a tennis racket, turning someone's body to point where to walk)
- Accidental touches (arms hitting while walking, feet bumping under the table)[10]

With all these forms of touch, we must be sensitive to other people's levels of comfort. We need to be sensitive to what part of the body we touch, how long we sustain the touch, the intensity of the touch, and the frequency of the touch.[11] Remember that people vary in terms of their attribution of meanings, so what you intend as a nonsexual touch may be interpreted sexually by someone else.

Ask Yourself

To what degree is it okay for a first-grade teacher to touch students on the arm? The head? The shoulder or back? What if a college instructor did those things? What makes it different?

When, if ever, is it all right to hug people with whom you work? What forms of touch are okay at the workplace, and what forms of touch are not?

Is it sexual harassment if you are made uncomfortable by a superior at work who touches you on the shoulder, arm, or knee every time you have a conversation?

Vocal qualities (vocalics or paralanguage) and vocalizations. Think of words as the outlines of pictures in coloring books and vocal qualities as the colors with which you fill in those outlines. **Paralanguage,** or **vocalics,** includes all those voice qualities that shade the meanings of our spoken words. These qualities include rate, pitch, volume, tone, accent, fluency, inflections, articulation, and pauses. Each of these qualities adds meaning to the spoken words and adds to the impression someone has of us.

Vocal qualities, in fact, are the primary way that we convey emotions in our words. We raise our voice to show anger. We speak softly to be seductive. We speak rapidly to show excitement. Read aloud each of the following sentences, emphasizing the word in capital letters:

"THAT dog bit me!"
"That DOG bit me!"
"That dog BIT me!"
"That dog bit ME!"

Notice how the change in vocal emphasis changes the meaning of each sentence, even though the words are the same.

We also attribute personal characteristics to individuals on the basis of their vocal qualities. Think of how important the voices of the characters can be in animated movies. Robin Williams's voice as the genie in *Aladdin* matches perfectly with the nature of the character, and James Earl Jones provides the vocal qualities one would expect for Darth Vader in the first *Star Wars* trilogy. People used to attribute some of the Beatles' success in the United States to their accent, which their fans found very attractive. What impression does your voice convey to others? And are you biased for or against any particular quality? Do you view people who speak slowly as unintelligent? Are you suspicious of people who talk fast? Do you have a positive or negative reaction to certain accents?

Vocalizations are the nonsymbolic sounds we make, such as yawns, coughs, "ums," and "ahs." The sounds we make, like "um" and "ah," are sometimes called vocalized pauses because they represent the production of sound where silence might have occurred. Vocalizations slow down our fluency and generally create a negative impact, depending on the context. You will rarely hear vocalized pauses in presidential addresses, national newscasts, or newsmagazine reports. On the other hand, you might hear vocalized pauses on TV talk shows or in sports interviews.

Consider your own tendency to add vocalized pauses in your conversations or presentations. How do you react to other people's vocalizations? What impression do you form of a public figure who speaks fluently with few vocalized pauses, compared to one who speaks with many vocalized pauses?

Written language lacks the advantage of being accompanied by vocal qualities. Log on to a chat session and review the comments made by the participants. In what ways do people try to add vocal qualities to typed messages? What emotional qualities are most easily added to what you type? What role does punctuation play? Are there some equivalents to vocalizations?

Use of space/territoriality (proxemics). We stand closer or farther from people, depending on our relationship with them.[12] Edward T. Hall, motivated by his work in directing training for the State Department, knew how important it was to understand how cultures differed in the way they used "the silent language." One area of interest for him was the physical distance maintained between people when they talked.[13] He found that Latin Americans preferred a much closer distance for conversing than did North Americans. He observed that as Latin Americans moved closer, North Americans became uncomfortable and pulled away, which caused the Latin Americans to view the North Americans as distant and cold.

Hall identified four ranges of distance that seemed to reflect distinctive communication relationships in the United States:

Intimate: 6 to 18 inches
Personal: 18 inches to 4 feet
Social: 4 to 7 feet
Public: 12 to 25 feet

For example, Hall saw the intimate distance being used when people were telling someone something confidential and the public distance for group announcements or presentations. Naturally, these distances vary from culture to culture. The distance in a particular conversation is also affected by such things as the nature of the relationship, status differences, the sex and age of the people, and the subject matter.

Each of us walks around with an invisible bubble that represents our "space." We become uncomfortable when someone violates this space by moving too close. We look for ways to counterbalance these intrusions. We look away as we pass someone on a narrow sidewalk—a response that seems to make the intrusion less

How do these people seem to be dealing with the personal space violations that are being forced upon them as they ride in this crowded elevator?

obvious to us. When we stand in a crowd on an elevator, we all face in the same direction, making ourselves small by folding our arms in and looking up at the display of floor numbers overhead, apparently to reduce the impact of having our space violated. As relationships become more intimate, however, we are more comfortable sharing our space, as shown by two friends who walk closely side by side.

Territoriality is our tendency to stake out our claim to a particular space. Our territories include our homes, apartments, and bedrooms. There are several ways we can stake out and maintain our territories.[14] We can "mark" temporary space by using such things as books or jackets spread out over table tops or chairs. (At least we don't mark our territories the same way dogs do!) We also use symbolic markers or signs to indicate territory, labeling parking places "Reserved for Mr. Smith" or putting placards on tables that say "Reserved." We can use offensive displays such as scowls or unfriendly looks to discourage anyone from invading our space. How do you discourage someone from sitting next to you on a bus?

One scholar, who sees the drive to create territories as one of the strongest human drives, refers to it as the "territorial imperative."[15] Fighting for territory occurs at the global level in border disputes and wars. Similarly, in our own homes we draw imaginary lines to mark "our" side of a bedroom. Our vernacular has even been influenced by this need through the creation of such phrases as "I need my space" and "Get out of my space."

Examples of territoriality can be seen in almost every aspect of our life. Look, for instance, at seating behavior in a classroom. Even when seating is not assigned, after the first few days students generally keep choosing the same seat for each class period. Try sitting in someone else's seat in a class and watch the domino effect as each student sits in someone else's territory. One of the strongest statements of acceptance and intimacy we can share with someone is living together. In essence, we are accepting someone else sharing our territory. Interestingly, even long-term marriage partners still seem to need individual territories and therefore develop their own spaces, such as sewing rooms, workshops, and studies.

Environment, time (chronemics), and smell (olfactics). Chapter 2 identified the environment as one of the contexts that affects all communication. You have had enough experience in different types of rooms to see how variations in size, shape, furnishings, color, lighting, and temperature can all affect the communication and interactions. Time and odors also contribute to the environmental context and influence the way we communicate.

As mentioned in Chapter 2, we can manipulate the environment as a way of affecting other people and as a way of communicating. Consider the arrangement of furniture. Groups meeting in a circle communicate differently than those sitting at a rectangular table that gives a power advantage to those sitting at the ends. Instructors often rearrange classroom seating in an attempt to alter the typical power structure created by having all of the students' chairs in nice rows facing the teacher's desk at the front of the room. Think about how communication has been affected in your classes when the instructor has arranged all the chairs in a large circle.

Now consider the use of time to communicate information. Suppose you are meeting with a salesperson to purchase some important computer equipment for your company. You want to get the best deal you can. Showing up early might convey an overeagerness to buy, while showing up late might signal a more laid-back attitude. However, if you show up too late, the salesperson might be gone.

Lateness is sometimes perceived as a power move. Keeping people waiting means that you are exerting control over them and in essence are threatening their self-esteem. Our U.S. culture is very time conscious: We believe in promptness and punctuality for arranged meetings. However, other cultures are more flexible about time. A U.S. citizen would consider it rude and disrespectful to be forty-five minutes late for an appointment. In Latin America, however, this would not be a problem. Such cultural differences often create stress and challenge effective communication.

The use of air fresheners, incense, colognes, and perfumes relates to our final nonverbal category—olfactics, or smell. Smell is one of the senses we sometimes take for granted, despite its significant impact. In U.S. culture, we have certain norms about body odors, and our impressions of other people are influenced by these odors. We try to control odor through showering, deodorants, and perfumes. People from the United States sometimes react negatively to the smells emitted by people from other cultures, where water is scarce and bathing is not an everyday activity. The multimillion-dollar industries for producing and marketing perfumes, colognes, air fresheners, deodorants, and breath fresheners attest to the importance we place on olfactics. We try to manipulate our personal smell to make ourselves more attractive and acceptable to other people, thereby enhancing communication.

■ Principles of Nonverbal Communication

Now that you have a sense of the different types of nonverbal communication, we can focus on some of the principles of nonverbal communication. Each of the six principles of attribution of meaning discussed earlier applies to nonverbal communication as well. A quick review of a few should make the point.

- Each of us attributes slightly different meanings to what we perceive. This is why a man might smile at a woman as a gesture of friendship, only to have her get angry because she sees the smile as forward and impolite.
- Like language, nonverbal meanings are influenced by the culture in which they are learned. Symbolic gestures are extremely culturally bound. A gesture that is harmless in one culture might be obscene in another. For instance, putting your thumb up to signal "well done" in the United States is obscene to an Iranian.
- The context in which we use and respond to nonverbals affects their meanings. Holding the hand of someone you just met would probably be perceived as negative and inappropriate. On the other hand, holding that same person's hand after your relationship has become more intimate would be seen as positive and appropriate. As contexts change, so do the meanings attributed to the nonverbals.

Now let's look at some specific principles that are unique to nonverbal communication.

1. *We expect certain nonverbal behaviors.* We have a set of expectations about the way nonverbals should be used in our interactions with others. Those expectations are defined both by our specific culture and by our own personal experiences and desires. Our emotions become aroused when people excessively violate our nonverbal expectations.[16] Learning about such expectations will improve your ability to adapt your own nonverbal behaviors to the situation.

Nonverbal expectancy violation theory was developed to explain how violations of our nonverbal expectations impact our behavior and regard for the violator. To investigate what this theory involves, look at Figure 4.5, which illustrates different degrees of violation of nonverbal behaviors.

The horizontal line in the figure represents the range of potential nonverbal behaviors. Let's assume that it represents how much eye contact a person has with you. In the middle of the continuum, section C indicates the amount of eye contact you expect and feel comfortable with. Suppose the other person starts exceeding the amount of eye contact you expect. This is a *positive* violation (the person is doing more of the nonverbal behavior than you expected). Your reaction to this violation depends on a number of factors, including attraction, familiarity, power, status, and the other person's ability to reward or punish you.[17]

Section D represents a range of positive violation behavior to which you will have a positive reaction if the behavior is displayed by someone to whom you are attracted. You may feel flattered, for instance. However, you will view that same behavior negatively if it is displayed by someone you dislike. And there is a threshold at which the behavior crosses over to section E, where the amount of eye contact becomes excessive for you even if you are attracted to the other person. Your reaction in section E is obviously negative. You feel uncomfortable at the "staring" or "glaring" of the other person.

At the other end of the continuum, your reactions will be slightly different. Section B represents a negative violation in that the range of behavior reflects less eye contact than you would normally expect. If you are attracted to the person who displays this negative violation, you are disappointed. The negative violation evokes a negative reaction. However, if you dislike the person, you will probably discount the behavior or even respond positively ("Oh, good, he's not looking my way anymore"). A strong negative violation, as represented by section A, would probably just heighten the effects felt in the moderate violation. Imagine sitting in the front row to hear a lecture by a person whom you admire and highly regard. If the lecturer looks at the people seated around you from time to time during the course of the presentation, but totally avoids eye contact with you, you might feel strong disappointment.

Figure 4.5

Continuum of Potential Nonverbal Behaviors

Strong negative violation	Moderate negative violation	Expected nonverbal behavior	Moderate positive violation	Strong positive violation
A	B	C	D	E

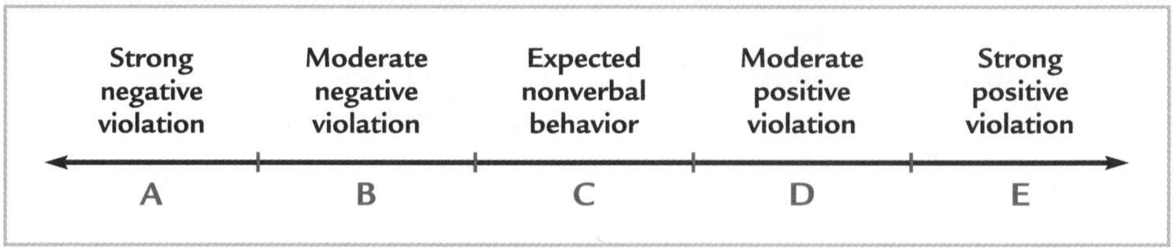

2. *Nonverbal communication is always present in human interactions.*
Each verbal message includes a nonverbal component. Our speech is accompanied by a number of paralinguistic features, such as pitch, tone, and rate, that color our message.

In fact, as soon as we see another person, nonverbal communication occurs. We are affected by an individual's body size, hair style, clothing, and movement. We are affected by such qualities whether we see the person approaching us on a sidewalk, standing in front of an audience giving a speech, or appearing on TV. We cannot escape nonverbal communication.

Erving Goffman, a theorist concerned with the process by which we form impressions of others, divided the way we get information about others into two categories: the expression one gives and the expression one gives off.[18] The **expression one gives** represents the intentional symbolic information that a person communicates. The **expression one gives off** represents the meaning that we attach to the actions and nonsymbolic qualities associated with the person. I can tell you that I am a nice guy (expression one gives), or you can watch me help an elderly lady across a busy street and conclude that I am a nice guy (expression one gives off).

Goffman originally intended the expression one gives off to reflect those kinds of qualities we observe about others that they don't control. However, he realized that we can indeed feign different behavior by putting on *masks* in an attempt to manage impressions. Masks are limited in how well they disguise some qualities; in most cases, for instance, they can do little to disguise skin color, height, and age. Nonetheless, we try to create masks through clothing selection, hair dyes, wigs, weightlifting, and even plastic surgery.

We are generally aware of the information we give through self-disclosure, but less conscious of the expression we give off. You should recognize that people are reacting to that information about you. Is the impression people are drawing from your nonverbal cues the way you want to be perceived? Do you wear clothes that make you appear different than you would like? You can benefit from developing a sensitivity to your own nonverbal presence and behaviors.

You might also try to develop an awareness of how surrounding nonverbal stimuli affect you. You meet someone new and decide you don't like him. Why? Unless you examine your response, you may not discover that your impression has been unduly influenced by a relatively insignificant nonverbal cue, such as a tendency to avoid eye contact, an accent, a stutter, or an unusual laugh.

Look at yourself right now. How much of the way you are presenting yourself have you attempted to modify as a way of managing impressions? Did you think about how others would react to your clothing choices, hair style, makeup, and so on? What impression did you want to make?

---

3. *Nonverbal communication varies in its degree of ambiguity.* Consider the meaning you would attach to the nonverbals in each of these scenarios:

A. A friend waves at you from across the street.
B. A friend smiles at you, pats you on the shoulder, and says, "You moron."

C. Your boss calls you into her office. You stand in front of her desk while she examines a document on the desk without looking up at you.

D. A classmate looks away from you, frowns, and says in a quiet voice, "One more final to go."

Which of the four scenarios do you feel you could most accurately interpret? Which of the four do you feel you could least accurately interpret? Your level of confidence is directly linked to the amount of ambiguity in the nonverbals.

You would probably feel most comfortable betting on scenario A because it is the least ambiguous. A wave from a friend is usually a show of friendship and greeting. The meanings of the other three scenarios are not so clear. Many interpretations are possible, depending on the context and on what else you perceive. Nonetheless, you would attribute meaning to each interaction.

There is a tendency to treat nonverbal cues as though they are as well defined as words in a dictionary, but there is no dictionary of nonverbals. In 1970, a highly successful book was published called *Body Language.* Its premise was that nonverbal communication had specific identifiable meanings just like verbal language. For example, the author described the nonverbals a man should use if he wanted to enter a room and signal "I'm available, I'm masculine, I'm aggressive and knowledgeable," as well as the nonverbals a woman could use to signal that she was "available."[19] However, the ambiguity intrinsic in nonverbal cues makes such global prescriptions unreliable. Nonverbal cues do not appear in isolation, and they depend on many other pieces of information for their meaning.

How can you guard against misinterpreting ambiguous nonverbal cues and making potentially embarrassing responses? Try to check out your interpretations of nonverbal cues to reduce the problems associated with ambiguity. Don't assume that you know what other people's nonverbal cues mean all the time, and don't assume that other people know your meaning. As with words, two people never reach total shared meaning. The degree of overlap in two people's meanings determines the amount of misunderstanding. Tell other people what you think you have perceived in a qualified way, and ask them to correct you.

Suppose that an instructor spends the last ten minutes of a class talking in a rather casual and noncommittal fashion. Your interpretation may be that the material will not be on a test. You would be wise to confirm your reading of the instructor's nonverbals by asking if the material will be on the exam.

4. *Nonverbal communication is the primary means for communicating information about emotions and relationships.* Here's another experiment for you, probably one you have done before. Turn on the TV to a drama (soap operas count) and turn off the sound. What is communicated? Surprisingly, you can still follow quite a bit of what is going on simply by watching the nonverbal action. What you notice are the emotions, expressions, and reactions of the actors. What you miss are the facts and information regarding the plot line.

As this example illustrates, people use nonverbal communication as the primary method for expressing emotions. You might say the words "I love you," but you probably spend considerably more time expressing this emotion nonverbally—through facial expressions, eye contact, touch, and other behaviors. This may be why people are inclined to believe emotional nonverbal statements more

than spoken words. You are likely to doubt the sincerity of a person who says "I love you" but fails to show affection or caring.

As you watch a TV program without sound, you should also be able to tell a lot about the relationships between the characters. You can tell who has the most power, who has the least power, who is attracted to whom, and who is dependent on whom. You can understand these relational issues because relational dimensions such as power and intimacy are communicated primarily through nonverbals. If you reach out and hold someone's hand as you walk together, this gesture is a nonverbal way of communicating your feelings and your definition of the relationship.

5. Nonverbal communication varies in immediacy, power, and responsiveness.[20]   By now you may have some understanding of what these three qualities mean. **Immediacy** involves communicating our liking or dislike of someone through nonverbal behaviors. We try to get "closer" nonverbally to those we like and distance ourselves from those we dislike. Immediacy behaviors include increased eye contact, leaning forward, smiling, touch, and close proximity.[21]

Power, as a dimension of nonverbal communication, is the use of nonverbal behaviors to communicate control over another person or acceptance of submission and dependence.[22] We communicate power through posture, body position and movement, artifacts, furniture arrangement, use of space and territory (having the larger office), and eye contact. One study found, for example, that high eye contact and close proximity conveyed dominance and control.[23]

Responsiveness is nonverbal communication that reflects awareness of the other person and reactiveness to him or her.[24] We have some degree of emotional or visceral response to almost everything we perceive. Turning your head toward the sound of screeching tires and feeling alarmed, reflects a form of responsiveness. We might listen to a speaker advocating mammograms talk about the death of her mother from breast cancer and be moved to respond with nonverbal behaviors showing sadness and fear. Some of us might be more moved than others and therefore display a greater degree of responsiveness. Speakers are in turn affected by the responsiveness cues that listeners display. Responsiveness can be displayed through any of our nonverbal behaviors, especially through facial expressions, eye contact, and vocal qualities (pitch, rate, tone, and volume).

6. ***We adapt our nonverbal behavior to other people's nonverbal behaviors.*** Our nonverbal behaviors change in response to our perceptions of other people's nonverbals. We change in one of two ways: reciprocation or compensation.

Reciprocation means adapting our nonverbal behaviors in a similar direction to other people's nonverbal behaviors.[25] You could reciprocate the smile and nod of a speaker by smiling and nodding back. **Compensation** involves adapting our nonverbal behaviors in the opposite direction to other people's nonverbal behaviors.[26] You would compensate for someone's moving closer to you on a bench by moving farther away.

Our nonverbal behaviors form a part of our response that the other person observes and adapts to as well. You might start to fall asleep in response to a lecturer who speaks slowly and with little energy (compensation). Your sleeping might motivate the speaker to pick up his pace and speak with more enthusiasm (compensation), which in turn might awaken you and draw your attention (reciprocation).

We adapt to both positive and negative nonverbal expectancy violations through reciprocation and compensation. For example, if someone you are attracted to moves away (negative violation), you might try to move closer to compensate. The process of adapting and reacting to each other's nonverbal behaviors is one of the ways people negotiate the definition of relationships.

7. ***We vary in our abilities to express and perceive nonverbal communication.*** The ability to use nonverbal cues to express ourselves and the ability to perceive other people's nonverbal cues are skills that some people have in greater measure than others. One author goes so far as to describe those who have difficulty expressing or perceiving nonverbals as "nonverbally handicapped."[27]

To get an idea of your own skill level, complete the following Test Yourself. The items in the test reflect some of the different categories of nonverbal behavior. Which items reflect your strengths? Which reveal your weaknesses?

Decide how much each item describes your behavior, and record your responses on a scale from 1 (doesn't describe me at all) to 5 (describes me very well).

Nonverbal Expressiveness

1E. I am very good at expressing my emotions through my facial expressions.	1 2 3 4 5
2E. I use a lot of variation in my voice when talking.	1 2 3 4 5
3E. I have been told that I am very animated in my use of gestures.	1 2 3 4 5
4E. My body is very flexible, and I frequently lean toward people when they talk.	1 2 3 4 5
5E. I touch people when I care about them a lot or when I'm comforting them.	1 2 3 4 5

| 6E. My physical appearance accurately reflects who I am. | 1 2 3 4 5 |
| 7E. I consciously arrange my furniture and belongings to influence others. | 1 2 3 4 5 |

Nonverbal Perceptiveness

1P. I am very good at reading people's facial expressions.	1 2 3 4 5
2P. I listen closely for changes in people's vocal expressions.	1 2 3 4 5
3P. I am very good at interpreting people's gestures.	1 2 3 4 5
4P. I am sensitive to whether someone is leaning toward me when talking.	1 2 3 4 5
5P. I am very aware of when someone is touching me and why.	1 2 3 4 5
6P. I can tell a lot about people by what they wear and how they look.	1 2 3 4 5
7P. I am sensitive to how people arrange their office or home furniture.	1 2 3 4 5

Total your scores for each set of items. A score of 28 to 35 for each set indicates that you are expressive or perceptive. A score of 7 to 14 indicates that you are not very effective in expressing yourself nonverbally or picking up on others' nonverbal cues.

Because nonverbal expressiveness and perceptiveness are skills, you can improve them. Throughout this text, you will receive advice on ways to improve your nonverbal communication skills. You can even improve your skills within ongoing relationships if you are open to learning other people's nonverbal patterns. You can become more familiar with the meanings behind various nonverbal cues you receive from those you know well. Even if your general nonverbal skills are relatively weak, you can be effective at reading your boss's mood or your best friend's emotions.

■ The Relationship Between Nonverbal and Verbal Communication

Nonverbal communication works in conjunction with verbal communication in a number of ways. In fact, communication scholar Mark Knapp has identified six ways in which nonverbal and verbal communication relate: substituting, repeating, contradicting, complementing, accenting, and regulating.[28] These relationships were imbedded in the examples already discussed in this chapter, but now will be examined specifically.

In Knapp's classification, **substituting** occurs when nonverbal communication is used in place of verbal communication. If you give someone a hug instead of saying "I love you" or if you hang up the phone in the middle of a conversation because you are angry, these actions substitute for verbally expressing your feeling.

Substituting frequently involves the use of nonverbal gestures that have a specific symbolic meaning. These gestures, which fit within quadrant 3 in Figure 4.1, are called **emblems.** Emblems include such gestures as giving the okay sign with your fingers and waving hello to a neighbor. As you have learned, these gestures are culture specific.

What if a person waves and says hello at the same time? Presenting the same message nonverbally that we state verbally is called **repeating.** Repeating increases the likelihood of understanding because we are using two channels to communicate the same message.

Sometimes nonverbals appear to conflict with the accompanying verbal message. **Contradicting** occurs when the meaning associated with the nonverbal message contradicts the verbal meaning. Hearing someone say "I'm really excited about this project" in a quiet, monotonic, lifeless manner would produce contradicting cues. You probably would infer from the nonverbals that the person is not really excited about the project at all. Generally, we give more credibility to a person's actions (the nonverbal message) than to the words.

What if the project participant in the preceding paragraph had said "I'm really excited about this project" in an energetic, excited tone and behaved in a highly animated way? In that case, the nonverbals would have complemented the verbal message. **Complementing** occurs when nonverbal messages add to the meaning of the verbal message.

An energetic tone and animated movements in and of themselves are not content specific. They don't convey the same meaning as the words; they are not just repeating the verbal message. Instead, the verbal meaning is given depth and color through the accompanying nonverbals.

Raising the volume of your voice to make a point during a presentation is an example of accenting. **Accenting** is the use of nonverbal cues to focus attention on a particular verbal message. The written word can be accented with CAPITAL-IZATION, **bold print,** *italicization,* underlining, and punctuation!!!! The same things can be done with spoken messages through paralanguage (increased or decreased volume, changes in rate, use of silence, and so on), gestures, body movement, and facial expressions. People who accompany their words with frequent hand movements are using a lot of accenting.

Finally, nonverbal communication is used to regulate verbal communication. **Regulating** involves using nonverbal cues to manage the flow of communication. We use nonverbals to signal initiation of interactions, to signal turn taking, and to terminate interactions. These cues are often subtle. For instance, as you walk by someone you know, you usually signal to each other whether you have time to stop and talk. You can signal an interest in talking by slowing your gait, increasing your eye contact, smiling, and turning your body.

Instructors don't need watches to tell when a class period is nearing the end because students display leave-taking behaviors such as closing their notebooks, putting things in their backpacks, and donning their jackets. What happens when instructors ignore these signals? Usually, students grow more anxious and more bold in their behaviors, ultimately standing up and moving toward the doorway, even with the instructor still talking.

This chapter has alluded to some of the problems that arise in communication when individuals misinterpret or misunderstand the meaning behind verbal and nonverbal messages. The next chapter deals specifically with factors that interfere with listeners' understanding of messages and speakers' representation of information. In addition to discussing the challenge of achieving understanding, Chapter 5 addresses how deception and conflict stifle effective communication.

This chapter has focused on the process of attributing meaning to what we perceive, particularly words and nonverbal stimuli. Stimuli can be categorized as either symbols or signs and as either vocal or nonvocal. The type of communication that is symbolic and vocal is called verbal communication. Nonverbal communication refers to all other types.

According to the principles of attributing meaning, each person attributes meaning to what he or she perceives but does so in different ways. The meanings associated with perceptions are drawn from people's psychological contexts. The amount of overlap or shared meaning with other people's attributions varies, but two people's meanings are never exactly the same. Meanings are influenced by the culture in which the communication occurs and by other contextual elements as well.

These principles apply to all our interactions with others, including ones involving language. Language is a set of words and the rules that govern how the words are connected. Words possess power, vary in their level of abstraction, affect and are affected by thought, and have both connotative and denotative meanings.

Besides attaching meaning to the words we perceive, we attach meaning to nonverbal behaviors. Nonverbal communication encompasses the following categories: physical characteristics, clothing, and possessions; use of the face and eyes; gestures and body movement; touch; vocal qualities and vocalizations; the use of space and territoriality; and environment, time, and smell. Nonverbal expectancy violation theory helps explain the various ways we react when people violate our expectations by making too much eye contact, moving too close, and so on. Here are some other principles guiding our understanding of nonverbal communication: Nonverbal communication is always present in human interactions; varies in ambiguity; is the primary means for communicating information about emotions and relationships; reflects immediacy, power, and responsiveness; is adapted to other people's nonverbals; and requires skills of expressiveness and perceptiveness.

Verbal and nonverbal communication occur at the same time during our interactions with other people. Nonverbal communication can substitute, repeat, contradict, complement, accent, and regulate our verbal communication.

Key Terms

symbols   Stimuli with abstract, learned, arbitrary, flexible, and changing meanings.

signs   Stimuli with fixed and concrete meanings.

vocal stimuli   All sounds that emanate from the mouth.

nonvocal stimuli   All stimuli except oral sounds.

verbal communication   Communication based on vocal symbols.

nonverbal communication   Communication based on signs or nonverbal symbols; communication that is not verbal.

social decentering   The degree to which we understand the other person's psychological context.

egocentric communication   Communication in which we fail to recognize differences between ourselves and others and therefore fail to adapt our communication.

shared meaning   The degree to which you and another person have the same interpretation for a word or act.

language A set of words and the rules that govern the connection of those words.

Whorfian hypothesis A hypothesis that maintains that how we think is determined by the language with which we think.

polarization The tendency in language to divide things into two groups.

overgeneralizations Statements that claim broader truth than is reasonable to assume.

allness statements Statements that claim the existence of a common characteristic for an entire category.

qualifiers Words or phrases that indicate probabilities, tendencies, restrictions, and limitations.

denotative meanings The objective, cognitive, dictionary-like, commonly defined meanings associated with words.

connotative meanings The nonobjective, intrinsic responses associated with or implied by words.

paralanguage Voice qualities that shade the meanings of our spoken words; vocalics.

vocalics Voice qualities that shade the meanings of our spoken words; paralanguage.

vocalizations The nonsymbolic sounds we make, such as yawns, coughs, "ums," and "ahs."

nonverbal expectancy violation theory A theory that explains how violations of our nonverbal expectations impact our behavior and regard for the violator.

expression one gives The intentional symbolic information that a person communicates.

expression one gives off The meaning that we attach to the actions and nonsymbolic qualities associated with a person; in essence, our impression of someone.

immediacy Communicating our liking or dislike of someone through our nonverbal behaviors.

power In nonverbal communication, it is the way we use nonverbal behaviors to communicate control over another person or acceptance of submission and dependence.

responsiveness Nonverbal communication that reflects awareness of the other person and reactiveness to him or her.

reciprocation Adapting our nonverbal behaviors in a similar direction to other people's nonverbal behaviors.

compensation Adapting our nonverbal behaviors in the opposite direction to other people's nonverbal behaviors.

substituting Using nonverbal communication in place of verbal communication.

emblems Nonverbal gestures that have a specific symbolic meaning.

repeating Presenting the same message nonverbally that we state verbally.

contradicting Using a nonverbal message with an associated meaning that contradicts the verbal meaning.

complementing Using nonverbal messages that add to the meaning of the verbal message.

accenting The use of nonverbal cues to focus attention on a particular verbal message.

regulating Using nonverbal cues to manage the flow of communication.

Review Questions

1. What are the differences between symbols, signs, verbal communication, and nonverbal communication?
2. Explain three of the general principles that explain how we attribute meaning to what we perceive.
3. Discuss the relationship between language and thought.
4. Explain the differences between two categories of nonverbal communication.
5. Discuss three principles that apply to nonverbal communication.
6. How do verbal and nonverbal communication relate to each other?

Chapter 5

Challenges to Communication

Objectives

Studying this chapter will allow you to:
1. Explain three types of needs we seek to satisfy through communication.
2. Understand the process and strategies involved in saving face when confronted with failed expectations.
3. Define several types of deception: equivocation, concealment, half-truths, diversions, and lies.
4. Explain the difference between aggressive and assertive messages.
5. Identify ways for a listener to improve understanding.
6. Identify ways for a speaker to improve representation.
7. Discuss various methods of managing conflict.

S*cenario 1:* The discussion during a group meeting has grown very heated. Everyone is tired, and the group does not seem to be getting anywhere. You suggest that the group adjourn and start fresh the next day. Another group member immediately chastises you, saying, "You're an idiot!! You've made no contributions the whole time, and now you try to boss us around. What a jerk you are." You shout back that the other person is an idiot and that you have been listening very closely to what is going on. You continue that your being quiet doesn't mean you can't suggest that the group adjourn. You turn to the other group members to see their reactions.

Scenario 2: Your boss asks you to help a new employee, Chris, learn some of the procedures that need to be followed on the job. You explain to Chris in great detail how things work. While you talk, Chris nods understandingly but says little. You ask Chris if she understands what you've said. She says, "Yeah, I, um, think so." A week later your boss complains to you that you did a poor job of training Chris. Chris has not followed any of the procedures correctly. You are exasperated.

Scenario 3: You and a friend decide to go out Saturday night. You are ready to go at eight, but your friend has not shown up. Around half past nine, your friend calls and says he's at a party and can't get away; he'll see you Monday. On Monday, you tell your friend that you no longer want to be friends. He asks why. You start telling him how selfish and immature he is, but he interrupts and claims that you are being unreasonable. For an hour you go back and forth, arguing about what happened and about the future of the relationship. Eventually, your friend apologizes and vows to be more diligent in following through on commitments. You accept the apology and express your willingness to continue the friendship.

Chapter 1 offered seven reasons why we communicate. The first reason was to satisfy needs. Each of the three scenarios represents a different kind of challenge that we encounter in our effort to satisfy three particular types of needs: identity, instrumental, and relational.[1]

Satisfying **identity needs** involves using communication to present who you are to other people, to have that presented self accepted and confirmed by other people, and to confirm other people's identities. Rejection of a presented self thwarts your effort to satisfy your identity needs. In the first scenario, your identity needs are challenged by the group member who criticizes you and calls you names. Your "face" (discussed in Chapter 2 and later in this chapter) is being threatened by what the other group member has declared about you. People often respond to attacks with counterattacks and attempts to defend or justify their behaviors. Sometimes people even lie. You can address the challenge of dealing with aggressive behavior, attacks to your face, and lying by improving your communication skills.

The second scenario reflects communication that is used to meet **instrumental needs**—that is, to accomplish a task or perform a job. However, the new employee does not understand your instructions, and so the task is not performed correctly. Even though you ask if she understands you, Chris probably does not want her face threatened by having to admit that she doesn't understand. She wouldn't want to threaten your face either by telling you that your explanation isn't clear. In general, we are able to satisfy our instrumental needs through understanding and through effective use of persuasive strategies. However, satisfying instrumental needs can be hampered by problems in perception, listening, expressing ideas, and strategic decisions.

The third scenario focuses on satisfying your need for healthy relationships. Communication is used to satisfy **relational needs** through the management of relationships from initiation to termination. In this scenario, communication is used to maintain the relationship by effectively managing a conflict. This involves satisfying both your identity and your relational needs. Ineffective use of communication, on the other hand, can intensify conflicts.

These scenarios reflect the types of challenges we must deal with in our interactions with other people. Knowing how to communicate effectively can help us resolve many problems and satisfy our needs. However, communication can also be a problem in and of itself or can worsen a problem. One popular myth is that we could solve all our problems with other people if we would just sit down and talk. Indeed, there are some problems that can be helped by constructive communication. However, there are also times when communication is the wrong action to take.

For instance, if you are having a major fight with a friend, it might be best to retreat awhile, cool down, and distance yourselves from the situation. If you continue to talk, you both might regret things spoken in a fit of anger. Communication has to be used strategically to be effective. Knowing *when* to say something is just as important as knowing *how* to say it.

This chapter will examine a variety of factors that inhibit our ability to satisfy our needs. To use communication effectively to satisfy our needs, we must overcome the challenges created by threats to our face, by misunderstandings and misrepresentations, and by conflict. By the end of this chapter, you will have gained a variety of suggestions on how to recognize and adapt to such communication challenges.

■ The Challenge of Maintaining Face

Each time you communicate with other people, you present a conception of yourself (face), and you seek confirmation and acceptance of that presented self.[2] As you stand in front of an audience to give a presentation, for example, you have a particular image you are trying to convey. You want the audience to confirm and accept that image. You probably want to be seen as intelligent, articulate, informed, and likable. What happens, though, when you get lost in the middle of your presentation? You start muttering and apologizing as you search for your next point. You feel embarrassed by your behavior.

In situations like this, you have threatened your own face; that is, you have displayed behaviors that contradict the image you were trying to present. Apologies are a way of helping us **save face,** that is, restore the image that we were originally trying to convey. In our example, you find your place in the speech again and continue on, trying to do better and forget what happened. When you finish your presentation, the audience applauds, and your friends tell you that you did a great job and that they found the presentation very informative.

The audience's positive reaction to the speaker helps the person maintain a positive face.

Why do your listeners make a point of complimenting you and ignoring your stumbles? Because, generally, other people will try to help us **maintain face** by providing support, confirmation, and acceptance of the self-conception we are presenting. Some of the ways people can help us maintain face involve expressions of understanding, friendly advice, pardons, compassion, offers of help, and laughing with us.[3] By not raising the issue of your getting lost in the middle of your presentation, your listeners are helping you maintain your image as an articulate and intelligent speaker. Obviously, this example depends on your having a self-concept that includes being articulate and intelligent. If that is not how you think of yourself, getting lost in the speech might not be a threat to your face.

There are times when rather than helping us maintain our face, people threaten and challenge it. Face-threatening acts include name-calling, arguing, disapproval, criticism, ridicule, teasing, insults, accusations, disagreements, contradictions, reprimands, complaints, blatant noncooperation, threats, orders, and ignoring. However, when people make face-threatening statements, they put their own face on the line as well. For example, suppose I accuse you of not turning in an assignment, but in fact you did turn it in and I simply misplaced it. My accusation threatens your face, and you are likely to try to save face by a strong declaration that you turned in the assignment. By accusing you, I have put my face on the line—my self-concept of being a diligent and fair instructor. After finding your paper, I have to come back to you and admit my error, which causes me to lose some face. I will probably present some excuse for my error in an attempt to minimize my loss of face.

One way we protect ourselves from face threats is to use the powerless language discussed in Chapter 4. We can "waffle" a bit in presenting our face, so it becomes more difficult to threaten. Statements like "I might be wrong, but . . ." or "I think, maybe, we could do it this way" are a way of presenting an idea without commitment or ownership. If someone says, "No, we shouldn't do it that way," we can save face by saying, "Yeah, I didn't think that was the best way either."

We can also indicate that we are aware of a social code and ask for indulgence while we violate it.[4] My family has a rule about not burping loudly at the table. One of my sons is particularly adept at shaking the walls with his belches. He knows the rule and abides by it; however, he occasionally asks permission to violate the rule and let it rip, which is sometimes granted. He knows that if he did not ask permission and just belched loudly, he would be acting impolitely and disrespectfully, which is not the face he wishes to present.

Cultures differ in terms of the importance of face. Think about your own cultural background. How important is it in your culture to save face and to help others do so? What factors in your upbringing have influenced the way you think about face?

Compare your thoughts with those of your classmates. To what degree do you find differences by race, sex, age, or hometown?

Ask ? Yourself

■ *Failure Events*

Human communication and interactions are filled with expectations about behaviors. Failing to fulfill an obligation or expectation produces a **failure event**.[5] Failure events relate to communication in two ways: First, failure events occur in your communication behavior; and second, communication can be used as a tool for managing failure events.

Imagine that your boss expects you to deliver a well-prepared presentation to a group of managers. When you are ill prepared, it is a failure event. Your friends expect that when you say you will help decorate for a party, you will be there. Not showing up is a failure event. So what will you do in these two failure events? Part of your reaction depends on the other people. You may choose not to say or do anything if your boss or friends don't mention your failure. On the other hand, if you know that the other people are really upset, you may choose not to wait for them to say something—you may raise the issue yourself and apologize.

Failure events involve threats to people's face, and the management of failure events is an exercise in "face work." Giving an ill-prepared presentation could reflect an image of someone who is unprofessional and incompetent, and thus it would threaten your face (unless that's how you want to be perceived). Your boss's face is also threatened by your action. Your boss's abilities to make decisions, judge personnel, and manage effectively are undermined by your performance.

It is challenging to resolve such situations while preserving both parties' face. Sometimes one person's face is maintained through the loss of the other person's face.[6] Apologizing to your boss helps your boss maintain face but causes some loss

Maintaining Face: Sex Differences in Communication Styles

A popular author of gender and communication texts, Deborah Tannen explains some of the differences in the way men and women respond to face-threatening situations such as apologizing, fighting, and criticism. As you read this article, see if the descriptions match the way you react to these face-threatening situations.

Unfortunately, women and men often have different ideas about what's appropriate, different ways of speaking. Many of the conversational rituals common among women are designed to take the other person's feelings into account, while many of the conversational rituals common among men are designed to maintain the one-up position, or at least avoid appearing one-down. As a result, when men and women interact—especially at work—it's often women who are at the disadvantage. Because women are not trying to avoid the one-down position, that is unfortunately where they may end up. Here are the biggest areas of miscommunication:

Apologies

Women are often told they apologize too much. The reason they're told to stop doing it is that, to many men, apologizing seems synonymous with putting oneself down. But there are many times when "I'm sorry" isn't self-deprecating, or even an apology; it's an automatic way of keeping both speakers on an equal footing. For example, a well-known columnist once interviewed me and gave me her phone number in case I needed to call her back. I misplaced the number and had to go through the newspaper's main switchboard. When our conversation was winding down and we'd both made ending-type remarks, I added, "Oh, I almost forgot—I lost your direct number, can I get it again?" "Oh, I'm sorry," she came back instantly, even though she had done nothing wrong and I was the one who'd lost the number. But I understood she wasn't really apologizing; she was just automatically reassuring me she had no intention of denying me her number.

Even when "I'm sorry" is an apology, women often assume it will be the first step in a two-step ritual: I say "I'm sorry" and take half the blame, then you take the other half. At work, it might go something like this:

A: When you typed this letter, you missed this phrase I inserted.
B: Oh, I'm sorry. I'll fix it.
A: Well, I wrote it so small it was easy to miss.

When both parties share blame, it's a mutual face-saving device. But if one person, usually the woman, utters frequent apologies and the other doesn't, she ends up looking as if she's taking the blame for mishaps that aren't her fault. When she's only partially to blame, she looks entirely in the wrong. . . .

Unfortunately, not apologizing can have its price too. Since so many women use ritual apologies, those who don't may be seen as hard-edged. What's important is to be aware of how often you say you're sorry (and why), and to monitor your speech based on the reaction you get.

Criticism

A woman who co-wrote a report with a male colleague was hurt when she read a rough draft to him and he leapt into a critical response—"Oh, that's too dry! You have to make it snappier!" She herself would have been more likely to say, "That's a really good start. Of course, you'll want to make it a little snappier when you revise."

Whether criticism is given straight or softened is often a matter of convention. In general, women use more softeners. I noticed this difference when talking to an editor about an essay I'd written. While going over changes she wanted to make, she said, "There's one more thing. I know you may not agree with me. The reason I noticed the problem is that your other points are so lucid and elegant." She went on hedging for several more sentences until I put her out of her misery: "Do you want to cut that part?" I asked—and of course she did. But I appreciated her tentativeness. In contrast, another editor (a man) I once called summarily rejected my idea for an article by barking, "Call me when you have something new to say."

Those who are used to ways of talking that soften the impact of criticism may find it hard to deal with the right-between-the-eyes style. It has its own logic, however, and neither style is intrinsically better. People who prefer criticism given straight are operating on an assumption that feelings aren't involved: "Here's the dope. I know you're good; you can take it." . . .

Fighting

Many men expect the discussion of ideas to be a ritual fight—explored through verbal opposition. They state their ideas in the strongest possible terms, thinking that if there are weaknesses someone will point them out, and by trying to argue against those objections, they will see how well their ideas hold up.

Those who expect their own ideas to be challenged will respond to another's ideas by trying to poke holes and find weak links—as a way of helping. The logic is that when you are challenged you will rise to the occasion: Adrenaline makes your mind sharper; you get ideas and insights you would not have thought of without the spur of battle.

But many women take this approach as a personal attack. Worse, they find it impossible to do their best work in such a contentious environment. If you're not used to ritual fighting, you begin to hear criticism of your ideas as soon as they are formed. Rather than making you think more clearly, it makes you doubt what you know. When you state your ideas, you hedge in order to fend off potential attacks. Ironically, this is more likely to invite attack because it makes you look weak.

Although you may never enjoy verbal sparring, some women find it helpful to learn how to do it. An engineer who was the only woman among four men in a small company found that as soon as she learned to argue she was accepted and taken seriously. . . .

THERE IS NO "RIGHT" WAY TO TALK. When problems arise, the culprit may be style differences—and all styles will at times fail with others who don't share or understand them, just as English won't do you much good if you try to speak to someone who knows only French. If you want to get your message across, it's not a question of being "right"; it's a question of using language that's shared—or at least understood.

of face for you. Potentially, neither of you would suffer a loss of face if your reason for being ill prepared was out of your control, such as a computer crash that destroyed all your material right before your presentation.

Reproaches. A failure event may be followed by a reproach. A **reproach** is an indication by someone (usually the person toward whom the failure event is directed) that a failure event has occurred. The reproach can be either implicit or directly stated.

Reproaches fall along a continuum from mitigating to aggravating.[7] A **mitigating reproach** reflects only mild irritation with the failure event (for instance, stating rather matter-of-factly, "I thought you were going to be here ten minutes ago"). An **aggravating reproach** is a severe, intense declaration of the occurrence of a failure event (such as loudly stating, "Once again, you've kept me waiting! Do you think I don't have anything better to do? You are so irresponsible!").

Accounts. Usually, a reproach is followed by an account. An **account** is a stated response to a reproach by the person accused of the failure event. Early researchers identified five types of accounts: apology, excuse (the most common), justification, denial, and silence.[8]

- An **apology** is a statement in which the person admits the failure event, accepts responsibility for it, and expresses regret.
- An **excuse** reflects an admission that the failure event occurred but contends that nothing could have been done to prevent it (because, for example, it occurred through unfortunate circumstances).
- **Justification** involves accepting responsibility for the failure event but then trying to redefine the event as not being a failure.
- **Denial** involves stating that a failure event never took place.
- **Providing no account,** or **silence,** occurs when an individual either offers no response or ignores the reproach by changing the subject.

Examples of these five types of accounts are given in Table 5.1. Which of the accounts do you think would create the most negative reaction from a reproacher? Which would evoke the most positive reaction?

Like reproaches, accounts can be placed on a continuum of mitigating to aggravating. Table 5.1 lists them in this order, with apology being the most mitigating and silence, or no account, the most aggravating. There is also a connection between how aggravating an account is and how threatening it is to each

Table 5.1 Examples of the Five Types of Accounts

	Reproach: "Your presentation today really needs some work. You didn't seem very prepared."
Apology	"You're right. I'm sorry. I've already got some ideas for improving it."
Excuse	"Yeah, I know. My computer crashed while I was putting together my notes. I lost a lot of what I was planning to use."
Justification	"Well, I had a choice: finish the research report that the president wanted, or prepare for this presentation. You know how the president feels about late reports."
Denial	"Hey, everybody else seemed to like it. I think it went really well."
No account	"So next week we're going to be working on that new computer project, right?"

participant's face. For example, an apology causes the greatest loss of face for the accounter while preserving the most face for the reproacher. Silence, on the other hand, protects the accounter's face the most, but represents the greatest threat to the reproacher's face.[9] In general, mitigating reproaches are likely to evoke mitigating accounts, while aggravating reproaches are likely to evoke aggravating accounts.[10]

The give-and-take of failure events. After an account is given, it is up to the reproacher to decide whether the account is acceptable and whether to dismiss the failure event. When the account is rejected, we often try to provide another account. We might initially give an excuse for our failure event, but if the reproacher doesn't buy the excuse, we might decide to apologize. A give-and-take occurs that sometimes develops into a conflict.

Each party must decide how far to push his or her point of view. A number of factors influence this process, such as the perceived severity of the failure event, the importance of other issues (such as the relationship), and the consequences for future behavior.

Think about a recent significant event in which you failed to meet someone else's expectations and were reproached. How did the other person reproach you? How did this reproach affect you, and what account did you give?

How else might the other person have reproached you, and in that case, how would you have reacted?

Embarrassment. Sometimes we fail to meet our own expectations for our behaviors (we threaten our own face) and thus feel embarrassed.[11] For example, walking into class and spilling a can of soft drink all over the place means you have threatened your own face by appearing clumsy and uncoordinated. Research on how we manage embarrassing situations indicates that we use the account strategies already discussed, plus four additional strategies: humor, remediation, escape, and aggression:[12]

- *Humor* involves laughing off the issue or making light of it. After spilling your soft drink, you might say something like "I didn't really need the caffeine anyway."
- Through *remediation*, people make restitution, repair the damage, or simply re-collect themselves. Using this strategy, you might quickly get some paper towels and wipe up the spilled soda, particularly if no one else is around to know that you have made the mess.
- *Escape* allows people to distance themselves from the situation. If you were the only person in the room when you spilled the soft drink, you could use escape as a strategy by leaving the room and coming back later. Upon your return, you would act as if you didn't have anything to do with the spill.
- Finally, *aggression* involves a verbal or physical attack on the other people involved. You might lash out at the other students who watched you spill your drink: "What's the matter? Haven't you seen anybody spill something before?" A particularly aggressive response might be to knock over other students' drinks as a way of disguising the initial embarrassment.

Managing failure events and embarrassment. Your communication interactions are filled with failure events and embarrassing situations. Understanding the likely patterns in these events can help you use communication to manage them better.

You can handle failure events better if you appreciate, for example, how your reproaches affect other people. If you threaten a person's face too aggressively, you are unlikely to gain admission of guilt, apology, or restitution. Thus, you need to consider what your goal is in reproaching the other person. Reproaches can be used to correct behavior that you find inappropriate, unsatisfactory, or damaging. But reproaches that are presented simply to belittle the other person are unproductive and can ultimately backfire.

Likewise, in providing an account to another person, you should examine your culpability. You should also consider the reproacher's objectives and desires so that you can understand his or her reason for the reproach. Sometimes it is best simply to admit your failure and make a genuine effort to correct it.

In many situations, unfortunately, attempts to save face lead to lying or deceit. You might create false excuses or justifications to gain acceptance of your account and get yourself off the hook. In the next section, we'll look at different types of deception and some of the reasons people resort to them.

■ *Deception*

One of the unique characteristics of human communication is that we can manipulate symbols and create messages that are false, misleading, and deceptive. We cannot believe everything we hear, and consequently we must evaluate messages for their veracity. Guarding against deception in communication is a regretful necessity.

Deception can be thought of as the intentional disguising, avoiding, hiding, or falsifying of the truth. There are a number of types of deceptive communication, including equivocation, concealment (secrets), half-truths, diversions, and lies.

Equivocation. Given the ambiguity of language, messages are often equivocal—that is, suggestive of more than one interpretation. The term equivocation, however, adds the sense of intention, or purpose, as mentioned in Chapter 4. **Equivocation** involves purposely sending vague, unclear, or ambiguous messages.

Politicians are often stereotyped as exemplars of equivocation. The rest of us, too, use equivocation as a way of avoiding the truth, often because we are afraid of hurting another person's feelings. For example, a friend going out on a date asks you, "What do you think of my new outfit?" You think to yourself that the outfit is unflattering, but you don't want to threaten your friend's face. On the other hand, you don't want to threaten your own face by lying (after all, you have an honest relationship). So what do you say? You probably equivocate, saying something like "It's interesting." You are being deceptive because you are not disclosing your true reaction; however, you are not telling an outright lie if you think the outfit is indeed interesting.

Sometimes other people realize that we are sending ambiguous messages. In that case, they have two options. They can move on to another topic, realizing that we are trying to help them save face. Or they can ask us to give them more specific feedback. In the situation of your friend's new outfit, your friend may use a "disclaimer" that in essence gives you permission to threaten her face: "No, really, tell me what you think, I know this might not be my best look." At this point, you may be more "honest" but still try to limit the threat to your friend's face by saying something like "I think your blue jeans and navy blue sweater are a better look."

Concealment. In our example of equivocation, your response was meant to hide your true reaction to your friend's new outfit. A similar technique is **concealment,** which involves holding back information so that the other person reaches erroneous conclusions.

Suppose you are in an employment interview. As the interviewer examines your transcript, she comments, "Wow, you got an A in statistics, that's really good, we need people with good math and statistics skills." You remain silent, concealing the fact that the course involved hardly any math and that everyone in the class got an A because the instructor was an easy grader. This is deception by concealment.

Half-truths. Half-truths are similar to concealment in that some information is withheld. **Half-truths** involve leaving out information or modifying or qualifying the message to lessen the impact or reaction. Suppose your computer crashes for an hour one night while you are working on a class assignment. After you get it running again, you decide to go out with some friends. The next day you tell your professor, "My computer crashed last night in the middle of working on today's assignment, so I don't have it done. Can I turn it in tomorrow?" Your statement is only half true; it is deceptive because you are intentionally trying to create the impression that the computer failure prevented you from finishing the assignment.

Some half-truths are created by qualifying. For example, a boss might mislead her employees about a cutback in funds that she knows is going to happen by saying, "I know some of you are upset about these proposed cutbacks, but you know, sometimes the company ends up not making the cuts, so don't panic."

Diversions.   Sometimes deception involves simply dodging the matter. **Diversions** are attempts to change the focus of the communication to another topic to avoid discussing the issue at hand. After outlining a quality-control plan that requires employees to meet in groups to develop their ideas, a manager fields the following question: "Will we be meeting on company time or on our own time to discuss our ideas for improvements?" The manager uses diversion to respond: "That's a good question. There will be lots of opportunities to improve the production facilities, for example. . . ." The manager at first seemed willing to address the question, but actually diverted the answer to a side issue. The manager was hoping to deceive the listeners into believing that the question was answered.

Unless we are effective listeners, we might not even realize that someone hasn't responded to our query. And even if we do realize, we are usually hesitant to requestion the speaker after a diversion because that would challenge the speaker's face and potentially our own. How would you tactfully get someone who is using diversions back on track? Which of the following two follow-ups to the manager's response would be more effective?

A. "You didn't answer my question. Are we doing this on our own time or not?"
B. "I'm not sure I understood you. Are you saying we will be doing this on our own time?"

Statements that are qualified and that put the responsibility for misunderstanding on you rather than on the other person are less threatening to the other person. Therefore, option B would be the better choice.

Lies.   Lies are probably viewed more negatively than any other form of deception because there is little doubt about the speaker's intention. **Lies** are the deliberate presentation of false information. Lies are probably the most common form of deception.[13] Lies take on many forms, and they are sometimes categorized by their degree of falseness or harm.

The term **white lie,** for instance, is used to describe a lie that is viewed as fairly close to the truth and fairly insignificant in its impact. Sometimes we lie as part of teasing, kidding, joking, bluffing, or playing a hoax. We kid others with statements like "You know those new CDs you lent me? Did you know they melt?" After watching for a horrified reaction, the "teaser" usually breaks out laughing and admits, "I was just kidding."

We also lie through exaggeration or embellishment, overstating the case or adding information that is inaccurate. The famous line in fishing, "You should have seen the one that got away—it was this big" (at which point the speaker's arms spread wide apart), is a good example of exaggeration. Exaggeration is generally used to emphasize a particular point, ensure the listener's attention, add credibility to a story, impress the listener, or heighten the effect. A narrow escape from a wild bear sounds much more exciting if the teller says the bear was only two feet away rather than admitting that it was thirty feet away.

Exaggerations are not to be taken lightly when the intention is to deceive and gain advantage over the listener. Commercials are monitored for false claims in which the value of a product is exaggerated. Almost every week an investigative report on *60 Minutes* or *20/20* details exaggerated claims for get-rich schemes or products such as miracle-cure mineral waters.

Think about an instance of deception you have engaged in recently. What type did you use? Why did you do it? What were the effects for you? What were the effects for the other person? Did you get caught?

Reasons for deception.   Research shows that deception is fairly pervasive in our communication.[14] Most of the time we use it for selfish reasons, such as the following:

- We sometimes use deception to gain or protect resources. Those resources can be material things, such as money or possessions. But resources can also include relationships and self-esteem.
- We might use deception to improve our ability to persuade or gain compliance from other people. One research study found distinct differences in the way truthful and deceptive persuaders tried to get something from someone.[15] Deceptive persuaders offered more explanations and rationales for granting the request than did the truthful persuaders. On the other hand, truthful persuaders were more likely to use reward or punishment as a means of persuasion.
- We use deception to protect ourselves. For instance, after a failure event, we might lie to save face. We might falsify information in our excuse or justification to reduce the damage to our face. We also try to protect ourselves by avoiding conflicts through deception. The manager who used diversion when responding to an employee's question was probably motivated by a desire to avoid conflict.
- We might use deception for our amusement. Deceptive teasing or kidding allows us to gain some pleasure from watching other people's reactions. The TV shows *Candid Camera* and *Bloopers* often involve filming people's reactions to a deceptive situation for the entertainment of the audience.

LEMONT BROWN by Darrin Bell

©1998 Darrin Bell, all rights reserved. Visit www.lemontbrown.com

■ Finally, we use deception to protect others (although there is often a degree of self-serving in such acts as well). For example, we might not reveal information to friends that we expect would upset or depress them.

Under what circumstances do you feel deception is acceptable? Within which of the following categories of communication do you feel deception is least unethical? Most unethical? Explain.

interpersonal communication	presentational communication
interviewing	organizational communication
small group communication	mass communication

Detecting deception.   Research on detecting deception has produced contradictory results.[16] Some research suggests that as relationships become more intimate, we develop a truth bias; that is, we are more apt to believe what we are told by those closest to us. One study found that being a participant in an interaction decreases our ability to detect deception as compared to those who simply observe the interaction.[17] In contrast, other researchers in a noninteractive study found that lovers could tell when their partners were lying 65 to 70 percent of the time.[18]

In some research studies, ironically, "experts" (such as military intelligence officers) were less accurate in determining truth than were novices.[19] Nonetheless, other research has found that deception detection training is sometimes effective. One study, evaluating a training program that had participants focus on six behavioral causes of deception, found that the training did increase the participants' accuracy in judging other people's statements.[20]

We do tend to give some clues when we are telling lies. **Leakages** are subtle behavioral changes that accompany deception. The degree to which these leakages occur depends on the level of anxiety felt by the deceiver: the less anxiety, the less leakage. This is one reason that lie detection machines are not infallible.

Leakages involve various types of behavior. Compared to nondeceivers, deceivers generally exhibit more adaptors (such as scratching, rubbing, picking, handling a pencil), hand gestures, and speech errors. Deceivers also pause more often, take a longer time to respond to questions, and provide shorter responses.[21]

What happens when we suspect that someone isn't being honest with us? If it's an interpersonal encounter, we might decide to probe for more information to determine the person's veracity. Our probing behavior, though, can potentially alert the deceiver to our suspicions, thus causing the deceiver to alter his or her behavior to cover up.[22]

A significant problem in communicating with strangers on the Internet is the presentation of false information and the attempt to detect it. Log on to a chat session for a while and see what cues you can identify that might lead you to believe a deception is occurring. What can you do to determine if other people on the Net are being honest with you? How important is honesty over the Internet?

■ *Aggressive Versus Assertive Messages*

We have discussed teasing as both a face-threatening act and a form of deception. Teasing can also have another impact, that of making the recipient feel put down and belittled. When this is the speaker's intent, teasing becomes an aggressive message.

Aggressive messages are verbal attacks on the self-concepts (face) of individuals for the purpose of making them feel less favorable about themselves.[23] Four reasons have been identified for the use of verbal aggressiveness: frustration (a response to having goals blocked), social learning (the way someone has learned to deal with situations), psychopathology (lashing out at other people who symbolize unresolved personal issues), and argumentative skill deficiency (lack of verbal skills to constructively deal with issues)[24]. Most of us have been outargued or otherwise frustrated in our interaction with someone, and we may have responded by verbally attacking the other person through name-calling, putdowns, insults, and so on. Such attacks to another person's face often result in a corresponding attack on our own face and/or escalation of the interaction into a conflict.

How aggressive are you? Complete the following Test Yourself to see what the aggressiveness scale indicates about you. How does your score compare with the way you generally regard your level of aggressiveness?

This verbal aggressiveness scale is concerned with how we try to get people to comply with our wishes. Indicate how often each statement is true for you personally when you try to influence other people. Use the following scale: (1) almost never true, (2) rarely true, (3) occasionally true, (4) often true, (5) almost always true.

Test Yourself

_____ 1. I am extremely careful to avoid attacking individuals' intelligence when I attack their ideas.

_____ 2. When individuals are very stubborn, I use insults to soften the stubbornness.

_____ 3. I try very hard to avoid having other people feel bad about themselves when I try to influence them.

_____ 4. When people refuse to do a task I know is important, without good reason, I tell them they are unreasonable.

_____ 5. When others do things I regard as stupid, I try to be extremely gentle with them.

_____ 6. If individuals I am trying to influence really deserve it, I attack their characters.

_____ 7. When people behave in ways that are in very poor taste, I insult them in order to shock them into proper behavior.

_____ 8. I try to make people feel good about themselves even when their ideas are stupid.

_____ 9. When people simply will not budge on a matter of importance I lose my temper and say rather strong things to them.

_____ 10. When people criticize my shortcomings, I take it in good humor and do not try to get back at them.

_____11. When individuals insult me, I get a lot of pleasure out of really telling them off.

_____12. When I dislike individuals greatly, I try not to show it in what I say or how I say it.

_____13. I like poking fun at people who do things which are very stupid in order to stimulate their intelligence.

_____14. When I attack peoples' ideas, I try not to damage their self-concepts.

_____15. When I try to influence people, I make a great effort not to offend them.

_____16. When people do things which are mean or cruel, I attack their character in order to help correct their behavior.

_____17. I refuse to participate in arguments when they involve personal attacks.

_____18. When nothing seems to work in trying to influence others, I yell and scream in order to get some movement from them.

_____19. When I am not able to refute others' positions, I try to make them feel defensive in order to weaken their positions.

_____20. When an argument shifts to personal attacks, I try very hard to change the subject.

Scoring instructions: Sum the scores of the 20 items after reversing the scoring for items 1, 3, 5, 8, 10, 12, 14, 15, 17, and 20 (change 1 to 5, 2 to 4, 4 to 2, and 5 to 1).

One study found the average score to be 49.10. How does your score compare to this number? A score greater than 59 probably indicates strong verbal aggressiveness. A score less than 39 probably reflects verbal nonaggressiveness.

Source: From D. A. Infante and C. J. Wigley, III, "Verbal Aggressiveness: An Interpersonal Model and Measure," *Communication Monographs,* 53 (1986): 61–69. Reprinted with permission.

We sometimes use aggressive messages in the mistaken belief that we are simply asserting our own rights. However, we can assert our rights without attacking others. **Assertive messages** are messages in which we argue for our own rights while recognizing the rights of others. Assertive messages involve a forthright yet socially appropriate expression of our rights and feelings.

Being assertive is a complex task that requires the ability to express one's self verbally and nonverbally in such a way as to minimize hostility or defensiveness on the part of other people. Let's go back to the employee who asked the manager about the quality-control plan. Underlying the interaction is the question of whether the employee is going to have to forfeit his or her own time. An assertive response would be: "I would not be happy if I had to do this on my own time. I believe that my time is *my* time, not the company's. However, I'd be happy to participate while I'm on the clock." This statement includes an honest expression of feelings, a claim of personal rights, and a recognition of the manager's rights.

You might choose not to be assertive because you are concerned about how you will be seen. You wouldn't want to voice an assertive message that conveyed an image contrary to your positive face. Also, you might be concerned about the threat to another person's face caused by your assertive message. The key is to make statements that are both consistent with your face and minimally damaging to the other person.

How would you handle the following situation? You are in a busy restaurant and your order is messed up. You get a spinach salad when you ordered a tossed salad. Do you go ahead and eat the salad, or do you call the waiter over to correct your order? If you don't ask to have the order corrected, why not? If you do ask, are you aggressive (hostile) or assertive (recognizing that the waiter is busy)? Telling the waiter that the order is incorrect challenges the waiter's face. He wants to be seen as a good waiter and get a good tip. How can you help him maintain his image as a good waiter while getting what you want?

■ The Challenge of Misunderstandings and Misrepresentations

Chapter 4, in discussing the notion of shared meaning, pointed out that two people never really have a 100 percent overlap in the meaning they assign to messages. But the fact that you and I don't share exactly the same meanings doesn't mean that we can't communicate effectively. Human communication is flexible enough to tolerate most deviations from shared meaning without causing significant breakdowns in our interactions. Misunderstandings occur only when the differences reach a critical threshold.

Misunderstandings are instances in which a hearer's inability to comprehend the message results in confusion, failure events, conflict, or incorrect responses. Misunderstandings are problems in the way the hearer decodes messages or interprets perceptions. In addition to difficulties with the language in the message, misunderstanding can occur at several other levels:

- *Misunderstanding intentions.* You might understand the words people have spoken but misunderstand their intentions. For example, Lincoln asks Myron to leave. Myron doesn't leave, and Lincoln becomes irritated and says, "Why aren't you leaving like I asked you?" Myron responds, "I thought you were kidding. I didn't really think you meant it." Myron understood Lincoln's words but misunderstood his intentions.
- *Misunderstanding the relationship.* You may believe that a certain relationship exists between you and the person speaking to you, but that person may have a contrary perception. In this case, you have a misunderstanding of the relationship.
- *Misunderstanding the situation.* Showing up in shorts and a T-shirt for a Sunday afternoon brunch at which everyone else is in skirts and suits reflects a misunderstanding of the situation. Usually, this kind of misunderstanding results in socially inappropriate behavior.
- *Misunderstanding the culture.* Misunderstanding the cultural factors that underlie another person's behavior can lead to incorrect attribution of meaning, as you saw in Chapter 4.

Speakers themselves also contribute to incomprehension. **Misrepresentations** are instances in which a speaker produces an incomprehensible message. Like misunderstandings, misrepresentations lead to confusion, failure events, conflict, and incorrect responses. Suppose you have been invited back to your elementary school to give a presentation to the sixth graders about college life.

During part of your presentation, you say, "Higher education exposes you to a heterogeneous group of pedagogical purveyors who enjoin you to ratiocinate in neoteric ways." Do you think the sixth graders will understand what you have said? You have chosen language beyond their level of understanding and created incomprehension. A more effective statement would have been, "In college you have a lot of different teachers who make you think in new ways."

Some of the other ways speakers create misunderstandings are through the use of confusing nonverbal communication, insensitive or threatening statements, and lack of clear explanation. Sometimes the message might be clear but the speaker has caused the listener to quit listening. There are ways in which both listeners and speakers can reduce the amount of misunderstanding and misrepresentation. Underlying such efforts must be a desire by the listener to achieve understanding and a desire by the speaker to have the message accurately received. The following sections offer suggestions for making yourself both a better listener and a better speaker.

Suppose you are interacting with someone from another country who is not particularly fluent in your language. What can you do to minimize misunderstanding? What can you do to minimize misrepresentation?

■ *Improving Understanding: Things a Listener Can Do*

Thus far, you have read about a number of factors that interfere with your ability to accurately receive, decode, and interpret what you perceive. The problems include perceptual distortion, the ambiguity of words and nonverbal cues, and confusion about intentions. In this section, you'll find a number of suggestions for reducing misunderstandings. Ultimately, of course, the success of any of these suggestions rests on your desire and commitment to work actively toward better understanding.

Improve perception. Understanding requires gathering complete and accurate information. If your field of perception is too narrow, you will miss information. Challenge yourself to look beyond the obvious.

Perhaps you are listening to a speaker who talks in a quiet monotone. As a result, you conclude that the speaker must not have anything important to say and you tune out. Such behavior could cause you to miss important information. Instead, try applying the suggestions in Chapter 3 for improving your perception. Rather than tuning out, seek additional information. Make more observations before reaching conclusions. You will need to monitor and correct for perceptual biases. Are you attending only to the first and last information you receive? Are you drawing conclusions too quickly? Are you weighting negative information too heavily? What preconceptions did you bring to the situation? Are you focusing too much on irrelevant points (the speaker's monotone, fidgeting, poor eye contact, and so on)?

Improve listening. Part of misunderstanding stems from a failure to hear the complete message. The intermittent nature of listening, discussed in Chapter 3, almost ensures that you will miss part of the message. The question is whether you miss critical elements during your "vacation" time. You need to minimize the amount of time that your focus wanders away from the message.

You can consciously remind yourself to return your focus to the speaker and to ignore both external and internal distractions. You can also use your vacation time to focus on other aspects of what is being said that will aid you in understanding. You can organize what you are hearing so that it is easier to retain and recall. You can compare what is being said with how it is being said, seeking to capture deeper meanings.

Finally, you can apply the active listening skills discussed in Chapter 3, putting yourself in the role of cocreating understanding. Ask yourself what you understand. Tell the other person what you understand. Tell the speaker what you think has been said in your own words (paraphrasing). Don't just parrot back the words, but rephrase them. In that way, you add your interpretation to what was said and allow the other person to correct you if necessary.

Improve self-understanding. Understanding your own self helps to ensure understanding others. That is, a clear understanding of your psychological context helps you identify the factors that might distort what you hear—for example, your culture, your emotional state, your needs.

It is important to be conscious of your biases and how they affect your interpretations. You should examine and compensate for any communication preconceptions you might have. You need to identify your tendencies to impose expectations on what is actually heard and observed. Finally, you can try to desensitize yourself to words that might create overemotional reactions, interfering with your comprehension of the message.

Improve social decentering (perspective taking). Social decentering was presented in Chapter 4 as a way to help you understand other people's attributions of meaning. Social decentering involves knowing people's psychological contexts—their backgrounds, needs, cultures, and so forth. This enhances your ability to understand their meanings and behaviors.

You also need information about the situation. Understanding where people are "coming from" and the influence of the situation lets you put yourself in their shoes. You can comprehend their messages because you understand their feelings, thoughts, and behaviors. In one episode of the TV show *Star Trek: Deep Space Nine*, an electronic alien entity invaded the space station's computer system and began shutting down life-support systems. The entity had been alone on a spacecraft for decades. The alien's behavior was seen as hostile, and the more the protagonists tried to defeat it, the more aggressive it became. The solution to saving the station came when the engineering chief realized that the creature was like a puppy dog, longing for attention and caring. Imagining how attention craved the alien "puppy" must have been, cooped up on the spacecraft, the engineering chief created an electronic "doghouse" where the alien could be played with and cared for. An initial misunderstanding of behavior was corrected by the use of imagination-based social decentering. You can do the same thing when interacting with people.

Admit and correct misunderstandings. You must judge the significance of a misunderstanding and decide if it should be corrected. If you decide that it could cause problems, then the misunderstanding should be addressed as soon as possible. Waiting often intensifies the problems and makes addressing the misunderstanding a more burdensome task.

We sometimes ignore a misunderstanding or delay addressing it because we are afraid of losing face or of threatening another person's face. Don't be afraid to admit confusion or misunderstanding. People generally prefer to work on achieving shared understanding during the initial interaction, rather than correct errors caused by the misunderstanding at a later time.

■ Improving Representation: Things a Speaker Can Do

Just as you can work to improve your comprehension of messages as a listener, you can work to improve the degree to which your own messages are understood. Again, there is an assumption here that you want your message to be understood rather than to baffle your listeners. A sincere commitment to improving the comprehensibility of your messages relies on understanding your listeners, being

What do these two people need to know about one another to enhance their understanding of one another's messages?

sensitive to feedback, creating clear messages, and double-checking that listeners understand.

Improve social decentering.   How will the other person interpret what you are saying? What other interpretations are possible besides the one you intend? Your goal is to get your message through clearly. Are the words you choose or the accompanying behaviors you display creating any "noise," or interference, that will cause miscomprehension for the listener?

The more you know about your listener, the more effectively you can choose language that will be understood. Most of us intuitively change the words we use when talking to children because we realize they won't understand many of our "adult" words. With other adults, however, egocentric communication is a significant contributor to misrepresentation. We fail to recognize that the listener is different from us and has different reactions to what we say. Consequently, we may use language that, from the other person's perspective, is ambiguous or misleading. Our intercultural interactions are often marred by a failure to appreciate the effects of culture on another person's understanding of our messages.

You can engage in social decentering by listening to your message from the other person's perspective. Suppose you want your roommate to turn down the stereo so you can study. You could say, "Hey! I'm trying to study." But your roommate enjoys having the stereo playing loudly when studying and therefore doesn't comprehend your statement as a request to turn down the stereo. You failed to take your roommate's perspective when considering how your message would be heard. Taking into account your roommate's habits means creating a more developed request: "I'm studying for a big exam tomorrow and I really can't study very well with the stereo on. Would you be willing to listen through the headset?"

Improve perception of feedback.   Speakers sometimes ignore the fact that they are receiving continual reactions to their messages. You need to monitor the feedback you receive from those with whom you are interacting. This includes watching nonverbal behaviors and being sensitive to the undertones of verbal messages.

In scenario 2 at the beginning of this chapter, the employee you are training gives contradictory feedback, nodding her head to show understanding while responding to your question about whether she understands you by saying, "Yeah, I, um, think so." The way the scenario is written, the hesitancy and uncertainty the employee conveys is not picked up. How close is this to your real behavior?

To improve your skills, you need to be sensitive to the verbal and nonverbal feedback you receive that might indicate miscomprehension. You may need to ask listeners more than once if they really understand you. And you need to ask in such a way that they know you are receptive to questions and it's okay to admit confusion. One rule of presentational speaking is this: After asking if there are any questions, slowly count to three before continuing. The use of silence and waiting is one way to signal that you really are open to questions. Teachers sometimes think that all the students must have understood what was said at a lecture because there were no questions. Effective teachers, however, are constantly scanning the students' faces for signs of confusion.

Improve message delivery. You have many options for encoding your messages, and this means that some messages will be more comprehensible than others. Several points germane to this principle have already been covered, such as adapting the language and avoiding ambiguous or equivocal language. Here are some other suggestions.

- Organize information in a manner that facilitates retention.
- Keep your message interesting so that listeners will be less likely to tune out.
- Repeat what you have said.
- Rephrase what you have said and say it again.
- Try to keep your nonverbal behaviors consistent with your verbal message, avoiding contradictory cues that create confusion.
- Use nonverbal cues to emphasize important points.
- Include examples relevant to your listener.

Seek paraphrases. A final way you can help comprehension is by asking your listener to paraphrase what you have said. Listeners may be reluctant to volunteer a restatement of what you have just said, so they may need encouragement from you. Sometimes, however, asking for paraphrasing can put people on the spot. There is an implicit threat to face: "All right now, let's see if you were really listening." You have witnessed teachers calling on students who aren't paying attention, a technique that usually results only in laughter and embarrassment. The request for paraphrasing needs to be made in a way that minimizes threat to face. You might say something like "I don't know if I said that very clearly. Why don't you tell me what you heard, and I'll try to clear up any parts that might be confusing."

Which of the skills for improving understanding are your strongest? Which skills need the most improvement? How might you go about improving them?

Similarly, which of the skills for reducing misrepresentation are your strongest? Which need the most improvement? How might you go about improving them?

■ The Challenge of Managing Conflicts

Misunderstanding and misrepresentation can lead to conflicts as individuals try to allocate blame for problems or deal with the fallout from the miscomprehension. The manifestations of conflict can vary, but there are fundamental commonalities, which we will review here. Later in the text, you'll find more specific advice that is appropriate for each communication category. In general, conflicts need to be managed in such a way as to reduce the debilitating effects they have on effective and healthy communication.

■ *Defining Conflict*

Conflict is the interaction of interdependent people over real or falsely perceived incompatible goals and/or interference from each other in achieving goals.[25] This definition may seem complicated, so let's take it apart and examine each component.

Conflict involves interaction.   You may be upset with a decision made by your boss, but it is not a conflict unless you actually raise the issue with your boss, directly interacting with your boss about the decision. Your feelings may affect your communication with your boss, but unless you voice your concerns, what occurs is more appropriately considered negative, hostile, aggressive, or defensive communication rather than conflict.

There are many cases in which we decide we are better off ignoring an issue of potential conflict or finding some alternative way of reaching our goals. We are likely to apply social exchange principles to reach a decision about whether to initiate a conflict. That is, we evaluate the value of winning the conflict (achieving our goal) as well as our potential for winning the conflict (likelihood of success). We weigh these against the costs of engaging in the conflict—the damage that might be caused and the cost to us if we lose. We then decide whether the rewards outweigh the costs. There are times, however, when we act more impulsively and charge right into conflict situations. Also, we are sometimes drawn into a conflict by other people's actions.

The management of conflict can vary. It can be direct and focused on resolving the matter, or it can be indirect and sustained. Once the conflict is initiated, the parties involved may attempt to resolve it with dispatch, or they may continue the conflict for some time because of a failure to find a way of overcoming the issues (as in a feud). Sometimes conflicts are best managed by simply deciding to move on without reaching any final resolution. In that case, the parties recognize each other's points of view and accept that their views are different; they agree to disagree.

Conflict involves people who are interdependent.   The second part of the definition, interdependence, means that the conflicting parties are dependent on each other for something. Differences in their level of dependence can have a dramatic effect on their actions. A student's conflict with an instructor, for example, usually reflects a significant difference in dependence, with the student being more dependent than the instructor. As a result, the student is limited in the strategies or actions that can be used to resolve the conflict.

Sometimes only one party is dependent on the other. In such cases, there is no *inter*dependence, and conflict doesn't really happen, though hostility and frustration certainly do. Perhaps you have been in a romantic relationship that you wanted to maintain (making you dependent on the other person), but your partner was no longer interested (no dependence). In this circumstance, your attempts to raise issues of conflict would usually be ignored by your partner, who would feel no compulsion to deal with the issues.

Conflict involves the parties' goals.   The last part of the definition of conflict focuses on goals. Goals can be classified as indivisible or opposing. **Indivisible goals** are goals that only one party can attain. In essence, they are winner-take-all goals. Most sports, for example, allow only one person or team to be victorious, so the goal of winning the game is an indivisible one. **Opposing goals** are goals that prevent each other from being attained. When one party sees his or her goals blocked by the goals of the other party (or both parties see their goals blocked by the other's goals), it is a case of opposing goals. Parents attempting to accomplish their goal of protecting their children may set a curfew of eleven o'clock for a sixteen-year-old. The young person, who has the goal of having a good time with friends, wants to stay out till one o'clock. The ensuing conflict occurs because the teenager and the parents perceive themselves as having opposing goals.

A distinction is made between real and falsely perceived goal differences. *Real goal differences* exist when the parties are vying for a goal that is indeed indivisible or for separate goals that are truly blocked by each other. *Falsely perceived differences* exist when the parties see their goals as being in conflict although in reality they share similar goals. Conflicts over falsely perceived differences usually occur because people have misunderstood or misrepresented their goals or the situation.

Resolution of falsely perceived goal differences is usually easier to manage than resolution of real differences, and it often depends on the methods for improving comprehension skills that were discussed earlier. You and a friend might have a conflict over plans for Saturday night. You want to go dancing at a club, but your friend wants to go to a movie. You see your goals as opposing one another. One solution would be for each of you to do your own thing, but this is usually not desirable because the underlying goal that you both share is to spend time together. Another solution is to recognize that your goals don't have to be perceived as opposing; you could actually do both activities. You could go to a movie and then go out dancing afterward. (Of course, this is an expensive solution and might conflict with a goal of fiscal restraint. I don't have all the answers!)

■ Categories of Conflict

Conflict can occur anytime people communicate, because communication involves attempting to achieve goals. Most of the time, fortunately, our goals are compatible or the differences are not significant enough to warrant conflict.

When conflicts do occur, they can appear in any of the communication categories identified in Chapter 1.

- Intrapersonal conflicts occur when we have to make decisions for which there are several choices. For example, do you go to a party tonight or study for tomorrow's exam? This creates a conflict between the goal of having a good time and the goal of being a good student. In a sense, the parties to the conflict are different aspects of your self.
- Interpersonal conflicts are probably the most common. They occur in interpersonal relationships in which interdependence is a defining element.
- In small groups, conflict occurs among group members (intragroup conflict, which is a form of interpersonal conflict) and among groups (intergroup conflict).
- Organizational conflicts include interpersonal conflicts and group conflicts as well as interorganizational conflicts (between organizations). If an environmental group challenges a manufacturing company's plans to build a factory in a wetland, the result is interorganizational conflict.
- In mass communication, the conflicts are generally interorganizational conflicts in which one organization, such as a consumers advocacy group, challenges a mass media organization. For instance, a consumers group might

challenge television networks in connection with the TV rating system, children's programming, or the preponderance of sex and violence on TV.

- In presentational communication, you may think conflicts are unlikely, but speakers often find themselves confronted by resistant or belligerent audiences and even hecklers. Many presentations also involve question-and-answer periods that have the potential to spawn conflicts.

■ Conflict Management Styles

Good conflict management does not necessarily mean that the conflict is resolved. Rather, it means that we choose the best option for handling a conflict—that is, the way that best protects our interests. The basic options, which we can call *conflict management styles,* include avoidance, accommodation, competition, compromise, and collaboration.

Figure 5.1 shows how these styles differ in terms of concern for your own goals (competitiveness) and concern for the other person's goals (cooperativeness). The competitive axis ranges from having no real concern for your own goals to an extremely strong commitment to getting what you want. The cooperative axis ranges from no concern for the other person's goals to a strong desire to provide the other person what he or she wants. The five styles reflect different combinations of the two types of concern. The conflict management style you choose depends on the nature of the conflict, your needs, and your relationship to the other party.

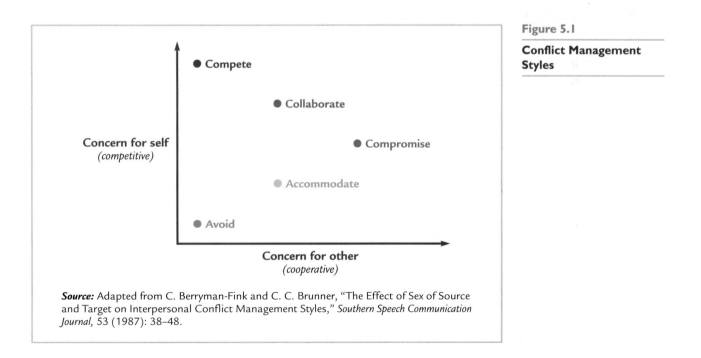

Figure 5.1

Conflict Management Styles

Source: Adapted from C. Berryman-Fink and C. C. Brunner, "The Effect of Sex of Source and Target on Interpersonal Conflict Management Styles," *Southern Speech Communication Journal,* 53 (1987): 38–48.

- *Avoidance* involves strategically evading direct discussion of the conflict. This might be the most useful strategy when a situation becomes emotionally charged. Avoidance lets you put the conflict aside until everyone is calm. You also might use avoidance when the issues are not particularly important and when focusing on the conflict could damage the relationship.[26]
- *Accommodation* means that you let the other party fulfill his or her goal while your immediate goal is set aside. This strategy would be effective when the issue is not as important for you as you perceive it is for the other person. Accommodation is also a good way to show your reasonableness and commitment to the health of the relationship. Accommodation on one issue can be used as a strategy for gaining accommodation by the other person on a later issue: "I let you have your way last time, now it's my turn."
- *Competition* is an appropriate strategy when you really are dealing with an indivisible goal that is important to you and when the relationship is much less important. Competition sends a clear message about your commitment to the goal, and it works best when there is a need for quick, decisive action.
- *Compromise* is also an effective way to reach quick decisions and overcome stalemates. It is particularly useful when the parties are fairly equal in power. You may also decide on compromise if you are losing a competition. Compromise lets both parties feel as though they have fulfilled part of their goals (though it also means they have given up part of their goals).
- *Collaboration* is an attempt to reach an agreement in which both parties' goals are fulfilled. The earlier example of going to a movie and then dancing is an example of collaborative management of a conflict. Collaboration takes time, energy, and respect by each party for the other party's goals; therefore, its application is limited.

How ethical is it to use deception as a way of resolving conflict? Or to overstate your needs in hopes of reaching a compromise that gives you what you really wanted all along? Or to use face-threatening tactics as a way to resolve a conflict in your favor?

■ General Conflict Management Skills

Each conflict presents unique challenges. There are, however, some general guidelines you can follow to manage conflict more effectively. One critical factor is to maintain effective communication. You have probably witnessed more than one conflict, such as a labor-management dispute or an interpersonal confrontation, in which communication broke down and the conflicting parties refused even to talk with each other. Keeping communication flowing during a conflict requires managing emotions, managing the information, and managing the flow of the conflict itself.

Managing emotions.   Conflicts threaten your negative face by preventing you from accomplishing your goals. Conflicts can also include direct threats to your positive face ("You're an idiot, and you don't know what you are talking about!"). Threats to either your positive or your negative face evoke emotions, and becoming too emotional can hamper your ability to manage a conflict effectively. Here's an example of such a process:

JACKIE   We really need to add another salesperson to my district. I can't get the coverage I need with just the four people I have.

JACE   Everybody thinks they need more staff. Maybe your staff is full of goof-offs and deadbeats.

JACKIE   (raising her voice) You're an idiot! My people are working their butts off. You just don't want me to be successful.

JACE   (also raising his voice) Then maybe it's their manager that's the problem!

JACKIE   (louder) Are you saying I'm not doing my job? You're a moron!!

JACE   (also louder) You can't call me names. *You're fired!!*

In this scenario, both parties should have called time out and broken off the interaction when their emotions started to get out of control. The use of avoidance would have helped both Jackie and Jace calm down. Both individuals had their face threatened and responded by further threatening the other's face, rather than helping each other maintain face.

The following suggestions can help you manage the destructive impact of unbridled emotions:

- Avoid aggressive messages—name-calling, personal attacks, and other direct face-threatening acts.
- Avoid emotional exaggerations and extremes. It's okay to be intense—emotions are unavoidable—but you don't have to be belligerent.
- Describe your emotions and ask the other people to describe their emotions when the situation calls for it. There are times when emotions are part of the conflict and need to be discussed. Hiding or ignoring emotions can result in destructive, volcanic eruptions of emotion.
- Listen to and watch yourself. What emotions are you displaying? How will the other person respond to those displays? You've probably been told things like "Don't look at me that way!" or "Quit smiling at me, I'm really upset." Our nonverbal cues can heighten emotional tension.
- Choose a time and place that are most conducive to a relaxed interaction. Being called into the dean's office in school or the boss's office at work can immediately raise a person's anxiety. Likewise, trying to discuss a conflict with people at the end of the day when they are tired or when they are swamped with work increases the likelihood of emotional interference.

Managing information.   We also manage conflicts by the way we manage information. Jace's comment about Jackie's sales staff evoked her defensiveness. Jace should have been aware that his offhand remark would upset her. He should have either stated the issue in a more constructive manner or dealt with the issue of Jackie's staff on another occasion. A number of rules apply to managing information during a conflict.

1. *Plan your message.* You can more easily state your concern about a point of conflict if you have planned in advance what you are going to say, rather than addressing the issue on the spur of the moment. Planning the message lets you consider how the other person might react and lets you choose language that is least likely to evoke a strong emotional reaction.

2. *Approach the issue from a problem-oriented perspective rather than an evaluative one.* Evaluative statements evoke defensiveness, whereas statements that focus on specific behaviors or issues tend to be supportive.[27] Jace could have approached the issue of Jackie's sales staff in a problem-oriented manner by saying, "Why don't we look at what your current staff is doing and see if there are any ways to improve their effectiveness?"

3. *Separate the issues from the person, and deal only with the issues.* We sometimes are lured into criticizing and evaluating the individual rather than dealing with the point of conflict. Jace and Jackie needed to deal with the issues of Jackie wanting to be more successful and Jace feeling the need to keep employee costs down. Instead, Jackie began focusing on Jace and drifted away from her own needs and goals.

4. *Seek information to understand the conflict more fully.* This includes seeking information from outside sources and directly from the other party. It also means listening effectively to what the other party is telling you and applying active listening skills.

5. *Share information with the other party.* Hiding information undermines trust and encourages the other party to hide information from you as well. Openly sharing information helps the other party learn about your position and establishes a climate of cooperation.

Managing the conflict.   Managing emotions and information puts you in a position to manage the conflict effectively. Each of the five styles mentioned earlier is a possible way of managing conflicts. There are also rules you can follow to improve the process for all the parties.

1. *Define and focus on the problem.* This might seem like an obvious thing to do, but we often lose sight of the issues during conflicts. In addition, the parties in the conflict often have different definitions of the problem. In either case, it becomes important to mutually define the problem. In defining the problem, both parties need to present their goals and needs. Both parties need to listen to and appreciate the needs and goals of the other person. Sometimes we dismiss the other person's goals because we don't see them as valid or important. Such judgments only serve to heighten tensions and raise the ire of the other party.

2. *Analyze the problem.* Analysis of the problem again involves both parties' presenting their perspective on what created the problem, the impact of the problem, and the reasons the problem persists. This discussion should include an attempt to find similarities between the conflicting parties. In the conflict described earlier, Jackie and Jace both want to see high sales and good profits in Jackie's territory. In analyzing the problem, they would have realized that Jackie saw the problem as too large a territory for the number of staff, and Jace saw the problem as an inefficient staff. This would have led them to explore the question of staffing efficiency.

3. *Define a mutually acceptable goal.* The conflict is practically over once this step is accomplished. However, this is much easier said than done. At this point, both parties must be willing to cooperate in defining a goal that is acceptable to both. This can be accomplished by integrating the goals and needs of both

parties, often creatively. Jackie and Jace probably could agree on the goal of maximizing sales while minimizing costs in her district.

4. *Generate multiple solutions to the problem.* Once a common goal has been identified, the parties should work to generate a number of alternative solutions. At times we are sucked into focusing on only one solution—just as Jackie saw the addition of a staff member as the only solution to her problem. Even if one solution seems apparent, try to generate as many other possibilities as you can. Valuable, innovative ideas often arise during the process of brainstorming alternatives. The best solution might be one that has integrated components of various alternatives.

5. *Select the best solution.* Once a list of alternative solutions has been generated, the parties can begin to analyze each choice in terms of how well it fulfills their mutually agreed-on goal. At this point, details are needed about how to implement the solution and monitor its effectiveness, as well as agreement on what steps to take if the selection does not seem to be working.

Think of a current conflict you are having. What are your goals and needs? What are the other party's goals? What commonalities are there in your goals and interests? What do you see as the underlying causes of the conflict? How would the other party describe the causes of the conflict? What would happen if you approached this person using the method we have just described?

Remember, the challenges to communication discussed in this chapter apply to all communication situations. Each time we interact with others, we risk threats to our face, the possibility of miscomprehension, and the development of conflict. Fear of such possibilities should not cause us to avoid communication; rather, knowledge of how to manage these challenges should lead us to be more effective in our dealings with other people.

Summary

This chapter has focused on three aspects of communication that are particularly challenging: maintaining face (self-image), dealing with misunderstandings and misrepresentations, and managing conflict. These challenges directly relate to the three basic types of communication needs (identity, instrumental, and relational). We enter communication interactions with a need to have our identity accepted and confirmed, but often we find it threatened. Our instrumental needs are met by using communication to accomplish and perform tasks. Finally, we have relational needs that are satisfied through communication with other people.

A variety of communication events pose threats to our face. We then use communication to try to save, maintain, or restore our face. Sometimes we cause failure events when we act in an unexpected manner or fail to meet an obligation. These events threaten both our face and that of the other people involved. Another person might point out our failure through a reproach, and we then respond with an account. Reproaches and accounts affect each other and vary in terms of how threatening they are.

Our face is also threatened by other people's deception. Deception occurs when a person intentionally tries to hide or falsify the truth. It can take the form of equivocation, concealment, half-truths, diversions, or lies. Deception is used for a variety of reasons, including gaining resources, gaining compliance, protecting face, having fun, and protecting others. Sometimes we can detect deception when we are able to observe leakages, the subtle behavioral cues that accompany deception.

Some attacks on our face come from aggressive messages, such as name-calling and insults—messages designed intentionally to threaten our face. In contrast to aggressive messages, assertive messages can be used to present a claim for one's own rights while acknowledging the rights of others.

Another major challenge to effective communication stems from misunderstandings and misrepresentations. Both of these communication events result in miscomprehension by the listener of what the speaker is trying to communicate. Misunderstanding is listener based, while misrepresentations are speaker based. Misunderstanding can be minimized through improved perception, improved listening, better self-understanding, improved social decentering, and admitting to and correcting misunderstandings. Misrepresentation can be minimized through improved social decentering, improved perception of listeners' feedback, improved message delivery, and asking for paraphrased feedback from listeners.

The final section of this chapter focused on conflict. The definition of conflict includes the following components: interaction; interdependence of the parties; and real or false perception of incompatible goals and/or interference in achieving goals. Goals can be classified as either indivisible (winner-take-all) or opposing. Conflict management styles include avoiding, accommodating, competing, compromising, and collaborating, and these five styles vary in terms of concern for self and concern for the other person.

Conflict management involves effectively managing emotions, information, and the conflict itself. Among the rules for managing emotions are avoiding aggressive messages, choosing a place and time conducive to a relaxed interaction, and being willing to discuss emotions. Information management involves planning a problem-oriented message, separating the issue from the person, and directly seeking and openly sharing information. Managing the conflict requires defining and analyzing the problem, finding a mutually acceptable goal, and then generating and selecting the best solutions.

Key Terms

identity needs   The needs we satisfy when we present who we are to other people, have that presented self accepted and confirmed by other people, and confirm other people's identities.

instrumental needs   The needs we satisfy when we accomplish tasks or perform jobs.

relational needs   The needs we satisfy when we manage our relationships.

save face   Restore the image that we were originally trying to convey before our face was threatened.

maintain face   Prevent loss of face. Other people can help us maintain face by providing support, confirmation, and acceptance of the self-conception we are presenting.

failure event   An instance of failure to fulfill an obligation or expectation.

reproach   An indication by someone that a failure event has occurred.

mitigating reproach   A reproach that reflects only mild irritation with a failure event.

aggravating reproach   A severe, intense declaration of the occurrence of a failure event.

account   A stated response to a reproach by the person accused of the failure event.

apology   A statement in which the person admits a failure event, accepts responsibility for it, and expresses regret.

excuse   An admission that a failure event occurred combined with an assertion that nothing could have been done to prevent it.

justification   Accepting responsibility for a failure event but then trying to redefine the event as not being a failure.

denial   Stating that a failure event never took place.

providing no account   Either offering no response to a reproach or ignoring it by changing the subject; silence.

silence   Either offering no response to a reproach or ignoring it by changing the subject; providing no account.

deception   The intentional disguising, avoiding, hiding, or falsifying of the truth.

equivocation   Deception by purposely sending vague, unclear, or ambiguous messages.

concealment   Deception through the holding back of information so that the other person reaches erroneous conclusions.

half-truths   Deceptions that leave out information or modify or qualify the message to lessen the impact or reaction.

diversions   Deceptions that change the focus of the communication to another topic to avoid discussing the issue at hand.

lies   Deception through the deliberate presentation of false information.

white lie   A lie that is viewed as fairly close to the truth and fairly insignificant in its impact.

leakages   Subtle behavioral changes that accompany deception.

aggressive messages   Verbal attacks on the self-concepts (face) of individuals for the purpose of making them feel less favorable about themselves.

assertive messages   Messages in which we argue for our own rights while recognizing the rights of others.

misunderstandings   Instances in which a hearer's inability to comprehend a message results in confusion, failure events, conflict, or incorrect responses.

misrepresentations   Instances in which a speaker produces an incomprehensible message.

conflict   The interaction of interdependent people over real or falsely perceived incompatible goals and/or interference from each other in achieving goals.

indivisible goals   Goals that only one party can attain.

opposing goals   Goals that prevent each other from being attained.

Review Questions

1. Define identity, instrumental, and relational needs.
2. Explain the process of dealing with a failure event.
3. Explain the differences between the different types of deception.
4. Distinguish between an aggressive message and an assertive message.
5. Identify several ways of improving understanding and representation.
6. Explain how conflict management involves the management of emotions, information, and the conflict itself.

Part Two

Communication in Everyday Life:
From Theory to Practice

Chapter 6

Interpersonal Communication: Theories of Relationships

Objectives

Studying this chapter will allow you to:

1. Identify the types of relationships and relational dimensions.
2. Explain how social penetration theory and dialectical theory apply to relational development.
3. Identify the stages of relationship escalation and de-escalation.
4. Discuss several theories of attraction.
5. Explain some of the principles related to self-disclosure.
6. Construct a Johari window and identify the quadrants.

You go into work. You and the receptionist, who is on the phone, smile and nod at each other as you pass his desk. You stop to get a cup of coffee in the employee lounge, where a good friend of yours from accounting is sitting at a table going over some forms. You and she spend a couple of minutes talking about the party you both went to Friday night. As you head to your office, your boss sees you and calls you into her office. She asks how your weekend was, and you tell her about a movie you saw Saturday night. You ask in turn about her weekend, and she talks about a purchase she made Sunday at a flea market. She then starts to talk to you about the work still to be done on the department's annual report. When you finish chatting with her, you go to your office.

Your interactions with the receptionist, with your friend from accounting, and with your boss all represent interpersonal communication. But they differ in many ways. Each reflects a different relationship. The interactions vary in terms of such qualities as how personal the interaction is and the kinds of things you talk about. These are some of the ways that interpersonal communication and interpersonal relationships affect one another. That mutual effect is the focus of this chapter.

■ Understanding Interpersonal Communication and Relationships

We often take our personal interactions with other people for granted. We usually don't realize the important role that communication is playing in our interpersonal relationships until something goes wrong. Communication, in fact, is an essential element of interpersonal relationships. We use communication to initiate, develop, maintain, and terminate relationships. The very nature of our relationships is reflected in the way we communicate.

Communication within personal relationships is called interpersonal communication. **Interpersonal communication** was defined in Chapter 1 as communication in which two or more people transactionally influence one another. This definition reflects the fact that interpersonal communication involves all of the parties in the interaction having an effect on one another simultaneously.

The definition indicates the very minimum conditions that must be present to call a situation interpersonal. Interpersonal communication actually represents a continuum of situations, as shown in Figure 6.1. On one end of this continuum are instances in which individuals have a minimal effect on one another, as when they merely make eye contact. At the other end of the continuum are instances in which individuals are focused intensely on each other, sharing information about themselves and providing confirmation of each other's self-concepts. In essence, this continuum reflects how "personal" the interaction is. For example, telling your best friend, "My shoe size is 10½" is not as personal as saying, "My father used to spank me with his belt when I was a kid, and I don't think I've ever forgiven him."

We use interpersonal communication to fulfill the three general needs discussed in Chapter 5 (instrumental, identity, and relational needs.) Interactions in which we are primarily seeking to meet our instrumental goals tend to fall on the left side of the continuum in Figure 6.1. Our communication is usually more personalized when we are seeking to achieve relational and identity goals. The far

Low degree of "personalness"			High degree of "personalness"
Simultaneous eye contact	Impersonal interactions	Personal interactions	Mutual confirmation of selves
Two strangers catching each other's eye across a room full of people	*Asking for a "Big Mac and fries"*	*Telling another person about your career interests*	*Two people being themselves with each other and conveying acceptance of each other*

right of the continuum reflects the situation in which the people involved have a strong intimate relationship and confirmation of their identities.

This chapter will help you understand the different types of relationships, how they develop and decline, how people become attracted to one another, and how the information we disclose about ourselves changes according to the nature of the relationship. Let's begin by looking at the basic types of relationships.

▊ Relationship Types

Interpersonal communication shapes the nature of your relationships, and your relationships in turn shape your communication. To understand interpersonal communication, therefore, you need to understand interpersonal relationships.

Think of all the terms that describe relationships: *friends, best friends, lovers, classmates, coworkers, parents, brothers, bosses, spouses, subordinates, acquaintances,* and dozens of others. How can you classify these many different relationships? One way to classify them is by the degree that the participants choose them or, conversely, the degree to which they occur because of circumstances:[1]

Relationships of choice are those relationships that you have chosen to form and maintain. You can also choose to terminate these relationships. **Relationships of circumstance** are those relationships that exist because of situational influences. You don't choose your siblings, bosses, or classmates, for example. Table 6.1 lists further examples of each type of relationship.

You can convert relationships of circumstance into relationships of choice. You can be friends with your siblings, bosses, or classmates. However, when you end a relationship of choice, such as being friends with your sister, terminating the friendship doesn't mean that the relationship is over. It simply reverts to being a relationship of circumstance. She is still your sister. On the other hand, most relationships of circumstance are not wholly devoid of choice. You can choose to quit a job if you don't like your boss or coworkers.

In Table 6.1, why does "roommate" appear as both a relationship of choice and a relationship of circumstance? Examine your own relationships of circumstance and decide if any of them are also relationships of choice. What happens when you want to end a relationship of choice and maintain it only as a relationship of circumstance?

Table 6.1 Examples of Basic Relationship Types

Relationships of Choice	Relationships of Circumstance
Friend	Sister/brother
Best friend	Uncle/aunt
Lover	Mother/father
Acquaintance	Boss
Wife/husband	Coworker
Buddy	Classmate
Boyfriend/girlfriend	Subordinate
Partner	Customer
Significant other	Teacher
Confidant	Teammate
Roommate	Roommate

■ Relational Dimensions

We often classify our relationships by how long they have lasted ("We've been dating now for six months"), how much we have disclosed about ourselves ("He knows more about me than even my mother"), how close we feel toward the other person ("We're really not that close"), and the roles each partner plays ("This is my girlfriend, Mary"). Another way of classifying relationships is according to the dimensions of interpersonal trust, intimacy, and power.[2]

■ *Trust*

We mentioned trust in Chapter 2 as one of the factors affecting the relational context of communication. More precisely, **interpersonal trust** is a reflection of how secure we are that a partner will act in a predicted and desirable manner. When we trust someone's actions, we have faith that he or she will behave in the way we expect (for example, "I trust you will be here at eight"). When we tell people personal information, our trust is reflected in our expectation that they will not use that information in a way that might harm us.

Interpersonal trust manifests itself in different ways. In very close relationships, you trust that your partner will remain committed to the relationship. You expect to see the person again whenever you need. And in your relationship with instructors, you trust that they will grade you fairly and objectively.

Trust is the product of your interpersonal interactions. As you interact and learn more about the other person, you reduce your uncertainty. As you gain a stronger sense of what to expect from the other person through communication, your trust builds. And as trust grows, your communication changes. You discuss more topics more openly as you feel more trust toward the other person.

■ *Intimacy*

Intimacy is strongly related to trust. **Intimacy** is the degree to which two people rely on each other to accept and confirm each other's self-concept. In essence, the more intimate the relationship, the more we can be ourselves without fear of rejection or of losing the relationship.

Think about how a relationship changes as you move from being a stranger to being best friends. At first you are guarded about what you share about yourself. You put on a positive mask that you think will be attractive to other people, but that mask reflects only part of who you really are. As the relationship becomes more intimate, you are able to share more of your "real" self with your partner until finally you are able to just "be yourself."

How intimate is your relationship with your parents or other close relatives compared to your relationship with your close friends? Because most of us tend to be on our good behavior in front of our parents, we don't really get our complete self confirmed in those relationships. Our drive to find people who will accept us as we are (part of our identity needs) leads us to seek out more intimate relationships. As you can tell, the term *intimacy* is not being used here as a reference to sexual activity. We can have very intimate relationships that have no sexual component—for instance, the relationship we form with our best friend.

Part of being ourselves means that our communication is much more free flowing and unrestricted. We don't feel that we need to be as guarded about what we say or how we say it. As relationships become more intimate, communication becomes more efficient. We get to know each other so well that we can send abbreviated, vague, and ambiguous messages that are still understood.

■ *Power*

We can also distinguish our relationships by the dimension of power. Unlike trust and intimacy, which normally increase as a relationship grows closer, power does not necessarily change.

Power is the ability of people to influence other people in order to accomplish their goals. Power exists in all relationships, and both parties in a relationship have power. Power is neither positive nor negative, but simply a quality that is present. However, power can be *used* both positively and negatively.

As you examine your own relationships, you can probably think of some in which you have more power than your partner, some in which your partner has more power than you, and others in which power is fairly equal. In your relationship with your instructor, the instructor probably has more power over you than vice versa. However, you are not powerless. The instructor needs you and the other students to come to class, and if you don't like something your instructor has done, you usually have some recourse, such as talking with the department chair or college dean.

Power over other individuals is usually based on the ability to control resources that affect the other person. In the case of your instructor, you may control course evaluations that affect the instructor. Thus, you have power to the degree that the instructor cares about getting positive course evaluations. However, once course evaluations are completed, you no longer control that resource and no longer have that as a basis of influence on the instructor.

Think about close relationships that you have wanted to maintain. The more dependent you are on a relationship to meet your interpersonal needs, the more power your partner has. But when you find some other source of satisfaction and no longer "need" the relationship, your partner has lost that source of power. Such an imbalance leads to inequitable relationships in which the person with more power has the potential to abuse and exploit the difference.

Power and relational styles.   The different balances of power in relationships create three potential styles: complementary, symmetrical, and parallel.[3]

The **complementary style** represents an imbalance in power such that one person is dominant and the other is submissive. This might sound like a terrible arrangement, but such relationships are satisfactory if both parties are agreeable to the arrangement. Your relationship with your instructors is probably complementary. The instructor gives you assignments and exams and you comply. Think about your personal relationships. Some of them are probably complementary in that either you or your friend is always the one who initiates interactions, calls the other, and decides when to go out together and what to do.

A **symmetrical style** is a relational style in which both parties have fairly equal power. If you and your friend are both active in initiating interactions and deciding when to go out and what to do, that is a symmetrical style. You may be inclined to think that symmetrical relationships are inherently better than complementary relationships. However, imagine what happens in a marriage if both parties want to be responsible for deciding how to spend their money. Reaching a decision about what to buy and how much to spend would sometimes produce

REAL LIFE ADVENTURES by Gary Wise and Lance Aldrich

© 1998 GarLanCo/Distributed by Universal Press Syndicate

www.uexpress.com

HERE. LET ME SHOW YOU.

The best marriages combine people who don't know how to say no with people who do.

conflict and a need for negotiation. Having two individuals with equal power can produce problems when they have different goals.

In a **parallel style** relationship, one partner sometimes has more power or less power than the other, and sometimes both partners are equal. The style varies according to the situation and the needs and skills of each person. Working out who has power in a given situation is one of the relational dynamics that couples must negotiate as they develop a more intimate relationship. Parallel styles are continually developing as couples encounter new situations and decide whether to approach them in a complementary or symmetrical manner.

Each of the styles related to power is reflected in interpersonal communication. In a complementary relationship, we would likely hear one partner giving commands or directions and the other asking questions of clarification; communication would almost seem unbalanced. Symmetrical relationships and parallel relationships would incorporate a fair amount of disagreement and conflict as the partners tried to work out decisions. Well-developed parallel relationships would eventually resolve many issues, and the amount of conflict could be expected to subside.

■ Stages of Relational Development

Relationships go through a series of stages as intimacy escalates; they go through another series of stages if intimacy de-escalates. Of course, most of our encounters with people end without the relationship moving past the initial stages. But if we do move on to later stages, each stage represents a filtering process whereby we decide either to abandon the relationship, maintain it at its current level, or escalate it to the next stage. Each stage can be identified by changes in the way we communicate[4] and by changes in our relational expectations.[5]

Before examining how researchers have defined the various stages, let's look at theories that try to explain why people move from one stage to another.

■ *Theoretical Perspectives on Relational Development*

Various theoretical approaches have been used to explain how and why relationships develop. In this section, we'll explore two major theories, social penetration theory and dialectical theory, as well as the key concept of process trajectory cognitions.

Social penetration theory.   According to Altman and Taylor's **social penetration theory,** we move from one relational stage to another as a result of deciding that such a move would be more rewarding than costly.[6] That is, we try to assess how "profitable" it would be to have a closer relationship with someone. Similarly, we retreat from relationships when the costs begin to increase more than the rewards.

For example, suppose you have a friend with whom you have had a rewarding relationship, and he moves two hundred miles away. You continue to talk on the phone, send email, and occasionally visit on the weekends. But when you do get together, instead of doing all the fun things you used to do, you sit around and listen to him complain about his life. In this situation, you would probably reach a point at which you felt that the costs of maintaining the relationship (including travel costs, phone bills, and emotional stress) exceeded the rewards (friendship and fun times), and you would be motivated to ease out of the relationship. In general, decisions about pursuing relationships are based on such factors as what our previous relational experiences have been, what our experience is in the current relationship, and our ability to predict what we might attain in the future.

In its reference to rewards and costs, social penetration theory draws from the social exchange theory described in Chapter 2, and it uses the same notion of a savings account. Even if we see that costs exceed rewards in a certain relationship, we may remain in the relationship for a while if we have built up a sufficient "savings" from our previous interactions—or if there are no real prospects for greater reward.[7]

Dialectical theory.   Another theory, **dialectical theory,** suggests that we move from one relational stage to another as a result of resolving certain tensions inherent in forming relationships. These tensions are autonomy versus connection, openness versus closedness, and novelty versus predictability:[8]

- Our desire to connect and form close relationships with other people creates tension with our desire to remain autonomous.
- Our desire to be open and to share who we are with other people creates tension with our desire to protect ourselves by being closed about ourselves.
- Our desire to reduce uncertainty and to be able to predict what will happen contrasts with our desire for new, novel, and unpredictable situations.

According to dialectical theory, each escalation stage represents a point at which we have overcome some of the tension associated with becoming more intimate. For instance, moving from remaining strangers with someone to engaging in a getting-acquainted conversation means following our desire to be open while overcoming our desire to remain closed. Similarly, deciding to get married often requires a lot of soul-searching to determine if we are willing to give up certain freedoms and to accept certain relational commitments.

Think about some of your interpersonal relationships. How have the dialectical tensions affected the development of those relationships? How comfortable were you in giving up some of your independence to become closer? How open or closed have you been in sharing information about yourself? What has happened in relationships when they became very predictable?

Process trajectory cognitions.   In the next section, you'll find a model of relational development. When you study this model, or any other model based on stages of involvement, it may seem that relationships proceed in only one way toward intimacy. Remember, though, that most of the interpersonal relationships we form don't reach intimacy. Moreover, there are many different paths we can take to reach an intimate relationship.

For instance, we might know someone for a long time as a friend before we ever start dating. This pattern has been called "friendship first."[9] On the other hand, we sometimes meet people with whom we develop a close relationship very quickly. We can be "swept off our feet" and engulf ourselves immediately in an intimate relationship, spending hours and hours together after the first meeting. Or we can become fairly intimate, have a falling out, return to being friends, and then once again move toward intimacy.

Partly on the basis of our own experiences, each of us develops different conceptions about how relationships progress. These are called process trajectory cognitions.[10] In essence, **process trajectory cognitions** are the set of thoughts and expectations that we have about how relationships progress.

Think of a relationship trajectory in terms of taking a bus to get downtown. Suppose we are taking the Red Route for the first time and we don't know the streets it will take. After we ride the red bus several times, we learn the route and develop expectations about what we will see along the way. But perhaps one day we take the Blue Route bus instead. At first we might get nervous when it travels an unfamiliar route, and we are relieved when we eventually end up downtown. With a few more trips on the Blue Route, though, we will have learned another way of reaching our destination. Each route represents a trajectory, just like the routes we take in relationships. As we experience more and more relationships, we can potentially learn more and more of these relational routes—these process trajectory cognitions.

We develop process trajectory cognitions for each type of relationship we form: for example, the path to forming a close same-sex friendship or the path to forming a positive coworker relationship. We use these preconceived views of how relationships progress to assess where a given relationship is. For instance, where would you say your relationship was if the person you were dating invited you home for the weekend to meet his or her family? For many people, this could be a strong indication that the relationship was getting very serious, perhaps moving toward marriage. On the other hand, some people wouldn't think much about the matter because they view meeting the family as part of an early relational stage.

Each of us has our own unique process trajectory cognitions (though there are lots of similarities).[11] Part of relational development involves the two partners' coordinating their process trajectory cognitions—a subject we will return to in Chapter 7.

■ *A Model of Relational Development*

As mentioned earlier, relationship development can be viewed as a series of stages that reflects the escalation toward and de-escalation from intimacy. Many models have been developed to describe and explain such stages. The models vary in their orientation and in the number of stages they include.

For instance, a model based on Altman and Taylor's social penetration theory emphasizes how self-disclosure changes through four escalation stages.[12] Another model by communication scholars Knapp and Vangelisti focuses on changes in communication.[13]

The model presented in Figure 6.2, which combines the elements of several other models, emphasizes changes in the communication and in the relationship as the partners move toward or away from intimacy. As the figure suggests, relational development is like an elevator ride. As you move toward intimacy, you ascend in the elevator from one floor, or stage, to another. At times you will stop at a

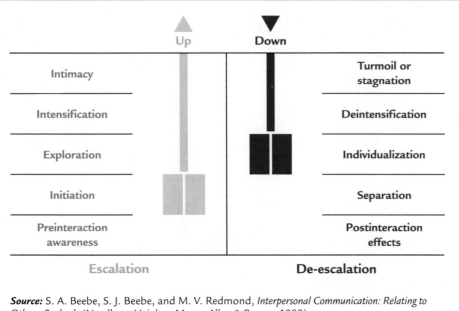

Figure 6.2

A Model of Relational Development

Up **Down**

Intimacy	Turmoil or stagnation
Intensification	Deintensification
Exploration	Individualization
Initiation	Separation
Preinteraction awareness	Postinteraction effects

Escalation De-escalation

Source: S. A. Beebe, S. J. Beebe, and M. V. Redmond, *Interpersonal Communication: Relating to Others,* 2nd ed. (Needham Heights, Mass.: Allyn & Bacon, 1999).

given floor and remain there. Sometimes you will decide to take the elevator back down—that is, to de-escalate the relationship. The higher you ascend toward intimacy, the more floors you generally go through when descending.

The model may seem to reflect a linear progression in which we methodically ride the elevator up or down from stage to stage. However, movement through the stages varies in several ways:

1. The rate of movement changes. Sometimes we move quickly through the stages, and at other times we move very slowly. For example, you may terminate a relationship by descending stage by stage. Or you may take an express elevator down, ending a relationship abruptly (as when a partner dies).
2. We can stabilize the relationship at a given stage and choose to remain at that stage indefinitely. This happens, for example, with many work-related relationships, which remain at a relatively low level of intimacy.
3. Relationships can change direction repeatedly. Most intimate relationships move up and down through the same stages several times during their life span.

Escalation stages. As shown in Figure 6.2, the process of escalation toward intimacy can be divided into five stages: preinteraction awareness, initiation, exploration, intensification, and finally intimacy.

1. Preinteraction awareness occurs when you have an opportunity to observe or learn about people before you actually interact with them. The amount of information you learn before interacting with someone can vary a great deal. Think about your first day in class. An unfamiliar student sits next to you and starts talking to you. You have had only a few seconds to observe that student, but

What cues do you notice in this photograph that indicate this relationship is in the early stages of development?

you will have acquired some information. You can probably tell the student's sex, race, and approximate age. You also have had a brief moment to examine other nonverbal cues, such as his or her clothing, and to form an initial impression.

Now, fast-forward to the end of the term. Perhaps there is a student in the same class with whom you have never directly spoken but whom you have watched throughout the term. You have also listened as that student asked and answered questions of the instructor. You have probably formed a fairly extensive impression of that student. You might have formed enough of a positive impression that you decide to move to the next stage of relational development. Both situations involve some level of **preinteraction awareness.**

2. Initiation is the first part of an interaction with someone we don't know. The **initiation** stage usually follows an initiation *script* (an expected and enacted pattern of interaction) in which we exchange a series of brief questions and answers, such as "Where are you from?" "What's your major?" "What kind of work do you do?" "How long have you lived here?" and "Can you believe the weather we're having?"

Even though the initiation stage is fairly scripted, we can learn a lot about the other person from his or her behavior. The way people communicate in this stage is as important as what they communicate. You assess people's friendliness, sense of humor, interest in you, intelligence, articulateness, and so forth. Depending on your impression, you might decide to stop any further development of the relationship and politely terminate your interaction. You might continue discussing only inconsequential topics. However, you might find the interaction rewarding and decide to move to the next stage of relational development.

3. Exploration occurs as you and your partner go beyond the initiation script and start looking for areas of commonality, or mutual interest. During this stage, you make a decision to share another level of information about yourself and to seek more information from your partner. There is little physical contact at this stage, with an appropriate social distance maintained during interactions. The interactions are generally pleasant, low-key, polite, casual, and uncritical.[14] Interactions are often limited to one context, such as classroom encounters, bar conversations, going to movies together, or talking after a team sport activity.

Exploration can be extended over a long period of time, and most relationships never move past this stage. Your continued interactions with individuals with whom you have formed only an explorative relationship tend to stay on the same topics and at the same depth of disclosure.

4. Intensification is the stage in which you decide to move into a more intimate relationship and disclose both more breadth of information and more depth of information about yourself. Movement to this stage is reflected in the way you talk.[15] You use more informal forms of address, such as nicknames. The language changes from "I" and "you" to "we": Instead of "Would you like to go with me to a movie?" you say, "Why don't we go to a movie?" You are more likely to talk directly about the relationship, what it means, and where it's going.[16]

At the **intensification** stage, you and your partner also increase the amount of time you spend together and the variety of activities you engage in together. You become more adept at understanding each other's verbal and nonverbal messages, and your messages become better adapted to each other. It takes fewer words to convey meaning. You introduce each other to people as "my friend."

5. Intimacy is the peak stage of relational development, epitomized by a feeling of mutual acceptance and confirmation of each partner's self-concept. This is the relationship stage at which both you and your partner feel free to be yourselves, knowing that the other person accepts and values who you are. The relationship is typified by a sense of codependence, with both partners equally dependent on each other for confirmation. Communication is free flowing and generally effortless. It takes less talk to understand what the other person is saying, and nonverbal communication is more accurately understood. You and your partner communicate "in sync" with one another.[17] Marriage is one way that people seek public recognition of an intimate relationship and declare mutual commitment.

De-escalation stages. Like escalation, de-escalation can be divided into five stages, as indicated in Figure 6.2. These are turmoil or stagnation, de-intensification, individualization, separation, and postinteraction effects.

1. Turmoil or stagnation is the first stage that occurs when intimate relationships begin to move toward termination or less intimacy. **Turmoil** is an increase in conflict and a tendency for more and more conflicts to remain unresolved. Partners raise more complaints about each other, and the complaints lead to countercomplaints. Communication can become filled with stress and emotional outbursts. Conflicts that were once resolved by a willingness to reach some resolution now linger on without either partner being willing to collaborate, compromise, or accommodate.

Yet, relationships do not have to experience conflict to begin moving toward termination. They can also stagnate. **Stagnation** occurs when the partners decrease the effort they put into maintaining the relationship and reduce the degree to which they turn to each other for self-confirmation. Stagnation can be thought of as a "tired" relationship; neither partner wants to invest any more in the relationship, but at this stage neither feels compelled to terminate the relationship.

2. Deintensification reflects a backing down from the relationship accompanied by a marked decrease in intensification behaviors. Partners interact less, increase their physical distance from each other, and have less physical contact (including less sexual activity in sexual relationships) as **deintensification** happens. They have longer periods of silence and generally decrease positive affiliative nonverbal behaviors such as smiling, laughing, eye contact, and direct body orientation.[18] Fewer topics are discussed, and the discussion is generally short and to the point. Less information, particularly about oneself, is shared. The partners engage in a smaller variety of activities together, and there are fewer spontaneous shared activities (for instance, going out to dinner or lunch or going on a picnic). In short, the relationship is being recast as a nonintimate relationship.

3. Individualization occurs when the partners see themselves as independent from one another and no longer look to each other as a prime source of self-confirmation. They no longer define themselves as a couple. Things that were once done together are now done separately. With **individualization,** communication is fairly superficial and routine. Interaction is kept to a minimum. "Ours" is replaced with "mine" and "yours." Each partner now dwells on his or her dissimilarities rather than similarities with the other.

4. Separation is the point at which the relationship is formally terminated and the partners proceed on their own paths. In living-together situations, **separation** is the point at which one partner moves out. There is a termination of shared social engagements; there may be a total cutoff of interaction between the former partners. Divorced couples with children are often forced to continue interacting, though the nature of their interaction is more formal and less social than in the past.

5. Postinteraction effects are the residual impacts that terminated relationships have on the partners, even when the intentional interactions have ceased. Our relational experience becomes part of who we are and affects our other relationships, current and future. We learn from our relational experiences, and we use those experiences to plan and interpret communication activity in other relationships. Perhaps you have initiated a relationship with someone who has just ended a destructive and disheartening relationship. That person was probably cool to your attraction, reacting to you on the basis of the previous relational experience.

Postinteraction effects are likely to inhibit our next relationship if the previous relationship was terminated in a detrimental, face-threatening way. On the other hand, ending a relationship in a constructive and face-saving manner promotes a positive attitude toward relationships. It is possible to de-escalate or terminate relationships and still remain on good terms with our partners. (Chapter 7 covers more on this topic.)

Think Twice Before Renewing a Relationship

You've just broken up with someone, and you're in so much pain, as a blues singer might say, it even hurts to change your mind. A thought keeps hounding you: "If only we could give it another chance." Well, it turns out your mate is miserable, too. The next time you talk to each other, one of you brings up maybe starting over. After all, what was so bad? It couldn't be worse than "this," right?

It's a proven phenomenon that people who've had painful breakups may suffer from two conditions: short-term memory loss and a remarkably increased capacity for rationalization. I'm not saying broken relationships "can't" be fixed. I know someone who broke up with her boyfriend three times—and ended up marrying him. And their marriage is great.

But I can't help thinking about poor Barry Switzer. For those of you who aren't football fans, Switzer is [the former] head coach of the Dallas Cowboys. [In 1996] he was widely ridiculed for something that became known as "The Call." He called an Emmitt Smith running play at a critical time—and the play went nowhere. But a technicality gave Dallas a second chance. So what did they do? Come up with something different and better? Nope. Switzer called the same play—and it had the same outcome. Dallas lost.

I viewed that game as a warning, since its lessons seemed to relate directly to my own life. An old flame who had rejected me in the past had reappeared, making overtures, giving me another chance—just like that penalty flag had given Switzer another chance. I was being "un-rejected." I figured: Time had passed, people change. So I went for it. Ouch. Game over—again.

Aina Abiodun, a 23-year-old creative writing student at the University of Miami, once pulled a Switzer, too. For 2½ years, she kept dating and breaking up with the same guy. "There was a honeymoon period, but it was continuous fighting," she says. "After a while, the same things were coming up over and over again." But, for some reason, they kept trying. "Usually, those kind of relationships are based on something about the person you find attractive," she says, "but it's not substantive enough to have a relationship."

Tony Ramos says he didn't fool himself about why he spent five years going back to the same woman even though he knew it couldn't last. "This was a situation

Ending relationships can be a difficult task and we often end up second-guessing our decision to breakup. In this article, the author discusses why people try to resurrect relationships following an initial separation. As you read this article, think about your own process trajectory cognitions for what happens after a relationship ends the "first" time.

where, yes, I know this person is bad for me, but the sex was so good, there was no way I could give it up," says Ramos, 45, who works for a Miami mortgage company. "I was in my early-to-mid-20s then, and I still think about her. Finally, I was able to break the cycle." How? Maturity, he says. So when another woman, his ex-wife, came to him a year after he granted her a divorce and suggested starting over, he knew better. (They'd been married five years.) He believed she was returning because she valued his friendship and knew she could count on him—but not because she really wanted to get married again.

"Norman," a 49-year-old university researcher in Miami, says it's not impossible to revisit an old relationship—if you give it time. Rebuild the friendship first, he says. Then, if something blossoms later, fine. But you have to find a way to move beyond old hurts. "Someone, in a passionate moment of anger, is going to bring up something from the past," he says. "Certain scars will never clear up. Certain healing will never take place."

That was part of my problem when I tried to take a second run at a courtship. I'd never gotten over the first one. Say your pet peeve was that your partner was always late for appointments with you: Sure, your partner may try to improve, but now even "one" tardiness will be a pinprick, reawakening old anger. As much as you may both try to change the way you behave, you'll still be the same people. You may be in a forgiving mood now, but what about later?

The problem is, sometimes we do just blow it. We break up, and we know it was a mistake. We were being unyielding, or unfair, or selfish, and we're willing to fix that for the sake of the relationship. And our partner is willing to accept us and move on. More often, though, it's plain old wishful thinking. If you're trying again, something has to be different. Not just promises, but truly different. You can't just ignore and tiptoe around what went wrong before. You have to knead it until the poison is gone. And you have to do that "before" you start again.

If you can't, you'd better just punt. As Switzer could tell you, nobody gets far running the same failed play, changing nothing, magically expecting to win the game.

Source: Tananarive Due, *Charleston Gazette,* January 7, 1997. Copyright 1997 Charleston Newspapers. ©Tribune Media Services, Inc. All Rights Reserved. Reprinted with permission.

▌ Interpersonal Attraction and the Forming of Relationships

Think about someone you have just met that you find "attractive." Why are you attracted to that person? Now think about one of your best friends. Why are you attracted to your friend? The answer to the first question is probably something like "I thought we could become friends," "He was cute," "She had a nice sense of humor," or "She seemed to like me." Answers to what attracts you to your friend might include "We have a lot in common," "I can be myself around her," "I can tell him anything," or "She makes me feel special."

Look at the differences between these two sets of answers. As they indicate, our reasons for first being attracted to someone are usually not the reasons we choose to maintain a relationship. In the first situation, short-term **initial at-**

traction reflects an initial desire to interact and potentially develop a relationship with someone. In friendships, on the other hand, we develop **enduring attraction** that represents the basis for liking or loving another person. Enduring attraction sustains relationships after the initial phases.

A typical pattern of development involves initial attraction toward someone, leading to interaction, leading in turn to the development of enduring attraction that accompanies an ongoing relationship. However, you have probably had experiences in which you were initially *not* attracted to someone, but because of the circumstances, you continued to interact with that person and eventually formed an enduring attraction. In those instances, your relationship began as a relationship of circumstance and evolved into a relationship of choice. This happens, for example, when you become friends with a coworker you didn't like initially.

Sometimes, too, you are initially attracted to someone but don't act on that attraction: for instance, seeing people you find physically attractive at a party but never talking to them. But probably the most common course of events is to interact with someone for whom you have initial attraction but then never move beyond that stage to an enduring attraction. You probably have experienced the disappointment of approaching a person you found physically appealing, only to discover that he or she had the personality of wet paint. In such cases, the relationship doesn't go beyond the initiation and exploration stages to enduring attraction.

■ *Theories of Attraction*

A number of theories and research projects have been developed to explain personal attraction. However, these theories have failed to provide a completely adequate explanation. For one thing, the theories sometimes fail to differentiate between initial and enduring attraction. In addition, the research tends to depend heavily on manipulating paper-and-pencil descriptions of people and then assessing attraction. Such methods fail to recognize the importance that communication has on attraction.[19]

The following review of attraction theories is divided into three categories. The first, attraction based on preinteraction influences, focuses on factors that affect our perception of prospective relational partners. These preinteraction influences act as the impetus for interaction and the possible formation of enduring attraction. The second category, attraction based on interaction, discusses how attraction emerges because of the opportunity to interact with another person. The third category, attraction based on needs, best explains the reasons we develop more enduring attraction as we learn more about other people.

The following scenario will serve as an example throughout our discussion of attraction. You arrive early for a training session, where you find thirty people you have never met already milling around. The participants are all of the same sex as you (either all males or all females), ranging in age from eighteen to eighty and racially and ethnically diverse. With whom will you talk?

The question may be hard to answer without actually seeing the crowd of participants, but in such a situation, you will probably pick out someone who looks like you—someone whom you see as physically attractive (not in a sexual sense). If you are forty years old, African American, short, and wearing a business suit, and you notice someone else standing a few feet away who has similar attributes, you will probably talk to that person.

To turn the question around, if you were this forty-year-old African American, why wouldn't you be likely to approach the participant who is eighteen years old, white, tall, wearing a muscle shirt, and standing on the other side of the room? The following theories provide possible explanations.

■ *Attraction Based on Preinteraction Influences*

The theories of attraction based on preinteraction influences generally focus on two principal elements: physical attraction and proximity.

Physical attraction.   **Physical attraction** occurs when we are drawn to interact with people because of their physical attributes. More specifically, we tend to interact with people who we perceive as physically similar to us. In the training session scenario, you would be drawn to talk with those people you saw as physically attractive, but that physical attraction would actually be an extension of your self-image.

Physical attraction is different from physical attractiveness. Our notions of physical attractiveness represent an idealized image of other people, but we don't necessarily expect to interact or develop relationships with people who correspond to that image. In the training session, you might see individuals whom you regard as having physical attractiveness because of their physique, but with whom you do not choose to interact.

We probably interact with those we see as physically similar to us because we assume that they will be similar in other ways as well. A forty-year-old African American in a business suit has a greater likelihood of finding similarities to discuss with another person of the same age, race, and attire than with the eighteen-year-old. This does not mean that the presumed similarities will actually turn out to exist. Nor does it mean that the forty-year-old and the eighteen-year-old couldn't become friends. It's more a matter of playing the odds.

Proximity.   We often form relationships with those who are physically closest to us—that is, with those who are within close **proximity** to us. You are more likely to form a friendship with the person living across the hall from you than with someone on another floor. You are more likely to become friends with your next-door neighbor than with someone who lives a block away. You are also more likely to become attracted to students sitting around you than to students on the other side of the classroom.

In these cases, it isn't the close distance that creates the relationship and attraction. Rather, it's the opportunity to interact. Think about what happens in each of the situations of proximity just described or in the training scenario described earlier. The close proximity increases the likelihood that you will cross paths and have a chance to talk. Talking means that you gain information about the other person. Gaining information means that you reduce uncertainty and can make better predictions about the prospects of continued positive interactions.

In short, proximity means more communication, and communication increases the likelihood of becoming attracted and developing a relationship. If you don't get a chance to interact, you can never move beyond initial attraction to enduring attraction.

■ Attraction Based on Interaction

Theories of attraction based on interaction usually take one of two approaches: a focus on the phenomenon known as reciprocity of liking or an emphasis on people's use of predicted outcome value.

Reciprocity of liking. **Reciprocity of liking** is the tendency to like those who like us; that is, we reciprocate (return) liking. Our face tends to be supported and endorsed by the indication that someone likes us, and in turn, we generally feel positive toward that person. After all, if someone is smart enough to recognize what a good person we are, that person must be okay.

Our dependency on reciprocity of liking provides a partial explanation for why you might seek out individuals who are similar to yourself in the training session scenario. As a rule, we try to make a guess about who would be most likely to like us, and we usually assume that someone similar to us would like us. We want to be liked, and we want to like those who like us. However, some people are not very good at making these predictions, and they often find themselves confronted with trying to save face when they are rejected.

Predicted outcome value. According to **predicted outcome value** theory, we formulate a personal hypothesis about the likelihood that a given relationship will be rewarding.[20] In initial attraction, this is based on the limited information we have: physical appearance, observed behaviors, and information that other people have told us. We approach those people with whom we think we can have a rewarding interaction. As we gain more information and reduce our uncertainty about people, we are able to make more accurate and complete predictions that can lead to enduring attraction. Or, as a relationship escalates, we may decide that there would be no real positive outcome in pursing the relationship, and so we end it.

Predicted outcome value theory draws on the social exchange theory concepts of costs and rewards discussed in Chapter 2. We seek to develop relationships that are more rewarding than costly. As a relationship develops, our decision to pursue the relationship is based on our ability to predict the potential outcome. Our success in developing satisfactory relationships is a reflection of our competence at predicting outcome values.

■ Attraction Based on Needs

Our needs affect attraction in a number of ways. We seek out relationships with people who can satisfy our needs; we are attracted to those who have similar needs; and we are also attracted to those whose needs complement our own.

Need satisfaction. In Chapter 2, you learned that needs are a primary motivation for communicating. We are attracted to people who we believe can satisfy our needs. In the training session scenario, your need is simply to find someone to engage in a conversation that validates your identity; and your best guess is that someone who looks like you will do that.

Relationships can be developed to satisfy any of the needs in Maslow's hierarchy of needs (see Chapter 2). For instance, we might find ourselves attracted to a manager who we believe will help us be successful in our career, thus satisfying our need for money to pay for food and shelter. Higher up the hierarchy, we also have **interpersonal needs** that lead us to form relationships. According to theorist William Schutz, these interpersonal needs can be described as the needs for inclusion, control, and affection.[21] That is, we develop relationships as a way to satisfy our need to be included and to include others (inclusion), our need to make decisions and share decision-making with others (control), and our need for emotional involvement (affection). Each of us varies in terms of the strength of these various needs. When a need is being satisfied by current relationships, we are not as likely to seek new relationships to satisfy that need.

Similarity. In thinking about what attracts you to your friends, one quality you may have identified is the degree to which you and your friends are similar. As you have seen, the notion of similarity comes up often in theoretical explanations of attraction. Two reasons why similarity fosters attraction should be apparent from what you have already read.

First, similarity helps reduce uncertainty. Initially, we can predict the behavior of people who are similar to us better than we can predict the behavior of those who are different.[22] This point has especially strong implications for intercultural interactions, in which we are apt to associate with and be attracted to those from our own culture while avoiding those who are different. (Over time, of course, as we gain information about another person, we can develop the ability to predict the behavior of someone who is dissimilar from us.)

Second, similarity attracts us to other people because it helps us find something in common to do and to talk about. Many times, for instance, we develop friendships with those we have met while engaging in some activity we enjoy (for example, involvement in a church, athletic team, or interest group like a bicycle club or the Sierra Club).

Relating similarity directly to needs, researchers have identified another reason that similarity leads to attraction. We are attracted to individuals when their needs match our own needs—a phenomenon called **similarity of needs.** For instance, we are likely to be attracted to someone who has a need for a close relationship similar to our own need. And those who have similar needs to include others or be included are likely to be more attracted to each other, just as those who have similar needs for affection are more inclined to develop a relationship with one another. On a more instrumental level, two students who both need to pass a difficult course might decide to spend time studying together.

Complementarity of needs. Besides attraction based on similarity of needs such as inclusion and affection, you can also be attracted to and form relation-

One basis for enduring attraction is when individuals have similar interests.

ships with those whose needs complement your own. In **complementarity of needs,** attraction occurs because one person needs what the other person has to offer.

Control is a good example of how needs can be complementary. Suppose you don't like to make decisions; instead, you like it when others decide things for you, such as what to do on Friday night. Your control need would be most compatible with someone who likes to make decisions, not with someone who is similar to you in avoiding decision-making. Earlier in this chapter, relationships were described in terms of a complementary style of power; in essence, this is another basis for enduring attraction. Having needs that complement one another explains the adage that opposites attract.

Think of two of your best friends. In what ways are your needs similar to theirs, and in what ways are they complementary? Are there areas where your dissimilarities or lack of complementarity occasionally causes friction and conflict? How are those problems resolved?

For each of the following vignettes, identify the attraction theory that is most applicable:

1. Marci has turned Jarrod down for a date. The next day, Marci gets flowers and a card from Jarrod asking for a date again. The day after that, she receives a balloon bouquet with another note. When Jarrod calls to get her answer, she accepts his invitation.

2. Mitch is standing in a long line behind Jennings waiting to buy tickets to a concert. They begin talking to each other, and during the hour that they stand in line, they talk the entire time. When they get to the ticket window, they decide to get tickets next to each other at the concert.

3. Rachel is struggling in her communication course. She notices that Matiana has gotten the highest grade in class so far. Rachel approaches Matiana about studying together. Matiana, who is somewhat shy, admires Rachel's outgoing nature in class, so she agrees. Matiana helps Rachel learn the material and begins to be included in Rachel's social circle.

▌ Self-Disclosure

One of the elements of proximity that leads to attraction is the communication of information about ourselves. Learning about each other is necessary for the development of intimacy in relationships.

As you have seen in earlier chapters, there are several ways we acquire information about other people.[23] For example, a lot of information is gained simply by observing a person. We can also gain information about a person from other people, especially from friends or family members. Such methods often provide us with a great deal of information about the person, but the information is limited in depth. Deeper information generally has to come from the person's own self-disclosure.

Self-disclosure is the intentional sharing of personal information. As such, self-disclosure is a specific communication activity that also conveys information about how we perceive the relationship. We generally disclose to people as a way of conveying a certain level of trust and confidence in the relationship.

Self-disclosure can be thought of as a verbalized presentation of your face; you tell another person who you are and how you see yourself. You usually do this only when enough trust has been established in the relationship so that you don't fear rejection of your face. Occasionally, though, you may self-disclose to strangers when no relational development is anticipated (for example, conversations between strangers on airplane trips).

▪ *Qualities and Principles of Self-Disclosure*

The kind of information we disclose varies from the sharing of simple facts about our background to the sharing of our deepest fears. In addition, there are several principles that help explain the process of self-disclosure and its connection to the development of intimacy. Let's examine some of these qualities and principles of self-disclosure.

We disclose descriptive and evaluative information.   The information we disclose about ourselves can be classified as either descriptive or evaluative:[24] **Descriptive information** can be thought of as biographical and factual information about who we are. Descriptive information would include things like where we are from, what our major is, and how many siblings we have. **Evaluative information** includes our feelings, emotions, judgments, and reactions to experiences.

Different levels of risk are associated with descriptive and evaluative information. Most people are more comfortable telling a stranger descriptive information like their names, hometowns, or majors than sharing evaluative information like their views on abortion or drug use or their feelings toward their parents.

Self-disclosure varies in breadth and depth.   According to Altman and Taylor's social penetration theory, the amount of "self" you disclose to others can be described in terms of breadth and depth. **Breadth** reflects the variety of qualities or elements you share about yourself. **Depth** reflects the level of intimacy or risk associated with self-disclosures.

The model in Figure 6.3 shows a number of concentric circles, each representing a different level of information. The outer circles are predominantly descriptive information, and the inner circles are more evaluative. As disclosure moves toward the inner circles, greater *depth* of disclosure is occurring.

As you examine the figure, you'll see that the circles are divided into pieces like a pie. Each pie piece represents a particular facet of your personality or self. For example, one piece might be you as a student, another might be you as a basketball player, and yet another might be your approach to intimate relationships. *Breadth* of disclosure refers to the number of pieces of the pie that you choose to disclose. Of course, your self is divided into many more pieces than can be shown in the figure.

You can define your relationships with other people according to the breadth (how many different facets of your self you disclose) and depth (how intimate the information is). Some relationships have a fair amount of breadth but little depth,

Figure 6.3

The Social Penetration Model of Self-Disclosure

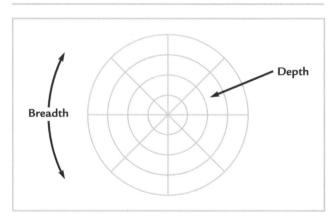

as shown in Figure 6.4A; essentially, these are casual relationships. Other relationships might have depth on one or two issues but not much breadth, as in Figure 6.4B; an example might be your relationship with your boss at work or with your parents. Finally, your most intimate relationships reflect a high degree of both breadth and depth, as shown by Figure 6.4C.

We self-disclose when we feel that the rewards will outweigh the costs. A core notion of Altman and Taylor's social penetration theory is that we self-

Figure 6.4

Relationships Described by the Social Penetration Model

(A) A casual relationship, with some breadth but little depth.
(B) A specialized relationship, with depth in two areas but little breadth. (C) An intimate relationship, showing both depth and breadth.

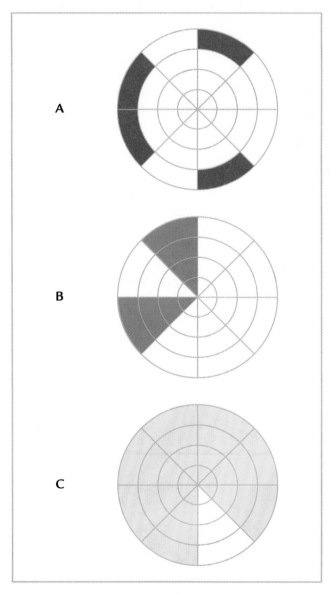

disclose when we feel that the rewards for doing so will outweigh the costs of self-disclosure. Those rewards are generally the escalation of a relationship to a more intimate level.

According to social penetration theory, a relationship develops in proportion to the amount of self-disclosure that has occurred. In Altman and Taylor's model of relational development, which uses four stages of escalation, each stage represents a significant increase in the amount of self-disclosure. We disclose on the presumption that we will be rewarded with a more satisfying relationship. We reduce or terminate self-disclosure if we feel that its costs are not or will not be balanced by sufficient reward. You probably would be reluctant to give your phone number (a type of self-disclosure) to someone you just met at a party if you had a negative reaction to this person and did not see the further development of a relationship as rewarding.

Disclosure does not increase liking, but is necessary to achieve intimacy. Simply self-disclosing doesn't cause someone to like us more; indeed, we might reveal information that causes a person to become less attracted.[25] Likewise, just liking someone doesn't mean that we will be inclined automatically to reveal more about ourselves. We are generally cautious about telling people we are attracted to about ourselves because we don't want them to dislike us. We begin to disclose more as we see rewards in self-disclosing and develop trust in the other person.

Perhaps you have experienced a relationship in which you or your partner was hesitant to self-disclose (unwilling, for instance, to share feelings). Such restraint prevents a relationship from reaching the last stages of relational escalation, and it often leads to relational de-escalation. As Altman and Taylor's model suggests, we need to disclose more and more information, in terms of both breadth and depth, if we are to move to the most intimate relational stage.

Self-disclosure is reciprocated.   Can you think of times when you have disclosed information about yourself and a friend has responded with information about himself or herself? **Reciprocity of self-disclosures** is the tendency of one person to respond to another person's disclosure by disclosing similar information.

One study indicated that such reciprocation was limited to evaluative disclosures.[26] That is, the researchers found that people were more inclined to reciprocate intimate disclosures, even with strangers, than to reciprocate factual and biographical information. In essence, we feel more compelled to reciprocate when our partner is revealing more intimate information. Thus, when people tell us their names and hometowns, we might not necessarily tell them ours. On the other hand, if they discuss the recent death of a parent, we would probably disclose some similar emotional experience.

However, reciprocation also depends on the appropriateness of the disclosure to the situation. Telling a stranger about your first sexual encounter would probably not be reciprocated because it is an inappropriate disclosure in that relationship. Telling your best friend about that same experience is more likely to be reciprocated because it is more appropriate to the intimacy of the relationship.

Log on to a chat session. You don't have to participate; simply read the messages as people chat with one another. How much variety of self-disclosure is occurring (breadth)? How evaluative are the self-disclosures that are taking place (depth)? In what ways is self-disclosure on the Internet the same as disclosing face to face? In what ways is it different? To what degree does the type of chat group affect self-disclosure?

■ *A Model of Self-Disclosure: The Johari Window*

Self-disclosure can be described in terms of the amount of information about yourself that is known or not known to you and to another person. This is the basis of a model of self-disclosure called the **Johari window,** developed by Joseph Luft and Harry Ingham (thus the name "Joe-Harry").

The Johari window has four quadrants, similar to window panes, as shown in Figure 6.5. Think of the window as the sum total of who you are: your "self." The four quadrants represent four conditions that can exist in terms of information known or unknown to you and to another person:

1. The *open* quadrant is that part of yourself that you know and that the other person also knows about you.
2. The *blind* quadrant is information that the other person has about you but that you are not aware of about yourself. Sometimes other people can be more objective in making observations about us than we ourselves are. Perhaps you think of yourself as a funny person—but others know that is not the case. As relationships develop, we often share our perceptions of our partners with them and help them to see themselves more completely, thus moving information from the blind quadrant to the open quadrant.
3. The *hidden* quadrant is information that you know about yourself but that is unknown to the other person. The information can be hidden because you

Figure 6.5

The Johari Window

	Known to you	Unknown to you
Known to other	Open 1	Blind 2
Unknown to other	Hidden 3	Unknown 4

have not chosen to share it or because the other person has not been able to observe it (through weak perceptual ability, lack of opportunity to observe, or disguise on your part).

4. Finally, the *unknown* quadrant is information about yourself that neither you nor the other person sees. This is information that you both have yet to discover. What kind of a parent or grandparent are you? What kind of a boss are you? How effective are you at consoling individuals who are in deep crisis? Unless you have experienced these situations, you can only make guesses about how you will respond to them. You are continually learning more and more about yourself and thus reducing your blind and unknown quadrants.

The Johari window can be drawn to reflect a given relationship. A lot can be told about a relationship when we examine its accompanying window. Figure 6.6 shows three Johari windows. Look at each window and describe what you think it tells about the person and the relationship. Then read the following analysis.

- The relatively large blind and unknown quadrants in Figures 6.6A and B are often typical of younger people who still have a lot to learn about themselves (though there are older people who don't have a clue as to their identities).
- Large hidden areas (Figure 6.6A) are found in new relationships.
- A large open area, small hidden area, and large blind area (Figure 6.6B) might occur in a relationship in which one person knows the other very well but is not comfortable telling the other about the blind information he or she has perceived. This might be typical of parent-child relationships in which the parents don't want to discourage their children by telling them about their shortcomings or weaknesses. Most of us have probably overheard our parents telling their friends something about us that they did not directly share with us. Sometimes it is amusing, sometimes disheartening.
- Figure 6.6C reflects someone who knows himself or herself very well. This person has openly disclosed a lot of personal information, and the partner in the relationship has shared information to which the first person was blind.

Figure 6.6

Johari Windows for Three Different Relationships

(A) A large hidden area, typical of a new relationship. (B) A large open area, small hidden area, and relatively large blind area, often seen in parent-child relationships. (C) An intimate relationship in which most of the information about the person's self is shared.

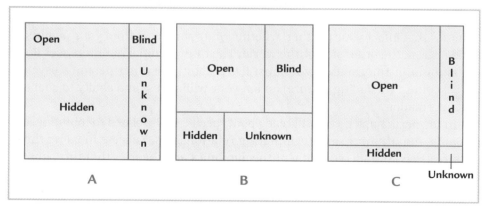

■ Developing Intercultural Relationships

All of the material you have been reading about interpersonal communication has dealt primarily with developing relationships within U.S. culture. You need to realize that the rules that govern interpersonal relationships are culture specific. The rules that apply in the United States don't apply in every culture.

For example, the idea of having a marriage arranged for you is probably not one of your process trajectory cognitions. Yet, in many places in the world, this is the expectation. Because of such cultural differences, the development of cross-cultural friendships requires the two parties to blend their cultures and develop a culture specifically for their relationship—a third culture (as discussed in Chapter 2).

One of the most obvious barriers that must be overcome in forming intercultural friendships is language. Surprisingly, people who don't even speak the same language do form friendships and sometimes even get married. Their interactions are limited, though, in how much self-disclosure occurs, and they depend on non-verbal communication as a primary method of communicating.

Besides language differences, intercultural friendships must overcome differences in cultural norms, attitudes, rituals, and customs. Because of all these differences, there are often times when one member of the pair violates the expectations of the other (a failure event). The development and maintenance of intercultural friendships depend on a strong commitment to the relationship, an understanding and appreciation of the cultural norms of the partner, an ability to discuss and resolve cultural differences, and flexibility.

Of course, the very dissimilarity that creates problems in intercultural friendships is also one of the major attractions.[27] There is an attraction to the novelty and unpredictability that exist in developing relationships with people from different cultures. We enjoy the opportunity to learn about others whose customs are alien to us. However, this is not usually enough on which to form a friendship; there must also be some degree of shared interest or similarity. Think about movies you have seen in which people from different cultures develop relationships (for example, *My Giant* or *The Air Up There*). The friendship develops because the people share some common interest such as sports or music, and some common attitudes, such as an appreciation for freedom, family, or friendship.

The principles underlying the development of intercultural, interracial, or interethnic relationships are essentially the same as those that underlie homogeneous relationships. For instance, you should try to appreciate the unique qualities that affect your partner, whether your partner is from your neighborhood or from the other side of the world. The most significant differences lie in the amount of information you must learn about the other person's psychological context (including culture) and in your willingness and ability to adapt to that information.

In the next chapter, you will read about specific skills related to initiating, developing, maintaining, and terminating relationships. Success in using those skills rests on an understanding of the dynamics and theories that this chapter has presented. Understanding the process by which interpersonal relationships develop and move toward intimacy will improve your ability to make appropriate relational decisions.

Summary

Relationships can be placed on a continuum of personalness that reflects their degree of intimacy. Relationships also fall into two broad categories: relationships of choice and relationships of circumstance. Three dimensions that further distinguish relationships are interpersonal trust, intimacy, and power. Different power balances create different styles of relationships: complementary relationships, with one dominant and one submissive member; symmetrical relationships, in which the two people have equal power; and parallel relationships, in which the power balance varies with the situation.

Relationships move through identifiable stages, perhaps because of an analysis of the rewards versus costs (social penetration theory) or because of the resolution of such tensions as autonomy versus connection (dialectical theory). For the escalation of relationships, this chapter identified five stages: preinteraction awareness, initiation, exploration, intensification, and intimacy. Relationships go through a similar series of stages as they de-escalate: turmoil or stagnation, deintensification, individualization, separation, and postinteraction effects. Movement among these stages can be forward or backward, and a given relationship may remain stabilized in any given stage.

Relationships develop because of initial attraction and are maintained through enduring attraction. Physical attraction and proximity are two qualities that lead us to initiate interactions with other people. As a result of these initial interactions, we gain information that lets us formulate predicted outcome values about the likelihood that a relationship will prove rewarding. In addition, because of reciprocity of liking, if we feel that another person likes us, we are likely to like him or her. Finally, needs satisfaction provides the basis for more enduring attraction as we look to other people to fulfill our needs, either because their needs are complementary to ours or because they are similar to ours.

Self-disclosure, the intentional sharing of personal information, is necessary for relationships to move toward intimacy. Self-disclosures are either descriptive (factual) or evaluative (involving feelings and judgments). Self-disclosures vary in the breadth and depth of the information that is shared. We tend to disclose when we think it will be rewarding, as a requirement for movement toward intimacy, and to reciprocate another person's disclosures. The Johari window divides self-information into four quadrants, or categories, that reflect how much we know or don't know about ourselves, as well as how much another person knows or doesn't know. These quadrants are labeled open, blind, hidden, and unknown.

The rules governing interpersonal relationships are culture specific. To develop an interpersonal relationship with someone from another culture, we must overcome the cultural barriers and create a third culture. In any cultural setting, however, understanding the dynamics of interpersonal relationships, the stages, the reasons for attraction, and the principles of self-disclosure will help us develop effective communication skills.

Key Terms

interpersonal communication   Communication in which two or more people transactionally influence one another.

relationships of choice   Those relationships that you have chosen to form and maintain.

relationships of circumstance   Those relationships that exist because of situational influences.

interpersonal trust   A reflection of how secure we are that a partner will act in a predicted and desirable manner.

intimacy   The degree to which two people rely on each other to accept and confirm each other's self-concept; as a relational stage, the peak of relational development.

power   The ability of people to influence other people in order to accomplish their goals.

complementary style   A relational style reflecting an imbalance in power such that one person is dominant and the other is submissive.

symmetrical style   A relational style in which both parties have fairly equal power.

parallel style   A relational style in which power varies between two people, depending on the situation.

social penetration theory   A theory that suggests that we move from one relational stage to another as a result of weighing the rewards and costs associated with self-disclosure.

dialectical theory   A theory that suggests that we move from one relational stage to another as a result of resolving certain tensions inherent in forming relationships.

process trajectory cognitions   The set of thoughts and expectations that we have about how relationships progress.

preinteraction awareness   The first stage of relational escalation, when you have an opportunity to observe or learn about people before you actually interact with them.

initiation   The first part of an interaction with someone you don't know.

exploration   The stage of relational escalation at which you and your partner go beyond the initiation script and start looking for areas of commonality, or mutual interest.

intensification   The stage of relationship escalation in which you decide to move into a more intimate relationship and disclose both more breadth of information and more depth of information about yourself.

turmoil   An initial stage in relational de-escalation, characterized by an increase in conflict and by a tendency for more and more conflicts to remain unresolved.

stagnation   An initial stage in relational de-escalation during which the partners decrease the effort they put into maintaining the relationship and reduce the degree to which they turn to each other for self-confirmation.

deintensification   A stage of relational de-escalation that reflects a backing down from the relationship accompanied by a marked decrease in intensification behaviors.

individualization   The stage of relational de-escalation when the partners see themselves as independent from one another and no longer look to each other as a prime source of self-confirmation.

separation   The stage of relational de-escalation at which the relationship is formally terminated and the partners proceed on their own paths.

postinteraction effects   The residual impacts that terminated relationships have on us, even when the intentional interactions have ceased.

initial attraction   An initial desire to interact and potentially develop a relationship with someone.

enduring attraction   Attraction that represents the basis for liking or loving another person.

physical attraction   Being drawn to interact with people because of their physical attributes.

proximity   Nearness or closeness that facilitates communication; a reason for attraction.

reciprocity of liking   The tendency to like those who like us; we reciprocate (return) liking.

predicted outcome value   A personal hypothesis about the likelihood that a given relationship will be rewarding.

interpersonal needs   Needs that drive us to seek relationships, such as the needs for inclusion, control, and affection.

similarity of needs Other people's needs matching our own needs; a reason for attraction.

complementarity of needs One person's needs matching what another person has to offer; a reason for attraction.

self-disclosure The intentional sharing of personal information.

descriptive information Biographical and factual information about who we are.

evaluative information Information about our feelings, emotions, judgments, and reactions to experiences.

breadth In self-disclosure, the variety of qualities or elements you share about yourself.

depth The level of intimacy or risk associated with self-disclosures.

reciprocity of self-disclosures The tendency of one person to respond to another person's disclosure by disclosing similar information.

Johari window A model of self-disclosure consisting of four quadrants (open, hidden, blind, and unknown) that reflect the degree to which information is known or unknown to you and to another person.

Review Questions

1. Distinguish between relationships of choice and relationships of circumstance.
2. Briefly explain the three dimensions of relationships: interpersonal trust, intimacy, and power.
3. Identify and discuss the escalation stages of relationships.
4. Identify and discuss the de-escalation stages of relationships.
5. Identify and explain three of the theories of attraction.
6. Define self-disclosure and explain two related principles.
7. Construct and label the probable Johari window for a very intimate, well-developed relationship involving individuals who know themselves well.

Chapter 7

Interpersonal Communication:
Skills and Strategies

Objectives

Studying this chapter will allow you to:

1. Identify several ways of initiating an interaction.
2. Explain how you can use affinity seeking, process trajectory cognitions, and self-disclosure to develop a relationship.
3. Explain several ways of maintaining a relationship.
4. Describe some strategies for gaining compliance from another person.
5. Discuss strategies for ending a relationship.

Leslie has gone to a party being held by Alisha, one of her friends from work. She begins talking to Eric, whom she just met. She finds herself attracted to him and therefore acts particularly friendly toward him. She asks him questions about himself, laughs at his jokes, and suggests that they go into the kitchen to get something to eat. She excuses herself to go to the bathroom, and while there makes sure her makeup and hair are just right before returning to Eric.

Fast-forward now a few weeks. Leslie and Eric are on their third date. Leslie finds her attraction growing for Eric, and she wants to develop the relationship even further. She remains very responsive to him during their conversations. She actively listens, self-discloses relevant information about herself, and continues to seek more information about him. She wants to invite him to a party that she has been invited to, but does not want to seem too pushy because she has learned that Eric doesn't like domineering women. She tells him about the party and describes a mystery game the people will be playing (she knows Eric likes mystery movies and books). He says that it sounds like it would be a lot of fun. Nonchalantly, she suggests that he might want to come along. He agrees.

Fast-forward a few more weeks. Things aren't going so well for Leslie anymore, and she wants out of her relationship with Eric. She knows that he doesn't want to break up. She decides just to start avoiding him, making excuses why she can't get together with him. Finally, Eric asks what is going on, and Leslie tells him that she wants to date around a bit, but that she and Eric can still be friends. They stop seeing each other.

This saga of Leslie and Eric illustrates the application of a number of interpersonal communication skills throughout the progress of a relationship. Leslie uses specific strategies to initiate the relationship, to escalate and maintain the relationship, to gain compliance from Eric for things she wants, and finally to terminate the relationship. In this chapter, you will read about these strategies and other interpersonal communication skills that you can use in your relationships. Remember, however, that the skills and strategies presented here are meant to provide you with options. None of these skills by themselves represent a magic formula for relational success.

■ The Impact of Your Goals

Chapter 6 and earlier chapters discussed the use of communication to satisfy needs. Interpersonal communication is used to satisfy those needs that can be met through personal interactions with other people. Among those needs is the need for personal confirmation through intimate relationships.

Most of our relationships, however, are not very intimate. Only a few relationships of the hundreds that we form in our lifetime reach the intimate stage. Most of our interpersonal relationships are more casual, of the friend and colleague variety. Our goals in these relationships are often instrumental ones. Because these relationships don't have to be intimate to be satisfying, they tend to stabilize at the second or third stage of relational development (for a reminder of the stages, look back at Figure 6.2 on page 151). Even though not intimate, these relationships are important to us. Creating positive relationships of this type can aid us in achieving our instrumental goals and provide the additional benefit of meeting some of our social needs.

Our goals play an important part in determining what skills are necessary for managing our interpersonal communication effectively. An intimate relationship requires different communication skills than a relationship that is primarily instrumental. The focus of this chapter will be on the skills needed for developing intimate relationships; however, this does not mean that the skills are not applicable to nonintimate relationships as well. For instance, you may develop compliance-gaining skills that help you determine the best strategy for convincing an intimate partner to visit your parents on Thanksgiving. The same skills might help you find a way to ask your boss for a raise.

▮ Approaching Others

First encounters with other people occur in a myriad of ways. Your first encounter with someone may occur while the other person is standing behind you in a grocery line, walking out of class the same time as you, mingling at a party, sitting next to you at a company meeting, or working in the office next to yours. In each of these situations, there is an initial decision to engage in an interaction, making it a relationship of choice. However, the fact that one person starts a conversation doesn't mean that it will proceed. You have probably had the exper-

Which woman do you think would be the most open to starting a conversation with you? Why?

ience of trying to talk to someone who is nonresponsive—who isn't interested in carrying on a conversation. It's usually a rather awkward and uncomfortable episode, and it typically occurs because you have misread the other person's **approachability cues**—indications that a person is receptive to interpersonal communication.

Most of our approachability cues rely on nonverbal communication and thus are often open to misinterpretation. Clearly, people working at a library table with their heads buried in their books are not signaling a desire for social interaction. However, students sitting at that same library table who are leaning back in their chairs, gazing around the room, making eye contact with those who pass by, and smiling as they do so are displaying an assortment of approachability cues. In general, we signal approachability through eye contact, body position, facial expressions, and use of space. We also signal approachability in our first responses to other people's initial communication attempts. We return a smile, a wave, a head nod, a wink, or a greeting (saying "Hello" or "Hi").

To improve your skill with first encounters, you need to develop sensitivity to the cues you are receiving from other people. When deciding whether or not to approach someone, you need to answer two basic questions:

Is this person open to social interaction?
Is this person open to interacting with *me*?

◾ Initiating Relationships

Once you have decided to approach someone, there are a variety of ways to initiate the conversation. There are jokes about men developing the perfect come-on line. There are books and web pages that promise to provide the perfect opener. In reality, though, it is hard to predict how another person will react to your opening. There are women who will respond positively to a man who attempts to initiate a conversation with the line "Your place or mine?" However, such a line is likely to be rejected 99 percent of the time.

Do a search on the Internet using key words for initiating statements. Look under "conversation starters" or "conversation openers." After that, look under "pickup lines" or "opening lines." Do you think that any of these "lines" are useful in real life?

You'll notice a significant difference in the level of directness and sexual explicitness associated with "pickup lines." What does this tell you about the connotation of the term? (Be cautioned that some of the material you find may be offensive.)

◾ *Using Free Information and Common Elements*

If you try the Internet search suggested in Connect Yourself, you may reach the same conclusion as many communication experts: that the best opening line is no line at all, but rather an effort to be sincere and honest. One fairly safe and acceptable way to initiate interactions is to incorporate free information into an opening statement. **Free information** includes things that are apparent or obvious about the person you are approaching. Noticing that the person is wearing a Harley-Davidson T-shirt might prompt you to ask, "I noticed your T-shirt, do you own a

Harley?" Asking about the cast on someone's arm would be another example of using free information.

Another way to initiate an interaction is to make reference to some surrounding common element. For instance, as inane as it might seem, talking about the weather can be an effective way to begin a conversation. While standing at a corner in the rain waiting to cross the street, you might say, "I can't believe all the rain we're having. I hope we get some sunshine soon." Or, while standing at a bus stop, you could comment to another person who is waiting that the bus really seems to be late today.

At this point, for validation of your initial assessment of approachability, you should watch for additional signals about the other person's receptiveness to your opener. When people ignore your comments or provide only minimal response, they are generally signaling an unwillingness to interact. On the other hand, if they provide a fuller response, that is usually a positive indicator. After your comment on the Harley-Davidson T-shirt, a positive response might be, "No, I can't afford to own one, but I have a number of friends who give me rides all the time." Or, after your comment on the late bus, the person might respond, "I know, and I'm going to be late for a job interview I have downtown."

Each response provides additional "free information" that you can use to continue the conversation. You now have the opportunity to continue by asking for more information about what the person has said, as well as by providing information about yourself. For example, "I've always wanted to own a Hog. I have a friend who has an Electra Glide Road King that is really great." Or "What kind of job are you interviewing for?"

■ Asking Questions

Asking questions as part of the opener is an effective way to elicit interaction. When I was hiking up out of the Grand Canyon one time, I switched from saying "Hi" to those going down to saying "How's it going?" or "How's the hike?" This often led to a more extended response that involved stopping for a minute or two to visit. My motivation wasn't to develop relationships; it was simply to have an excuse to stop and catch my breath. Nonetheless, I learned how important the initial greeting could be, both in signaling my interest in talking and in eliciting conversation from others.

Often, of course, people respond to a question out of politeness, not because of interest in extending the conversation. These responses are usually short and to the point and are accompanied by nonverbal cues showing little immediacy. It is generally easy to tell when the person does not really want to talk.

■ Following the Initial Interaction Script

As Chapter 6 noted, the general pattern that initial interactions follow is fairly "scripted" and predictable. This pattern allows you to reduce uncertainty and feel relatively confident about what to expect. Because breaking away from the script might increase the uncertainty and discomfort for your partner, you should generally stick to the conventional pattern.

Here is the pattern as identified by one researcher:[1]

Phase	Examples
Greetings: social statements of greeting	"Hi," "Hello,"
Introductions: exchange of names	"My name is Mark. What's yours?"
First topic: discussion of the present situation	"Pretty hot for this time of year, isn't it?" "Yeah. I'm not ready for it to be this hot. What happened to spring?"
Second topic: discussion of residences	"Where are you from?" "I'm from Pella." "How long have you lived there?" or "What's it like in Pella?"
Third topic: finding people known in common	"Do you happen to know Shirley Jones? I think she's from Pella." "Yeah, she's a good friend. How do you know her?"
Fourth topic: discussion of majors/jobs	"Where do you work?" "At Penney's. I'm the assistant manager." "Really, I used to work at a Penney's in my hometown."
Fifth topic: discussion of TV, movies, music, family, sports, books, or travel	"My brother and I both worked at Penney's." "How many kids are there in your family?"
Future Meeting: discussion about getting together	"You should stop by Penney's sometime. I'll show you around." "I'd like that. How about next week?" "Sure."
Pleasantries: polite ending statements exchanged	"It was nice talking to you." "I enjoyed our conversation, too. I'm glad we met."
Conversation closure: signaling the end of the conversation	"See you later." "Yeah, don't forget to stop by sometime." "I won't."
Farewells and good-byes: traditional exit lines	""Bye." "So long." "Take care." "You too."

■ Further Suggestions for Initial Interactions

Besides following the script for initial interactions, there are several other suggestions that can help you enhance this stage of relational development, such as providing information about yourself, presenting yourself in a positive manner, asking questions, and listening actively.[2] These suggestions essentially involve applying what you have learned about perception, self-disclosure, and attraction.

1. Providing information about yourself. According to the rules of self-disclosure, you need to disclose appropriately—not too much and not too little. Most people are uncomfortable with too much openness in an initial interaction, so it's best to share fairly safe and noncontroversial information. Notice that the disclosures in the sample initiation pattern followed this rule. The disclosures were about where the people were from, what jobs they had, where they worked, how many children were in their families, and so on—all fairly safe descriptive information.

2. Presenting yourself in a positive manner. One typical perceptual bias is an overinfluence of negative information. To counteract that bias, you initially should focus primarily, if not exclusively, on your positive attributes.

3. Asking questions and listening actively. Remember that people tend to like those who like them. This means that you should display your liking for the other person by asking questions, showing interest, and exhibiting the other qualities of an active listener: having positive eye contact, leaning forward, and so on. (See Chapter 3 for a review.)

Use the following summary of initiation strategies to identify your skill at using each one. Record your responses on a scale from 1 (for a strategy you find very hard to use) to 5 (for a strategy you are adept at using):

1.	Be honest and sincere.	1	2	3	4	5
2.	Use free information in opening remarks.	1	2	3	4	5
3.	Look for some common element to discuss.	1	2	3	4	5
4.	Watch for signals of a willingness to interact.	1	2	3	4	5
5.	Follow up on the other person's responses.	1	2	3	4	5
6.	Ask questions, and then watch and listen to the answers for cues about the person's willingness to talk.	1	2	3	4	5
7.	Follow the traditional, expected pattern for initial interactions.	1	2	3	4	5
8.	Provide an appropriate amount of information about yourself.	1	2	3	4	5
9.	Present yourself in a positive manner.	1	2	3	4	5
10.	Listen actively.	1	2	3	4	5

Add up the numbers you have circled. If your total score is less than 30, look at the strategies that you marked with less than a 3 and try applying them in your interactions.

■ Developing Relationships

After the initiation stage of a relationship, you might decide to escalate the relationship to the next stage; after that, you might continue to advance the relationship. There are a variety of strategies you can employ in developing your relationships. This section will cover three of them: affinity seeking, coordinating you and your partner's perspectives and process trajectory cognitions, and self-disclosing.

■ *Affinity Seeking*

In the scenario that opened this chapter, Leslie enacts several strategies to encourage Eric's interest in her. She pays attention to him, shows interest in him by asking questions, includes Eric in her activity of getting food, and makes sure that her appearance is positive. All of these are examples of affinity-seeking strategies. **Affinity-seeking strategies** are behaviors we enact in an attempt to increase another person's liking for us. Usually, if we are attracted to someone but remain uncertain about his or her feelings toward us, we will use affinity-seeking strategies.

Think about the various behaviors you use to try to get someone to like you more. Communication researchers Robert Bell and John Daly identified twenty-five different strategies commonly employed for this purpose. They can be organized into seven categories.[3]

1. Self-presentation. Presenting yourself as physically attractive, interesting, dynamic, in control, and independent/freethinking.

2. Mutual trust. Showing yourself to be trustworthy, as well as showing trust in the other person.

3. Politeness. Following good conversational rule behavior and conceding control of the conversation to other people in an attempt to gain their favor.

4. Listening. Being attentive, being supportive, confirming the other person's self-concept, seeking disclosures, and being sensitive. This category depends on displaying other-centered behaviors.

5. Other involvement. Including the other in your activities, facilitating the other's enjoyment, and displaying nonverbal immediacy. (Nonverbal immediacy, as you may recall from Chapter 4, includes such behaviors as good eye contact, leaning toward your partner, smiling, being animated in response to your partner's comments, and orienting your body so you are directly facing the other person.)

6. Self-involvement. Trying to include yourself in the other person's activities (for instance, asking if you can tag along) or trying to influence the other person's perception of closeness (to suggest that the relationship is closer than he or she has realized).

7. Commonalities. Pointing out or focusing on commonalities, creating a sense of equality between you and your partner, and presenting yourself at ease.

What strategies do you use the most when you are first developing a relationship? One researcher found that people claim to use commonalities, mutual trust, and other-centered behaviors (like listening and sensitivity) the most.[4] This researcher, who was also interested in how these strategies are used to maintain intimate relationships, found that people use a wider assortment of affinity-seeking strategies in those relationships than in more casual ones.[5] Other research on ongoing relationships has found additional categories of affinity strategies, such as faithfulness, honesty, and affection.[6]

■ *Coordinating Relational Perspectives and Process Trajectory Cognitions*

In any of your relationships, you and your partner need to be on the same page, so to speak, when it comes to knowing where the relationship is. Each person behaves according to his or her perception of the relationship, and each interprets the partner's behaviors on that same basis.[7] In a dating relationship, for example, you might see the relationship as having escalated to the intensification stage, a point at which you think it is appropriate to share information about your previous romantic partners. Your partner, still seeing the relationship as being in the exploration stage, might see these disclosures as inappropriate and be offended.

To avoid such problems, you need to coordinate your expectations and perceptions with your partner's. You need to share not only your sense of where the relationship is, but also your ideas about where it is going. You and your partner may have substantially different process trajectory cognitions, as defined in Chapter 6—that is, different assumptions about how a relationship like yours will normally progress.

But sharing your relational perspectives and cognitions can be a problem in itself. Depending on the situation and the stage of the relationship, such "meta-relational" conversation can be face threatening and inappropriate. Let's look at how the stage of the relationship influences the choice of an appropriate strategy.

Initial stages.   In the initial stages of a relationship, it is usually risky to discuss the relationship directly. Instead, we depend on indirect cues to inform us about where the relationship is and where it is going. Such indirect cues allow each person to protect his or her face.[8]

Imagine how you would feel if you asked a new acquaintance if he or she was attracted to you, and the person said no. Such a direct request would put your face directly on the line. On the other hand, your face would be less threatened if you called up to ask about going to dinner sometime, and the reply was "Thanks anyway, but I'm really busy these days."

Most people recognize the implicit message "The attraction is not shared" without being told so explicitly. However, the use of indirect messages often makes it difficult to coordinate perceptions of a relationship. People easily misread indirect messages, misinterpreting their partner's level of interest in the relationship.

Later stages.   As relationships develop, we are more and more likely to discuss the nature and definition of the relationship with our partners. We become more direct as the relationship becomes more intimate. Such discussions can facilitate achieving what one scholar has labeled "perceived symmetry of involvement."[9] One study of romantic relationships found that only about 20 percent of the identifiable points during the "get-to-know time" involved relational talk. On the other hand, after couples moved to an exclusive dating arrangement, over 90 percent of the couples reported the occurrence of relational talk.[10]

This pattern is not universal, of course. Every once in a while, there's a news story about a man who has hired a plane to circle a football stadium trailing a sign that says "Ginny, will you marry me?" as a TV crew focuses on her for her reply. When interviewed, Ginny indicates that she is totally surprised by the proposal. As you might suspect, being surprised by a marriage proposal is not a very good indication that the couple has coordinated their process trajectory cognitions. Generally, couples discuss the prospect of marriage long before the relationship reaches that stage. These discussions reflect explicit relational talk so that both parties know each other's perception of the relationship.

Sometimes, relational talk is necessitated by the occurrence of failure events or conflicts. We often seek clarification from our partners when they behave differently than we expected. This clarification helps to align our relational perceptions with theirs.

Think of a particular close relationship that you have. What are your expectations in this relationship? What are your partner's expectations? When was the last time you actually talked about the relationship with your partner? What, in particular, did you talk about?

Rules for coordinating relational perspectives.   Three general rules can be identified for coordinating your relational perspective with that of your partner:

"You always complain that I don't know how to show my emotions, so I made these signs."

1. Know when it is appropriate to discuss the nature of the relationship, including your feelings for the other person.
2. Be willing to share your expectations and perceptions of the relationship.
3. Be receptive to your partner's sharing similar information.

When you engage in relational talk, you may find that you thought the relationship was a lot further along than your partner did. This can be disappointing. However, which is better: facing eventual disappointment earlier than you might have, or proceeding in a relationship in which you are out of touch with its true nature? Accurately knowing where the relationship is allows you to adjust your communication behaviors and strategies, thus increasing your interpersonal effectiveness.

■ Self-Disclosure

As discussed in Chapter 6, to move toward intimacy, partners must be willing to self-disclose. Yet, too much self-disclosure too early will generally create a level of imbalance, signaling a rapid movement toward intimacy for which the other partner may not be ready. On the other hand, too little self-disclosure will cause the relationship to stagnate and remain at a superficial level. Generally, you are best served by disclosing in measured steps as the relationship continues to develop. You must be willing to self-disclose (relative to your comfort level) and also be willing to accept your partner's self-disclosures.

The best rule of thumb is to try small amounts of self-disclosure and then carefully listen to your partner's response. Typically, your partner will reciprocate the self-disclosure if he or she is comfortable with your initial self-disclosure. When that reciprocation occurs, you can then escalate the self-disclosure, again watching for reciprocation. If the information is not reciprocated, that could signal too high a level of discomfort for your partner. You probably should back away from further disclosing at that time. Effective self-disclosing thus depends on your ability to assess the situation, the relationship, your partner's perception of the relationship, and the amount of risk associated with such disclosures for both you and your partner.

Summary and Self-Analysis:
Skills for Developing Relationships
Use the following summary of skills for developing relationships to identify your strongest skills and those that you could improve.

Affinity Seeking: Getting Another Person to Like You

- Self-presentation: Present an attractive and interesting image.
- Mutual trust: Show yourself to be trustworthy and trusting of the other.
- Politeness: Display good conversational behavior.
- Listening: Be attentive, supportive, and sensitive.
- Other involvement: Include the other in your activities.
- Self-involvement: Get yourself invited to be included in the other person's activities.
- Commonalities: Point out how similar you are to the other person.

Coordinating Relational Perspectives and Process Trajectory Cognitions

- Be willing to discuss your expectations and perceptions.
- Be receptive to your partner's expectations and perceptions.
- Appropriately time relationship talk.

Self-Disclosure: Sharing Information About Yourself

- Appropriately time when and what you disclose.
- Watch for reciprocation of your disclosures as a signal for further disclosing.

Maintaining Relationships

The model of relationship development in Chapter 6 included the prospect of stabilizing a relationship at any of the escalation stages. In essence, you can choose to maintain a relationship as an acquaintance, a casual friend, a friend, a close friend, or even a best friend. But relationships are not self-perpetuating; they require constant effort and skill to maintain. Keeping the relationship at a certain stage requires the use of various communication strategies.

Your partner might try to escalate or de-escalate the relationship contrary to your desires. Such attempts by your partner require counterbalancing behaviors on your part. For instance, say you've met a person with whom you wish to remain casual friends, seeing each other every couple of weeks or so. However, this person wants more from the relationship and tries to increase the amount of time the two of you spend together. To counter these attempts, you must continually restrict the time you spend with this individual. The commonality of this dilemma is one reason it so often formed the basis for episodes of the TV show *Seinfeld.*

Besides using strategies to keep a relationship from escalating, you can implement communication strategies to keep a relationship vibrant and stable. For example, you can use the affinity-seeking strategies described earlier to maintain a partner's interest and attraction. Buying flowers for no reason at all, treating a friend to dinner, calling long distance to friends or relatives regularly—these are all affinity strategies that can help you maintain stable relationships. The following sections examine several other types of strategies that are useful for maintaining relationships at a steady level.

Using Maintenance Strategies

There are times when we consciously attempt to "recharge" a relationship that seems to be losing its energy, or to slow its de-escalation. We strategically attempt to rekindle waning relational involvement and commitment. Some of the relational **maintenance strategies** that have been identified include positivity/romance, openness, assurances, sharing tasks, and avoidance of antisocial behavior.[11] Although these strategies have primarily been applied to marital relationships, they have their parallels in less intimate relationships as well.

- *Positivity/romance strategies* are those in which you are cheerful and positive, surprise the other, give sentimental gifts, and celebrate and create romantic situations.

- *Openness* involves having explicit relational talks in an attempt to repair problems or decide mutually how to maintain the relationship.
- Another strategy involves giving *assurances* to your partner about your commitment to the relationship. This can include statements of how much you still like or love the other person as well as physical displays of affection.
- You can *share tasks* as a way of maintaining togetherness, as when couples do the dishes together or cook dinner together. These activities provide a way of simply maintaining a sense of togetherness.
- *Avoidance of antisocial behavior* involves strategically choosing not to engage in behaviors that are known to be disruptive. This means avoiding arguments, refraining from criticizing the other person, restraining yourself from being impolite, rude, or sarcastic, and waiting through a cool-down period when you are angry.

The last strategy in the list deserves further comment. One scholar suggests that one characteristic of satisfied couples is that they are selective in what they disclose and discuss with their partners; that is, they don't feel compelled to voice every negative feeling or thought.[12] A study I conducted on my own university campus obtained parallel results. Of the various ways in which students reported adapting their communication in conversations, the most common way was to avoid certain topics or to leave out information that might offend or disturb the other person.[13]

■ *Communicating and Interacting*

The strategies just discussed deal with specific behaviors in which people engage. However, the strategy that couples have most frequently identified as a way to maintain their relationship is simply spending time together and interacting.[14] The amount of time spent interacting with another person usually relates to the health and success of the relationship. One study of interpersonal rituals found that "couple time" was the most commonly reported form of interaction for married couples.[15] Couple time included jointly participating in enjoyable activities, spending time together, and special escape or getaway episodes. Similar interaction rituals were reported for friendships as well.

What we communicate about is also important. If we interact on a very impersonal level, the interaction will have minimal impact on the maintenance of the relationship. On the other hand, communication can have a substantial impact when we personalize our messages, self-disclose, respond spontaneously, and confirm the other's self-concept. One study found a positive correlation between married couples' satisfaction and their tendency to discuss their sexual relationship, home life, and vacations.[16] In addition, a correlation existed between women's satisfaction in the relationship and the tendency to discuss religion, relatives, and work. The authors of this study point out that it is unclear whether we increase our communication because we are satisfied or whether we are satisfied because we have increased communication.

Whatever the cause and effect may be, it is likely that if you are not satisfied in a relationship, you probably will not seek to interact as much with the other person. On the other hand, increasing your communication with a dissatisfied partner will probably not improve the relationship unless the problem your partner is having is simply a need for more interaction.

■ *Using Social Decentering: Being Other-Centered*

In Chapter 4, social decentering was presented as a process by which we come to understand another person's psychological context. We can also see social decentering as a *skill* by which we take into consideration another person's thoughts, feelings, perspectives, and so on, usually within the context of a given situation.[17] In essence, social decentering involves trying to think and feel about something the way the other person would.

You could probably predict pretty well how your best friend would feel after winning a million-dollar lottery. You could do this because you know your friend so well that you would be able to imagine his or her reaction. If you had the same predictive skill with other people in other situations, you'd be remarkably effective at managing your interpersonal relationships. You could adapt your behavior, communication strategies, and requests much more effectively because you would be able to predict how the other person would react.[18] In most of your relationships, you will never reach that degree of predictive ability. But there are several guidelines you can follow to improve your ability to socially decenter.

1. *Obtain as much information as you can about the person and the situation.* The more you learn about people, the better able you are to predict their behavior. This step requires effective listening and perception as discussed in Chapter 3. In addition to perceiving the information, you must be able to remember it and to incorporate relevant information in your analysis.

Understanding the dynamics of the surrounding situation also enhances your social decentering because it helps you know what factors are influencing the other person's reactions. For instance, finding out that a friend has just done poorly on an exam might lead you to believe that your friend will be bummed out. However, if you know that the class has five exams, that your friend has gotten an A on four of them, and that students are allowed to drop one exam grade, then you will probably reach a different conclusion about your friend's reaction.

2. *Use your understanding of yourself and people in general to reach an understanding of a specific person.* You can reach some level of understanding of people you don't even know by drawing on your own experiences and reactions. For instance, you can use your own experience of having bungled an exam as a means of predicting another student's reaction. This works to the degree that you and the other student are similar. You might also realize important distinctions between yourself and the other student and therefore increase your effectiveness. If the exam you messed up was in an elective course but the other student's was in a course required for his or her major, you could take that difference into account in predicting the other student's reaction.

In situations that go beyond your personal experiences, you can use your understanding of people in general, derived from your years of observation. Even if you have never messed up an exam in your life, you probably have some notion of how students in general react to such an event. You can use that general knowledge to reach an understanding of a specific student's reaction. Improving your ability to use such general knowledge about people requires being open to interactions with all kinds of people in all kinds of situations. Isolating yourself from opportunities to interact with members of various cultures and ethnic groups will limit your ability to understand and predict behavior.

3. *Learn from your errors.* Social decentering does not always lead us to an accurate prediction of another person's reactions. When a prediction of yours is inaccurate, you should examine what caused the inaccuracy. Suppose you learn that Bryan, a student you don't know very well, has done poorly on an exam, and you assume that he will be angry and upset because you believe that students in general would be. However, you observe Bryan acting upbeat and positive about the situation. Just as with attribution theory, the deviation of the behavior from your expectation should cause you to seek more information to explain the discrepancy. You might have to revise your beliefs about how students in general behave. More likely, you will probably find out some additional information about Bryan that will explain his positive reaction. Perhaps he has a personal philosophy of taking everything in stride.

To learn from your errors requires, first of all, recognizing that you are in error. Sometimes people fail to realize that they have made an inaccurate conclusion because of perceptual biases. Once you have recognized your inaccuracy, you need to collect information that will allow you to understand how you reached the erroneous conclusion. You can usually get this information directly from the person with whom you are interacting or by talking with others who have first-hand information. In the exam scenario, you might ask a friend of Bryan's why he is so upbeat after the debacle. Bryan's friend might tell you, "Oh, he's always like that. Nothing ever really seems to get him down." By actively seeking information to correct your errors, you can improve your ability to be accurate in the future.

4. *Consider your choices and adapt your communication to the understanding you have reached.* Social decentering puts you in the position of anticipating a person's reaction and selecting the appropriate response or strategy. The ideal strategies are those that let you accomplish both instrumental and relational goals; in essence, you get what you want while still maintaining the relationship. Consider the following progression:

- *Your goals:* To borrow a friend's car (instrumental) and to maintain your friendship (relational).

- *Anticipated reaction to the request:* Denial because your friend fears that someone borrowing her car will get drunk and wreck the car—an outcome that would also jeopardize the relationship.

- *Possible strategies:*

    a. "I'll fill the gas tank when I bring the car back."
    b. "I'm taking your car, and too bad if you don't like it."
    c. "I let you borrow my notes for the communication class lectures you missed."
    d. "I just need the car to go shopping at the mall. I'll be back by dinnertime."

- Consider your friend's reaction to each request through social decentering:

    a. She doesn't really worry about having to fill the car with gas.

    b. This might get me the car but cost me the relationship.

    c. I had to borrow some notes from her before, so she won't feel any obligation.

    d. This will let her know that I won't be drinking and should allay her fear of my having an accident.

- *Implement the best choice:* "Can I borrow your car to drive to the mall? I need to do some shopping, and I'll be back before dinnertime."

■ *Being Flexible and Adapting*

Social decentering puts you in a position to adapt your strategies to the particular person and situation you are dealing with. You must also be able to be flexible and adapt to changes—changes in your partners and changes in your interpersonal relationships. Flexibility and adaptability increase your ability to be effective with a wider and more divergent group of people.

If you are rigid and inflexible, you can still have effective interpersonal relationships, but they are generally going to be fewer in number because you are dependent on finding a compatible match to your set personality and communication style. Being adaptable means getting along with more people. However, you can be too adaptable and in essence lose your own sense of identity. The key is in finding a balance between maintaining your own sense of self (and achieving your goals) and adapting to the needs of other people.

When relationships are too inflexible, the partners start to take each other for granted, failing to recognize that both they and their relationship continue to change. Being successful in a relationship means being in tune with changes in your partner and adapting to those changes. Think, for instance, about people who get married when they are eighteen. At this age, a lot of information will still remain in the hidden, unknown, and blind quadrants of each partner's Johari window. (See Figure 6.5 on page 166.) As the partners age, each will undoubtedly be faced with new information about the other that was not known at the time of the marriage. Perhaps the woman discovers a strong need for achievement and success that she previously had not realized. This discovery would require the husband to adapt to his wife's need. Failure to adapt in this instance could lead to conflict and relational termination.

Flexibility and adaptability require an openness on your part to new information. Periodically, you need to assess yourself, your partner, your relationship, and the situation. For instance, after dating someone for a year, you should ask yourself these questions: How have I changed in the last year? How has my partner changed in the last year? How has our relationship changed? In what ways have I adapted to the changes? What changes could I make that would improve the relationship? and How do I feel about those potential changes? You might find this analytic process difficult, but by continually trying to answer these questions, you can improve your ability to conduct such analyses.

After you have analyzed the situation, you are in a position to adapt if you choose. Sometimes the amount of adaptation required may be more than you are

Lifelong relationships usually involve being flexible and adapting to changes in the relationships and the partners.

willing to undertake, and you may decide either to try to get your partner to adapt or to end the relationship. One experience that you will likely have is being in a job where you are assigned a new boss. Perhaps your former boss was relaxed and let you have a great deal of independence, whereas the new boss wants to see everything you do and requires his approval for all decisions. What options are open to you? You can be inflexible and continue to act independently, hoping that the new boss will eventually adapt to your style. You can adapt your style to comply with your new boss's way of conducting business. Or you can quit your job and seek another position that lets you maintain your independent ways.

■ Gaining Compliance

The earlier example of figuring out how to borrow a friend's car was an illustration of compliance gaining. **Compliance gaining** is essentially interpersonal persuasion; it is an interpersonal process of overcoming another person's resistance to a request. The request reflects a desire to meet some need, and the resistance usually occurs because the request conflicts with the needs of the other person.

As relationships progress, the amount of resistance to various requests often decreases because the nature of an intimate relationship involves a greater willingness to accommodate our partner's needs. Suppose you need to borrow five dollars. The amount of resistance you might expect from classmates you barely know is considerably greater than the amount you expect from your best friend. In this situation, what would you say to get the money from your classmates? You might appeal to their sense of charity by telling them you need lunch money. You might say that you will give them six dollars tomorrow in repayment. Or you might offer to lend them the notes from the class they missed last week. Each of these options reflects a compliance-gaining strategy.

Compliance-gaining strategies are specific communication approaches for overcoming resistance. Table 7.1 lists several compliance-gaining strategies that are often used. The goal you want to fulfill will affect your choice of strategy.[19] For example, if you are eager to sustain a relationship (your relational goal), you will eliminate strategies that damage the relationship (such as threats or coercion).[20] You will often need to request things from other people, but the strategies you choose to gain compliance can directly affect whether the relationship is maintained or not.

Table 7.1   Compliance-Gaining Strategies

Strategy	Definition	Example
Rationality	Use of explanation and logic; use of supportive evidence	I forgot to bring any money with me today. Could you lend me $5?
Coercion/threat	The use of threat or punishment	If you don't lend me $5, I won't be your friend anymore.
Promise/reward	The use of reward or reimbursement	If you lend me $5, I will wash your car for you.
Pregiving	Doing a positive act for the other before making a request	You know how I did your dishes for you this morning? How about lending me $5?
Debt	Calling in a previously accrued debt	You know how I loaned you my car last week? Well, I need to borrow $5.
Manipulation of negative feelings	Making the other person feel bad about not complying (coercion)	True friends are always willing to lend $5 to their friends.
Manipulation of positive feelings	Making the other person feel good about complying (reward)	You're such a nice person and so charitable. Could I borrow $5?
Altruism	Appealing to the other person's kindness	I really need you to help me. I need $5.
Indirect appeal	Hinting at the request; use of subtle and covert strategies	Boy, I wish I had $5 so I could go to lunch today with you.

Source: Adapted from G. Marwell and D. R. Schmitt, "Dimensions of Compliance-Gaining Behavior: An Empirical Analysis," *Sociometry,* 30 (1967), 350–364; and M. J. Cody, D. J. Canary, and S. W. Smith, "Compliance-Gaining Goals: An Inductive Analysis of Actors' Goal Types, Strategies, and Successes," in *Strategic Interpersonal Communication,* ed. J. A. Daly and J. M. Wiemann (Hillsdale, N.J.: Lawrence Erlbaum, 1995), pp. 33–90.

Tactics developed over time.   A special quality of compliance-gaining strategies is that they can take advantage of the ongoing nature of interpersonal relationships.[21] People don't just use one compliance-gaining tactic on a one-shot basis. Rather, they employ a series of tactics over an extended period of time.

For instance, because you know that you will see your boss each workday, you might extend the approach you use in requesting specific vacation dates. You could adopt a tactic of *persistence* (or chiseling) to wear away your boss's resistance to your vacation request. Suppose your boss rejects your initial request for vacation time because of the high volume of work that occurs during the period you requested. You could make an effort to get a lot of work done over the next few days and then make your request again. Failing again, you might wait another week and then approach your boss with complaints about how depressed you're becoming and how disappointed you are that you can't get the vacation time you want. Through persistence and the use of a variety of compliance-gaining tactics, you eventually get your vacation time. You have chiseled away at your boss's resistance.

Two other tactics that take advantage of the continual interaction inherent in interpersonal relationships are foot-in-the-door and door-in-the-face.[22] You've probably used both of these techniques already. **Foot-in-the-door** involves making an initial small request that meets minimal resistance. Having gained that, you return later with a larger request, and you continue to escalate the request until you achieve what you want. Suppose you are from Indiana and you want to go to Mexico for spring break, but you know your parents will resist. You start out by asking if you can go with friends to Chicago for spring break, and your parents agree. Later you go back and indicate that your friends are thinking of going skiing in Colorado instead, and you ask if that would be okay, since your parents have already agreed to let you travel. Still later, you tell your parents that the snow isn't very good this year, so everyone has decided to go to Mexico. Once you receive the initial compliance, it is a matter of slowly increasing the size of the request.

Door-in-the-face uses the opposite effect. You initially make a very large request and then bargain down to a much smaller request, which is actually the one that you wanted. Suppose you want to go to Chicago for spring break but anticipate resistance from your parents. You start by asking permission to go to Mexico, then request Colorado, and finally ask for Chicago. This technique works because it prompts your parents to feel guilty about denying the larger request and at the same time makes the Chicago request seem minimal relative to the alternatives of Mexico and Colorado.

Compliance gaining as a transactional process.   Social decentering provides you with insights that help you develop effective compliance-gaining strategies. The more information you have about a partner, the more you can predict his or her reactions and prepare appropriate strategies. However, your partners also know you and can often muster effective counterstrategies.[23]

Thus, compliance gaining is not a linear process in which you act unilaterally. Given the transactional nature of interpersonal communication, compliance gaining is a process in which you give and take during your interactions about a given request.

Compliance gaining and relational maintenance. Any request can potentially disrupt the balance of a relationship. That's one reason for the old adage that you should never borrow money from a friend—it can redefine and destroy the friendship. Therefore, you need to know how to seek compliance effectively while still maintaining a relationship. You can improve your effectiveness in gaining compliance and maintaining the relationship by utilizing social decentering, considering multiple strategies, taking advantage of the ongoing interaction opportunities, and adapting to the transactional nature of interpersonal communication.

At times, compliance gaining will focus directly on relational maintenance issues. Suppose that you and a friend haven't been able to spend much time together in the last few weeks. You call up your friend and invite her out to a movie, but she tells you she has too many other things to do. You might apply various compliance-gaining strategies to overcome her resistance to going out. Your effort is essentially aimed at spending time together to maintain the relationship.

Think about times you have successfully gained compliance in a highly resistant situation. What strategies did you employ? Which ones worked most effectively? Least effectively?

Now think about a time when you were unsuccessful. What strategies did you employ? Why didn't they work? What other strategies might you have employed?

■ *Constructively Managing Interpersonal Conflict*

Conflict is inevitable in relationships, since your goals and your partner's goals are bound to seem incompatible from time to time. Maintaining satisfying interpersonal relationships often depends on how skilled you are at managing interpersonal conflicts.

The impact of conflict on a relationship is not necessarily bad if the conflict is managed constructively. For instance, as relationships develop, conflict sometimes occurs because of a lack of clearly defined roles. Productive conflict leads to clarification and agreement about relational roles, and this can strengthen the relationship.[24]

The conflict management style you choose can have a significant impact on the productiveness of the conflict. Remember the five styles of conflict management outlined in Chapter 5? To recap, the styles are avoidance, accommodation, competition, compromise, and collaboration. Consider how these styles might affect a conflict between two people who are dating.

- The use of a *collaborative* conflict management style would validate their relationship, showing that each person could be concerned about the other's welfare without abandoning his or her own needs.
- *Compromise* might also be effective, although it would mean that neither party would achieve entirely what he or she wanted.

Other styles of conflict management, however, could jeopardize the relationship.

- Being *competitive* would place one person's needs above those of the partner and emphasize goal achievement over the maintenance of the relationship.

- *Accommodating* (one partner's giving in to the other) might initially preserve the relationship but potentially at great personal cost.
- *Avoiding* means that the issue would continue to fester and potentially undermine the stability of the relationship.

You should review the material in Chapter 5 about managing emotions, managing information, and managing the conflict. Briefly:

1. *Managing emotions.* You need to be willing to share your feelings and be receptive to hearing your partner express his or her feelings.
2. *Managing information.* You need to seek information about your partner's needs and goals and create an atmosphere in which your partner will listen to you express your own needs and goals.
3. *Managing the conflict.* Finally, you need to seek solutions that are respectful of both parties' needs.

One objective of any conflict situation should be to strengthen the relationship rather than weaken it. Successful conflict management leads to a stronger sense of trust and commitment and in some ways greater freedom to express yourself, knowing that the relationship will continue. Remember, however, that through relational development, you will experience many relationships that really aren't viable. Some conflicts may reflect an inherent problem that cannot be resolved and for which dissolution of the relationship is the best course of action. If you are continually having to sacrifice your own goals and needs to maintain a relationship, you might reach a point where the costs of the relationship exceed the current or projected benefits. At that point, you need to implement termination strategies.

Summary and Self-Analysis:

Skills for Maintaining Relationships

Use the following summary of skills for maintaining relationships to identify your strongest skills and those that you could improve.

Using Maintenance Strategies

- Positivity/romance strategies: Be cheerful and positive, give gifts, and be romantic.
- Openness: Engage in explicit talk about the relationship and its problems.
- Assurances: Explicitly state your commitment to the relationship.
- Sharing tasks: Work with your partner in completing tasks.
- Avoidance of antisocial behavior: Avoid arguing or being sarcastic, rude, or critical.

Communicating and Interacting

- Spend time with your partner talking and doing enjoyable activities.

Using Social Decentering

- Obtain as much information as you can about your partner and the situation.
- Use your understanding of yourself and other people as a basis for understanding your partner.

- Learn from your errors.
- Adapt your communication to reflect what you have learned.

Being Flexible and Adapting

- Adjust to changes in your partner and in the relationship.

Compliance Gaining

- Use strategies to fulfill your needs in such a way as to avoid harming the relationship.
- Use strategies to maintain the relationship by overcoming your partner's attempts to redefine or change it

Constructively Managing Interpersonal Conflicts

- Manage emotions: Be willing to express your emotions and let your partner express his or hers.
- Manage information: Share and seek relevant information.
- Manage the conflict: Seek solutions that respect each party's needs.

■ De-escalating and Ending Relationships

Although you may not realize it, there are certain skills associated with ending relationships successfully. The theme of Paul Simon's song "Fifty Ways to Leave Your Lover" is that people have lots of options open to them for terminating relationships. Sometimes you may not want to end a relationship but merely de-escalate it—redefine it as less intimate—and this also requires certain skills.

Changing the definition of a relationship involves varying degrees of threat to each party's face. For instance, telling people you don't want to see them anymore implicitly conveys a message that there is something wrong with them and that they are no longer valued or important. At the same time, such an interaction might result in your partner's attacking your face by either challenging your self-worth or by attempting to block you in accomplishing your goal of redefining the relationship. To deal with these challenges effectively, you have to consider the impact of various strategies.

■ *Mutual Versus Unilateral De-escalation*

The decision to redefine or end a relationship can be either mutual or unilateral. Both parties might desire to de-escalate the relationship to the same level. This **mutual de-escalation** involves each party's expressing his or her needs and appreciating the other person's needs.

Unilateral de-escalation, on the other hand, is an effort by just one party to redefine or dissolve the relationship. This can be more difficult than mutual de-escalation, depending on the resistance of the other partner. A high degree of disharmony can exist if one person has a strong desire to end the relationship while the other party has a strong desire to maintain it.[25] The person who wants out of the relationship often utilizes compliance-gaining strategies in an attempt to end the relationship.[26]

Closure of a Relationship After a Breakup

This excerpt appeared in a newspaper advice column written by Dr. Neil Rosenthal, a licensed marriage and family therapist. In his response, Rosenthal provides a list of questions that is meant to help a person learn from the experience of leaving a partner. How many of these questions have you asked yourself following the end of a relationship?

Dear Neil:

I was in a two-year relationship with a 50-year-old man who asked me to marry him. But Bob had both second thoughts and anxiety attacks, and eventually he ended the relationship, saying: "I don't want to talk anymore, and I don't have to tell you why I don't want to marry you." I had no feedback from him about what happened, and subsequently there was no closure for me. It's now been 11 months, and I still don't understand what happened. Not only do I want closure for myself, but I want some closure for my 2-, 3- and 4-year-old nieces who visited us frequently when we were living together. The girls still ask about him and why he's not around. I've answered these questions as best I can, but finally I asked Bob to talk to them. His response was "just distract them."

Can you write about the importance of closure in a relationship and how to achieve it? —Ruth, Milwaukee.

Dear Ruth:

Putting closure to an intimate relationship that has ended is essential if you are wanting to move on. Closure consists of four components: figuring out what happened or what went wrong between the two of you; making peace with the relationship ending; figuring out what you can learn from the experience so you don't repeat the same scenario; and envisioning a positive future for yourself with someone else.

The following questions are designed to assist you in gaining greater awareness of what happened, and how to make sense of your experience. On paper write:

What you will miss about the relationship and about the person.

What you will not miss.

Acknowledge what your role was in causing the problems in the relationship, or in assisting the relationship to fail.

Lessons this experience has taught you.

Concerning this relationship, what are you sad about?

Concerning this relationship, what would you do differently if you had to do it over again?

What relationship skills do you need to develop or perfect in the future?

Explore each of the following emotions carefully: anger, passion, loneliness, happiness, grief, pain, joy, guilt, shame, fear, terror, love, hate, resistance, depression, blame.

What did you gain from the relationship? How are you richer, deeper or wiser because of the experience? What did the relationship give you that you are grateful for?

What did your "ex" give you that you are grateful for?

Concerning the relationship with your former mate, what are you willing to forgive?

What are you wanting to be forgiven for?

What are you willing to forgive yourself for?

Breaking up destroys the idea that if you only try hard enough—or love more—you will be able to fix or solve the problems so that things will get better again. Letting go of the dream we create about a relationship—and about the future—is a whole lot harder than letting go of the person. Be willing to do this unfinished business of the heart.

> "Seldom, or perhaps never, does a marriage develop into an individual relationship smoothly and without crisis; there is no coming to consciousness without pain."
> —Carl Jung
> "When you're in love, you put up with things that, when you're out of love, you cite."
> —Miss Manners (Judith Martin)

Source: Neil Rosenthal, *The Denver Post*, May 15, 1997. Copyright © 1997 The Denver Post Corporation. Reprinted by permission of the author.

One unfortunate problem associated with weak communication occurs when both parties want out of the relationship but think the other person wants to continue it. As a result, the relationship may be maintained needlessly until their mutual perspective is discovered.

■ Direct Versus Indirect Strategies

Regardless of whether you are de-escalating or terminating a relationship, you can choose between direct and indirect strategies. **Direct de-escalation strategies** involve an explicit statement about your desire to redefine or end the relationship. **Indirect de-escalation strategies** avoid any specific indication of your intentions. Most people prefer to be told directly if their partner intends to end a relationship, but prefer to use indirect strategies when they themselves want to end a relationship.[27]

Using indirect strategies.   Probably the most common indirect strategy is behavioral de-escalation. *Behavioral de-escalation* simply means reducing the behaviors associated with a given relationship level. Typically this involves reducing the frequency and duration of interactions. You might choose, for example, to avoid any further interaction with the other person. This approach does provide for some face-saving because your partner is never directly rejected; but your partner is left with uncertainty about what is happening, particularly if he or she fails to recognize your intentions.

Another indirect strategy, *cost escalation*, involves making the relationship more costly for your partner, to the point that your partner wants to redefine it. You might make yourself a nuisance as a way of making the relationship undesirable.

Finally, you can engage in *pseudo-de-escalation,* in which you tell your partner that you want to redefine the relationship at a less intimate level, but your true intention is to terminate the relationship. In essence, this is a form of compliance gaining through foot-in-the-door, because you start with a small request and eventually move to the larger one.

All of these indirect methods run the risk of inaccuracy. For example, if you try behavioral de-escalation to reduce the level of intimacy with someone, with the intention of still maintaining a friendship, your partner might misperceive your behavior as indicating a desire to end the relationship altogether. Your partner might then totally withdraw.

Using direct strategies.   Direct strategies include various ways of indicating your desires while also trying to protect your partner's face. The most straightforward technique is justification. *Justification* is essentially the use of a rational compliance-gaining strategy. (See Table 7.1 on page 189.) In justification, you provide a full and rational explanation to your partner about why you want to change the relationship.[28]

In *positivity,* another direct strategy, you attempt to put a positive spin on the change in the relationship. You indicate why you think the change is for the best for both you and your partner. This involves the use of reward compliance-gaining strategies, which can include such statements as "We'll both be a lot happier if we have a chance to date around a while" and "I think we both know that we are only bringing each other down."

Finally, you can use *emotional tone* as a way of directly changing a relationship. Through emotional tone, you express your sorrow, fears, concerns, desire to create a positive ending, and even your caring for your partner.

■ *Choosing a Strategy*

The way you de-escalate or terminate a relationship depends on your goals and on your desire to protect both your face and your partner's. Clearly, each strategy discussed has certain advantages and disadvantages, depending on whose perspective is taken. Some strategies are more partner focused, and others are more self-focused.

Usually, in long-term relationships, people feel an obligation to be more direct and up-front with their partners about their feelings and thoughts. In carrying on such relational discussions, though, you need to consider the impact that your messages will have on your partner's face. You want to adopt strategies that help your partner maintain his or her face.

Overall, your ability to manage relational de-escalation or termination will be enhanced if you utilize many of the interpersonal skills discussed in this chapter, such as social decentering, flexibility and adapting, and compliance gaining.

Look at the following summary of termination strategies. Which are you most likely to use yourself, and why? Which would you most prefer that other people use if they were to terminate relationships with you?

Indirect Strategies

- Behavioral de-escalation: reducing interactions, communication, affection, and so forth
- Cost escalation: making the relationship more costly
- Pseudo-de-escalation: telling your partner you want to become less intimate, with the unspoken intention of eventually ending the relationship

Direct Strategies

- Justification: providing a rational explanation of why you want out of the relationship
- Positivity: making it sound like ending the relationship will be positive for both you and your partner
- Emotional tone: disclosing feelings of concern, fear, sorrow, and a desire for a positive ending

Summary

Your goals dictate your reasons for approaching others and initiating relationships. In a particular relationship, your goals play an important part in determining what skills you need for managing your interpersonal communication.

You should look for approachability cues that signal another person's willingness to interact. After approaching someone, you can draw on several initiation strategies. These include using free information and common elements to start the conversation, asking questions, following the expected pattern, or script, for an initial interaction, and listening actively.

Once you have begun a relationship, you can use a variety of strategies to help the relationship develop. You can use affinity-seeking strategies, which are ways of increasing another person's attraction to you. These include presenting yourself as attractive, displaying trust, being polite, and listening. Coordinating you and your partner's relational perspectives and process trajectory cognitions helps ensure that your behaviors are appropriate and beneficial to relational development. Finally, self-disclosure is necessary to reach intimacy but requires appropriate choices concerning when and what to disclose.

Interpersonal communication is also an essential element in maintaining relationships. Relational maintenance strategies include being positive and/or romantic, being open, providing assurances about your commitment to the relationship, sharing task responsibilities, and avoiding antisocial behaviors like arguing or criticizing. Spending time with your partner and communicating on a personal level also aid in relational maintenance. Being other-centered through the use of social decentering allows you to obtain information about your partner and adapt your communication appropriately. This leads to the need to be flexible and willing to adapt. Getting what you want from your partner involves utilizing compliance-gaining strategies that achieve your purpose without harming the relationship. Some conflict is inevitable in relationships, however, and relational maintenance depends on how the conflict is managed. Constructive conflict management often involves finding a collaborative solution that meets the needs of both you and your partner.

Many relationships eventually end, and it is important to know how to end them effectively. The effort to terminate or de-escalate a relationship can be mutual or unilateral. Direct strategies reflect an explicit statement of the intent to de-escalate the relationship, while indirect strategies avoid such specificity. The challenge is to maintain face for both you and your partner while still accomplishing your goal.

Key Terms

approachability cues   Indications that a person is receptive to interpersonal communication.

free information   Information that is easily observed about another person and utilized in conversations.

affinity-seeking strategies   Behaviors we enact in an attempt to increase another person's liking for us.

maintenance strategies   Conscious attempts to "recharge" a relationship or help a relationship remain at a given level of intimacy.

compliance gaining   Interpersonal persuasion; the interpersonal process of overcoming another person's resistance to a request.

foot-in-the-door   A compliance-gaining strategy that involves making an initial small request that meets minimal resistance. Having gained that, you escalate your requests until you achieve what you want.

door-in-the-face   A compliance-gaining strategy in which you initially make a very large request and then bargain down to a much smaller request, which is actually the one that you wanted.

mutual de-escalation   An effort by both parties to terminate a relationship or reduce its level of intimacy.

unilateral de-escalation   An effort by only one party to terminate a relationship or reduce its level of intimacy.

direct de-escalation strategies   Relational de-escalation efforts that involve explicitly stating a desire to terminate or redefine the relationship.

indirect de-escalation strategies   Relational de-escalation efforts that avoid any specific indication of the desire to terminate or redefine the relationship.

Review Questions

1. Explain what an approachability cue is.
2. Discuss three ways you can initiate an interaction.
3. Explain affinity seeking.
4. Why do you need to coordinate your relational perspectives and your process trajectory cognitions with your partner's?
5. Describe some of the strategies for maintaining a relationship.
6. In what ways can social decentering help you maintain a relationship?
7. Discuss two strategies that might be used to gain compliance.
8. Briefly explain the difference between indirect and direct strategies for ending a relationship.

Chapter 8

Interviewing: Theory and Principles

Objectives

Studying this chapter will allow you to:

1. Explain the definition of interviewing.
2. Identify and define several types of interviews.
3. Distinguish between nondirective and directive interview formats.
4. Identify several factors that interfere with gaining accurate and complete information in interviews.
5. Explain the relationship between questions and thought processes.
6. Differentiate closed questions from open questions.

GEORGE	Hi, Helen. Do you have a couple of minutes?
HELEN	Hi, George. Sure, come on in.
GEORGE	I understand you just bought some new computers for your division.
HELEN	Yes, I did. We're really happy with them.
GEORGE	I'm checking into buying some new computers for my division, too, and I thought you might have some good information to share.
HELEN	I'd be happy to.
GEORGE	What were some of your main considerations in deciding what to purchase?
HELEN	Well, cost was certainly a factor, but more important was trying to find machines that had enough memory to handle the increasingly complex software that's coming out.
GEORGE	Anything else?
HELEN	I wanted machines that had a lot of software preloaded and that we could simply take out of the boxes, plug in, and use. We didn't have time for a long setup.
GEORGE	That's a good point. We'll have the same issue to consider. What kind of service arrangements did you get?
HELEN	I was really pleased to get a three-year extended on-site warranty for only one hundred dollars more per machine.
GEORGE	Did you have to order a certain number of machines to get that deal?
HELEN	Yes, they gave me the deal because I was ordering more than six machines.

In this interaction, George is conducting a fairly informal interview with Helen. In Chapter 1, **interviewing** was defined as a goal-structured form of interpersonal communication in which one party plays the role of interviewer and the other party plays the role of interviewee. Defining an interview as an interaction that has an interviewer and an interviewee may seem rather circular. As you will see, however, these roles distinguish interviewing from other forms of interpersonal communication.

We can see the various elements of our definition reflected in George's interaction with Helen.

- The interaction is goal structured in the sense that George came in with a predetermined goal—to find out information about Helen's computer purchase. George has at least an informal agenda of questions for which he is seeking answers.
- Even from the short excerpt, we can see that this interaction reflects interpersonal communication. George and Helen know each other and appear to have a friendly working relationship.
- Both individuals know their roles. In his role as interviewer, George asks questions and decides on the direction and focus of the interaction. In her role as interviewee, Helen lets George set the agenda and direction of the interaction, responds to his questions, and provides information and clarification. We can easily imagine the roles being reversed, with Helen seeking information from George about some other issue.

■ The Components of an Interview

For a better understanding of interviewing, let's go through the components of an interview in more detail.

■ *Goal-Structured Communication*

To say that interviews are goal structured essentially means that the interaction has a specific beginning, middle, and end. That structure is created to advance the interview toward the fulfillment of one or both parties' predetermined goals.[1] Having a predetermined goal means that we have engaged in some degree of planning and preparation. George, in the sample interview, had a predetermined reason for seeking out and interacting with Helen.

The interaction itself is structured and elicits a set of expected behaviors—most significantly, that of the interviewer and the interviewee. These two roles create expectations for how the interaction should proceed and give it further structure.

■ *Interpersonal Communication*

Interviews fit the definition of interpersonal communication (See Chapter 6.) in that two or more people transactionally influence one another. Both the interviewer and the interviewee are influencing each other simultaneously. The development of a question occurs while the interviewee is watching and nonverbally affecting the interviewer. The interviewer's communication during the interviewee's spoken response affects how the interviewee responds.

Reporters, for instance, can unconsciously direct an interviewee's responses through note-taking. By actively taking notes during some responses and failing to take notes during others, the reporter signals what he or she is really interested in hearing. These signals can potentially bias the interviewee's responses.

Interpersonal relationships are also part of interviewing. Would George's questions be the same if he were asking them of someone he didn't already know? Would George be able to trust the responses? George is able to use his existing relationship with Helen as the foundation for his interview with her. He can be confident in Helen's credibility because they already have a trusting relationship.

When no such previous relationship exists, part of the interviewing process involves establishing an appropriate relationship. For instance, to conduct an effective counseling interview, the counselor must first establish a trusting relationship that is conducive to openness and honesty. One study looked at interviews with victims of incest. The interviewer's verbal and nonverbal behaviors, the study found, contributed to creating a supportive relationship in which the interviewees felt enough trust to discuss their experiences.[2]

■ *The Parties*

No, this part of the definition doesn't refer to fun-filled get-togethers, but rather to the notion that there may be more than one person acting as interviewer or interviewee. Sometimes interviews are conducted by panels, and sometimes there is more than one person responding to the questions. So the definition uses the term *party* rather than *person* or *individual.* Still, interviews involve only two parties: those acting as interviewers, asking the questions; and those acting as interviewees, responding.

Having multiple participants adds additional dynamics to the interview process. You will probably experience the situation of being in an employment interview conducted by several people on a selection committee. If so, you may find that you are more anxious than in a one-on-one interview because it becomes more difficult to develop personal relationships with three or four people at one time. Special dynamics also come into play when more than one person acts as interviewee. You have probably observed a political debate in which a panel of reporters asks questions of opposing political candidates. Each candidate hears the other candidates' responses and alters his or her responses as a result.

■ *Role of Interviewer*

A *role* is a set of expected behaviors associated with a particular position. The phrase *role of interviewer* means that there are certain expected behaviors associated with the party conducting the interview.

The most obvious expectation of the interviewer is to ask questions. The interviewer is engaged in gaining information. The interviewer generally controls the focus, pace, and direction of the interview (although some kinds of interviews, such as problem-solving and counseling interviews, may use an approach that lets interviewees set the direction). The interviewer usually has the responsibility for creating a supportive atmosphere, trust, and the appropriate relationship needed to enhance the flow of information.

In our opening scenario, George clearly plays the role of interviewer. He has specific information he is looking for. He asks questions and directs the focus of the interaction. He assumes responsibility for managing the interview.

■ *Role of Interviewee*

The interviewee's role consists of providing answers to the questions asked by the interviewer. There is an expectation that interviewees will answer questions honestly and to the best of their ability. The interviewer sees the interviewee as possessing needed information. In this way, the interviewee has some degree of power over the interviewer. The interviewee must assess the reasonability of sharing the requested information and determine how that information might be used.

Interviewees provide answers because they believe that there is some benefit to them by doing so. What does Helen gain by answering George's questions? She probably feels confirmed by his request for information, and she is probably creating a social exchange situation in which she can expect him to return the favor sometime. Helen's actions also help maintain the relationship. If she refused to answer, George might feel slighted, might consider the relationship to be deteriorating, or might threaten her face.

Purposes and Types of Interviews

The most general purpose of an interview is to gain information. Interviews differ, however, in how the information is used. In this section, we'll examine several different types of information-gaining interviews that stem from different purposes. Then we'll take a brief look at interviewing outcomes that go beyond the collection of information.

Information Action Interviews

Information action interviews involve collecting information that helps the interviewer in taking some action, specifically decision-making, problem solving, or report writing. This is the type of interview that George has with Helen, and it is probably the most common type of interview, though it varies in formality. The casual interaction between George and Helen is fairly typical.

Think about all the times you engage in interviews of this sort. For instance, you need information about an assignment and go to see the instructor. You may not think of this as an interview, but it is. Your purpose is to gain information; you consider what you need to know and what questions you will ask.

Employment (Selection) Interviews

Employment, or **selection, interviews** involve making decisions about the appropriateness of a given individual for a particular job. Interviewers seek information from the various applicants in an attempt to decide which applicant would do the job the best. Employment interviews often include an opportunity for the applicant to turn the tables by interviewing the company representative. The applicant will usually ask questions to collect information that will aid him or her in deciding whether to accept a job offer.

In addition to employment interviewing, organizations often use exit and appraisal interviews. *Exit interviews* provide an organization with feedback about itself. Some universities and colleges, for example, interview graduating students as a way of assessing the performance of the school. *Appraisal interviews* provide for

GRANTLAND®

NOW REMEMBER, THESE ANNUAL REVIEWS ARE SUPPOSED TO BE A TWO-WAY PROCESS.

SO FORGET THAT I'M YOUR BOSS. FORGET THAT I CONTROL YOUR JOB.

DON'T EVEN THINK ABOUT THE FACT THAT YOUR SALARY AND CAREER ARE COMPLETELY IN MY HANDS.

JUST TELL ME HOW YOU REALLY THINK I'M DOING AS A MANAGER.

an assessment of a person's performance and sometimes evolve into problem-solving interviews.

■ Problem-Solving and Counseling Interviews

Besides seeking information for our own purposes, we can seek information as a way of helping interviewees come to an understanding of their problems. This is the case in problem-solving and counseling interviews. The interviewer's goal is not to gain information for the interviewer's benefit, but rather to aid the interviewee in becoming self-informed.

Problem-solving interviews are designed to help the interviewee analyze some problem and/or develop a plan of action. In this type of interview, the interviewee is the one who has the predetermined purpose to solve a problem, and the interviewer adapts to that purpose. Such interviews are often conducted by employers who are seeking to resolve employee problems. One outcome of a problem-solving interview might be a decision for the employee to seek professional counseling.

Counseling interviews typically require a higher degree of skill, expertise, and training. They often involve an in-depth personal analysis that requires the establishment of a trusting, disclosive relationship. The goal is to lead to greater self-understanding for the interviewee.

The following scenario is a typical problem-solving interaction between an academic advisor and a student, in which the information is for the student's (interviewee's) benefit:

ADVISOR From what you've told me so far, you're not sure why you're having trouble in your courses this semester.

STUDENT That's right. I think I'm studying just as much, and I mostly like the courses I'm taking.

ADVISOR How does your studying compare to previous semesters?

STUDENT Well, I'm living in an apartment now, and I used to live in a dorm.

ADVISOR How does that affect your studying?

STUDENT I love the apartment, but my roommates are pretty noisy, and they're always dragging me out to the bars with them. Not that they have to twist my arm much.

ADVISOR Sounds like it's gotten harder for you to find any quality study time.

STUDENT Yeah, I guess that's true. I hadn't really thought about how living in the apartment has affected my studying, but I guess it has.

ADVISOR In a minute let's talk about ways you can improve your study conditions, but first I want to follow up on something else you said. You mentioned that you "mostly" like your courses this semester?

STUDENT Well, I actually hate the biology and statistics courses I have to take. I've skipped them a few times, but I don't ever miss anything important.

ADVISOR How do you think skipping classes might be contributing to your troubles this semester?

STUDENT I suppose I have missed some information that was on the exam. I did okay on the parts of the exam that covered the course material I took notes on.

In this interview, the advisor is gaining information that is really helping the student understand and come to grips with the problems affecting the student. The role of the interviewer is to ask questions that bring out information that is helpful to the interviewee.

■ *Persuasive Interviews*

Persuasive interviews are really interactions in which the interviewer seeks to influence the interviewee. Persuasive interviews follow the principles of interviewing while also drawing on the principles of persuasion that will be discussed in Chapter 12.

Sometimes the persuasive interview utilizes information gaining in the development of persuasive strategies. For example, good computer salespeople start by asking customers about their computer needs, future use requirements, the amount of money they have to spend, and their level of computer ability. With that information in hand, the salespeople can then tailor their recommendations and persuasive strategies to the customer.

Questions can also be used as a tool for manipulating the interviewee's analysis of an issue, decision, or solution. Some telephone solicitations start with a survey in which the questions are aimed at creating a need for the product. Some persuasive interviews don't even involve questions; rather, they represent directed conversations in which the interviewer is offering information in an attempt to overcome the interviewee's resistance and objections.

■ *Complaint Interviews*

Complaint interviews are similar to problem-solving interviews in that they are usually initiated by the interviewee and they often involve trying to resolve a problem. Unlike problem-solving interviews, however, the complaint interview revolves around an issue specifically concerning the interviewer or one or more parties affiliated with the interviewer.

You might approach your boss to complain that you weren't given the days off you requested. During this interaction, your boss could use complaint interviewing to gain information about the nature of your complaint, why you thought you had been treated unfairly, and possible solutions or ways to address your frustration.

Table 8.1 summarizes the various types of interviews that we have discussed.

Think about some of your experiences as an interviewee. In which categories did the interviews fall: information action, selection, exit, appraisal, problem-solving, counseling, persuasive, or complaint? What was different about the various interviews? What was similar about them? Which did you enjoy the most? Why? Which did you enjoy the least? Why?

■ *Beyond Information: Other Outcomes of Interviews*

Gaining information is the main purpose of interviewing. However, there are a number of other outcomes besides gaining information. Asking for information

Table 8.1 Summary of Interview Types

Type of Interview	Purpose
Information action	Gaining information to aid in reporting, deciding, or problem solving
Employment/selection	Gaining information to make a decision about the appropriateness of an individual for a job
Problem-solving/counseling	Gaining information that helps the interviewee understand and solve problems
Persuasive	Influencing the interviewee, often by acquiring information that can be used in developing persuasive strategies
Complaint	Gaining information about a complaint levied against the interviewer or a third party to increase understanding and possibly develop corrective action

from people makes them feel important and valued. A boss who interviews her employees about their suggestions for modifying the vacation policy empowers the employees and makes them feel involved in the organization. Contrast that behavior with that of a manager who simply announces a new vacation policy without consulting her employees. The interview situation is likely to lead to more acceptance of the final policy.

Interviewing someone shows the interviewer's respect for the knowledge and information that the interviewee possesses and can therefore enhance the relationship. Think back to the scenario at the beginning of this chapter. George could probably make his computer purchases without interviewing Helen, but by choosing to interview her, he shows his respect for her knowledge and confirms the value of their relationship.

■ Interview Formats

One of the significant ways that interviews vary is in terms of how much the questions are prepared in advance. In **directive interviews,** the interviewer prepares a list of specific questions in advance. In **nondirective interviews,** the interviewer considers the objective, prepares the opening, but plans just one or two questions.

The directive interview gives control to the interviewer, while the nondirective interview gives the interviewee more control. The directive interview is also more restrictive, since the questions are primarily developed in advance of the interview. Nondirective interviews are very flexible, and the interviewer has a great deal of latitude concerning the direction of the interview. There aren't really just two formats, however, but rather a full range from highly directive to highly nondirective, as illustrated in Figure 8.1.

■ Classifying Interviews by Format

Interviews can be classified according to their level of directiveness. Surveys in which respondents choose from among the prescribed answers represent the most

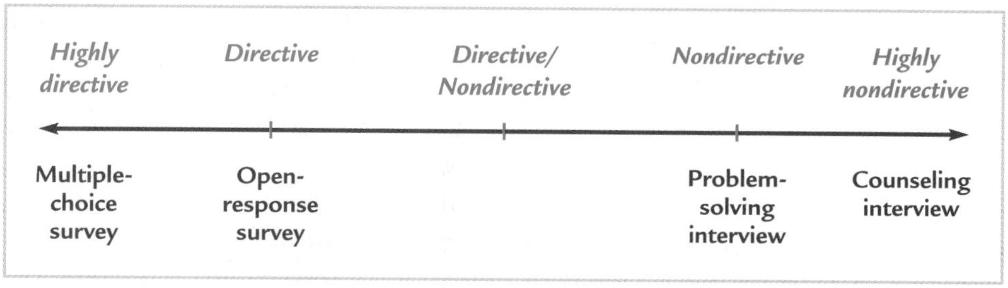

Figure 8.1

Continuum of Interview Formats

Highly directive	Directive	Directive/ Nondirective	Nondirective	Highly nondirective
Multiple-choice survey	Open-response survey		Problem-solving interview	Counseling interview

directive interviews, shown at the left side of Figure 8.1. Surveys can also be designed in which the answers are more open-ended and give the interviewee more latitude in his or her responses. These open-ended, less directive surveys are shown farther to the right in the figure.

A selection interview can be highly directive if it consists of a fairly closed set of questions, almost like a survey. On the other hand, a selection interview can be based on one open-ended question: "Tell me about yourself." Because such a highly nondirective approach would make it difficult to compare the responses of the various interviewees, most selection interviews follow a more "criteria-based" format. Criteria-based selection interviews depend on a schedule of questions that allows for comparisons of the different respondents. These interviews may have ten or fifteen prepared questions, but the interviewers also do a lot of following up and adapting to the interviewee's responses.

Problem-solving and counseling interviews generally fall toward the nondirective side of the continuum in Figure 8.1, but they vary in terms of the number of predetermined questions. In some instances, there might be only one predetermined question: "Tell me what's on your mind." Or the interviewer might just wait for the interviewee to start talking. In such cases, everything the interviewer says follows up on the interviewee's first comments.

■ Choosing a Format

The choice of format is determined by a number of factors. A highly directive approach is appropriate when you need to compare the answers from different respondents or statistically analyze the responses. If a pollster wants to know, for example, what percentage of the U.S. public approves of the president's job performance, a directive multiple-choice format is appropriate. Such surveys permit general statements about patterns of responses: "The president's job approval ratings rose from 55 percent to 68 percent in the past two years." Such information has limited value, however. It doesn't tell us, for example, *why* the president's approval ratings rose. Directive interviews do not capture much in-depth information.

Nondirective interviews allow more depth but make comparisons and generalizations more difficult. Suppose your department is failing to meet its sales quotas, and you decide to interview your staff. As a result of a nondirective interview, you might find out that one employee's difficulty in making his monthly sales quota stems from recent marital problems. This information might help you understand that employee, but it won't help you improve the sales performance of the rest of the staff. Overall, the decision to use a directive or nondirective approach depends on the kind of information you need.

■ Information in Interviewing

So far in this chapter the term *information* has been used a good deal in relation to interviews, but what precisely does it mean? **Information** can be thought of as anything we perceive that reduces our uncertainty.[3] Uncertainty reduction was discussed in Chapter 2 as one of the basic elements of communication. We seek information to help reduce uncertainty and increase predictability.

In essence, information is all the stuff we don't know, all the uncertainties that we possess. We can tell something is information because we recognize it as new to us. There is a lot of information out there in the world that we never learn. Even in our everyday interactions, we continually miss information that is available to us because we don't perceive it. Interviews represent specific, conscious efforts to find out particular information, which we can then use to reduce the uncertainty associated with decisions, problems, and so forth.

■ *Information and Perception*

The discussion of perception in Chapter 3 is particularly relevant to interviewing effectiveness. We are constantly involved in perceiving both verbal and nonverbal messages and deriving meaning from those perceptions. This perceptual process provides us with information. We examine the verbal messages in the context of the accompanying nonverbal cues in an attempt to determine the veracity of the messages. Yet, this process is prone to a variety of perceptual and attributional biases, as you learned in Chapter 3.

Interviews are also extremely prone to the challenges of communication discussed in Chapter 5, especially deception, misunderstanding, and misrepresentation. Is the person we are interviewing telling us the truth? Can we accept the responses as valid information?

Suppose we ask someone, "Hey, Bob, what did you have for dinner last night?" and he replies, "A turkey sandwich and potato salad." Have we gained information? We have learned something we didn't know before, so, yes, we have gained information. However, what if Bob is lying to us? In that case, we have gained false information, but we don't know that it is false. Our reaction to the information—our reduction of uncertainty—is the same whether the information is true or false. Suppose we find out later from someone else that Bob actually had pepperoni pizza. The information we received from Bob's "turkey sandwich" statement is no longer about what he had for dinner. Now it is information about Bob's character and propensity to lie to us.

This scenario leads us to an important distinction. Direct statements in response to a question represent **explicit information. Implicit,** or **derived, information** results from conclusions that we make on the basis of our perceptual processes, including inferences, impressions, and attributions.

Even with apparently explicit information, people are inclined to hear what they want to hear. Sometimes an interviewer simply misunderstands a response.

Our perceptions of other people influence the way we interpret their behaviors and responses to questions in an interview.

All the problems of misunderstanding discussed in Chapter 5 can undermine accurate information acquisition in an interview. Some of the ways to overcome those problems in interviewing will be discussed in the next chapter.

The problems of perception are compounded when we conduct intercultural or interracial interviews. These interviews can often lead to erroneous conclusions when we generate implicit information. For example, in employment interviews, we might be making an incorrect inference if we interpreted the laid-back and apparently unenthusiastic behavior of a Native American applicant as lack of interest in the job.[4] Such behaviors could reflect a culturally learned way of interacting. (See the feature "Cultural Bias in the Employment Interview.")

■ Determining Fact or Opinion

When we act as interviewers, we must judge whether a statement is a fact or an opinion. If it is an opinion, we must decide how much weight to give it.

Sometimes it's easy to tell that a statement is an opinion because the interviewee uses a qualifier like "I think," "it might be," or "maybe." When those indicators are not present, the interviewer might have to ask specifically whether the person is stating a fact or an opinion. In the movie *My Cousin Vinny,* lawyer Vinny Gambini is interviewing a witness—his girlfriend and auto expert Mona Lisa Vito. In his direct examination, he asks her to identify the make of a car based on a photo of tread marks over a curb. After she identifies the car, he pointedly asks, "Is that your opinion or is that a fact?" to which she replies that it's a fact and proceeds to explain why. The opposing attorney, of course, has the option of challenging the supposed "fact," but even if her testimony is classified as "opinion," the follow-up questions and explanation add weight and credibility to it. Even outside a courtroom, statements with the most credibility, believability, and importance have the greatest impact on us.[5]

Cultural Bias in the Employment Interview

This article excerpt demonstrates why interviewers need to be sensitive to the cultural background of interviewees. The article describes the difficulties that Native Americans, specifically Navajo students, face in a typical U.S. employment interview.

It's important to understand the unfortunate dynamic of interview bias and how it impacts judgments made of traditional Native Americans. Some typical criteria used to evaluate students during on-campus interviews are:

■ Self-Confidence: Strong handshake, good eye contact.
■ Goal Orientation: Able to express short- and long-term goals.
■ Enthusiasm: An animated conversationalist with an easy smile.
■ Leadership: Able to provide examples of specific individual achievements and strengths.

What many recruiters fail to consider is that these may be false indicators of the desired qualities and more a matter of style than of substance. Despite the American "ideal," traits of confidence, commitment to the job, and even leadership can be deeply woven into a quiet and unpresumptuous character. The challenge for recruiters is to discover the qualities that are really there, perhaps hidden by cultural norms.

Before an interview even begins, traditional Navajo students from a rural environment might find themselves at a disadvantage. From their cultural perspective, it might appear aggressive to firmly grip a person's hand. They are accustomed to greeting people by gently touching palms with a light grasp. Additionally, to give direct eye contact to a person in authority is considered discourteous. They may be paying a compliment to a recruiter by treating him or her with respect, but the recruiter who evaluates Native American candidates by Anglo standards would make the assumption that they are insecure or shy.

The frequently asked questions pertaining to goals such as "Where do you see yourself in three to five years?" are another area in which a traditional native student could fail to shine. In their culture, making specific plans for the future and then talking about them is a strange concept. They live more in the present and value the wisdom of the past. In their framework, it makes no sense to try to establish long-term goals because the ability to make them happen is not in human hands. Therefore,

Native Americans do not often talk about achieving specific goals in given timelines. Instead, they tend to think more holistically about the type of person they want to be and the kind of life they are destined to live They will then choose paths open to them that allow fulfillment of their personal vision.

Enthusiasm is always listed as a crucial element in prospective candidates, but few people can explain how to measure enthusiasm objectively. When asked to be more specific about that quality, several employers on our campus cited behaviors such as smiling, talking in an animated manner, and asking numerous questions. These are not behaviors typical of traditional Native American students, who tend to be quiet, reserved in expression of feelings, nonassertive, and nonaggressive. Often their tone of voice and pace of speech is lower and slower than that to which recruiters are accustomed.

Leadership skills demonstrated through personal achievements and the ability to discuss individual strengths are uncomfortable areas for many Native Americans. Traditional Navajo culture emphasizes community, family, and collective tribal achievements rather than individual accomplishments. They are reluctant to discuss their own strengths because they do not wish to put themselves above others or to appear boastful. In their culture, these are unappealing characteristics. In addition, they have different criteria for success. Professional, economic, and academic success might not be as important as are the virtues of generosity, sharing, and the development of wisdom. They do not seek to be singled out for praise and reward because they have been taught not to compete but to act instead with a spirit of. cooperation. Native people who achieve personal success are not held in as high esteem by their peers as those who have made a success of helping others. . . .

In order to drive home more clearly how awkward the Anglo interviewing process can be for Native Americans, shift paradigms and imagine an interview based on very traditional Navajo values. The criteria might look something like this:

- Respect: A tactful handshake and limited eye contact.
- Harmony: At ease with self and the world; able to be comfortable with silence, and be more intent on listening than talking.
- Cooperation: A history of working with others for the good of the group; avoids making boastful statements about self.
- Leadership: Follows the concept that true leadership is through quiet example—deeds, not words.

The interview setting would also be vastly different. It would take place in a remote natural environment, far from the noises of traffic and ringing phones. It would last a minimum of two hours, during which the recruiter would appear to have all the time in the world. Instead of direct questions and rhetoric, the interviewer might tell stories and use analogies to describe the hiring organization. The polite candidate would be expected to listen, reflect, and respond only when urged to do so.

Sound like a curious system? This process would seem no more foreign to majority students than the on-campus interview system practiced today feels to many traditional Native Americans.

Source: F. Mahoney, "Adjusting the Interview to Avoid Cultural Bias," *Journal of Career Planning & Employment,* 52 (1992), 41–43. Reprinted from the Spring 1992, *Journal of Career Planning & Employment,* with permission of the National Association of Colleges and Employers, copyright holder.

■ Redundancy

Another characteristic of the way we communicate is that we are redundant in conveying information. We include a lot of superfluous stimuli that really aren't informative, and we often repeat our message (for instance, saying hi while waving to someone). Redundancy refers to a lack of informative value in a message—in other words, the message does not reduce uncertainty. The person already knows what is being conveyed. **Redundancy** is that part of a message that is predictable because of the application of language or repetition; it's extraneous and superfluous information.

Redundancy is more a matter of degree than of absolute presence or absence. Much of our language includes verbiage that is unnecessary to accurately convey meaning. Look at the following sequence of sentences:

1. The man who called yesterday, Bob, called again and said that he would like to buy the '97 blue Chevy van.
2. Man who called yesterday, Bob, called, said he would buy Chevy van.
3. Bob called. He buy van.

While the third line might not be correct grammatically, it conveys essentially the same meaning as the first two because of the redundancy built into the language.

We also repeat ourselves. We also repeat ourselves. The second "We also repeat ourselves" was redundant and conveyed little information to you unless you skipped the first sentence. Although little information is conveyed, repetition does provide emphasis and clarification. In interviews, we often repeat questions or ask for the answer to be repeated to ensure accuracy. The more redundant a message, the less information is conveyed, but the more likely the message will be received in spite of competing noise, and thus the greater the overall accuracy.[6]

Sometimes, too, we ask questions to which we already know the answers because we are seeking implicit rather than explicit information. For example, after conducting an appraisal interview with an employee, a supervisor might ask the employee to summarize the plan of action they have developed to improve the employee's performance. The answer should be redundant with what the supervisor already knows. However, the supervisor wants a chance to infer whether the employee truly understands the plan. Any errors in the employee's summary can then be corrected.

■ The Right Questions and the Right Answers

The successful interview depends on two key principles: asking the right questions and receiving the right answers. This sounds like stating the obvious, but there is more to these two principles than you might first think. Let's examine each principle in turn.

Asking the right questions.   In most interviews, it may seem a simple process to frame your questions and ask them. However, a number of things can go wrong. For instance:

- You might ask a question that leads in the wrong direction.

- You might ask a question in an unclear manner.
- You might ask a question that requires a more trusting relationship with the interviewee than you have established.

Sometimes you have the right question, but you ask the wrong person. Careful analysis of what you need to know and who is likely to know it will help you ask the right person the right question.

Getting the right answers.   Getting the right answer depends on the interviewee's understanding what you are asking, possessing the appropriate information, being willing to be honest, and having the ability to convey that information effectively. All of these requirements sometimes present difficulties.

Interviewees may be confused by a question and therefore provide irrelevant or even inaccurate information. Thus the interviewers must be certain that the questions are phrased clearly, often asking the interviewee if the question is understood. You've seen courtroom dramas in which an attorney rephrases a question to a witness in a number of different ways, trying to get a clear and precise response.

In some cases, the interviewee may truly not have the answers you are seeking. When I first started advising students, the students often asked me questions for which I didn't know the answers. Fortunately, I usually knew whom to ask to find the answers the students needed. Sometimes, however, interviewees are so anxious to please the interviewers that they make up answers, even when they don't have the information. To determine when the interviewee is just guessing or giving an opinion, skilled interviewers watch the nonverbal cues that accompany the verbal response.

Misrepresentation and deception always undermine the accuracy of information, and many interviewers almost seem to invite these problems. For example, in an appraisal interview, what do you think employees are likely to say in response to their boss's asking, "Well, how do you think your performance has been?" The employees are likely to sing their own praises and equivocate about any shortcomings. In other situations, too, interviewees may have specific reasons for hiding the truth or deceiving the interviewer. Creating the proper interview environment to gain accurate information requires planning and skill.

In some interviews, people's reluctance to answer questions may reflect learned cultural behavior rather than avoidance or deception. One study of intercultural interviews examined a visa application process in which citizens of a West African country were interviewed by consulate members from a Western culture. The applicants often displayed broken, nonassertive speech patterns and limited eye contact, which in fact were typically displayed in their culture when dealing with higher-status individuals. However, the interviewers responded to those behaviors as though they reflected potential deception.[7] The researchers emphasized the need for interviewers to understand the cultural norms affecting interviewee behavior.

There are a number of additional issues related to developing and asking questions, as you will see in the next section.

Questions: Tools of the Interview

The most distinguishing and critical feature of an interview is the question. However, the term *question* is used here in a very global sense. A **question** in this discussion, refers to any behavior (usually spoken words) designed to elicit information from other people. As this definition indicates, we are concerned with more than grammatical questions that have a question mark at the end. Here are some examples of questions that fit the definition:

- "What are some of your favorite courses you've taken?"
- "Tell me about some of your favorite courses."
- "I really like my communication courses." (Relying on a reciprocated disclosure such as "I had one, but I didn't get much out of it. The textbook was pretty hard.")
- "Our company is looking for individuals with strong communication backgrounds." (Stated for the purpose of hearing how the interviewee responds.)
- "I'd like to know about any courses you have had that you see as relevant to this job."
- Interviewee: "I had courses in interpersonal communication and public speaking." The interviewer nods and remains silent—an invitation for the interviewee to continue by describing the courses and their relevance to the job.

As these examples indicate, a statement or even a nonverbal behavior like a nod can constitute a question in an interview.

■ *The Psychology of Questions*

To understand how questions work in interview situations, we need to explore several points concerning the psychology of questions.

Questions influence thought. Chapter 4 dealt with how meaning is attributed to what is perceived, particularly spoken words. All of the information contained in that chapter is relevant to understanding the dynamics involved in asking questions in an interview. It's particularly important to realize, though, that the questions an interviewer asks affect the way the interviewee is thinking.

"Don't think about a big pink elephant with large, flopping pink ears!" As you read that line, what happened? You probably thought about a large pink elephant. Despite the word "Don't," your mind couldn't help but envision the elephant image. In a like manner, questions affect the thoughts of the interviewee. When communication occurs, a reaction is triggered in the interviewee.

Interviewers usually have a pretty good idea of what the reaction is going to be, and that is why they choose the words they do. But they can't always predict what is going on in the mind of an interviewee, especially if they don't know the person very well. Suppose you were interviewing a job applicant and you asked him, "How would you feel about having to relocate to Duluth?" You would probably expect the applicant to say "Fine" or "I guess that would be okay," but what if the applicant became teary-eyed and unable to answer the question? According to attribution theory, you would try to explain this unexpected behavior. You might ask the applicant what was wrong, not realizing that his father was killed last week in a car accident while driving through Duluth.

While this is a rather dramatic example, it is important to remember that each question evokes a response from the interviewee. Mentioning Duluth might evoke memories of the times the applicant passed through that city with his family on summer vacations. Or it might call up images of a good friend he knew from Duluth. Each question can potentially evoke a number of associated meanings and memories that affect the interviewee.

Cultural norms also affect the appropriateness of questions and the underlying meaning of words and phrases. A question that is appropriate to ask in the context of one culture might be totally inappropriate in another. For example, a typical Japanese employment interview might include questions about your family and about your commitment to previous organizations—questions that a typical American might react to as overly personal. In an intercultural situation, the interviewer also needs to be attuned to language issues. Those who have learned English as a second language may be unfamiliar with many U.S. idiomatic phrases. The question "What type of people rub you the wrong way?" may elicit some bewilderment and perhaps even embarrassment, especially if followed with "How do you feel about starting at the bottom?"

Questions can be sequenced to direct thought.   The way questions are sequenced can direct the interviewee's thinking. Sometimes this principle is used intentionally in a persuasive interview, in which the interviewer is trying to influence the conclusions that the interviewee reaches. You've seen this done in many courtroom dramas. The lawyer asks a series of questions, trying to get the witness to reach a conclusion supporting the lawyer's case.

LAWYER	You've testified that you saw my client stab the deceased at 8:00 P.M. as you looked outside your window into the window next door on December 31. I want you to think back to that day. Okay?
WITNESS	Okay.
LAWYER	Do you remember what you were doing from around 6 till 8?
WITNESS	Sure.
LAWYER	What?
WITNESS	I had dinner around 6:30 and then I watched TV.
LAWYER	What did you watch on TV that night?
WITNESS	Let's see, I usually watch the news at 6:30 and then, that was a Thursday night, so I was probably watching *Crime-Stoppers*.
LAWYER	*Crime-Stoppers*—that's the show where they re-create crimes with actors and then ask people to call in with tips, is that right?
WITNESS	Yes, that's right.
LAWYER	What crimes were they depicting that night?
WITNESS	I'm not sure.
LAWYER	Take a little time. Do you remember a crime about a stabbing victim?
WITNESS	Yes, I know I've seen one like that.
LAWYER	What do you remember about that?

WITNESS	A man was seen through his living room window to be stabbing a woman.
LAWYER	Just like in this case?
WITNESS	That's right.
LAWYER	Here's a photo of the actor who played the part of the stabber. Doesn't he look a lot like my client?
WITNESS	Well, I guess he does, sort of.
LAWYER	Do you think that maybe that's the image you remember because you really couldn't make out enough details of the man through the darkness and two sets of windows?
WITNESS	I guess it's possible, maybe, I just don't know.

Questions arouse questions.   Questions not only stimulate thoughts concerning the specific subject; they also stimulate other cognitive reactions in an interviewee. Often these reactions lead to questions in the interviewee's mind.

Imagine your boss calling you into her office after you have been working at a new job for two weeks and asking you, "How do you think you are fitting in here?" You would try to figure out why she was asking you that question. You

Effective lawyers know that the way they sequence their questions affects the witnesses' thoughts and subsequent responses.

would try to determine what she wanted to hear, and you would probably attribute implicit meanings to her question. You might ask yourself, Is she planning on firing me? Have I done something I wasn't supposed to? Does she want me to tell her I love my job and she's a great boss?

The boss's question stimulated your thinking about her motives and the underlying meaning of her questioning. Because of this phenomenon, one rule presented in the next chapter is that interviewers should clearly state their purpose for the interview. Your boss could have reduced a lot of your uncertainty and anxiety by indicating that after two weeks, every new employee meets with the boss to discuss how things are going, to determine if the training has been sufficient, and to decide on any additional training that might be helpful to ensure the employee's success.

Questions vary in the thought required to answer them.   Read the following set of questions and think about how you would answer them.

1. What jobs have you had in your life?
2. Describe a task that you were assigned in your last job.
3. What did you learn about yourself through your job experiences?
4. Explain why you would prefer a job that paid very well but that you didn't like or a job that didn't pay very well but that you really liked.

As you read the questions, you probably noticed that some were easier to answer than others. Each question differed in terms of the kind of thought required of you.

1. *Questions of fact or recall* simply require you to recollect a certain piece of information and repeat it. **Questions of fact or recall** are generally the easiest to answer. In our set of four questions, the first was a question of fact or recall requiring you simply to remember and list your previous jobs.
2. *Convergent thinking questions* require you to translate, explain, draw a conclusion, or make some association. **Convergent thinking questions** focus your thinking into a narrow channel (your thoughts converge on one issue). Although these cognitive activities depend on the facts you have at hand, they require more effort than simple questions of fact. If you were asked to explain a process, that would be a convergent thinking question. So would being asked to phrase complicated instructions in terms that another person without your expertise could understand. Question 2 in the list of examples required you to provide an explanation and thus demanded convergent thinking.
3. *Divergent thinking questions* require you to elaborate, synthesize, analyze, or solve a problem. In essence, you are required to expand your thinking beyond a narrow scope (your thoughts diverge from a focus point). Answering a **divergent thinking question** requires more time than the first two types of questions; you must consider the facts and think through the analysis. Question 3 in the list of examples was a divergent thinking question because it required you to analyze a variety of job experiences and reach some conclusions.

4. **Evaluative questions** involve assessing the conditions surrounding some issue and coming to conclusions based on your values and preferences. **Evaluative questions** usually involve all the other types of thought—recalling, convergent thinking, and divergent thinking. Question 4 in our list of examples required you to make an evaluation that reflected how you would regard money as opposed to contentment in your job.

In our examples, any of the last three questions could actually be questions of fact or recall if you had previously thought about the issue. For instance, you might have previously considered whether you preferred a job you liked doing or a job that paid well. In that case, answering the question would simply involve recalling the conclusion you had previously reached.

If an interviewee has not considered a question before, the interviewer must provide time for the interviewee to think. Sometimes it is helpful to have the interviewee think aloud. This lets the interviewer understand which issues the interviewee is taking into consideration and helps reduce misunderstanding. In answering question 4 for the first time, you might share the following with the interviewer:

> Well, I went to college in the hopes of finding a job that paid really well. I do have a lot of loans to pay off, and I have a whole list of things I want to buy as soon as I have the money. On the other hand, it could be really depressing doing a job every day that I hate. I did that one summer and promised myself never to stay in a job I didn't like. On the other hand, there are so many things I like that I can't imagine being unable to find things I liked in a job that paid well, so I guess I'd choose "paid well."

Think about a time when you have been interviewed—for a job, by your advisor, by a supervisor, or by a pollster. What questions were asked that you found particularly difficult to answer? What made them difficult to answer? What questions were the easiest for you to answer? Why?

■ Phrasing Questions

Because questions have a direct impact on the thoughts and subsequent responses of interviewees, to be an effective interviewer you need to understand the options available in phrasing questions. The goal of a good question is to gain valid information. The way you phrase a question influences your chances of achieving that goal.

Ideally, you want to phrase questions in such a way as to make them easily understood without unduly influencing the response. But a number of language-related problems can affect your interview questions. You need to choose words that are understandable, avoid jargon or unfamiliar technical terms, and avoid emotionally laden terms (such as vulgarities or swearing) that might distract, embarrass, or otherwise inhibit the interviewee.

Ambiguity and confusion.   You need to be particularly careful about ambiguous or misleading language as exemplified in Table 8.2. To overcome such problems

Table 8.2 Ambiguous and Confusing Questions

Sample Question	Problem
Have you had this trouble often?	How many times is often?
Did you find that report difficult?	Difficult in what way—to read, to understand, to digest?
Tell me about your education.	Does the question include kindergarten, grade school, college? What does the interviewer want to know about each stage?
Have you been working with this type of computer for a while?	How long is a while?
Tell me about your work experience. What jobs did you like the most and why, and what supervisory experience did you have in those jobs?	Which question should be answered first? Can the interviewee keep track of all these questions while formulating the answers?

in large-scale surveys, pilot studies are often conducted in which respondents are asked to circle any words that are confusing or ambiguous. This allows the questions to be rewritten before the full-scale survey is conducted. Table 8.2 lists some examples of ambiguous questions and indicates what makes them ambiguous.

A similar problem occurs when you run questions together, asking more than one question at a time. Not only does this confuse interviewees, but it makes it difficult for them to remember which questions they've answered and which questions they haven't. The last entry in Table 8.2 is an example of a confusing sequence of multiple questions.

Leading questions.   One particular type of phrasing problem is the use of leading questions. **Leading questions** are questions in which the interviewer conveys the expected or desired answer to the interviewee. When leading questions are used intentionally, they aren't really questions at all because they are not sincere attempts to gain information. However, most leading questions are unintentional; they occur because the interviewer is careless in phrasing questions.

Your desired response is evident when you ask a friend, "Would you rather go see this really exciting new adventure film or sit home and watch another night of boring reruns?" or when you ask your boss, "I don't suppose you would let me have Friday night off, would you?" If you're truly looking for information, your questions should be designed to elicit the interviewee's own genuine thoughts.

■ *Types of Questions*

In addition to creating problems in the way you phrase a question, you can inadvertently hamper information acquisition by asking questions that are too narrow or too broad. You might get a yes or no response when you really need elaboration, and vice versa.

Questions can be placed on a continuum according to the number of options for answers available to the interviewee. The options can range from just one answer to a nearly infinite number of possibilities. Communication researchers refer to these extremes in terms of openness and closedness. As shown in Figure 8.2, questions can be placed anywhere along the continuum, from highly closed to highly open.

Closed questions.   As you can gather from Figure 8.2, **closed questions** are questions in which the interviewee is restricted in the choice of potential answers. Multiple-choice exams are good examples of a closed-question format, since the respondents are forced to choose from among a limited number of choices.

Bipolar questions are closed questions for which there are only two choices. True-false questions are bipolar questions. So are questions that must be answered yes or no, right or wrong, or agree or disagree. These questions are the type used in highly directive interviews. The amount of information gained from such questions is very limited. Sometimes, in fact, bipolar questions force individuals to give answers that do not really reflect their thoughts. Courtroom dramas on TV and in the movies again offer a handy example. Frequently you've seen a witness trying to explain a point of view or a complicated situation, but the lawyer (who does not want this information presented) interjects, "Your honor, please direct the witness to answer only yes or no."

Here are some examples of closed questions:

Did you watch TV last night?
Do you have a favorite TV show?
Which show do you like better, *Baywatch* or *60 Minutes*?
Have you ever been to Brown County?
Do you agree or disagree with the statement "Everybody should have the opportunity to go to college"?
On a scale of 1 to 5, with 1 being the highest, how much did you like that movie?

Even though the choices might be narrow, the thought required to reach an answer can be difficult. Making a choice between two options can involve all the forms of thinking previously described.

Open questions.   In contrast to closed questions, for which the choice of answers is provided, **open questions** are questions for which the interviewee is

Figure 8.2

Continuum of Question Openness

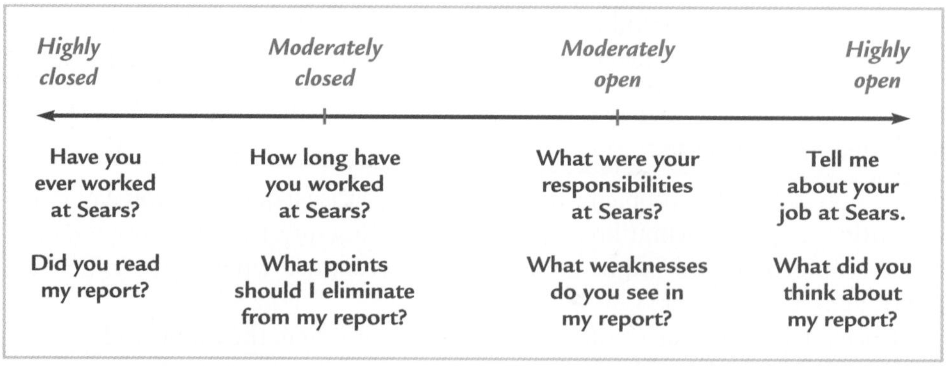

Highly closed	*Moderately closed*	*Moderately open*	*Highly open*
Have you ever worked at Sears?	How long have you worked at Sears?	What were your responsibilities at Sears?	Tell me about your job at Sears.
Did you read my report?	What points should I eliminate from my report?	What weaknesses do you see in my report?	What did you think about my report?

given freedom and responsibility for creating the answer. As the authors of an interviewing text have put it, open questions allow the interviewee "considerable freedom in determining the amount and kind of information to give."[8]

Because the interviewee is unrestricted in terms of the specific information to be shared, open questions give greater control to the interviewee than to the interviewer. Open questions also have the potential to evoke more depth and breadth of information than closed questions. Open questions usually begin with words like *What, Who, How, Why, Where, When,* and *Tell me.*

A question like "Where were you at 10:15 last night?" represents only a slight degree of openness. Because the question directs the interviewee to focus on providing a location at a particular day and time, there are a limited number of real choices. On the other hand, "Tell me about last night" is a more open question because the interviewee has greater freedom to choose what to focus on.

People frequently ask closed questions even when they really want the interviewee to respond more openly. When we ask something like "Did you see *Melrose Place* last night?" we often expect more than yes as a response. We expect people to tell us what they thought about the show, whether they liked it, and so on. Still, closed questions implicitly communicate to the interviewee that we don't want a very long answer. Therefore, they generally evoke a shorter response than open-ended questions.[9] As an interviewer, you need to consider carefully the effect your type of question has on the response.

Decide where to place each of these questions on the continuum shown in Figure 8.2.

Test Yourself

1. Have you been waiting very long?
2. What do you see as the best feature of this new computer?
3. Do you have any advice on how I can improve my performance?
4. How many times have you had to redo that report?
5. Would you like me to assign someone to help you with the year-end review?
6. Tell me a little about how the new production schedule works.
7. You don't really need to resubmit that, you know?

Primary and probing questions.   Another way of classifying questions is in terms of their relationship to the topic and to previous responses. **Primary questions** are questions that introduce a new issue or topic. Primary questions reflect the directive influence of the interviewer because the interviewer is making a choice about the interview's focus.

Imagine yourself conducting an employment interview in which the focus has been on the applicant's schoolwork and courses taken. Then you say, "Tell me about your job at Sears." That would be a primary question, changing the direction of the interview. Primary questions can be prepared in advance if the interviewer develops a schedule of issues to be covered.

To signal to the interviewee that the topic is about to change, effective interviewers use **transitions.** In the employment interview, you might use the following transition: "I think we've covered your college education fairly well. Let's talk about your work experience now."

Probing questions are questions that are created in response to an answer that the interviewee has presented. Probing questions are responses to responses. They usually involve asking for more information, explanation, elaboration, or clarification. Probing questions are a form of confirming response, as discussed in Chapter 3, because they let the interviewee know that the interviewer has heard the answer.

Table 8.3 presents a sample interview excerpt that uses both primary and probing questions. Probing questions are usually spontaneous, developed in direct response to the answers. You can plan on probing, but it is difficult to decide on specific probes because you don't generally know what the interviewee is going to say. Suppose you decided in advance to probe the applicant's job experience at Sears to find out if the applicant did any supervision. But in answering your open question about his job experience at Sears, the applicant might talk about his supervisory duties before you even got a chance to probe. Your planned probe would then become unnecessary.

Probes are a key element in effective interviews because they allow the interviewer to gather valuable information by adapting to the interviewee's responses. Primary questions are based on what interviewers assume they want to know, whereas probes allow for gathering information in areas that the interviewer

Table 8.3   Interview Excerpt with Primary and Probing Questions

Situation: A boss is visiting with an employee who has been with the company for only two months.

Speaker	Remarks	Type of Question
Interviewer	How have you been adjusting so far?	Primary question
Interviewee	Pretty well. I really like what I'm learning and getting to do.	
Interviewer	What problems have you encountered so far?	Primary question
Interviewee	I'm still not sure about how much information to include in my weekly reports.	
Interviewer	What have you been including so far?	Probing question
Interviewee	Well, I've put in a list of the contacts I made and the hours spent on each project, plus a description of what I did on each project that week and my plans for the next week.	
Interviewer	How much time is it taking to write all that up?	Probing question
Interviewee	About three hours.	
Interviewer	I don't really need the extensive descriptions or plans for the following week. Why don't you skip those for a while?	
Interviewee	That will help a lot.	
Interviewer	How are things going on the McPherson campaign?	Primary question
Interviewee	I've almost got all the data entered, but I'm still waiting for two marketing reports.	
Interviewer	Which reports are those?	Probing question

might not have considered. Being skilled at probing requires strong listening skills, especially because the interviewer's attention is divided between listening to the interviewee's response and developing the next question.

The Internet is filled with transcripts of interviews. Type in "interview" in a search engine and locate an interview (there are a lot with popular rock artists). What connection do you notice between the quality of the question and the quality of the response? Can you identify the type of thinking required by different questions? Can you identify different types of questions: closed, bipolar, open, leading, primary, and probing?

Summary

Interviewing is a goal-structured form of interpersonal communication in which one party plays the role of interviewer and the other party plays the role of interviewee. In this definition, the term *goal-structured* implies a predetermined purpose and a particular set of expectations about how the interview will progress. As *interpersonal* communication, interviews involve a transactional influence between the parties as well as the presence of a relationship. The term *party* is used to indicate that there can be more than one interviewer or interviewee. Among the *role* behaviors expected of the interviewer are asking questions, seeking information, and controlling the pace and direction of the interview. Interviewees are expected to provide answers to the questions.

In general, the major purpose of an interview is to gain information. Information action interviews involve collecting information for the purpose of decision-making, problem solving, or report writing. Employment, or selection, interviews involve collecting information for the purpose of making a decision about an individual's appropriateness for a certain job. Problem-solving and counseling interviews are aimed at helping individuals better understand personal issues and develop a plan of action. In persuasive interviews, interviewers manipulate or seek information to help them influence the interviewee. Complaint interviews, usually initiated by the interviewee, deal with some problem related to the interviewer or parties affiliated with the interviewer.

Interviews can be either directive or nondirective in their format. Directive interviews involve preparing a list of specific questions in advance. They give the interviewer a lot of control over the direction and focus of the interview. Nondirective interviews attempt to give the interviewee the control over the direction and focus of the interview. In the nondirective interview, the interviewer may have prepared an objective, an opening statement, and only one or two questions.

Since gaining information is a frequent goal of interviews, you need to understand how information relates to interviewing. There is a strong connection between the perceptual abilities of the interviewer and the ability to gain accurate and complete information. Explicit information comes from direct responses to questions, whereas implicit, or derived, information consists of the conclusions the interviewer reaches by means of the perceptual processes discussed in Chapter 3. The interviewer must determine whether the interviewee's responses are statements of fact or opinion. Redundancy involves responses that are not informative and that do not reduce uncertainty, however it can help ensure accuracy.

Gaining relevant information involves asking the right questions and receiving the right answers. We may ask questions that are poorly worded or addressed to the wrong person. Interviewees may be reluctant to share information or may attempt to deceive us, meaning that we are not getting the right answers. To ensure open and honest responses, interviews require the establishment of a trusting relationship.

Questions, the basic tools of the interview, can be broadly defined as any behavior designed to elicit information from other people. Questions affect a person psychologically. They spawn a number of associated thoughts in the interviewee of which the interviewer may not even be aware. This means that the interviewee may respond in an unexpected manner. Interviewers need to be sensitive to cultural and racial differences in the wording and selection of questions as well as in the interpretation of answers. Interviewees' thoughts can also be directed by the manner in which questions are sequenced. Interviewees are stimulated, too, to form their own mental questions; they may wonder about interviewers' motives and about possible repercussions of certain answers.

Questions vary in terms of the thought required to answer them. Questions of fact or recall simply require remembering stored information. Convergent thinking questions require interviewees to explain or translate some piece of information, whereas divergent thinking questions require analysis, synthesis, and problem solving. Evaluative questions, which require assessment and judgment, usually involve all three other types of thought.

Interviewers need to consider how the language and phrasing of a question can impact the response. Using language that is confusing or ambiguous will hamper the interviewer's ability to gain accurate and complete information. A leading question can even convey the interviewer's desired answer to the interviewee.

Questions can be placed on a continuum of closed to open, reflecting the degree to which an interviewee simply chooses from a narrow set of answers (closed questions) or enjoys freedom in deciding what to say (open questions). Bipolar questions are a specific type of closed question from which the interviewee selects from only two choices, such as yes and no. Questions can also be categorized as primary or probing. Primary questions introduce a new issue or topic and signal a change in the direction of the interview. Probing questions are follow-up questions that seek more information about the last response given by the interviewee.

Key Terms

interviewing   A goal-structured form of interpersonal communication in which one party plays the role of interviewer and the other party plays the role of interviewee.

information action interviews   Interviews that involve collecting information that helps the interviewer in taking some action, specifically decision-making, problem solving, or report writing.

employment interviews   Interviews that involve making decisions about the appropriateness of a given individual for a particular job; selection interviews.

selection interviews   Interviews that involve making decisions about the appropriateness of a given individual for a particular job; employment interviews.

problem-solving interviews   Interviews designed to help the interviewee analyze some problem and/or develop a plan of action.

counseling interviews   Interviews designed to help interviewees analyze and better understand themselves.

persuasive interviews   Interviews in which the interviewer seeks to persuade or influence the interviewee.

complaint interviews   Interviews usually initiated by the interviewee in response to a problem with the interviewer or a party affiliated with the interviewer.

directive interviews   Interview format in which the interviewer prepares a list of specific questions in advance and maintains primary control of the interaction.

nondirective interviews   Interview format in which the interviewer considers the objective, prepares the opening, and plans one or two questions but allows the interviewee to have primary control over the interaction.

information   Anything we perceive that reduces our uncertainty.

explicit information   Information based on direct statements made in response to a question.

implicit information   Information not explicitly presented but based on inferences, impressions, and attributions.

derived information   Information not explicitly presented but based on inferences, impressions, and attributions; implicit information.

redundancy   That part of a message that is predictable because of the application of language rules or repetition.

question   Any behavior (usually spoken words) designed to elicit information from other people.

questions of fact or recall   Questions that require you to recollect a certain piece of information and repeat it.

convergent thinking questions   Questions that require you to translate, explain, draw a conclusion, or make some association.

divergent thinking question   Questions that require you to elaborate, synthesize, analyze, or solve a problem.

evaluative questions   Questions that require you to assess the conditions surrounding some issue and come to conclusions based on your values and preferences.

leading questions   Questions in which the interviewer conveys the expected or desired answer to the interviewee.

closed questions   Questions in which the interviewee is restricted in the choice of potential answers.

bipolar questions   Closed questions for which there are only two choices, such as yes and no.

open questions   Questions for which the interviewee is given freedom and responsibility for creating the answer.

primary questions   Questions that introduce a new issue or topic.

transitions   Statements that signal to the interviewee that a change is about to take place, usually from one topic area or issue to another.

probing questions   Questions created in response to an answer that the interviewee has presented.

Review Questions

1. Define interviewing and explain the components of the definition.
2. Briefly explain the five major types of interviews described in this chapter.
3. Explain how interviews can be placed on a continuum from highly directive to highly nondirective.
4. In what ways do opinions and redundancy affect an interview?
5. What is the relationship between questions and thought?
6. Identify and describe several different types of questions.

Chapter 9

Interviewing: Skills for Interviewers and Interviewees

Objectives

Studying this chapter will allow you to:

1. Explain why a clear purpose is necessary in planning an interview.
2. Explain the major question sequence patterns.
3. Identify the elements that make up an effective opening.
4. Identify the elements that make up an effective closing.
5. Describe some of the basic skills needed to be an effective interviewer.
6. Describe some of the basic skills needed to be an effective interviewee.

Chapter 8 described a number of different types of interviews: information action interviews, employment (selection) interviews, problem-solving and counseling interviews, persuasive interviews, and complaint interviews. There are entire texts devoted to each of these types, so this chapter obviously cannot cover all the skills and procedures needed. Instead, this chapter will focus on the most general form of interview—the information action interview. In fact, the skills needed to gather information effectively provide the basis for many of the other types of interviews. We'll look at the skills required for both of the roles you'll play—interviewer and interviewee.

■ The Interviewer

Like most students, you probably think about interviewing primarily in terms of getting a job after graduation. You are most interested in how to be a good interviewee. However, during your life, you will probably play the role of interviewer much more often than the role of interviewee (unless you really, really have a hard time holding down a job!). For this reason, you need to learn how to conduct an interview effectively.

Most of your interviews will be fairly informal, and they won't require the extensive amount of preparation described in this chapter. However, studying the fundamental principles will improve your interviewing technique regardless of the degree of formality. In information action interviews, interviewers need to know their goals; develop an appropriate sequence of questions; plan the opening, body, transitions, and closing; and apply appropriate interviewing skills throughout the interaction.

Think about two times when you needed certain information from someone: one time when things went very smoothly and another time when the going was rough. What factors contributed to the smooth information-gathering experience? What made the other one difficult? What did you do differently? What was different about the interviewees?

■ *Planning and Preparation*

Interviews vary in terms of the amount of preparation needed to conduct them successfully. Sometimes interviews are fairly spontaneous and involve little planning. You might bump into a colleague in the hall and take the opportunity to get feedback about a recent report—in essence conduct an informal interview. On the other hand, you might spend a considerable amount of time investigating an issue, developing a schedule of questions, and arranging for interviews with carefully selected interviewees. But regardless of how formal or informal they are, all interviews require a consideration of the objectives and potential questions.

Determining your purpose and objectives. Preparing for an interview requires clearly thinking out the reason for the interview. You can start by completing the following statement:

When this interview is done, I want to be able to . . .

Your response should be something like this:

> . . . decide which computer system will be best for our division.
> . . . decide if this candidate is the best one for the job.
> . . . write a report on the market outlook for next year.
> . . . develop a plan for handling the company's high turnover.

Each of these responses indicates the focus and direction that the interview should take.

Defining your purpose in such a fashion is essential to developing an appropriate set of questions. What kind of information are you looking for? Remember from Chapter 8 that if you want highly quantifiable and comparable information, you may decide to use relatively closed questions. On the other hand, if you want a better sense of depth and detail, you'll want to incorporate open questions.

To define your interview's purpose requires some additional considerations, including an assessment of what you already know. You need to take an inventory of the information you already have. This inventory will allow you to deter-

Interviewing can be an effective way of gaining important information even in an informal setting, as long as there is a clear purpose.

mine what you don't know. Imagine that you have twenty-five pieces of an unassembled thirty-piece jigsaw puzzle. You are told that the five missing pieces are mixed in with a box of miscellaneous jigsaw pieces. How do you know what to look for? The easiest way is to assemble the twenty-five pieces you have and get a sense of the shapes and colors of the missing pieces. Once you've done that, you can more efficiently find the missing pieces. Similarly, knowing what information you are missing before conducting an interview will help you clarify your purpose and pinpoint your objectives.

Once you know what information you are seeking, you can start investigating potential interviewees. Many times, interviews are conducted with the wrong person. Whom would you want to talk to if you were trying to determine how to reduce employee turnover in the manufacturing division of your company? You wouldn't talk to the sales staff or to the research and design division. You would want to talk to the employees who have left, the employees who have stayed, their managers, and perhaps a specialist in organizational psychology. In other words, you can't decide whom to interview until you have defined your purpose clearly and decided what information you need.

Research.   In preparation for the interview, you need to gain enough understanding of the issues so that you can develop a coherent and relevant set of questions. Ironically, you sometimes have to conduct interviews to be able to conduct interviews. That is, you may have to conduct some preliminary interviews to help you understand the issues.

For example, suppose you were in charge of interviewing employees who had chosen to leave your company. What would you ask them? What issues would be important to cover? You would need to talk with various members of your organization to determine the kind of information they would like collected. After talking with a number of managers, you would be in a better position to develop a productive set of questions to ask during the exit interviews.

Part of the research process involves learning about issues through more conventional means. For instance, you can search books, journals, reports, or online articles for background information. This background work will allow you to ask more "educated" questions of your interviewee, rather than devoting valuable interview time to preliminary information that was available elsewhere.

Depending on the type of interview, you may also need to conduct research about the interviewee. Television talk shows and news magazine shows, for example, have staff members who collect and feed information to the show's host about the background of the guest—information the host can use to enhance the quality of the interview. Knowing the background of your interviewee can be useful in establishing rapport, developing relevant questions, and gaining insight into the answers.

Arranging the interview.   Before you get too far along in the planning process, you will need to contact the potential interviewee and request an interview. The best time and location depend on the type of interview you are conducting and the relationship you have with the interviewee. As a general rule, you want to make arrangements that are most convenient for the interviewee and that minimize his or her anxiety and reluctance to be open. For instance, you might conduct an employee problem-solving interview in the employee's own office.

Essentially, the process of setting up the interview is part of the interview opening, because you provide some initial information to the interviewee, such as the purpose of the interview and how much time is needed. If interviewees are reluctant to participate, you may have to engage in compliance-gaining and persuasive strategies. You need to convey to the interviewees how important their participation is to you and convince them (when possible) that they, too, will benefit.

Once you have secured the interviewee, you can adapt the rest of your planning and preparation to that particular person. For example, once a potential job candidate has agreed to an interview, the interviewer can thoroughly review the candidate's résumé or portfolio and develop specific questions related to those materials.

Developing a schedule of questions. Knowing the interviewee and researching the topic allow you to pinpoint the information you want to acquire in the interview. Knowing what you don't know allows you to develop appropriate and specific questions.

In interviewing employees who have quit, for instance, you might not know their feelings about the company, supervisors, colleagues, wages, or benefits. As a result, you would develop questions to explore each of these areas. Your interview purpose would dictate whether you prepared closed or open questions or some combination of the two.

Knowing that the sequence of questions affects the way people think, you can construct a schedule of questions that follows a relevant organizational structure. There are four organizational sequences often seen in interviews: the funnel, the inverted funnel, the tunnel, and the quintamensional design.

The **funnel sequence** (Figure 9.1) begins with broad, open-ended questions and then, through a process of probing questions, narrows to more focused, closed questions. Thus, the potential scope of answers looks like a funnel. Here is an example from an interview with an employee who has quit:

Figure 9.1

The Funnel Sequence of Interview Questions

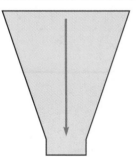

1. Tell me about your experience working here.
2. What was your supervisor like?
3. What problems did you have with your supervisor?
4. What was your supervisor's response to your request for time off?
5. Was your poor relationship with your supervisor the main reason you quit?

The funnel sequence is an effective format when the interviewer needs specific details from the interviewee but wants to let the interviewee control the initial direction of the interaction. The funnel sequence reduces the impact of any prejudgment by the interviewer. If the interviewer's first question was, "Was your poor relationship with your supervisor the main reason you quit?" the interviewee's thinking and responses might be prejudiced, as discussed in

Chapter 8. In addition, the interviewee might feel put on the spot and respond deceptively. If the supervisor relationship wasn't the problem, the interviewer would then have to develop a long series of guesses about the person's reasons for quitting.

There are times, however, when the reverse sequence is appropriate: starting with closed and narrow questions and then moving to more open questions. This is called an **inverted funnel sequence** (Figure 9.2) because the shape is like an upside-down funnel. Here is an example:

1. Who was your supervisor?
2. How often did you meet with your supervisor to discuss concerns?
3. How did your supervisor react to your concerns?
4. How did you feel about the way you were treated by your supervisor?
5. What could your supervisor have done to make your job more satisfying?

Inverted funnels help to get reluctant interviewees to open up. Can you see why? The inverted funnel moves from questions that demand little thought (questions of fact or recall) to more open, higher-order questions (divergent or evaluative questions). The interviewee has a chance to become comfortable with the interview process before being challenged with the harder questions.

The sequence used in surveys and other highly directive interviews involves a series of questions of approximately the same scope. This is called a **tunnel sequence** (Figure 9.3). The tunnel sequence does not usually involve much probing and is therefore not very amenable to the use of open questions. This format works when the interviewer has a good sense of the specific information that is desired, as in the following example:

1. Did you like your supervisor?
2. Did you like your fellow employees?
3. Were you happy with the responsibilities you were given?
4. Did you feel your wages were fair?
5. Did you feel you received raises that reflected your work performance?

The **quintamensional design sequence** involves five dimensions, as the name indicates. This design was developed by the creator of the Gallup Polls, George Gallup, primarily as a survey interview method.[1] The aim of the sequence is to determine the respondent's attitudes without undue influence by the interviewer. In Chapter 8, you read that you have to ask the right person the right question. Therefore, the first question in the quintamensional design seeks to find out if the interviewee even knows about the subject. The questions then pursue four other dimensions: what the interviewee thinks or feels about the subject, reaction to specific issues, reasons for the reaction, and finally the intensity of the attitude.

1. *Filter questions* (awareness of the issue): What do you know about the level of turnover in your division?
2. *Free answer* (open questions, uninfluenced attitudes): How do you feel about this level of turnover?

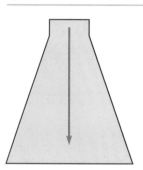

Figure 9.2

The Inverted Funnel Sequence of Interview Questions

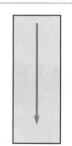

Figure 9.3

The Tunnel Sequence of Interview Questions

Table 9.1 Question Sequences and Their Potential Applications

Sequence Type	Use
Funnel	When interviewees are comfortable, confident, and eager to talk about the issues; when you are concerned about possibly influencing the interviewee's responses
Inverted funnel	When the interviewee is reluctant to talk openly; when you need to focus the interviewee on particular issues; when the interviewee's memory needs prodding
Tunnel	When the interview is part of a survey in which quantifiable answers are desired; when there is a known set of issues that needs to be covered; when the questions are all fairly similar in scope
Quintamensional design	When collecting attitudes and opinions is the primary goal; when you want to screen out those who don't have knowledge related to the issues; when you need to know the underlying reasons for a person's attitudes and the intensity of those attitudes; when you want to gain both open and specific responses

Source: Adapted from C. J. Stewart and W. B. Cash, Jr., *Interviewing: Principles and Practices,* 6th ed. (Dubuque, Iowa: Brown, 1991); and G. Gallup, "The Quintamensional Plan of Question Design," *Public Opinion Quarterly,* Vol. 11, (1947), 389–393.

3. *Specific issues* (closed or bipolar questions): Do you think higher wages would significantly reduce turnover?
4. *Reason why:* Why do you feel that way?
5. *Intensity of attitude:* How strongly do you feel about the need to address the turnover problem?

Each of the four types of question sequences has certain advantages and lends itself best to certain applications, as summarized in Table 9.1. Yet, the actual progress of an interview is not likely to follow any one sequence exactly. Rather, your typical interview will probably be a combination and variation of different patterns.

In fact, just as the quintamensional design sequence was created for a specific purpose, you can design sequences that meet your own needs. For instance, you might begin with a series of questions that follows the funnel sequence, then move to a tunnel sequence, and finish with the inverted funnel. In other words, you would start out with open questions to discover the general attitudes of the interviewee, shift to a series of planned specific questions, and then seek commentary on the issues discussed (for instance, by asking for suggested solutions). This progression is illustrated in Figure 9.4.

Develop a series of nine questions, dealing with any topic you like, that follows the pattern illustrated in Figure 9.4. Use three questions for each of the three segments.

Planning the opening. Interviews are effective only if the interviewee is comfortable enough to share the information you seek. The level of comfort is often established in the first few moments of an interview. Thus, getting the interview started in a positive manner will significantly enhance your chances for a productive interview. For this reason, you need to plan your opening carefully.

Because your questions will evoke questions in the interviewee's mind, you should allay any initial concerns the interviewee may have by explaining the purpose of the interview, the manner in which the interview is to be conducted, and what will be done with the information. You should write a few notes for yourself about the opening to ensure that you cover all these points. Remember, the interviewee may be uncertain about what to expect from you, and you should do your best to reduce that uncertainty.

The need to reduce uncertainty must be balanced, of course, with your need to avoid prejudicing the interviewee's answers by providing too much information. For instance, you would not want to say something like the following: "I'm going to be asking you questions about the food service here on campus. I want to get the administration to change the way things are done. I need to show that other students have the same complaints about the lack of variety and the poor quality that I do." This opening would bias any subsequent answers.

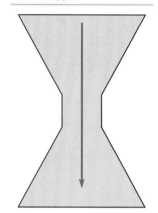

Figure 9.4

A Question Sequence Combining the Tunnel, Funnel, and Inverted Funnel Types

■ *Conducting the Interview*

Careful planning and preparation make the process of conducting the interview relatively easy. The actual interview generally progresses along the schedule you have developed, starting with the opening, moving through the body of questions, and finally reaching the closing.

The opening.   The **opening** is the initiation phase of the interview. Examine the following examples of an interview opening:

1. Hey, I need you to answer a few questions. First, what do you think of the food service?
2. Would you have about ten minutes to talk about the food service?
3. Hi. My name's Alicia Grover, and I'm part of a team of students doing a survey on students' views of the food service. If you could spare about ten minutes to answer a few questions, it would really help us out. Your answers will help in improving any food service problems.
4. Hello, Juan, I'm Angela Peabody, senior vice president for operations. I want to find out a little about your work experience and your major. I'll be making a recommendation to the company president about your job application. I guess you've already met with several other staff members and had a tour of our facilities. I noticed on your résumé that you were pretty active in intramural sports. What did you think of our company recreation center?

How would you respond to each of the four openings? If you're like most people, the first two openings wouldn't be very effective. The first opening would leave you feeling rather cold. You'd probably make some excuse for not answering the questions; after all, why should you answer? The second opening at least lets you know how long the interviewer wants to talk and what the subject will be, but it leaves several questions unanswered. Who is this person talking to you? What will be done with your responses? Why should you respond? The third and fourth openings, in contrast, include many of the elements that are needed in a good opening. The interviewers introduce themselves, making the process feel personalized. Both openings include a statement of purpose and let the interviewee know what will happen with the information. The third opening also includes a statement of how long the interview will last, and it attempts to solicit the interviewee's participation by indicating the value of the answers. The fourth opening adds another technique: It attempts to establish rapport by beginning the interview on an unrelated but positive topic, recreation and sports.

For an effective opening, you need to do the following:

- Explain the purpose of the interview and your role.
- Preview the interview.
- Motivate the interviewee as needed.
- Establish rapport (a positive and supportive relationship).
- Indicate how the information will be used.
- Follow norms of etiquette (introductions, shaking hands, and so forth).

The body. The **body** is the central part of the interview, the part in which you focus on collecting information by using your schedule of questions. The form of the body depends on how directive or nondirective you are, as well as on how precisely you have scheduled your questions.

Whatever form of questions you use, you will have to adapt to the interviewee. You can plan your half of the interaction only partially because each interviewee has different information to share and will respond uniquely to your questions. Don't let a well-scheduled set of questions get in the way of gaining valuable information.

Your question schedule lets you know where you are going, but the interviewee tends to be flying blind. Just as you gave a preview in the opening to help the interviewee understand the scope and direction of the interview, you should provide further directional signals throughout the body. As mentioned in Chapter 8, effective interviewers use *transitions* to signal their shifts from one significant issue to another (one primary question to another). You should also use transitions from the opening to the body and from the body to the closing. Transitions are like automobile turn signals; they let the interviewee know when you are about to change direction.

For instance, in our fourth sample opening, Ms. Peabody and Juan might talk for several minutes about the new recreation facilities and how beneficial they are to the employees. Before Ms. Peabody begins asking questions about Juan's work experience, she needs a transitional statement like this: "Your interest in intramural sports certainly fits in with a lot of our other employees. Let's talk a little now about some of the work experiences you've listed on your résumé."

As you progress through the body (particularly in a nondirective format), it is important to assess periodically the quality of the information you are receiving. Are you getting information that fulfills your purpose? Are you following up sufficiently to provide the depth of information you need? Sometimes, when interviews come to an end, the interviewer discovers that he or she never got to the meat of the issue. This can be particularly true with reluctant or evasive interviewees.

You need to be sensitive to the interviewee and adapt to his or her behavior. Besides assessing the information, you should assess the emotional and cognitive state of your interviewee. Some questions will be more challenging than others, both emotionally and cognitively. You may have to change your questions if the interviewee becomes distraught, angry, upset, or confused. You may have to provide opportunities for the interviewee to relax and regain composure. This can be done by engaging in a general conversation for a while or even by taking a break from the interview.

Showing sensitivity toward the interviewee is one way to maintain rapport. Throughout the interview, you want to continue to develop and nurture your relationship with the interviewee. Maintaining a positive, confirming atmosphere will enhance the flow of information and help you accomplish your interview goals. You can help maintain a positive relationship by periodically engaging in nontopical conversations, letting the interviewee ask questions, and freely offering information to the interviewee.

Finally, you need to consider issues of ethics and legalities in how you conduct the interview. For employment interviews, there are specific guidelines about what questions are considered illegal. Before conducting an employment interview be sure you are aware of these rules. Most companies have materials that spell out what questions are illegal. The general rule of thumb is that you can only ask questions regarding bona fide job requirements. This means that in general you cannot ask questions about a person's age, sex, race, ethnicity, sexual orientation, religion, physical appearance, marital status, family, or other personal issues because they don't relate to job skills.

Besides questions being deemed illegal, there are questions that can be considered unethical. As you learned in Chapter 8, questions are a powerful tool because of the psychological impact they can have. In any information action interview, asking questions that serve no purpose other than to embarrass, harass, or threaten the interviewee can be considered unethical. As with most questions of ethics there are many gray areas.

Some employers practice guerilla or stress interviewing in which they intentionally try to threaten interviewees' faces to see how they handle the pressure. Their tactics include openly criticizing the interviewee, asking rude or intimate questions, interrupting the interviewee, long periods of silence, and direct challenges of what the interviewee has said. The strategy is based on the belief that if interviewees can't handle a stressful interview, they can't handle a stressful job. But, is such interviewing ethical?

There is no absolute answer to this question. In a strict sense, violating the expectation that interviewees have for the way an interview is to be conducted could be considered unethical; and most people certainly don't expect a stress interview. In addition, asking questions that go beyond the areas previously agreed to by both parties could be considered unethical. However, you see this done sometimes on such television shows as *60 Minutes*, or *20/20*, when interviewers prod into areas that they had promised to avoid.

In sum, in an effective body, you should do the following:

- Follow a prepared schedule of questions.
- Adapt your questioning as needed.
- Use transitions to signal a change from one topic to another and from one major segment of the interview to another.
- Periodically assess the quality of the information you are receiving.
- Monitor the emotional and cognitive state of the interviewee and adapt accordingly.
- Display sensitivity to the interviewee.
- Be sure to engage in legal and ethical forms of questioning.

The closing.   In most situations, you want to maintain a positive relationship with the interviewee, even after the interview is over. Your interviews will often be with people with whom you have an ongoing relationship: coworkers, teachers, and clients, for instance. Hence, you need an effective **closing,** the final phase of the interview.

In closing, you want the interviewee to feel good about the interaction and to be willing to interact with you again if necessary. If, for example, you have to write a report based on your interviews, you may find that you need to contact interviewees again for additional clarification or elaboration. They will be resistant to providing that additional information if the interview ended negatively.

For an effective closing, do the following:

- Express your thanks and appreciation.
- Reconfirm the value of the interviewee's participation.
- Restate what will be happening with the information you have collected.
- Summarize what you have learned from the interviewee and ask for any corrections.
- Invite and respond to questions from the interviewee.
- Follow norms of etiquette (shake hands, escort the interviewee to the door or out of the building, and so on).

■ *Postinterview Follow-Up*

The postinterview stage is when you act on the information you have collected. That action may include developing a report or making a decision. This stage also includes actions designed to maintain a positive relationship with the interviewee. Concern for the interviewee doesn't stop with the end of the formal interview.

Depending on the formality of the interview, you may want to send a note of thanks to the interviewee. In addition, you may want to forward a copy of any report or document in which you incorporate information from the interviewee. You may choose to send a preliminary draft and ask for feedback or corrections of factual error. In some cases, as already mentioned, the postinterview process may include further discussion with the interviewee to gain additional information or clarification.

If the interviewee is an expert who would add credibility to your recommendations or decisions, you would probably identify her or him by name. Including

Table 9.2 Checklist of Steps for Conducting an Information Action Interview

After conducting an interview, either an actual one or a practice exercise, you can use this checklist to determine whether you completed all the steps.

_____ 1. Purpose: When this interview is done, I want to be able to . . .

_____ 2. List the issues or topics to be covered.

_____ 3. Decide on the best sequence of topics.

_____ 4. Decide who can best answer your questions and then arrange the interview.

_____ 5. Prepare your schedule of questions:
    _____ Develop primary questions to cover topics.
    _____ Develop secondary/follow-up questions.

_____ 6. Plan your opening:
    _____ State your purpose.
    _____ Motivate your interviewee.
    _____ Preview the interview.

_____ 7. Conduct the interview:
    _____ Open.
    _____ Ask primary questions.
    _____ Probe as necessary.
    _____ Close.

_____ 8. Develop a written summary of the responses.

_____ 9. Follow up appropriately with the interviewee.

the names of your sources—giving them proper credit for the vital information they have provided—also helps you maintain a positive relationship with them. If the information is treated collectively, however (for instance, if you summarize the reasons why ten former employees left the company), identifying the people by name is less important. Interviewees should be informed in the opening and reminded during the closing whether their responses will be handled anonymously.

Table 9.2 offers a short checklist of what an effective interviewer should do, from the preparation stage through the postinterview follow-up.

The Internet offers many advice pages for interviewing. Use a search engine and type in "employment interview" or "interviewing tips." Each page will have a wide variety of suggestions. In what ways is the advice similar to the principles discussed in this section? In what ways is it different?

■ General Interviewer Skills

The discussion thus far has dealt with the tasks involved in planning and conducting an interview. However, each interview is unique and variable, and there are a few fundamental skills that will help you carry out an interview effectively in many different situations. Effective interviewers know how to ask questions, probe, listen, record information accurately, adapt, and understand the interviewee.

Question formation and probing.   Not everyone has a knack for asking just the right question at just the right time. There is a definite skill to knowing what to ask and how to ask it. Many TV shows include scenes of detectives or investigators interviewing witnesses and suspects (for example, *NYPD Blue, Law and Order,* and *X-Files*). These scenes usually show the investigators skillfully asking carefully worded questions in an attempt to gain information. In reality, investigators spend years developing their interviewing skills to such a high degree.

Many employment interviews in the United States are conducted by managers or assistant managers, who often lack formal employment interviewing training. Not surprisingly, they often lack effective questioning skills.[2] They ask poorly worded, inappropriate, and even ridiculous questions ("If you were a piece of fruit, what would you be and why?").

These examples point up the need to think carefully about how you word your questions. Pay particular attention to the interviewee's responses to see if the interviewee has understood what you are asking for. Do this both for your primary questions and for your follow-up, probing questions. Probing effectively, which requires spontaneous adaptation to an interviewee's responses, demands even more skill than asking primary questions.

Listening.   Asking the right question won't do you any good if you don't hear or remember the response. Effective interviewers listen well. Each of the types of listening discussed in Chapter 3 can be applied to interviewing.

- *Listening objectively* ensures that you accurately gain the information the interviewee has to offer. This means listening to key points, maintaining your attention on the interview and the interviewee's responses, seeking clarification, summarizing, probing, and perception checking.
- At times you might have to *listen critically* to determine whether the information is reliable, valid, and consistent. Critical listening means that you evalu-

"How can I listen to you if you don't
say the things I want to hear?"

ate and analyze what you hear. In addition, you ask probing questions to eliminate any contradictory conclusions or impressions.

■ You might have to *listen personally* when you are involved in helping the other person or establishing rapport.

■ *Listening actively,* besides enhancing all the other types of listening, lets interviewees know that you are sincerely interested in their responses. Attending closely, probing, perception checking, paraphrasing, and summarizing are confirming responses that make interviewees feel valued and thus enhance the flow of information.

Recording the responses.   Many times you will be incorporating the information you gather in a report or other document. This means that you need some way to record the responses so that you don't forget them or recall them incorrectly. Also, interviewees do not like to be misrepresented, and you can increase their sense of security by carefully recording their responses.

There are three common options for recording interview information: memory, note-taking, and taping (usually audiotape).

1. Memory.   Although relying solely on your memory can cause you to lose specific information, it is an appropriate option if you need to remember only generalities and impressions. Employment interviews usually depend on the interviewer's memory, but this increases the likelihood of a biased selection. Usually, employment interviewers write themselves notes or fill out an evaluation form immediately after the interview. If you are going to use your memory as the primary way of retaining information, try to schedule your time so that you have a few minutes immediately after the interview to record the most important information.

2. Note-taking.   Compared to memory, note-taking provides a more accurate method of recording information; however, it is less efficient. Note-taking can slow down the interaction because the interviewee must sit and wait while you write yourself notes before asking the next question. By signaling the interviewee about what you consider important, note-taking can also bias the responses.

Note-taking works well if you are using a highly scheduled and standardized set of closed questions. Then you may simply have to make a mark by the choice the interviewee has made. In more open-ended interviews, you can learn to record key words and phrases rather than writing down a word-by-word response. Then, after the interview, you should find time as soon as possible to flesh out your notes.

3. Taping.   Tape-recording the interview is the most effective way to gain a complete and accurate transcript. Videotaping is even better than audiotaping because it captures more of the interviewee's nonverbals. However, audio or videotaping can increase the anxiety of the interviewee. The more obtrusive (obvious and visible) the recording device, the more it reminds interviewees that every word is being recorded. They may worry that someone will study the tape to analyze their every hesitation or slip of the tongue. Taping also prevents interviewees from saving face later by claiming that they were misquoted or misunderstood.

Thus, the less obtrusive the recording device, the better. Small tape recorders that rest on a table may come to be ignored by the interviewee as the interview proceeds. (There are some great examples of this phenomenon in the movie *All the President's Men.*) Whatever the taping device, however, ask the interviewee for permission before you begin taping.

Adapting. The process of adapting your behavior to a specific interviewee begins as soon as you decide whom to interview. Skilled interviewers use all the information they obtain about the interviewee during the research phase to adapt both the questions they plan and the manner in which they will conduct the interview.

The process continues during the interview itself. As a result of effective listening and astute observing, you will receive many cues from the interviewee to which you should adapt. In the exit interview scenario, imagine that you notice the interviewee getting upset when you begin asking about the impact of salary on turnover. This should lead you to modify your questioning. Adapting during the interview involves the ability to revise your schedule of questions and generate new questions in response to unexpected reactions or replies.

Social decentering. Social decentering provides one of the tools you need for adapting effectively. Chapter 7 discussed how being other-centered helps maintain interpersonal relationships. It provides a similar benefit in an interview situation.

Social decentering in interviewing involves putting yourself in the interviewee's shoes and considering his or her feelings, perspectives, and thoughts. This process aids you in developing appropriately adapted strategies. Suppose you are a manager conducting an appraisal interview with a new employee. You might consider asking, "How well do you think you are fitting in?" Through social decentering, however, you would predict that the new employee would probably feel very nervous about being evaluated. In such a face-threatening situation, your question might be taken as implying that the employee has had trouble getting along with coworkers. So you would reconsider the question, trying to imagine what type of inquiry you would feel comfortable answering if you were the new employee. You might change your question to "What aspects of your job seem to be going the best for you right now?"

The more different someone is from you, the more challenging it will be to decenter effectively. Chapter 8 offered some examples of how cultural differences can affect the interpretation of interviewee behavior. Cross-sex, interracial, and intercultural interviews require heightened social decentering skills. You need to be especially sensitive to how the differences affect communication.

Think of it this way: The greater the cultural difference, the more information you need. That information might come from your previous intercultural experiences related to the interviewee's background. If not, part of your preparation for the interview should include gaining additional cultural information. However, you may find yourself interviewing individuals of whom you have limited cultural understanding. In this case, you may have to depend on direct questioning of the interviewee to gain the necessary information. In essence, a new objective arises: to collect background information that helps you understand the primary information you are seeking.

Summary and Self-Analysis:

Interviewer Procedures and Skills

Use this summary list to assess your previous experience as an interviewer or your expectations about how well you would perform in each area.

Planning and Preparation

- Carefully determine the purpose and objectives of the interview.
- Conduct the necessary background research.
- Strategically arrange the time and place.
- Develop a well-prepared and thoughtful schedule of questions using the funnel, inverted funnel, tunnel, or quintamensional design sequence or an appropriate combination of these forms.
- Thoughtfully plan the opening.

Conducting the Interview

- Use an opening that previews, motivates, establishes rapport, informs, and is polite.
- Incorporate transitions to signal changes in the interview's direction.
- Periodically assess the information you are receiving and be sensitive to the interviewee's reactions.
- Use a closing that confirms the value of the interviewee's participation, informs, summarizes, invites questions, and is polite.

Postinterview Follow-Up

- After the interview, engage in appropriate follow-up behavior: Send a thank-you note; give proper credit; seek additional information, clarification, or feedback.

General Interviewer Skills

- Ask appropriately phrased questions.
- Ask probing questions that strategically follow up on responses.
- Apply a full range of listening skills.
- Accurately and discreetly record responses.
- Adapt to the unique aspects of the interviewee and the situation.
- Utilize understanding of other people (social decentering).

■ The Interviewee

Just as being an effective interviewer requires certain skills, so does being an effective interviewee. The interviewee is involved in this interpersonal, transactional process and therefore has a direct impact on the success of the interview. There is more to being a good interviewee than just answering questions.

In employment, appraisal, and counseling interviews, the interviewee has a vested interest in the outcome of the interview. A successful interview in these instances results in a tangible, positive outcome for the interviewee. However, vested interests can also undermine the effectiveness of an interview. In employment interviews, for instance, interviewers want honest and open answers, but answering openly and honestly can sometimes work against the interviewee's chance of getting the job. Regretfully, these interviews often violate a number of rules for effective interviewing. They become "games" in which interviewers paint a very positive picture of the job and the company (even when things are really miserable) and interviewees present themselves as ideal for the position (even when they really aren't). The result of such a game is usually high turnover: The employees aren't happy with the actual conditions they find in the workplace, and the supervisors find that employee performance falls short of the claims made in the interview.

Table 9.3 presents some tips for achieving success in an employment interview without engaging in such games. The rest of this section will discuss the kinds of skills and behaviors you need to be a "good" interviewee in a variety of interview situations.

Think about two times when someone sought information from you (these can be employment interviews, if you choose): one time when things went very smoothly and another time when the interaction was problematic. What factors contributed to the smooth interview? What made the other one difficult? What did you do differently? What was different about your interviewers?

■ *Planning and Preparation*

When you know in advance that you are going to be interviewed, there are a number of things you should do to prepare. There is usually some initial contact between the interviewer and the interviewee, at least to make arrangements about when and where the interview will take place. As the interviewee, you should try at this time to clarify the goal of the interaction. The more you know in advance, the more you can think about the issues and your possible answers and the more relevant information you can collect.

Goal clarification.   As the interviewee, you should determine the purpose of the interview as soon as possible—if not before the interview takes place, then during the opening segment. Knowing the purpose allows you to prepare yourself and gather relevant information.

Good interviewers, as you learned earlier in this chapter, present their purpose clearly, but not everyone is a good interviewer. This means that you might have to be assertive, asking the interviewer directly what the objectives are. For employment interviews, this may seem silly, but sometimes the interview is only a first step in a prolonged screening process. On-campus recruiting interviews, for instance, primarily serve to inform interested candidates about the position or company, and they aren't really selection interviews at all. In such an interview, you would want to seek information actively rather than try to provide a lot of information about yourself.

You must consider your own reasons for participating in the interview and what you hope to gain. In information action interviews, the benefit may simply be the attention—confirmation of your value. We feel important when people seek out our advice or input. (This is one reason an interviewer should give proper credit to the interviewee's contributions.)

You must also consider the negative consequences of participating. There is always some cost incurred by participating in an interview. Minimally, that cost is the time and energy expended. Perhaps you've been gracious enough to respond to a telephone research interview. The interviewer probably said, "This will only take about ten minutes." Twenty minutes later, you become irritated because the cost (time) has exceeded what you were willing to spend.

There is also a cost in forfeiting control of information. Kenneth Starr's investigations of President Clinton, which resulted in the impeachment trial of 1999, demonstrated how important the control of information is for self-protection.

Table 9.3　Interviewee Tips for an Employment (Selection) Interview

Preparing for the Interview

- Analyze yourself. What are your strengths and weaknesses?
- Think about potential questions and potential answers, but don't prepare canned responses.
- Research the company and the position as much as possible. Use that information to develop questions or show your interest in the position.

Participating in the Interview

Impression management: Focus on creating a positive first impression.
- Be early.
- Dress appropriately. Keep it simple and clean.
- Introduce yourself—first and last name. Pay attention to the interviewer's name.
- Shake hands, smile, wait to sit until you are invited to.
- Take along extra copies of your résumé, references, and other materials.
- Be nonverbally expressive. Be animated. Be energetic and show interest nonverbally.

Responding to the questions
- Be specific in your answers. Provide examples and evidence to support claims.
- Relate your answers specifically to the job and the company.
- Use each question to tell additional information about yourself. Avoid redundancy.
- Promote yourself. Don't be shy about your accomplishments and strengths. Show confidence.
- Keep yourself in the answer. Use "I" and "me."
- Pause and think before answering. Avoid sounding (or being) canned.
- Organize your answers and enumerate points when possible. ("My three strengths are: one . . . two . . .")
- Use powerful language. Instead of "I think I'm good at," use "I am good at."

Closing and follow-up
- Have questions ready that reflect your interest in and knowledge of the position.
- Seek any additional information or clarification you need. ("When will the selection be made?")
- Follow appropriate etiquette. Shake hands.
- Restate your interest in the position and the company.
- Send a thank-you letter.

Only after getting immunity did key witnesses agree to share information. The immunity allowed them to provide information that would otherwise be self-damaging and therefore costly. You will be faced with a similar, though less dire, situation when you are asked during an employment interview to divulge some of your weaknesses. This question puts you on the spot. If you are too open about your frailties, you may not get the job. The question creates a dilemma because you want to be honest and you also want the job. One way to handle such a question is to provide an answer that shows you are aware of certain weaknesses but are working to improve them.

There are times when you will want to excuse yourself from participating in an interview because participation is not worth the risk. Suppose you are working at a company that has come under public scrutiny for some mistake or controversial policy decision (for instance, an oil spill, contaminated food, or a decision to lay off workers). If a newspaper reporter calls you for an interview, you may not want to compromise your position in the company by participating. Most large companies have clear procedures for directing outside inquiries to the appropriate company spokespeople.

Information collection and self-preparation.　Interviewees need to do their homework in preparation for an interview. Once the general purpose is known, interviewees should gather relevant information so that they can provide informed answers. For example, after a student calls to set up an advising appointment, I examine his or her record of course work and determine what the student still needs to take to satisfy requirements for a degree. As the student asks me questions, my advance preparation saves us time and increases the effectiveness of our interaction. Sometimes, interviewers go so far as to provide interviewees with a schedule of the questions they will be asking. This helps ensure that the interviewee will be able to collect the necessary information prior to the interview.

Preparation for an interview can also include research about the interviewers and who they represent. Acquiring information about interviewers can help you understand their behavior, attitudes, inclinations, and so on. For example, if you are a new employee about to go for your first appraisal interview with your boss, you might ask other employees what to expect. Knowing that the boss generally says very little and expects the employee to direct the interview will help you prepare for this interaction. In employment interviews, the more knowledge of the company and position that you display, the more you will impress the interviewer with your interest in the job.

In addition to collecting information, you should anticipate questions and think about their answers. This is particularly true for employment interviews, in which most questions are fairly predictable. You should not be stuck for an answer when an employment interviewer asks you, "What are your strengths?" You should have anticipated this question and thought about possible answers. The feature "Ten Tough Interview Questions and Ten Great Answers" discusses some of the typical employment questions and suggests possible ways to answer.

Anticipating questions doesn't mean scripting or memorizing a pat answer. Lack of spontaneity in a response raises questions about its genuineness. In preparing for the question "What are your strengths?" you simply need to think about what your strengths are so that you are able to respond intelligently. Thinking through the possible questions increases your confidence and comfort. It also improves the quality of the information you are able to provide. For example, when an advisee who has fallen short of the needed credits to graduate makes an appointment with me, I anticipate a question about what the student should do next. In preparing to answer, I consider what I know about the student's confidence, financial concerns, academic strengths, and so on. Without such anticipation, my spontaneous response might prove to be poorly adapted to the student's particular situation.

■ *Participating in the Interview*

The way interviewees conduct themselves in an interview is a determining factor in the interview's effectiveness. An interviewer can prepare a great schedule of questions, but if the interviewee is unwilling or incapable of providing appropriate responses, little will be accomplished. You have witnessed numerous television interviews in which the interviewee simply responds with "No comment" or engages in equivocation. Problems are more likely to arise, however, when the interviewee lacks certain interviewing skills. Inter-viewees need to be able to express themselves clearly, take an active role in the interview, listen well to the questions, and send appropriate nonverbal messages.

Responding.   The most obvious thing an interviewee needs to do is to respond to the questions. However, this is not enough to ensure an effective interview. The answers need to be relevant, informed, informative, comprehensive, understandable, concise, and honest. The following is an example of ineffective responding. Can you tell why?

1. Student reporter: What kinds of careers can you pursue with a communication degree?
2. Communication teacher: There are lots of possibilities. Our students take a variety of courses and have been very successful at finding jobs after graduation.
3. Reporter: What kind of jobs?
4. Teacher: Just about anything.
5. Reporter: What percentage of your students go on to graduate school?
6. Teacher: A pretty high percentage.
7. Reporter: What graduate programs do they go into?
8. Teacher: Communication and other things.

The teacher is responding to the questions, but the responses are not very informative. The teacher's response to the question in 1 is vague and tangential. The teacher fails to elaborate even when asked the probing question in 3. Then in 6, the teacher uses ambiguous language that is likely to create confusion and misunderstanding. How much is a "pretty high" percentage? And in 8, the response is almost as vague as in 2.

As this example illustrates, effective responding involves more than just making noise after a question is asked. Good responses address the question and provide the desired information. But how do you know what information is desired if the interviewer is not very good at asking questions? That leads to our next topic, transactional participation.

Transactional participation. There is a tendency to assume that the sole responsibility for the interview's success lies with the interviewer. But as you know

Ten Tough Interview Questions and Ten Great Answers

This excerpt is from an article designed to help college graduates with employment interviews. It offers strategies for answering ten frequently asked questions.

The following answers are provided to give you a new perspective on how to answer tough interview questions. They are not there for you to lift from the page and insert into your next interview. They are there for you to use as the basic structure for formulating your own answers. While the specifics of each reply may not apply to you, try to follow the basic structure of the answer from the perspective of the interviewer. Answer the questions behaviorally, with specific examples that show clear evidence backs up what you are saying about yourself. Always provide information that shows you want to become the very best _____ for the company and that you have specifically prepared yourself to become exactly that. They want to be sold. They are waiting to be sold. Don't disappoint them!

1. **Tell me about yourself.**
   My background to date has been centered around preparing myself to become the very best _____ I can become. Let me tell you specifically how I've prepared myself . . .

2. **Why should I hire you?**
   Because I sincerely believe that I'm the best person for the job. I realize that there are many other college students who have the ability to do this job. I also have that ability. But I also bring an additional quality that makes me the very best person for the job—my attitude for excellence. Not just giving lip service to excellence, but putting every part of myself into achieving it. In _____ and _____ I have consistently reached for becoming the very best I can become by doing the following . . .

3. **What is your long-range objective? Where do you want to be 10 or 15 years from now?**
   Although it's certainly difficult to predict things far into the future, I know what direction I want to develop toward. Within five years, I would like to become the very best _____ your company has. In fact, my personal career mission statement is to become a world-class _____ in the _____ industry. I will work toward becoming the expert that others rely upon. And in doing so, I feel I will be fully prepared to take on any greater responsibilities that might be presented in the long term.

4. **How has your education prepared you for your career?**
   As you will note on my résumé, I've taken not only the required core classes in the _____ field, I've also gone above and beyond. I've taken every class the college has to offer in the field and also completed an independent study project specifically in this area. But it's not just taking the classes to gain academic knowledge—I've taken each class, both inside and outside of my major, with this profession in mind. So when we're studying _____ in _____, I've viewed it from the perspective of _____. In addition, I've always tried to keep a practical view of how the information would apply to my job. Not just theory, but how it would actually apply. My capstone course project in my final semester involved developing a real-world model of _____, which is very similar to what might be used within your company. Let me tell you more about it . . .

5. **Are you a team player?**
   Very much so. In fact, I've had opportunities in both athletics and academics to develop my skills as a team player. I was involved in _____ at the intramural level, including leading my team in assists during the past year—I always try to help others achieve their best. In academics, I've worked on several team projects, serving as both a member and team leader. I've seen the value of working together as a team to achieve a greater goal than any one of us could have achieved individually. As an example . . .

6. **Have you ever had a conflict with a boss or professor? How was it resolved?**
   Yes, I have had conflicts in the past. Never major ones, but certainly there have been situations where there was a disagreement that needed to be resolved. I've found that when conflict occurs, it's because of a failure to see both sides of the situation. Therefore, I ask the other person to give me their perspective and at the same time ask that they allow me to fully explain my perspective. At that point, I would work with the person to find out if a compromise could be reached. If not, I would submit to their decision because they are my superior. In the end, you have to be willing to submit yourself to the directives of your superior, whether you're in full agreement or not. An example of this was when . . .

7. **What is your greatest weakness?**
   I would say my greatest weakness has been my lack of proper planning in the past. I would overcommit myself with too many variant tasks, then not be able to fully accomplish each as I would like. However, since I've come to recognize that weakness, I've taken steps to correct it. For example, I now carry a planning calendar in my pocket so that I can plan all of my appointments and "to do" items. Here, let me show you how I have this week planned out . . .

8. **If I were to ask your professors to describe you, what would they say?**
   I believe they would say I'm a very energetic person, that I put my mind to the task at hand and see to it that it's accomplished. They would say that if they ever had something that needed to be done, I was the person who they could always depend on to see that it was accomplished. They would say that I always took a keen interest in the subjects I was studying and always sought ways to apply the knowledge in real-world settings. Am I just guessing that they would say these things? No, in fact, I'm quite certain they would say those things because I have with me several letters of recommendation from my professors, and those are their very words. Let me show you . . .

9. **What qualities do you feel a successful manager should have?**

The key quality should be leadership—the ability to be the visionary for the people who are working under them. The person who can set the course and direction for subordinates. A manager should also be a positive role model for others to follow. The highest calling of a true leader is inspiring others to reach the highest of their abilities. I'd like to tell you about a person who I consider to be a true leader . . .

10. **If you had to live your life over again, what would you change?**

That's a good question. I realize that it can be very easy to continually look back and wish that things had been different in the past. But I also realize that things in the past cannot be changed, that only things in the future can be changed. That's why I continually strive to improve myself each and every day and that's why I'm working hard to continually increase my knowledge in the _____ field. That's also the reason why I want to become the very best _____ your company has ever had. To make positive change. And all of that is still in the future. So in answer to your question, there isn't anything in my past that I would change. I look only to the future to make changes in my life.

In reviewing the above responses, please remember that these are sample answers. Please do not rehearse them verbatim or adopt them as your own. They are meant to stir your creative juices and get you thinking about how to properly answer the broader range of questions that you will face.

Source: This information is copyright 1999 by College Grad Job Hunter, Inc. and is used by permission of the author, Brian Krueger. You may review further career information online at http://www.collegegrad.com.

by now, the interview is a transactional process, and this means that the interviewee shares the responsibility for making the interview effective. For instance, if the interviewee doesn't understand a question, then he or she should ask for clarification. Too often though, interviewees try to answer questions regardless of whether they understand them, a pattern that leads to irrelevant responses or misunderstanding.

In line 7 of the previous sample interview, the phrase "what graduate programs" could mean which schools or which degrees. Perhaps the student reporter doesn't know that there are graduate degrees in communication. The teacher interviewee should take a more transactionally active role and ask for clarification of the question. After doing so, the teacher would be more likely to respond appropriately.

Being an active participant in the interview means asking questions to understand what the interviewer is after. The interviewee should seek clarification and feedback. This can include seeking acknowledgment that an answer given was appropriate: "Does that answer your question?" Paying attention to probing questions can also give the interviewee a hint as to whether the previous responses were adequate, relevant, and understood. Look at this example:

INTERVIEWER Will the new program be able to handle statistical analysis?
INTERVIEWEE It does have all of the appropriate scientific notation available as inserted symbols.
INTERVIEWER So it can calculate things like correlations?

The interviewer's probing follow-up question indicates that the interviewee did not answer the first question in the way the interviewer had sought. The use of the phrase "able to handle" was taken by the interviewee to mean the mere representation of scientific symbols, whereas the interviewer was asking about actual performance of statistical analysis. The probe should cue the interviewee to the misunderstanding and allow him or her to provide the relevant information.

Listening. You won't know if a question is signaling misunderstanding unless you listen closely to the interviewer. As an interviewee, you have a responsibility to use your skills of objective listening. You must pay attention to the interviewer and consider each question within the context in which it is asked. A supervisor who, during an appraisal interview, asks the employee, "What kinds of problems are you having?" is not expecting the employee to talk about his brother's being arrested, his marital troubles, or his recent speeding ticket. Within the context of an appraisal interview, the question seeks information about on-the-job problems.

Sometimes you simply may not hear all of a question because of noise or distractions. Usually, it is better to admit that you didn't hear and ask the interviewer to repeat the question. To save some face and reduce embarrassment, you can show you were trying to listen by repeating the part of the question you did hear: "I'm sorry, I'm not sure I heard your question completely. You asked something about the zoning waiver?"

Active listening demonstrates your interest and commitment to the interview and will help maintain a positive relationship. Being a good listener creates a positive impression. Of course, creating such an impression is particularly beneficial in an employment interview. Interviewers usually respond well to interviewees who carefully check that they understand a question before providing a response. This helps the interviewer feel confident about the quality of the information gained throughout the interview.

Nonverbal responsiveness. The astute interviewer not only listens to the words you use to answer questions, but also attends to your nonverbal communication. Your body language, eye contact, tone of voice, and other nonverbal cues can provide information. Thus, you should be aware of the information you are communicating nonverbally. Are you communicating information that you don't intend (desperation for a job possibility or anger toward your supervisor)? Are your nonverbals contradicting your verbal message and therefore undermining your credibility (for instance, telling someone, "Oh yeah, that new computer program is really great" in a quiet voice with a weak and unconvincing tone)?

Use nonverbal communication to fully express yourself, to convey your emotions, and to enhance your verbal statements. Giving a firm handshake while greeting people, smiling, leaning forward during interesting questions or discussion, being animated, and using your full range of vocal qualities—all these techniques will add to your effectiveness in the interview.

■ Postinterview Follow-Up

Like interviewers, interviewees often have some follow-up duties after the interview.

- In employment interviews, it is a good idea to send a thank-you note to the interviewer as a demonstration of politeness and interest in the position.
- After the interview, you may think of additional information that might have been helpful in response to a question. In these instances, consider offering that information to the interviewer—by a phone call or note, for example.
- In other instances, specific arrangements may have been made for you to find out additional information and forward it to the interviewer. Make every effort to follow through on such a commitment. If you fail to follow

Who is the interviewee in this photograph? What is your impression of the interviewee's nonverbal expressiveness?

through, the interviewer will probably ask why, creating a face-threatening situation.

- Most interviews occur within the bounds of ongoing relationships (such as interviews between coworkers). Therefore, as the interviewee, you want to engage in behaviors that continue to support a positive relationship.

Summary and Self-Analysis:

Interviewee Procedures and Skills

Use this summary list to assess your previous experience as an interviewee or your expectations about how well you would perform in each area.

Planning and Preparation

- Seek clarification about the goals and objectives of the interview.
- Consider your reasons for participating and the consequences of participating.
- Effectively collect any necessary information that will be needed in the interview.
- Thoughtfully consider possible questions and responses prior to the interview.

Participating in the Interview

- Provide answers that are relevant and responsive to the questions.
- Provide sufficient detail and specificity in your responses.
- State responses in clear and unambiguous language.
- Be actively involved in ensuring the success of the interview.
- Seek clarification of questions as needed.
- Seek feedback about the adequacy of answers.
- Actively and objectively listen to the questions.
- Be sensitive to the nonverbal messages you are sending.
- Send clear and consistent nonverbal messages.

Postinterview Follow-Up

- Send an appropriate note of thanks after employment interviews.
- Convey any additional information that you recall after the interview.
- Follow through on any commitments to collect and convey additional information.

This chapter has focused on the skills necessary for participating in an information action interview. Interviews involve, first of all, planning and preparation by the interviewer. The effective interviewer uses a clearly determined purpose to decide what information is needed and whom to interview. Some research may be necessary to learn more about the issue or the interviewee. At this point, arrangements can be made for conducting the interview, including contacting the interviewee and selecting the best time and place. The next step in preparing the interview is to develop a schedule of questions. These questions may be organized in a typical sequence, such as the funnel, inverted funnel, tunnel, or

Summary

quintamensional design sequence or a combination of these sequences. Finally, the opening is planned to ensure that the interview begins successfully.

Conducting the interview involves beginning with an opening that establishes the purpose, previews the interview, creates rapport, and motivates the interviewee. The body of the interview is where the majority of questions are asked and answered. The prepared schedule of questions is followed, using appropriate flexibility and probing as needed. Transitions signal the interviewee when the interview is changing direction. The closing makes it clear that the interview is coming to an end. An effective closing involves expressing appreciation, confirming the value of the interviewee's participation, summarizing and clarifying, inviting interviewee questions, and restating what will happen to the information. Finally, the interviewer acts on the information—by making a decision or writing a report, for instance.

A number of specific skills can enhance the effectiveness of interviewers. One essential skill is the ability to develop effective questions and probe effectively. Asking questions is effective only if the interviewer hears the answer; therefore, listening skills are also critical. Retaining the responses involves either a good memory, effective note-taking skills, or the audiotaping or videotaping of the interview. Each method has its advantages and disadvantages. The final two skills are adapting and social decentering. Adapting involves being able to adjust to the uniqueness of each interview situation. Social decentering leads to greater sensitivity and increased understanding of the interviewee's behavior and responses.

Interviewees also have a set of skills that lead to more effective information sharing. Interviewees need to understand the purpose of the interview and what is expected of them. Interviewees may need to collect information in advance about the topic and about the interviewer. During the interview itself, interviewees should provide responses that are clear and informative. They should also become active participants in the transactional process of interviewing. This means that interviewees should seek clarification from the interviewer if questions are confusing or ambiguous. Just like interviewers, interviewees must have good listening skills, since they cannot answer a question effectively if they really haven't heard it. Interviewees need to be effective in their nonverbal expressiveness, too. After the interview, the interviewee should follow up with appropriate activities that help maintain a positive relationship with the interviewer.

Key Terms

funnel sequence A way of organizing questions that begins with broad, open-ended questions and then, through a process of probing questions, narrows to more focused, closed questions.

inverted funnel sequence A way of organizing questions that starts with narrow questions and then moves to more open questions.

tunnel sequence A way of organizing questions that involves asking a series of questions of approximately the same scope.

quintamensional design sequence A way of organizing questions around five dimensions, ranging from awareness of the issue to attitude intensity.

opening The initiation phase of an interview.

body The central part of an interview, in which you focus on collecting information by using your schedule of questions.

closing The final phase of an interview.

Review Questions

1. Why is it necessary for an interviewer to have a clear purpose and objectives?
2. Distinguish the funnel, inverted funnel, and tunnel sequences of questions.
3. Describe the quintamensional design sequence of questions.
4. What should an interviewer try to accomplish in the interview opening?
5. What should an interviewer include in a closing?
6. Identify and describe two skills that an effective interviewer should have.
7. Identify and describe two skills that an effective interviewee should have.

Chapter 10

Small Group Communication: Theories of Group Process

Objectives

Studying this chapter will allow you to:

1. Explain the elements that define small group communication.
2. Identify several types of small groups.
3. Identify some of the advantages and disadvantages associated with groups.
4. Discuss the factors that affect the development of group structure.
5. Distinguish among various theories of leadership.
6. Describe the stages of group development.

The following is a hypothetical discussion about how to increase membership in a club devoted to environmental issues. The following students are present: Joe, Nancy, Lincoln, Maria, Jawan, and Monica.

JOE   The real problem seems to be student apathy. Nobody wants to be involved anymore.

NANCY   I don't think it's apathy; it's just that students are too busy with classes and work and things.

LINCOLN   Yeah, Nance has a good point. It's hard for people to find time to get involved in a new organization like ours.

JOE   If students really cared about what happened to the environment like we do, they'd join us.

MARIA   I think we need to think about ways to get more students involved, not just complain about the students.

JOE   But we need to understand why they aren't involved so we can overcome their reluctance.

MARIA   Maybe, instead of dealing with the negatives, we could focus on why people are involved, like us.

LINCOLN   I got involved because I've seen a lot of negative effects from pollution and exploitation of natural resources. I was excited to find a group like this doing something about it.

NANCY   I got involved because I like a lot of the other people who were involved in this group and I found that I had interests similar to theirs.

JOE   How can we use that information to increase our membership?

MARIA   We can increase student awareness of the problem and show them how students just like them are doing something about it.

LINCOLN   We probably need to show how we've been successful at some things, like creating the new prairie area north of town.

This short excerpt from the interaction of a group of students illustrates a number of principles about small group communication that will be discussed in this chapter. You've probably had similar interactions with friends or coworkers. Usually, working with other people in groups or teams is both very satisfying and very frustrating. Over the years, you may have developed a dislike for working in teams because of negative group experiences, or you may love working in teams because you've enjoyed the camaraderie and success. Regardless of your previous experiences, you will find it difficult to avoid working in teams or groups as you progress in your professional career. Almost all organizations use teams of individuals for one thing or another.

Whether a group experience turns out positive or negative is not just a matter of chance. You can enhance the likelihood of a positive group experience by increasing your understanding of small group dynamics and improving your own group communication skills. This chapter and the next will provide some fundamental information to help you in both respects.

Defining Small Group Communication

The students in our scenario are involved in small group communication. Can you identify what is occurring that makes it small group communication?

Consider these elements:

- For one thing, there is clear interaction among four of the individuals. But you may have noticed that two of the people present, Jawan and Monica, never speak. Would you consider them members of the group? Why or why not?
- You might also assume that this is small group communication because it involves six people. Size is one factor that is sometimes used to distinguish a small group from an interpersonal dyad or an audience.
- You might observe that the individuals obviously know each other and have some sort of interpersonal relationship. Relationships are certainly a component of small group interactions.
- The final quality you may have noticed is that all the participants are talking about the same issue; that is, they share a common goal.

Small group communication can be defined as interpersonal communication among three or more people who view themselves as a group and who are working toward a shared purpose or goal. As with some of the other communicaton definitions covered in this text, examining the component parts helps to more fully understand the term.

■ *Interpersonal Communication*

In interpersonal communication, people are mutually and simultaneously influencing each other. Our transcript of the environmental group does not reflect all of the mutual influence that is occurring because a lot would be nonverbal. As each member takes a turn making a comment, he or she is affected by the nonverbal communication of the other group members. That is, he or she is either receiving or not receiving eye contact, head nodding, a leaning toward or away, and so on. This mutual influence is one of the elements that limits how large a small group can be.

You've probably been at a party where you were one of the first people to arrive. The first three or four people usually stand together talking, and they are joined by the guests who arrive later. At some point the group becomes too large for each person to be aware of and influenced by all of the other members, and the group splits into smaller, more manageable groups. How large the group gets before this split occurs depends on the people, but usually the group grows no larger than fifteen or twenty people.

In larger groups, you no longer are influenced by individual members. Individual reactions are buried in the "audience." In a group of twenty, you probably won't notice that someone has lost interest in what you are saying, but you will notice in a group of three or four. The larger the group, the more the rules for communicating become formalized in order to handle the increasing communication management problems. In a large group, for example, members may raise their hands to get the floor, or the group may use Robert's Rules of Order to dictate how the members offer motions, amendments, and so forth.

■ *Three or More People*

The requirement of mutual and simultaneous influence restricts how large a group can be, but why is three the minimum and not two? Two people can share a common goal and engage in a project together, acting like a dyadic work group. However, having three or more people involved produces a number of dynamics that are not present with just two people.

Look at what happens, for instance, with the balance of power. In a dyad, two people can become stalemated in a fight for control and dominance. Suppose you wanted to go see *Titanic II* and your friend wanted to see *Star Wars III*. You could argue with each other all night and end up not seeing anything. Now add a third person. Suddenly there is the potential for a majority view. If the third person also wants to see *Star Wars III*, you are put in a minority position. The balance of power has shifted because of group dynamics.

The size of a group also has an effect on such things as conformity, cohesion, communication networks, relationships, conflict, leadership, and roles—concepts discussed later in this chapter and the next.

■ *A Shared Purpose or Goal*

In the opening example of this chapter, the students share a goal of improving the quality of the environment. This goal brings them together and keeps them together.

The goals of groups are widespread and varied, but they generally fall along a continuum from **task orientation** to **social orientation.** (See Figure 10.1.) You may serve on a committee formed by your boss to develop a new vacation policy; that group would have a task orientation. On the other hand, you may be in a group that merely enjoys spending social time together, such as a gourmet-dinner club; that group, clearly, has a social orientation.

It is important to realize, however, that no group is entirely devoid of either quality. When groups of friends get together to satisfy their social needs, they face certain tasks, such as deciding what movie to rent, where to eat, and who's driving. Similarly, the members of task-oriented groups also have social needs and goals. As Nancy mentions in our example, she liked the people in the group, so socializing was one of her reasons for joining. When we say that a group has a task orientation or a social orientation, we are merely indicating which quality is dominant.

A significant factor in group dynamics is the tension that inherently exists between the group goal and each member's individual goals. In our scenario, Joe

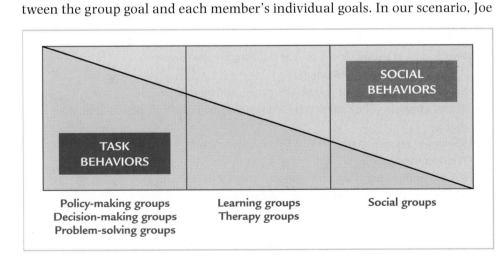

Figure 10.1

The Continuum of Groups from Task Orientation to Social Orientation

SOCIAL BEHAVIORS

TASK BEHAVIORS

Policy-making groups
Decision-making groups
Problem-solving groups

Learning groups
Therapy groups

Social groups

may share the goal of improving the environment with the other members, but he also may have the goal of being leader of the group. He may drop out of the group if his individual goal is not met, or he may create conflict if someone else vies for leadership. Participation in groups often involves making individual goals secondary to commitment to the group's goal.

■ People Who View Themselves as a Group

This part of the definition has been left until last because it may seem like a circular notion: You are a group because you think you are a group. However, remember that the three other qualities just discussed must also be present.

People must feel a sense of "groupness" for the collection of people to be a real group. That feeling or perception involves recognizing who is in the group and who isn't. In the environmental group, if Joe, Nancy, Lincoln, and Maria don't think of Jawan and Monica as being members of the group, and neither do Jawan and Monica, then those two aren't part of the group, even though they are in the same room. The four active individuals probably have a good idea of who is in and who is out. The need for such a perception distinguishes groups from other bodies of people who share a common goal but who do not interact and do not perceive themselves as a group. Ten people waiting in line to buy tickets to a concert share a common purpose, but they will not usually perceive themselves as a group.

The perception of "groupness" also includes a sense of the relationships among the members and an identification of roles. When you recognize that you are in a group, you can usually describe the relationships among the members and identify who is playing such roles as leader, follower, deviant, and harmonizer. The relationships do not necessarily have to be positive; sometimes you may find yourself disliking another member in the group, but you still recognize that person as a member.

Remember from Chapter 3 that perception has a direct impact on how people communicate with others. For example, if Jawan and Monica are not perceived as members of the group, comments may not be directed toward them. Perhaps they are just friends of Nancy's who are waiting for her to finish the meeting.

Identify which of the following scenarios qualify as small group communication and which do not, according to the definition.

1. Five people standing at a bus stop waiting for the same bus
2. A classroom of twenty students
3. Six people playing coed volleyball against another six people
4. Those same six volleyball players enjoying a pizza and soft drinks after their match
5. Seven city council members discussing recent zoning waiver requests
6. A twelve-person jury watching the testimony of witnesses during a trial
7. A jury deliberating the guilt or innocence of a defendant
8. Four people in a chat session on the Internet
9. Four people playing a game of cards
10. A therapy session involving a counselor and five teenagers with drug problems

Types of Groups

Groups are often classified by their goals. Groups vary according to how much the task is social or task oriented as shown in Figure 10.1. The following section identifies some of the specific types of groups within this framework.

Groups with High Task Orientation

At the left end of Figure 10.1's continuum are groups that are high in task orientation and relatively low in social orientation. These include policymaking groups, decision-making groups, and problem-solving groups.

Policymaking groups are charged with developing the principles by which future decisions and actions will be guided. An example would be a city council that is formulating a zoning policy for the community. Policymaking groups sometimes develop policy in response to specific problems, but generally they are not charged with problem analysis.

Decision-making groups are faced with having to make a choice between alternatives. For instance, a purchasing team may be trying to decide whether the company should buy twenty Macintosh computers or twenty IBM-type computers. The decision may be guided by established policies, or the decision itself may set a precedent that becomes policy.

Problem-solving groups focus their attention on analyzing some problem, trying to determine its causes and effects, and developing the best solution. The environmental group in our example is trying to solve the problem of low membership in the organization. Problem-solving groups engage in both decision-making and policymaking as they work through the process of choosing the best solution.

Groups with Combined Task and Social Orientations

Toward the middle of the continuum in Figure 10.1, balancing task and social orientation, are learning groups and support groups.

Learning groups have as their purpose the sharing or discovery of information. One popular variety is study groups, in which the members seek to learn from one another. Study groups depend heavily on each member's having some information to contribute to the others. Besides student study groups, Bible study groups and book discussion groups are common. These groups usually have some central element that each group member examines before sharing insights and reactions with the rest of the group.

Support, or **self-help groups** are a type of learning group in which individuals are attempting to learn more about themselves. The advantage of being in a group setting is that each member receives honest and supportive feedback from a variety of perspectives. Toastmasters, for instance, are groups of individuals who get together to practice giving speeches and provide feedback to one another.

Support groups provide a cathartic atmosphere in which there is a feeling of belonging and succor. People can also learn a lot about themselves by learning about others. The current proliferation of such groups is a testament to their effectiveness and value. There are groups for cancer survivors, alcoholics, people

What kind of group do you think is pictured here? To what degree do you suspect the group is task and/or socially oriented?

with drug dependencies, sexual assault victims, children of alcoholic parents, and so on. When they are formed by a professional counselor to address client issues, these groups are often known as *therapy groups.*

■ Groups with High Social Orientation

Toward the right side of the continuum in Figure 10.1 are groups whose primary orientation is social and relational. **Social groups** exist to satisfy members' needs for companionship, belonging, and self-confirmation. Family and friends are the best examples of social groups.

Social groups can be thought of as expanded networks of interpersonal communication. The reason for the group's existence is to foster the social welfare of its members. Social groups are not devoid of task responsibilities, but those are secondary to fulfilling the social needs of the members. We spend a lot of time in these groups because they are effective in satisfying our social needs.

There are both informal and formal social groups. Informal groups are those we create by developing a network of friends and family. Formal groups are those specifically established to meet people's social needs, like the Girl Scouts, fraternities, intramural teams, and coffee clubs.

▌ Advantages (Benefits) and Disadvantages (Costs) of Groups

Groups represent potential. The advantages that accrue from the use of groups are only potential advantages; they depend on the group's working effectively. Correspondingly, there are always costs involved in the use of groups, and the costs may escalate when the group fails to follow appropriate principles.

▪ *Factors Affecting Group Benefits and Costs*

One significant factor affecting group benefits and costs is the degree to which the members are appropriately cooperative. U.S. culture tends to be competitive and individualistic.[1] Competition generally involves placing one's own goals ahead of other people's. Winning a competition means that you get what you want while the other participants lose. This value is in direct opposition to the collectivistic cultural value in which individuals place the group's goals above their individual goals. Actually, in genuine collectivism, the group goals *become* the individual goals, and individuals feel successful only if the group is successful. Asian countries like Japan and China are examples of collectivistic cultures that traditionally value cooperation above competition.

Think about your own experiences in groups that had individuals with different cultural values concerning competition and cooperation. What impact did these differences have on the group?

How would you rate yourself on a scale of 1 to 10, with 1 being highly competitive (individualistic) and 10 being highly cooperative (collectivistic)? What impact does that have on your attitude and behavior in groups?

In addition to cooperation, groups need diversity and participation to maximize their potential benefits. Diversity is needed not just in racial or ethnic terms but in terms of perspectives. Imagine two groups charged with developing a new advertisement campaign for selling Cheerios. Group 1 is made up of four 25-year-old Caucasian male college graduates from Ohio. Group 2 is made up of a 25-year-old African American male from New York, a 40-year-old Asian American woman from California, a 30-year-old Hispanic woman from Illinois, and a 45-year-old Caucasian male from Florida. Which group do you think will generate the best list of possible ideas?

The homogeneous group 1 may not be much more effective than a single person in developing the ad campaign because all the members are likely to see things the same way. On the other hand, the diversity of group 2 should enhance the ability to generate a wide variety of ideas.

However, there is a downside to diversity. Diversity can increase the likelihood of misunderstandings and misperceptions among the members. Cultural, ethnic, age, and sex differences affect the ways the members communicate. Hence, the problems associated with language and perception discussed in Chapters 3 and 4 might undermine the effectiveness of group 2.

Global Teams: The Ultimate Collaboration

This article provides some real-world evidence in support of the use of diverse group memberships. In addition it describes the general process by which diverse individuals become a collaborative team.

You think team-building in the United States is challenging? Companies such as Maxus and Intel have gone even further. They've built cross-functional teams that comprise different cultures, languages, locations and time zones.

The scene is one of sharp contrasts. Ten people—geophysicists, geologists, engineers, oil-drilling pros and production experts—meet in a modern boardroom looking out onto a lush, equatorial garden of palm trees, ferns and tropical shrubs. But the tropical paradise isn't all it appears to be. A tall brick wall topped with jagged pieces of broken glass surrounds the compound.

The team of people inside mirror the contrasts of the environment. They're from Dallas-based Maxus Energy (a wholly owned subsidiary of YPF, the largest Argentinean corporation in the world) and Maxus-Southeast Sumatra (SES). Teaming up are Americans, Dutch, British and Indonesians—people whose cultures are as contradictory as the serrated wall to the tropical garden of the office complex. Some of these people believe in individualism, others believe in collectivism; some believe in equal opportunity based on achievement, others believe status is inherited. Politically, culturally, religiously—this group is composed of disparate elements.

The team is one example of how two Maxus groups formed a cross-functional, cross-cultural unit to pursue a common goal: to maximize oil and gas production. As if working together wasn't formidable enough, they faced an enormous business challenge—to stave off the typical drop in production that occurs after the first few years on an oil field. The companies expected a 15% decrease in production.

Could the team stabilize production and avoid the dramatic decline that was anticipated? Working together, they did. Capitalizing on Maxus's technical expertise and SES's cultural tradition of teamwork and worldwide experience, the team not only avoided the 15% reduction, but leveled off production and even helped the companies add oil reserves to their stockpiles—an almost unprecedented achievement.

Indeed, work teams already have become an established institution domestically, and now they're making their way into international projects. It's little wonder. Global teams address certain problems and affect the bottom line in ways that are fundamentally different from the ways individuals approach the same situation. They maximize expertise from a variety of people, provide companies a more accurate picture of international customers' needs, and profit by the synergy necessary to unify the varying perspectives of different cultures and different business functions. It all adds up. "You've got to utilize your human resources much more efficiently today if you're going to stay on top of it. That's why everyone is heading toward the team concept," says Steve Ginsburgh, manager of Organization Services and Employee Development at Maxus Energy. "When a project requires brain power, teams are much more efficient."

Because of these factors, global teams will become as prevalent as Hondas manufactured in America, Motorola beepers marketed in China, and Big Macs™ made and served in Saudi Arabia. HR managers with international responsibility know that global teams will become an integral part of the developing global work force. The fundamentals of global-team success aren't very different from the practices that work for domestic work teams. But there are more variables. Overlay cultural behavior and expectations on the roles of communication, team leadership and group dynamics, and you immediately understand. Moreover, there are logistics to overcome: challenges inherent in working in different time zones, lots of travel and busy, conflicting schedules.

"The beauty about global teams is that they're reaching for the next stage," says Tony Barnes, director of human resources development at the Japan Center in England. Barnes, who worked for decades with Edward Demming on team process in Japan, believes that global teams are the next wave of corporate development. "I think corporations as we've known them have actually run their course and are beginning to break into autonomous business units, so the decisions are in the hands of the people carrying out the work. Global teams are one way of cross-pollinating—they move people who are successful in one branch of the organization to work with people in another country and another branch of the organization."

In these situations, people develop themselves as well as help develop others. "It's a program of both learning and teaching that enhances the ability and taps into the creativity of all people in an organization," says Barnes. And like any other successful organization, teams evolve as business conditions change, and as their members' comfort levels with one another grow.

To become productive units, global teams must evolve. Sylvia B. Odenwald, chief executive officer of Odenwald Connection Inc., a Dallas-based international consulting firm, knows about global teams. As author of "Global Solutions for Teams," she has studied them for years. Her analysis: GlobalWork teams (her phrase) move from being an assortment of individuals on a chaotic collision course through a state of coexistence into a collaborative phase where they truly work together as a team.

There are four phases. In Phase One, each team member comes with his or her own expectations, culture and values. Most people take their cultural values for granted—they often do not think of them as being specific to their society and different from other people's expectations. So the first step involves team members recognizing that values are merely a set of norms particular to their society; they're not universals.

Phase Two comes after this self-awareness. Individuals begin to respect the cultures of other team members. While acknowledging problems and differences, they're willing to listen to others and move into a neutral zone where they appreciate others and work together.

During Phase Three, team members begin to trust each other. They start to share knowledge. At this time, they begin to focus on achieving team goals. And then, in Phase Four, the team begins to work in a collaborative way. Corporate vision and strategy infuse the team with energy. Cross-cultural differences become a competitive advantage. "During this phase, people begin to truly work together. They learn day by day how to negotiate team milestones, develop reporting procedures and meet deadlines. The real challenge is to find something that works for everybody. It might not be exactly what everybody wants, but it allows the team to accomplish its goals in a collaboration that works," Odenwald says.

Source: "Global Teams: The Ultimate Collaboration," by Charlene Marmer Solomon, copyright September 1995. Used with permission of ACC Communications, Inc./*Personnel Journal* (now known as *Workforce*), Costa Mesa, CA. All rights reserved.

One effect of diversity may be to limit the participation of some members. For a group to reach its full potential, each member must participate. Cooperation means a pooling together of resources; that pooling together requires member participation. Group 2 would not reach its full potential, for instance, if the Asian American woman remained quiet throughout the group interaction. The absence of her input, knowledge, and feedback would keep the group from tapping all its available resources.

■ Advantages: The Upside of Groups

If a group meets the conditions we have just outlined—appropriate cooperation, diversity, and participation—the group can potentially have a number of advantages, compared to a single person or a dyad:

- An increased body of knowledge and information to be tapped and shared
- An increased potential for generating ideas
- The ability for members to feed off each other's ideas
- The offering of valuable feedback about ideas
- An increased likelihood of correcting members' errors of fact or perception
- More perspectives and insights into problems and issues
- A greater satisfaction of social needs and confirmation of self-value
- Development and enhancement of interpersonal relationships
- Enhancement of individuals' motivation and commitment to the issue and solutions
- The development of a collective memory, increasing the retention of information and of the interaction

■ Disadvantages: The Downside of Groups

Many of the advantages of groups depend on the group's working to its full potential. But various factors, as you have seen, may limit a group's ability to reach that potential. For example, domination by one or two members can undermine full participation. Partly because of these limitations, groups can have disadvantages, including the following:

- Expenditure of time
- Expenditure of energy and money (for instance, five executives meeting for two hours constitute a sizable financial cost to an organization)
- Straining of relationships and creation of ill will among members
- Potential loss of face when some members challenge others' ideas or information
- Conflicts resulting in harm to individuals (such as the psychological harm of being demeaned)
- Failure to stay on track, as when work groups become too social
- Conformity when some members give in to group pressure
- Loss of individual perspective (groupthink)

As we explore group structure and dynamics in the remainder of this chapter, you'll get a better idea of how such problems arise and how to prevent them.

The Development of Group Structure

Put five strangers together, give them a problem to solve, and some interesting things happen. Over the course of their interaction, they will develop preferences among the members as to whom they like the most. They will eventually establish patterns of behavior that amount to different roles for different people, and members will come to expect continuation of these same behaviors. Among the more significant roles that might develop is that of leader. A communication network will evolve that reflects who talks to whom. A set of rules and norms will be adopted, informally and perhaps formally as well, prescribing the manner in which the group is to operate and communicate.

All these occurrences are part of the process of **structuration,** by which a group develops its own unique structure and corresponding culture.[2] The principle of **duality of structures** reflects the fact that group structures are the product of the group interaction and also dictate the nature of the interaction.[3] A group might find that people keep interrupting one another. Therefore, the group decides to create a norm that nobody should interrupt the other members. In this way, communication is used to create the structure, and the norm that is created then dictates the manner of the subsequent communication.

In the following sections, we'll examine several key components of group structure: relationships, communication networks, norms, membership composition, roles, and leadership.

■ *Relationships in Groups*

A group can be thought of as a set of interpersonal relationships. Look at the interaction in the environmental group at the beginning of this chapter. Who do you think likes whom the most? What clues do you pick up that lead you to your conclusion? The way the students talk and respond to each other provides some evidence about the relationships among the members.

Figure 10.2 shows possible relationships among the members of the environmental group, as defined by what can be told about their attraction to one another. Shorter lines indicate a closer relationship. Nancy, Lincoln, and Maria are all closer to one another than any of them is to Joe. The two people who don't speak, Jawan and Monica, are on the sidelines; you can't tell what relationships they have with the other four.

Relationships among group members are affected by all of the factors discussed in Chapter 6, including attraction (liking), trust, intimacy, and power. Figure 10.2 illustrates the environmental group's relationships according to attraction, but it doesn't necessarily reflect member power. Maria seems to have the most influence among the members: She suggests directions for the group

Figure 10.2

Possible Levels of Attraction

Possible levels of attraction among the members of the environmental group in the scenario at the beginning of the chapter. The shorter the line, the greater the attraction and the closer the relationship.

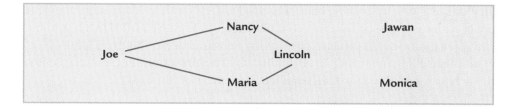

discussion, and her ideas tend to be followed. Joe attempts to control other members, but his efforts prove fruitless.

Cohesion and groupthink.   Positive relationships significantly enhance the quality and effectiveness of a group. People are more likely to be motivated to participate when they like the other group members. When group members are attracted to the group and to each other, the group has **cohesion.** If you are in a group of six people and each member enjoys working with only one other member, then the group will not be very cohesive and is unlikely to reach its full potential. The more secure and confident members are about the existence of positive relationships with other members, the more open and disclosing they can be. Positive relationships facilitate communication and thereby improve group performance.

Groups can become too cohesive, however, and as a result suffer from groupthink. **Groupthink** is the phenomenon in which belonging to a group creates a tendency in members to accept the group's way of thinking, even when realism or common sense would dictate otherwise. Groupthink occurs when group members get so caught up in reaching unanimity that they fail to appraise other courses of action realistically.[4] Preserving the group becomes the focus of group effort, and deviance, nonconformity, individuality, and conflict are not tolerated. Groupthink can result in the group's ignoring morals, feeling invulnerable, stereotyping other groups, and engaging in self-censorship.[5]

■ *Communication Networks*

A consistent pattern of interaction among group members creates a **communication network.** Large organizations often create formal networks that dictate the flow of communication, as you will see in Chapter 15. In small groups, though, the networks that develop are generally informal ones, reflecting the relationships, attractions, power, and roles of the group members.

Figure 10.3 shows some of the most identifiable patterns in group communication networks. In actual groups, the pattern of interaction is usually not quite as simple and clear-cut as those illustrated in the figure, but the impact on communication and group effectiveness is just as real. Look at the patterns in Figure 10.3. What position in each network do you think has the most influence on the group's productivity? Which members do you think would be most isolated and have the least influence? Which position would you most like to occupy?

In general, people feel most alienated when they have few communication opportunities with the rest of the group. The all-channel pattern (Figure 10.3E), which keeps each member in contact with everyone else, is typically best at reducing alienation. Networks sometimes develop outliers, however, because certain individuals are uncomfortable being involved with the other group members and prefer a more passive role. In this case, they might be quite satisfied in a less interactive position, such as an end position in a chain pattern (Figure 10.3A). Networks also follow the principle of duality of structures: Communication creates the network, and the network then affects communication.

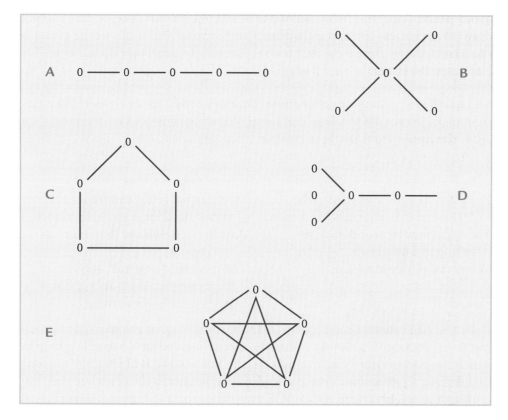

Figure 10.3

Typical Communication Networks in Small Groups

(A) Chain network
(B) Wheel network (C) Circle network (D) Y network
(E) All-channel network

■ *Norms*

A group's behavior is dictated by a set of norms that the group adopts. Earlier chapters have mentioned the widespread norms established by society, but it's important to realize that even small groups have norms. In the most general sense, **norms** are rules that prescribe what is appropriate and inappropriate behavior. In a small group, the norms in operation come both from society at large and from the group itself.

Social norms.   Each of us has a set of norms that we follow, ones we have acquired through socialization. From your parents you may have learned not to talk with food in your mouth; you may have learned to raise your hand in class if you have a question for the teacher; you may have learned to stop your car when you see a red light. Each of these behaviors reflects a different social norm that you have acquired. These norms were acquired within the context of your culture; people from different cultures have different norms. As you have seen in earlier chapters, intercultural interactions are sometimes problematic because the participants operate from different sets of norms that may be in conflict with one another.

When a group gets together, each member brings the norms that he or she has acquired outside the group. Each member begins operating on the basis of these norms. To the degree that the group is similar, communication and interaction can flow fairly easily. For instance, all the members may have the same norm about not interrupting while someone is talking. In this way, **social norms** drawn from society are applied within a given group. But as far as the group is concerned, these norms exist only to the degree that the group follows them. This leads us to the subject of group norms.

Group norms.   Suppose one member has not learned the rule governing interrupting or chooses not to follow that norm. What happens? Violating a norm is an act of **deviance.** Here are three possible outcomes:

Result of Violating a Norm	Example
Punishment may be applied to the deviant until the norm is followed.	Members act coldly toward an interrupter until the interrupting stops.
The norm may be abandoned, resulting in a new norm.	A norm is established that interrupting is okay.
The norm may be modified.	The modified norm indicates that interrupting is okay, but only if the point is really important.

The modification of social norms to fit the unique circumstances of the group results in group norms. **Group norms** are norms created for the specific group in which they occur. Here's an example: In the movie *Good Will Hunting,* the four friends have a particular norm about seat assignments in the car when they are cruising the neighborhood. When Will leaves the group, the norm immediately is changed as Morgan moves from the back seat to take Will's spot in the front passenger seat.

This is also an example of an implicit norm. **Implicit norms** are norms that are followed even though the group has never discussed them. Implicit norms arise through a process of observation, reinforcement, and punishment. **Explicit norms,** in contrast, are created when groups discuss the rules that govern their behavior. In *Good Will Hunting,* Chuckie, the driver of the car, might have questioned Morgan's move to the front seat. The ensuing discussion might have led to the creation of an explicit norm legitimizing Morgan's move to Will's seat.

Think about some of the groups you belong to and the specific norms that exist for them.

Search your school's Internet web sites for rules about appropriate Internet usage. Most schools have a formal, explicit set of norms (sometimes described as codes of ethics) that users are supposed to follow. Do you and your friends follow these rules? What implicit norms do you follow when emailing or instant-messaging?

Conformity.   Norms are necessary for groups to accomplish their goals.[6] Norms help to create order in a situation that could be quite chaotic. Norms are part of the culture and identity of a group. Groups feel threatened when the norms are challenged, ignored, or eliminated. As a result, groups seek to maintain and protect their norms.

Putting pressure on individuals to follow group norms that they would otherwise not follow creates **conformity.** Group members who ignore or act coldly to an interrupter are attempting to pressure that individual into conforming to the norm. At times, conformity is valuable as a way to maintain stability and cohesiveness in the group. On the other hand, conformity can lead to blind acceptance and the failure to adequately examine and analyze an issue—in essence, a lemming effect (those little critters that follow each other over a cliff).

Members are more likely to conform under certain conditions.[7] Conformity is increased in highly cohesive groups in which members don't want to disturb the harmony. The more attracted a member is to the group, the less likely that member will question group norms. The more structured a group is, the more likely the members will conform.

As the size of the group increases, the ability to create conformity increases, up to a point. The impact of size depends on the amount of interaction and pressure that can be directed toward the deviant. A nonconformist can hide in a large group. In smaller groups, the members know when one person is not conforming. It is more difficult to skip out of a class of five students than a class of five hundred.

■ *Membership Composition*

Each group reflects a merging of the psychological contexts of its members. That process of merging is affected by each of the elements that make up each person's psychological context. As discussed in Chapter 2, these elements include needs, personality, values, sex, age, culture, race, and ethnicity. **Membership composition** is a term often used to represent the collection of group members' individual characteristics, and it can have a large impact on how the group functions.

For instance, a group composed of five females will function differently than a group of five males. A group of five Hondurans will function differently than a group of five Swedes. A group of five twelve-year-olds will function differently than a group of five eighty-year-olds (maybe). The infinite number of possible combinations of individual members' qualities makes it challenging to predict group outcomes.

Differences among group members impact group behavior in two primary ways. First, these differences lead to real variations in the way people behave. People's behaviors are a reflection of their culture, sex, age, and so on. In Chapter 2, you saw how differences in the cultural values of masculinity/femininity and individualism/collectivism affect the way people communicate. These differences can be expected to affect group performance. Members of a collectivistic culture, for instance, are more likely to work collaboratively in teams, while those in individualistic cultures (such as the United States) are more likely to be competitive.

The second impact of member differences on group behavior involve stereotyping and bias. Members may view those who are different from themselves in a prejudicial manner and behave accordingly. For example, a study of diverse groups of professional workers in a state government found that minority members and women (who were in the minority by number) were viewed as less effective team members than the white males.[8] In addition, when people were asked how many people contributed to the project, the all-white groups reported higher team contributions than did the diverse groups. And in the racially mixed groups, white males perceived significantly less overall team contributions than did the racial minority members.

■ Roles

A **group role** is a set of specific behaviors associated with each member of a group. The exact role each member plays reflects a merging of assigned roles and emerging roles.

Sometimes a group member is assigned a particular position within a group. An **assigned role** is a set of expected behaviors typically associated with that position (for example, being the chair, the vice chair, or the secretary). For each position there is a set of preexisting expected behaviors, usually defined by society or by the organization. You expect certain duties to be performed by a person who has been assigned the role of committee chair. Knowing that a person has this role provides you with information about how you should behave, a yardstick by which to measure the chair's performance, and a base from which to develop your own role.

Whether or not roles are assigned, the roles that members actually perform are the product of their conception of what behaviors are appropriate and the influence of other members' behaviors. This results in the development of expected, or emerging roles that are unique to that group. An **emerging role** is the role that evolves for each group member as the group interacts. That is, the group develops expectations about each member's performance. For example, in a group of very influential people, you might emerge in the role of follower; but in a group where you have the most influence, you might emerge in the role of leader.

Table 10.1 lists specific types of roles often found in groups. Usually, though, the roles that people take represent a unique mixture of several of these identified roles.

Because of the transactional nature of small groups, each person's ability to enact a given role depends on the other members. What happens if two different people in the group want to be chair? A conflict arises between the appointed chair and the other person who was seeking that role. Similar conflicts may occur in the process of establishing each member's role. Each member's role is created as a direct product of the roles that other group members seek.

Table 10.1   Some Typical Roles Within Groups

Roles	Description
Task	
Coordinator	Pulls together related ideas or suggestions; clarifies the relationships between various ideas or suggestions; tries to coordinate the activities of various members or subgroups
Elaborator	Expands on suggestions; offers a rationale for suggestions previously made; tries to figure out how an idea or suggestion would work out if adopted by the group
Energizer	Tries to prod the group to action or decision; attempts to stimulate or arouse the group to greater or higher quality activity
Evaluator-critic	Gives a critical analysis of a suggestion or idea; evaluates or questions the practicality, logic, or facts of a suggestion; holds the group up to a standard of accomplishment
Information giver	Offers facts or opinions; relates one's own experience directly to the group task or problem
Information seeker	Asks for facts, opinions, or interpretations; seeks clarification of suggestions made
Initiator-contributor	Proposes tasks, goals, or actions; suggests solutions, procedures, or ways of handling difficulties; helps to organize the group
Opinion giver	States beliefs or opinions pertinent to a suggestion made or to alternative suggestions; emphasizes what should become the group's view of pertinent values, not primarily relevant facts or information (combined with information giver role)
Opinion seeker	Asks not primarily for the facts of the case but for a clarification of the values pertinent to what the group is undertaking or of values involved in a suggestion made or in alternative suggestions (combined with information seeker role)
Orienter-clarifier	Defines the position of a group with respect to its goals by summarizing what has occurred; points to departures from agreed on directions or goals; raises questions about the direction that the group discussion is taking
Procedural technician	Does things for the group; performs routine tasks such as distributing materials, taking notes, typing, photocopying
Recorder	Writes down suggestions, makes a record of group decisions, or writes down the product of discussion; provides group memory (combined with procedural technician role)
Maintenance	
Compromiser	When one's own idea or position is involved in a conflict, tries to offer a compromise (for example, by yielding to status, admitting error, maintaining harmony, or meeting the group halfway)
Encourager	Praises, agrees with, and accepts the contributions of others; friendly, warm, and responsive to others; offers commendation and praise, and acceptance of other points of view, ideas, and suggestions
Follower	Passively goes along with the ideas of others; serves as an audience in group discussion and decision
Gatekeeper and expediter	Attempts to keep communication channels open; encourages the participation of others; tries to make sure that all group members have the chance to participate

continued

Roles	Description
Harmonizer	Attempts to reconcile disagreements among group members; reduces tension; gets people to explore differences
Observer and commentator	Comments on and interprets the group's internal process
Standard-setter/ ego-ideal	Expresses standards for the group to attempt to achieve in its functioning or applies standards in evaluating the quality of group processes (combined with evaluator-critic role, as both involve standards of achievement)
Individual	
Aggressor	Expresses disapproval of the acts, values, or feelings of others; attacks the group or the group's problem; shows envy toward another's contribution or tries to take credit for it; jokes aggressively
Blocker	Tends to be negative; resists the direction the group is headed in; tends to disagree and oppose beyond reason; attempts to bring back an issue the group has bypassed or rejected
Dominator	Tries to assert authority or superiority and to manipulate the group or certain members of the group (for example, through flattery, giving directions authoritatively, or interrupting the contributions of others)
Evader and self-confessor	Uses the audience that the group setting provides to express personal interests, feelings, or opinions that are unrelated to the group's purpose; stays off the subject to avoid commitment
Help seeker	Attempts to call forth sympathy responses from other group members by expressing insecurity, personal confusion, or self-deprecation
Playboy/girl	Makes a display of one's lack of involvement in the group's processes (for example, through cynicism, nonchalance, horseplay, and other more or less studied forms of out-of-field behavior)
Recognition seeker	Works in various ways to call attention to oneself (for example, through boasting, referring to personal achievements, or acting in unusual or inappropriate ways)
Special-interest pleader	Speaks for the small business person, the grassroots community, the housewife, labor, and so forth, usually cloaking any prejudices or biases in the stereotype that best fits one's own individual needs

Source: P. E. Mudrack and G. M. Farrell, "An Examination of Functional Role Behavior and Its Consequences for Individuals in Group Settings," *Small Group Research,* 26, No. 4 (1995), 542–571, copyright © 1995 by Sage Publications, Inc. Reprinted by Permission of Sage Publications, Inc.

The identification and casting of roles usually occurs early in a group's life. However, roles change during the course of the group's progress as the task changes or as the membership changes. For instance, what happens to a five-member group when the person who has taken on the role as chair is unable to attend a meeting? The other four members' roles must be reconfigured to handle this change in circumstance. Perhaps the person who has been secretary for the group takes the chair; then someone else takes on the note-taking role, and so on.

▪ *Leadership*

Of all the roles in a group, the leadership role is probably the most critical to the manner in which the group functions. The **leader** is the group member who positively influences the group the most in accomplishing its goal. Typically, group members bestow the role of leader on one or more group members who display behaviors usually associated with leadership. The leaders then influence the direction and development of the group.

Notice that the definition of a leader assumes that leadership behaviors move the group toward accomplishment of its goal. Because the initial stages of group development often involve defining the group goal, the leader plays an important part in determining this goal. One danger is that a leader can create a goal that is self-serving and not necessarily the one the group would have selected of its own accord.

The importance of group leadership is reflected in the number of theories and amount of research on how leaders emerge and how they influence their groups. Each theory of group leadership tends to focus on a particular aspect of leadership. Hence, no one theory is totally correct or incorrect. As you read the following brief survey of theories, think about how they might be combined to explain the dynamics of leadership in your group experiences.

Trait theory. One of the first theories to explain why someone emerges as a leader was based on identifying certain leadership traits. According to the theory's predictions, people who are taller, heavier, smarter, stronger, and more physically attractive will emerge as group leaders. However, for each trait that was identified, there were always exceptions, thus undermining the theory.

Current research along these lines has found that people who talk the most are most likely to emerge as leaders.[9] This effect reflects the obvious fact that people who don't say anything in a group minimize their ability to influence other members.

Functional theory. Another theory of leadership involves identifying the functions performed by those who are seen as leaders. This theory is based on the premise that certain functions must be performed in a group for it to accomplish its goals. These functions include initiating, coordinating, summarizing, elaborating, reducing tension, encouraging members, and managing conflict.[10] Notice that these functions are essentially the same as some of the roles identified in Table 10.1.

The functions are then categorized as either task functions or social/relational functions. (Social/relational functions are sometimes known as maintenance functions, referring to the desire to maintain the group.) A task leader is someone who is particularly adept at task functions, while a social/relational leader is adept at social functions. A task leader would be likely to initiate proposals, while a social leader would encourage other members and mediate conflicts.

When leadership is analyzed according to these functions, some research indicates that task leaders are more likely than social/relational leaders to be perceived as the leader by the other group members.[11] This could be why women, who are generally relationally oriented, are less likely than task-oriented males to be considered leaders.

Research shows mixed results about women emerging as leaders in groups. Why do you think women do or do not emerge as leaders?

What have you observed about the likelihood of a woman emerging as the leader in a group of about five people? What happens (or what would you expect to happen) in groups made up of three men and two women? Two men and three women? One man and four women? One woman and four men?

One problem with functional theory is that it has not proved widely effective in predicting who will emerge as a group leader. Which of the functions leads to leadership emergence? A person might perform the same function in two groups, emerging as the leader in one group but not in the other. How many of the functions does a member have to fulfill to be viewed as the leader? What happens when typical leadership functions are performed by more than one person?

Actually, the performance of leadership functions by multiple members reflects an approach called *shared leadership*. Groups of this sort are also sometimes known as *leaderless groups*, because they don't have a single member identified as "the leader."

Situational theory: Fiedler's contingency theory.   A **situational theory of leadership** recognizes that different people emerge as leaders under different circumstances. According to this type of theory, the nature of the task, the group composition, and other group factors will dictate the kind of leadership that is best suited for the group.

Researcher Fred Fiedler developed a **contingency theory** based on the premise that predicting who will be the most effective leader is "contingent" on

Who do you think the leader is in this group? What cues did you draw from to make your choice?

three situational factors[12] that determine whether the situation favors a task-oriented leader or a relationally oriented leader.

1. *Leader-member relations.* The most important situational factor concerns the interpersonal relationship between the leader and the other group members. This includes the amount of loyalty, attraction, confidence, and acceptance the members feel toward the leader. Leader-member relations can be regarded as either good or bad.

2. *Task structure.* The second quality deals with the complexity and clarity of the task. The more structured and less complex the task, the less confusion there will be among the group members about what needs to be done. A simple math problem of adding four two-digit numbers is a highly structured task. Deciding what to do about the homeless in America is a much more unstructured task because of its complexity and the multiplicity of possible answers.

3. *Position power.* The final situational factor is the amount of influence a person has by being in the role of assigned leader. This quality doesn't really apply to emergent leader situations, but rather to those situations in which a person is placed in charge of a group. Think of assigned leadership positions like committee chair, drill sergeant, teacher, and boss. Those positions vary in terms of how much influence is associated with them. The drill sergeant and boss probably have strong position power, whereas a peer who is appointed as the chair of a committee would have weak position power.

Figure 10.4 shows how these three situational factors result in eight possible combinations. Fiedler's research has found that cells 1, 2, 3, and 8 favor a leader who is task oriented for these reasons:

- When relationships are good (as in cells 1, 2, and 3), the leader can usually concentrate on the task regardless of his or her position power.
- A group in a fairly tumultuous state (cell 8) needs the strong guidance and direction of a task-oriented leader.

Cells 4 and 5 favor relationally oriented leadership for these reasons:

- In cell 4, the leader is liked (good leader-member relations). But with weak position power and an unstructured task, he or she has to depend on

☐ Favors task-oriented leader

■ Favors relationally oriented leader

Figure 10.4

Fiedler's Contingency Model of Leadership

Leader-member relations	Good				Poor			
Task structure	Structured		Unstructured		Structured		Unstructured	
Position power	Strong	Weak	Strong	Weak	Strong	Weak	Strong	Weak
Cell number	1	2	3	4	5	6	7	8

Source: Reprinted by permission.

member cooperation to be effective. Therefore, the leader needs to be relationally oriented.[13]

■ In cell 5, the situation favors the leader who can improve the relationships.

In the two remaining cells (6 and 7), neither style is more advantageous than the other.

Situational theory: Hersey and Blanchard's readiness theory. Another situational theory of leadership, developed by Paul Hersey and Ken Blanchard, focuses on the readiness of the members or followers.[14] That readiness will dictate the degree of task or relational behavior the leader should emphasize.

Readiness, is the degree to which the members are willing and skilled enough to perform the group's task. New employees may be willing to perform a task but may lack the necessary skills. On the other hand, a team that is discussing a change in marketing strategies may have the skills but be unwilling to generate solutions because they want to continue discussing the underlying issues.

Hersey and Blanchard's situational leadership model identifies four leadership styles for four readiness levels of the members. Each style represents a blend of task and relational behavior. These styles are really most applicable to managerial situations in organizations. However, the underlying principle has valuable applications to teams and small groups: Leaders who wish to maintain their leadership role must adapt their style to the changing conditions of the group or situation.

Figure 10.5 shows a curving arrow representing the typical path that groups travel as they develop. Notice the four corresponding leadership styles.

1. The first style, *telling,* is effective when groups are new, are uncertain about the tasks, and lack ability. The telling style is a high task leadership style in which the leader provides direction, instructions, training, and so on.

Figure 10.5

Leadership Style as a Function of Member Readiness

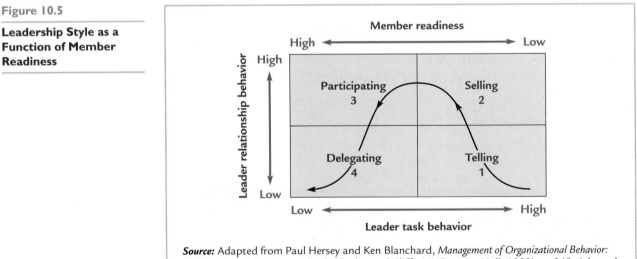

Source: Adapted from Paul Hersey and Ken Blanchard, *Management of Organizational Behavior: Utilizing Human Resources,* 6th ed. (Englewood Cliffs, NJ: Prentice-Hall, 1982), p. 248. Adapted with permission of Center for Leadership Studies, Escondido, CA. Situational Leadership ® is a registered trademark of the Center for Leadership Studies. All rights reserved.

2. The second style, *selling,* involves a high degree of both task and relational behavior. This style is usually appropriate with a group that has gained some degree of confidence in its skills. In this situation, the effective leader must use more persuasion to accomplish tasks. This means that the leader must be aware of both relational and task issues.

3. The third style, *participating,* involves greater task responsibility and independence for the group members. The leader becomes more equal to the other group members. Decision-making is shared rather than solely the responsibility of the leader.

4. The final style, *delegating,* involves letting the group provide its own leadership. This style is appropriate when a group has developed the confidence and skill to accomplish the task without the intercession of an outside leader. In this situation, the group generally provides its own leadership from among the members.

■ The Development of Groups Over Time

Groups change over the course of time. The exact nature of those changes depends on a variety of factors, such as the nature of the group task, the group membership, and the context in which the group is operating. Several models have been created in an attempt to capture the specific stages of group development. The research on these stages is often contradictory and unclear because the groups used often varied in their functions.[15] Nevertheless, understanding the stages that have been identified can give you a greater appreciation of the dynamics of group development.

Each stage reflects a change that has occurred in the task and social/relational dimensions. On the task dimension, development depends on the nature of the task but generally reflects the kind of readiness process described by the Hersey and Blanchard model. As the group develops, it should gain confidence, expand its understanding of how to perform a given task, and increase its task focus and effectiveness. On the social dimension, since group development involves developing interpersonal relationships, groups can be expected to progress through the interpersonal stages discussed in Chapter 6. That is, as individuals feel more secure in the relationships, more and more disclosure can be expected with a concurrent increase in intimacy. Of course, groups do not have to form intimate relationships to accomplish most tasks.

The following sections describe five typical stages that have been identified.

■ *Orientation (Forming)*

New groups experience a **primary tension** caused by the uncertainty associated with the forming of a new group. People feel initial discomfort in groups because they don't know what to expect. They don't know how the other members will behave, and they don't know what roles they or other members will be able to play. This uncertainty exists even when the group is made up of people who already know one another, because they are not sure how they will interact with one another in the context of the group. There is also uncertainty about the task. This uncertainty can vary a great deal, depending on how clearly the task and the procedures for accomplishing it are defined.

During the *orientation*, or *forming*, *stage*, groups try to reduce primary tension by finding out information about the other members and about the task. Sometimes groups focus on one or the other rather than trying to accomplish both at the same time. Some groups, for instance, will spend time socializing, going through introductions, and discussing members' backgrounds. (This disclosure will be limited, however, because of the lack of any significant trust or intimate relationship.) Orientation toward the task often involves each member's sharing his or her understanding of the task or seeking clarification about it.

■ *Conflict (Storming)*

One of the more stressful aspects of working in groups is that they often seem to face conflict. This is sometimes unavoidable, and it should not be viewed as destructive. The *conflict*, or *storming*, *stage* is part of the natural growth of the group and its process of developing group structure.

Group conflicts can be categorized by their degree of task or social orientation. Task conflicts arise as discussion focuses on the definition of the task and the best strategy for accomplishing it. Social-emotional and relational conflicts occur as group members begin defining their roles. Competition for similar roles may cause conflict. For instance, two individuals may struggle for sole possession of the leadership role. Personal relationships that rise and fall over the course of the group may also occasion conflicts. Chapter 11 will return to the subject of group conflicts and offer some advice for dealing with them.

■ *Emergence (Norming)*

As conflicts are resolved, the group structure begins to appear. In this stage of *emergence*, or *norming*, roles are defined, leaders emerge, decisions about the task

GLASBERGEN

"My new approach to effective team development will take a bit longer. In my plan, we raise them from birth."

process are made, and norms are established. This stage represents the creation of the working structure that will allow the group to accomplish its task.

By this point, individuals have resolved personal issues, such as seeking independence and being competitive, and have accepted the group's need for interdependence and cooperation. Members are more comfortable disclosing personal information; they form closer bonds both with the group as a whole and with other members. The group has begun to form a sense of identity, and the individuals begin to identify with the group.

The members have also reached a point where they are committed to the task and feel confident about their ability to accomplish it. The group works at developing the necessary resources and skills. Members collect information, seek outside expertise and advice, and work on improving individual skills that might be needed to complete the task.

■ *Production (Performing)*

With a structure in place, the group is now ready to accomplish its goals. In the *production*, or *performing, stage*, the group operates more smoothly than in earlier stages, though not without conflict. Differences of opinion about the issues under investigation create a **secondary tension,** but this type of conflict reflects a healthy group. The individuals have reached a high enough level of comfort with one another that they can challenge each other's ideas without fear of being personally attacked or ostracized.

Intimacy has grown, and the group has a high level of cohesion and strong positive group feelings. In this stage, though, the group is confronted with an equilibrium problem: It must balance feelings of group solidarity and interest in socializing with absorption in the task.[16] Groups can become overly concerned with relationships and thus fail to adequately address the task, or they can become overly absorbed in the task and forget the individual needs of the members. Ideally, the group reaches a peak, both in terms of the development of personal relationships and in terms of the ability to accomplish the shared task.

■ *Termination (Mourning/Adjourning)*

Ending a group can be as simple as saying good-bye at the last meeting, or it can be a more prolonged process. In the *termination*, or *adjourning, stage*, the group may continue to get together for socializing even though its task has been completed. Group members who have spent a lot of time working together and who have formed strong bonds often find it hard to let go after the completion of the task. In these cases, the term *mourning stage* may be appropriate.

Groups sometimes even seek out a new task rather than face adjournment. In my classes, students sometimes have to work on two consecutive team projects with the stipulation that the second project will involve a new grouping of students. Frequently, the groups that were cohesive and successful in the first project plead with me to let them stay together for the second one. This desire is understandable because by staying together, they would reduce the uncertainty and effort involved in forming a new group.

Small group communication is interpersonal communication among three or more people who view themselves as a group and who are working toward a shared purpose or goal. The interpersonal communication component reflects the transactional nature of groups: Each member is mutually and simultaneously influencing the others. Group members have a sense of identity that leads them to perceive themselves as a group; that is, members have a sense of who constitutes the group and who doesn't. Finally, working toward a shared goal distinguishes small group communication from general gatherings of people.

Group goals fall along a continuum of task versus social orientation, and this provides one way of classifying different types of groups. Among the highly task-oriented groups are policymaking groups, decision-making groups, and problem-solving groups. Learning groups and support, or self-help, groups are a blend of task and social orientation. Groups primarily concerned with satisfying social and relational needs, such as friends and family, represent the social end of the goal continuum.

For groups to reach their full potential, they need cooperation, diversity, and full participation of the members. Cooperation can be difficult to achieve in U.S. culture, which tends to be competitive and individualistic. Diversity is important because it increases the variety of perspectives and the information base. However, diversity can also be a source of problems because of increased misunderstandings and perceptual differences. Among the advantages of groups are increased knowledge, ability to feed off others' ideas, sharing of feedback, correction of errors of fact or perception, and satisfaction of social needs. Among the disadvantages of groups are the time and energy they require and the potential risks of participation.

A number of factors contribute to the development of group structure. Groups can be thought of as a network of relationships. As members interact, they form attractions for other members that affect their communication. Strong overall attraction leads to a cohesive group. The pattern of communication results in a communication network that then influences the subsequent interactions. Typical communication network patterns include the chain, wheel, circle, Y, and all-channel.

Norms also create structure by providing guidance about the appropriateness of behavior. Deviation from group norms can result in punishment of the deviant or changes to the norm. Members are encouraged to conform to the norms. Conformity can help a group be efficient but can also undermine adequate analysis of the group's task and the problems it faces.

Membership composition—the collection of individual members' characteristics —is another influence on group structure and behavior. Differences in characteristics such as age, sex, and culture lead to differences in the way members behave and also sometimes to stereotyping and bias.

Group roles represent the set of expected behaviors that become associated with each group member. We each settle on a set way of interacting that is affected by the roles chosen by other members. The most significant role is that of leader. Leaders are those individuals who have the most influence on the group's accomplishing its goals. Theories of leader emergence include trait theory, functional theory, and situational theory. Among the situational theories are Fielder's contingency theory and Hersey and Blanchard's readiness model, both of which identify factors that mediate the emergence of a leader. These approaches are based on matching the leader's style with various aspects of the situation or membership.

Groups go through a development process as they seek to accomplish their goals. This development often progresses through a series of stages: orientation, conflict, emergence, production, and termination. Each stage reflects some blend of task and social orientation. As a group progresses through the stages, its social development parallels the stages of interpersonal relationships. Increasing trust, self-disclosure, and intimacy are reflected in a movement toward stronger interpersonal relationships. Task orientation also increases as groups grow in confidence and skill.

Key Terms

small group communication Interpersonal communication among three or more people who view themselves as a group and who are working toward a shared purpose or goal.

task orientation A focus on accomplishing a group's goals.

social orientation A focus on meeting the social and relational needs of group members.

policymaking groups Groups charged with developing the principles by which future decisions and actions will be guided.

decision-making groups Groups faced with having to make a choice between alternatives.

problem-solving groups Groups that focus their attention on analyzing some problem, trying to determine its causes and effects, and developing the best solution.

learning groups Groups whose purpose is the sharing or discovery of information.

support, or **self-help groups** Learning groups in which individuals are attempting to learn more about themselves.

social groups Groups that exist to satisfy members' needs for companionship, belonging, and self-confirmation.

structuration A process by which a group develops its own unique structure and corresponding culture.

duality of structures The principle that a group's structure is the product of the group interaction while at the same time dictating the nature of the interaction.

cohesion Attraction of group members to the group and to each other.

groupthink A phenomenon in which belonging to a group creates a tendency in members to accept the group's way of thinking, even when realism or common sense would dictate otherwise.

communication network A consistent pattern of interaction among group members.

norms Rules that prescribe what is appropriate and inappropriate behavior.

social norms Norms drawn from society that can be applied within a given group.

deviance Violating a norm.

group norms Norms created for the specific group in which they occur.

implicit norms Norms that are followed without any group discussion of them.

explicit norms Norms created when groups discuss the rules that govern their behavior.

conformity Following group norms because of group pressure, even if those norms would not otherwise be followed.

membership composition The collection of group members' individual characteristics.

group role A set of specific behaviors associated with each group member.

assigned role A set of expected behaviors associated with a particular group position.

emerging role   A role that evolves for a group member as the group interacts.

leader   The group member who positively influences the group the most in accomplishing its goal.

situational theory of leadership   A theory of leadership that recognizes that different people emerge as leaders under different circumstances.

contingency theory   A situational theory of leadership that claims the effectiveness of a task or relational leader depends upon leader-member relations, task structure, and position power.

readiness   The degree to which group members are willing and skilled enough to perform the group's task.

primary tension   The uncertainty and uneasiness associated with the forming of a new group.

secondary tension   Uneasiness in a group caused by conflicts.

Review Questions

1. Explain what it means for a small group to be defined as a form of interpersonal communication.
2. How do problem-solving groups differ from support groups?
3. Identify three advantages and three disadvantages of groups.
4. In what ways do roles and norms affect relationships in groups?
5. In what ways is a diverse membership both advantageous and disadvantageous for groups?
6. Compare the functional theory of leadership with situational theories.
7. How do the stages of group development relate to group structure?

Chapter 11

Small Group Communication: Skills for Members and Leaders

Objectives

Studying this chapter will allow you to:

1. Explain the role that analysis of the situation, goal and role clarification, and research play in preparing to participate in a group.
2. Identify the basics of the reflective thinking process, the creative problem-solving sequence, and brainstorming.
3. Describe essential group communication skills.
4. Identify and describe four task skills relevant to group work.
5. Identify and describe the four social skills that help create a positive group climate.

magine that your boss has asked you to serve on a team made up of managers from various departments. The team will be examining ways of increasing the company's share of the market. After reading Chapter 10, you should have a pretty good idea of what to expect in terms of the interaction dynamics. You know that each person will be developing a particular role and that your group will go through a developmental process. But what can you and your colleagues do to make the group as effective as possible?

This chapter will discuss four areas of skill development that you can work to improve: (1) planning and preparation, (2) essential group communication skills, (3) task skills, and (4) social skills.

■ Planning and Preparation

Planning and preparation are significant factors in group success. They occur at an individual level before the group meets and also at the group level as part of the group process. The elements of good planning and preparation include analyzing the situation, clarifying goals and roles, doing any needed research, and considering the possible approaches.

■ *Analyzing of the Situation*

The process of joining a new group is filled with uncertainties and apprehension. To help reduce your uncertainty, try to gather as much information as you can in advance of the group's first meeting. Among the first questions to ask are these:

- What are the goals of the group?
- What is the purpose of the group?
- To whom is the group responsible?
- What will happen with what the group produces?
- What are the expectations facing the group?

The next set of questions concerns what you will bring to the group:

- What knowledge or expertise can you offer the group?
- What role are you expected to play?
- What role do you want to play?

Next, you should consider the other members. You have probably seen many TV shows in which a new cast member has been added, as in *NYPD Blue, Law and Order, ER,* or *Chicago Hope.* There's usually a scene in which the new person is talking to a friend about what to expect from the people in the existing group. The new member tries to find out as much as possible about the members, the atmosphere, the work ethic, and so on. You will need to find out similar information.

- What does each member contribute?
- What problems exist among the members?
- How will you need to behave in reaction to the other people?

If you know, for instance, that one member is extremely dominant and talkative, you might plan on being a bit more forceful in trying to include other members in the discussion. One challenge of analyzing the other members is that your dyadic interactions with each member might not be very representative of his or her behavior in a group. Sometimes people are more outgoing or more introverted when they are in a team situation.

Finally, examine and understand the agenda and consider any changes you might want to propose. An **agenda** is an outline of the issues to be covered in a meeting, including the order in which they will be considered. If no agenda has been circulated, you might suggest to whoever is convening the meeting that one be prepared. If you are in charge of the group, you will want to prepare and disseminate an agenda. Agendas offer a number of advantages.

- They help members reduce uncertainty by letting them know in advance the nature of the meeting.
- They let members assemble any necessary information that might be relevant to the discussion.
- They form the basis for the initial organization of the discussion and help the group stay focused.

■ *Clarifying Goals and Roles*

People often enter groups with only vague notions about the group's purpose. If the goal is not defined clearly before the group meets, then it is essential for the group to spend time clarifying the goal. There are three types of goals that operate in groups.

1. **Individual goals.**   Think back to the scenario at the beginning of this chapter, in which you are assigned to a team that will analyze ways to increase the company's market share. You will probably have an individual goal of participating in the group in a way that makes your boss happy and ensures your continued employment, raises, and promotion. You will also want to be liked by the other group members and to be regarded as a valued member.

2. **Group goals.**   In our scenario, your group will probably have a goal of producing a written proposal that outlines some plan of action for the company to increase its market share. The group also has a goal of creating something that is praised by the company and that brings recognition and reward to the group. Even if a group's original goal is dictated by other people, that goal will be refined and redefined as the group develops.

3. **Organizational,** or **external, goals.**   The group is influenced by the organization in which it operates. The organization itself has goals for the group. In our scenario, the company expects some plan that can be implemented to increase profitability and market share. These organizational goals will influence the decision-making of the group.

The individual, group, and organizational goals are sometimes in conflict, and this can lead to group ineffectiveness. Clarifying all these goals can help you understand what is expected of you as a member. Table 11.1 offers a checklist for goal clarification that can be useful in many group situations.

Table 11.1 Goal Clarification Checklist

Questions	Sample Answers
What are your goals in this group?	Friendships, raise, minimal time.
What motivates you to be a member of this group?	Other members, honor, job security.
How well is the group meeting your goals?	Others seem to value my ideas.
What are the individual goals of other group members?	Some want friends, some want power.
What are the goals of the group?	A written report in two weeks.
How compatible are your individual goals with the group goals?	I can improve my relationships with these workers and add to the project.
What are the organization's goals and expectations for the group?	Give us something that is feasible and easy to implement.
How well is the group meeting its own goals and the goals of the organization?	Our initial report was on time, and we are receiving good feedback.

In addition to clarifying goals, it's important to clarify the roles to be played, both your own and those of other members. Understanding the role you are expected to play lets you know the type of research, information, functions, and actions that will be expected of you. Knowing other members' expected roles helps reduce initial tension and improve your ability to adapt to the situation.

For example, suppose you are asked to join a committee that is examining student life at your school. You would want to clarify the group goal, but you would also want to know what is expected of you. Are you there just to tell about your own experiences or as a representative of the student body? Are you expected to collect any data from other students or to find and read relevant materials? Who are the other members, and what are their roles? Whenever you are asked to join or lead a group, you will want to clarify the roles as much as possible so that you can prepare yourself effectively.

■ Research and Preparation

There are times when groups are composed of informed individuals who already possess all the information they need for making decisions or solving problems. Many times, though, groups must postpone their progress till they collect the necessary information. Thus, having a group of individuals who are adequately prepared to participate can enhance the group's efficiency dramatically.

You can do some of the research needed before the group meets for the first time. The group's goal and agenda provide direction for starting your research. In the scenario at the beginning of this chapter, you already know that you will need information about the company's current sales activity, its market share, its competitors' market shares, product lines, and so on. Gathering this information beforehand will facilitate group meetings.

Sometimes, appointed group leaders will take the lead by collecting and disseminating background information to all the members in advance of their meeting. This provides a level playing field for each member. However, it can also create a homogeneous and narrow perspective on the issue if no one seeks any other information. Each member usually has access to some unique information, and it is the sharing of that information that makes each member so valuable to a group's success.

The nature of the task dictates the type of information needed before and during group decision-making. For example, analyzing your company's market share would depend primarily on in-house data, interviews with marketing experts, and trade publication reports. Typical sources of information would include the library (books and journals), organizational reports, information-gathering interviews, surveys, and the Internet. The information would need to be up-to-date, credible, and clear. (You may want to jump ahead and review the specific suggestions for gathering information provided in Chapter 13.)

Sometimes the information you need doesn't exist. In this case, you might have to design a project to collect such data. Suppose you were on a community committee dealing with race relations, and you wanted to know if minority members in your community felt discriminated against. Your group might conduct an attitude survey to create representative information that was not otherwise available.

■ Considering the Approaches

Although the task will dictate the exact nature of the group process, there are several common approaches that groups can use to arrive at a decision. Each approach has its own benefits, and research results are mixed about whether one is better than another. Research suggests, in fact, that groups naturally cover all the necessary decision-making steps without being told to follow a preset format.[1] However, following a structured approach appears to have several advantages.

- Members have a clearer picture of where the group is and where it is going.
- It is easier to tell when the group is diverging from its format (although divergence isn't necessarily bad).
- The probability is greater that each necessary step will be covered.
- Time spent in deciding what comes next can be reduced.
- The efficiency of the group is generally improved (less time is spent going in circles).

The following sections describe some of the typical structured approaches. The format does not have to be complex, nor are groups limited to one of these prescribed formats. Certainly, the group may create its own procedure for dealing with the issues it faces.

The reflective thinking process. John Dewey, a noted philosopher and scholar, proposed in his 1910 book *How We Think* that individual decisions could be improved if decision-makers followed the steps in his **reflective thinking**

"My team has created a very innovative solution,
but we're still looking for a problem to go with it."

process. The format involves three significant components: problem, criteria, and solution. The following steps represent an adaptation of his approach to decision-making or problem solving:

1. Define, locate, and describe the problem.
2. Analyze and explore the problem. How significant and widespread is the problem? What are the symptoms? What are the causes? Who and what are affected?
3. Establish explicit criteria by which to select the best solution. What are the minimum requirements of any solution that is generated (for example, cost limitations, quickness of implementation)?
4. Develop a list of solutions.
5. Evaluate the possible solutions by applying the criteria.
6. Select the solution that seems to best meet the criteria and that fares best in comparison to the other solutions.
7. Plan how to implement the solution and how to evaluate its effectiveness.
8. Implement the solution.
9. Evaluate the solution's effectiveness. If the solution is not effective, examine why it is failing and repeat the appropriate reflective thinking steps.

The reflective thinking process attempts to ensure that all the relevant issues are considered before a decision is made. Nevertheless, groups attempting to follow this process or a similar one often encounter some pitfalls. One common tendency is to jump right to solutions. In the classic movie *Twelve Angry Men*, the jurors take a vote as soon as they get to the jury room without first discussing the merits of the case. In other words, the jury moves right to the decision point. Such haste increases the risk of a terrible decision or of a solution that has little to do with the true nature of the problem.

However, when the problem is already understood, focusing directly on solutions can be an appropriate action. Imagine that your company has a product that is 30 percent more expensive than the competition and therefore does not sell as well. Assuming that the company is making the product as inexpensively as possible, the team can focus immediately on developing a plan for marketing the more expensive product in the same way that the manufacturers of Cadillacs, Mercedes Benzes, and BMWs plan how to sell their expensive cars.

The creative problem-solving sequence. Another tendency of groups is to skip the stage of establishing criteria for choosing a solution. Sometimes this is actually advocated. The possible inhibiting effect produced by discussing the criteria can be avoided by generating a set of solutions first.[2] This sequence—discussing solutions first and then the criteria—is called a **creative problem-solving sequence.**[3]

What generally happens is that *implicit criteria* are generated in support of each solution but are not specifically identified. If the group is fortunate, it will eventually recognize the need to establish *explicit criteria,* ones that are specifically discussed and agreed upon. The following excerpt shows this process at work.

RALPH	Increasing the training of our sales staff will help us get more market share.
NONA	We need an advertising campaign that stresses the quality of our product.
ALTON	I think we need to emphasize the service we provide after the sale of the product.
SHANNA	Before we decide on any of these solutions, we should establish some criteria. For instance, I think we can't afford to spend a lot of money because our profit margin is so low right now.
NONA	Okay, whatever plan we come up with has to be relatively inexpensive.
RALPH	Right.
ALTON	Okay.
NONA	Any plan we develop needs to be one that we can implement quickly because the problem is so immediate.
ALTON	I agree. Are there any more criteria?
RALPH	Sure, it's got to increase sales.
ALTON	Good. Then we've got three criteria: The solution needs to be inexpensive, quick to implement, and increase sales.

As this excerpt demonstrates, it can sometimes be useful for group members to suggest solutions before they have established the criteria for judging them. It's important, though, that the criteria be identified before the final decision is made. Deciding on a solution without applying any criteria can turn decision-making into a political power struggle. Without criteria, group members tend to fight for the solutions they favor without adequate analysis of the merits of each solution.

Proponents of the creative problem-solving sequence stress the role of creativity throughout the process. Generating solutions and criteria requires creativity, and creativity requires openness. For example, individuals need to feel comfortable enough in the group to make risky suggestions without fear of embarrassment or loss of face. Problem analysis requires creativity as well. Often, individuals approach problems with a number of preconceptions about the causes and effects. Creative problem analysis means having an open mind and thinking broadly about the problem.

Suppose you were on a team that was asked to explain why a large number of students drop out of your college after their first year. Your first response might be that they didn't like the campus or couldn't afford it. But there are other potential causes that should be explored as well: for instance, a weak high school education, immaturity, lack of friends, poor advising, being in the wrong major, and culture shock. Creative problem solving would require that you and other team members keep an open mind while you explore the possibilities.

Brainstorming.   One method that helps generate creative input is called brainstorming. **Brainstorming** is a method of producing ideas by emphasizing quantity over quality. The sole objective of brainstorming is to generate as many responses to a question as possible in as short a time as possible.

In a group setting, brainstorming is a high-risk activity for individuals because of the potential threat to their face. People may worry about sounding foolish presenting off-the-wall ideas or thoughts they haven't fully considered. The biggest deterrent to effective brainstorming is self-censorship, when members decide not to voice an idea because they fear it isn't good enough. To overcome this danger, there are a number of rules that should be followed.

1. Put aside judgments and evaluations. Avoid reacting to the ideas. Save evaluation until all ideas are generated.
2. Adopt a "try anything" attitude. No ideas are too weird. Be willing to suggest anything.
3. Use each idea as a catalyst for other ideas. The most ridiculous idea can trigger someone else's practical suggestion.
4. Encourage piggybacking on each other's ideas. Each member should feel comfortable adding to or editing other members' ideas.
5. Recognize that once an idea is presented, it no longer belongs to the individual but becomes the property of the group. Set aside ownership and ego involvement.
6. Make sure that *all* ideas get recorded.
7. Make sure that everyone participates. A quiet member means that the group is not tapping its full potential. Ask for and encourage ideas from everyone.
8. Encourage and reward the most off-the-wall ideas. This helps stimulate creativity.
9. Remember, brainstorming success is measured in quantity, not quality.

For each of the following situations, decide which approach—reflective thinking, creative problem solving, or brainstorming—would be best to use:

1. A group trying to decide on a theme for a dance
2. A neighborhood group looking at ways to reduce crime in the area

3. A committee, made up of members from many departments, charged with the job of improving employee morale
4. A group of union members trying to decide how they can get higher wages from their employer
5. A group of employees deciding on a retirement gift for their boss
6. A group of coworkers who have been asked to come up with a way to reduce costs while maintaining the quality of their product

Flexibility of approach. Considering various strategies and techniques that can be adopted during a group interaction is a valuable component of planning and preparing. However, what happens when the group actually convenes might be totally different from what you anticipated. You might develop a logical and effective method for the group to follow only to have that method abandoned because of the political nature of group interactions.

For this reason, your planning and preparation must be accompanied by an ability to adapt and be flexible. The most effective team members are those who can abandon their plans and adopt a new strategy in light of the unique dynamics encountered in each new group. Flexibility is actually an essential skill in groups, and we'll have more to say about it in the next section.

Think about the task groups in which you have participated. How well did they follow a particular format or method? To what degree did following or not following a format influence their effectiveness? The final product? The group satisfaction?

▌ Being an Effective Team Member and Leader

In the simplest terms, leaders are those group members who exhibit more leadership qualities than anyone else. In general, leaders are those members who take on the greatest responsibility for moving the group toward its goal. They tend to display such behaviors as initiating, clarifying, seeking input, giving input, providing direction, keeping on task, and showing concern for members' welfare.

But individuals do not have to aspire to leadership to play an important role in the group. Being an effective member requires providing appropriate input; listening actively, objectively, and critically; and being flexible and adaptive.

Actually, the skills that make someone an effective team member are not very different from those that make an individual an effective leader. Chapter 10 mentioned shared leadership, in which all members provide leadership as each performs needed functions. That arrangement helps us recognize that all members share responsibility for a group's success. This section will discuss skills needed by both leaders and team members.

▪ *Essential Group Communication Skills*

Some skills are needed by all participants if a group is to be effective. These are not skills that deal directly with accomplishing the task or maintaining a positive social atmosphere. Rather, they are essential group communication skills that all group members must exhibit. As you read through these skills, consider the degree to which you possess each one.

Providing appropriate input and information. The full potential of a group is met only when every member contributes. The information that each member has is like a piece of a jigsaw puzzle. If one member sits quietly throughout a group meeting, then there will be a hole in the final puzzle where that member's piece is supposed to be. The group may not even be aware of the hole. To avoid contributing to such problems, you need to be an active participant, providing relevant information, ideas, suggestions, and opinions as appropriate.

Deciding what is "appropriate" is not an easy task, however. Read the following interaction between Arielle, Brian, and Cleo, who are discussing how to reduce college student costs. Decide whether each member is providing appropriate input.

ARIELLE Books keep getting more and more expensive. Even used books cost a fortune.

BRIAN I know. My books cost me over $350 for this semester alone.

ARIELLE I usually try to find friends who are in classes I'm going to take and buy their books.

BRIAN That's a great idea. If we did that campuswide, everyone could save money.

CLEO I like to buy a lot of the bestsellers to read during the summer. Usually I can find them in paperback at the discount stores and save a lot of money that way.

ARIELLE If everyone traded books, though, would the bookstores lose a lot of money?

BRIAN Who cares?

CLEO Some of those authors, like Danielle Steel, make millions of dollars from their books.

All three members of the group are making contributions. However, Arielle's and Brian's comments focus on the cost of textbooks, while Cleo deals with recreational reading. Cleo's comments are actually inappropriate because they don't relate to the discussion.

The nature of the task will determine the type of contribution that you can make. Some of your contributions will be in the form of information based on the knowledge you have acquired through your experiences and studies. This knowledge base can be supplemented by the research you do prior to and during the group's deliberations. When the task is more value oriented, you are likely to share opinions and personal insights. These contributions involve a degree of self-disclosure and reflect your values and beliefs.

You can be a valuable participant even if you don't have any knowledge of the issue under discussion. You can listen to others' comments, ask questions, and provide feedback. Just because you don't know anything about the issue being discussed doesn't excuse you from participating. Participation can come in the form of asking for more information, seeking clarification, and keeping the discussion focused.

Listening actively, objectively, and critically. Making appropriate contributions depends on maintaining an awareness of the group interaction. Listening provides you with that awareness. In the discussion of college costs, Cleo did not demonstrate very effective listening skills.

Chapter 3 discussed a number of principles concerning listening, including the nature of active, objective, and critical listening. All of these types of listening are necessary in group discussions.

1. *Listening actively.* As you learned in Chapter 3, this means that you ask questions, seek clarification, display attentive behaviors, and provide confirming responses. Each member has a responsibility to play an active role in understanding what the other members are saying. This means asking questions to gain more information. It also means asking for clarification when you don't understand what has been said, rather than remaining silent. From time to time, you should also summarize what you have been hearing to ensure that you are in tune with the group discussion. Remember that confirming responses let others know that you value them and what they are saying. Active listening promotes continued input from other members.

2. *Listening objectively.* This means seeking to learn the information that the other members have to offer. Your goal is to try to learn and retain information

Group members need to be able to listen actively, objectively, and critically if they are to be effective.

that will help you contribute to informed group decisions. There is a balance that must be reached between retaining your own opinions and being open to differing views. You can be so tied to your own views that you fail to listen objectively to contrary opinions. You can also be so open that you are unwilling to form or voice your own views. Chapter 3 offered several suggestions for listening objectively: listening for key points, listening to both the big picture and the supportive details, focusing on the message rather than the speaker, avoiding mental arguing, and listening actively.

3. *Listening critically.* It serves as the basis for one of the important qualities of group interactions—being able to provide immediate feedback and constructive criticism. Listening critically involves analyzing the information and opinions provided by other members. Nobody's ideas are perfect; however, groups can easily fall prey to blind acceptance of a dominant member's proposals. Critical listening guards against such blind acceptance and against the emergence of groupthink.

You need to systematically evaluate the information you hear and share your evaluation with the group. This evaluation includes weighing the validity and applicability of the evidence as well as examining the logic and reasoning used to support claims. In sharing your evaluation, you want to do so in a constructive and confirming manner. When each member does this, the group maximizes its strengths because the final conclusions are based on a careful analysis of the issues. Listening critically does not mean criticizing personal characteristics of other members, but rather sharing your questions and concerns about the arguments supporting their claims.

Being flexible and adaptive. Group success depends on a cooperative spirit. Cooperation requires flexibility in the way members approach both the issue under investigation and the group. Groups fail when the members refuse to adapt to the task or to the other members. Suppose two members are vying for the role of leader, with each advocating a different approach to the task. The group will be stuck at an impasse as long as neither member is willing to be flexible and adapt.

Flexibility means adapting your communication behaviors to meet the changes in the group. Remember that groups go through phases, and communication changes in the group, with each phase. If you are inflexible, your style may work well during one stage but become inappropriate and dysfunctional during another.[4]

Leaders, too, must demonstrate flexibility if they wish to remain leaders. The most successful leaders are those who are able to adapt their leadership style to changes in the group.[5] For instance, an effective leader will use one strategy to deal with primary tension, such as some initial social event, and then adopt a different strategy to get the group to focus its attention on the task. In the last chapter, we studied a model of leadership (Hersey and Blanchard's) that was based on members' readiness to perform a task. That model implicitly tells us that leaders have to adapt their style as the members' skills and readiness develop.

Part of being flexible involves balancing cooperation with resistance to conformity. You can be *too* flexible and adaptive. There is a song about being a successful poker player that goes, "You've got to know when to hold them and know when to fold them." Likewise, as a group member, there are times when you need to maintain a stable and consistent role and other times when you need to be flexible. You don't want to simply agree to a certain position because it is the "fashionable" one to take. You should present your case while the other members listen objectively. If they still reject your position, then you should consider adapting to the majority position.

In essence, you need to put the group's goals ahead of your individual goals; you need to adopt a collectivistic attitude rather than an individualistic one. However, when accepting the group's position means abandoning your basic values or beliefs, dropping out of the group is sometimes the best course of action.

There are many skills that you will need to be an effective team member. Use a search engine to search the World Wide Web for any of the following terms: "team building," "team skills," or "leadership skills." You will find a large number of consulting and training companies. Look at some of their pages. What kind of training seems to be offered the most? What skills do they suggest they can improve or develop in their clients? Why do you suppose there are so many companies offering these services?

The Era of Mason, Matlock Is Over

The traditional model of the lawyer is the strong, all-knowing individual who single-handedly guides the client through the legal maze. You know—Matlock, or Mason. Now filtering in from the business world is something completely different—the concept of "team lawyering." This is a dynamic model of strategic alliances of lawyer groups which are designed to bring enhanced resources and synergism to a particular case or transaction without adding organizational layers or overhead.

. . . The business world is increasingly turning to teamwork as a solution to the productivity problem. Quality circles can lower costs and ensure quality. Strategic partnerships can permit entry to new markets. As a result of these developments, clients are increasingly familiar with business arrangements that involve assembling effective teams. No wonder, then, that clients want lawyers who can assemble cooperative combinations of legal expertise when the situation merits it. Joan Haratani, a litigator with Crosby, Heafy, Roach & May handling breast implant work, frequently finds herself a member of a team composed of lawyers from several different firms. She reports that litigating with an effective team is invigorating, powerful and stress reducing.

Here's an example of how groups are being utilized in the legal profession. This article includes a list of skills and suggestions that parallel many of those included in this chapter.

Team Players

Mutual respect is a key, she says. "I take care to select people who won't let me down and who communicate well with each other," says Haratani. "This reduces monitoring and follow-up activities. Effective teams require effective team players."

Pat Kayajanian, now head of the six-office legal department of Farmers Insurance Exchange, remembers a case in which her former law firm, an insurance defense firm, teamed up with Johnnie Cochran in a sizeable personal injury matter. Her firm handled all the discovery and motion work, which they were well-equipped to do, while Cochran handled the jury trial. "It's crucial to have your roles and responsibilities well defined," says Kayajanian.

But wait. It's no secret that the typical lawyer's approach to teamwork goes something like this: "Everybody do as I say and no one will get hurt."

Competitive Behavior

American culture in general emphasizes competitive rather than cooperative behavior. The training of American lawyers focuses almost exclusively on the mastery of self and of subject matter, not on cooperative processes.

While being an effective team player may not come naturally to American lawyers, the experts say it can be learned. What makes a good team? What makes a good team player? Don't assume your high school football or debate team experience will help you much. In *Team Players and Teamwork, The New Competitive Business Strategy* (Jossey-Bass, 1990), Glenn M. Parker explores 11 characteristics of an effective team.

A Good Team

1. The "atmosphere" tends to be informal with no obvious tensions and no boredom.
2. There is a lot of discussion and participation, which remains pertinent to the task.
3. The task or objective of the group is well understood and accepted by the members.
4. The members listen to each other.
5. There is disagreement which is not suppressed but is carefully examined with the expectation of finding a solution.
6. Most decisions are reached by a kind of consensus.
7. Criticism is frequent, frank and relatively comfortable and without personal attack. Criticism is oriented toward removing an obstacle to the group's objective.
8. There are few "hidden agendas." Everybody appears to know how everybody else feels about any matter under discussion.
9. When action is taken, clear assignments are made and accepted.
10. The chairman of the group does not dominate it. Leadership may shift as different members act as "resources" for the group.
11. The group is self-conscious about its own operations. It will stop to examine how well it is doing or what may be interfering with its operation.

Source: Donna Beck Weaver, "The Era of Mason, Matlock Is Over" *California Bar Journal*, Online. May 1996. Reprinted from the *California Bar Journal*.

■ Task Skills

Sharing information, listening effectively, and adapting are essential group communication skills, but there are additional skills that deal directly with the task and social processes unique to groups. The failure of some group members to display specific task and social skills will not necessarily undermine the effectiveness of the group. However, these skills need to be exhibited by at least some of the group's members,[6] and a person who displays several of them may well gain recognition as a team leader.

This section considers task skills, which directly concern behaviors that provide direction, guidance, and structure to group decision-making and problem solving. Task skills include initiating, managing goals, managing procedures and promoting involvement.

Initiating. "Now that everyone has gotten to know each other a little, let's talk about how each of us defines the problem." This statement reflects initiation on the part of the speaker. *Initiation,* in a group setting, means being the first member to propose a direction or idea that has not yet been considered. Groups can't move forward unless members display initiative.

There are two types of initiation. The first, **information initiation,** involves being the first to offer a new idea or piece of information. The second, **procedural initiation,** involves suggesting a change in the direction or course of action that the group is following, as in the sample statement at the beginning of this section.

Initiation at first seems like a rather easy behavior to display, but there are risks. Making a comment that is innovative or different from previous ones puts your face at risk. Sometimes people laugh at something that is new, different, or unusual. You can also initiate at the wrong time. You might suggest moving to a discussion of problem solutions when other members of the group don't feel they have adequately discussed criteria. This can result in the group's rejecting your initiative and a possible weakening of your influence.

Making a comment that changes the direction of the discussion may prove to disconfirm the previous speaker:

SANDY   I think a major question we need to discuss is whether we can afford the proposal.

LYNN   Let's take a look at the calendar and plan how we can implement the proposal.

Lynn's comment shows initiative because it offers a new suggestion about the group's direction. However, Lynn has ignored Sandy's previous comment, thus disconfirming the value of Sandy's contribution. Sandy's suggestion about discussing cost might get lost because of Lynn's initiative, and Sandy might become reluctant to offer additional comments. Lynn should have waited until later to suggest discussing the implementation or should have first acknowledged Sandy's suggestion.

Managing goals. Groups often fail to identify their goals adequately. Even when they do identify their goals, these goals sometimes are forgotten or misconstrued during the course of the group interaction. Members can help groups avoid these pitfalls by effectively **managing goals** and periodically directing the group discussion toward goals.

Initially, groups need to discuss their objectives so that all the members have shared understanding. As the group proceeds, there need to be "goal watchdogs" who are able to identify times when the group is drifting away from its goals or has implicitly changed its goals. Goals do change as groups proceed with their tasks, but such change needs to be deliberate and conscious. Individuals who are skilled at goal management must decide whether a given tangential discussion is leading to potential revelations and insights or whether it is simply taking the group further from its goals.

Managing procedures. Groups are fluent entities, always moving and changing, and as a result they need direction. Group efficiency can be improved by establishing and following specific procedures, such as the methods discussed earlier for approaching a decision. **Managing procedures** involves helping the group decide on a course of action and then helping the group stay on course. Groups need to be put back on course periodically when they go adrift.

Group members need to decide, for instance, when they have finished a particular issue and are ready to move on to the next issue. This can be accomplished either by suggesting that it is time for the next issue or by asking if there are any additional points that need to be covered before moving on: "We've been talking a lot about the problem, and maybe we should move on to discuss possible criteria for a solution. Does anyone have anything else we should discuss about the problem before we do?" Table 11.2 lists a number of procedures that can be followed as part of managing a meeting.

Table 11.2 Ten Procedures to Follow to Create a Successful Meeting

1. Arrange for the best time and the best location.

2. Develop and disseminate an agenda before the meeting. Consult with other members in advance about the content of the agenda.

3. Secure any necessary supportive materials, supplies, equipment, or nourishment that might be needed during the meeting.

4. Start the meeting promptly.

5. Start by asking for any additions or changes to the agenda. Let the group approve changes.

6. Use the agenda as the guide for the issues that are discussed and the order of discussion. Keep to the agenda as much as possible. The majority should agree on any alteration.

7. Manage the time fairly for each agenda item. Don't spend too much time on early issues and shortchange later issues. The group should decide if the intent is to meet again to complete unfinished items or to establish a time line for the agenda (for instance, fifteen minutes on each of four issues that need to be discussed in an hour).

8. Make sure minutes of the meeting are kept and later disseminated to the participants.

9. Before the meeting ends, make a plan for dealing with any unresolved issues, such as scheduling another meeting. Don't let unfinished business items get lost.

10. End the meeting as scheduled.

Promoting involvement.   Not all group members have the same level of group skills. Some members, for instance, will be reluctant to engage in the three essential skills discussed earlier. Remember Jawan and Monica in the environmental group in Chapter 10? They did not provide appropriate input or information; in fact, they didn't speak at all. The other group members should be getting them involved.

You can help others participate by asking for their input. Simply asking individuals by name for their thoughts is often enough to prompt their participation. Try to value the input of everyone. Let everyone know that his or her input is desired and needed. As the group is reaching a conclusion on a particular issue, be sure to canvass all members to see if they feel comfortable with the decision. Larger groups do this by using Robert's Rules of Order, which call for making motions and voting on those motions.

Participating involves putting your face on the line. You can help create an environment in which individuals feel secure enough to voice their thoughts and share information without fearing a loss of face. The use of confirming responses, encouraging remarks, and praise are effective ways to create such an atmosphere. When challenging an idea, you need to provide constructive criticism that confirms the value of the contributor: "Arielle, that's a good point about rising book prices, but to analyze student costs overall we might want to focus on the more expensive items like tuition and housing."

To what degree do these students seem involved in the team? What cues are there that support your impression?

Think about any group-related experiences you've had on the Internet. If you haven't already, you may soon participate in a "virtual" task group that meets in cyberspace. What skills are you likely to need to be effective both in face-to-face groups and in "virtual" groups? What skills are needed in face-to-face groups that aren't needed in virtual groups? What skills are needed in virtual groups but not in face-to-face groups?

■ Social Skills

The social and emotional atmosphere of a group can have a dramatic impact on the group's effectiveness and the satisfaction of the members. Ignoring the social and relational needs of members can hamper a group's ability to deal with the task and lead to low motivation, poor morale, and a high member dropout rate. In the early stages of a new group's development, there is a particularly strong need to help define roles, create trust, and establish positive relationships. Some individuals are particularly adept at forging a positive atmosphere, managing interpersonal conflicts, and ensuring that social needs are met.

Developing and maintaining personal relationships. Chapter 10 identified meeting social needs and having interpersonal relationships as two advantages of groups. People like to have positive and healthy relationships in groups. Some individuals, though, become so wrapped up in the task that they neglect the need to form and maintain relationships.

Positive relationships actually improve a group's task performance. In the TV series *NYPD Blue,* there is a marked improvement in the effectiveness of the detective unit when newly added characters join the other members for dinner or drinks. As the writers of this series recognize, the development of good personal relationships enhances work relationships.

Developing positive personal relationships with group members requires the type of strong interpersonal communication skills discussed in Chapter 7. Here are some ways you can help develop and maintain positive group relationships:

- Show an interest in the other group members as people.
- Find out about each member's background, interests, values, beliefs, and attitudes.
- Share information about yourself.
- Work to develop sufficient trust within the entire group so that everyone feels comfortable and willing to self-disclose.
- Be friendly, warm, considerate, and helpful.
- Express genuine concern for members' welfare.
- Listen actively and express confirming responses.
- Suggest that group members initially spend time introducing themselves and sharing information about themselves.
- Plan social events in the beginning and throughout the group's existence to aid the development of relationships.

Creating a positive atmosphere.   The activities that help develop relationships will also help create a positive, supportive atmosphere. A positive atmosphere promotes the development of group cohesion, and cohesive groups are more productive.[7]

You can help other group members develop a positive regard for the group. Part of this process involves finding a balance between the group's need to have fun and its need to produce. Not all members have the same needs, and this makes creating a positive atmosphere more challenging. Some members will be highly task oriented and will feel that socializing is inefficient. Other members will be highly relationally oriented and would rather spend time socializing than addressing the issue. You need to adapt the group activities to meet everyone's needs.

Here are some steps you can take to help create a positive atmosphere:

- Help members identify with the group. Create a group name, a logo, T-shirts, customs, and norms.
- Develop pride in group membership. Express your own pride in being a member of the group. Make the group attractive: Publicize accomplishments, activities, and so forth.
- Recognize and praise group members' work, both within the group and to others.
- Look for fun things for the group to do together. Create group events.
- Let group members know you enjoy working with them.
- Openly address problems, crises, or conflicts confronting the group.

Reducing tension.   You've experienced the value that a well-timed joke can have during a tense moment in a group. The very nature of human interaction leads to moments of high tension. That tension can immobilize groups. Providing comic relief (even without Robin Williams, Whoopi Goldberg, or Billy Crystal) is one way to reduce the tension and move the group forward.

Not everyone is good at knowing how to be funny at the right time. Tension can also be reduced by having the group take a break, changing to another topic for a while (though the original issue needs to be addressed again later), or conducting a social event. In the TV series *M*A*S*H*, surgeon Hawkeye Pierce constantly helped reduce the tension of the operating room with his jokes and antics. The group also engaged in events designed to raise morale and relieve tension, such as a mock Olympics, a spectacular bonfire, a mouse race, an interunit bowling competition, and a Kentucky Derby party.

Sometimes tension is best handled by directly discussing it. Individuals in a group may experience a high level of stress as they approach a deadline, and at such moments, they may engage in face-threatening activities like name-calling and backstabbing. Talking about the tension that everyone is feeling and why they are feeling it often helps defuse the situation. A certain amount of catharsis is experienced when everyone realizes that they share the same feelings.

Managing conflict collaboratively.   A final skill you can bring to a group is the ability to help members address and manage conflict in a collaborative manner. There are two situations in which you might find yourself needing such a skill: when you are a mediator in a conflict among other group members and when you are one of the parties involved in the conflict.

As a mediator you can attempt to get both parties to address the conflict according to the principles outlined in Chapter 5. As a party in the conflict, you can apply these same principles. Mediators usually have an easier time maintaining objectivity and keeping their emotions in check. That's not as easy when you are one of the parties in the conflict. Regardless of your role, the conflicting parties need to manage their emotions and openly share information. The focus should be on the issues, not on the individuals. The underlying problem causing the conflict needs to be clearly identified and agreed upon.

Resolving conflicts follows a format similar to the reflective thinking process.

1. Clearly define the problem.
2. Analyze the problem and identify the wants and needs of the parties.
3. Define a mutually acceptable goal. This works only if the parties are genuinely committed to the overall group goal, which provides a common starting point for discussion.
4. Generate multiple solutions.
5. Select the solution that best meets the needs of all parties.

Ultimately, resolving conflict issues in groups involves placing the good of the group above individual interests. When personal conflicts can't be resolved and when they interfere with the group's achieving its goals, they need to be put aside. For instance, if you are in the minority on an issue, rather than continuing to fight for your way, you should eventually accept and even support the group's decision. Cooperation instead of competition should be the rule applied to managing conflict in groups.

Summary and Self-Analysis:

Small Group Skills

The items below are based on the skills that have just been discussed. Read each item and decide how well it applies to your normal performance in groups. Use the following scale to assess yourself:

> **1** Not at all true   **2** A bit true   **3** Sort of true
>   **4** Often true   **5** Always true

_____ 1. I'm comfortable sharing my ideas and opinions in a group. (providing input)

_____ 2. I readily share any information with a group that I feel is relevant. (providing input)

_____ 3. There are times when I stop myself from saying something because I realize that it is not the appropriate time to share it. (appropriate input)

_____ 4. I actively listen to others in groups, asking for clarification and elaboration. (listening actively)

_____ 5. I listen carefully to others so that I can remember the information they have provided. (listening objectively)

_____ 6. As I listen to other group members, I evaluate the quality of their input and then provide them with feedback and criticism. (listening critically)

_____ 7. I am able to work effectively in all kinds of groups. (adaptability)

_____ 8. If a group calls for me to be the leader, I can be, or if they need me to be more of a follower, I can do that, too. (flexibility)

_____ 9. I am often the group member who offers new ideas and suggestions. (initiation)

_____ 10. I am often the one who offers different strategies or approaches. (initiation)

_____ 11. I try to make sure a group knows where it's going and what its goals are. (goal management)

_____ 12. I usually point out to the group when it starts getting off track. (goal management)

_____ 13. I like to help groups develop a good method or approach to deal with their tasks. (procedural management)

_____ 14. I am effective at organizing meetings—scheduling time and location, preparing and disseminating an agenda, and running the meeting. (procedural management)

_____ 15. When members have been quiet for a long time, I usually ask them for their thoughts. (promoting involvement)

_____ 16. Before a group assumes that there is unanimous agreement, I ask each group member by name if he or she agrees. (promoting involvement)

_____ 17. Forming personal relationships with the other group members is just as important to me as accomplishing the task. (developing personal relationships)

_____ 18. I seek personal information about the other group members and share personal information about myself. (developing personal relationships)

_____ 19. I like to have fun in groups and try to keep the atmosphere light. (creating a positive atmosphere)

_____ 20. I suggest and organize fun things for the group to do. (creating a positive atmosphere)

_____ 21. When I notice that the group is getting too uptight, I usually suggest a pizza break or something similar. (reducing tension)

_____ 22. When things get too tense, I interject some humor or try to get the group to talk about how it's feeling. (reducing tension)

_____ 23. When I'm having a conflict with another group member, I try to find common ground for a solution, listen to his or her needs, and share my own needs. (conflict management)

_____ 24. I tend to take the lead in resolving conflicts between group members. (conflict management)

Total your score for items 1 through 8:　　　_____ (your essential skills score)

Total your score for items 9 through 16:　　　_____ (your task skills score)

Total your score for items 17 through 24:　　　_____ (your social skills score)

Now add up your score for all three sections:　　_____ (your overall score)

The overall score potentially ranges from 24 to 120, with 72 being the midpoint. How does your score compare with that of others? What skills are your strongest? What skills might you try to improve?

Summary

Effective participation in groups and teams requires planning and preparation. You need to analyze the group situation, including who else will be in the group, the role you will be able to play, your goals, the group's goals, and the larger organization's goals for this group. Part of your preparation will involve researching the issue so that you can be an informed member. There is a certain amount of research you can do in advance of the first session, but you will probably need to accumulate additional information throughout the life of the group.

As you prepare for the group session, you should consider the approach that might work best in dealing with the issue. The Dewey reflective thinking process is one method that can be used. It begins with a careful analysis of the problem, proceeds to the generation of solution criteria, and moves on to selection of the best solution. The creative problem-solving sequence follows a similar procedure but involves generating solutions first and creating criteria afterward. Brainstorming is another method used by groups to generate creative input.

A number of skills can help you become an effective group member or leader. Three essential skills needed by all group members are providing appropriate input and information; listening actively, objectively, and critically; and being flexible and adaptive.

Specific task skills can help a group achieve its goals and increase your likelihood of emerging as leader. Initiation skills include proposing new directions or ideas. Goal management skills help the group identify and pursue its goals. Procedural management involves helping the group apply the most appropriate methods and helping to manage group meetings. The final task skill, promoting involvement, focuses on getting other members to provide input.

Social skills are also important because participants want to have their relational and social needs meet through group interaction. You can play an important role by helping group members develop and maintain personal relationships. You can also contribute to the creation of a positive atmosphere by supporting the development of a group identity and nurturing group social events. When groups become stressed, they need individuals who are skilled at reducing tension. Tension reduction includes knowing when to provide comic relief or to call for a break in the discussion. The final social skill is the collaborative management of conflict. You might need to manage a conflict that you yourself are in or to mediate a conflict between other members.

Key Terms

agenda An outline of the issues to be covered in a meeting, including the order in which they will be considered.

individual goals The reasons each member has for participating in a group.

group goals The reasons a group exists; its purpose.

organizational or **external goals** The reasons an organization has for forming a group.

reflective thinking process A decision-making method that involves an analysis of a problem, development of criteria, and evaluation of solutions.

creative problem-solving sequence A group procedure that involves discussing possible solutions first, then discussing and applying the criteria for choosing a solution.

brainstorming   A method of producing ideas by generating as many responses to a question as possible without evaluating them, thus emphasizing quantity over quality.

information initiation   Being the first to offer a new idea or piece of information.

procedural initiation   Being the first to suggest a change in the direction or course of action that the group is following.

managing goals   Efforts that help a group develop and maintain clear goals.

managing procedures   Behaviors that help a group decide on its procedures and then help the group maintain those procedures.

Review Questions

1. Describe some of the issues you need to consider in preparing to participate in a group.
2. Explain the difference between the reflective thinking process and the creative problem-solving sequence.
3. What are some of the rules for brainstorming? Why are those rules important?
4. Explain how listening helps improve a person's effectiveness in a group.
5. Discuss the two task skills that are your strongest.
6. Discuss the two social skills that you could improve the most.

Chapter 12

Presentational Communication: Purposes, Theory, and Principles

Objectives

Studying this chapter will allow you to:

1. Explain the three main purposes of presentational communication.
2. Understand the questions you need to answer in preparing a presentation.
3. Explain at least three ways to organize your information.
4. Explain how values, beliefs, and attitudes relate to persuasion.
5. Briefly explain how emotional appeals, logical proofs, and credibility contribute to persuasion.
6. Explain the difference between need appeal strategies and the use of cognitive dissonance in persuasion.
7. Briefly outline the process for analyzing the audience and the situation.

S tudents often wonder why they need to learn to give a speech. They don't see themselves ever having to give one. Perhaps you feel the same way. That perspective is probably based on the idea that public speaking is a formal address given to hundreds of people in an audience. However, presentational communication involves a much broader range of situations. As the following scenarios demonstrate, there are a variety of presentational situations in which you might find yourself.

Presentational Scenarios

A. The Chamber of Commerce has invited you to give the thirty-minute keynote address at its annual awards ceremony.

B. The class you are taking requires that students do a fifteen-minute presentation to the rest of the class about their research projects.

C. You are in a team meeting with ten other managers, developing priorities for the coming year. You have been particularly involved in examining the company's record of hiring women and minorities. At one point in the meeting, the team coordinator turns to you and asks you to tell everyone what you have learned.

D. You are visiting one-on-one with a potential software client. For fifteen minutes you explain the merits of your company compared with the competition. You try to convince the person that the higher cost for your company's service is outweighed by such advantages as dependability and good service.

Each of the these scenarios represents a form of presentational communication. The first two reflect settings commonly associated with giving a speech. The other two scenarios might not seem to you like public speaking, but they share a common definitional element with the first two: They are primarily actional (linear) communication in which one person speaks most of the time and the other people listen.

The variation, or differences, in the four scenarios reflects the range of communication activities that can be labeled presentational communication. We will explore several of these differences in this chapter. The differences have an impact on the decisions you make as a presenter. Among other things, the four scenarios vary in these respects:

1. Goals. The basic purpose of the presentation can be entertainment (scenario A), the conveying of information (scenarios B and C), or persuasion (scenario D). This variation is reflected in the topic that is presented.

2. Context. The setting and occasion can vary from formal (scenarios A and B) to informal and personal (scenarios C and D).

3. Planning. The presentation can be highly planned and structured (scenarios A and B) or more spontaneous and flexible (scenario D) or even impromptu (scenario C).

4. Audience size. The number of listeners may vary from over one hundred (scenario A) to just one (scenario D).

5. *Interaction opportunities.* The size of the audience has a strong impact on how much opportunity there is for the audience to interact and ask questions of the speaker.

6. *Length.* Presentations typically vary from thirty minutes or more (scenario A) to just a few minutes (scenario C).

During your lifetime, most of your presentations will be of the types reflected in scenarios C and D. Although such presentations are informal and spontaneous, you will still need strong presentational skills and an understanding of what is required if you are going to be successful. Learning the material in this chapter and in Chapters 13 and 14 will enhance the quality of your presentations regardless of their degree of formality.

■ The Purposes of Presentational Communication

In presentational communication, speakers have a particular message that they want a given audience to hear. Generally, **presentational communication** is an actional (linear) form of communication in which one person speaks most of the time and other people listen. The most obvious advantage of presentational communication, compared with other forms of communication, is the ability to deliver the same message to a large number of people at one time. This is why we think of public speaking as usually having audiences in the range of twenty to one hundred people. Yet, a message similar in design can be presented to just one person at a time. Presenting to fewer people creates more opportunity for interaction, thus reducing the speaker's control of the presentation.

Knowing the purpose of your speech is critical to effective preparation and design. Besides knowing your general purpose, you will need to develop specific objectives concerning what should happen as a result of your presentation. The success of a presentation can be assessed by how well both the general purpose and the specific objectives were achieved.

Now let's examine the three major purposes for presentations: to entertain, to inform, and to persuade.

■ To Entertain (Emotional Impact)

Sometimes, speeches are delivered essentially for their entertainment value—for the pleasure they bring the audience. The keynote speech at an awards banquet might have as its goal simply to entertain the listeners. The audience's enjoyment of the presentation would indicate how successful it was.

Speeches to entertain create an emotional response from the audience, and this is their primary objective. These presentations are frequently on the light side, incorporating jokes and funny anecdotes. Yet, speeches to entertain are not necessarily stand-up comedy routines. They can also be dramatic presentations that involve sharing personal stories that move an audience to tears.

■ To Inform (Cognitive Impact)

Presentations can be used as an effective way to share information with other people. They have a *cognitive* impact because they affect the way people think about something–usually by providing information that the audience did not know. The goal of an informational presentation is to have the audience reach a targeted level of understanding and to retain that information.

Instructional presentations, such as classroom lectures, are a common type of informational speaking, and the audience is usually motivated to learn the information. In other informational presentations, however, the audience is usually not as motivated to memorize or retain the speaker's message. One of the challenges facing the informational speaker, then, is to create an interest to learn, understand, and retain the message.

Types of informational presentations. Informational presentations fall within a wide range of categories.

1. ***Narratives*** are stories, or tales, that people tell, often about their own life experiences.

2. ***Reports*** are summaries that are usually generated in response to someone's inquiry or directions.

3. ***Instructions*** are explanations of how to do something. The goal is for the audience to be able to perform some task after hearing the presentation.

4. ***Coaching*** often involves providing instructions about the method to be followed in accomplishing some task. A boss might provide coaching instruction to a new employee about how to fill out the end-of-the-month report.

Providing information to others is one purpose of presentations.

5. Demonstrations are narrated examples in which the speaker typically displays how something works: for example, using words and corresponding actions to demonstrate the operation of the new computer scanner to a computer class.

6. Analyses involve a report of some examination that has been conducted for a particular reason. They are similar to reports because they involve sharing the product of work or effort. You might give a report on your sales, but you could also provide an analysis of why the sales have dropped in your district.

7. Descriptions are straightforward presentations of details and information that help create a mental image in your audience's mind. For instance, you might describe the habitat of the Australian wombat.

8. Examples are informational presentations that give a detailed description of a single item or instance that is representative of other items or instances.

9. Comparisons can include analyses and descriptions in which the similarity between two or more things is presented.

10. Contrasts are presentations that focus on the differences between two or more things.

■ To Persuade (Cognitive or Behavioral Impact)

The third use of presentational communication is to persuade an audience. The impact of persuasion can be on the cognitive level or on the behavioral level. That is, persuasion can involve changing the listener's *attitudes* or stirring the audience to *action*. This distinction, however, is not always a clear one, because changes in attitudes and behavior often accompany one another.

Imagine that you are addressing an audience that has a negative impression of your school. You want to persuade your listeners to adopt a more positive view by providing evidence that your college or university offers an excellent education. The goal of your speech is to change the audience's attitude. Indirectly, though, changing the listeners' attitude will affect their behavior. Before your speech, they may have made fun of your school in conversations with other people. After your speech, their change in attitude may result in their stopping this behavior, even though that was not your goal.

You might also give a speech trying to convince your listeners to attend your school. This would be a speech aimed directly at behavior. Your intention would be to recruit new students, and your success could be measured by the number of students who decided to apply to your school after hearing your presentation. Of course, getting students to apply to your school would usually be preceded by some change in their attitudes or opinions. Even those who didn't apply might leave your presentation with a more positive attitude, even though that was not your ultimate goal.

Think of some instances when you debated the very existence of something: for example, UFOs, life on other planets, or the existence of ghosts. How did you attempt to convince others to adopt your opinion?

Also think of some times when you debated the goodness or badness of something: the desirability of going to graduate school, the original *Star Wars* movies, the best nightclub in town, or country music. How did you attempt to convince others?

Finally, think about times when you debated what should be done to resolve a problem: for instance, improving the school basketball team, making it easier to graduate, making your workplace more enjoyable. How did you attempt to convince others?

Types of persuasive presentations. You may have noticed in the Ask Yourself section that the three types of issues were considerably different. The first involved the factuality of something; the second, the merit of something; and the third, the need for action. These differences reflect three specific types of persuasive presentations: speeches of fact, speeches of value, and speeches of policy.

Speeches of fact attempt to convince the audience of the existence of something or that something is true. Trying to convince someone that UFOs really exist involves presenting data that are seen as valid, incontrovertible, and confirming of your conclusion.

Speeches of value argue for the worth or correctness of something. These speeches usually involve evidence that something is good or bad, desirable or undesirable, or morally right or wrong. Value can be based on either comparison with something else (relative) or comparison with a standard (absolute). A *relative* claim compares one thing with another: for example, claiming that getting a job is more important than completing a college degree or that *Titanic* is a better movie than *Armageddon.* An *absolute* claim applies an established standard to demonstrate the value of something: for example, arguing that getting a college degree is a good thing to do or that *Titanic* is a great movie.

Speeches of policy advocate the adoption of a particular plan of action. Just as with value speeches, speeches of policy can be either relative or absolute. From a relative perspective, you can argue the value of your proposal against other proposals: for example, arguing that plan B is far less expensive than either plan A or plan C. You can also argue the absolute value of a policy relative to some criterion: for example, arguing that raising tuition will generate the necessary revenue to improve the school. Speeches of policy typically provide an answer to the question, What should be done?

■ Information Theory and Principles

This section will focus on presentational communication that aims to inform—to convey information to other people. Think for a moment about what it means to inform someone.

As you have been reading this text, you have been learning information. Your instructor probably has assessed how well you have learned by giving you an exam. That exam asked questions about the information included in the text. Your exam grade was supposed to indicate how well you had learned the information. Some of the questions you had to answer probably required simple recall, while other questions might have required you to show a deeper understanding by applying the concepts you had learned. Depending on how you studied, you might have done better in recalling facts or in applying concepts.

As this example shows, people can think and learn in two basic ways. *Recall* involves memorization and playback—learning facts and remembering them accurately. *Understanding* is reflected in the ability to translate, analyze, synthesize, apply, and evaluate the information being read.

As a speaker, you need to decide whether you want your audience simply to be able to recall information or to understand and apply it. The way you present your information, just like the way you study for an exam, will depend on which objective is more important to you.

By thinking about your own experiences in listening to informational presentations, you can probably identify other fundamental issues. The following questions and answers deal with some of these issues. You may also want to review what you learned in Chapter 3 about perceptual factors in gaining information and in Chapter 5 about dealing with misunderstanding and misrepresentation.

■ *Answering the Question, Why Should the Audience Listen to You?*

Why do audiences listen to speeches to inform? Why would they put effort into learning the particular information you are sharing? The answers to these questions are part of the challenge you must address when you prepare an informational presentation.

Generally, we listen to information that we see has value to us, and we tune out information that we don't see as relevant or beneficial. Therefore, you must convince the members of your audience that listening and learning the information you are sharing has relevance to them. This will help increase their attention and their desire to understand and retain the information.

Showing relevance means helping the audience members see that the information you are presenting has a direct value or application to their lives. The more direct this connection, the more they are motivated to listen. Making a presentation relevant begins with choosing a topic and selecting points to talk about that are most applicable to your audience. Giving a talk to eighth graders about the hole in the ozone layer might not generate a lot of interest if you can't tie the topic to the life of an eighth grader. On the other hand, telling an audience of salespeople that you are going to speak about three proven ways to increase their sales will motivate them to listen to the information you are presenting. Specific ways to analyze your audience and adapt to audience characteristics are discussed later in this chapter.

■ *Answering the Question, What Do the Listeners Need to Know from You?*

Sometimes, speakers try to convey all the information they know to the audience. In such cases, the audience is usually overwhelmed. On the other hand, sometimes there is information that the audience wants to know that the speaker does not include. In making informational presentations, you will need to think from the audience's perspective and consider what and how much information the audience needs to know.

The problem of not enough new information. Right now, you are reading a book about communication. You are reading a chapter about presentational communication.

"Duh," you may be thinking; you already know that you are reading a book about communication and a chapter about presentational communication, so the preceding two sentences were not very informative. If this section continued with statements that you already knew, you would probably stop reading. You would no longer see any informational value in the activity. As this example illustrates, information may be relevant, but if we already know it, then it isn't really information.

As a speaker, you will need to find out what your audience members know and what they don't know. A significant problem you'll face is that some audience members usually know more than others. Teachers in upper-level courses made up of both majors and nonmajors often face the challenge of trying to find the appropriate information level. They are faced with the problem of either covering material for nonmajors that is not informative to the majors or covering material for majors that is too abstract for the nonmajors. You will be faced with similar dilemmas in your presentations.

The problem of too much new information. An excess of new information can be as problematic as a lack of new information. Consider this sentence:

> The obsequious amanuensis asseverated to the brummagem Xantippe that the syncretistic screed was indecorous.

The sentence probably didn't make much sense to you because many of the words were unfamiliar. Now read the same sentence with synonyms substituted for all the unusual words except one:

> The submissive secretary asseverated to the phony nag that the reconciling criticism was inappropriate.

What do you suppose *asseverated* means? If you guessed something like *declared, contended,* or *asserted,* you were right.

The problem with the original sentence is that there was too much new information, too much that you couldn't comprehend. But when only one unfamiliar word was present, you were better able to understand the sentence. Now imagine that each of these words represented an idea or concept that you were sharing with an audience. The same principle would apply. With too much new information, the audience would likely feel confused and uncertain. But with a measured amount of new information, the audience could learn.

Finding the right balance. As a general rule of thumb for judging how much new information to present, you can follow the *70/30 rule,* which recommends that 70 percent of the information be familiar (already known) and 30 percent be new.[1]

Judging how much new information a person can learn and recall depends on a lot of variables. While the 70/30 rule isn't absolute, it can be a helpful guideline. In general, you want to provide a base of familiar information on which you add new information. We know that people are unable to remember a lot of unfamiliar information;[2] with too much new information, they get lost and confused. On the other hand, people get bored listening to a complete repetition of information they already know.

Following the 70/30 rule should be achieved by integrating the 30 percent new information throughout a presentation. You can do this by providing examples, analogies, metaphors, demonstrations, and illustrations that draw from what the audience already knows as you introduce new information. Imagine that you're trying to convey the nature of radio waves. You might explain that radio waves are like ripples in the water that keep flowing until they reach the shore or become too weak to go any farther. On long car trips, when my children had not yet developed a sense of time, my wife and I would explain how long it was to our destination by saying, "We'll be there in the amount of time it takes to watch two *Sesame Street* shows." This put information into a context that was familiar and understandable.

■ Answering the Question, How Can You Stimulate Listeners to Attend and Learn?

One of the principles of listening presented in Chapter 3 was that listening takes energy and effort. As a speaker, you are asking listeners to spend some of their energy on you and your message. While you may have created motivation by explaining why they should listen, you also need to present a message that is easy to listen to, easy to understand, and capable of maintaining the audience's attention. You can stimulate interest by the way you present the information. Let's look at some of the factors that influence your success in keeping the audience attentive.

Perceptual factors.   Several perceptual factors that influence an audience's attention and retention of information were introduced in Chapter 3. These factors can be used to your advantage when you are organizing and presenting a speech.

For example, according to the **primacy** and **recency** effects, people tend to remember the first things they hear (primacy) and the last things they hear (recency). Thus, you can increase the likelihood that important information will be retained by putting it toward the beginning or end of the presentation.

People also tend to be influenced by **novelty.** That is, they remember the unusual or unique. If you can find some way to increase the novelty of your presentation, you will increase the chances that the audience will attend to the information and retain it. You've probably seen a science teacher put a rose or balloon in a container of liquid nitrogen and then smashes it to the ground after it has been superfrozen. This novel display leaves a lasting impression on students.

You can also emphasize important points that you wish your audience to retain. **Emphasis** can be accomplished in several ways, including a change in your delivery style (such as raising or lowering your voice), writing the key points on a chalkboard or overhead transparency, or handing out an outline of the main points.

In addition, presenting information in written form on transparencies or handouts reflects the use of multiple communication channels; that is, you are using not just the sound channel, but also the visual channel. Because people learn information in different ways, presenting information through multiple channels increases the potential match between your presentational choice and your audience's learning styles.

Another way to emphasize the importance of a particular point is through repetition, repetition, and repetition. **Repetition** of key information signals to your audience that they should pay attention to the point. Repetition is also a way to ensure that those who are listening intermittently will at least hear the message one of the times you repeat it. Repetition can take the form of repeating a key point several times in a row or repeating the information several times throughout the presentation.

Structural factors.   Several qualities in the structure of the presentation can enhance information acquisition. These include the use of previews, summaries, transitions, and keywords. These help because their impact is directly linked to the perceptual factors we have just discussed.

A **preview** is a brief overview of the key information that you will be elaborating on within the body of your presentation. According to the primacy effect, the preview is a part of your speech that the audience is likely to remember. You will therefore want to have an effective preview.

Similarly, a **summary,** which recaps the information covered in the main body of the presentation, takes advantage of the recency effect. An effective summary focuses on repeating the information that is most important for the audience to retain. Presenting the same information in the preview, the body, and the summary means that the audience will hear the most important information three times. This repetition increases the likelihood that the audience will learn and remember the points you have deemed most important.

As you learned in the discussion of interviewing in Chapter 8, a **transition** is a statement signaling that you are completing one point and about to move to another. Transitions are much like car turn signals. They let people know that you are about to make a turn. Here is a sample transition statement:

> "Now that I've explained the *motives* of European Americans to push West, let me talk about the *impact* on Native Americans."

This statement serves as a transition by repeating the main point that was just discussed and previewing the coming issue. It also takes advantage of keywords.

Keywords are specific terms or phrases used as constructs that the audience can easily recall. If the speaker used the terms *motives* and *impact* several times while discussing the surrounding issues, the audience would be more likely to recall them, and those terms might stimulate the recollection of additional information. Keywords should be concise and should be repeated the same way each time. Saying "impact" one time and "effect" the next time fails to establish a clear keyword.

■ *Answering the Question, How Can You Organize the Information?*

Research evidence is contradictory about whether presenting information in an organized fashion helps an audience's retention.[3] But whether or not organization helps the audience, it can definitely help the speaker.

You have probably had occasion to explain the rules of some game to another person. Usually, you describe the rules in a logical fashion, explaining how the game begins, what happens next, and then how the game ends. This may make it easier for your listener to follow along and retain the rules. Even if it doesn't help the listener, it helps you in figuring out the next thing to cover so that you don't leave anything out.

Think about a time you may have watched a football, baseball, or basketball game with someone unfamiliar with the sport and proceeded to explain the rules. You probably explained the rules as the situation dictated, without any overall organization to your explanation. The listener was probably still able to learn the

Information that is particularly important can be emphasized by using the visual channel.

rules. But you probably found yourself having to say, "Oh, yeah, by the way, another rule I forgot was. . . ." Following a specific order increases the likelihood that you've covered everything you intended.

Generally, the organization you follow in an informational presentation is dictated by the topic. You will need to examine the nature of the issue you are presenting to determine the best organizational pattern. The following are some of the more common presentational organizations you can use.

Topical organization. In a **topical organization,** the key points associated with a topic are identified and then organized as the points seem to dictate. The points may be arranged in order of importance (ascending or descending), familiarity to the audience, or complexity.

Central Idea	Possible Main Points	Topical Organization
The future of personal computing	Future hardware, future software, the Internet, impact on education, impact on the home, impact on business, games, DVD, voice recognition	I. Hardware and software developments II. Impact in the home III. Impact in the schools IV. Impact in the office
The reasons people are attracted to one another	Relational development, needs satisfaction, attraction of opposites, similarity, proximity, compatibility, opposites, physical attraction, reciprocation	I. Physical attraction II. Attraction of similars III. Attraction of opposites IV. Attraction to those in close proximity

Chronological organization. Some topics involve presenting a history or time line of occurrences and therefore can be organized in a chronological manner. **Chronological organization** can move either from the first occurrence to the most recent or from the most recent to the first.

Central Idea	Chronological Organization
The development of electronic TV games	I. 1972: The Odyssey from Magnavox II. 1974: Atari Home Pong III. 1979: Intellivision from Mattell IV. 1984: PCs take over V. 1985–1986: Nintendo, Sega VI. 1989: 16-bit machines VII. 1994–1996: 32-bit and 64-bit machines; Sony Playstation
Michael Jordan: basketball's greatest	I. 1981–1984: college years at North Carolina; college Player of the Year II. 1984–1985: NBA Rookie of the Year with Chicago Bulls III. 1991: First NBA championship IV. 1992: Olympics V. 1993: First retirement from basketball; plays minor-league baseball VI. 1994–1995: midseason return to the Bulls VII. 1996–1998: more championships VIII. 1999: second retirement

Spatial organization. Some topics can be organized according to the spatial relationship between the main points. **Spatial organization** involves taking your audience on a journey that follows some logical pattern based on the relative proximity of the main points to one another.

Central Idea	Spatial Organization
The Oregon Trail	I. Beginning the journey: St. Louis to "jumping off" cities II. Traveling through Nebraska: Fort Kearny III. Gateway to the Rockies: Fort Laramie IV. South Pass: Halfway point; Continental Divide V. Crossing the Snake River in Idaho VI. Reaching the Columbia River: The Dalles VII. End of the Trail: Oregon City
The *Titanic,* from top to bottom	I. Boat deck: the bridge, officers' quarters, lifeboats, wireless room II. Promenade deck (A): first-class lounge, smoking room, staterooms III. Bridge deck (B): first-class cabins and À La Carte Restaurant IV. C deck: second-class promenade and cabins V. D deck: first- and second-class dining facilities VI. Bow and stern compartments for third-class passengers VII. E deck: crew's quarters VIII. Orlop deck and tank top: boiler rooms, coal storage, baggage, fresh water

Dimensional organization. You might choose to organize your topic according to some ascending or descending pattern that is apparent in the main points, such as an arrangement by size or scope. With such a **dimensional organization**, you might begin, for instance, at the microscopic level and then cover points in ascending size until you reached the macroscopic. Or you might reverse the order, beginning with the largest and moving to the smallest.

Central Idea	Dimensional Organization
The drug problem	I. Drug dealers on my block II. The drug problem in our town III. The drug problem in the state IV. The drug problem nationally V. The drug problem internationally
Best automobile buys	I. Full-size sedans II. Mid-size sedans III. Compacts IV. Subcompacts

Cause-and-effect organization. In speaking about your topic, you may want to discuss factors that constitute the causes of a certain situation and then describe their subsequent effects. Or you may use the reverse order, discussing effects first and then their underlying causes. Either of these structures is called a **cause-and-effect organization.** In an informational presentation, the connection between causes and effects should not be a point of controversy or uncertainty.

Central Idea	Cause-and-Effect Organization

Divorce in the United States	*Cause to Effect:*
	I. Causes of divorce
	  A. Spousal incompatibilities
	  B. Growing financial independence of women
	  C. Changing social mores
	II. Effects of divorce
	  A. Effects on the psychological well-being of children
	  B. Effects on the psychological well-being of the couple
	  C. Effects on social institutions and the workplace

The improving health of Americans	*Effect to Cause:*
	I. Signs of improvement
	  A. Decline in diseases such as tuberculosis, polio, measles, and mumps
	  B. Increase in average life expectancy
	II. Causes
	  A. Better availability of health care
	  B. Better drugs and inoculation against diseases
	  C. Advances in medical diagnosis and treatment

Connect to a few home pages that include listings of subcategories of information that you can access. For example, look at the home page for a college or university; for *U. S. News & World Report* (notice the headings and how they are organized); for a professional sports team; for *Consumer's Digest.* Click on a hyperlink and keep following the links till you get to a final set of information choices. What organizational pattern is followed? Can you find pages that follow organizational patterns like the ones discussed in this chapter?

■ Persuasion Theory and Principles

Understanding the principles of information will help you make more effective informational presentations, but frequently your goal is to do more than inform other people: You want to move them in some direction—to persuade them. Your ability to make effective persuasive presentations can be enhanced by understanding the theories explaining what causes people to change.

Persuasion is a direct influence on another person's attitudes, beliefs, values, or behaviors. To understand this definition, consider the issue of increasing federal funding for the national parks. On this issue there is a continuum of possible positions, as shown in Figure 12.1. Individuals' attitudes could fall anywhere

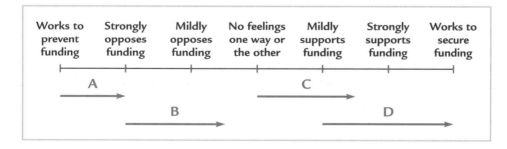

Figure 12.1

A Continuum

A continuum of potential positions on the issue of increased funding for national parks. Lines A, B, C, and D represent possible outcomes of persuasion.

along this continuum; that is, people could range from being active opponents of funding for national parks to being active proponents. Persuasion would cause a person's position on this continuum to move from one place to another. If no movement occurs, then no persuasion has occurred.

Lines A, B, C, and D show some possible results of successful persuasion. All four lines represent success at persuasion, even though each results in a different outcome. The persuasion reflected by line A involves convincing opponents to stop their direct actions against funding, though their attitude is still opposed to funding. Line B shows a situation in which the audience moves from strong opposition to a more neutral stance. Line C shows a neutral audience being moved to a strong supportive attitude. And line D represents convincing audience members who are already in favor of funding to commit themselves to action.

As this figure suggests, effective persuasion involves knowing your audience's initial stance toward the topic and then adapting your goals accordingly. Suppose you were speaking to an audience of highly conservative activists who opposed funding for national parks. Their view would put them toward the far left on the continuum in Figure 12.1. It would not be a very realistic goal to move them all the way to the far right on the continuum and expect them to work in support of increased federal spending for parks. Instead, you would tailor your goal to the audience's predisposition by trying merely to temper their opposition to funding, as reflected by line A or B. Keeping your goal realistic would allow you to develop a more effective persuasive presentation.

The strategies used for changing attitudes often differ from the strategies used for changing behavior. Lines B and C, which represent persuasion aimed at changing an attitude, might require different approaches than lines A and D, which represent attempts to change the audience's behavior. In the following sections, we'll look more closely at persuasive strategies and the factors that affect them.

■ Values, Beliefs, and Attitudes

Values, beliefs, and attitudes were discussed in Chapter 2 as components of a person's psychological context. They are key elements that make up who we are, and for that reason they become key factors in accomplishing any change in a listener. Recall what you learned in Chapter 2:

- *Values* are deep-rooted conceptual responses about the worth or importance of something.
- *Beliefs* are judgments concerning how things are or how they should be— basically convictions about what is true.[4]
- *Attitudes* are predisposed evaluative responses that have been developed toward a person, object, or issue.[5]

In developing a presentation, you need to identify which elements of the audience's predispositions you are attempting to change. As Chapter 2 pointed out, the three kinds of predispositions differ in their stability: Values are the most stable, beliefs next, and attitudes the least stable. This means that you are more likely to succeed in changing audience members' beliefs than in changing their values, and even more likely to succeed in changing their attitudes.

In addition to knowing the values, beliefs, and attitudes of the audience, you need to know the intensity and level of entrenchment of these predispositions. An audience might have a positive attitude toward an issue, but it might not be very intense or deeply rooted. This means that you have a better shot at changing it. Imagine that you are trying to persuade a client to buy a Gateway computer. Your task will be easier if the client has used many different PCs and currently owns a Dell than if the client has never used anything but Apple computers.

Besides knowing where your audience members stand on the specific value, belief, or attitude you are attempting to change, you should try to grasp their other values, beliefs, and attitudes as well. You will be able to use those other predispositions as a basis for your appeals. For example, if you know that the audience values education, you can appeal to that value as the basis for changing an attitude against increasing property taxes by showing how the revenues will improve the school system.

■ Traditional Strategies of Persuasion

Persuasion is one of the oldest areas of theory and research in the social sciences. The ancient Greeks and Romans were keenly sensitive to how politicians might change their audiences through persuasive strategies. In his *Rhetoric,* the Greek philosopher Aristotle identified three particular strategies that have stood the test of time: pathos (emotional appeals), logos (logical proofs), and ethos (credibility, or belief in the speaker).

Emotional appeals. **Emotional appeals** depend on arousing an audience's emotions and then providing a method for alleviating them. Telethons, like the one for muscular dystrophy, seek to arouse the viewers' feelings of sympathy and caring. Then they provide an outlet for those emotions, offering viewers an opportunity to help by contributing money. Similarly, while I was writing this section of the text, the local public radio station was engaged in its semiannual fund-raising drive. The announcers tried to make the listeners feel guilty for listening to the station but not contributing to its financial support. The listeners' guilt could be alleviated by making a pledge.

One way to arouse emotions is to provide a detailed description of an emotionally laden situation. For example, you might talk about your personal bout with cancer while asking someone to donate funds to a cancer drive. Emotional appeals often use highly charged language and imagery. Yet, the impact of the emotionally generated motivation can be expected to diminish quickly once the audience is removed from the situation. This necessitates getting immediate action from audience members—while their emotions are heightened. Urging listeners to sign a pledge card now (without actually having to contribute the money till a later date) is one way to secure a commitment while they are still emotional.

Logical proofs. Putting together a set of logical arguments and supportive evidence is the basis for a **logical proof.** Aristotle pointed out that a speaker could persuade an audience either by providing real proof or by creating the appearance of proof. He recognized that sometimes arguments appear logical when they really aren't. Audiences therefore need to employ critical listening to discover if there are significant fallacies in a speaker's message.

Logical proofs can take the form of either inductive or deductive reasoning. **Inductive reasoning** involves making generalized conclusions on the basis of a few specific examples. **Deductive reasoning** involves making specific conclusions based on a generality. Here are examples of the two types of reasoning:

Induction

Evidence 1: John got a degree in communication in 1997 and started a new job at $25,000.

Evidence 2: Mary got a degree in communication in 1997 and started a new job at $25,000.

Evidence 3: Enrico got a degree in communication in 1997 and started a new job at $25,000.

Claim or conclusion: A degree in communication in 1997 resulted in a starting salary of $25,000.

Deduction

Evidence 1 (general premise): The estimated average starting salary for communication graduates in 1997 was $25,224.[6]

Evidence 2 (minor or specific premise): Jill received her communication degree in 1997.

Claim or conclusion: Jill's starting salary was probably around $25,224.

Do you accept the final claims of the two proofs? Which one would you be more willing to bet is correct?

Your confidence in the inductive claim is probably affected by how many pieces of evidence or how many individual cases were presented to support it. If only John were listed as evidence, you would probably be very uncomfortable about accepting the claim. The use of three cases increases your confidence, and still more cases would help. The problem is that there are a lot of other variables that could affect the conclusions. At best, induction rests on a probability, or likelihood, that the conclusion is true.

Reasoning from induction "sounds" logical and can result in an audience's accepting the speaker's claims. Sometimes, however, people try to present inductive logic as though it were deductive. In that case, critical listening will usually result in more resistance from an audience. You probably tried to disguise inductive logic with your parents when you were younger. You may have said, for example, "May I stay out till midnight? Everybody else my age gets to." If you ever spoke in this way, you were attempting to claim a generality (everybody gets to stay out till midnight) when in reality your claim was based on only two or three people you knew. You were disguising an inductive conclusion by claiming a general, deductive conclusion. If your parents asked you for specific names and you failed to provide more than one or two, they probably saw through your disguise and spotted your use of inductive reasoning.

Deductive proofs are usually regarded as stronger than inductive, but finding the initial evidence is more difficult. In our example of deductive reasoning, the general premise requires evidence that the average starting salary for communication graduates in 1997 was indeed $25,224. For evidence of this sort, surveys, polls, and samples are used to try to tap general trends, and they often provide averages, correlations, and other statistics that can be taken as a mathematical basis for deductions. Even so, an "average" salary of $25,224 means that there were probably some individuals making $10,000 and some making $40,000. Applying the general number to a specific case involves a chance of error.

Deductive reasoning is often presented in the form of a classical syllogism. The **classical syllogism** claims that if the major and minor premises based on shared elements are true, than a concluding relationship must also be true.

Proposition	General Form	Example
Major premise	If A = B	All humans are mortal. (This can be stated as: If human, then mortal.)
Minor premise	and C = A,	Socrates was a human. (If Socrates, then human.)
Conclusion	then C = B.	Therefore, Socrates was mortal. (If Socrates, then mortal.)

In using a syllogism, the speaker attempts to provide evidence that the major and minor premises are both true. If the speaker can convince the audience of the validity of the premises, then the conclusion is proven as well.

Credibility: belief in the speaker.   Aristotle also recognized that people were often persuaded simply because of the character of the person delivering the presentation. **Credibility** is the personal quality or character of a speaker that leads people to accept what the speaker says as true. Credibility, essentially, is how much you trust the speaker and how much you are willing to change your attitudes or actions because of him or her.

Logic: another thing that penguins aren't very good at.

Being credible in one context, however, doesn't mean that the same speaker is credible in another context. Research suggests that we make different judgments about a person's credibility, depending on the context or topic.[7] For example, a police officer telling you about the dangers of drug addiction would be less credible than a former drug user giving the same presentation.

Credibility is often conceptualized as being composed of several components, or dimensions.[8] These dimensions reflect the different reasons we might put our trust in someone. Among the dimensions that have been identified are competence (expertise), trustworthiness (positive intentions), and dynamism (charisma and attractiveness).

1. Competence.   You've just taken your car into the repair shop for an oil change, and the service manager informs you that you need a thousand dollars worth of repair work on the engine. Do you believe the service manager? Do you have the repair work done? Your decision rests on how much credibility you assign to the service manager's claim. One question in this regard is how competent or skilled the repair shop is. You will probably accept the message as credible if you believe that the employees know what they are doing and are expert mechanics.

This example illustrates how we judge a speaker's competence to be speaking on a particular topic. **Competence** is the expertise, knowledge, and skills we perceive a speaker to have. We tend to discard the opinions of individuals we perceive as uninformed. If a speaker claimed that your favorite food was bad for you, you would not be persuaded to stop eating it if you knew that the speaker had no expertise in food, nutrition, or health.

Sometimes, as a speaker, you may need to inform your audience directly about the basis of your expertise and knowledge. Suppose you were trying to convince a group of managers to implement team management in their company. You might start your talk by saying: "Let me tell you a little about myself. I received my M.B.A. from Harvard in 1994. I then began training with Anderson Consulting in team management. I became a senior consultant and have worked on the successful implementation of programs for Ford Motor Company, Microsoft, and John Deere Manufacturing." This introduction would give the managers confidence in your qualifications to talk about the topic.

2. Trustworthiness.   You may have confidence in the competence of a speaker but still not be persuaded if you don't trust the speaker. For instance, you would be unlikely to have your car repaired if you knew that the shop had a reputation for pushing unnecessary repairs. You would not consider the manager trustworthy. On the other hand, if you had been taking your car to this same shop for several years and had always felt that the mechanics were honest and straightforward with you, you'd probably have the repairs done.

Trustworthiness, then, is the degree to which we perceive a speaker as honest, ethical, dependable, consistent, and open. Establishing trust often requires an extended period of time, during which we develop a relationship. We have all felt the trust that develops as a relationship moves toward intimacy. Speakers generally don't have the luxury of creating a long-term relationship with their audience, but they can establish trustworthiness by showing that they are concerned with the audience's interests and by speaking in a consistent manner.

- *Concern for the audience's interests.* We can assess people's trustworthiness by the degree to which they look out for our interests, sometimes at the expense of their own. In the movie *Miracle on 34th Street*, Kris Kringle is working as Santa Claus for Macy's Department Store. He tells parents where they can get the best deals on toys, even when it's at competing stores. This act of looking out for the parents' interests increases his trustworthiness and his credibility.

- *Speaking consistently.* Besides avoiding self-serving messages, speakers should maintain internal consistency in what they say to an audience. The old phrase "speaking out of both sides of his mouth" reflects our tendency to believe that speakers who are inconsistent are untrustworthy. We probably would not regard as credible a speaker who said, "I support change in our organization. We need to seek new solutions to our problems and new ways of doing business. Of course, right now we need to leave things alone until the right time arrives."

3. Dynamism. You might be persuaded to have your car repaired if the service manager were friendly, attractive, outgoing, and energetic. Personal qualities such as these influence the degree to which we regard someone as credible, and a person with these qualities is often said to be dynamic. **Dynamism** is the ability to gain credibility by being enthusiastic, energetic, and likable. Speakers can display their dynamic character through their nonverbal behaviors. These include eye contact with the audience members, animated gesturing, effective body movement and posture, smiling and pleasant facial expressions, and variation in vocal qualities such as pitch, volume, and rate.[9]

Researchers have posited that dynamism has a curvilinear relationship with credibility, meaning that a medium amount of dynamism will produce the maximum amount of credibility.[10] In essence, being too listless or being too exuberant might turn an audience off and have a negative impact on credibility.

Another aspect of this character influence is the degree to which we are attracted to the speaker. The more we like people, the more we are apt to believe and trust them and therefore be persuaded by their messages. This attraction to a speaker is often referred to as *charisma*. Charismatic speakers are dynamic speakers who affect us with their charm and personal appeal.

The next time you watch television, see if you can identify the three traditional persuasive strategies—emotional appeals, logical proofs, and credibility—in the commercials you see. Which type is used the most? Are certain products associated with one strategy rather than another?

■ Need Appeal Strategies of Persuasion

As you know from earlier chapters, individuals are motivated to satisfy their needs. Appealing to those needs is one strategy that can be used in persuasive presentations. You can motivate your audience to accept your proposed change if you can show that by doing so they will be able to satisfy their needs.

In Chapter 2, you read about Maslow's hierarchy of needs:

- Physiological needs (food, water, sex)
- Safety needs (security, protection)
- Belonging and love needs (interpersonal relationships, organizational membership)
- Self-esteem needs (status, worth, appreciation)
- Self-actualization needs (need to find one's true self)

In a presentation, you can develop appeals to any level of this hierarchy or to more than one level.

In developing such need appeal strategies, you can use **reward appeals**, showing how adopting the proposed change will help satisfy a need. You can also use **fear appeals**, showing how failing to adopt the proposed change will threaten a need. The basic approach involves clearly identifying the audience's needs, explaining your proposition, and then connecting the two in a logical fashion. Consider the following examples of reward and fear appeals:

Reward appeal

- Identify audience need: The desire to be attractive to members of the opposite sex (meeting needs for sex and relationships)
- Speaker's proposal: Sign up for our fitness program to reduce your weight.
- Reward connection: Being fit and trim will make you more attractive to members of the opposite sex and meet your needs.

Fear appeal

- Identify audience need: The desire for security and for protection of family members.
- Speaker's proposal: Vote for me for governor, and I will crack down on crime.
- Fear connection: My opponent wants to cut funding for law enforcement, which will put more criminals on the streets and in your neighborhood. Your family will be in danger.

The success of need appeal strategies depends on the strength of your arguments and how well you connect them. You have to identify real needs that the audience clearly feels. Then you must make a strong connection between your proposal and the audience's needs. This connection can be fostered by the use of supporting evidence and illustrative examples. You've seen ads for diet products in which several satisfied customers provide testimony that their lives have improved because they used the product and lost thirty pounds.

■ Cognitive Strategies of Persuasion

People usually strive for consistency in their attitudes, beliefs, values, and behaviors. According to cognitive theories of persuasion, the human desire to maintain this consistency can be used as a persuasive tool.

Cognitive theories. Two well-known theories, **balance theory** and **cognitive dissonance theory,** focus on people's drive to maintain balance or consonance (agreement) in their thoughts and actions.[11]

Figure 12.2 An Example of Imbalance or Cognitive Dissonance

You are attracted to a job with the company (a positive attitude, indicated by +), and you support environmental protection (+). Yet the company has a poor reputation on environmental matters (−). The result is an imbalance or dissonant state.

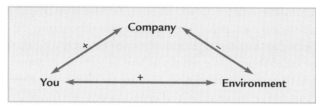

Suppose you are very interested in working for a company because the job will pay well and it comes with a great benefits package. However, you are a strong supporter of environmental protection, and the company has a reputation for polluting the environment. Do you take the job? This situation is out of balance, as illustrated in Figure 12.2. Your positive regard for two things that are in opposition to each other creates an *imbalance*, or a *dissonant* state.

Faced with this dilemma, you have a number of options for eliminating the imbalance. You can create balance, or consonance, by adopting a negative attitude toward the company and the job. In this way, you would establish a consistent pattern of beliefs: You would have a positive regard for the environment (+), the company would have a disregard for the environment (−), and you would maintain your regard for the environment by disliking the company (−). You might also change your attitude about environmental issues and disregard them, thus sharing the same view as the company to which you are attracted. Or you can convince yourself that the company is really trying to rectify its pollution problem.

Using cognitive strategies.   You can apply the principles of balance theory and cognitive dissonance theory to a strategy for gaining compliance in a persuasive situation. Essentially, you can create dissonance by showing an audience how its attitudes, beliefs, values, or behaviors are contradictory to other, more important attitudes, beliefs, values, or behaviors.

1. First identify a particular predisposition shared by the audience members.
2. Then show how another attitude, belief, value, or behavior contradicts the first.
3. Finally, provide a way to eliminate the imbalance, or dissonance.

Suppose you are trying to convince an adult audience to buy life insurance. Using a cognitive strategy, you can take the following steps in your presentation:

1. Focus on a value that the audience members consider important: providing for their family and protecting their family's future welfare.
2. Show how their behavior contradicts this value: They don't have insurance and thus are putting their family's future at risk. If they were to die in an accident, you make them realize, their family would be left with little income. You are arousing a state of dissonance: Their values are contradicted by their behaviors.

3. Now, in the most important part of your appeal, provide a way to eliminate the contradiction: The audience members can change their behavior and buy your life insurance.

Success with cognitive strategies depends on the same degree of visualization as with need appeal strategies. You must accurately identify the audience's values, beliefs, attitudes, or behaviors that are out of balance. Then you must convince the audience that what you propose will bring about balance and that it is the best course of action. In the insurance example, the audience members may discard your first proposition because they believe that they are healthy and that nothing catastrophic will happen to them. Or, even if you are successful in arousing their feelings of dissonance, they may find another avenue for alleviating their dissonance, such as buying mortgage insurance and creating college funds for their children rather than buying your life insurance. Thus, to use balance theory and cognitive dissonance theory in an effective persuasive strategy, you need evidence and convincing arguments.

Ask Before You Tell

This article illustrates the importance of learning about the characteristics of an audience before you begin a presentation.

I was preparing for a major presentation of 401(k) retirement plans to a corporate committee. As usually happens, there was one person, in this case the Vice President of Human Resources, who was my principal contact. When the VP faxed me a list of the people who would attend my presentation, I was concerned to notice that three of the people were strangers to me. And two of the others I had met only briefly.

My challenge was this: Since I had already spent a great deal of time with the VP and her assistant, I didn't want to spend too much time in the meeting repeating things they already knew. At the same time, I had to consider all those other people I didn't know. How could I make sure they came away satisfied from my presentation, without talking them all to death? If only I knew what everyone wanted from me.

And that was the key.

I had an easel set up at the front of the room and kicked off the meeting with: "We have prepared a number of things to present to you today which we believe you will find both valuable and interesting. But to make absolutely sure we cover all of your questions, before we begin I'd like to go around the room and ask each of you what you would like to get out of today's meeting."

I started with the VP, whose goals I already knew pretty well, and then went on to each person on the committee. As they spoke, I acknowledged their requests by writing them on the easel. Throughout my presentation, I referred back to the easel to make sure every point I made was connected to something the group wanted. At the end of the meeting, I asked everyone whether I had covered all of their points. They agreed that I did. As they agreed I had covered each point, I put a check next to the item on the easel.

When I look back at the meeting, I covered pretty much what I had planned to talk about. But starting with the attendees' wish list got them more involved in my presentation, made them understand I truly cared about their needs, and helped me clarify how every one of my points related to their needs. It also alerted me to a few hidden issues I hadn't known about.

A week later I got the call from the VP telling me I had won. And the main reason—my competitors had delivered hard-driving canned presentations. Mine was the only presentation that really answered everyone's questions.

Source: J. Dolittle, "Ask Before You Tell," *SalesDoctors Magazine*, from *SalesDoctors Magazine* http://www.salesdoctors.com.

■ Analysis of the Audience and the Situation

The success of both informational and persuasive presentations depends on how well you have adapted to your audience and the situation. Adaptation requires gaining as much information as you can in advance. Knowledge of the audience will allow you to:

- Select appropriate need appeals.
- Incorporate examples and illustrations to which your audience can relate.
- Choose appropriate language.
- Adapt the topic and objectives to the needs of the particular audience.
- Decide on the most appropriate informational and persuasive strategies to use.

■ *Before the Presentation*

Gaining information about your audience requires research. The research can involve a wide variety of sources. For large audiences, you may be able to rely on formal sources, such as an organization's brochures, information from its web site, and perhaps even news reports. If you were asked to address a convention of the National Organization of Women, for example, you could use the library and the Internet to learn about the organization's membership, the positions it has taken on recent issues, and so on.

For smaller-scale presentations, the sources are often informal. One important source of information is your own experience. Perhaps you have been a member of the same audience to which you will be speaking—for instance, when you make a presentation to a class in which you yourself have listened to other speakers. Or you may have interacted with the audience previously; for a presentation to members of your work team, you could use your knowledge about the team and its members.

If you are presenting to an unfamiliar group, you may be able to talk with members of the group beforehand. In preparing for workshops, I spend a considerable amount of time talking to the person who is making the arrangements, and I ask many questions about the audience. The major problem with this approach is that you are getting only one person's perspective about the audience, and that perspective is likely to be somewhat distorted. To combat distortions, you can focus on

Table 12.1   Audience and Situation Analysis Questionnaire

Question	Sample Answers and Factors to Consider
What does the audience want from me?	Facts, information, help, answers, proposals
What does the audience expect from me?	Energy, professionalism, entertainment
What motivates the audience?	Money, sex, advancement, recognition
What are the reasons the audience will be there?	Forced to be there, choose to be there, wish to pass the time
What is the occasion for the presentation?	Invitation to speak, training session, staff meeting
What restrictions are there?	Time, location, facilities, size of audience
What do you have in common with the audience that you can include in the presentation?	Similar interests, experiences, education, goals, needs
What is the audience's likely attitude toward the topic?	Apathetic, supportive, opposing
What is the audience's likely attitude toward you?	Respectful, challenging, neutral
What are some of the values, beliefs, attitudes, and needs held by this audience?	Inferred from ages, occupations, educational background, ethnicity, race, economic status, gender, political affiliations, religious affiliations, organizational affiliations, hometowns/origins, family background

questions of fact, such as how many people will be there, the sex composition of the audience, and audience members' job descriptions and occupational backgrounds.

Table 12.1 provides some guidelines for conducting audience analysis before a presentation.

■ During and After the Presentation

Audience analysis is important not only in preparation for your presentation but also during and after your presentation. During your presentation, you need to be sensitive to nonverbal cues from your audience. Watch, for example, for nonverbal reactions that signal misunderstanding or confusion. If you notice these cues, you can immediately alter your presentation to include additional explanation or examples. If you pick up signs of hostility or disagreement, you may have to change the nature of your presentation to address the audience's concerns. You can also tell a lot about your audience by the questions the members ask.

After a presentation, you should try to analyze the audience's reaction. You can make some judgment about your effectiveness on the basis of the audience's comments or actions, and the conclusions you draw can help you plan your future presentations. Believe it or not, some instructors actually use their students' performance on examinations as a measure of their own ability to convey information effectively.

■ Presentations and Ethics

A presentation has the potential to affect everyone in the audience—potentially a lot of people. The use of that power and influence is subject to ethical standards. The following sections describe some of the ethical standards that you will be expected to adhere to in your presentations.

■ *Speaking Honestly and Truthfully*

Audiences tend to believe what they are being told by speakers. There is an underlying ethic that presenters speak honestly and truthfully. The various forms of deception discussed in Chapter 5—equivocation, concealment, half-truths, lies—are all considered unethical in a presentation. Being honest and truthful applies to speeches in a number of ways.

1. Speakers must present their credentials honestly, not claiming undue expertise or knowledge. Overstating your knowledge or expertise as a way of increasing your credibility is a form of deception.
2. Like newspaper reporters, speakers are obliged to try their best to ascertain the validity of the information they are conveying to the audience. This includes finding a second or third source for a piece of information to provide verification of its validity.
3. Speakers need to explain the nature of their sources. Failure to adequately explain the source and validity of the information should be a signal to listeners to be wary.
4. Speakers should not knowingly convey false or inaccurate information. This would seem like an easy rule to follow, but ethics is filled with gray areas. Suppose your boss told you that he heard that your company's major competitor was way behind in filling its product orders. Should you include that information in a presentation you were making to a group of prospective buyers for your company's product? How credible could you consider the information? What if you knew that your boss was prone to exaggerate facts and start rumors?

■ *Speaking Respectfully*

As a speaker, you need to respect your audience and display that respect in your presentation. In addition, you need to be respectful of all individuals and all groups of people, whether they are present in the audience or not. You should avoid derogatory, libelous, offensive, malicious, and defamatory comments.

"Putting down" others is a poor reflection on the speaker and can be considered unethical. Our society has developed an intolerance for bigotry, racism, sexism, and other forms of class degradation. Even jokes are seen as unethical if they make fun of a particular group of individuals.

■ *Crediting Your Sources*

Failing to put quotes around written material that was created by someone else is considered plagiarism. This is unethical, and so is failing to credit borrowed words or ideas in a presentation you make. The audience will likely consider anything you say as original and attributable only to you unless you indicate otherwise. Thus, you need to indicate clearly to your audience the source of any idea or words that are not your own. From an ethical perspective, failing to credit another source is tantamount to stealing. Here are three examples of how to give appropriate credit:

- "In a staff meeting last week, Joan Lungrave offered a great idea about how we should address this problem, and I would like to share it with you. She suggested that we. . . ."
- "According to a Gallup poll conducted in 1997, the people seen as being in the most honest and ethical occupation were pharmacists."
- "The movement to increase volunteer efforts was epitomized in the words of President John F. Kennedy when he said, and I quote, 'Ask not what your country can do for you, ask what you can do for your country,' unquote."

In the next chapter, as you learn about specific ways to collect information and develop your presentations, keep in mind the need to apply ethical principles throughout the entire process, from the initial research through the final delivery.

For each of the following scenarios, decide which choice would be the ethical one to make.

1. You have notes from your library research about some data that fit your speech perfectly, but you have lost the citation. Do you use the data in your speech anyway?

2. You are giving a speech in favor of the right to own firearms. During your research you find a claim that if certain states had not outlawed the carrying of concealed firearms in 1992, there would have been 1,600 fewer murders because people would have been better able to protect themselves. The source of this information is the National Rifle Association (NRA). Do you use it? Do you cite the NRA? Would it be okay to simply say, "I have this from a reliable source?"

3. You have data indicating that your company will increase its profits by $13 million in the next five years. However, this represents only 2 percent growth per year. You'd like to be optimistic in your presentation, so can you stress the total profits and avoid mentioning the slow growth rate?

4. You are trying to convince some clients to invest in a particular firm. You have evidence showing that the firm's profits increased by 5 percent two years ago, 8 percent one year ago, and 10 percent in the fiscal year just completed. You also have incomplete data suggesting that profits will decline by 2 percent in the current year. Can you legitimately ignore the possible loss?

Summary

Presentational communication primarily involves one person talking and other people listening. The major purposes for presentational communication are to entertain (make an emotional impact), inform (make a cognitive impact), and persuade (make a cognitive or behavioral impact). Persuasive presentations can be further categorized as speeches of fact, value, or policy.

In informational presentations, the speaker wants the audience to learn, understand, and retain knowledge. Because people listen for information that they feel has value to them, an effective informational presentation includes motivating the audience to listen by showing the relevance of the information. A balance must be struck between overwhelming the audience with too much new information and boring the audience with not enough new information. You can stimulate audience attention through the use of perceptual elements such as primacy, recency, novelty, emphasis, and repetition. You can also use structural methods such as previews, summaries, transitions, and keywords. Organizing the information may help the audience retain the information and will definitely help you cover all points systematically. Organizational patterns include topical, chronological, spatial, dimensional, and cause-and-effect patterns.

Persuasive presentations try to influence the listeners' attitudes, beliefs, values, or behaviors. Values are the most basic element of a person's psychological context, followed by beliefs, attitudes, and behaviors. The persuasive speaker needs to be clear about what change is being sought. Traditional strategies for persuading listeners depend on emotional appeals, logical proofs, and credibility (belief in the speaker). Emotional appeals involve arousing the audience's feelings and then providing some outlet for them. Logical proofs use induction and deduction as ways of proving the speaker's claims or conclusions. Credibility develops when the speaker displays competence, trustworthiness, and dynamism. Need appeal strategies involve the speaker's demonstrating that the desired change will meet important audience needs. Reward appeals show how a need can be fulfilled, while fear appeals show how needs are being threatened. Cognitive strategies depend on demonstrating an imbalance, or dissonance, in the values, beliefs, attitudes, or behaviors of the audience. The persuasive speaker provides the audience with a way of creating balance and consonance.

The most effective presentations are those based on a careful analysis of the audience and the situation. The speaker can incorporate more effective strategies, examples, and language when the audience's background is more clearly understood. The speaker needs to analyze the audience before, during, and after the presentation.

Communication is subject to ethical standards. Speakers are expected to provide honest and truthful information. The ethical speaker speaks respectfully, not making fun of others or using derogmatory language. Finally, ethics dictates that all sources be clearly identified for any material that is not original to the speaker.

Key Terms

presentational communication An actional (linear) form of communication in which one person speaks most of the time and other people listen.

speeches of fact Presentations that attempt to convince the audience of the existence of something or that something is true.

speeches of value Presentations that argue for the worth or correctness of something.

speeches of policy Presentations that advocate the adoption of a particular plan of action.

primacy The tendency for people to recall the first things that they hear.

recency   The tendency of people to recall the last, or most immediate, things that they hear.

novelty   The tendency to recall the unusual or unique.

emphasis   Giving certain points prominence, such as by raising or lowering the voice or writing items on a chalkboard.

repetition   Use of repeated words, phrases, or sentences to emphasize a point.

preview   A brief overview of the key information that you will be elaborating on within the body of your presentation.

summary   A section at the end of your presentation that recaps the material covered in the main body of the presentation.

transition   A statement that signals to the audience that you are completing one point and about to move to another.

keywords   Specific terms or phrases used as constructs that the audience can easily recall.

topical organization   An organizational pattern in which the key points associated with a topic are identified and then organized as the points seem to dictate.

chronological organization   An organizational pattern that follows a historical sequence or time line of occurrences.

spatial organization   A pattern of organization that follows a logical pattern based on the relative proximity of the main points to one another.

dimensional organization   A pattern of organization in which the material is placed in some ascending or descending order based on factors such as size or scope.

cause-and-effect organization   An organizational pattern based on discussing causes and their effects.

persuasion   A direct influence on another person's attitudes, beliefs, values, or behaviors.

emotional appeals   Persuasive appeals based on arousing an audience's emotions and then providing a method for alleviating them.

logical proof   A persuasive appeal based on a set of logical arguments and supportive evidence.

inductive reasoning   A form of logical reasoning that involves making generalized conclusions on the basis of a few specific examples.

deductive reasoning   A form of logical reasoning that involves making specific conclusions based on a generality.

classical syllogism   A form of deductive reasoning that claims that if a major and minor premise based on shared elements are true, a concluding relationship must also be true.

credibility   The personal quality or character of a speaker that leads people to accept what the speaker says as true.

competence   The expertise, knowledge, and skills we perceive a speaker to have.

trustworthiness   The degree to which we perceive a speaker as honest, ethical, dependable, consistent, and open.

dynamism   The ability to gain credibility by being enthusiastic, energetic, and likable.

reward appeals   Persuasive appeals that show how adopting a proposed change will help satisfy a need.

fear appeals   Persuasive appeals that show how failing to adopt a proposed change will threaten a need.

balance theory   A cognitive theory stating that people have a drive to maintain balance in their thoughts and actions.

cognitive dissonance theory   A cognitive theory that claims that people strive to maintain consonance (agreement) in their thoughts and actions and avoid dissonance (disagreement or contradictions).

1. Explain what is meant by presentational communication.
2. Briefly review some of the types of informational and persuasive presentations.
3. Explain how you can affect a listener according to the continuum of persuasive impact.
4. Develop examples of inductive and deductive logical appeals.
5. Define credibility and its three components.
6. How can cognitive dissonance be used to persuade someone?
7. Briefly explain the guidelines for speaking ethically.

Chapter 13

Presentational Communication: Research and Preparation

Objectives

Studying this chapter will allow you to:

1. Explain the importance of developing a purpose for a presentation.
2. Describe some of the sources for researching a topic and collecting support material.
3. Identify some of the important guidelines for developing an effective introduction.
4. Identify some of the important guidelines for developing an effective body.
5. Identify some of the important guidelines for developing an effective conclusion.

One of the most important aspects of making an effective presentation is the preparation. Presentations vary in the amount of specific preparation they require, ranging from relatively little specific preparation for spontaneous speeches to a great deal for highly prepared manuscripts.

Impromptu speeches are presentations made on the spur of the moment, without benefit of a detailed outline. Impromptu speeches rely on the general preparation and readiness of the speakers. Speakers must draw from their reservoir of knowledge and adapt to the specific audience and situation. This is the type of presentation that commonly occurs in the context of meetings and discussions. For example, you might need to respond to a new proposal just made by another speaker. You would draw on your general knowledge relevant to the proposal. The spontaneous nature of impromptu speeches means that they generally are not rehearsed. Despite the inability to prepare extensively, impromptu speeches should, as much as possible, follow the speech guidelines discussed in this chapter and the next.

At the other end of the spectrum from impromptu speeches are memorized speeches and manuscript speeches, which involve writing down word for word what is going to be said. Speakers delivering **manuscript speeches** essentially read directly from the full text in front of them. Speakers presenting **memorized speeches** have committed the written text to memory and thus do not need to read it. Sometimes, speakers memorize their presentations because they are uncomfortable reading them. Memorized and manuscript speeches run the risk of sounding impersonal. In addition, if something is forgotten in a memorized speech the speaker is often thrown off track. Whether memorized or not, these highly prepared speeches are usually reserved for major addresses, for which the speaker needs to carefully consider every aspect of the text. Presidential addresses are examples of such speeches. Moreover, even though the exact text is worked out in advance, a great deal of skill is needed to deliver the speech effectively. These presentations generally are rehearsed several times before being delivered.

Extemporaneous speeches fall between impromptu and manuscript speeches in terms of preparation. **Extemporaneous speeches** involve careful preparation of the introduction, main ideas, evidence, appeals, and conclusion. Extemporaneous speeches are also rehearsed. However, the exact wording used in explaining the points is essentially impromptu. Extemporaneous speeches maintain spontaneity of delivery within the bounds of a considered and strategic approach.

Sometimes, in an extemporaneous speech, the introduction may be written out word for word to ensure that all of the important points are covered. A well-developed introduction also helps reduce speech anxiety, giving the speaker confidence in how the presentation begins. Another key to effective extemporaneous speaking is having a comprehensive set of notes from which to speak. These notes provide a framework for the presentation and help ensure that the speaker does not forget important information. The notes are usually well organized, and they include the outline that the speaker has developed in advance of the presentation.

The extemporaneous speech will be the primary focus in this chapter and the next. Because it falls midway on the continuum of preparation, the extemporaneous speech shares some of the qualities of both the manuscript speech and the impromptu speech. Therefore, learning to be an effective extemporaneous speaker can help you with other forms of presentation as well. This chapter focuses on preparation, from determining your purpose through outlining and making notes. Chapter 14 then presents guidelines for delivering your presentation.

Think about some speeches you have listened to on TV or in person (other than lectures). Which one did you like the best? What type of speech was it—memorized, manuscript, extemporaneous, impromptu? Can you think of speeches you have heard that are good examples and bad examples of each of these types?

■ Developing the Purpose and Selecting the Topic

Imagine that you have graduated and are gainfully employed. You receive a call from the alumni association of your former college or university inviting you to make a presentation during alumni week. You say, "Great!"

Now what? Let's explore how you will prepare your speech.

■ *Initial Questions to Answer*

A number of questions need to be answered if you are to prepare an effective presentation—questions about your objectives, the situation, your audience, and yourself. The following list details the questions to ask as well as the answers you might give in the alumni presentation scenario.

	Questions	Sample Answers
Your objectives	1. What is the objective of my presentation?	1. I want to inspire my audience to achieve success in their lives, even if their college careers haven't been stellar. I want to persuade them to go on to graduate school.
	2. What change do I want in the audience?	2. I want the audience to gain confidence and to consider applying to graduate school.
The situation	3. What do the people who invited me expect from my presentation?	3. They want me to make the audience feel good about having attended the session. They want the audience to learn any relevant information that I might have to share.
	4. How long am I expected to speak?	4. It could be any amount of time, let's say fifteen minutes.
	5. How will my presentation relate to other activities or presentations?	5. I am one of three speakers in a morning session about careers.

The audience	6. Who will make up the audience?	6. The audience will consist mainly of senior and junior undergraduates in addition to a few faculty and administrators.
	7. What are the audience's reasons for listening to me?	7. The students hope to learn something that will help them make career decisions. The faculty and administrators want validation of information they feel they already know.
The speaker	8. What am I comfortable and qualified talking about?	8. I am qualified to talk about getting a master's degree or Ph.D. and about pursuing careers in liberal arts and sciences, especially in communication.
	9. What am I interested in talking about with the audience?	9. I like talking about my career. I like talking about communication and graduate education. I feel strongly about encouraging students to seek advanced degrees.
	10. What work will I need to do to prepare for this speech?	10. I will need to do some research on graduate education and careers related to a variety of majors.

■ From Topic to Central Idea

Look again at the sample answer to question 1. Do you see any problem there? One of the most fundamental errors made in presentations is not clearly identifying a specific (narrow) purpose. After identifying the topic about which you want to speak, you need to narrow your focus by identifying a specific purpose. Trying to accomplish too many different goals in one presentation often confuses and overwhelms the audience and diffuses your efforts.

With that principle in mind, you can see that the answer to question 1 is rather broad. Though it does identify the general topic area for the presentation, it names two objectives that might get in each other's way and effectively neutralize each other. So you might focus on just trying to persuade the audience to go to graduate school and leave out the broader, less clearly defined goal of inspiring the audience to achieve success.

You can set a well-defined, specific goal for your presentation by completing the following statement:

"When I'm done with my presentation, I want the audience to. . ."

For our specific scenario, you might complete the statement this way:

"When I'm done with my presentation, I want the audience to seriously consider going to graduate school."

Developing a Topic for a Classroom Presentation

Students are often puzzled about what to choose for a topic for a classroom assignment. You already know a lot about some things and have an interest in others. Those are good places to start. Don't assume that other people will find your topic boring. Learning about new things, people, and places generally fascinates people.

Here's a little brainstorming activity to help you generate some possibilities.

First Stage

- Make a list of your hobbies, activities, pastimes, and so on (quilting, volleyball, TV, reading).
- Make a list of any local, state, national, or international issues in which you have interest (zoning issues, overcrowding of national parks, cloning, urban sprawl).
- Make a list of any topics of conversations you have found provocative and fun (life on other planets, overpaid professional athletes, corrupt politicians, best bar in town, favorite movies).
- Make a list of those things you know a lot about (your hometown, your major, working at Disneyland, motocross, the American Revolution, Martin Luther King, Jr.).

Second Stage

- Look over these lists and select a few items that are the most interesting to you.
- Create a list of topics related to each of the items on your list. For example, if you choose TV as one of your pastimes, what topics about TV could you explore? TV ratings, TV violence, interactive TV, dish TV, the history of situation comedies, the effectiveness of commercials?
- Select a couple of topics and analyze the potential audience interest in each issue. Ask your classmates or other college students how interested they might be in hearing about the topic.
- If you're preparing a persuasive presentation, turn the topic into a question, a statement of policy, or a call for action. For instance, "TV shows should not be subject to a national rating system" or "Why should you consider buying a TV dish?" Be sure to consider where your audience falls on the continuum of support for or opposition to the issue. You may want to conduct an informal survey of classmates or friends.

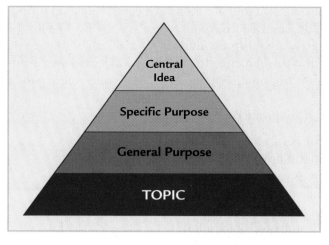

Figure 13.1   The Process of Building a Presentation from Topic to Central Idea

The process of developing a speech is depicted in Figure 13.1. Thus far, you have identified a **topic** (graduate school), a **general purpose** (to persuade), and a **specific purpose** (to persuade students to consider going to graduate school). Eventually you will need to develop a central idea, or thesis. The **central idea,** or **thesis statement,** is a thematic statement that reflects the topic, general purpose, specific purpose, and major focus of what you plan to say. The central idea is formulated after you have sufficiently researched the topic, explored the variety of potential themes, and selected the theme you plan to develop. The central idea is a carefully worded statement that serves as your guide in making decisions about what to include or exclude in your presentation.

Speakers often explicitly present their central idea to the audience, but there are some dangers in that approach: It may come across as trite or dull. You generally want to be more creative and provocative than starting your presentation with a statement such as: "The purpose of my speech today is persuade you to go to graduate school by showing you the merits of such a decision." In the following sections, you'll see how the process of preparation will lead you to your central idea and help you decide how to present it most effectively.

■ Researching the Topic and Collecting Evidence

You will frequently need to supplement your own knowledge of the topic with additional information. Regardless of whether you are informing or persuading the audience, you want to provide the strongest, most reliable, and most relevant information possible. This means conducting research. Finding the best information depends on using a variety of techniques and searching a variety of sources.

■ *The Need for Research*

Researching a topic should begin early in speech preparation. In fact, your research may help you determine your topic. Research will help you decide whether a particular topic is worth pursuing, and it can lead you to discover other topics.

Even if you stay with the topic you initially choose, research helps you formulate the specific purpose and the central idea. Your research provides you with the substance you need for the body of your presentation—the information you will share with your audience and the evidence to support your persuasive arguments. Citing outside sources of information also increases the audience's trust in you and your message.

The value of research can be summed up as follows:

- Research helps you narrow and clarify the topic.
- Research creates a reliable information base.
- Research generates supportive and persuasive evidence.
- Research improves audience trust in you and your message.
- Research helps you emphasize your points.
- Research provides clarification and illustration.

■ Types of Evidence and Support

You have probably watched enough courtroom-drama TV to learn some of the legal rules of evidence. For instance, hearsay evidence (repeating what someone else has said) is usually ruled inadmissible in court. The idea is that the information is likely to be distorted in being repeated. Similarly, in presentations, you need to present information that the audience will believe is free of distortion. To support your statements, you can use either direct evidence or indirect evidence.

Direct evidence.   **Direct evidence** is evidence that an audience can view or hear firsthand. By examining this evidence, audience members can reach their own conclusions. Direct evidence includes physical evidence, firsthand evidence, and expert evidence.

- **Physical evidence** can be in the form of objects, such as photographs, diagrams, and maps, or it can involve demonstrations. The use of physical evidence depends on the topic. For example, telling an audience how easy it is to surf the web would be enhanced with an actual demonstration of web surfing.
- **Firsthand evidence** is a report by a witness about facts that he or she knows personally, usually from having observed some occurrence. The person providing this testimony appears in front of the audience, thus making this a form of direct evidence. As a speaker, you might use your own firsthand observations as firsthand evidence.
- **Expert evidence** is presented by a person who is recognized as possessing a credible body of knowledge on some topic or issue. Lawyers typically have to establish the credibility of a witness whom they want to characterize as an expert. In the movie *My Cousin Vinny*, Ms. Vito (the girlfriend of lawyer Vinny) is presented as an expert witness on automobiles. She is able to prove her expertise because of her experience and her demonstration of knowledge. In presentations, the rules for expert evidence are not as stringent as in a courtroom. Often, you yourself can provide expert testimony when you draw from your own experiences, education, and knowledge.

Audience members evaluate the credibility of the evidence a speaker presents.

Indirect evidence. Most of the time, you don't have the opportunity to bring in other people to provide testimony as part of your presentation. Therefore, you will likely be using quotes or statistics to support your statements. Because the audience cannot directly judge the evidence firsthand and depends on a second party (you) to convey the information accurately and honestly, it is called **indirect evidence.**

- **Indirect firsthand evidence** consists of quotations from individuals who have personal experience or knowledge of the issue but are not regarded as experts. This is essentially reported eyewitness testimony. For example, to evoke a sympathetic response from your audience, you might quote comments from people whose homes were destroyed by a flood. In this case, they would not be considered experts on floods, but they would provide testimony about their personal experiences.
- **Indirect expert evidence** takes the form of quotations from individuals or sources known to have knowledge on the issue being presented. Because you typically can't bring in an expert the way a lawyer might, you can rely on quotes from published sources or from personal interviews. To have this testimony accepted as expert, you need to establish the credibility of the experts you are quoting, just as you would with direct expert evidence.

- **Statistical evidence** represents a numerical manipulation and simplification of raw data. Statistical evidence invariably results in some degree of distortion. For instance, reporting that the average on a final exam for six students was 85 percent (a B average) creates a very different picture than reporting that four of the students scored 100 percent and two scored 55 percent.

■ *Judging the Quality of the Source*

The material cited in your presentation needs to be reliable and trustworthy. The audience not only judges your credibility as a speaker, it also judges the credibility of your sources. For that reason, you must be a critical researcher when you begin collecting supportive data. You need to find impartial, objective, honest, relevant, and timely information. You must make the initial judgment about the reliability and validity of the information that you will be advancing to your listeners.

Table 13.1 offers a checklist for judging source credibility. On the basis of the table's guidelines, examine the following sources of information and decide which ones would be acceptable and which should be rejected:

1. The National Rifle Association (NRA) as a source of information in support of the right to bear arms
2. "Bernie's Personal Home Page" on the World Wide Web as a source of information about nuclear weapons
3. A 1991 *U.S. News Online* report as a source of information about trends in job opportunities
4. The American Medical Association (AMA) as a source of information about the current spread of AIDS
5. Your personal talk with Dr. Mildred Hanshear, a professor of biochemistry, as a source on genetic engineering
6. A quote from Mr. Conrad Pels, a witness to a tornado in Norwich, Canada, about what he saw

The first source would not be an effective one because the NRA has a vested interest in the topic—they have something to gain. Sources are more credible when they are seen as objective and not self-serving. Sources are even more credible when they are viewed as speaking against their own interests. In a recent election, a woman who identified herself as a mainstream Republican wrote in support of the Democratic candidate for governor. Her endorsement carried more

---

Table 13.1 Checklist for Judging the Credibility of a Source

_____ Is the source protecting some self-interest or vested interest?
_____ Is it reliable?
_____ Is it believable?
_____ Is it generalizable?
_____ Is it valid?
_____ Is it relevant?
_____ Is it up-to-date?

weight than it would have if she had been a Democrat, because she was seen as speaking against her own previous affiliation.

As for the second reference in our list, remember that one of the dimensions of credibility is expertise. Citing Bernie's home page would not enhance your presentation if Bernie were just an ordinary person who happened to have an interest in nuclear weapons. This lack of expertise would undermine the credibility of information drawn from Bernie. However, the assessment of credibility would change if Bernie were the late Dr. Bernard T. Feld of MIT, a noted physicist who worked to end nuclear weapons. In other words, you need to do research on the source of the information and provide the results of that search to your audience.

The third reference is a news source that is considered reliable and objective, the web site of *U. S. News & World Report.* However, the information is not particularly relevant to a current presentation because it is from 1991. Clearly, the date of the information can have a bearing on its value and relevance. Trends in job opportunities change quickly; therefore, this source would be of minimal value if you were trying to persuade your audience to pursue a given career. On the other hand, a quote from 1991 might be perfectly acceptable from a historian discussing the impact of the assassination of President Lincoln.

The last three references in our list generally would be considered credible. Each reference can be considered reliable and truthful, and each has relevant expertise. However, all three references have limits, and the speaker would have to be cautious about what conclusions to draw from their statements. Regarding the fifth reference, for example, if your presentation on genetic engineering focused on the ethics of the matter, you would want to quote philosophers and social scientists as well as a biochemist.

■ Conducting the Search

As shown in Figure 13.2, the process of collecting information can be thought of as a progression shaped like an hourglass. Initially, you look at many sources, collecting a broad spectrum of information. This information helps you narrow your focus from the broad topic to your central idea. Once you have a central idea, you

Figure 13.2 The Process of Collecting Information

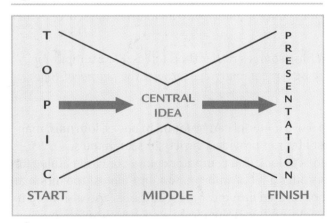

then begin expanding your search again, focusing now on information related exclusively to your central idea. In the beginning, your search is wide open and unrestricted, with any information you find of potential value. In the end, you are looking for particular, focused, and well-defined information.

Creative detective work. Conducting successful research involves being a cross between Sherlock Holmes and Maya Angelou. You need to be part detective and part artist. You need to be clever in thinking about what to look for and where to look for it. You need creativity in your search so that you look in places that might otherwise be missed.

Suppose you were doing a speech on mixed-race marriages. What keywords would you examine? You might not find much information under "mixed-race marriages." You would need to brainstorm words and concepts that might be related to this topic: interracial marriages, mixed-race relationships, interracial relationships, interracial couples, cross-cultural marriages, intercultural relationships, and black-white marriages. You also might look for related information about dating, interracial conflict, families, and so on.

For almost every question you can ask, there is a response floating around in the world of information. The challenge is finding it. You need to pursue the trail of an answer like Holmes pursuing the clues in a mystery. You also need to maintain an open mind and a willingness to examine a lot of paths that might lead nowhere, as Angelou would do in writing a poem.

Efficient research. Efficient research is probably an oxymoron. By its very nature, research is *in*efficient. There are some methods, however, that can help you zero in on relevant information.

1. Start wide—cast a large net. Use the most encompassing and general terms as your keywords.

    A. If you don't get much, try different terms.
    B. If you get too much, add more terms to your search.

2. Use a variety of terms and synonyms when conducting your search.
3. Use each source as a possible clue or link to other sources.

    A. Consider the references cited in the source as potential sources.
    B. Consider the keywords, concepts, and issues included in the source as further search terms.

4. When stumped, try searching sources rather than topics. For example, for possible articles related to interracial marriage, browse the *Journal of Black Studies*.

The library search. Supportive material can be found in books, journals, magazines, and newspapers. Most libraries provide a variety of search tools.

The traditional approach is to look in a computer catalog or card catalog for books on a given topic. Books offer a lot of information, but almost too much at times, to be digested and incorporated into most presentations. You also need to be careful about whether the information drawn from a book is out-of-date.

Newspapers and periodicals (both professional journals and popular magazines) contain an abundance of information. There are a large number of abstracts and indexes—collections of sources cross-referenced by topic or keywords—that can help you locate relevant information. Here are some of the most common.

- For newspaper searches: *Lexis-Nexis, Academic Universe,* and *National Newspaper Index*
- For popular magazines: *Reader's Guide Abstracts*
- *AGRICOLA* (agriculture)
- *Business Abstracts*
- *Current Contents-Abstracts*
- *ERIC* (education)
- *General Science Abstracts*
- *Humanities Abstracts*
- *Social Sciences Abstracts*

Besides these general indexes, almost each area of academic pursuit has an index or abstract that can help you: for instance, *Psychological Abstracts, Entomology Abstracts, Communication Abstracts, Toxicology Abstracts,* and *World Ceramic Abstracts.* Some abstracts are available online through various libraries around the country. In addition, a growing number of newspapers are making their archives available through the Internet.

The Internet search. The Internet offers access to an incredibly large amount of information. Unfortunately, most of it is usually irrelevant to your research on a particular topic. There are many search engines, however, and they continue to evolve. The search engines differ in the manner in which they create their indexes; therefore, different engines will produce different results. Most of them use web crawlers that enter web sites and create indexes of the content.

The manner in which you enter your request is also evolving rapidly. You can conduct a **keyword search,** in which you enter a variety of possible terms to locate relevant information. Usually, you enter the keywords of interest and some logical operators (such as "and", "or", or "not") or text operators (such as "near" or "followed by"). The manner in which you enter the keywords greatly affects the search output.

Recent developments based on artificial intelligence and fuzzy logic have made the search engines more user-friendly. Now you can simply type in a question, and the search engine identifies the keywords. Each engine provides guidelines on how to use it most effectively. There are also online tutorials to help you develop search skills.

Besides using search engines, you can also consult Internet subject directories. A **subject directory** is a hierarchical listing of various resources. Each time a topic is chosen, another list of subtopics appears. When a subtopic is chosen, another set of topics is revealed. And so on. At the end, you receive a list of possible Internet sites to visit, sometimes numbering in the hundreds or thousands.

Suppose you were using a directory to look for information on interracial marriages. You might start with the category "society and culture." Clicking on

Supportive material is increasingly available through computer searches of CD-ROM indices or the Internet.

that topic might give you a list of thirty subtopics. You might choose the subtopic "relationships," where you would find the sub-subcategory "interracial." Clicking on that category would then give you a list of sites that had something to do with interracial relationships.

One problem with Internet searches is the sheer volume of information that can overwhelm you. Internet searches take time, patience, skill, and luck to be productive. Another problem lies in the credibility or trustworthiness of the information. Anybody can create a home page and put any information they choose on it. To find out if the information you have accessed is reliable, you need to address the following questions:

1. Do you recognize the source of the information? Is the web page hosted, for instance, by a company or organization you know? Look for organizational identifiers of legitimate servers. For example, the extension "edu" stands for an educational institution (although particular pages within the site can be created by individual faculty members and students); "org" is the extension for registered organizations, and "gov" for government agencies.

2. Who are the author and publisher? Is there any evidence that they have expertise on the subject in question? Are they biased? Use the information on the site to help you determine the legitimacy of the information.

3. Is there an email address for contacting the webmaster or person in charge of the site? You can feel a bit more trusting of those pages that have email addresses for contacting the source.

4. Is the information from the primary source? Be careful about sites that are posting information that is not original, because this increases the likelihood of inaccuracy. As much as possible, information should be taken from the primary source.

Choose a topic of interest and conduct a keyword search on one of the Internet search engines. How many hits did you get? Try entering various synonyms for your keywords. Did you locate other sources?

Now use an Internet subject directory such as Yahoo! (http://www.yahoo.com/) or Metacrawler (http://www.go2net.com/search.html) to look for sources related to the same topic. How many links did it take to get to the final listing of sites? How many sites were there?

Which search method gave you better results: keyword or directory?

Interviews and surveys.   Interviews and surveys provide another way of finding information that can help you develop the presentation and provide evidence to support your claims.

Discussions with individuals who are knowledgeable about a given topic can give you insights into aspects that you might not have considered. On the topic of interracial marriage, for instance, talking with people you know who are married to someone of another race might help you identify relevant issues. Their testimony could also be used to support the points you cover in your presentation. Your interviewing can also involve expert testimony. You could talk to a sociology professor known for studying the social impact of interracial marriages. In such a case, you might need to do two interviews: an exploratory interview as you developed the presentation, and a second interview that sought specific answers to questions you decided to address. For any interviews you conduct as research for a presentation, the material in Chapters 8 and 9 of this book can help you be an effective interviewer.

Informal surveys can help you gain a better understanding of your audience or the topic. You might discuss some of the points you are going to cover in a presentation with several of the audience members prior to the presentation. More formal surveys can be beneficial in providing the precise information you need. Before a managers' meeting to discuss strategies for reducing employee turnover, you might conduct a survey of the employees to find out what issues are important to them. These data could then be used as evidence in your presentation, with appropriate qualifications about the nature of the survey.

Creating a fully reliable and valid set of data through the use of surveys requires some degree of expertise and knowledge. Therefore, you need to be cautious about claiming generalizability of your own survey data unless you followed accepted survey methodology.

■ *Referencing Information in the Presentation*

As noted in Chapter 12's discussion of ethics, you need to provide a full citation of the information you have included in your presentation. Failure to indicate the source of your material is equivalent to plagiarism.

Your reference should include as much information as needed for the audience to judge the credibility of the source. This usually includes the name of the source, the location of the information, the credentials of unfamiliar sources, and the date when the material was originally created. It is not necessary to give a complete oral bibliography, but you should be prepared to provide audience members with a full citation after the presentation, should they request it.

■ Developing the Structure and Preparing an Outline

You have chosen a topic, you have researched it, and now you have a lot of information about various aspects of your topic. You are ready to start developing the structure and content of the presentation. You should have a lot more information than you can actually include; therefore, you need to decide what to include and what to exclude. You need to review the material and see if there are logical groupings of information that might be used as the basis of your presentation.

There are five steps in developing an initial rough draft of your outline.

1. Write down all of the possible subpoints, keywords, and issues that you have identified with the topic.
2. See how that information falls into the organizational patterns discussed in Chapter 12.
3. Look for categories or main points that you can use to group the subpoints or issues.
4. Create several possible arrangements, and write a central idea for each arrangement.
5. Analyze each option in terms of these criteria:
   a. how well it fits your purpose
   b. how the audience might respond
   c. how much information you need to fully develop the presentation and how much you have obtained in your research

The following example illustrates this process:

Topic: Going to Graduate School

Step 1: List possible subpoints, keywords, and issues.

Getting a better job	Learn more in an area of interest
Find a specialty	Improve yourself
Costs	Assistantships
Change career path	Delaying work
How to apply	Deciding where to go
Taking the GRE (Graduate Record Exam)	Master's degrees and doctorates
Intellectual stimulation	Higher standards

Adjustment shock	Heavy study load
New people	Less direction
Preparing while an undergraduate	Isolation
Life as a graduate student	Feeling inadequate or intimidated

Step 2: See how the information might fit organizational patterns.
Chronological Organization

Preparing as an undergraduate	Financing
Taking the GRE	Life as a graduate student
Deciding where to go	Getting a job after graduate school
Applying	

Step 3: Look for ways to categorize subpoints within an organizational pattern.
(Step 3 may be performed before step 2, depending on the nature of your material. Here, for the sake of illustration, we'll use a different organizational pattern than in step 2.)
Topical Organization

Advantages	Disadvantages
Get a better job	Costs
Improve yourself	Higher standards to meet
Learn more	Heavy study load
Intellectual stimulation	Feeling intimidated

Step 4: Create several arrangements (like those in steps 2 and 3), and write a central idea for each.
Chronological organization (using the outline from step 2):
Central idea: I want my audience to know the sequence of events they will experience when pursuing a graduate degree so that they can better plan their futures.

Topical organization (using the outline from step 3):
Central idea: I want my audience to learn the advantages and disadvantages of getting a graduate degree and thus be able to make an informed decision about pursuing one.

Step 5: Analyze each option in terms of (a) how well it fits the purpose, (b) how the audience might respond, and (c) how much information is needed and how much is already obtained.
Chronological Organization

a. Doesn't really motivate audience to pursue a graduate degree.
b. The audience will probably find the information somewhat boring and irrelevant.
c. I've got personal experience in all the steps, and I can use the additional information I have found on current costs, financing, and job opportunities.

Topical Organization

a. Showing the advantages should encourage audience members to think about a graduate degree, but covering all the disadvantages might discourage them.

b. The issues covered should be of interest to students, especially in regard to getting a better job. They will also have genuine concerns about the costs and difficulty.

c. I can use myself as an example for each advantage and disadvantage, and I can use the information I have collected about costs and job opportunities.

▮ Preparing the Introduction, Body, and Conclusion

The structure of a presentation has three main components: the introduction, the body, and the conclusion. Each part has a particular function that enhances the effectiveness of the presentation. The following simple cliché reflects the relationship between these three parts:

> Tell them what you are going to tell them (introduction).
> Tell them (body).
> Tell them what you have already told them (conclusion).

This adage is based on using repetition, emphasis, primacy, and recency to enhance the audience's attention to and retention of what you have to say.

▪ The Introduction

The **introduction** sets the stage for the rest of your presentation. Usually, the audience members will be attentive to you as you begin. You need to take advantage of their attentiveness to create interest in listening to your entire presentation. That is, you want to make them willing to continue expending their energy in listening to you. This means carefully and strategically planning your introduction. Know what you are going to say in the introduction and have it well organized.

Speakers often begin their presentations with a statement acknowledging the significance of the occasion, a graphic story, an illustration, a detailed example, a

"If you can wait a few hours, I'll clear a path to the main point of my presentation."

quotation, a critical question, or a humorous anecdote. Using a humorous anecdote can help build rapport with your audience, but be sure you are able to tell a joke effectively and that the joke has a point that relates to your topic and is not offensive to the audience. Whatever technique you use to start, there should be a connection between the initial statements you make and the topic of your presentation.

There are a number of guidelines to follow when creating an effective introduction. These are not the steps or components of an introduction; rather, they are goals you should seek to accomplish. Sometimes one statement will accomplish several of these objectives.

Eight Guidelines for an Effective Introduction

1. Build rapport.   Establish a rapport, or relationship, with the audience members. Connect with them and establish your concern for them.

2. Introduce the topic.   Let the audience know what you will be talking about.

3. Make the topic relevant to the audience.   Show how the topic relates to the people in the audience and why it should be important to them.

4. Establish your credibility or interest.   Explain your expertise or interest in the topic. If necessary, present your credentials.

5. Create a need to listen.   Answer the question, Why should we listen to you?

6. Provide background information.   Sometimes you may have to get your audience up to speed about an issue before beginning a fuller discussion.

7. State the expected outcome.   Let the audience members know what is expected of them.

8. Preview.   Orient the audience to the presentation by giving a detailed, enumerated preview of your presentation. (Tell them what you are going to tell them.)

The following sample introduction accomplishes these goals. In this case, there is no need for goal 6, so that is omitted. Notice, too, that the other goals are addressed in a somewhat different order. Remember, these are objectives to aim at, not a precise format into which you should plug your words.

Build rapport	"Good afternoon. I appreciate the nice introduction from Mr. Green. It's really great to be back on campus. It brings back a lot of memories—some that I can't really talk about.
Establish your credibility	As Mr. Green mentioned, I received my bachelor's and master's degrees here. After my master's degree, I worked for a couple of years, trying to figure out what I wanted to be when I grew up. Eventually I decided to get my Ph.D. and be a college professor. I have been teaching now for almost twenty years and have been fortunate to work with a lot of outstanding students.

Introduce the topic	As you approach graduation, a lot of you are wondering what to do. Most of you have focused on the idea of immediately finding a job, but I'd like to talk to you this afternoon about considering graduate school.
Relate the topic to the audience	I know your first reaction is that the *last* thing you want to do is keep going to school. But I also know that you want to get the best income you can while also doing something you really enjoy.
Create a need to listen	I plan to cover a number of issues you may not have considered before. There are several advantages to getting your master's degree or even the Ph.D. Hopefully, when I am done talking, you will at least be able to make a more-informed decision about your career choices.
Preview	I'm going to focus on three major advantages. First, improving your marketability. Second, learning more. And third, finding a better job. There are some downsides, too, so I will talk about two major disadvantages: one, the financial cost, and two, possible feelings of intimidation. However, I will also tell you how to overcome those disadvantages.
State the expected outcome	When I'm done, I hope you will seriously consider finding out more about graduate school opportunities in your area of interest."

■ *The Body*

The **body** is the part of the presentation in which you present the major pieces of information or arguments. The body should be organized according to one of the organizational patterns described in Chapter 12.

In developing a presentation, you should start with the body. The body is the largest part of the speech. Once the body is completed, then developing the introduction and conclusion is a relatively straightforward process because they represent a preview and a review of what you say in the body.

To create the body, you need to decide what major elements you intend to cover. You need to organize these points and identify appropriate support for them. For an extemporaneous speech, your aim should be an outline that is a fleshed-out version of your rough outline, including the main points, the subpoints, and supportive materials and evidence. Your final outline of the body will look something like this:

I. First main point
    A. First subpoint
        1. Support/evidence/elaboration
        2. Support/evidence/elaboration
    B. Second subpoint
II. Second main point
    A. First subpoint
    B. Second subpoint

Just as there are guidelines to follow for an effective introduction, there are a number of guidelines that will help you succeed in developing the body of your presentation.

Thirteen Guidelines for a Healthy Body

1. Consolidate material. Try to group your material into subpoints within major points.

2. Limit the major points. Keep the number of major points as few as possible (two or three works well).

3. Control the number of subpoints. Too many subpoints can cause the audience to lose sight of the major point and can add confusion and undermine your focus. The number of subpoints will be determined by how much time you have and how much information you need to support each major point.

4. Use subpointing only when there are at least two. If you have only one subpoint, it is probably just a repeat of the major point. Either look for another subpoint or expand the major point to include the single subpoint.

5. Organize according to relationships. Your outline and use of major points and subpoints should reflect the relationships between the concepts and issues.

6. Keep major points equivalent. Major points should be similar in importance, scope, and impact. (Inevitably, though, you will have stronger and weaker arguments.)

7. Keep subpoints equivalent. The subpoints should be similar in importance, scope, and impact.

8. Coverage of points should be equivalent. The amount of time spent talking about each major point should be fairly consistent.

9. Connect the evidence to the issue. The evidence should be clearly linked to the point you are making.

10. Use parallel phrasing and terminology. Try to use terms and phrases that are similar and that the audience can easily recall; for example: "strolling through the past, walking through the present, and running to the future" or "I will discuss three aspects of training: training for learning, training for improvement, and training for success."

11. Enumerate your points. As you speak, refer to your points by number, and keep repeating the numbering: "There are three advantages. The first advantage is. . . . The second advantage is. . . . The third and final advantage is. . . ." Later in the presentation, you can then say, "As I discussed, there are three advantages. . . ."

12. Use keywords. Choose short keywords that reflect larger ideas. Keep repeating them throughout your presentation.

13. Use transitions. As mentioned in Chapter 12, transitional statements signal changes from one point in the presentation to another. Transitions are needed to make a smooth change from the introduction to the body, from one major point to another, and from the body to the conclusion. For example: "Now that I've covered the three advantages, let me talk about the two disadvantages."

■ *The Conclusion*

The **conclusion** is an important place to make one last impact on the audience. Here you have a final chance to review your most important information or most persuasive arguments.

Just as audiences have a natural tendency to tune in during the introduction, they also tune in when they hear a speaker announcing that the presentation is nearing its end. To take advantage of this tendency, you must let the audience know that you are in the conclusion. This can be done in many ways other than using the trite phrase "And in conclusion." For instance, you can use a transitional statement: "As I finish up my comments, let me go back for just a minute to review the advantages and disadvantages."

Like your introduction, the conclusion should be well thought out and prepared. A number of guidelines can help you develop an effective conclusion.

Seven Guidelines for a Strong Conclusion

1. Signal the conclusion.   Let the audience know that you are beginning to wrap up.

2. Review.   Provide a summary of the main points. Depending on your purpose, you may also review important subpoints, evidence, and arguments.

3. Finish strong.   Organize the summary to finish on the points that are most critical, taking advantage of the principle of recency. For example, you might review the disadvantages first and finish with the advantages.

4. Relate to the audience.   Reemphasize the relevance and importance of your topic to your audience.

5. Present final expectations.   Let the audience know what is expected of them. In persuasive presentations, this can include a final call to action.

6. Reconnect to the introduction.   If appropriate, reconnect to your starting point. You might make a reference to the anecdote, quote, or statistic that began your presentation.

7. Conclude.   Let the audience know you are done. Don't just fade away or keep talking as you return to your seat. Make it clear that you are done through your content and delivery: "I want to thank all of you for this opportunity to return and talk to you about continuing your education. Perhaps you, too, will get an invitation in twenty years to return and share stories of your success and insights. Thank you."

■ Preparing Extemporaneous Speaking Notes

Extemporaneous speaking allows you to maintain a personal and spontaneous speaking style to which most audiences are very responsive. To accomplish this

A Sample Speech: "Working Together to Meet the Future"

It is a pleasure to be here with you in the lovely and beautiful city of Victoria. It's also an honor to share my views as chairman of The Boeing Company and to sponsor this lunch.

First, I would like to congratulate Canada on its well-organized yearlong efforts to host a series of business events leading up to the APEC Economic Leaders Meeting this November in Vancouver. And to offer a special thank you to the Canadian National Committee for Pacific Economic Cooperation (PECC) for bringing us together for today's Industry Forum to coincide with the APEC Transportation Ministerial.

I'm always reminded that meetings like this one today simply can't take place without commercial airplanes and many other forms of transportation . . . a place where people can get together for discussion to make the world a better place. At Boeing, we're proud that we've been working for more than 80 years to bring people, products, and places a little closer together. In fact, in 1920 our founder Bill Boeing and his pilot Eddie Hubbard used the B-1, a flying boat with a wood veneer hull and biplane wings, to carry international mail between Victoria and Seattle. It was the beginning of making the world a smaller place.

Today I'd like to talk about my vision of how we might develop the infrastructure needed to support growth in the Asia Pacific. The region is rapidly growing and this presents both challenges and opportunities—especially for the infrastructure that supports the transportation sector.

I have three premises that I would like to offer:

First: Economic growth fundamentally follows transportation infrastructure.
Second: Transportation systems are no longer separate modes, but are integrated sets.
Third: A changing world and trade and investment liberalization create more opportunities to work together.

First premise: Economic growth fundamentally follows transportation infrastructure.

There is evidence that the great cities of the world grew up because of their transportation infrastructure. Initially, these cities were either ocean ports or on major rivers, or on major trading routes such as the silk trade route in Marco Polo's time.

A perfect example today of a water port is where I live: Seattle. Seattle is on Elliott Bay, a port. And that is why New York is where it is; and Hong Kong, Shanghai, and Singapore are where they are. They're all water ports and great cities.

In history, we had a relatively brief period on land where rail was the dominant mode of transportation and a few cities grew up around that form of transportation. Dallas and Chicago, for example, became railheads because of the need to ship commodities such as livestock to market.

I don't believe there are many cities that are truly growing up around air yet. But I can think of two examples. Orlando is one. It is where air is virtually the only way to

This speech was delivered by the chairman and CEO of the Boeing Company in Vancouver, British Columbia. His audience was a large group of people in the transportation industry. Read through the speech and see if you can identify the application, or lack of application, of the principles discussed in this chapter. Pay particular attention to the organization of the introduction, body, and conclusion.

keep the city vital and this may become a prototype for others. The other is Dallas/Ft. Worth. [The airport was] originally built between these two Texas cities, [but] the two places have literally grown into one center.

I believe that this trend will continue. And if the economies grow and it is to be fostered and sustained, it's absolutely crucial that the infrastructure be there to support the growth.

Second premise: The challenge we have is to think about transportation not just as separate modes, but as an integrated set.

When container ships arrive at their port of destination, we need to have the rail and highway structures—as an integrated part of the process—to move goods to their destination. In other words, a port that integrates what comes from the sea side to the land side and the land side to the sea side. The same goes for air; e.g., passenger and cargo on airplanes—we need to distribute them.

What you really would like is the ability to interconnect rail, auto, and bus on the land side of the airport in an efficient fashion. The new airport in Hong Kong is one example of where rail links right into the airport. Kansai International Airport is another. Zurich is superb: first level is for cars and taxis; second level is for light rail into the city; third level is for the Swiss National Railway. You move from the air side to the auto, light rail, and railroad without going outside. It's all integrated right into the terminal. These are good examples to emulate.

We also have to recognize it's total travel time that impacts the movement of people and goods. By integrating systems together for the ease of the passenger or movement of the products, we will have happier customers and faster delivery of goods. For example, I'll bet that many of you who travel may have had that "total travel" experience.

It goes something like this: drive to the airport, fly nine hours to a large coastal city, change airplanes, fly some more, arrive, get your luggage, get a cab or take a bus, check into your hotel, and go to a meeting that night or the next morning. The total travel time getting there was probably substantial. Certainly point-to-point air would have helped cut down on the air portion, but it's the total travel time that impacts people and freight.

That's why the recently completed Congestion Points Study, sponsored by the APEC Transportation Working Group, is such an important contribution. It identifies transportation bottlenecks and what can be done to resolve them.

Third premise: A changing world and trade and investment liberalization create more opportunities to work together.

We live in a changing world—a kaleidoscope of times. Last month, NATO signed a new partnership agreement with its former Cold War adversary Russia. Scheduled today, there's the MFN vote on China in the United States. Next month, Hong Kong reverts to China. Lots of change in our world; and lots of opportunity if we work together.

Land, air, and sea play a role here. Our transportation sectors can come together and provide the infrastructure we need in the 21st century. We can learn from our past, listen to each other, and work together by sharing our thoughts and ideas to solve the challenges of the Asia Pacific region. We can lead or we can follow. We can envision and implement, or we can wait and fret. We can come together and work together, or we can go our separate ways. We have tremendous opportunity to take advantage of our kaleidoscope of times by working together.

APEC exemplifies this working-together spirit, by embracing the concept of "open regionalism." The goal APEC has set for itself of achieving free and open trade and investment in the region by 2010 for its industrialized members, and 2020 for developing economies, has the potential to be the most far-reaching trade agreement in history—and one that companies like Boeing stand to gain from.

As a company, we strongly support free trade and the kind of objective that APEC represents. We believe that trade creates prosperity. A world that is free of trade barriers—not free trade blocs, but a world system—is one that offers the best hope for humankind.

The creation of such a system had its beginnings 50 years ago. On October 30, 1947, representatives of 23 countries, meeting in Geneva, signed the General Agreement on Tariffs and Trade (GATT). In four short months, just before the APEC Economic Leaders Meeting in Vancouver, we celebrate the 50th anniversary of the signing of the multilateral trading system.

Fifty years ago the scope of world trade was considerably smaller. The whole world was different. We didn't have jet airplanes, air express, high-speed rail, personal computers, CNN, cellular telephones, CDs, recycling, McDonald's, or parasailing. We were local economies then. Now we are global rather than just local, regional, or national. In fact, at the same time that our world has grown smaller because of advances in both transportation and communication, world trade has grown larger.

The reduction of barriers to trade, under successive GATT rounds, has helped manufactured exports to increase by a factor of 26 since 1950. Last year, world exports passed the $5 trillion mark for the first time. This expansion in world trade has benefited many companies around the world, including Boeing.

Our markets are international—the same as many other industries. At Boeing, for example, about 70 percent of our commercial airplanes now sell outside the United States. We project that the world's airlines will add more than 16,000 new jets, worth $1.1 trillion, during the next 20 years. In the Asia Pacific, we forecast that the region will require a total of about 4,500 units worth $380 billion over the next 20 years, making it the largest market in the world.

So on the eve of the 50th anniversary of the signing of that famous multilateral trade agreement in Geneva, we have an opportunity: to forge a renewal of how we will work together for the next 50 years on trade and how to build our transportation infrastructure.

As transportation executives and government leaders and representatives, our work on infrastructure comes first. Remember: build the transportation infrastructure and economic growth will follow. I believe we can succeed in meeting the challenges of congestion, the movement of large volumes of freight and numbers of passengers, bottlenecks at airports and marine terminals, and source financing by being innovative and working together.

I also believe we play a unique leadership role in building the infrastructure foundation that comes first. We have the opportunity to integrate land, air, and sea transportation sectors and become more efficient in the rapidly growing region of the Asia Pacific. We can act collectively and decisively to implement a vision and a plan. We might begin by working together more.

We can:

- Think differently.
- Look at different models that are working, such as Orlando and Zurich.
- Bring customers and suppliers together from all areas; e.g., designers, builders, planners, engineers, accountants, customs agents, people who use the systems and people who create the systems.
- Use computers and technology to create the systems we want on the skyways, waterways, and land-ways; e.g., use global positioning satellites more.
- Think about what the Asia Pacific region has naturally to build upon; e.g., the ability to move people and freight to myriad destinations.
- Make some new models of infrastructure and new ways to integrate—not just copy what existed in the past; e.g., figure the best way to link and integrate things together in a smaller world.

The list goes on and on. Opportunities are endless. But the opportunity to lead is "one of a lifetime." World trade offers us the opportunity for creative thinking and bold leadership—not just in the Asia Pacific but around the world.

Let's start on the 50th anniversary of the multilateral trading system to create the vision for the transportation infrastructure system needed for the 21st century "by working together." Then, I truly believe, we will make a difference.

Thank you.

Source: Phil Condit, chairman and CEO of The Boeing Company, speech to the Pacific Economic Cooperation Council (PECC) Transportation Industry Forum, Victoria, British Columbia, June 25, 1997. The Boeing Company.

style, you need to prepare an effective set of notes. Your notes will provide you with a sense of security, helping you keep track of where you are and what you should be covering. If you get lost during your presentation, you merely need to look at your notes to find the next point you should cover.

■ *Keyword Notes*

For extemporaneous speaking, the best notes are made up only of keywords. These keywords act as prompts, or stimuli, that evoke your memory of the points you developed in your final outline. The bulk of your speech essentially involves elaborating on each keyword. Excessive notes tend to make your speech sound less spontaneous, and they also make it difficult to find your place when you get lost. As you develop your speaking skills, you will find that notes made up of keywords are all you need for an effective presentation.

Think of your presentation as "organized conversation" in which you get to dominate the conversation for a few minutes. This means that your style should be conversational in terms of delivery, but that what you say has to have been carefully thought out and organized. The keyword notes help ensure that your part of the conversation covers all your points. Of course, to keep the speech flowing and to articulate your ideas completely, you will need to practice with your note cards so that the ideas associated with each keyword are clearly embedded in your mind.

If you are skeptical about your ability to elaborate on ideas from a list of keywords, try this experiment. What follows is a set of very general keywords organized around the topic "My Hometown"—that is, anybody's hometown. Find some place right now where you won't be bothered and start talking out loud about each point.

Topic: My Hometown

  I. Likes:
      A. Things to do
      B. Places to go
         1. Stores/restaurants
         2. Museums, historic places, entertainment
  II. Dislikes
      A. Location (weather, traffic, remoteness)
      B. Changes (growing or declining)

In the preceding Test Yourself, you should have been able to talk at least five minutes on the points listed. You could easily adapt this rough speaking outline to your specific hometown and expand the presentation. In a real presentation, the general keywords in these notes would be replaced with terms specific to your hometown. For example, if your hometown were Philadelphia, under stores and restaurants you might have King of Prussia, a reminder to discuss the biggest mall in the United States. Under historic places you might have Elfreth's Alley, a reminder to elaborate on the street that has been continuously inhabited longer than any other street in the country.

The keyword notes do not provide particular words to say, but they direct your speaking to the issue you want to cover. Each time you practice the presentation, it will be different, but the same main points and subpoints will be covered.

There are three exceptions to the exclusive use of keywords in your notes: the introduction, the conclusion, and evidence.

- To ensure that you get started on the right foot, you may want to write out the first line or two of your introduction word for word. You can also practice that opening several times so that you know the exact wording.
- The same principle applies to the conclusion. You may choose to write out the exact wording or practice it enough that you know it by heart.
- Quotations or statistics should also be written out on your speaking notes. Trying to recite quotes or statistics from memory invites disaster and sometimes causes the audience to question their accuracy.

■ *The Format of Note Cards*

Cards are generally more effective for your speaking notes than sheets of paper. Cards are easier to handle and can be kept easily in your hand. Sheets of paper will probably have to be placed on a podium.

The five-by-eight-inch card size works well for most presentations. Cards of that size are stiff enough to be easy to handle and large enough so that you can write in big legible letters that can be read with a glance. Don't try to cram a lot on a single card. Use space to make the information easily visible and accessible.

On your cards you can highlight important points and write additional reminders about delivery. These reminders can include when to use an overhead, when to hand out material, and when to increase your eye contact and energy level.

Figure 13.3 presents a set of sample speaking cards for illustration. To help you follow the content of the speech, some of the subpoints include more than just the keywords that would normally be there.

The use of note cards will be discussed in more detail in Chapter 14, which discusses how to actually deliver your presentation.

Figure 13.3

Sample Note Cards for a Presentation

I.   Good afternoon. I appreciate the nice introduction from Mr. Green. It's really great to be back on campus. It brings back a lot of memories—some that I can't really talk about.
II. My background
III. Consider graduate school
IV. Preview
     A. Three advantages
        1. Improve marketability
        2. Learn more
        3. Find a better job
     B. Two disadvantages
        1. Cost
        2. Intimidation

1

TRANSITION
V. Advantages
    A. Improve marketability
       1. More prepared than those with just B.A.s
       2. Impresses potential employers
    B. Learn more
       1. More specific training and education
       2. Explore areas in depth that were limited in undergraduate study
    C. Find a better job
       1. Provides access to advanced jobs that require either M.A.s or Ph.D.s
       2. Increased job offers provide better selection to match your interests

2

Figure 13.3 (continued)

VI. Disadvantages
  A. Cost
      1. Graduate school can cost up to twice as much as undergraduate
      2. Graduate debt added to any undergraduate debt already incurred
  B. Intimidation
      1. Graduate courses are demanding
      2. Other graduate students might be better than you
  C. Counterarguments
      1. Cost: There are ways to control the costs.
      2. Intimidation: You won't get into graduate school unless you are seen as good enough.

3

VII. Summary
    Disadvantages: cost, intimidation
    Advantages: marketability, learning, better job

VIII. I want to thank all of you for this opportunity to return and talk to you about continuing your education. Perhaps you, too, will get an invitation in twenty years to return and share stories of your success and insights. Thank you.

4

Summary

Presentations vary in their level of preparation from impromptu speeches to extemporaneous speeches and finally to highly prepared manuscript or memorized speeches. Regardless of the type of presentation, its development involves considering your objectives, the situation, the audience, and yourself as the speaker. Having a clear objective is critical to an effective speech. You should be able to complete the statement, "When I'm done with my presentation, I want the audience to. . . ." Speeches also require identifying the topic, a general purpose, a specific purpose, and a central idea (thesis statement).

Generally, research is needed to help you develop the points that you will cover in your presentation and to develop supportive evidence. Evidence can be either direct or indirect. Among the types of direct evidence are physical, firsthand, and expert evidence. The types of indirect evidence include indirect firsthand, indirect expert, and statistical. The evidence needs to be valid, reliable, credible, relevant, and up-to-date.

The process of finding evidence starts with a general search until a central idea has been established. At that point, specific evidence is sought that relates to that central idea. A wide variety of sources of information can help you, including the library, the Internet, personal interviews, and surveys. Outside material presented in the speech needs to be referenced so that the audience can judge its credibility.

Developing the structure of the presentation involves generating a list of potential points and subpoints and then weaving them into one of the organizational patterns discussed in Chapter 12. Once that is done, you are ready to develop the three major components of the presentation: the introduction, the body, and the conclusion. The general approach will be to tell the audience what you are going to tell them, to tell them, and then to tell them what you have told them.

The introduction should be carefully thought out. It should build rapport, relate the topic to the audience, establish your credibility or interest in the topic, introduce the topic, create a need to listen, provide any necessary background information, announce the expected outcome, and provide a detailed preview. The body of the presentation is where the majority of information is provided. Guidelines for constructing the body include keeping the points and their coverage equivalent, using keywords and enumeration, and using transitions. Finally, the conclusion should be as carefully prepared as the introduction, providing a review and another statement of the presentation's relevance to the audience.

For extemporaneous speeches, you can think of the presentation as "organized conversation." Your note cards should generally include only keywords, except that you may need to write out the introduction, the conclusion, and specific points of evidence.

Key Terms

impromptu speeches Presentations made on the spur of the moment, without benefit of a detailed outline.

manuscript speeches Speeches written down word for word in advance and delivered by reading from the text.

memorized speeches Speeches written down word for word in advance, memorized, and then delivered without reading from the text.

extemporaneous speeches Speeches for which the introduction, main ideas, evidence, appeals, and conclusion are prepared and rehearsed in advance, but for which the exact wording of the text is essentially impromptu.

topic The subject discussed in a presentation.

general purpose The goal of a presentation stated in broad terms: for example, to inform the audience or to persuade the audience.

specific purpose The goal of a presentation stated in narrow and specific terms, defining exactly what the speaker intends to accomplish.

central idea or **thesis statement** A thematic statement that reflects the topic, general purpose, specific purpose, and major focus of a presentation.

direct evidence Evidence that an audience can view or hear firsthand.

physical evidence Evidence that takes the form of an object or demonstration.

firsthand evidence A report by a witness about facts that he or she knows personally, usually from having observed some occurrence.

expert evidence Evidence presented by a person who is recognized as possessing a credible body of knowledge on some topic or issue.

indirect evidence Evidence that the audience cannot directly judge.

indirect firsthand evidence Quotations from individuals who have personal experience or knowledge of the issue but are not regarded as experts.

indirect expert evidence Quotations from individuals or sources known to have knowledge on the issue being presented.

statistical evidence Evidence that takes the form of numerical manipulation and simplification of raw data.

keyword search A search for information, usually on CD-ROM or the Internet, that relies on specific terms to locate relevant information on a topic.

subject directory A hierarchical listing of resources, usually on a computer or the Internet, in which the choice of one topic leads to a list of subtopics.

introduction The opening of a presentation, which sets the stage for the entire presentation.

body The part of a presentation containing the major pieces of information or arguments.

conclusion The final section of a presentation, during which the speaker typically reviews the most important information or most persuasive arguments.

Review Questions

1. Distinguish between the different types of speeches: impromptu, extemporaneous, manuscript, and memorized.
2. Distinguish between a topic, a general purpose, a specific purpose, and a central idea or thesis statement.
3. Briefly describe the major types of direct and indirect evidence.
4. How do you conduct a keyword search and a subject directory search?
5. What are the steps for developing the structure of a presentation?
6. Identify at least three guidelines that a good introduction should follow.
7. Identify four guidelines that should be followed in developing the body of the presentation.
8. In what ways is the conclusion similar to the introduction?

Chapter 14

Presentational Communication: Skills for Delivery

Objectives

Studying this chapter will allow you to:

1. Briefly describe the five general qualities of delivery style summarized by the acronym **GIVES**.
2. Explain how eye contact, facial expressions, gestures, body movement, paralanguage, and personal appearance contribute to an effective presentation.
3. Explain some of the rules for using notes, a microphone, and a podium.
4. Briefly explain some of the rules for designing and using visual aids.
5. Understand the best ways to handle questions after a presentation.
6. Explain three different ways of practicing a presentation.

Building on Chapters 12 and 13, this chapter takes you to the final stage of a presentation: delivery. Once you have done your research, organized your material, and developed your speaking notes, you are ready to think about the actual delivery of your presentation. Delivery includes your speaking style, your nonverbal communication, your use of visual aids or handouts, and your response to audience questions. While each speaker must find his or her own speaking strengths, this chapter explains the elements you will need for an effective style and the methods you can use to successfully manage your presentation.

■ Five General Qualities of Delivery Style: GIVES

There are really no absolute rules of delivery. For every rule, you can find examples of speakers who have violated the rule and yet been effective at achieving their goals. One reason is that each situation has its own unique demands and audience expectations. In addition, the rules that apply in one culture don't necessarily fit in another culture.

Despite these variations, there are five qualities of delivery style that will generally enhance your presentations. These qualities can be summed up with the acronym **GIVES:**

G	be **G**enuine
I	be **I**nterpersonal
V	use **V**ariety
E	display **E**nergy
S	speak **S**incerely

■ *G: Be Genuine*

Being genuine basically means being yourself. Your presentational style should be an honest reflection of who you are. Audiences are more likely to respond positively to a message from a source they perceive as genuine.

Sometimes speakers try to adopt a "speaking voice" that comes across as contrived and artificial. Such a style undermines credibility because audiences can usually tell when speakers are not presenting themselves honestly. To show that you are being yourself, go with the style that is most like your natural conversational style. Don't try to adopt a false image or play some theatrical role.

Being yourself is risky to some degree because you are putting your face on the line. You may be afraid that if the audience members reject your presentation, they will be rejecting you. This risk can be partially offset if you have adapted your presentation carefully to your audience analysis. That is, you can more easily be yourself if you have developed an effective strategy for dealing with the audience.

■ *I: Be Interpersonal*

The more personal and interpersonal you can be in making your presentation, the more the audience will feel involved in it. Listeners respond positively to speakers who seem to be talking with them instead of preaching or lecturing to them.

What is this speaker doing to enhance the interpersonal quality of her delivery?

In general, you want to adopt all of the qualities that typically accompany an interpersonal interaction. You want to have good eye contact, be friendly, be close to your audience, and connect with your audience. This style involves using a tone of voice that is conversational and personal. The use of keyword speaking notes for extemporaneous speaking, discussed in Chapter 13, is one way to achieve a feeling of conversationality. Overall, your delivery style should seek to maximize your attention to and connection with the audience and minimize the amount of time you spend looking at notes or other materials.

■ V: Use Variety

Varying your delivery style makes it easier for the audience to listen to your presentation. You should avoid a style that remains constant throughout. The most obvious violators of this principle are speakers who talk in a monotone, without any variation in their pitch or rate. Such a patterned delivery tends to evoke boredom and restlessness from the audience. Any sustained pattern of delivery will have a similar effect, even if it's one of high energy.

For these reasons, you should vary your rate, pitch, movement, volume, eye contact, and so on, using the variation to complement and accent the content of your presentation. Avoid talking to just one section of the audience the entire time, making the same gesture over and over again, and talking at a constant volume. You probably realize that raising the volume of your voice catches people's attention, but maintaining a high volume throughout is quickly irritating. You can also emphasize a point by dramatically reducing your volume.

■ E: Display Energy

Don't be afraid to let the audience see your excitement and enthusiasm for the topic you are discussing. Think about the teachers to whom you find it easiest to listen. One quality they probably share is a genuine excitement about their material. Their interest is reflected in the energy with which they deliver their presentations. Audiences find it easier to listen to speakers who are enthusiastic and energetic.

Don't confuse being enthusiastic with being bombastic, however. You don't have to act like a hyped-up MTV disc jockey. Just vary your delivery, use the full range of your voice, and be animated. If you receive feedback from the audience indicating that your listeners are getting bored or restless, try to boost your energy level.

All of this is much easier if you are genuinely excited about the topic and the opportunity to talk about it with others. Displaying energy is difficult when you don't care about the topic or your audience.

■ S: Speak Sincerely

Speaking sincerely means essentially that you display belief in your issue. This final style quality can offset a lot of other delivery weaknesses. Sincere speakers move audiences. People who talk from the heart gain the compassion and attention of their audiences. Most of us cannot, and ethically should not, manufacture or fake sincerity. We must believe in our message and let our delivery reflect that belief.

Sometimes you may be asked to present information on issues in which you have little genuine interest. For example, perhaps you lack any true interest in giving your sales report at the monthly staff meeting. This would make it difficult to exhibit interest, though you could still display energy. In such a case, you could identify aspects of your presentation for which you do have a strong feeling and sincerely display that feeling at the appropriate time. Maybe you had a really positive sales experience during the last month; you could describe it during your sales report.

Of the five general delivery qualities (GIVES), at which are you most effective? Which needs the most improvement?

■ Specific Nonverbal Delivery Qualities

The five general delivery qualities just discussed are accomplished through the strategic management of language and nonverbal communication. Your choice of wording, types of examples, and use of personal testimony can add to the perception of genuineness, sincerity, and interpersonalness. However, nonverbal communication plays an even greater role in helping you display these three presentational qualities. In addition, energy and variety are particularly dependent on nonverbal elements such as body movement, facial expressions, and paralanguage.

Learning to use all of the communication modes available to you takes time and practice. Taping yourself on either an audiotape or videotape and studying the replay is a good way to increase your awareness of how you are using nonverbal communication in your presentations. You must be cautious about becoming too "staged" in your delivery, however. Your nonverbal communication should complement your verbal message, not interfere with it. Developing an awareness of your style will help you become more effective at managing your nonverbals while still maintaining a natural delivery.

The following sections describe specific nonverbal qualities that you can try to improve. But don't try to change too many things at one time. Improving your delivery is a developmental process in which small, incremental changes will ultimately lead to significant gain.

■ Eye Contact

There are two major reasons for trying to maintain as much eye contact with your audience as you can. First, audiences are more likely to trust a speaker who is maintaining eye contact with them. Eye contact is particularly helpful in maintaining an interpersonal quality in your presentation; it lets the audience members feel more connected with you, as if you are talking "with" them, not "at" them. Second, eye contact keeps the audience's attention focused on you, since your listeners know that you will be looking at them. Sometimes audience members engage in unrelated activities (for instance, talking to someone or reading something) while the speaker talks. But if they think you will notice their inattention, they will likely avoid such distracting activities.

The larger the audience, the more difficult it is for a speaker to have eye contact with each audience member and the less control the speaker has on the audience's attention. You've probably noticed the marked difference in behavior between a class of fifteen students and a class of three hundred. In the larger class, because of the distance from the teacher and the lack of eye contact between students and teacher, students in the back rows are often sleeping, reading unrelated material, or having conversations. In that setting, effective instructors often walk up and down the aisles to maintain as much connection with the students as possible.

Maximizing eye contact means minimizing your time spent looking at notes, overhead transparencies, handouts, or other materials. One reason for using a keyword speaking outline is to reduce your dependence on reading from your notes. Even when using visual support, you should look at the audience as much as possible, not at the visuals. Speakers sometimes get sucked in by their own visual aids, focusing their attention on a transparency and forgetting the audience.

Ideally, you will slowly shift your eye contact around the audience so that all your listeners feel that you are maintaining contact with them. Be careful about continually looking at only one or two audience members or at just half of your audience. The more members of the audience you can make eye contact with, the more attention you will hold.

■ *Facial Expressions*

The face is an effective way to convey emotion. You can change your facial expressions to convey a wide variety of emotions, such as happiness, anger, confusion, interest, fear, sadness, disgust, and surprise.

Your facial expression should match the tone and intent of your message. Sometimes, contradictory messages are sent by speakers who say one thing while their facial expression and other nonverbals convey another. You are unlikely to be successful convincing an audience that you have a great product if you are displaying a deadpan face.

One study has found that facial pleasantness (smiling) and facial expressiveness relate to the perception of a speaker as credible, composed, competent, and sociable.[1] Another study of interpersonal interactions found that frequent smiling relates to greater intimacy, involvement, relaxation, and composure.[2]

Overall, your face is a tool that you can use to display your sincerity, genuineness, variety, energy, and interpersonalness. You probably know when you are "making a face"—the sort of expression that occurs when you are experiencing intense emotions. However, you may not be as sensitive to the more subtle expressions you may be giving off. Videotaping yourself is a good way to develop sensitivity to your facial expressiveness.

■ *Gestures*

Gestures can be an effective way to display your energy and maintain your audience's attention. Gestures can also be used to convey other information, as discussed in Chapter 4.

- You can use emblems (symbolic gestures)—for instance, making a thumbs-up gesture or showing two fingers while saying, "My second point is. . . ."
- You can also use pictographic illustrators—gestures that physically reproduce what you are talking about—to show the size or shape of something.
- You can use gestures to accent your verbal message. For example, you can clench your fist and wave it in the air to show power or determination while saying, "We are in this fight together."

Early textbooks on public speaking offered many guidelines for positioning hands and arms to reflect particular emotions or attitudes.[3] But trying to incorporate such planned gestures often makes your presentation appear "staged," thus undermining your genuineness. In addition, planned gestures can look rather comical when the gesture is out of sync with the material being discussed. Do use your hands, but try to make your gestures as natural as possible.

When not gesturing, speakers sometimes seem at a loss as to what to do with their hands. If you don't need your hands for gesturing, simply leave your hands hanging down by your sides. You increase the likelihood of natural gesturing if your hands are unencumbered. Try to avoid putting your hands in your pockets, holding the podium, clasping your hands behind your back, or holding your notes.

Sometimes, speakers get caught in a rut and continue to use the same gesture or same nervous motion over and over again during a presentation. Such repetitive motions can be distracting to your audience. Monitoring your gestures or watching a videotape of your presentation can help you develop an awareness of such problems.

■ Body Movement

Like gestures, body movement can be an effective tool to enhance a presentation—or it can become a major distraction. Movement can add meaning, variety, and interest to your presentation, as you can see by watching almost any televangelist on Sunday morning TV. However, movement can also be detrimental to a presentation. You have probably witnessed speakers who are pacers—walking back and forth like caged animals. The audience can become preoccupied with this kind of movement.

Gestures are one way of accenting the content of a presentation.

When used properly, movement can benefit your presentations in a number of ways.

- Movement toward the audience members increases their attention to you and thus can be used when you have an important point to share.
- Movement adds variety to your presentation and relieves the audience from having to stay focused on a single spot.
- Movement into the audience can help make the presentation more personal.
- Movement that parallels your content can accent or complement your meaning. For example, you might move from one spot to another as you make a transition from one major point to another.
- The rate of your movement can communicate information. Walking quickly from one spot to another might communicate urgency or importance, while slowly moving to another spot might signal a less significant shift in your message.

Sometimes your opportunity for movement is restricted. If you are seated at a conference table during your presentation, for instance, you have relatively few options. Even here, however, you can lean and turn your torso in appropriate ways to connect with your audience and emphasize your points.

■ *Paralanguage and Vocalized Pauses*

As you learned in Chapter 4, our spoken words are accompanied by a wide assortment of vocal characteristics that color our messages. *Paralanguage* includes volume, rate, pitch, tone, accent, inflection, articulation, and pauses, and *vocalizations,* or *vocalized pauses,* are nonsymbolic sounds such as "aah" and "um."

The way we talk is one of the primary ways we can display the five general qualities of delivery summarized by the acronym GIVES. Each paralinguistic quality can be managed to add effect to your presentation. For example, taking a long pause after you have finished a point emphasizes that point and increases the audience's attention to the next thing you are going to say. Raising the volume of your voice is another way to create emphasis and attention, and so is lowering your voice.

Generally, you want to speak energetically and with lots of vocal variation. Most of us tend to be reserved in the way we speak, failing to take full advantage of our voices. The most serious offense is to speak in a quiet monotone. This delivery style makes it difficult for the audience to stay focused on your message. Changing your volume, rate of speaking, pitch, and tone are ways of keeping the audience's attention.

Besides the vocal qualities that we use to add character to our message, we often add vocalized pauses, such as "um" and "ah." We seem to dislike having moments of silence, so we fill them with a word or sound. Besides "um" and "ah," perhaps you use "like," "okay," or "you know." Such vocalizations tend to undermine a speaker's effectiveness. Along with the various forms of powerless language discussed in Chapter 4, vocalized pauses probably have a negative impact on the audience's belief in the speaker. Speaking fluently adds to the impression of a speaker's credibility.[4]

Vocalized pauses are learned and can therefore be unlearned. Ask a friend to listen to you practice your presentation and to raise a hand every time you make a vocalized pause. Initially, you might get very frustrated, but you will become more aware of this tendency and learn to substitute a moment of silence. Learn to relax during your pauses. Audiences seem to have little problem with speakers who pause momentarily to gather their thoughts.

■ *Personal Appearance*

The audience's first impression of you will be based on what they see. Your personal appearance will have an initial impact on their willingness to listen to you. As much as possible, make choices about your personal appearance that will help you accomplish your presentational goals.

I remember a comedian who was performing at Purdue University. He came on stage dressed in a Purdue sweatshirt, wearing a Purdue cap, and waving a Purdue banner. His attire immediately won over the audience. He used attire as a strategy to gain the audience's acceptance.

Most of us recognize the need to "dress up" for formal occasions or when we are trying to impress someone. But there are also times when we need to "dress down." Politicians usually dress up in suits to enhance their credibility, but when attending local barbecues, they often try to be folksy by appearing in shirtsleeves and blue jeans.

Your decision about what to wear depends on what the audience expects you to be wearing. Determining the audience's expectation for dress should be part of your planning for the presentation. You may want to choose clothing that gives you options. For example, if you wear a suit and you discover that you look too formal, you can take off the coat. Wearing an elegant gown, on the other hand, would limit your ability to become more casual.

Your personal appearance is not limited to clothing. The audience will observe and respond to such things as your hair, makeup, jewelry, and briefcase, and these are items you should consider in your planning.

Of the six nonverbal delivery qualities just discussed (eye contact, facial expressions, gestures, body movement, paralanguage, and personal appearance), which do you manage most effectively? Which do you manage least effectively?

▌ Presentational Management

Giving a presentation is more than just standing up and talking. Presentations are a minor form of theatrical production, and they require learning to properly manage the "stage" and "props." **Presentational management** includes the way you use your notes, the podium, the overhead projector, multimedia equipment (slide projectors, video projectors, PowerPoint), and microphones. Knowing when to use a handout and how to handle questions also requires effective management.

■ Using a Podium

Podiums are a convenient place to keep your notes at a level that makes them easy to see. However, podiums can become fortresses that speakers use to psychologically hide behind. And if you develop a style that depends on a podium, you can find yourself ill at ease if you are forced to give a presentation without one. Thus, you need to learn to use a podium to best advantage.

During a formal presentation, such as at a commencement or other large gathering, the audience may expect you to remain behind the podium. In informal presentations, though, you are best advised to move from behind the podium as much as possible. Stepping out from behind the podium increases the interpersonal quality of your presentation and gives you more opportunity to use movement to enhance your presentation. Think about the podium as your home base, to which you return when you are ready to move to your next point. Avoid becoming a "clinger" who holds tightly to the top edges of the podium.

■ Using a Microphone

Microphones can be a great asset, ensuring that everyone is able to hear you, but they can also be a hindrance to your mobility.

You will probably have a choice about whether to use a microphone. The decision should be based on audience size, your vocal strength, the room's size and acoustics, and the nature of the equipment available. Amplification can make the presentation more formal and reduce your personal connection with the audience. On the other hand, you can't be effective if the audience can't hear you, no matter how personal you are.

Microphones can be either hard-wired or wireless. In terms of position, they can be stationary, such as those attached to podiums; they can be hand-held; or they can be attached to the speaker, such as lapel, tie-clip, and lavaliere mikes. These different types of microphones all have advantages and disadvantages. For example, stationary microphones don't need to be held, but they restrict the speaker to one spot. Movable, wired mikes increase the speaker's mobility, but the length of the line limits it. And if the line is too long, it gets easily tangled or caught. Wireless mikes provide the greatest mobility but vary a great deal in how well they pick up the speaker's voice. You will sometimes see speakers with their heads continually turned down so that the tie-clip mike will pick up their voice.

Remember that microphones amplify whatever they pick up. This means that the audience might be hearing you shuffle through your notes, mumble to yourself, or make side comments to others. Be sure that the system is operational and that you know how to turn the microphone on and off *before* you begin your speech. Don't put yourself in the position of irritating the audience by tapping on the microphone and saying, "Is this thing on?"

■ Using Notes

Notes play a vital role in helping you stay on track and reminding you of the points you planned to cover. However, notes can also get in the way of an effective presentation. You can easily find yourself buried in your notes if you have a lot of information on them or if they are unorganized. This means that you are less likely to maintain good eye contact with your audience.

There is a skill to using notes effectively. In general, you want to minimize the time spent looking at your notes but still check to ensure that you are covering what you intended. Your notes should be large enough and simple enough to read very quickly. Here are some general guidelines for the use of note cards:

- Put your notes down before you begin your presentation.
- Situate your notes so that you can look at them while you talk without holding them.
- If you have to hold your notes, try to hold them in only one hand—this will help increase your gesturing.
- If you read from your notes, hold them up so that you merely have to look over the top to see your audience.
- Maintain eye contact with the audience as much as possible.
- Number your cards to help keep them in the proper order.
- Add "stage directions" to your cards as reminders. For example, you might write "Energy" in the corner of one card or "Show Overhead #3" after your third point.
- Reading statistics or quotes from the note cards is acceptable, but continue to look up at your audience occasionally.

■ *Managing Mistakes*

Invariably, you will make mistakes during some of your presentations. Your initial reaction may be to try to save face by apologizing or ignoring the error. Sometimes this initial reaction is the best one, sometimes not.

The manner in which you manage a mistake depends on the type of mistake it is. If you muff the pronunciation of a word or get tongue-tied, it is usually best to just keep talking and not call attention to your slip. Audiences will usually correct the statement in their own minds without much fanfare. Apologizing or spending time trying to say the correct thing tends to exacerbate the mistake.

On the other hand, if the mistake is factual in nature and is likely to lead to misunderstanding, then you need to correct it. For example, if you were reporting days lost in the past month because of employee sick leave, you would need to correct yourself if you said "nine days" when the correct number was nineteen.

■ *Using Visual Aids*

Visual aids are support materials presented to the audience members for their own observation. Included in this category are charts, drawings on a chalkboard, models, and overhead transparencies. The key is that the audience can observe directly rather than depending solely on the speaker for a description.

Today, traditional visual aids such as chalkboards and flip charts are being replaced by multimedia technology. Computer-generated overheads, created through such programs as PowerPoint, are becoming increasingly popular. Given these developments, it makes sense to categorize visual aids according to whether they are unprojected or projected.

Unprojected visual aids are ones that the audience can directly observe without the use of any electrical projection aid. These include actual objects, physical models, flip charts, chalkboards, white boards, and felt boards. **Projected visual aids** require an electrical device to make them visible (or audible) to the audience. These include overhead projectors, electronic visual presenters, slide projectors, movie projectors, videotapes, and audiotapes.

The type of visual aid you should use depends on a number of factors, such as appropriateness to the issue, availability, quality demands, cost, and preparation time. The following sections discuss some functions and rules that apply to all visual aids, especially to projected visuals.

Functions of visual aids.   Visual aids can perform several useful functions in a presentation.

*1. **Visual aids convey visual types of information.***   Certain types of information are difficult to describe verbally and therefore need to be conveyed visually. Graphs, charts, images, and models often contain information that is essentially visual in nature. Look at the imaginary sales trends shown in Figure 14.1 and think about the difficulty of conveying the same information verbally.

*2. **Visual aids reinforce or emphasize verbal information.***   Visual aids can repeat the verbal message and thus signal the importance of that information to the audience. The audience hears the point and sees it at the same time. Suppose you are explaining three reasons why your listeners should consider going to graduate school. As you state the first reason, "the opportunity to learn more," you show an overhead image:

As you introduce your second and third reasons, you likewise summarize them with overhead images. With this device you reinforce and emphasize your words.

*3. **Visual aids stimulate interest.***   The process of displaying a visual aid raises the audience's attention. For this reason, you should be sure the visual contains information that will help you achieve your goal. A long series of similar visuals, however, may eventually become boring to the audience. Imagine how you would feel seeing the twelfth overhead image filled with nothing but dense text.

*4. **Visual aids can be used to guide the audience through the presentation.***   You can display an outline of the points you are covering as a way of leading your audience through the presentation. This will help ensure that the audience clearly understands your progress in the argument and the relationship between the points.

Figure 14.1

Sample Sales Figures for an Imaginary Company

This illustrates information best conveyed with a chart or graph. How long would it take you to explain this pattern with words alone? Would your audience understand a verbal description?

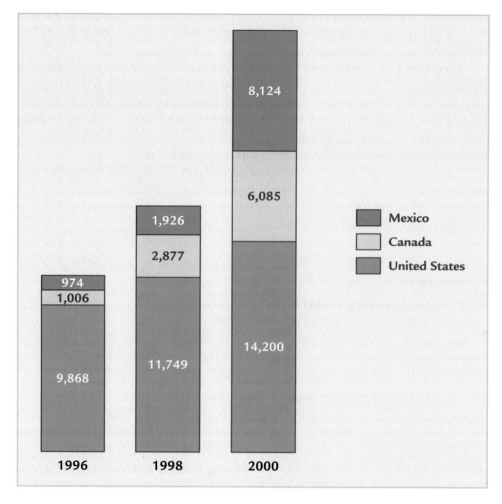

5. Visual aids can enhance the retention of information. People tend to remember images and visuals, especially if they are relevant and significant.

6. Visual aids can be used to effectively show visual comparisons. Describing the differences between a water molecule and a salt molecule is easier if there are two models to display. Charts and graphs often include comparative information, such as figures for two or three different years, as in Figure 14.1.

Rules for designing visual aids. Good design of visual aids can greatly increase their effectiveness. Here are some general guidelines for designing visuals:

1. Keep visuals simple. Try to restrict each visual to a single idea. Ask yourself if you can make the visual simpler. Create multiple visuals as needed rather than trying to cram a lot of information into one visual.

2. Limit the number of words in each visual. Having your audience read exactly what you are saying makes your speech rather superfluous. You can lose control of your listeners' attention if they are busy reading while you are talking—they can't really do both at the same time. To avoid such problems, try to use just keywords in the visuals. Avoid complete sentences, and place only four or five words on each line. Eliminate unnecessary words or figures. The information should be concise and quickly grasped.

3. *Use large images and easily readable fonts.* The visual should be large and plain enough to be seen by those seated in the last row. Make it clear, professional, neat, and LARGE.

4. *Use a visually stimulating and diverse design.* Use colors, font styles, variety, images, and novelty to add excitement and interest to your visuals. For instance, using colored fonts instead of black on an overhead adds some interest. However, don't create noise by having too much stimulation or by introducing visual impairments. For example, yellow letters on an overhead are generally hard to read. Figure 14.2 provides some examples of this rule.

5. *Make understanding the visuals dependent on what you have to say.* On the visuals, use abbreviations, keywords, fill-in blanks, or symbols that require the audience to listen to you to gain the full meaning. This creates a desirable interdependence between you the speaker and the visual aid.

Using an Internet search engine, search under "graphs" or "charts and graphs" to locate typical graphs that might be used in a presentation. Examine some of the examples you find, and evaluate how well they would work as visual aids in a presentation. Are they clear? Do they make visual comparisons? Are fonts and images large enough for use as a projected image? What could be done to make each chart or graph more effective as a presentational aid?

Rules for using visual aids. Besides understanding the effective design of visual aids, you should know the most effective way to use them in your presentations.

1. *Integrate the visual into the presentation.* This means that the visual should be relevant to what you are saying. Don't just display a visual and assume that the audience will understand its relevance. You need to explain the application of the visual. Consider these examples:

> *Weak:* "Our sales peaked in 1998." [Graph of ten-year sales activity displayed.] "I'd like to talk about why sales have dropped since then. First, the number of competitors has increased. Second, the market is somewhat saturated." [Graph removed.]

> *Strong:* "As this graph shows" [graph displayed], "our best year of sales was in 1998. After that time, you'll notice a steady decline in sales. I'd like to talk about why sales have dropped." [Graph removed.]

2. *Don't reveal the visual aid prematurely.* Don't display the visual until you are ready to talk about what is on it. If you show it early, the audience members will immediately start examining it. This means that their minds will be preoccupied with two different forms of information.

Figure 14.2

Effective Design in an Overhead Projection

(A) A plain but uninteresting design. (B) The same design improved with the use of color and varied fonts. (C) A design that has become too busy and confusing.

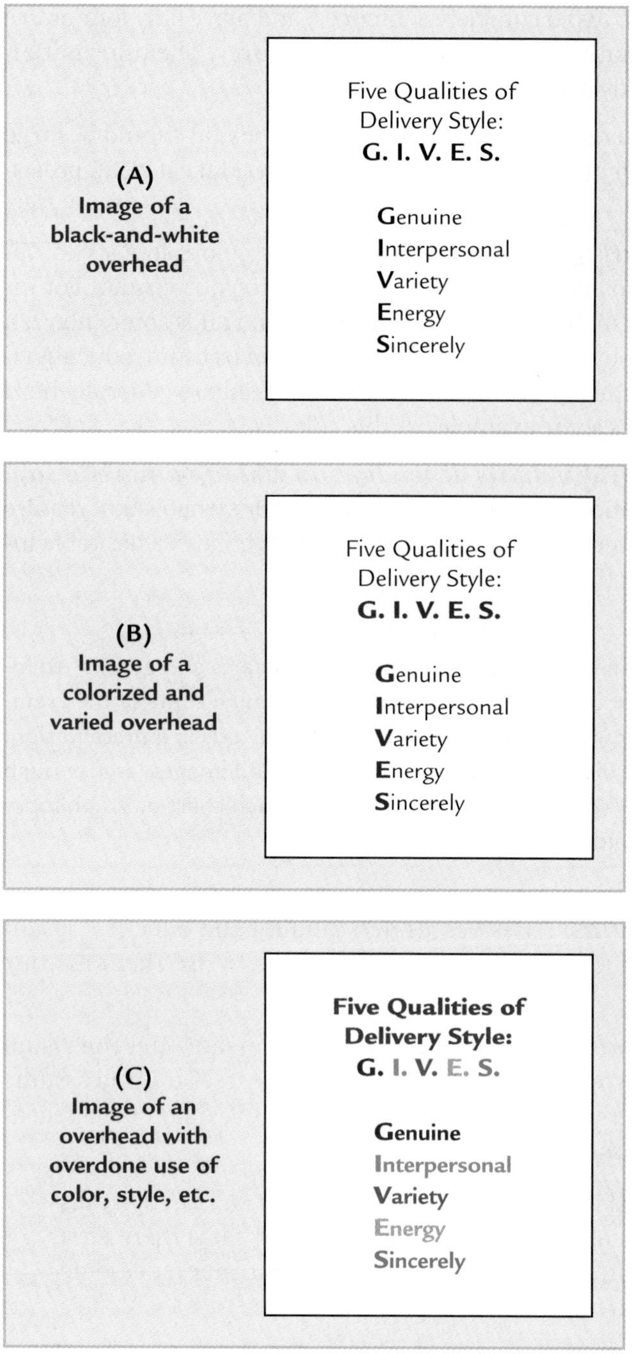

(A)
Image of a black-and-white overhead

Five Qualities of
Delivery Style:
G. I. V. E. S.

Genuine
Interpersonal
Variety
Energy
Sincerely

(B)
Image of a colorized and varied overhead

Five Qualities of
Delivery Style:
G. I. V. E. S.

Genuine
Interpersonal
Variety
Energy
Sincerely

(C)
Image of an overhead with overdone use of color, style, etc.

**Five Qualities of
Delivery Style:**
G. I. V. E. S.

Genuine
Interpersonal
Variety
Energy
Sincerely

3. Remove the visual from the audience's perception as soon as you are done with it. When you move on to other issues, take the visual aid away so that it doesn't become a distraction. Think of the visual aid as resembling a quote or a piece of evidence. It is meant to support what you are saying, not attract the audience's attention in and of itself. The visual should be used to support the point you are making and then be set aside.

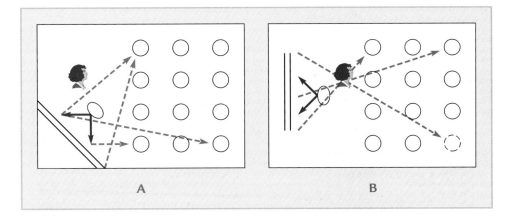

Figure 14.3

Two Arrangements for a Projected Visual Aid

(A) A corner projection, that allows all audience members a clear view. (B) A centered projection, in which the speaker partially blocks the audience's view.

4. Be sure the entire audience can easily see the visual.   Stand to the side of the visual as much as possible so that you don't block anyone's view. If you have the option of arranging screens and projectors, you may want to use the projection shown in Figure 14.3A. This arrangement produces the best visibility and least blocking. As you prepare for your presentation, put up your visuals and then sit in some of the seats the audience will occupy to gain a better sense of the audience's vantage point.

5. Minimize and control the amount of information shown to the audience.   Whatever information you place before the audience members, they will probably read it. Therefore you want to control carefully what they are seeing. If you have four main points to make, don't display all four when you are talking about just the first one. It's better to use a separate visual for each point or to use a technique like progressive reveal to slowly add information.

    Progressive reveal involves gradually revealing more and more of an image as you go along. With a manual overhead projection, you may simply use a sheet of paper to cover part of the information. As you move to each subsequent point, you pull the paper down, revealing more and more information on the transparency. Similarly, with a computer projection, as shown in Figure 14.4, you can use a series of images in which each subsequent frame introduces new information in a highlighted way and relegates the older information to a shaded background.

Assume that you will be giving a speech about the design and use of visual aids, explaining the rules you have just read in this text. You will have an overhead projector available during the presentation. Try designing or sketching out the projections you will use, and plan when and how you will introduce them.

Test Yourself

■ Using Handouts

Handouts are printed materials distributed to the audience in conjunction with a presentation. They are an effective way to distribute information that goes beyond the scope of the presentation.

Figure 14.4

Using the Technique of Progressive Reveal in a *PowerPoint* Presentation

The new information is highlighted. Older information, which the audience has already seen, remains visible but is relegated to the background.

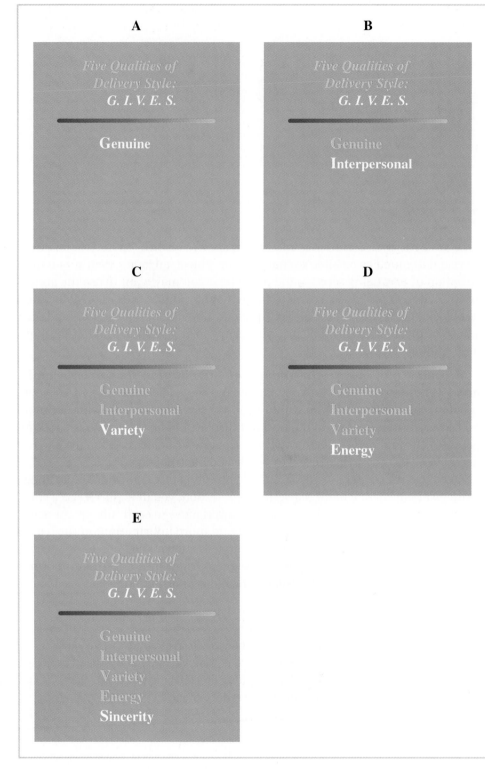

Handouts are often necessary when the information you are conveying is particularly complex or detailed. Handouts also reinforce the presentation, and they provide something for the audience members to review at a later time. Handouts can range from a copy of the outline of the presentation to a lengthy and detailed report.

The rules applying to the use of handouts are similar to those for overheads. You don't want the handouts to become a distraction, and you want to control the audience's attention to your spoken message. Distributing a handout during your presentation invites your listeners to turn their attention toward it. If it is a complicated and detailed document, many will start reading it and you will lose their attention. You can limit such problems by following some basic rules.

1. Whenever possible, distribute your material after you are done talking. Let your listeners know that they will be receiving a handout, and describe briefly what it will include. For instance: "After my presentation, I will be distributing a brief summary and outline of my main points."

2. Keep any material distributed during the presentation as simple as possible. Whatever you distribute, you want the audience to be able to read quickly, thus minimizing the distraction from your talk. This means handing out keyword, outlined material instead of full text. Any graphs, charts, or data should be simple enough to digest quickly.

3. Distribute your handouts to coincide with your oral message. Just as with visual aids, you want to time your handouts to correspond with the oral message you are presenting. If you hand out material too early or too late, the audience will be examining a document that is not relevant to what you are speaking about at that moment. You should talk your audience through the handout so that you can best direct their attention. This will help you know when to expect the audience to turn their attention back to you. For example: "On the chart I have just handed out, you'll notice that the first column lists the year of sales, and the second column gives the total amount. Notice our peak in 1997 when we had $25 million in sales."

4. Consider using more than one handout if you are distributing material during your presentation. Rather than handing out a packet that has four pages of data and graphs, hand out the pages one at a time. Use each handout as you would a piece of evidence. Distribute the material in the order that you want the audience to examine it. (If you have a lot of material, however, continually handing it out can become a distraction and nuisance, so you will probably want to save it until you are done speaking.)

5. Distribute complex or detailed material several days in advance. This method usually works when you are giving a report to a work group or committee. Letting your audience members have a copy of the report on which you will be briefing them gives them a chance to prepare informed questions and feedback.

■ Handling Questions, Conflict, and Confrontation

In most of the presentational situations you experience, you will be expected to answer questions from the audience.[5] The way you respond to questions can add

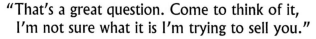

"That's a great question. Come to think of it,
   I'm not sure what it is I'm trying to sell you."

a lot to the overall effectiveness of your presentation. However, questions can also get in the way of your presentation by interrupting you in the middle of important points or by changing your focus. Questions can take away your control of the presentation.

To decide how best to respond, you need to understand the intent of the questioner. Some questioners are actually trying to confront you and engage you in conflict. On the other hand, you will also receive questions from supportive audience members who are trying to help you make your point more clearly or from audience members who genuinely want additional information. This distinction in questioning can be witnessed in almost any TV courtroom drama. The prosecutor, as a negative audience member, tries to trip up the defendant with difficult or subtle questions. The defense attorney, as a positive audience member, asks questions that let the defendant put the most positive spin on the message. The way the defendant handles both kinds of questions often makes a major difference in whether he or she is found guilty. Similarly, the way you handle questions from the audience can affect your ability to accomplish your presentational goals.

Even when you receive hostile questions or rebuttals, avoid getting into a conflict with audience members during your presentation. If necessary, indicate your willingness to meet people after the presentation to discuss their concerns. If people continue challenging you, you may have to use some of the conflict management skills discussed in Chapter 5. This would include openly listening to their perspectives, letting them know that you hear their concerns, asking them to explain what they want, restating your goals, and proposing ways to address the issues they have raised. Remember that other audience members are watching how you handle the situation.

When to take questions.   You control when you entertain and answer questions. You should let the audience know your preference; you will answer questions when you are done, or you will answer questions during your presentation.

What if you say that you'll take questions at the end but someone nevertheless interrupts with a question during the presentation? Don't ignore or discard the question. If possible, provide a short answer and indicate that you will give a more complete response at the end of your presentation. For example: "That's a good question. My first reaction is to say yes, but let me come back to that and explain a bit more at the end of my presentation." Of course, you need to remember to come back to the question; you can ask the questioner to remind you at the end.

Even if you are open to questions during your presentation, you will want to avoid being interrupted when you are in the middle of making a major point. In essence, you don't want the flow of your arguments or explanations disrupted. Most people are sensitive to this and will wait until you provide some indication that you are open to questions. If you do get interrupted in the middle of a major point, and it's a positive audience, you might say something like "Let me just finish this point and then I'll come back to answer your question about how we can implement the plan in six months." Notice in this response that the speaker is providing a confirming response to the questioner by restating the question. This lets the questioner know that the speaker has heard the question accurately.

Using your answers to reinforce or expand on important information. Each question is another opportunity to score points with the audience. The fact that a question is being asked usually means that the audience member is open to what you have to say. Use the opportunity to restate important information that relates to the question.

You might rephrase the question so that the answer can be grounded in your main points. For example, if an audience member asks, "Isn't this a risky plan?" you can respond, "Certainly there is risk, but let me go over the three potential benefits that I think offset any potential risk." Sometimes, responding to the question will give you an opportunity to include new information that you have not yet covered. If so, start by relating this new information to the points you have already made.

Answering questions straightforwardly.   Don't make up answers or pretend to know what you don't. Avoid beating around the bush when asked a difficult question. The audience will pick up on your evasiveness, and this can undermine what you have accomplished. If you don't know an answer, admit that straightforwardly, but also indicate your willingness to find out and get back to the audience member: "I don't know the breakdown in that territory, Jill, but I'll find out and email you the data."

You should answer each question directly, but end by restating important information from your presentation: "Ralph points out that he thinks the line employees will react negatively to any restructuring. He may be right. I think we'll need to monitor that closely, but let's review the benefits I've discussed."

Maintaining your genuineness, sincerity, and interpersonalness. Handling questions is part of the presentation. The audience is listening and evaluating your responses as they weigh what you have said in the body of your talk. Therefore, you need to maintain the same presentational qualities that have been important throughout.

Think of questions as an opportunity to really connect with the audience. Don't get antagonistic or defensive. Continue to be yourself, answer sincerely and with conviction, and use the opportunity to interact interpersonally with the audience. You need to talk to the questioner, but don't forget the rest of the audience. To make sure that everyone has heard the question, you may need to repeat it. If the question is not central to your presentation or of general interest to the audience, you can suggest that the questioner visit with you after the presentation for a more complete answer.

▌ Practice, Practice, Practice

The best presentations are those that seem fresh and spontaneous but have been rehearsed enough to provide the speaker with confidence. You are not ready to give your presentation when you have finished creating a set of speaking notes. You are ready when you have practiced the presentation several times.

Speakers who fail to prepare adequately are apt to experience anxiety, and they have a greater likelihood of failing to fulfill their objectives. These problems can be reduced by knowing thoroughly what you are going to cover and also by practicing the presentation.

Ten Techniques for Overcoming Speaking Anxiety

Anxiety before a presentation is normal. Even experienced speakers often feel some degree of "stage fright." The trick is to control your anxiety so that it doesn't interfere with your performance. Here are ten suggestions for overcoming speaking anxiety.

1. *Know the room.* Become familiar with the place in which you will speak. Arrive early and walk around the room including the speaking area. Stand at the lectern, speak into the microphone. Walk around where the audience will be seated. Walk from where you will be seated to the place where you will be speaking.
2. *Know the audience.* If possible, greet some of the audience as they arrive and chat with them. It is easier to speak to a group of friends than to a group of strangers.
3. *Know your material.* If you are not familiar with your material or are uncomfortable with it, your nervousness will increase. Practice your speech or presentation and revise it until you can present it with ease.
4. *Learn how to relax.* You can ease tension by doing exercises. Sit comfortably with your back straight. Breathe in slowly, hold your breath for 4 to 5 seconds, then

slowly exhale. To relax your facial muscles, open your mouth and eyes wide, then close them tightly.

5. *Visualize yourself speaking.* Imagine yourself walking confidently to the lectern as the audience applauds. Imagine yourself speaking, your voice loud, clear and assured. When you visualize yourself as successful, you will be successful.

6. *Realize people want you to succeed.* All audiences want speakers to be interesting, stimulating, informative and entertaining. They want you to succeed—not fail.

7. *Don't apologize for being nervous.* Most of the time your nervousness does not show at all. If you don't say anything about it, nobody will notice. If you mention your nervousness or apologize for any problems you think you have with your speech, you'll only be calling attention to it. Had you remained silent, your listeners may not have noticed at all.

8. *Concentrate on your message, not the medium.* Your nervous feelings will dissipate if you focus your attention away from your anxieties and concentrate on your message and your audience, not yourself.

9. *Turn nervousness into positive energy.* The same nervous energy that causes stage fright can be an asset to you. Harness it, and transform it into vitality and enthusiasm.

10. *Gain experience.* Experience builds confidence, which is the key to effective speaking.

Source: Excerpted from Lenny Laskowski, "Overcoming Speaking Anxiety in Meetings and Presentations," available online at http://www.ljlseminars.com/anxiety.htm. Byline: Lenny Laskowski. This article first appeared in *Presentations Magazine,* September 1998.

Practicing is actually part of the preparation process because you can continue to edit and modify your presentation as you get a sense of how the pieces fit together. Practice becomes particularly important when you are under time constraints and need to know exactly how long it will take you to present your speech. A spoken practice allows you to time the presentation and decide where to cut or elaborate. Practice also gives you a feel for using your presentational aids, such as overheads or handouts. Finally, practice gives you a chance to concentrate on questions of style, such as eye contact, rate of delivery, and gestures.

The types of practice vary from a mental run-through of the points you are going to cover to a full videotaped rehearsal with a mock audience. The former is not usually enough for beginning speakers, and the latter requires significant pre-arranging. In most cases you'll want to begin with a mental rehearsal, then proceed to practice the presentation aloud. Ultimately, for major formal presentations, you should try to arrange a full-dress rehearsal. The following sections explain what you can hope to accomplish with each type of rehearsal.

■ Mental Rehearsal

The first practice for a presentation is conducted in your head—a **mental rehearsal.** That is, you run through your presentation mentally. High divers get ready to make a dive by mentally thinking through it, and other athletes perform similar mental rehearsals.

Mental rehearsals help you make decisions about the components of the presentation as you are developing it. Often, for instance, the mental rehearsal will help you decide on the best introduction and conclusion. You can easily revise such elements until you feel confident about their effectiveness.

■ Vocal Rehearsal

Next, you should practice your presentation out loud. This **vocal rehearsal** should reflect the actual speaking conditions as much as possible. If you will be standing during your presentation, you should stand during your vocal rehearsal, and you should use your notes and visual aids.

You can gain valuable feedback for improving your delivery by either audio-taping or videotaping the rehearsal. The playback will provide you with insights as to the quality of your presentation and alert you to any problems of which you may have been unaware. Also, depending on the nature of the speaking situation, you may want to invite others to listen to your rehearsal and provide feedback.

Here are some additional suggestions for vocal rehearsal:

1. Plan on doing the vocal rehearsal more than one time.
2. Time yourself to get a sense of how long the presentation takes. This becomes particularly important if you have time restrictions. You may have to edit out material or expand some areas.
3. Don't try to change your delivery rate to match the time demands; this will undermine the effectiveness of your delivery style. You are better off taking your time and covering less material than speeding up and covering more.
4. As you practice, you may want to put some time cues on your speaking notes. For instance, as you practice a twenty-minute speech, make a note of where you are after ten minutes. You can use this as a cue to pace the second half of your presentation.

■ Full-Dress Rehearsal

Ideally, you will want to conduct a **full-dress rehearsal** of your presentation in the room in which you will be speaking, using all the equipment on which you will rely. Practice with a microphone if you plan on using it during your presentation. Be sure to practice using your visual aids as well. The rehearsed presentation should be just like the one you will be giving to the audience. Such a rehearsal can greatly increase your level of comfort and confidence.

There are many times when you will be unable to conduct a full-dress rehearsal. In such cases, try at least to come early enough to set up your materials and get a feel for how the room is arranged. Set up your materials and familiarize yourself with the layout before the audience members arrive.

■ Practice Again

The more familiar you are with your presentation, the less you will be tied to your speaking notes. Don't assume that one practice is all you need. The presentation will continue to evolve each time you practice. You will also gain confidence each time you run through it.

However, don't practice to the point of memorization. If you do this, you may find yourself getting stumped in the middle of your presentation, trying to recall exact words. Remember that extemporaneous speaking is essentially organized, one-sided conversation. Remain flexible and conversational.

Summary

There are five general qualities of delivery summed up by the acronym GIVES: Be genuine, be interpersonal, use variety, display energy, and speak sincerely. You should be yourself and remain genuine while delivering your presentation. Being interpersonal means being conversation-like in your delivery and making personal contact with the audience. Variety involves trying to use the full range of your nonverbals rather than being constant or patterned. You should be enthusiastic about your topic and let the enthusiasm come through in your delivery, trying to keep the presentation energized. Finally, sincerity means speaking from the heart and meaning what you say.

These five delivery qualities can be achieved by the effective management of specific nonverbal cues. These cues include eye contact, facial expressions, gestures, body movement, paralanguage and vocalized pauses, and personal appearance.

Presentational management involves developing skills for staging the speech. Podiums should not be used to shield the speaker. In informal presentations, you should try to speak without relying on a podium. Microphones are sometimes necessary for large audiences, but try to avoid a mike system that restricts your movement and interpersonal style of delivery. Notes should serve as a hedge against forgetting, but not as a script for the presentation. Mistakes of delivery can simply be ignored, but mistakes of fact should be corrected.

Visual aids can be either projected or unprojected. They are used in presentations to convey visual types of information, to reinforce or emphasize verbal information, to stimulate interest, to guide the audience, to help the audience retain the information, and to show visual comparisons. Visual aids should be kept simple, with the wording limited to keywords. They should be visually stimulating, with large images and fonts. The visuals should require that the audience listen to the speaker for a full explanation. Visual aids should be integrated into the presentation just like a piece of evidence; they should not be presented too early or remain displayed after the point has been made. Be aware of whether you are blocking the audience's view of the visual. Control the information that the audience is seeing by using techniques such as progressive reveal.

Supplemental material in the form of handouts is often used to reinforce the presentation. Ideally, such material should be distributed after the presentation. If you need to distribute something during the presentation, keep the handout simple. Distribute the handout only when you are ready to talk about the information it contains. Try to limit the amount of information on each handout, using several handouts if necessary to break up information into manageable pieces. Complex material should be handed out several days prior to the presentation.

Questions from the audience can interrupt the flow of the presentation and even challenge the speaker's face. Try to control the timing of questions by telling the audience when you will entertain questions. Answer questions either at the end of your presentation or after a major point. As you address questions, reinforce or expand on important information in your presentation. Answer the questions straightforwardly while maintaining your genuineness, sincerity, and interpersonalness.

Be sure to practice your presentation. You can practice your early drafts in your mind as you think about wording. Several vocal rehearsals should be made, with or without a friendly audience. Ideally, conduct a full-dress rehearsal, with all your visual aids, in the actual room where you will be making the presentation.

Key Terms

GIVES   An acronym designating five general qualities of delivery style that enhance presentations: being genuine, being interpersonal, using variety, displaying energy, and speaking sincerely.

presentational management   Managing those elements of a presentation that deal with its production, or performance, such as the use of notes, a podium, overhead projectors, multimedia equipment, and microphones.

visual aids   Support materials presented to the audience members for their own observation.

unprojected visual aids   Support materials that an audience can observe without the use of electrical projection, such as actual objects, physical models, flip charts, and chalkboards.

projected visual aids   Support materials displayed to the audience through electrical devices; for instance, slides, videotapes, and overhead projections.

progressive reveal   A visual aid technique in which more and more of an image is gradually revealed as the speaker progresses.

handouts   Printed materials distributed to the audience in conjunction with a presentation.

mental rehearsal   Practicing your presentation by running through it in your head.

vocal rehearsal   Practicing your presentation out loud.

full-dress rehearsal   A vocal practice conducted with visual aids and any necessary equipment in the room in which the presentation will be given.

Review Questions

1. Explain what each of the letters in the acronym GIVES means.
2. Explain how the five general qualities of delivery style relate to some of the specific nonverbal delivery qualities.
3. Explain at least three functions of visual aids.
4. Describe three rules for designing and three rules for using visual aids.
5. Explain some of the rules for using handouts in a presentation.
6. How does the handling of questions relate to the five general qualities of delivery style?
7. Explain the importance of practice.

Chapter 15

Organizational Communication: Descriptive and Prescriptive Theories

Objectives

Studying this chapter will allow you to:

1. Define and explain what is meant by organizational communication.
2. Explain the difference between formal and informal communication networks.
3. Describe the kind of communication that occurs in upward and downward communication.
4. Explain the differences between descriptive organizational communication theories and prescriptive organizational communication theories.
5. Briefly describe systems theory and the organizational culture approach.
6. Briefly describe classical theory, human relations theory, and human resource development theory.

This textbook began with sample phrases from job ads, illustrating the value that organizations place on communication skills among their employees. All the specific skills discussed in this text so far are relevant to effective organizational functioning: interpersonal communication, interviewing, small group communication, and presentational communication. These skills contribute to what is called micro-organizational communication. The *micro-organizational approach* involves examining the communication skills that you need as a member of an organization. Your abilities to interact effectively with others, to work in teams, and to present ideas all contribute to your individual success in an organization.

Another way of approaching the study of organizations is macro-organizational. The *macro-organizational approach* examines organizations in terms of the interactions and relationships between members, regardless of their individual communication skills. Macro-organizational communication includes the hierarchy that prescribes who should talk to whom and about what, whereas the micro-organizational level deals with how well those individuals are able to talk to one another. You could be extremely effective at making presentations (micro), but if the organization never asked you to make one (macro), your skill would add little to the organization.

This chapter will deal extensively with theories related to macro-organizational communication. Chapter 16 will then deal with issues related to micro-organizational communication.

▌ What Is Organizational Communication?

In Chapter 1, an organization was described as a group of interdependent individuals brought together in a hierarchical structure to perform a variety of structured tasks toward the accomplishment of some goal. Organizational communication was defined in a simple way as the communication that occurs in organizations. In this chapter, we'll refine that definition and say that **organizational communication** is the communication that occurs in the accomplishment of, or the attempt to accomplish organizational goals. In other words, just because communication occurs within an organization doesn't necessarily make it organizational communication. It has to connect in some way to the organization's goals. Let's look in more detail at what this means.

■ *Communication and Organizational Goals*

Imagine that as part of your job responsibilities, you are meeting with a colleague in your department to discover her reaction to a proposal to modify the department's computer net server. As your discussion ends, you ask her to email you a summary of her concerns and suggestions. This interaction obviously meets the definition of organizational communication, because the communication is directly related to the performance of each member's job. This interaction also reflects the formal communication network of the organization—that is, communication that occurs because of the defined roles of the organizational members.

But the connection between communication and an organization's goals isn't always so easy to establish. Suppose you are in your office, and one of your colleagues stops in and begins talking about her recent vacation. You spend ten minutes chatting about her trip, and then she leaves. Does that interaction constitute organizational communication?

Perhaps you've worked in a company where, if that interaction occurred, your boss would dock both employees ten minutes' pay for wasting time. That kind of reaction by a boss reflects a classical, or traditional, view of organizations. Such a boss would be considered a theory X type of manager—a concept we'll discuss in detail later in the chapter. Basically, for this boss, the ten-minute interaction is not seen as helping the organization accomplish its goals.

On the other hand, another type of boss might come and join your conversation. That boss might regard such an interaction as important to the development and maintenance of good employee relationships, which might be seen as beneficial in the organization's efforts to accomplish its goals. In this view, the easier it is for you and your colleague to interact, the more effectively you will both do your jobs. In addition, good relationships add to employee satisfaction, which in turn leads to better job performance and reduces employee turnover. This approach is typical of a human relations theory of organizations.

Are you now convinced that the interaction was part of organizational communication? Would you still feel that way if the person who visited with you was from a unit in the organization that had little to do with your job? This would mean that the interaction was almost exclusively social. Certainly, this interaction might provide personal gratification, but what about the organization's needs?

As these scenarios illustrate, the nature of organizational communication varies according to the way an organization defines its goals. In the broadest sense, some organizations have the goal of producing and selling products, while other organizations provide services. But whatever the principal goal, most organizations also have a variety of subgoals. McDonald's might have the goal of making as large a profit as it can in any given year, but it also has subgoals, such as having satisfied customers and happy employees, maintaining a strong, positive public image, providing safe and tasty food, and finding additional products that will add to profitability. The nature of these subgoals and the way managers interpret them will determine the types of organizational communication that are encouraged.

The connection of organizational communication to the organization's goals applies to both internal and external communication. **Internal communication** includes face-to-face interactions and group meetings that occur within an organization, as well as written memos, policy or procedure statements, and computer-mediated communication (such as email) directed to organizational members. **External communication** is communication from the organization that is directed to clients, the public, and others outside the organization's formal structure. External communication includes advertising and public relations, sales calls, press releases, speeches, and interaction with other organizations.

What about when members of the organization are simply interacting on a personal level with members of other organizations? Is that external organizational communication? The same considerations apply as for internal communication. Determining whether the communication is organizational depends on the degree to which it contributes to the accomplishment of the organization's goals, and that depends on how the organization defines its goals.

■ Evaluating an Organization's Communication

The effectiveness of an organization is usually assessed in terms of how well the organization is accomplishing its goals. This assessment is sometimes conducted relative to the organization's expectations or potential. Organizations continually look for ways to be more successful. They may look at how to produce the product more efficiently, how to increase their market share, how to improve the product, or how to generate more funds.

Most of the time, efforts to improve organizational goal fulfillment deal with tangible issues such as costs of raw materials and wages. Yet, to the degree that communication is seen as important to the accomplishment of goals, organizations also focus attention and resources on sustaining or improving communication. When there is a concern for communication, organizations seek answers to such questions as these:

- Are we communicating effectively with one another?
- Can we improve the way decisions are made and communicated throughout the organization?
- Are our members effective communicators?
- What factors are impairing effective communication between the members?

Communication consultants, training and development specialists, and human resource personnel are often called on to address these questions. One tool that may be used is the **organizational communication audit,** a formalized process of evaluating the effectiveness of communication within an organization, leading to a strategy for improving communication. During periods of instability and change, when enormous demands are placed on communication networks, organizations are especially likely to look to communication specialists to help them deal with the changes.

Ten Strategies for Managers in a Multicultural Workforce*

The following advice for managers, from an article published in a business magazine, offers suggestions for interacting with a multicultural workforce. Notice how many of the ideas involve aspects of organizational communication.

Most managers today are being challenged to improve their employees' productivity effectively. As more industries compete in a global marketplace, this issue will become even more crucial to business success. Industry leaders, however, should realize that achieving their goals will be more complex than ever. One reason for this increased complexity involves the ethnic composition of a future workforce that will be noticeably different from today's makeup. Managers now must decide how they will manage an ethnically diverse workforce.

The key to managing a multiculturally diverse workforce successfully is to realize that majority and minority cultures do not always share experiences. The following 10 strategies are recommended for managers.

1. *Develop programs that promote awareness of cultural differences.* Managers responsible for education and training budgets should include programs, seminars and workshops that will help make supervisors and employees aware of cultural differences. Corporate budgets should be sufficient to conduct training on a regular basis. These programs also need a high profile to ensure that employees understand the company's sincerity in building a positive working environment.

2. *Promote positive attitudes toward differences among ethnic groups.* Senior management should promote diversity awareness by acknowledging support for such efforts in company mission statements, memos or written correspondence from one or more of the organization's top executives. Post these communications in areas where all employees can read them. Seek out information regarding various special ethnic observances and events, and make this information known among all employees. Company newsletters, publications and bulletin boards are ideal promotion tools when used regularly. Various cultural events are observed each year, such as Black History Month (February), Asian Pacific Heritage Week (first or second week in May) and National Hispanic Heritage Week (second week in September).

3. *Recognize common links among different ethnic groups.* Managers should be aware that although many differences exist, there are common values and beliefs that cross all cultural and ethnic lines. Look for these similarities and discuss them openly with employees.

4. *Become a flexible communicator.* This goal involves using different channels of communications to establish maximum understanding of the message, such as sending a memo, conducting a one-on-one consultation or holding a group discussion. Studies have shown that certain modes of communications are more effective than others with various ethnic groups. Many African Americans, for example, come from an Afrocentric background and prefer oral communication over written communication.

5. *Express your concerns and confusions.* Methods commonly used to communicate, such as giving lavish praise to someone for doing good work or looking directly in the eyes of a person when speaking, will not be accepted positively by some ethnic groups. (Many Native Americans, for instance, out of respect, are taught not to look directly in the eyes of elders or those in authority when speaking. They also are taught to be humble in front of their peers.) When this happens, managers must express their concern, especially when they perceive that a problem exists.

6. *Identify concerns and needs of ethnic groups.* This can be achieved through an assessment survey or questionnaire, or facilitation of group discussions or one-on-one counseling sessions. Top management must support these initiatives fully.

7. *Involve representatives of all minority groups in the decision-making process.* It's important that executives establish free-flowing communication networks throughout their organizations that allow minority concerns to reach the levels where deci-

sions are approved. Managers need encouragement to solicit feedback from minority employees to obtain different perspectives regarding decisions that affect their performance at work.

8. *Recognize that no "one size fits all" solutions exist.* Some solutions may involve introducing policies for more flexible dress codes or allowing minorities to celebrate holidays, such as Martin Luther King Jr.'s birthday.

9. *Challenge all stereotypes and assumptions about minority groups.* Managers must learn to distinguish between characteristics based on intuition and overgeneralizations. Allowing arbitrary attitudes and stereotypes to linger in the workplace will only generate misunderstandings and possible declines in productivity. Personnel development courses or workshop discussions on cultural differences are the best tools to eliminate conflicts.

10. *Include minority groups in all after-work engagements and company-sponsored events.* Managers must make a sincere effort to encourage these groups to become involved in social organizations and activities that will enhance career development, as well as the planning of such events. These efforts will be seen as favorable to all employees and can help to build positive race relations.

Source: From Alvin C. Hill, Jr., and James Scott, "Ten Strategies for Managers in a Multicultural Workforce," *HR Focus,* 69, No. 8 (August 1992), 6. Copyright American Management Association 1992.

■ Communication Networks

The patterns of communication in an organization provide us with insight into an organization's nature, philosophy, climate, and effectiveness. We can learn about a company by how it prescribes interaction among its members and by how the members choose to interact among themselves. But first we need to distinguish between formal and informal communication networks.

Formal communication networks are patterns of communication prescribed by the organizational hierarchy or by members' job functions. **Informal communication networks** are patterns of communication that occur within an organization but outside the lines prescribed by job descriptions. Within both types of networks, individuals can fall into any of several roles.

- *Isolates* are those who have little or no interaction with other members. Salespeople who are on the road a lot and have little direct contact with the company can become isolates within the organization.
- A *dyad* consists of two people who form a connection primarily with one another. Office mates often form this kind of network relationship.
- *Groups* or *teams* of individuals gather as part of the formal organizational network. They have some goal or purpose that has been prescribed by the organization.
- *Cliques* develop in the informal network. They are composed of a small number of individuals who voluntarily interact among themselves regularly. These cliques often form among organizational members who work together and have a common bond, such as their position. Like groups, cliques have a definite sense of who is a member and who is not a member.

In any communication network, a tendency to form isolates rather than groups can reduce communication efficiency and undermine the organization's cohesion.

Connections between groups or cliques are made in three ways. One member of a group or clique may also be a member of another, thus becoming a *link* between the two. Sometimes the connection is made because members of two different groups or cliques have a dyadic relationship; these people are said to serve as *bridge links.* Finally, a person may have connections to two groups or cliques without being a member of either, thus serving as a *liaison.* Upper-level managers often play this role because of their responsibility as managers of several departments.

Think about organizations to which you belong. What roles do you play in them: isolate, dyad, link, liaison, or bridge? How do you feel about the roles you play? Why have you come to play the roles that you do?

Ask Yourself

■ Formal Communication Networks

Part of the intrinsic nature of organizations is that individuals are expected and required to communicate with certain other individuals. Supervisors are supposed to communicate with their subordinates, presidents are expected to interact with their vice presidents, salespeople are expected to talk with clients.

This formal chain of command, power, and communication is often summarized in an organizational chart. Each chart is essentially a communication map of how messages are supposed to flow in the organization, as well as a relational map that tells members with whom they are to interact. We can use generic organizational charts to describe the two primary structures in today's organizations. The first is the traditional **vertical (tall) hierarchy** of upward and downward communication between supervisors and subordinates (Figure 15.1A). The second is the **horizontal (flat) hierarchy,** which reflects more lateral communication between organizational members (Figure 15.1B).

Figure 15.1   Two Basic Types of Organizational Structure

(A) A vertical hierarchy, in which the communication flow is mostly upward and downward between supervisors and subordinates. (B) A horizontal hierarchy, reflecting a greater amount of lateral communication between organizational members at the same level.

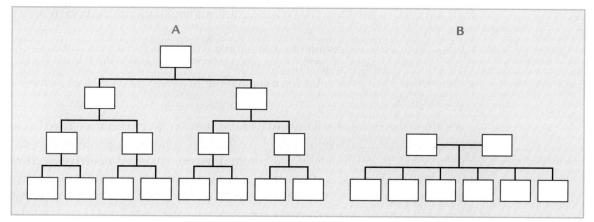

Such structures are not permanent. They continually change as an organization evolves and attempts to find its "ideal," or most productive, structure. Think about the organizations to which you belong. What does their hierarchy look like?

Do a search on the web using the phrase "organizational chart." Select a few charts from different kinds of organizations, such as government agencies, educational institutions, and corporations. How do the charts compare? On the basis of these charts, what would you predict about each organization's internal communication?

The effect of network structure on communication. An organization's hierarchical structure has a direct impact on the flow of information and communication efficiency. In vertical structures with many levels, information generally flows slowly and becomes more distorted. In highly horizontal networks, on the other hand, the flow of information is more happenstance, with some members never getting some information.

Real organizations are, of course, more complex than the two models reflect, often combining elements of both models. The overall structure of an organization might be vertical, but a particular unit within that organization might be horizontal. At each level, the structural pattern reflects and influences the communication that occurs.

Vertical communication is generally discussed in terms of supervisors' communication to subordinates, called **downward communication,** and the reverse process of subordinates' communication to superiors, called **upward communication.** The reason for this distinction is that the flow of communication is often unidirectional, with the supervisor being more likely to communicate to the subordinate than vice versa. A lot of research has been done on downward and upward communication in an attempt to determine the factors that influence it and the degree to which it relates to organizational effectiveness.

Types of downward communication. Most formal downward communication can be placed in one of the following categories:[1]

1. *Job instructions:* directives about how to perform a particular task
2. *Job rationale:* a description of how a person's job relates to others and its value to the organization
3. *Procedures and practices:* the policies, rules, and regulations that govern the organization
4. *Indoctrination:* the assimilation of members into an organization by communicating its values, goals, and objectives
5. *Performance feedback* communication about the quality of work displayed by a subordinate.

Of these five types of downward communication, **performance feedback** has been given particular emphasis by researchers. It has been identified as a key element affecting the quality of a subordinate's performance.[2] **Positive performance feedback** consists of favorable messages that indicate satisfactory or exceptional job performance. It includes praise, guidance or instruction, ongoing comments during the performance of a task, and reward for good outcomes.[3] **Negative performance feedback** consists of unfavorable messages that indicate unsatisfactory or problematic job performance. Negative performance feedback is more complex in nature than positive performance feedback and has direct face-threatening implications. Negative performance feedback has been found to vary on several dimensions: explicit versus ambiguous feedback; destructive versus constructive criticism; amount of knowledge of the conditions of performance; and clarity of the standards of evaluation.[4] The best approach to providing effective negative performance feedback is to play the role of coach instead of judge—that is, to offer explicit and constructive criticism based on clear evaluative standards and a thorough knowledge of the employee's performance.[5]

Information overload or deprivation in downward communication. Subordinates depend on those above them in the formal vertical network to provide them with information about the organization. This dependence sometimes creates situations in which subordinates feel either overwhelmed by information overload or uninformed because of information deprivation.

Information overload occurs when little information is filtered out by the network and all members are therefore given access to almost all the information.[6] While this may seem like a very democratic method of operation, eventually members begin ignoring information because there is too much to digest. This in turn results in important information being missed by members. This kind of problem is occurring with increasing frequency because of computer-mediated communication.

With the advent of email, more and more information is being disseminated among organizational members. Rather than working with improved efficiency, these members are spending more and more time filtering through information or else they are missing important information because they can't separate it from the clutter. For this reason, effective supervisors filter out what they see as

"And Frank, you'll be here, in charge of thinking up a better organizational arrangement."

unimportant information before passing on what is relevant to those down the network.

Sometimes, however, supervisors filter out information, either intentionally or unintentionally, that those lower in the hierarchy want to know. This produces *information deprivation,* which leads to employee dissatisfaction. Even though more communication flows downward than flows upward, those toward the bottom of the hierarchy are more likely to feel uninformed than those at the higher levels.[7]

Types of upward communication. Subordinates typically approach their superiors for certain specific reasons: to talk about themselves, their problems, and their coworkers; to complain; and to gather information about tasks or organizational policies and practices.[8] There are also times when the purpose of the communication is to define, clarify, or maintain the relationship between the subordinate and the supervisor. Think about those interactions with your boss in which you have engaged in "social" talk for the purpose of maintaining a positive relationship.

Factors that affect the flow of upward communication. Those in lower levels of the vertical hierarchy are often reluctant to initiate communication with those above them. Here are some typical reasons:

- Subordinates are less inclined to share information with superiors when they fear a personal impact or reprisal, such as being denied promotion.[9]
- Status differences between hierarchical levels tend to impede upward communication. For example, status differences cause information to be communicated more formally, usually in written form rather than in person.[10]
- Sometimes, subordinates are invited to share ideas, only to have them ignored by superiors. This creates a lack of trust and dissatisfaction on the part of the subordinate, which in turn reduces the likelihood of further upward communication.[11]

Research has shown that subordinates engage in direct and open attempts to influence their superiors when they (1) feel part of a high-participation group, (2) perceive a positive relationship with their superiors, and (3) have job autonomy.[12] In addition, subordinates are more likely to engage in attempts to influence superiors when they feel they are likely to be successful—in other words, when they feel that the superiors are open to considering input from subordinates.[13]

■ Informal Communication Networks

Unlike formal communication networks, informal networks are not prescribed by the organization. They emerge as a result of happenstance and members' attractions, preferences, and choices.

The members of an organization are free to choose with whom they will informally interact as well as what topics to discuss. Informal communication networks can be examined in terms of their characteristics—such as inevitability, emergence, complexity, overlap,[14] and technology—and also in terms of their functions.

Inevitability.   Inevitability refers to the fact that humans will form connections with various other members of an organization regardless of the formal structure that exists. We prefer to interact with some colleagues and not with others. Those preferences lead to the inevitable formation of informal interaction networks. You have probably experienced the formation of informal networks in your own jobs and among your classmates.

Emergence.   Networks emerge from the interactions that occur among organizational members. As you begin a new job, you slowly make connections with various members of the organization, and informal channels of communication begin to emerge.

One of my own strongest informal networks has been with a group of individuals with whom I play basketball—people from all different parts of the campus and community. This network has proven valuable because I have made connections with a variety of people whom I would not have otherwise known. From time to time, I call someone in this network for information needed in the performance of my job. I have been able to gain access to information more quickly and more completely than if I used the formal communication network.

An informal communication network depends a lot on chance for its development. Although organizations sometimes attempt to regulate informal networks, there is a great deal of unpredictability about who will connect with whom. You might be having lunch in the company cafeteria and begin a conversation with someone you've never met before. This could lead to more lunchtime conversations, and eventually you will have added a new member to your informal network. The emergence of informal networks take time, and our networks are constantly changing as new people are added, as relationships fade away, and as relationships change.

Complexity and overlap.   Informal communication networks are complex—they overlap and intertwine. The connections between members of informal networks do not follow the nice patterns found in formal organizational charts. Rather, the informal network is a complex web among a wide cross section of the organization and even reaching outside the organization. The complexity is further compounded by the fact that different informal networks are often connected, creating network constellations and galaxies.

Each organizational member belongs to several informal networks. Information in one network can be transferred to another because of the membership overlap. For example, during a recent noontime basketball game, a professor from the English department asked what I knew about a developing campus scandal. After I told him what I knew, he proceeded to share what I had said with his network in the English department. From there, it was only a matter of time until I heard the same information repeated by someone from agronomy. Interestingly, the information originally came to me from a person no longer at the university but who was still connected to his university networks through the Internet.

Technology.   Technology is having a dramatic impact on the development and maintenance of informal communication networks. We can now create electronic mailing lists and use them to communicate quickly with a large number of people. (Even my basketball group has a mailing list to keep everyone up to date on changes in the playing schedule.) Besides making connections easier, email makes them more regular and consistent. Many people who might previously have relied on chance meetings or occasional phone calls now maintain more frequent contact with the other members of their networks.

We are just beginning to see the impact of this technology on informal networks. Often the information shared is social, unrelated to organizational goals—for example, passing around the latest jokes or fun web sites to visit. However, such communication helps define and maintain the relationships that can be tapped later for more substantive information.

Functions. Informal communication networks serve a number of functions.[15] For one thing, they supplement the formal communication channels. A lot of information passes through the informal communication networks in an organization. The interactive nature of informal communication allows individuals to seek specific information and to clarify information while talking with other members.

Interacting with colleagues who are part of your informal communication network can be a safe way to get feedback and suggestions.

Individuals gain information they might otherwise have missed because their placement in the organizational structure would have left them out of the loop or would have delayed and distorted the flow of information.

But informal communication has its dangers. Rumors can run rampant through the informal network. False or distorted rumors can generate unnecessary anxiety and panic. This is one reason why informal communication is sometimes discouraged by those in power.

Informal communication networks can be used strategically to disseminate information "unofficially." Members in the organization can test the reaction to certain information by leaking it to their informal networks. The information can be disavowed if the reaction is negative or confirmed if the reaction is positive. Indirectly, this can help an organization make more effective decisions.

Besides simply testing the water, informal communication can be used to share ideas and gain feedback without the restrictions that occur when following formal procedures. Using informal networks, members are able to speak off the record, visit with colleagues about ideas they are considering, determine levels of support, and identify potential problems or roadblocks—all before putting an idea through the formal channels. For example, before making a formal proposal, a subordinate might ask his or her supervisor to float an idea by a vice president during an upcoming social gathering. This process can speed up innovation in an organization because it avoids the slower bureaucratic process. Subordinates are most likely to share innovations when they feel they have friendly and supportive relationships with their superiors.[16]

■ Organizational Theory

As a fundamental part of all organizations, communication networks provide one basis for describing the structure of an organization. There are also a number of theories that try to explain organizational behavior and process. These general theories will be examined with a bent toward the role that communication plays in each of them.

Organizational theory can be divided into two categories: descriptive and prescriptive. **Descriptive organizational theory** seeks to explain the dynamics of the organization. Such theories attempt to explain why things happen the way they do. Communication is one of the elements that contributes to these theories because of its importance to organizational functioning. **Prescriptive organizational theory** advocates a particular approach that organizations should follow. In essence, theories of this type prescribe a particular way of operating for an organization to achieve excellence.

A major problem underlying the prescriptive approach is the difficulty of defining excellence. Does it mean that the organization should be profitable? A great place to work? The largest, best known, or fastest growing? Defining excellence in different ways leads to different prescriptions. If excellence means making the most profit, then you have the classical, or scientific, approach: People are resources to be manipulated and maximized. If excellence means creating a place where the employees are happy, highly committed, and satisfied, then you have the human relations approach.

Descriptive and prescriptive theories have considerable overlap. A description of how organizations generally operate can lead to a prescription of what might be changed in an organization that doesn't fit the description. Similarly, prescriptions sometimes represent an attempt to generalize the way one organization has operated (descriptive) to the way all organizations should operate (prescriptive). Neither approach is stagnant. Over the years, each has changed as organizations have evolved. The following sections examine some leading examples of each type of approach.

■ Descriptive Approaches

The two primary approaches that are currently used to describe organizations are systems theory and organizational culture. These two approaches attempt to identify the elements and factors that constitute or define organizations. In addition, the increasing use of computer-mediated communication in organizations has led to attempts to extend these existing theories or develop new descriptive theories.

Systems theory. **Systems theory** is a meta-theory that can be applied to almost any process. It was originally developed by a biologist who was attempting to explain the interdependent nature of biological structures.[17] The basic tenet of systems theory is that organisms are made up of interconnected parts that influence one another. A change in one part of a system results in a change in all parts. The primary elements that make up a system are inputs, process (throughput), and outputs. Systems theory attempts to identify the relationships between these components.

Because organizations can easily be seen as equivalent to a biological organism, the application of systems theory seems logical. From a communication perspective, the inputs in an organization would include information, personnel, and materials. The communication network acts as the processing agent. The outputs are the decisions, actions, and products generated by the organization.

Let's use a college as an example. The inputs into the organization include the administrators, faculty, staff, students, finances, and the college's physical plant. The process involves interactions among the organizational members, including classroom activities, committee meetings, and network interactions among administrators, faculty, staff, and students. The outputs include educated students, research findings, and community outreach. Systems theory allows for an understanding of how a change in one of these components would affect all the other related components. If there were a drop in student enrollment, for example, the university might have to lay off faculty and staff, decrease support for research, or cut back class offerings.

Two other aspects of systems theory have proven to be particularly useful in the study of organizations: open versus closed systems, and homeostasis and feedback.

1. Open versus closed systems. A system is considered closed when it has a restricted number of elements and an identifiable boundary. A system is considered open when there is no definable boundary and the number of potential elements seems limitless. For instance, we can think of a tree as an open system, including the environment as an element because of its impact on the organism. An analysis of the tree would therefore include all those factors that influence the tree's environment.

One of the early applications of systems theories to organizations claimed that organizations should be considered open systems. The rationale for this claim was that outside forces (the environment) play a significant role in the organizational process.[18]

2. *Homeostasis and feedback.* Systems seek to maintain homeostasis, which means that they try to keep everything stable and in balance.[19] A disruption of one part results in an attempt to counter that disruption by changes in the other parts. This correction process makes use of positive and negative adaptive feedback.

In systems theory, **negative feedback** is information provided to the system that something is wrong and needs to be corrected. For instance, if employers complained to your college that graduating students lacked sufficient writing skills to be viable employees, your college would take that feedback and adopt corrective action. **Positive feedback** on the other hand, is information about an opportunity that can be met by some change in the system or by reinforcement of a system output. For example, many colleges have begun to offer courses over the Internet. Students have been quick to enroll in these courses, letting colleges know that they like the flexibility associated with Internet offerings. This positive feedback has resulted in the addition of more and more Internet courses.

Organizational culture. Culture is a concept used by sociologists and anthropologists to reflect the collection of values, beliefs, attitudes, rituals, and language associated with a given population. A number of principles have been developed to explain the development and evolution of cultures. Recently, many organizational theorists have studied **organizational culture** in the belief that organizations represent unique cultures in and of themselves.

Just as anthropologists approach the study of cultures from different perspectives, so do researchers who are studying organizations. In all approaches to organizational culture, however, communication plays a central part because of its critical role in sustaining, teaching, and modifying the organizational culture.

Sometimes anthropologists study the artifacts that exist within a culture. For an organization, this approach might involve collecting manuals, memos, email, minutes of meetings, and so on. Such artifacts provide insight into the "visible," or "concrete," manifestations of a culture, but they don't give much of a sense of the day-to-day interactions among its members.

Other organizational culture approaches focus on analysis of relevant written or spoken messages. Members of the organization might also be interviewed. Such approaches identify factors like these:

- *Fantasy themes,* that is, recurring themes or visions that reflect a core company perspective. For example, if organizational members continually mentioned that the customer is number one, this could be considered a fantasy theme. (In this usage, "fantasy" reflects concrete themes.)

- *Narrative stories* that members generate to describe life and events in the organization: for example, "Let me tell you about the time the boss got his comeuppance."
- Recurrent *metaphors,* used to describe the organization in terms of something else with similar properties: for instance, describing the company as "one big happy family" or "a well-oiled machine."

Another approach to organizational culture is called the *interpretive perspective,* meaning that it is concerned with how people think about or interpret their organization. In this approach, organizational reality is what the members of the organization say it is. Cultural rules are created and maintained by the members of the organization themselves. For example, a sales department's office manual might dictate that employees are to submit a written summary of a complaint before talking with a supervisor. However, everyone in the department simply goes directly to the supervisor, who is willing to listen to them and respond. In this instance, the subordinates have in their mind a particular way they believe the department handles complaints, regardless of the prescription in the manual. If we were studying this department, we would be mistaken if we depended only on the written manual as our guide.

Cultures are maintained through a process of *enculturation,* whereby new members are initiated into the culture by learning the values, beliefs, rituals, and language.[20] This means that a new member of the sales department would be taught by the other employees how complaints were handled in the department. The process of enculturation occurs through both the formal communication network and the informal network. The formal network often conducts training sessions in which new members can learn about the organization's history, values, and methods of operation. If you have ever worked for a large company like Sears, JC Penney, Target, Disney, or Macy's, you have probably sat through the obligatory new-employee orientation sessions that communicate organizational values.

The informal communication network also helps initiate new members. Sometimes, informal rules are more difficult to learn than the formal ones because few of them are explicitly communicated. Many of the informal rules are learned through trial and error. When you violate one of the rules, the other members let you know.

Cultures engage in distinct rituals, rites, and ceremonies. As cultures, organizations have their own such rituals, some of them formal and some informal. In a university, for example, the formal rituals include graduation ceremonies, the way committee meetings are run, and new-student orientation. Informal rituals vary greatly, and they are often specific to a single unit within a larger organization. You may have experienced informal rituals such as chipping in with others to buy a fellow employee a wedding or retirement present, going out to lunch to celebrate a person's birthday, and having a party to celebrate a promotion or retirement. A student once told me about a company in which people who were having a birthday were expected to bring chocolate chip cookies to share with everyone. Failure to bring cookies—or to bring the right kind of cookie—resulted in harassment by the other members. Obviously, bringing cookies was a ritual followed in this organization.

An organizational culture is the product of the interaction of all the members of an organization. Each member brings to the organization his or her own cultural values. Once formed, the organizational culture continues to evolve, imposing itself on new members but also being influenced by the addition of new members. Depending on the rigidity and size of the organization, the cultural values may be relatively fixed or quite fluid. Large organizations with deeply implanted values and highly homogeneous membership (with everyone coming from the same outside culture) are slower to change than smaller, more diverse organizations.

Suppose, for example, that you had been working for a year with two other people as part of a cooking staff for a restaurant. You would develop a very specific organizational subculture among the three of you. One value you might adopt is an acceptance of constant teasing and joshing with each other. If one member left and was replaced by a new employee, you would attempt to enculturate the new person into your group. However, since there were only two of you trying to sustain your cultural values, the new person could dramatically change those values. The new person might dislike teasing and cause you to abandon this value in your subculture. In this way, the culture evolves and develops new values.

In the last several decades, several factors have caused significant changes in the organizational cultures of U.S. businesses. These include increasing globalization, racial and ethnic diversification, and an increase in the number of women in the work world. The United States has historically been dominated by white males; that trend is changing, though somewhat slowly in some quarters. There are still a disproportionate number of white males in positions of power in organizations, and those in management have a disproportionate influence on organizational culture.[21] As women and members of minorities rise to management positions, they can be expected to have greater impact on the organizational values of tomorrow.

Watch a couple of television shows that take place in an organization: for example, *M*A*S*H*, *News Radio*, *The Drew Carey Show*, *ER*, or *Chicago Hope*. What instances can you find in which the cultural rules followed by the organizational members differ from those prescribed by the formal organizational culture? What impact does this have on new members or on those who fail to recognize these informal cultural rules?

Current trends.   Because the advent of email and other computer technology has resulted in changes in the traditional structure of organizations and their associated cultural values, organizational theory is being developed to reflect these developments. (See, for instance, the online *Journal of Computer-Mediated Communication*.) The increasing adoption of personal computers, email, servers, local area networks (LANs), the World Wide Web, web pages, and the Internet has already made a significant difference in the way many organizations operate. For example, organizational members can work from their homes with little face-to-face contact with colleagues, but they remain vital contributing members of the organization. This has led to the emergence of theories that describe virtual organizations.

Virtual organizations consist of individuals who are connected primarily through computer networks. Virtual organizations maintain the organizational properties of individuals interacting toward common goals and making coordinated work efforts, but they do so without the constraints of geography or time. Despite early speculation that virtual organizations would be decentralized and devoid of hierarchy, research has shown that a centralized hierarchy does emerge on the basis of easy access to experts and the need for efficient communication.[22] For example, a secretary who is highly knowledgeable about word-processing programs might receive a large number of emails from other members in the virtual organization who depend on the secretary's expertise. Other members would save themselves time by having one particular person to whom they could direct their inquiries.

The development and maintenance of an organization's communication network are greatly enhanced by email. Both formal and informal networks develop from listservers created both by the organization (formal lists) and by individuals (personal address books). Computer-mediated communication increases access across the hierarchy and allows for information dissemination to a wide range of organizational members.

However, the adoption of computer-mediated communication has a downside as well. The ability to access anyone else who has an Internet address has created increasing problems for users. The problems that arise include interpersonal abuse and what might be called slavery to email.[23] Information overload, mentioned earlier in the chapter, is a frequent difficulty because computer-mediated communication increases the ability to copy everyone in an organization with every message. Less discrimination is being made about who should get what information, leaving it to individual readers to make such determinations. This means that organizational members are likely to have too much email, most of it irrelevant to their jobs. This means that they must spend an increasing amount of time sorting through their email, looking for important or relevant messages. "Spam" (electronic junk mail) is also filling users' mail baskets. And even when organizational information is posted on web pages—an increasingly frequent occurrence—it can become overwhelming. These are some of the issues that newer organizational theories are addressing.

■ *Prescriptive Approaches*

There are a large number of prescriptive theories, each advocating a different way for organizations to achieve excellence. As discussed earlier, differences in the way excellence is defined result in different prescriptions. Here we will review three significant theories: classical and scientific management theory, human (industrial) relations theory, and human resource development theory. Each theory prescribes a different way for organizations to operate. Each theory advocates a variety of ways to address management and communication issues, including how much control should be held by management and how much shared with subordinates.

Classical and scientific management theory. The notion of a vertical hierarchy, described earlier, reflects classical theories of organizations. These theories were developed to prescribe ways of improving organizational efficiency. **Classi-**

cal theory assumes that each member of the organization has a specific set of duties and that the positions are ordered and structured. Managers make decisions, and the workers carry out the decisions. Such theories often blend issues of management, control, motivation, bureaucracy, and structure.

Max Weber and Henri Fayol developed some of the first theories of organizations during the early twentieth century. In their ideal, an organization represented a "well-oiled machine" that operated smoothly and efficiently. This conceptualization reflected a view of people as resources to be used for the good of the organization. Here are some of the principles they applied to organizations:[24]

1. Organizations are composed of individuals with specific, skill-based, titled positions.
2. The organization is hierarchically structured (ideally as a pyramid); each higher level has authority for the levels under it (the *scalar principle*).
3. The organization is structured by tasks, specialization, and expertise. The relationships between positions are clearly defined, with a distinct division between management and production.
4. Power is ascribed to positions. Individuals have legitimate authority because of the positions they hold. Decision-making is centralized and consolidated.
5. Decisions are to be made according to organizational policies and procedures (hence the basis of "bureaucratic red tape"). Decisions are to be impersonal.
6. A strong distinction is made between organizational life and personal life. Organizational power, possessions, time, and commitment are to be separated from personal dealings. Under this approach, there should be no personal phone calls or family visits during work hours.

One area in which Weber and Fayol differed was in how rigidly the structure should be followed. Rather than restricting communication absolutely to the chain of command, "Fayol's bridge" allowed for temporary connections between parts of the organization to handle crises or problems. Fayol advocated both stability and flexibility.[25]

During this same era, another theorist, Frederick Taylor, was developing his theory of scientific management, which eventually merged with the theories advocating organizational hierarchies. The general premise of **scientific management** is that people are rational, motivated beings who respond to reward (and punishment). Taylor advocated that managers analyze tasks scientifically and thereby develop the "best" way of doing each task. People were to be similarly analyzed for their capabilities and placed in situations best suiting their abilities. Taylor saw fair wages as a key factor in getting productivity out of workers; too little pay would lead to less production.

One outgrowth of Taylor's approach was the use of efficiency studies, also known as time-and-motion studies. These examined how much time and how much motion a worker used in accomplishing a given task. On the basis of such studies, the experts recommended ways to increase an organization's efficiency.

In both classical theory and scientific management theory, organizational communication is controlled. The formal communication network is an essential element in these approaches, and communication is expected to follow that structure. Communication is used for organizing, commanding, coordinating, and controlling.[26] Under the most restrictive guidelines, only communication that deals with organizational goals should occur. Human relations theory, which is examined next, developed as a direct challenge to the restrictive and impersonal nature of the classical approach.

Human (industrial) relations theory. A series of studies conducted from 1923 to 1933 to test scientific management theory instead provided support for a different approach to organizations. When researchers dimmed the lights on an assembly line, they anticipated a decrease in production. However, they found just the opposite: Production increased. The workers apparently responded more to the attention paid to them by the managers and researchers than to the light itself. This surprising result was named the *Hawthorne effect*, after the plant where the studies were conducted.

The Hawthorne studies gave rise to **human relations theory,** also known as industrial relations theory, which stressed that the quality of the relationships between workers and management was as important as wages in motivating productivity. Further studies identified three factors that have a positive influence on productivity: good interpersonal relationships with other employees, working in a cohesive team, and feeling positive about the supervisors.[27] Because of these factors, the human relations approach embraces the informal communication network as a valuable asset to organizational effectiveness.

A good relationship between supervisors and workers is one of the basic tenets of the human relations theory.

The basic tenet of the human relations approach is that the happy organizational member is a productive organizational member. Underlying this tenet is the belief that good relations with other members create positive morale and that positive morale makes members more compliant with managerial authority, which in turn leads to greater productivity.[28] Organizations would be effective, the advocates of this approach concluded, if they met the social needs of people through the use of groups, open communication, and democratic principles. Proponents of the classical and scientific approach saw human relations advocates as romantics with an overidealized perspective, too prone to view organizations as "one big happy family."

The human relations approach sounds very appealing, but its downfall lay in the intent underlying the approach. The approach was adopted by organizations not out of a concern for the workers, but in an attempt to maximize productivity, just like the classical approach. The result was that managers were trained how to "act" open and concerned for their subordinates, and the resulting changes in productivity were tenuous at best. Nevertheless, the movement toward human relations did temper the impact of the classical approach and make clear that employees did work for more than just wages. This set the stage for the human resource approach.

Human resource development theory.   After reading about the classical approach and the human relations approach to organizations, you may have reached the same conclusion that many organizational theorists did: Why not blend the two? The approach known as **human resource development theory** recognizes the need for a formal organizational structure, but also looks at individuals as having a variety of needs that can be met within the organization. To help explain what motivates members of an organization, Maslow's hierarchy of needs is applied. Human resource development seeks to help members realize their own goals and needs while effectively contributing to the organizational goals.[29]

Human resource development focuses on equipping members for success by offering training, education, and developmental opportunities. There are several key principles advocated by the proponents of this approach.[30]

1. Organizational members are a resource to the company, but they have a right to be satisfied with their role in the organization.
2. Members don't necessarily come totally prepared to handle the jobs they are assigned.
3. Changes in organization require providing members with retraining.
4. The organization should develop members who can take on responsibility and management.
5. Supervisors need to understand human behavior.
6. The quality of work life is an important concern.

Human resource development led Douglas McGregor to write *The Human Side of Enterprise*, a 1960 book that describes two types of managers, theory X and theory Y.[31] In McGregor's terminology, the **theory X** manager follows the principles of the classical approach to organizations. McGregor identified three assumptions underlying the theory X manager's approach to subordinates.[32]

1. People have an inherent dislike of work and will avoid it when possible.
2. Therefore, people must be manipulated, threatened, watched, and controlled in order to get any productivity from them.
3. People prefer to be directed, don't want responsibility, and have little ambition.

McGregor advocated a theory Y approach to managing people. **Theory Y** follows a principle of integration; people can achieve their own goals best when they direct their efforts toward the organization's success. This philosophy is reflected in the statement of the star athlete who claims, "I don't care about setting personal records. I just want to help the team win." Theory Y follows these assumptions:[33]

1. People take as much pleasure from a good job as they do from play or rest.
2. People can be left to self-direction when committed to a goal.
3. Commitment to organizational goals develops when there are personal rewards associated with their achievement.
4. Under the right conditions, people will accept and even seek responsibility.
5. The ability to generate creative and imaginative solutions exists in a broad section of the population.
6. Organizations generally fail to take advantage of the full intellectual potential of their members.

Theories X and Y differ in their use of communication. Theory X managers use communication to manipulate and control. Theory Y managers seek to gain and share information, using communication as a bridge between themselves and their subordinates. They communicate openly and honestly. They seek input and ideas from all members.

Current trends.   The success of Japanese industry after World War II led to a reevaluation of U.S. management methods and an attempt to adapt Japanese management techniques to the United States in the 1980s and 1990s. Cultural differences limited the effectiveness of such applications. (See, for instance, the Michael Keaton movie *Gung Ho*.) One particular difference is that Japan is a collectivistic society and the United States is individualistic.

A recent approach, **theory Z,** attempts to find a middle ground between the individualistic and collectivistic approaches. Theory Z focuses on increasing organizational members' participation in decision-making. The assumption is that people are more motivated to work for an organization in which they participate in the decision-making process. According to advocates of this approach, the divisions between management and labor have to be diminished. All organizational members must trust in the other members and believe in their commitment.

The philosophy underlying theory Z can also be seen in such movements as employee empowerment, shared management, and quality circles—approaches in which all members of the organization are involved in decision-making. Each approach attempts to create a flat, horizontal organizational structure. Quality circles provide a good example. Quality circles involve groups of five to fifteen organizational members who meet for the purpose of improving the quality of the organization, often focusing on the product. These groups have worked well in collectivistic Japan, but they have not been as dramatically effective in the United States. Quality circles require a commitment to organizational goals, a willingness to participate, and empowerment of the circles.

Despite the limitations of quality circles, the use of project teams and flexible organizational structures seems to be gaining momentum. Organizations are acting more organic as they create and disband groups of various members to handle issues on an *ad hoc* basis.

Decide whether each of the following statements reflects systems theory, organizational culture, classical and scientific management theory, human relations theory, or human resource development theory.

1. Managers expect an honest day's work for an honest day's pay.
2. People are basically lazy and will goof off if not carefully supervised.
3. All organizational decisions are to be made by higher administration.
4. The president of a company has more power than the vice president, who has more power than a departmental manager, who has more power than the line employees.
5. People want to be appreciated for the work they do for the organization.
6. People who belong to our organization are committed to excellence.
7. We need to improve the quality of our product because our customers are complaining about too many breakdowns.
8. You know the procedure: Fill out the appropriate form, have it signed by your supervisor, and submit it a week before you plan on being sick.

This chapter has focused on macro-organizational issues, such as the nature of organizations and communication networks. Although you now have an idea of the role that communication plays in the life of an organization, you still need to learn about the communication skills that you personally will need if you are to succeed in an organization. The next chapter will focus on the importance of micro-organizational communication skills—skills that will improve your ability to work with others, both as a subordinate and as a supervisor.

Summary

Organizations can be defined as interdependent individuals brought together in a hierarchical structure to perform a variety of structured tasks toward the accomplishment of some goal. Organizational communication is communication that occurs in the attempt to accomplish organizational goals. Organizational communication includes both internal communication, which occurs within the organization itself, and external communication, which is directed from the organization to those outside it. When companies are concerned about the effectiveness of their communication, they may conduct an organizational communication audit, a formal evaluation that leads to a strategy for improvement.

Formal communication networks are patterns of communication dictated by the organizational hierarchy, while informal communication networks are networks that naturally develop among members of the organization. Formal networks prescribe who talks to whom about what. They reflect the power and relationships defined by each person's position in the organization. Hierarchies can be vertical (tall) or horizontal (flat). Downward communication (supervisor to subordinate) often consists of instructions, rationales, descriptions of procedures and practices, indoctrination, and feedback. Upward communication (subordinate to superior) is more restricted than downward and is affected by status, trust, and anticipated impact.

Informal communication networks are complex, involving considerable member linking and overlap. These networks help supplement information flow from the formal network. They can be used strategically to "leak" information and test reactions. The informal communication network can also be used to expedite innovation, bypassing formal channels.

Organizational theory includes both descriptive theories that explain the dynamics of organizations and prescriptive theories that advocate how an organization should operate. Two prominent descriptive theories are systems theory and organizational culture. Systems theory describes organizations as interconnected parts that influence one another. The primary parts are inputs, process (throughputs), and outputs. Systems theorists also consider whether the system is open or closed and how it responds to both positive and negative feedback.

The organizational culture approach describes organizations as cultures with associated sets of values, beliefs, attitudes, rituals, and language. Organizational artifacts can be examined to provide insights into the culture. An organization's cultural rules evolve as a result of changes in membership and the outside environment.

As new technology changes the way members communicate, organizations are continuing to evolve. Computer-mediated communication, altering the traditional hierarchies, has led to the concept of virtual organizations, in which the members are linked primarily by computer networks. New theories are attempting to assess the advantages, disadvantages, and overall impact of email and other forms of electronic communication.

The important prescriptive approaches include classical and scientific management theory, human relations theory, and human resource development theory. The classical approach reflects strong adherence to a formal, vertical, hierarchical structure. Organizations are viewed as trying to emulate a "well-oiled machine." According to this approach, each member of the organization has prescribed duties and a prescribed position. Communication is restricted to the appropriate channels and organizational issues, though some theorists allowed for alternative channels to handle crises. Scientific principles are applied to try to maximize the performance of each organizational member. People's skills are carefully analyzed and matched with the scientifically determined requirements of a given position. In these approaches, communication is seen as being used for organization, control, command, and coordination.

Human relations theory is based on the premise that organizational members are motivated by more than just the desire for wages. Quality personal relationships, cohesion, and positive feelings about supervisors are seen as increasing productivity. Another approach, human resource development theory, seeks to integrate the organization's structural needs with means of producing satisfaction among organizational members. It stresses self-fulfillment, training, and developmental opportunities for employees. This approach is reflected in theory Y managers, who view people as capable of self-direction, willing to commit themselves to working toward a goal, and willing to take responsibility. They contrast with theory X managers, who reflect classical theory in that they see people as having a dislike for work, needing to be manipulated and controlled, and having little ambition or desire for responsibility.

Current trends in prescriptive approaches include the development of theory Z, which describes managers who involve subordinates in decision-making. Quality circles are one method of doing so. Other such trends include employee empowerment programs and shared management. The traditional hierarchy is being replaced by a more team-based or project-based orientation.

Key Terms

organizational communication   Communication that occurs in the attempt to accomplish organizational goals.

internal communication   Communication within an organization, including face-to-face interactions, group meetings, written memos, statements of policy or procedure, and email directed to organizational members.

external communication   Communication from an organization that is directed to clients, the public, and others outside the organization's formal structure.

organizational communication audit   A formalized process of evaluating the effectiveness of communication within an organization, leading to a strategy for improving communication.

formal communication networks   Patterns of communication prescribed by an organizational hierarchy or by members' job functions.

informal communication networks   Patterns of communication that occur within an organization but outside the lines prescribed by job descriptions.

vertical (tall) hierarchy   A pyramidal organizational structure in which communication primarily flows upward and downward between supervisors and subordinates.

horizontal (flat) hierarchy   An organizational structure that reflects lateral communication between organizational members.

downward communication   The communication that flows from supervisors to subordinates.

upward communication   Communication initiated by subordinates and directed to superiors.

performance feedback   Communication about the quality of work displayed by a subordinate.

positive performance feedback   Favorable messages that indicate satisfactory or exceptional performance.

negative performance feedback   Unfavorable messages that indicate unsatisfactory or problematic performance.

descriptive organizational theory   Organizational theory that seeks to explain the dynamics of the organization.

prescriptive organizational theory   Organizational theory that advocates or prescribes a particular approach that organizations should follow.

systems theory   An approach asserting that an organization is made up of interdependent inputs, process, and outputs.

negative feedback   In systems theory, information provided to a system that something is wrong and needs to be corrected.

positive feedback   In systems theory, information about an opportunity that can be met by some change in the system or by reinforcement of a system output.

organizational culture   The collection of values, beliefs, attitudes, rituals, and language inherent in an organization.

virtual organizations   Organizations consisting of individuals who are connected primarily through computer networks.

classical theory Organizational theory that assumes that each member of the organization has a specific set of duties and that the positions are ordered and structured.

scientific management A prescriptive approach to organizations based on the belief that people are rational, motivated beings who respond to reward (and punishment).

human relations theory A theory stressing that the quality of the relationships between workers and management is as important as wages in motivating productivity.

human resource development theory An approach to organizations that recognizes the need for a formal organizational structure, but also looks at individuals as having a variety of needs that can be met within the organization.

theory X A managerial approach grounded in the principle that people don't want to work and need to be manipulated and controlled to gain productivity.

theory Y A managerial approach grounded in the principle that when people are committed to a goal, they will work, be self-directive, be responsible, and offer creative solutions.

theory Z A managerial approach that seeks to involve organizational members in decision-making.

Review Questions

1. Explain the impact of formal organizational networks on communication.
2. In what ways are upward and downward communication similar? Different?
3. What factors influence the development of informal communication networks?
4. Describe organizations from a systems theory perspective.
5. How does culture relate to organizations?
6. How does classical theory differ from human relations theory?
7. Briefly explain theory X, theory Y, and theory Z.

Chapter 16

Organizational Communication: Skills for Employees and Managers

Objectives

Studying this chapter will allow you to:

1. Explain the process of assimilating into a new organization.
2. Explain how interpersonal communication contributes to your potential success in an organization.
3. Identify the types of teams and groups typically found in organizations.
4. Identify the elements that should be covered in a briefing.
5. Describe some of the advantages and disadvantages of email.
6. Describe the fundamental skills needed for effective managerial communication.

One chapter cannot possibly cover all the communication skills you will need to be successful in your professional career in an organization. But you have already made more progress than you may realize, because all the information you have read in this text has relevance to your organizational life.

The first five chapters, which discussed basic communication principles and theories, apply to the various types of communication that occur within organizations. For instance, understanding how words and nonverbal behaviors can create misunderstanding and confusion will help you deal with the inevitable breakdowns in communication with your boss. Similarly, the chapters on interpersonal communication, interviewing, small groups, and presentation all covered material pertinent to the types of communication you will encounter in any organization. This chapter will relate some of that material specifically to the nuances of organizations.

Required Skills

A recent newspaper article summed up a survey in which employers described the skills most needed by future employees. According to the survey, all future employees must have the ability to do the following things:

- Write technical reports.
- Read and analyze reports.
- Present ideas to co-workers and managers.
- Understand core business and financial operations.
- Communicate effectively with customers.
- Use word processing, spreadsheets, databases, and other software applications to compile and present information.
- Use e-mail, Internet, intranet, and other software to communicate.
- Use automated equipment or computer technology as it relates to a specific job or industry.
- Work in a team environment.
- Solve problems individually or in a group.
- Respond to change positively and effectively.
- Collaborate, negotiate, delegate.
- Deal with people, information, and processes with integrity.

As you can see, most of the skills listed relate to communication.

Source: "Required Skills," *Des Moines Register*, September 27, 1998.

■ Your Life Cycle in Organizations

Life in organizations is dynamic. Your experience in organizations is much like that of an interpersonal relationship; you meet as strangers, you begin developing a relationship, your roles change, you become interdependent, and sometimes you terminate the relationship.

Similarly, in organizations you go through a series of stages by which you become more integrated and involved. You begin as a rookie, learning the rules and cultural values of the organization. As you perform prescribed tasks, you begin to make contributions to the organization. As you demonstrate your skill and aptitude, you move into positions of greater responsibility and management. You play a more critical role in organizational decision-making as you become an "expert." Moving toward retirement, you can leave while at the peak of your influence, or you can continue as a member of the organization as your influence diminishes and you become less involved in decision-making.

This life cycle in an organization is accompanied by changes in communication. The communication skills you need and the contexts you encounter change as you move through an organization's hierarchy.

- When you enter an organization, your primary role is to gather information and learn. Therefore, you do a lot of listening and restrain yourself from offering suggestions.
- As you become more confident about your role, you offer suggestions and even seek out opportunities to influence and change things. You move from being a member of a team to being a team leader.
- As you gain supervisory responsibility, more and more of your communication involves formal interactions with subordinates. You become an information manager, transferring information between levels of the hierarchy.

Let's look more closely at these stages in your organizational life.

■ Initiation and Assimilation

Sometimes you interact with members of an organization as an outsider, developing a relationship with the organization even before you join as an employee. Usually, though, your life with an organization begins with the employment interview. This formal interaction begins the process by which you learn about the organization and the organization learns about you.

The greater the number of individuals in the organization with whom you have interviews, the more connected and informed you become. You develop expectations about your position and about the organization. The degree to which the organizational reality matches or contrasts with your expectations often determines your ease of assimilation, your satisfaction, and your likelihood of quitting.[1]

Some organizations have initiation rituals for newcomers. The ritual might be as simple as being introduced during a staff meeting or being taken from office to office to be introduced. At the other end of the spectrum, university Greek houses sometimes run into ethical problems when their initiation rituals involve cruel or dangerous forms of hazing.

Initiation is only the first step. There is usually a more formal training or indoctrination period that involves learning the procedures, filling out forms, getting keys, and so on. Training periods range from half a day with the personnel department to a year-long process involving dozens of people. This training process can also include an orientation to the organization's goals, values, and history. I remember being hired part-time by Sears. With the other new employees, I watched a filmstrip about the founding of Sears. I still remember the story of Mr. Sears working as a railroad station agent, selling pocket watches that he had bought when the receiver refused delivery. Obviously, the company's indoctrination of me worked pretty well.

The assimilation process. **Assimilation** is the process of aligning an individual's values and goals with those of the organization—in essence, having the individual adopt the organization's cultural values. Assimilation occurs through both formal and informal communication networks. You learn the organization's values, beliefs, rules, and policies, as well as its expectations for you.

You might experience role shock when your own expectations don't match the organizational reality. **Role shock** is the feeling you get when you find out that a job is not what you expected. At that point, you must decide whether to stick with it or quit. The discrepancy that occurs can be caused by a failure on your part to honestly evaluate your own needs and abilities, by a deception on the part of the recruiter or employer, or by the recruiter or employer's ignorance about the real demands of the position. Most of us have experienced role shock when we started working a job and found that it didn't match what we expected.

A large part of the assimilation process depends on the supervisor. Generally, the supervisor or training designate has the responsibility for seeing that newcomers are effectively assimilated. Assimilation is aided by the efforts of new members to fit in. Newcomers can actively modify their behavior and appearance so that they act and look the same as the more tenured members. When assimilation works well, new members gain the necessary information to perform their tasks, adopt the values of the organization, identify with the organization, and establish effective formal and informal network relationships. In essence, assimilation results in new members feeling like they are part of the organization and being accepted by others in the organization. If you have ever seen the Borg on the TV series *Star Trek: The Next Generation*, you've observed an extreme example of organizational assimilation.

Sometimes there are specific organizational markers that let you know you have been accepted into the organization. You may have been hired for a six-month probationary period, after which time you are considered a regular member. You acquire tenure or status the longer you remain in the organization. Typically, you remain the "new person" until another person is hired, at which time your role may change considerably as the new person turns to you for help in assimilating.

Dealing with uncertainty. Chapter 2 introduced the idea that we feel uncomfortable when faced with uncertainty and unpredictability. As newcomers in organizations, we experience high levels of uncertainty and stress. We seek information as a way of reducing uncertainty. This means that we are receptive to learning information about our job and the company. We are willing listeners to information from supervisors and colleagues.

The extent to which we actively seek information at this early stage can have implications for our later performance in the organization. Research has shown that those who are active in seeking information and who become critically involved in their workplace are likely to become more involved in making suggestions and in seeking to change the organization.[2] Once we "know the ropes," our information-seeking communication moves toward information-sharing communication.

Imagine starting a new job for which there was no formal orientation, assimilation process, or training period. Imagine not being taken around and introduced to others or having your job explained to you. Your level of uncertainty would be very high. You would probably feel lost and uncomfortable. Structured indoctrination and planned assimilation not only clarify a new member's role but also increase the new member's satisfaction, commitment to the organization, and confidence in the supervisor.[3]

■ *Individualization*

At the same time that the organization is attempting to assimilate you, you engage in **individualization,** a process in which you attempt to influence the organization to meet your needs. Organizations typically try to counter individualization because it is seen as detrimental to being a "team player." Under the classical approach to organizations, the organization requires everyone to wear the same type of clothing, have the same hairstyle, speak the same way, and behave the same way. Military organizations represent a good example of the attempt to reduce individualization. Military recruits get their hair cut the same way, wear the same clothes, get up at the same time, eat the same food, and talk to their superiors in the same manner.

Have you ever worked for an organization in which there were formal rules about what clothes you could wear and how you were to interact with others? Think, too, of

"Miss Whitney, cancel that memo requiring that personal appearance should reflect our corporate culture."

other organizations where such policies exist—for example, hospitals and fast-food restaurants that require employees to wear uniforms.

What impact is intended by the prescribed appearance and behavior? Do the rules work?

You may not get an organization to make major changes in its rules just to accommodate your needs. A military recruit is unlikely to get the army to change the style of clothing he or she is required to wear. Still, there are more subtle ways for you to individualize the organization: for example, putting family pictures on a desk, bringing in favorite pictures for your office walls, or wearing clothes that you particularly like. The longer your tenure in an organization and the more power that you accrue, the more you will be able to individualize the organization. Individuals can also work collectively to individualize an organization. For example, workers might seek to add on-site daycare centers, change work hours options, or add other benefits.

■ *Advancement to Information Manager*

Eventually, you gain more and more responsibility in an organization and take on the role of information manager. Whatever the formal title that goes with such a position, it means that you become more responsible for communicating information both upward and downward.

Becoming an information manager is accompanied by changes in communication, networks, relationships, and power. Instead of being responsible for acting on information passed down to you, you are now responsible for using communication to manage, coordinate, motivate, persuade, correct, teach, redirect, inspire, and control other employees. Each message you deliver as an information manager affects the progress toward organizational goals.

The purpose of information management is to fulfill the company's goals, the manager's goals, and the subordinates' goals. The manager often uses communication to clarify these goals, to convey the goals to each group, to negotiate differences in the goals, to persuade people to adopt changes in the goals, and to monitor progress toward the goals. In this kind of situation, you need to assess the needs and decide the type of message to deliver. Trying to persuade individuals when they need inspiration will accomplish neither. Trying to motivate when coordination is needed means that subordinates will be frustrated by the chaos. The effective manager will adapt the communication to the needs of the other people and the demands of the situation. This principle is illustrated in Hersey and Blanchard's model of leadership, described in Chapter 10. That model emphasizes that a leader or manager needs to adopt a style of management appropriate to the readiness of the workers.

■ Interpersonal Communication in an Organization

One of the more consistent qualities that organizations desire in their members is good people skills—the ability to interact interpersonally in an effective manner. The establishment, maintenance, and management of interpersonal relationships among coworkers and between subordinates and superiors will enhance organizational quality. Specifically, communication is improved when people have positive feelings about other people in the organization.

The organizational context creates relationships of circumstance because individuals are forced to interact with other people on certain tasks. Constant interaction increases the likelihood that a personal relationship will develop if there is sufficient attraction between the participants.[4] You shouldn't be afraid of making friends with coworkers, superiors, or subordinates, and you can increase your effectiveness in an organization by enacting the interpersonal skills you learned about in Chapters 6 and 7.

Can Managers and Employees Be Friends?*

Joan works as a manager for a manufacturing company. Every day, she interacts with Jack, the vice president of the firm. Jack's dealings with Joan are strictly business. He thinks she is a good worker, but neither likes nor dislikes her. He treats her cordially and with respect. Joan, on the other hand, doesn't like working for Jack because he is not friendly to her.

Could this relationship be improved if it were more friendly in nature? Most employers would shy away from the very notion that Jack and Joan might have a better working relationship if they were friends. After all, companies have long discouraged friendships between managers and subordinates for fear they will lead to biased performance appraisals and other problems.

The reality is that friendships in the workplace can be quite beneficial, both for the individuals involved and the organization. Friendships between managers and employees can improve communications and create a less stressful work environment. Despite the occasional problems that may arise, companies should encourage, not discourage, such relationships.

The author of this article lists a number of benefits to developing friendships with coworkers. How do these benefits compare with your experiences with workplace friendships?

Make New Friends

The value of friendship shows most clearly in our personal lives. In our childhood, adolescence and adulthood, they help define who we are. A friend is someone we know and like—and who provides us with support.

A variety of characteristics can form the basis of a friendship. These include age, sex, race, social class and location (that is, one's proximity to another). Other factors, such as similar attitudes, attractiveness, interests and personality style, also come into play in our choice of friends.

Friendships in the workplace are a natural occurrence because people constantly interact with one another. Two people who work side by side on an assembly line or in the same department may develop a friendship due to location. Two managers in the same company may become friends because they have similar positions. Friendships can and do form between managers and employees because they interact regularly, work on common projects and share common goals.

These friendships give us social support, which helps reduce psychological stress and enhance our mental and physical health. Social support comes from significant others—including friends—who provide us with esteem and help us interpret and clarify our feelings through social comparisons. Managers and employees who are friends provide this social support through direct feedback on the appropriateness of each other's actions.

Beyond that, on-the-job friendships allow people to compare their attitudes and work behaviors with those of others around them. Employees will copy the work behaviors and skills that appear to be successful for their friends and avoid those that are unsuccessful. These friendships also give employees a forum for sharing their work experiences—positive outcomes and complaints alike—with people who are having much the same experiences.

At a more formal level, managers and employees may form friendships through a mentoring process. As the senior employee assists the junior employee in building his or her career, he or she will share information, knowledge and skills. This investment of time and effort, along with the sharing that occurs between the two parties, can naturally lead to a friendship.

Either type of manager-employee friendship—formal or informal—can benefit the organization by creating a more open and positive culture. Managers who are "relationship-oriented" or have a helpful and supportive style provide a better working environment. Employees have fewer grievances about these managers and communicate better with them.

Source: William D. Marelich, "Can We Be Friends? (Managers and Employees)," *HR Focus*, 73, No. 8 (1996), 17.

■ *Interpersonal Dimensions*

The three dimensions of interpersonal relationships discussed in Chapter 6—trust, intimacy, and power—are particularly relevant to understanding organizational relationships. Think about your experiences in organizations in terms of these three dimensions. Your supervisors had power over you in their ability to control your employment, raises, and job assignments. Their power affected your communication and interaction with them. Despite the power differences, there were probably supervisors you trusted a great deal and on whom you could depend. With these people, you probably felt comfortable sharing personal information and having those disclosures reciprocated. You also formed relationships with coworkers, some of whom may have become your close friends and shared with you a high degree of intimacy.

Trust.   One way to think about trust is that it is present when a person believes in and depends on another person.[5] Another way of viewing trust is in terms of uncertainty reduction. The more information you learn about people, the more you can predict their behaviors. You feel comfortable knowing that you can trust another person to act consistently and predictably. Knowing what behavior to expect when you tell your boss about a mistake you made helps you make strategic communicative decisions, regardless of whether the boss will react positively or negatively.

Unlike the pattern in normal relational development, newcomers initially tend to trust their relationships in an organization. That is, newcomers usually enter organizations with a disposition to trust the people. This initial "institutional trust"—a feeling of security based on a faith in the organization—can be transferred to those who make up the organization.[6] There are times, however, when newcomers receive negative information, creating a different expectation.

Intimacy.   Once trust is established, we can feel comfortable disclosing personal information if we choose. The willingness to share personal information corresponds with the development of more intimate relationships and subsequently with a greater flow of information. Providing personal information to other people can help them in their decision-making with respect to you. For instance, disclosing your fear of flying to your boss lets your boss make an informed decision about sending you on an overseas assignment.

Power.   Power exists in all relationships to the degree that individuals influence the actions of their partners. Both parties in a relationship have power; a boss can threaten to fire an employee, leaving the employee without needed income, but an employee can threaten to quit, leaving the boss shorthanded and without that person's expertise. In all organizational relationships, the communication that occurs reflects people's perceptions of their power.

Some supervisors display their power continually in their relationships with subordinates, while others seek to minimize power differences. These contrasting styles are shown in their communication. A boss who wants to display strong power gives orders and commands, while a boss who wants to minimize his or her power makes requests and suggestions.

The organizational structure prescribes certain power relationships between its members. **Position power** stems from a position in the hierarchy that allows control over the distribution of rewards and punishments. Managers use position power to gain compliance from subordinates. **Interpersonal power** occurs when people are able to use the attraction or liking someone feels toward them as a source of influence. Interpersonal power is one way a leader of a small group or team gains compliance from other members.

Both types of power exist in organizational relationships, whether they are between peers or between superiors and subordinates. Theory X managers are

Table 16.1   Characteristics of Successful Influencers

Maintaining a positive attitude and a belief in what they are doing
Creating goals and realistic outcomes
Being flexible about how they achieve their outcomes
Using sensory acuity to help them "read" people from body language signals and other sub-conscious behaviors
Building and maintaining rapport to create strong interpersonal relationships with a large network of people
Treating others as potential allies rather than as enemies
Demonstrating integrity: that is, behaving in ways true to their own beliefs and feelings
Showing concern for the outcomes of others
Behaving "as if" they will succeed
Being known as successful influencers by those around them
Being a good listener

Source: R. Storey, "Influencing," in *Gower Handbook of Management Skills*, 3rd ed., ed. Dorothy M. Stewart (Brookfield, Vt: Gower, 1998), pp. 278–290.

more likely to wield such rewards as raises and promotions as a way of motivating others, while theory Y managers are more likely to try to get employees to like them and do things for them on that basis.

You can use a variety of strategies to influence others in an organization. The threat of punishment is not usually the most effective strategy because it tends to strain the relationship. When you use position power, offering rewards tends to be a more positive way to gain what you want. You can also influence others interpersonally by applying the persuasive strategies discussed in Chapter 12. You can use the knowledge you acquire through your ongoing interactions to develop the most effective compliance-gaining strategies.[7] In fact, you can develop strategies that take advantage of the repeated interaction opportunities you have in an organization;[8] for instance, you can conduct a compliance-gaining campaign that stretches over several days or weeks. Table 16.1 lists some of the characteristics of successful influencers in an organization.

■ *Organizational Friendships*

We carry our social needs with us into the workplace. After you leave college, the workplace will be a major resource for friendships. These relationships not only meet your social needs, but have professional benefits as well. Being friends with colleagues enhances communication, provides a support system, and helps in attainment of organizational goals. Look for opportunities to develop friendships with those who work near you or who have similar job responsibilities.

Just as your nonwork relationships go through developmental stages, so do your organizational relationships. One study found three significant changes in relationships with coworkers: acquaintance to friend, friend to close friend, and close friend to "almost" best friends.[9] Each of these shifts reflects an increase in intimacy, personalness, frequency of interaction, discussion of life events, and socializing. Workplace friendships provide support and help when our supervisors frustrate us, when we have a problematic coworker, and when we are faced with unwanted organizational change.[10]

■ Project Groups and Teams

Chapters 10 and 11 covered the basics you need to know about working effectively in small groups. To conduct their business, organizations use various forms of groups, such as standing committees, *ad hoc* committees, functional teams, quality teams, cross-functional teams, and project teams. The essential dynamics in organizational groups are the same as those discussed in the earlier chapters.

In recent years, organizations have increased their use of groups as a way of creating a more horizontal structure and empowering organizational members. The use of groups reflects a belief in the idea that all organizational members can contribute to solutions and innovations. Inevitably, you will be participating in groups and teams, and eventually, you'll be given the responsibility to manage them.

In this text, the term *small group* has been used to refer to individuals who interpersonally communicate, have a shared goal, and view themselves as a group. The term *team* has a slightly different meaning. A **team** is a coordinated group of individuals organized to work toward a common goal.[11] According to these definitions, teams are sometimes small groups and sometimes not. Teams may exist in name only (a nominal group), in which case the individuals never actually get together and interact interpersonally. For example, you might be a member of the "production team," a label your company applies to anyone involved in production. Whatever the designation, the following sections deal with principles and skills for working with a small group or team.

■ Types of Groups and Teams

Organizations make use of both permanent (standing) groups and temporary (*ad hoc*) groups. A **permanent group** is an ongoing group that is an established part of the organizational structure. There are two types of permanent groups: those in which you are a member as part of your job and in which you remain as long you hold that same position and those whose membership changes over time (for example, standing committees). A **temporary group** is a group that is established to deal with a particular issue and then disbanded (for example, *ad hoc* committees and special project teams). A group of engineers might be brought together to design an improved engine, but once they had developed it, the team would be dissolved.

Organizational teams can be organized on a functional or cross-functional basis. A **functional team** is made up of individuals within the same unit or individuals who have the same skills, expertise, or task responsibilities within the organization. An example would be a team of building managers from throughout a university who meet to discuss similar problems. Another example would be sales representatives who hold a meeting at the end of each week. A **cross-functional team** is made up of people who have different areas of skills, expertise, or task responsibilities. The diversity of these teams is meant to provide a variety of perspectives on a problem. A cross-functional design team, charged with developing a new product, might include a mechanical engineer, a designer, a manufacturing engineer, a market analyst, and a cost analyst.

■ Diversity in Teams

The diversity of cross-functional teams is both an asset and a liability. There is an increase in perspectives, but that also means more conflict and greater communication problems. In groups that are too diverse, the members have a hard time understanding each other and sometimes fail to appreciate perspectives that are different from their own.

As a member of a cross-functional team, you need to seek information from other members that will help you understand their take on an issue. Ask them for more information, seek clarification, try to relate their perspectives to knowledge you already have, and be willing to explain your own perspective. The team may need to take more time on each point than the members would like to ensure that each member has fully explained his or her perspective and understands the other members' perspectives. Each member also needs to reflect his or her understanding of the various other perspectives that have been offered.

Think about task-oriented teams or groups in which you have participated. How diverse was the membership? What impact did the diversity or lack of diversity have on the communication? What impact did it have on the success of the group? How do you think the group's functioning would have changed if the group had possessed more or less diversity?

■ Team Participation

Whatever the type of team or the diversity of the members, the following guidelines can help you be an effective participant:

- Know what is expected of you. Seek clarification of your role and the organization's reasons for wanting you to participate in the team, and prepare to make contributions that fulfill those expectations.
- Make a commitment to the group's goals. If you cannot commit yourself to the team goals, you should seek either to remove yourself or to change the goals.
- Participate fully. Your expertise and perspective are important to quality decision-making.
- Make sure that you, your supervisor, and the organization are aware of the impact your participation in the team will have on your other responsibilities. This may require negotiating a revision of your responsibilities and time commitments.
- Clarify how your performance in the team will be evaluated and how it fits within your individual performance appraisal.

- Be sure to meet deadlines for any contributions requested from you by the team or team leader.
- Check your ego at the door. Your contributions become the property of the team. Be aware that you may not receive individual recognition for your contributions.
- Accept gratification from the team's accomplishments.
- Avoid being competitive and strive instead to be cooperative.
- Seek help from other group members or the team leader whenever necessary.
- Don't be afraid to develop personal relationships with other members. Cross-functional teams are a great way to expand your informal network.

■ *Leadership in Teams*

Teams in organizations usually have an assigned manager. This is often someone who has been identified by the individual who formed the team as having the necessary skills to manage the team. Sometimes, though, the manager is simply the person with the longest tenure in the organization. However he or she acquires the position, the team manager is the official conduit between the group and the organization. Official messages will be channeled through this person.

If you have been made team manager, don't assume that the group members will automatically follow you. Remember that the manager of a team is not necessarily the team leader. Project management is bestowed by the organization, but the team members themselves bestow leadership. The emergence of a leader occurs as the members begin developing their roles. The leader in a group is the one the members turn to for direction, guidance, and advice. Group members give the leader influence over them because they view the leader as competent in managing the task and process.

One of the greatest challenges of new college graduates is being appointed team manager in a group in which other members are likely to emerge as leaders. These other people emerge as leaders because they have more experience and expertise and because they are viewed as leaders by the other team members. Such a situation might be intimidating to you as the manager if you are overly concerned about your status. The best approach is to work with the emergent leader to ensure a successful team. Rather than being threatened by the leader's influence over other members, secure the leader as an ally.

Here are some guidelines for managing a project team:

- Carefully select team members, taking into account their expertise and ability to work effectively in a team. Also consider the most appropriate size of the team for accomplishing its goals.
- Clearly establish the goals of your team with the organization, and communicate these goals to your team members.
- Establish a way of rewarding members' performance with the team. In the final appraisal of each member's performance, his or her participation, the team's success, and the quality of the product should all be considered.
- Gain the necessary commitment of resources from the organization. This includes allowing access to talent and providing time for team members to participate.

- Do as much preplanning as you can. Anticipate the needs of the team and make arrangements to have those needs met. (This can be as simple as arranging for lunch to be served during a team meeting.)
- Work to establish and maintain commitment and involvement from the members.
- Establish easy means of communication among the members, and be sure all members receive the same information. Encourage the members to communicate among themselves even when not in team meetings.
- Manage conflict effectively. Conflict will occur. The success of the team will often depend on establishing a collaborative way of managing conflict.
- Minimize domination by any one member.
- Keep the group focused on the task and on schedule.

■ Briefings and Reports

The theory and principles presented in the chapters on presentations (Chapters 12 through 14) apply to making presentations within the organizational context. Organizational presentations are part of the overall communication process utilized by organizations to get information from one segment to another. Members of organizations are often called on to provide presentations such as briefings, status reports, problem reports, and updates.

An oral *report* is usually detailed, while a *briefing* provides only essential information. Both of these presentational methods are meant to be informative rather than argumentative. They are often used in the context of a meeting in which the speaker may or may not be a participant. Briefings and reports frequently involve providing information to organizational members charged with decision-making. One goal, for example, may be to teach the audience about a particular topic. Table 16.2 offers a typical outline for a briefing.

Because briefings and reports occur within the context of an organization, the presentation isn't "public" speaking but rather "private" speaking "within the family."[12] As a presenter, you generally share organizational goals with your audi-

---

Table 16.2   Typical Briefing Outline

What did we hope would happen? State the key business issues. Present the goals for the month, quarter, or year.

What happened? Present the actual performance during the review period. Present a summary (often statistical in nature) of the performance during the period under review in relation to expected performance.

What is happening right now? Present the current status. This is a brief statement of the most current conditions.

Why did it happen? Present an analysis of the reasons for the performance. Provide a brief summary of the positive and negative factors that affected the results.

What is going to happen? Explain the future projections of performance, assuming that current circumstances continue.

What might be done? Present alternatives to decision-makers that can sustain or improve performance.

Source: Adapted from materials developed by Terry A. Pickett and Associates, Ames, Iowa.

ence and have considerable commonalities, and your presentation occurs in concert with other organizational communication. Before your presentation, you can visit with those who will be in the audience and determine the type of information they would like you to cover. You can accompany your presentation with written documents before, during, or after the presentation. Also, because the presentation takes place in-house, the audience members will have ready access to you afterward. They can seek more detail, challenge your facts, and provide feedback. In these ways, briefings and reports represent a dynamic component of multichannel organizational communication.

The organizational culture often dictates the style to be followed in giving a briefing or report. You will need to determine the organizational expectations for your presentation. Regretfully, the expected style is not always the most effective, but deviating from the norm with the intent of making the presentation better can undermine your presentation. Making changes in the presentational norms requires strategic action, such as clearing the change in advance or introducing your change gradually. For instance, the organization might expect that everyone use a large number of overheads, regardless of whether they add any true informational value. You might change your monthly briefings by slowly cutting back on the number of overheads until you reach the number you believe is most effective.

Remember, giving a briefing may be part of your job description, and your presentational performance may be evaluated. That evaluation can have a direct impact on raises, promotions, and other job assignments.

■ Computer-Mediated Communication: Email

One of the most significant recent changes in organizations has been the rapid adoption of email and the Internet. It is likely that you already use email in your personal life and perhaps to contact instructors, advisors, or other students. But there are distinct differences between official email and personal email.

In Chapter 2, you learned that every message has a relational dimension. Email messages are no different. For instance, we often use emoticons—graphic representations of emotions, such as the :) symbol, known as a smiley—in personal email messages, but should you do so in professional email communications? Email can seduce you into assuming a more personal relationship with other organizational members than is actually appropriate. It probably would be inappropriate to use a smiley in an email message to the president of an organization unless you were on very friendly terms and the message was not serious. An official email should follow the same basic guidelines as a hard-copy, typed memo. The tone and content should reflect the nature of the relationship.

As with any other form of communication, there are effective and ineffective ways of using email. Its primary advantages are speed, distribution, and interactivity; its primary disadvantages are speed, distribution, and interactivity.

Using any of the popular search engines, conduct a search using the keyword "effective email." There may be a lot of redundancy in the sites you find, but look through some of them and read some of the suggestions. What suggestions appear most

often? How many of these guidelines do you practice in your own emailing? Which ones do you violate?

■ Speed

A major advantage of email is the ability to compose a memo quickly and distribute it almost instantly. This is valuable when we need to get information to individuals in a timely manner. Taking advantage of speed means that we usually compose email more concisely than other messages. The ability to attach large documents to email messages also provides another advantage: We can quickly retrieve and forward requested documents.

Yet, the speed of email often leads people to distribute messages so quickly that they don't consider the impact carefully enough. You might communicate things you would rather take back; however, email can't be recalled. Using email for rapid communication also increases the chances of errors in spelling, content, and grammar. Despite the ease of running an email through a spell checker, many people are so absorbed with acting quickly that they fail to utilize this function or to proofread their messages for grammatical and factual errors. Your emails create an impression in the receiver, and errors reflect poorly on your knowledge and skills. Your email messages should reflect your professionalism and competence.

Speed can also lead to an escalation of emotions. In personal online settings, *flaming*—making derogatory remarks about another person—tends to escalate, especially in chat rooms, because users respond during fits of emotion. This same effect can happen to you within an organization. You might be upset with some news or decision that affects you and therefore be inclined to react vehemently. Sending a hot-tempered email might work against your ultimate objectives. In such a situation, write the email if you must, but don't send it until you have had a chance to walk away from it for a while. Go back to the message when you are more relaxed and then decide if what you have written will accomplish your overall goals.

■ Distribution

Email is easy to distribute to a wide variety of individuals. You can create mailing lists that distribute messages to a large number of readers. Many organizations create their own mailing lists that any individual can use to route messages. These lists are generally established because of some commonality among the list members. For example, a list might include the sales staff, middle managers, members of the accounting department, or clients.

The disadvantage of wide and easy distribution is that readers get inundated with email messages, many of which are of little interest to them. In addition, a message is sometimes sent without the necessary context. Suppose two members of a mailing list engage in a private dialogue that results in a decision to make a policy change. If a memo about the new policy is then distributed to everyone, it may seem to come out of the blue. The other readers may be confused because they lack the pertinent background knowledge. To avoid such a problem, email users should provide their readers with a summary of the necessary context, just as they would in a more formal memo or report.

■ *Interactivity*

Email can be used as written conversation. It has elements similar to an interpersonal interaction, though it takes place through deliberative correspondence. There is a certain amount of personalness fostered by the interactivity of email. This makes it an effective tool for negotiation, clarification, and the development of shared meaning, as illustrated in Figure 16.1.

The interactivity of email also means that some errors can be more easily corrected than in other written forms of communication. The receiver can quickly ask for clarification. For example, someone announces a meeting for Friday, February 12; however, February 12 is a Thursday. The recipient can quickly respond by asking if the meeting is on Thursday or Friday.

The interactivity of email often leads a sender to expect a quick response by the receiver. A colleague's mother recently got her own personal computer and email account to save on long-distance phone calls. However, she keeps calling her son about a half-hour after she sends an email, asking him why he hasn't replied. She views email as similar to a phone conversation and considers it rude if a recipient doesn't immediately reply to her message. In organizations, the

To: John@Ourcompany.com
From: Mary@Ourcompany.com
Re: Scheduling a meeting to discuss new hire

John:

Can you meet with me this Friday at noon to discuss the applicant pool?

Mary

- -

To: Mary@Ourcompany.com
From: John@Ourcompany.com
Re: Scheduling a meeting to discuss new hire

>Can you meet with me this Friday at noon to discuss the applicant pool?

I can't. I've got a prior commitment. I'm open at 10 and 2 on Friday.

John

- -

To: John@Ourcompany.com
From: Mary@Ourcompany.com
Re: Scheduling a meeting to discuss new hire

>I can't. I've got a prior commitment. I'm open at 10 and 2 on Friday.

John:

These times won't work for me. How about *Monday* at noon?

Mary

Figure 16.1

Sample Email Interaction

This is a series of messages between John and Mary, who are trying to arrange a meeting time. Note the use of the symbol > to mark lines quoted from an earlier message.

Table 16.3 Guidelines for Using Email

Use a spell checker and grammar checker, and proofread for errors in content.
Don't be too quick. Slow down and think before emailing.
Send some form of reply to emails that are directed to you individually.
The need to respond to emails from a mailing list depends on the nature of the message. Nonetheless, you may still want to provide feedback.
In responding to list-based email, decide whether you need to copy all the other recipients or reply just to the sender. Be careful that the email isn't forwarded automatically to people for whom you don't intend it.
Use the subject line—and keep the phrase you enter there short and to the point. People often prioritize their emails by subject and choose to ignore those seen as less relevant.
Include originators' subject lines when replying, so they know to what you are replying. You can include the entire original document for reference; or, if you are referring to individual lines, indicate these lines with the symbol > (see Figure 16.1).
Use spacing. Include space between paragraphs, not just indents. The way you type the message isn't necessarily the way it will look on the recipient's screen.
Keep the message short. Let the recipient ask for more information if necessary. Twenty-five lines (one computer page) is the general recommended maximum length.
Keep each message to one topic. You can create more than one email if necessary to cover more than one topic.
For light emphasis, you can use *asterisks* to surround a word, as shown by the last message in Figure 16.1.
Heavy emphasis can be achieved by CAPITALIZING the word you are emphasizing. You can use exclamation marks to emphasize an entire sentence!!!

situation may not be as dramatic, but nonetheless, there is often an expectation that email is part of an ongoing interaction. Failing to respond, or delaying the response, may be seen negatively by the sender.

Table 16.3 summarizes a number of guidelines for using email effectively.

■ Managerial Communication

Most of the skills discussed thus far apply to any position in an organization. When you begin taking on management responsibilities, however, there are particular communication skills that add to your effectiveness. Just as leaders assume different responsibilities in a group, so do managers assume different responsibilities than employees.

Numerous surveys have been conducted to find out what skills employers most need in their managers. One such survey of human relations managers conducted in 1996 found that the most significant skill deficiencies among management personnel were in listening and interpersonal communication.[13] The need for cross-cultural communication skills was also reported by 50 percent of the respondents. The ability to manage conflict was also frequently cited.

Before we explore some of these areas further, try the Test Yourself to evaluate your own potential communication skills as an organizational manager.

Effective organizational teams require clear goals and effective leadership.

Researchers have identified a number of areas in which organizational managers need to be skillful.[14] To what degree do you feel you are skilled in each of the following areas? Rate yourself on a scale from 1 (no skills) to 5 (highly skilled).

Test Yourself

1. Business writing	1	2	3	4	5
2. Interviewing	1	2	3	4	5
3. Group decision-making process	1	2	3	4	5
4. Oral presentations	1	2	3	4	5
5. Managing conflict	1	2	3	4	5
6. Leadership/management techniques	1	2	3	4	5
7. Interpersonal relationships	1	2	3	4	5
8. Computer-mediated communication	1	2	3	4	5
9. Listening	1	2	3	4	5
10. Motivating people	1	2	3	4	5
11. Handling grievances	1	2	3	4	5
12. Giving directions	1	2	3	4	5
13. Delegating authority	1	2	3	4	5

| 14. Negotiating skills | 1 | 2 | 3 | 4 | 5 |
| 15. Diagnosing organizational problems | 1 | 2 | 3 | 4 | 5 |

Total your scores. If you scored below 45, you should carefully review the areas that you need to improve. Even if your score is above 45, look at the particular items on which your score was low. Your experience in this course should have resulted in some improvements in many of these areas. However, you should consider ways that you can further improve any skills in which you are still deficient.

■ Listening

Listening and reading are important ways to acquire information. Gaining information reduces uncertainty, improves decision-making, and increases goal fulfillment. Most of us get caught up with feeling that we need to talk and contribute, and often we do so without a clear understanding of what is needed. Actively listening to others give us a foundation on which to be a more effective manager.

In Chapter 3, you read about the various types of listening as well as some of the problems that impede effective listening. In organizations, listening gives you information, which in turn gives you power. You need to listen objectively and actively seek information from the other person. Approach each of your interactions with organizational members as an opportunity to learn more and perform your job more effectively. Focus your energy and attention on the speaker. Remember that you need to show nonverbally that you are listening. Use confirming responses to communicate your willingness and commitment to listen. These techniques will help you nurture positive relationships so that individuals feel comfortable talking with you and sharing news. Listening to peers provides you with a rich source of information about organizational developments.

As for your superiors, listening effectively to them means that you increase the likelihood of performing tasks correctly. Active listening will help ensure that you completely understand what your superiors are telling you. People tend to assume that when you misunderstand them, it is not because they did not explain themselves well, but because you didn't listen well. Make sure you listen well.

Listening to subordinates allows you to seek changes that will help them accomplish their tasks more effectively. Up to 70 percent of workers don't express their disagreement with management because they fear that it will have a negative effect on their career.[15] You will need to build positive interpersonal relationships and establish trust, as discussed earlier in this chapter, to ensure the open flow of communication.

■ Conflict Management

Conflict is inevitable in organizations. Managers have the responsibility to address and manage conflict. However, conflict management is often an uncomfortable proposition, and some managers simply choose to ignore conflicts, hoping they will go away. Unfortunately, ignoring a conflict usually exacerbates the situation.

Constructive conflict, in which ideas are challenged in a positive way, is a healthy phenomenon. Destructive conflict, in which one party is simply attempting to threaten another party's face or undermine the other party's goal, reflects an unhealthy environment. Destructive conflict has to be addressed as a problem in and of itself. For example, if two of your subordinates are constantly backbiting each other, the group's overall effectiveness is undermined. As manager, you need to address this problem.

As a manager, you may be one of the parties involved in the conflict, or you may need to mediate other people's conflicts. In either situation, power differences may intimidate others into agreeing to a solution with which they are dissatisfied, thus creating long-term problems. Despite the power differences, conflicts with superiors or subordinates can all be handled effectively by using a collaborative approach. As you may recall from Chapter 5, this approach involves attempting to develop a solution in which both parties' goals are obtained.

Since Chapter 5 had a great deal to say about managing conflicts in which you are a participant, we'll concentrate here on your potential role in **third-party intervention**—that is, your role when you are not directly involved in the conflict but have to intervene between two parties. This is a position in which you may frequently find yourself as a manager.

As shown in Table 16.4, third-party interventions range from simply encouraging the disputants to talk about their problem to formal adjudication, in which you act like a judge rendering a verdict. The type of intervention depends on such variables as the importance of the issue, time pressures, the nature of the dispute, the relationship between the parties, and the likelihood of their commitment to a solution.[16] All of these factors will dictate which of the intervention options in Table 16.4 would be best for a particular situation.

No matter which method you choose, intervening in a conflict starts with deciding what the goals of your intervention should be. The following general goals provide a useful approach:[17]

Table 16.4 **Common Conflict Intervention Roles You May Play as a Manager**

Rule	How to Intervene
Encourager	You let the parties know that they must resolve the conflict, but leave it to them to find the means. This is the method parents use when they tell their children to go into a room and settle the issue for themselves.
Facilitator	You bring the parties together and facilitate the interaction. You actively ask questions and help focus the discussion. This role may include helping the parties collaborate on reaching a settlement.
Mediator	You listen to both sides, make suggestions, offer solutions, and eventually work to persuade the parties toward agreement.*
Arbitrator	Both parties voluntarily agree to have you make a decision after hearing both sides. The focus is on content, with limited regard for relational factors. Assuming your decision is binding, you risk alienating one of the parties. Ideally, though, you can find a solution that satisfies both parties.
Adjudicator	One party forces the other to have the issue addressed and judged, and you as manager serve as the judge. Adjudication is typically used to address issues such as disciplinary breaches and sexual harassment.

* J. L. Hocker and W. W. Wilmot, *Interpersonal Conflict*, 3rd ed. (Dubuque, Iowa: Brown, 1991).

1. You want to ensure that the organization's goals are being met. One of your responsibilities as manager is to have your unit contribute to the organization's goals as best it can. Any time a conflict interferes with that effort, you have a responsibility and a right to intervene.
2. You want, ideally, to resolve the conflict; but at the very least, you want to reduce its impact on the organization.
3. The process for resolving the conflict needs to be fair, equitable, impartial, and objective. Most of the time, people will accept a solution that might not include everything they would like as long as they feel that the solution was reached fairly. Dissatisfaction with interventions occurs when the participants feel that the process was tainted and biased.
4. A balance needs to be struck between (a) resolving the conflict quickly and with minimum expense and (b) resolving the conflict effectively. As a manager, you could simply tell the parties what to do. While that might be efficient, it generally would prove ineffective. Resolving conflicts effectively may take considerable time and energy.
5. The participants need to be committed to the solution. That commitment can take the form of willing acceptance and support or simply an acceptance of your authority to impose the solution. The former is preferable, because imposing a solution requires much more monitoring and enforcement on your part.

Summary

Your progress through an organization parallels the development of an interpersonal relationship. As you move from your first interview to executive management, you will be faced with changes in communication. The initiation stage may include rituals that you experience as you are accepted into the organization. Training periods vary in length from organization to organization as newcomers are indoctrinated into the company's culture. Assimilation into an organization involves aligning your values and goals with those of the organization. This process uses both the formal and informal communication networks. Supervisors often have the primary responsibility for assimilating newcomers.

Newcomers are motivated to learn about the organization and about their roles in order to reduce uncertainty and accomplish their own goals. At the same time, newcomers begin their attempts at individualization, which involves trying to change the organization to meet their own needs.

As you advance to the role of a manager in the organization, you become more responsible for communicating information both upward and downward. You have to adapt your communication to the needs of your subordinates and the demands of the situation.

Effective interpersonal communication skills can significantly improve your organizational life. Positive relationships help facilitate communication with other organizational members and satisfy basic social needs. The interpersonal dimensions of trust, power, and intimacy all have an impact on the flow of communication within organizations. Trust and power provide a basis for influencing other people and fulfilling goals. Newcomers seem to transfer an initial "institutional trust" to the members of the organization. Power can be either position power, which derives from the ability to control rewards and punishments, or interpersonal power, in which attraction toward the person gives him or her a base for influence.

In your organizational life, you probably will find yourself in both permanent groups and temporary groups. Permanent groups are part of the organizational structure, while temporary groups are created on an *ad hoc* basis to address a particular issue. These groups can be either functional (made up of members with similar expertise) or cross-functional (made up of people with different fields of expertise). Each type has advantages and disadvantages: Diversity increases the likelihood of group creativeness but increases the potential for conflict and communication problems.

The guidelines for participating in organizational teams include knowing what is expected of you, participating fully, and clarifying how your performance will be evaluated. At some point, you are likely to be made the manager of a team. The guidelines for effectively managing a project team include establishing clear goals, selecting the right participants, managing conflict effectively, and keeping the team on schedule and focused on the task.

Organizations frequently use presentations such as briefings, reports, and updates. The goal is typically informative, with the information directed toward decision-makers. The style of the presentation is often dictated by organizational cultural rules. The typical briefing involves answering the following questions: What did we hope would happen? What happened? What is happening right now? Why did it happen? What is going to happen? What might be done?

Another facet of the communication process in organizations is email. Email provides speed, easy and wide distribution, and interactivity. These are both advantages and disadvantages. Official email needs to be composed with care to reflect professionalism and competence. You should consider thoroughly what you want to say and to whom. Email invites rapid and broad distribution that at times is counterproductive. Proper use of email involves using spell checkers, keeping each message to one topic and to no more than twenty-five lines, and referencing appropriate previous email messages.

Among the communication skills needed by managers, listening and conflict management are especially important. Effective listening is absolutely necessary for the acquisition of information. Active listening is recom-mended for effective management because it encourages the open flow of information.

Managers must manage conflicts in which they are participants and also conflicts in which they begin merely as observers. You are encouraged to use a collaborative conflict management style, focusing on solutions that meet the needs of all the parties involved. Conflicts need to be managed in such a way as to protect the goals of the organization and its members. In intervening in conflicts between your subordinates, you may be called on to play the role of encourager, facilitator, mediator, arbitrator, or adjudicator.

assimilation The process of aligning an individual's values and goals with those of the organization.

role shock The feeling you get when you find out that a job is not what you expected.

individualization A process in which you attempt to influence the organization to meet your needs.

position power The ability to influence others stemming from a position in the hierarchy that allows control over the distribution of rewards and punishments.

interpersonal power People's ability to use the attraction or liking someone feels toward them as a source of influence.

team A coordinated group of individuals organized to work toward a common goal.

permanent group An ongoing group that is an established part of the organizational structure.

temporary group A group that is established to deal with a particular issue and then disbanded.

functional team A team made up of individuals within the same unit or individuals who have the same skills, expertise, or task responsibilities within the organization.

cross-functional team A team made up of people who have different areas of skills, expertise, or task responsibilities.

third-party intervention Intervention in a conflict by a person who is not one of the conflicting parties.

Review Questions

1. Explain the stages that are likely to occur in your life cycle in an organization.
2. Explain how the three dimensions of interpersonal relationships (power, trust, and intimacy) relate to your relationships in an organization.
3. Identify some of the guidelines you should follow as a member of organizational teams or groups.
4. Discuss some of the topics that are usually addressed in giving a briefing.
5. Identify some of the guidelines that should be followed in sending email in an organization.
6. In what ways are listening and conflict management important in managerial communication?

Notes

Chapter 1

1. Olsten Forum survey of human resource issues and trends, 1996.
2. F. E. X. Dance and C. E. Larson, *Speech Communication: Concepts and Behavior* (New York: Holt, Rinehart & Winston, 1972).
3. W. W. Wilmot, *Dyadic Communication: A Transactional Perspective* (Reading, Mass.: Addison-Wesley, 1975).
4. D. K. Berlo, *The Process of Communication: An Introduction to Theory and Practice* (New York: Holt, Rinehart & Winston, 1960).
5. These components include some elements first identified in a model of electronic communication developed at Bell Telephone Laboratories by mathematician Claude Shannon and explained by Warren Weaver. The resulting theory is referred to as the Shannon-Weaver model of communication. See C. Shannon and W. Weaver, *The Mathematical Theory of Communication* (Carbondale: University of Illinois Press, 1949).
6. D. Berlo, *The Process of Communication.*
7. Ibid.
8. P. Watzlawick, J. H. Beavin, and D. D. Jackson, *Pragmatics of Human Communication* (New York: Norton, 1967).
9. Dance and Larson, *Speech Communication.*
10. Ibid.
11. L. S. Vygotsky, *Thought and Language* (Cambridge, Mass.: The MIT Press, 1962).
12. S. Beebe, S. Beebe and M. V. Redmond, *Interpersonal Communication: Relating to Others* (Boston, Mass: Allyn & Bacon, 1999).
13. S. A. Beebe and J. T. Masterson, *Communicating in Small Groups: Principles and Practice* 5th ed. (New York: Longman, 1997). See also J. D. Rothwell, *In Mixed Company: Small Group Communication,* 3rd ed. (Forth Worth, Tex.: Harcourt Brace, 1998).
14. Rothwell, *In Mixed Company.*
15. C. Conrad, *Strategic Organizational Communication,* 3rd ed. (Fort Worth, Tex.: Harcourt Brace, 1994).
16. T. L. Albrecht and B. Wackernagel Bach, *Communication in Complex Organizations: A Relational Approach,* (Fort Worth, Tex.: Harcourt Brace, 1997).
17. Definitions of intercultural communication often reflect the author's conception of communication and culture.

For example, "Intercultural communication is a symbolic process in which people from different cultures create shared meanings," from M. W. Lustig and J. Koester, *Intercultural Competence: Interpersonal Communication Across Cultures,* (New York: Longman, 1999), p. 52. Compare that definition with the following: "Intercultural communication is a transactional, symbolic process involving the attribution of meaning between people from different cultures," from W. B. Gudykunst and Y. Y. Kim, *Communicating with Strangers: An Approach to Intercultural Communication,* 2nd ed. (New York: McGraw-Hill, 1992), pp. 13–14.

Chapter 2

1. A. Maslow, *Toward a Psychology of Being,* 2nd ed. (New York: Van Nostrand, Reinhold, 1982).
2. D. Ehninger, *Influence, Belief, and Argument: An Introduction to Responsible Persuasion* (Glenview, Ill.: Scott, Foresman, 1974).
3. P. Zimbardo and E. Ebbesen, *Influencing Attitudes and Changing Behavior* (Reading, Mass: Addison-Wesley, 1969).
4. S. Bem, "The Measurement of Psychological Androgyny," *Journal of Consulting and Clinical Psychology,* 42, (1974), 155–162.
5. G. Hofstede, *Culture's Consequences* (Beverly Hills, Calif.: Sage Publications, 1980).
6. Ibid.
7. W. Gudykunst and Y. Y. Kim, *Communicating with Strangers* (New York: McGraw-Hill, 1992).
8. Ibid.
9. D. Harris, "How Does Your Pay Stack Up?" (Salary Survey 1996), *Working Woman,* 21, No. 2 (1996), 27.
10. E. Hall, *The Hidden Dimension* (Garden City, N.J.: Doubleday, 1966).
11. M. W. Lustig and J. Koester, *Intercultural Competence: Interpersonal Communication Across Cultures,* 3rd ed. (New York: Longman, 1999), 30.
12. B. J. Broom (1991). Building shared meaning: Implications of a relational approach to empathy for teaching intercultural communication. *Communication Education,* 40, 235–249.
13. R. A. Clark & J. G. Delia (1979). Topoi and rhetorical competence. *Quarterly Journal of Speech,* 65, 187–206.

14. P. Brown & S. Levinson (1978). Universals in language usage: Politeness phenomena. In E. N. Goody (Ed.), *Questions and politeness: Strategies in social interaction.* Cambridge: Cambridge University Press.

15. C. R. Berger & J. J. Bradac (1982). *Language and social knowledge: Uncertainty in interpersonal relations.* Baltimore, MD: Edward Arnold.

16. Berger & Bradac (1982).

Chapter 3

1. M. Argyle, *The Psychology of Interpersonal Behaviour,* 2nd ed. (Baltimore: Penguin Books, 1972).

2. F. Hieder, *The Psychology of Interpersonal Relations* (New York: Wiley, 1958).

3. H. H. Kelley, "Attribution Theory in Social Psychology," in *Nebraska Symposium on Motivation,* ed. D. Levine (Lincoln: University of Nebraska Press, 1967), pp. 192–238. Also see H.H. Kelley, "Attribution in Social Interaction," in *Attribution: Perceiving the Causes of Behavior* ed. E. E. Jones, D. E. Kanouse, H. H. Kelley, R. E. Nisbett, S. Valins, and B. Weiner (Morristown, N.J.: General Learning Press, 1972), pp. 1–26.

4. D. J. Schneider, A. H. Hastorf, and P. C. Ellsworth, *Person Perception,* 2nd ed. (Reading, Mass.: Addison-Wesley, 1979).

5. M. S. Hanna, "Speech Communication Training Needs in the Business Community," *Central States Speech Journal,* 29, (1978), 163–172.

6. A. D. Wolvin and C. G. Coakley, "A Survey of the Status of Listening Training in Some Fortune 500 Corporations," *Communication Education,* 40, (1991), 152–164.

7. L. O. Cooper, "Listening Competency in the Workplace: A Model for Training," *Business Communication Quarterly,* 60 (1997), 75–85.

8. M. V. Redmond, "The Functions of Empathy (Decentering) in Human Relations," *Human Relations,* 42 (1989), 593–605.

9. L. O. Cooper, "Listening Competency in the Workplace."

10. K. N. Cissna and E. Sieburg, "Patterns of Interactional Confirmation and Disconfirmation," in *Rigor and Imagination: Essays from the Legacy of Gregory Bateson,* ed. (New York: Praeger, 1981), pp. 253–282.

11. Adapted from K. N. Cissna and E. Sieburg, "Patterns of Interactional Conformation and Disconfirmation."

12. R. B. Adler, L. B. Rosenfeld, and N. Towne, *Interplay: The Process of Interpersonal Communication,* 4th ed. (New York: Holt, Rinehart & Winston, 1989).

13. K. N. Cissna and E. Sieburg, "Patterns of Interaction Confirmation and Disconfirmation."

Chapter 4

1. F. E. X. Dance and C. E. Larson *Speech Communication: Concepts and Behaviors* (New York: Holt, Rinehart & Winston, 1972).

2. C. K. Ogden and I. A. Richards, *The Meaning of Meaning* (London: Kegan Paul, Trench, Trubner, 1923).

3. N. Chovil, "Equivocation as an Interactional Event," in *The Dark Side of Interpersonal Communication,* ed. W. R. Cupack and B. H. Spitzberg, (Hillsdale, N.J.: Lawrence Erlbaum, 1994), pp. 105–123.

4. D. Bolinger and D. A. Sears, *Aspects of Language,* 3rd ed. (New York: Harcourt Brace, 1981). See also A. G. Smith, *Communication and Culture* (New York: Holt, Rinehart & Winston, 1966).

5. T. J. Harris, "I know It was the Blood: Defining the Biracial Self in a Euro-American Society, *Our Voices: Essays in Culture, Ethnicity, and Communication* ed. A. Gonzalez, M. Houston, and V. Chen, (Los Angeles: Roxbury, 1997), pp. 149–156.

6. C. E. Osgood, "Studies on the Generality of Affective Meaning Systems," *American Psychologist,* 17 (1962): 10–28.

7. M. L. Knapp, *Nonverbal Communication in Human Interaction* (New York: Holt, Rinehart & Winston, 1978), p. 285.

8. See, for example, E. H. Hess, *The Tell-Tale Eye: How Your Eyes Reveal Hidden Thoughts and Emotions.* (New York: Van Nostrand Reinhold, 1975).

9. J. K. Burgoon, T. Birk, and M. Pfau, "Nonverbal Behaviors, Persuasion, and Credibility," *Human Communication Research,* 17 (1990): 140–169.

10. S. E. Jones and A. E. Yarbrough, "A Naturalistic Study of the Meanings of Touch," *Communication Monographs,* 52 (1985): 19–56.

11. Knapp, *Nonverbal Communication in Human Interaction.*

12. E. T. Hall *The Hidden Dimension,* (Garden City, N.Y.: Doubleday, 1966).

13. E. T. Hall, *The Silent Language,* (Greenwich, Conn.: Fawcett, 1959).

14. V. P. Richmond and J. C. McCroskey, *Nonverbal Behaviors in Interpersonal Relations,* 3rd ed. (Boston: Allyn & Bacon, 1995).

15. R. Ardrey, *The Territorial Imperative,* (New York: Dell, 1966).

16. J. K. Burgoon and J. Hale, "Nonverbal Expectancy Violations: Model Elaboration and Application to Immediacy Behaviors," *Communication Monographs,* 55 (1988): 57–79.

17. Ibid.

18. I. Goffman, *The Presentation of Self in Everyday Life,* (Garden City, N.Y.: Doubleday Anchor, 1959).

19. J. Fast, *Body Language,* (New York: Pocket Books, 1970), pp. 83–84.

20. A. Mehrabian, *Silent Messages* (Belmont, Calif.: Wadsworth, 1971).

21. J. K. Burgoon, et. al., "Relational Messages Associated with Nonverbal Behaviors," *Human Communication Research,* 10 (1984): 351–378.

22. Mehrabian, *Silent Messages.*

23. Burgoon et al, "Relational Messages Associated with Nonverbal Behaviors."

24. Mehrabian, *Silent Messages.*

25. J. K. Burgoon, and L. Dillman, and L. A. Stern, "Adaptation in Dyadic Interaction: Defining and Operationalizing

Patterns of Reciprocity and Compensation," *Communication Theory*, 3 (1993): 295–316.

26. Ibid.

27. Mehrabian, *Silent Messages*.

28. Knapp, *Nonverbal Communication in Human Interaction*.

Chapter 5

1. R. A. Clark and J. G. Delia, "*Topoi* and Rhetorical Competence," *The Quarterly Journal of Speech*, 65, (1979): 197–206.

2. W. R. Cupach and S. Metts, *Facework*, (Thousand Oaks, Calif.: Sage, 1994).

3. Ibid.

4. Ibid.

5. M. L. McLauglin, W. J. Cody, and H. D. O'Hair, "The Management of Failure Events: Some Contextual Determinants of Accounting Behavior," *Human Communication Research*, 9 (1983): 208–224.

6. Cupach and Metts, *Facework*.

7. McLauglin, Cody and O'Hair, "The Management of Failure Events."

8. Ibid.

9. Ibid.

10. Ibid.

11. S. Petronio, "The Use of Communication Boundary Perspective to Contextualize Embarrassment Research," *Communication Yearbook/13*, ed. J. Anderson (Newbury Park, Calif.: Sage, 1990), pp. 365–373.

12. S. Metts, and W. R. Cupach, "Situational Influence on the Use of Remedial Strategies in Embarrassing Situations," *Communication Monographs*, 56 (1989): 151–162. See also W. R. Cupach and S. Metts, "The Effects of Type of Predicament and Embarrassability on Remedial Responses to Embarrassing Situations," *Communication Quarterly*, 40 (1992): 149–161.

13. D. B. Buller and J. K. Burgoon, "Deception: Strategic and Nonstrategic Communication," in *Strategic Interpersonal Communication*, ed. J. A. Daly and J. M. Wiemann, (Hillsdale, N.J.: Lawrence Erlbaum, 1994), pp. 191–223. See also H. D. O'Hair and M. J. Cody, "Deception," in *The Dark Side of Interpersonal Communication*, ed. W. R. Cupach and B. H. Spitzberg (Hillsdale, N.J.: Lawrence Erlbaum, 1994), pp. 181–213.

14. Ibid.

15. J. W. Neuliep and M. Mattson, "The Use of Deception as a Compliance-Gaining Strategy," *Human Communication Research*, 16 (1990): 409–421.

16. J. K. Burgoon, et al. "Interpersonal Deception: V. Accuracy in Deception Detection," *Communication Monographs*, 61 (1994): 303–325. Also see S. A. McCornack and T. R. Levine, "When Lovers Become Leery: The Relationship Between Suspicion and Accuracy in Detecting Deception," *Communication Monographs*, 57 (1990): 219–230.

17. D. B. Buller, K. D. Strzyzewski, and F. G. Hunsaker, "Interpersonal Deception: II. The Inferiority of Conversational Participants as Deception Detectors," *Communication Monographs*, 58 (1991): 25–40.

18. McCornack and Levine, "When Lovers Become Leery."

19. Burgoon et al., "Interpersonal Deception."

20. M. A. deTurk and G. R. Miller, "Training Observers to Detect Deception: Effects of Self-Monitoring and Rehearsal," *Human Communication Research*, 16 (1990): 603–620.

21. M. A. deTurk and G. R. Miller, "Deception and Arousal: Isolating the Behavior Correlates of Deception," *Human Communication Research*, 12 (1985): 181–202.

22. D. B. Buller, K. D. Strzyzewski and J. Comstock, "Interpersonal Deception: I. Deceiver's Reactions to Receiver's Suspicions and Probing," *Communication Monographs*, 58 (1991): 1–24.

23. D. A. Infante and C. J. Wigley, III, "Verbal Aggressiveness: An Interpersonal Model and Measure," *Communication Monographs*, 53 (1986): 61–69.

24. Ibid.

25. J. L. Hocker and W. W. Wilmot, *Interpersonal Conflict*, 3rd ed. (Dubuque, Iowa: Brown, 1991).

26. Discussion of the advantages and disadvantages draws from J. L. Hocker and W. W. Wilmot, *Interpersonal Conflict*, 2nd ed. (Dubuque, Iowa: Brown, 1985).

27. J. Gibb, "Defensive Communication," *Journal of Communication*, 11 (1961): 141–148.

Chapter 6

1. S. A. Beebe, S. J. Beebe, and M. V. Redmond, *Interpersonal Communication: Relating to Others*, 2nd ed. (Needham Heights, Mass.: Allyn & Bacon, 1999).

2. F. Millar and L. Rogers, "A Relational Approach to Interpersonal Communication," in *Explorations in Interpersonal Communication*, Miller (Beverly Hills, Calif.: Sage, 1976), pp. 87–104.

3. Ibid.

4. M. Knapp and A. Vangelisti, *Interpersonal Communication and Human Relations*, 3rd ed. (Needham Heights, Mass.: Simon & Schuster, 1996).

5. L. A. Baxter, "Cognition and Communication in the Relationship Process," in *Accounting for Relationships: Explanations, Representation, and Knowledge*, ed. R. Burnett, P. McGhee, and D. Clarke, (New York: Methuen, 1987), pp. 192–212.

6. I. Altman and D. A. Taylor, *Social Penetration: The Development of Interpersonal Relationships* (New York: Holt, Rinehart & Winston, 1973).

7. G. Miller and M. Parks, "Communication in Dissolving Relationships," in *Personal Relationships*, ed. S. W. Duck (New York: Academic Press, 1982), pp. 127–154.

8. L. A. Baxter, "A Dialectical Perspective on Communication Strategies in Relationship Development," in *Handbook of Personal Relationships*, ed. S. Duck (New York: Wiley, 1988), pp. 257–273.

9. Baxter, "Cognition and Communication in the Relationship Process."

10. Ibid.

11. Ibid.

12. D. A. Taylor and I. Altman, "Communication in Interpersonal Relationships: Social Penetration Processes," in *Interpersonal Processes: New Directions in Communication Research*, ed. M. E. Roloff and G. R. Miller (Beverly Hills, Calif.: Sage, 1987), pp. 257–277.

13. Knapp and Vangelisti, *Interpersonal Communication and Human Relations*.

14. Ibid.

15. Ibid.

16. L. A. Baxter and C. Bullis, "Turning Points in Developing Romantic Relationships," *Human Communication Research*, 12, (1986), 469–493.

17. M. Knapp, D. G. Ellis and B. A. Williams, "Perceptions of Communication Behavior Associated with Relationship Terms," *Communication Monographs*, 47 (1980), 262–278.

18. Miller and Parks, "Communication in Dissolving Relationships."

19. M. Sunnafrank, "A Communication-Based Perspective on Attitude Similarity and Interpersonal Attraction in Early Acquaintance," *Communication Monographs*, 51 (1984), 372–380.

20. M. Sunnafrank, "Predicted Outcome Value During Initial Interactions: A Reformulation of Uncertainty Reduction Theory," *Human Communication Research*, 13 (1986), 3–33.

21. W. Schutz, *Interpersonal Underground* (Palo Alto, Calif.: Science & Behavior Books, 1966).

22. C. R. Berger and R. J. Calabrese, "Some Explorations in Initial Interaction and Beyond: Toward a Developmental Theory of Interpersonal Communication," *Human Communication Research*, 1 (1975), 99–112.

23. C. R. Berger and J. Bradac, *Language and Social Interaction: Uncertainty in Interpersonal Relations*, (Baltimore, Md: Edward Arnold, 1982).

24. K. Dindia, M. A. Fitzpatrick, and D. A. Kenny, "Self-Disclosure in Spouse and Stranger Interaction: A Social Relations Analysis," *Human Communication Research*, 23 (1997), 388–412.

25. A. P. Bochner, "On the Efficacy of Openness in Close Relationships," in *Communication Yearbook* 5, ed. M. Burgoon (New Brunswick, N.J.: Transaction Books, 1982), pp. 109–124.

26. Dindia, Fitzpatrick, and Kenny, "Self-Disclosure in Spouse and Stranger Interaction."

27. J. N. Martin and T. K. Nakayama, *Intercultural Communication in Contexts* (Mountain View, Calif.: Mayfield, 1997).

Chapter 7

1. K. Kellerman, "The Conversation MOP: II. Progression Through Scenes in Discourse," *Human Communication Research*, 17 (1991), 385–414.

2. S. A. Beebe, S. J. Beebe, and M. V. Redmond, *Interpersonal Communication: Relating to others*, 2nd ed. (Needham Heights, Mass.: Allyn & Bacon, 1999).

3. R. A. Bell and J. A. Daly, "The Affinity-Seeking Function of Communication," *Communication Monographs*, 51 (1984), 91–115.

4. J. H. Tolhuizen, "Affinity Seeking in Developing Relationships," *Communication Reports*, 2 (1989), 83–91.

5. Ibid.

6. D. J. Canary and L. Stafford, "Preservation of Relational Characteristics: Maintenance Strategies, Equity, and Locus of Control," in *Interpersonal Communication: Evolving Interpersonal Relationships*, ed. P. K. Kalbfleisch (Hillsdale, N.J.: Lawrence Erlbaum, 1993), pp. 237 –260.

7. L. A. Baxter, "Cognition and Communication in the Relationship Process," in *Accounting for Relationships: Explanations, Representation, and Knowledge*, ed. R. Burnett, P. McGhee, & D. Clarke (New York: Methuen, 1987), pp. 192–212.

8. Ibid.

9. Ibid.

10. L. A. Baxter and C. Bullis, "Turning Points in Developing Romantic Relationships," *Human Communication Research*, 12 (1986), 469–493.

11. E. P. Simon and L. A. Baxter, "Attachment-Style Differences in Relationship Maintenance Strategies," *Western Journal of Communication*, 57 (1993), 416–430. See also Canary and Stafford "Preservation of Relational Characteristics."

12. A. P. Bochner, "On the Efficacy of Openness in Close Relationships," in *Communication Yearbook* 5, ed. M. Burgoon (New Brunswick, N.J.: Transaction Books, 1982), pp. 109–124.

13. M. V. Redmond, "Content Adaptation in Everyday Interactions." Paper presented at the annual meeting of the National Communication Association, Chicago (1997).

14. Baxter, "Cognition and Communication in the Relationship Process."

15. C. J. S. Bruess and J. C. Pearson, "Interpersonal Rituals in Marriage and Adult Friendship," *Communication Monographs*, (1997), 25–46.

16. V. P. Richmond, "Amount of Communication in Marital Dyads as a Function of Dyad and Individual Marital Satisfaction," *Communication Research Reports*, 12 (1995), 152–158.

17. M. V. Redmond, "The Functions of Empathy (Decentering) in Human Relations," *Human Relations*, 42 (1989), 593–605. See also M. V. Redmond, "A Multi-dimensional Theory and Measure of Social Decentering," *Journal of Research in Personality*, 29 (1995), 35–58.

18. Redmond, "The Functions of Empathy (Decentering) in Human Relations."

19. M. J. Cody, D. J. Canary, and S. W. Smith, "Compliance-Gaining Goals: An Inductive Analysis of Actors' Goal Types, Strategies, and Successes," in *Strategic Interpersonal Communication*, ed. J. A. Daly and J. M. Wiemann (Hillsdale, N.J.: Lawrence Erlbaum, 1995), pp. 33–90.

20. G. R. Miller and F. Boster, "Persuasion in Personal Relationships," in *A Handbook of Personal Relationships*, ed. S. Duck (New York: Wiley, 1988), pp. 275–288.
21. Ibid.
22. Ibid.
23. Ibid.
24. S. Duck, *Understanding Relationships*, (New York: Guilford Press, 1991).
25. G. R. Miller and M. R. Parks, "Communication in Dissolving Relationships," in *Personal Relationships 4: Dissolving Relationships*, ed. S. W. Duck (New York: Academic Press, 1982), pp. 127–154.
26. Ibid.
27. D. DeStephen, "Integrating Relational Termination into a General Model of Communication Competence." Paper presented at the annual meeting of the Speech Communication Association, Denver (1985).
28. M. J. Cody, "A Typology of Disengagement Strategies and an Examination of the Role Intimacy, Reactions to Inequity, and Relational Problems Play in Strategy Selection," *Communication Monographs*, 49 (1982), 148–170.

Chapter 8

1. C. J. Stewart and W. B. Cash, Jr., *Interviewing: Principles and Practice*, 6th ed. (Dubuque, Iowa: Brown, 1991).
2. S. M. Varallo, E. B. Ray, and B. H. Ellis, "Speaking of Incest: The Research Interview as Social Justice," *Journal of Applied Communication Research*, 26 (1998), 254–271.
3. F. E. X. Dance and C. E. Larson, *Speech Communication: Concepts and Behavior* (New York: Holt, Rinehart & Winston, 1972).
4. F. E. Mahoney, "Adjusting the Interview to Avoid Cultural Bias," *Journal of Career Planning and Employment*, 52 (1992), 41–44.
5. S. W. Littlejohn, *Theories of Human Communication*, 5th ed. (Belmont, Calif.: Wadsworth, 1996).
6. W. J. Severin and J. W. Tankard, Jr., *Communication Theories*, 2nd ed. (New York: Longman, 1988).
7. B. A. Olaniran and D. E. Williams, "Communication Distortion: An Intercultural Lesson from the Visa Application Process," *Communication Quarterly*, 43 (1995), 225–240.
8. Stewart and Cash, *Interviewing*, p. 55.
9. C. D. Tengler and F. M. Jablin, "Effects of Question Type, Orientation, and Sequencing in the Employment Screening Interview," *Communication Monographs*, 50 (1983), 245–263.

Chapter 9

1. G. Gallup, "The Quintamensional Plan of Question Design," *Public Opinion Quarterly*, vol. II, (1947), 389–393.
2. A. H. Church, "From Both Sides Now: The Employee Interview—The Great Pretender," *The Industrial-Organizational Psychologist*, July 1996 (online version).

Chapter 10

1. G. Hofstede, *Culture's Consequences* (Beverly Hills, Calif.: Sage, 1980).
2. M. S. Poole, D. R. Seibold, and R. D. McPhee, "Group Decision-Making as a Structurational Process," *Quarterly Journal of Speech*, 71, (1985), 74–112. See also M. S. Poole, D. R. Seibold, and R. D. McPhee, "The Structuration of Group Decisions," in *Communication and Group Decision Making*, 2nd ed., ed. R. Y. Hirokawa and M. S. Poole (Thousand Oaks, Calif.: Sage, 1996), pp. 114–146.
3. Ibid.
4. I. Janis, *Victims of Groupthink* (Boston: Houghton Mifflin, 1972).
5. Ibid.
6. Rothwell, *In Mixed Company*.
7. M. E. Shaw, *Group Dynamics: The Psychology of Small Group Behavior*, 2nd ed., (New York: McGraw-Hill, 1976).
8. S. G. Baugh and G. B. Graen, "Effects of Team Gender and Racial Composition on Perceptions of Team Performance in Cross-Functional Teams," *Group & Organization Management* 22 (1997), 366–384.
9. D. C. Baker, "A Qualitative and Quantitative Analysis of Verbal Style and the Elimination of Potential Leaders in Small Groups," *Communication Quarterly*, 38 (1990), 13–26. See also C. Pavitt, G. G. Whitchurch, H. Siple, and N. Peterson, "Communication and Emergent Group Leadership: Does Content Count?" *Communication Research Reports*, 14 (1997), 470–480.
10. S. A. Beebe and J. T. Masterson, *Communicating in Small Groups*, 5th ed. (New York: Longman, 1997).
11. K. W. Hawkins, "Effects of Gender and Communication Content on Leadership Emergence in Small, Task-Oriented Groups," *Small Group Research*, 26 (1995), 234–249.
12. F. E. Fiedler, "Personality and Situational Determinants of Leadership Effectiveness," in *Group Dynamics: Research and Theory*, 3rd ed., ed. D. Cartwright and A. Zander (New York: Harper & Row, 1968), pp. 389–398. See also F. E. Fiedler, *A Theory of Leadership Effectiveness*, (New York: McGraw Hill, 1967), and F. E. Fiedler and M. M. Chemers, *Leadership and Effective Management*, (Glenview, Ill.: Scott, Foresman, 1974).
13. Fiedler, "Personality and Situational Determinants of Leadership Effectiveness." See also Fiedler, *A Theory of Leadership Effectiveness*, and Fiedler and Chemers, *Leadership and Effective Management*.
14. P. Hersey and K. Blanchard, *Management Organizational Behavior: Utilizing Human Resources* (Englewood Cliffs, N.J.: Prentice Hall, 1988).
15. For example, see: R. F. Bales and F. L. Strodtbeck, "Phases in Group Problem-Solving," in *Group Dynamics: Research and Theory*, 3rd ed., ed. D. Cartwright and A. Zander, (New York: Harper & Row, 1968), pp. 389–398. W. G. Bennis and J. A. Shepard, "A Theory of Group Development," *Human Relations*, 9 (1956), 415–437; B. A.

Fisher, *Small Group Decision Making: Communication and the Group Process* (New York: McGraw-Hill; 1974); B. W. Tuckman, "Developmental Sequence in Small Groups," *Psychological Bulletin*, 63 (1965), 384–399.

16. A. P. Hare, *Handbook of Small Group Research*, 2nd ed. (New York: The Free Press, 1976).

Chapter 11

1. Susan Jarboe, "A Comparison of Input-Output, Process-Output, and Input-Process-Output Models of Small Group Problem-Solving Effectiveness," *Communication Monographs*, 55, (1988), 121–142. See also R. Y. Hirokawa, L. Erbert and A. Hurst, "Communication and Group Decision-Making Effectiveness," in *Communication and Group Decision Making*, 2nd ed. ed. R. Y. Hirokawa and M. S. Poole (Thousand Oaks, Calif.: Sage, 1996), pp. 269–300.

2. John K. Brilhart and Gloria J. Galanes, *Effective Group Discussion*, 8th ed. (Madison, Wis.: Brown and Benchmark, 1995).

3. Brillhart & Galanes, *Effective Group Discussion*.

4. J. Anderson, "Communication Competence in the Small Group," in *Small Group Communication: A Reader*, 5th ed. ed. R. S. Cathcart and L. A. Samavor (Dubuque, Iowa: Brown, 1988), pp. 450–458.

5. B. A. Fisher, "Leadership: When Does the Difference Make a Difference?" in *Communication and Group Decision-Making* ed. R.Y. Hirokawa and M. S. Poole (Beverly Hills, Calif.: Sage, 1986), pp. 197–215.

6. Fisher, "Leadership: When Does the Difference Make a Difference?"

7. See review by J. D. Rothwell, *In Mixed Company*, 3rd ed. (Fort Worth, Tex.: Harcourt, 1998).

Chapter 12

1. I was taught the 70/30 rule by Dr. Frank E. X. Dance at the University of Denver, in 1977.

2. D. A. Sousa, *How the Brain Learns* (Reston, Va.: National Association of Secondary School Principals, 1995).

3. T. D. Daniels and R. F. Whitman, "The Effects of Message Introduction, Message Structure, and Verbal Organizing Ability upon Learning of Message Information," *Human Communication Research*, 7 (1981), 147–160; A. W. Johnson, "A Preliminary Investigation of the Relationship Between Message Organization and Listener Comprehension," *Communication Studies*, 21 (1970), 104–107; A. W. Johnson, "The Effect of Three Message Organization Variables upon Listener Comprehension,"(paper presented at the International Communication Association Annual Conference, 1971); E. Thompson, "Some Effects of Message Structure on Listeners' Comprehension," *Communication Monographs*, 34 (1967), 51–57.

4. D. Ehninger, *Influence, Belief, and Argument: An Introduction to Responsible Persuasion* (Glenview, Ill.: Scott, Foresman, 1974).

5. P. Zimbardo and E. B. Ebbesen, *Influencing Attitudes and Changing Behavior* (Reading, Mass.: Addison-Wesley, 1969).

6. P. Sheetz, *Recruiting Trends 1996–1997* (East Lansing, Mich.: Michigan State University, 1996).

7. R. F. Applbaum and K. W. Anatol, "The Factor Structure of Source Credibility as a Function of the Speaking Situation," *Communication Monographs*, 39 (1972), 216–222; J. Liska, "Situational and Topical Variations in Credibility Criteria," *Communication Monographs*, 45 (1978), 85–92.

8. J. C. McCroskey and T. J. Young, "Ethos and Credibility: The Construct and Its Measurement After Three Decades," *Central States Speech Journal* (now *Communication Studies*), 32, (1981), 24–34.

9. J. K. Burgoon, T. Birk, and M. Pfau, "Nonverbal Behaviors, Persuasion, and Credibility," *Human Communication Research*, 17 (1990), 140–169.

10. Burgoon, Birk, & Pfau, "Nonverbal Behaviors, Persuasion, and Credibility," 140–169.

11. L. Festinger, *A Theory of Cognitive Dissonance* (Evanston, Ill.: Row, Peterson, 1957); F. Heider, *The Psychology of Interpersonal Relations* (New York: Wiley, 1958).

Chapter 14

1. J. K. Burgoon, T. Birk, and M. Pfau, "Nonverbal Behaviors, Persuasion, and Credibility," *Human Communication Research*, 17 (1990), 140–169.

2. J. K. Burgoon, D. B. Buller, J. L. Hale, and M. A. deTurk, "Relational Messages Associated with Nonverbal Behaviors," *Human Communication Research*, 10 (1984), 351–378.

3. See, for instance, Henry David Northrop, *The Modern Speaker or Complete Manual of Elocution* (Philadelphia: J. H. Moore Company, 1896).

4. Burgoon et al., "Nonverbal Behaviors, Persuasion, and Credibility."

5. I am indebted to Dr. Terry Pickett for his insights into handling questions.

Chapter 15

1. D. Katz and R. L. Kahn, *The Social Psychology of Organizations* (New York: Wiley, 1966).

2. F. M. Jablin, "Formal Structural Characteristics of Organizations and Superior-Subordinate Communication," *Human Communication Research*, 8 (1982), 338–347; F. M. Jablin, "Task/Work Relationship: A Life-Span Perspective," in *Handbook of Interpersonal Communication*, ed. M. L. Knapp and G. R. Miller, 615–654; D. Geddes and F. Linnehan, "Exploring the Dimensionality of Positive and Negative Performance Feedback," *Communication Quarterly*, 44 (1996), 326–344.

3. Geddes and Linnehan, "Exploring the Dimensionality of Positive and Negative Performance Feedback."

4. Ibid.

5. Ibid.

6. Jablin, "Formal Structural Characteristics of Organizations and Superior-Subordinate Communication."

7. K. J. Krone, "A Comparison of Organizational, Structural, and Relationship Effects on Subordinates' Upward Influence Choices," *Communication Quarterly*, 40 (1992), 1–15; K. J. Krone, "Structuring Constraints on Perceptions of Upward Influence and Supervisory Relationships," *The Southern Journal of Communication*, 59 (1994), 215–226.

8. Katz and Kahn, *The Social Psychology of Organizations.*

9. C. Conrad, "*Strategic Organizational Communication: Toward the Twenty-first Century*, 3rd ed. (Fort Worth, Tex.: Harcourt Brace, 1994).

10. F. M. Jablin, "Formal Organizational Structure," in *Handbook of Organizational Communication*, ed. F. M. Jablin, L. L. Putnam, K. H. Roberts, and L. W. Porter (Newbury Park, Calif.: Sage, 1987), pp. 389–419.

11. T. D. Daniels, B. K. Spiker, and M. J. Papa, *Perspectives on Organizational Communication*, 4th ed. (Madison, Wisc.: Brown & Benchmark, 1997).

12. Krone, "Structuring Constraints on Perceptions of Upward Influence and Supervisory Relationships."

13. Ibid.

14. Conrad, *Strategic Organizational Communication: Toward the Twenty-first Century.*

15. See Conrad, for a more extensive discussion of functions.

16. T.L. Albrecht and B. J. Hall, "Facilitating Talk About Ideas: The Role of Personal Relationships in Organizational Innovation," *Communication Monographs*, 58 (1991), 283–288.

17. L. von Bertalanffy, (1940). "Der Organismus als Physikalisches Sytem Betrachtet," *Die Natruwissenschaften*, 28 (1940), 521–531.

18. Katz and Kahn, *The Social Psychology of Organizations.*

19. Ibid.

20. M. E. Pacanowsky and N. O'Donnell-Trujillo, "Organizational Communication as Cultural Performance," *Communication Monographs*, 50 (1983), 126–147.

21. S. Suzuki, "Cultural Transmission in Internal Organizations: Impact of Interpersonal Communication Patterns in Intergroup Contexts," *Human Communication Research*, 24 (1997), 109–146.

22. M. K. Ahuja and K. M. Carley, "Network Structure in Virtual Organizations," *Journal of Computer-Mediated Communication*, 3, No. 4 (1998).

23. H. Berhel, "Email: The Good, the Bad, and the Ugly," *Communications of the ACM*, 40 (1997), 11–16.

24. Conrad, See also R.W. Pace, *Organizational Communication: Foundations for Human Resource Development*, (Englewood Cliffs, N.J.: Prentice Hall, 1983).

25. Conrad, *Strategic Organizational Communication: Toward the Twenty-first Century.*

26. Ibid.

27. Ibid.

28. Daniels, Spiker, and Papa, *Perspectives on Organizational Communication.*

29. Pace, *Organizational Communication: Foundations for Human Resource Development.*

30. Ibid.

31. D. McGregor, *The Human Side of Enterprise* (New York: McGraw-Hill, 1960).

32. Ibid.

33. Ibid.

Chapter 16

1. F. M. Jablin, "Assimilating New Members into Organizations," in *Communication Yearbook 8*, ed. R. N. Bostrom and B. H. Westley (Newbury Park, Calif.: Sage, 1984), pp. 594–626.

2. J. T. Mignerey, R. B. Rubin, and W. I. Gorden, "Organizational Entry: An Investigation of Newcomer Communication Behavior and Uncertainty," *Communication Research*, 22, No. 1 (1995), 54–85.

3. Ibid.

4. P. M. Sias and D. J. Cahill, "From Coworkers to Friends: The Development of Peer Friendships in the Workplace," *Western Journal of Communication*, 62 (1998), 273–299.

5. D. H. McKnight, L. L. Cummings, and N. L. Chervany, "Initial Trust Formation in New Organizational Relationships," *Academy of Management Review*, 23 (1998), 473–491.

6. Ibid.

7. G. R. Miller and F. Boster, "Persuasion in Personal Relationships," in *A Handbook of Personal Relationships*, ed. S. W. Duck (New York: Wiley, 1988), pp. 275–288.

8. Ibid.

9. Sias and Cahill, "From Coworkers to Friends."

10. Ibid.

11. S. A. Beebe and J. T. Masterson, *Communicating in Small Groups*, 5th ed. (New York: Longman, 1997).

12. P. R. Timm, *Functional Business Presentations* (Englewood Cliffs, N.J.: Prentice Hall, 1981).

13. The Olsten Forum on Human Resource Issues and Trends, survey report published by the Olsten Corporation, Melville, N.Y., 1996.

14. C. C. Staley and P. Shockly-Zalabak, "Communication Proficiency and Future Training Needs of the Female Professional: Self-Assessment vs. Supervisors' Evaluations," *Human Relations*, 39 (1986), 891–902.

15. G. L. Cellini, "Enhancing Two-Way Communication: A View from the Trenches," *Managers Letter*, (Melville, N.Y.: Olsten Corporation, 1998).

16. A. R. Elangovan, "Managerial Third-Party Dispute Intervention: A Prescriptive Model of Strategy Selection," *Academy of Management Review*, 20, No. 4 (1995), 800–831.

17. This discussion draws on A. R. Elangovan, "Managerial Third-Party Dispute Intervention."

Photo Credits

(continued)

Chapter 3: p. 55, Jeff Greenberg/Photo Edit; p. 62, Randy Glasbergen; p. 72, Lemont Brown. Copyright 1998 Darrin Bell. www.lemontbrown.com and www.editorialcartoons.com.

Chapter 4: p. 93, Copyright © 1975 Paul Ekman. p. 97, David Young Wolff/Photo Edit; p. 103, DILBERT reprinted by permission of United Feature Syndicate, Inc.

Chapter 5: p. 112, A Ramey/Photo Edit; p. 121, Lemont Brown. Copyright 1998 Darrin Bell. www.lemontbrown.com and www.editorialcartoons.com; p. 128, Tony Savino/The Image Works.

Part Two: p. 141, Tom McCarthy/Photo Edit.

Chapter 6: p. 147, REAL LIFE ADVENTURES © GarLanco. Reprinted with permission of UNIVERSAL PRESS SYNDICATE. All Rights Reserved.; p. 152, R. Lord/The Image Works; p. 161, Frank Siteman/Photo Edit.

Chapter 7: p. 174, Larry Mangino/The Image Works; p. 181, Randy Glasbergen; p. 188, Myrleen Catfe/Photo Edit.

Chapter 8: p. 203, Grantland; p. 209, Richard Lord/The Image Works; p. 216, Julie Houck/Stock Boston.

Chapter 9: p. 228, Mark Richards/Photo Edit; p. 238, Ted Goff; p. 250, David Young Wolff/Photo Edit.

Chapter 10: p. 260, Bob Daemmrich/Stock Boston; p. 270, Grantland; p. 274, Cindy Charles/Photo Edit; p. 278, Randy Glasbergen.

Chapter 11: p. 288, Randy Glasbergen; p. 293, Steve Rubin/The Image Works; p. 299, Gary Conner/Photo Edit.

Chapter 12: p. 309, Elizabeth Crews/The Image Works; p. 316, Esbin Anderson/The Image Works; p. 323, Randy Glasbergen.

Chapter 13: p. 343, Matthew Berkoski/Photo Edit; p. 348, Gary A. Connor/Photo Edit; p. 352, Ted Goff.

Chapter 14: p. 368, Charles Gupton; p. 372, Rob Crandall/Stock Boston; p. 384, Ted Goff.

Chapter 15: p. 399, Ted Goff; p. 402, Bob Daemmrich/Stock Boston; p. 410, Michael Newman/Photo Edit.

Chapter 16: p. 421, Carol Simpson Productions; p. 435, Jeffery W. Myers.

Index

Absolute claims, 311
Abstract language, 87
Abstracts, research using, 347
Accenting, 106
Accommodation, 133, 134, 192
Accounts, 116–117, 118
Accumulated rewards, 45–46
Actional model of communication, 4–5, 6
Active listening, 70, 73, 127, 239, 249, 293
Activity dimension, of language, 91
Adaptability, 187–188
Added baggage, 86
Adjourning stage, of groups, 279
Advertising, 29–31, 67
Affinity-seeking strategies, 179–180, 183
Age, 33
    relational context and, 38
    shared meaning and, 83
Agendas, of groups, 285
Aggravating reproaches, 116, 117
Aggression, 117, 118
Aggressive messages, 124–125, 135
All-channel network, 266, 267
Allness statements, 90
Altman, Irwin, 150, 164–165
Analyses, 310
Antisocial behavior, 184
Anxiety, in presentations, 386–387
Apologies, 113, 114, 116
Appraisal interviews, 203–204, 212, 213, 242, 249–250
Appreciative listening, 67–68
Approachability cues, 175
Aristotle, 321–322, 323
Assertive messages, 124–125
Assigned roles, in groups, 270
Assimilation into organization, 420
Assurances, in relationships, 184
Attending, 52–53
Attitudes, 31–32, 35
    of audience, 320–321
    relational context and, 38
Attraction, 156–162
    complementarity of needs and, 160–161

enduring, 157
initial, 156–157
interaction and, 157, 159
needs and, 157, 159–161
predicted outcome value theory of, 159
preinteraction influences and, 157, 158–159
reciprocity of liking and, 159
similarity and, 160
theories of, 157–161
Attribution theory, 57–61, 78–84
    biases in, 58–61, 89–90
    causal theory of, 57–58, 59–60, 61
    complexity in, 61
    context of communication and, 84
    culture and, 81–83, 125
    individual differences in, 80
    interpretation and, 56–57
    nonverbal communication and, 99
    obvious, irrelevant, and negative in, 58–59
    overcoming biases in, 60–61
    perception and, 59, 78–79, 99
    preconceptions in, 59, 61
    from psychological context, 79–80
    shared meaning and, 80–81, 83
    subtle, relevant, and positive information in, 60–61
Audience, 307, 320–321
    analysis of, 328–330, 339
Audit, of organizational communication, 394
Avoidance, for conflict management, 133, 134, 192

Background information, 353
Balance theory, 326–328
Behavioral de-escalation, of relationships, 195
Behavioral uncertainty, 46
Beliefs, 31, 32, 35
    of audience, 320–321
    relational context and, 38
Bell, Robert, 179
Biases
    attributional, 58–61, 89–90

in employment interviews, 58–59, 209, 210–211
    in language, 89–90
    in listening, 65
    misunderstandings from, 127
    in selection, 53
Bipolar interview questions, 220
Birds, communication with, 16–17
Blanchard, Ken, 276–277, 422
Body movement, 94, 372–373
Bosrock, Mary Murray, 82
Brainstorming, 290–291
Breadth, of self-disclosure, 163
Bridge links, 397
Briefings, 430–431
Bush, George, 82

Caldwell, Neal, 69–70
Card catalog, research in, 346
Categories, 53, 54–55
Categorization, 53, 54–55
Causal theory of attribution, 57–58, 59–60, 61
Cause-and-effect organization, 318
Central idea, 339, 341
Ceremonies, 406
Chain network, 266
    in groups, 267
Channels of communication, 15
Choice, relationships of, 144, 145
Chronemics, 99
Chronological organization, 317, 351
Circle network, in groups, 267
Circumstance, relationships of, 144, 145
Claims, in speeches of value, 311
Classical syllogisms, 323
Classical theory, of organizations, 403, 408–410
Classroom, presentational communication in, 340
Cliques, 396, 397
Closed questions, 207, 220, 221, 228
Closed systems, 404–405
Closing, of interviews, 236
Coaching, 309
Cognitive dissonance theory, 326–328